American
LITERATURE

Cultural Influences of Early to Contemporary Voices

James P. Stobaugh

HIGH SCHOOL LEVEL
STUDENT

First printing: November 2012
Fourth printing: July 2015

Master Books®, P.O. Box 726, Green Forest, AR 72638

Master Books® is a division of the New Leaf Publishing Group, Inc.

ISBN: 978-0-89051-671-3
ISBN: 978-1-61458-266-3 (ebook)
Library of Congress Catalog Number: 2012951014

Cover design by Diana Bogardus.
Interior design by Terry White.

Please consider requesting that a copy of this volume be purchased by your local library system.

Printed in the United States of America

Please visit our website for other great titles:
www.masterbooks.com

For information regarding author interviews, please contact the publicity department at (870) 438-5288

Dedication

This Book is gratefully dedicated to Karen and our four children: Rachel, Jessica, Timothy, and Peter.

He has given us a ministry of reconciliation . . . (2 Corinthians 5:18).

Master Books®
A Division of New Leaf Publishing Group
www.masterbooks.com

Contents

The following is a list of additional books and texts not included within the study that are needed for this course. It is strongly suggested that students read most, if not all these titles during the summer before taking this course. Most will be available at local libraries or as free downloads at The Online Books Page (online-books.library.upenn.edu/lists.html), Project Gutenberg (www.gutenberg.org/wiki/Main_Page), or Bartleby (www.bartleby.com/).

Of Plimoth Plantations by William Bradford

Religious Affections by Jonathan Edwards

The Autobiography of Benjamin Franklin by Benjamin Franklin

Narrative of the Life of Frederick Douglass by Frederick Douglass

The Scarlet Letter by Nathaniel Hawthorne

The Adventures of Huckleberry Finn by Mark Twain

A Farewell to Arms by Ernest Hemingway

The Red Badge of Courage by Stephen Crane

The Unvanquished by William Faulkner

The Pearl by John Steinbeck

Walden by Henry David Thoreau

Billy Budd by Herman Melville

The Emperor Jones by Eugene Gladstone O'Neill

The Little Foxes by Lillian Hellman

The Glass Menagerie by Tennessee Williams

The Crucible by Arthur Miller

Ethan Frome by Edith Wharton

Cold Sassy Tree by Olive Anne Burns

Their Eyes Were Watching God by Zora Neale Hurston

The Chosen by Chaim Potok

Using Your Student Textbook

How this course has been developed:

1. **Chapters:** This course has 34 chapters (representing 34 weeks of study) to earn two full credits; writing and literature.

2. **Lessons:** Each chapter has five lessons, taking approximately 45 to 60 minutes each.

3. **Student responsibility:** Responsibility to complete this course is on the student. Students must read ahead in order to stay on schedule with the readings. Independence is strongly encouraged in this course, which was designed for the student to practice independent learning.

4. **Grading:** Depending on the grading option chosen, the parent/educator will grade the daily concept builders, and the weekly tests and essays. (See pages 7 and 8.)

5. **Additional books and texts:** A list of outside reading is provided after the table of contents. Students should try and read ahead whenever possible. Most readings are available free online or at a local library.

Throughout this book you will find the following:

1. **Chapter Learning Objectives:** Always read the "First Thoughts" and "Chapter Learning Objectives" in order to comprehend the scope of the material to be covered in a particular week.

2. **Daily warm-ups:** You should write or give oral responses for the daily warm-ups to your educator/parent. These are not necessarily meant to be evaluated, but should stimulate discussion.

3. **Concept builders:** You should complete a daily concept builder. These activities take 15 minutes or less and emphasize a particular concept that is vital to that particular chapter topic. These will relate to a subject covered in the chapter, though not necessarily in that days lesson.

4. **Assigned readings:** Remember to read ahead on the required literary material for this course. Students should plan to read some of the required literature the summer before the course.

5. **Weekly essays:** You will be writing at least one essay per week, depending on the level of accomplishment you and your parent/educator decide upon. These are available in the teacher guide.

6. **Weekly tests:** These are available in the teacher guide and online.

7. **Author Worldview Watch:** Because every writer in this book has a unique worldview (see chapter 1), including the author himself, this brief section gives a simple framework to help the student know what might be behind the words of the text. Many classic authors were not Christians, and so their views and beliefs often flow into their works. (Be aware of this with anything you hear or read, including blogs, news updates, and books or movies.)

Earn a bonus credit!

Easily integrate related history curriculum for an additional credit, a combination study done in less than two hours daily! History Connections are shown on the chapter introduction page in order to help a student study these texts consecutively, exploring literature and history in unison. (The *American*, *British*, and *World History* curriculum is also written by James Stobaugh and published by Master Books®.)

What the student will need each day:

1. Notepad/computer: for writing assignments.
2. Pen/pencil: for taking notes and for essays.
3. A prayer journal. As often as you can — hopefully daily — keep a prayer journal.

Increasing your vocabulary:

Part of the reason for reading so many challenging literary works is for you to increase your functional vocabulary. Your best means of increasing vocabulary is through reading a vast amount of classical, well-written literary works. While reading these works, you should harvest as many unknown words as you can, and try to use five new words in each essay you write.

Create 3x5 Vocabulary Cards

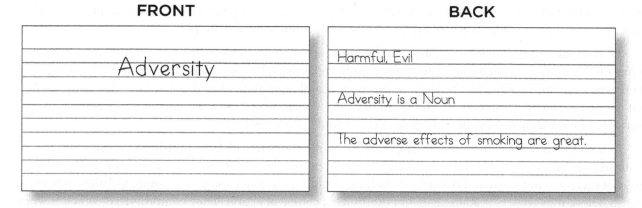

FRONT

Adversity

BACK

Harmful, Evil

Adversity is a Noun

The adverse effects of smoking are great.

When you meet a strange word for the first time,

- Do your best to figure out the word in context,
- Check your guess by looking in the dictionary,
- Write a sentence with the word in it.

Use the illustration above to formulate your vocabulary cards of new words.

About the Author

James P. Stobaugh and his wife, Karen, have four homeschooled adult children. They have a growing ministry, For Such a Time As This Ministries, committed to challenging this generation to change its world for Christ.

Dr. Stobaugh is an ordained pastor, a certified secondary teacher, and a SAT coach. His academic credentials include: BA, cum laude Vanderbilt University; Teacher Certification, Peabody College for Teachers; MA, Rutgers University; MDiv, Princeton Theological Seminary; Merrill Fellow, Harvard University; DMin Gordon Conwell Seminary.

Dr. Stobaugh has written articles for magazines: *Leadership, Presbyterian Survey, Princeton Spire, Ministries Today,* and *Pulpit Digest.* Dr. Stobaugh's books include the *SAT Preparation Course for the Christian Student,* the *ACT Preparation Course for the Christian Student,* the *Skills for Literary Analysis,* the *Christian Reading Companion for 50 Classics,* as well as the *American History, British History,* and *World History* high school curriculum.

Preface

In the World but Not of It. Reading, studying (analyzing), and evaluating (judging) American literature presents Christian students with the good, the bad, and even the ugly. First, American literature, especially in the short story genre (type), represents some of the best, most sublime literature written by humankind. Edgar Allan Poe, a tortured, conflicted poet, wrote what is arguably the best short story in world history: "During the whole of a dull, dark, and soundless day in the autumn of the year, when the clouds hung oppressively low in the heavens, I had been passing alone, on horseback, through a singularly dreary tract of country. . ." ("The Fall of the House of Usher") A credible American literature anthology would be remiss if it ignored Edgar Allan Poe, yet, Poe was certainly no follower of Christ.

Still, an American literature anthology can ignore the bad and this author will. The iconic, profane, and poorly written *Catcher in the Rye*, by J. D. Salinger, for instance, is easily ignored. The equally profane, but better written *A Farewell to Arms*, by Ernest Hemingway, is not so easily ignored.

Thus, at the beginning of this century, in the midst of a hostile culture, Christian scholars find themselves on the horns of a dilemma: How do they study the classics, the best literature, without offending, even damaging their spiritual walk? The truth is, this is an age-old question: How do Christians live in the world, but not be consumed, tainted by it? The Word of God commands us, "Do not conform to the pattern of this world, but be transformed by the renewing of your mind." (Romans 12:2)

At least this is not a new problem. There are hints that the practical, layman fisherman Peter and the Plato scholar Pharisee Paul had words several times about these issue. The Council at Jerusalem (Acts 15) was not merely about dogma, it concerned clashing world views. Peter sought to require Gentiles to become Jewish before they were Christian. Paul opposed such a course of action. They compromised, which is what we will do in this course: there are some excellent, but controversial literature choices we will skip because they go too far, or, we wish not to offend the sensibilities of our readers.

The inspired, inerrant Bible is without equal in authority or worth. In fact, it is unique among all cultural artifacts and transcends all nationalities and time. It is immutable. In fact, the only legitimate comparison to the Bible is the Bible itself. The Bible is without equal. All literary works pale in comparison.

The truth is, however, studying challenging, classical, secular literature may be necessary to connect to a culture. Augustine, Eusebius of Caesarea, Clement of Alexandria, John Milton, and C. S. Lewis were all students of the classics and advocated the same for all their followers. After all, the great apologists of the twentieth century were not theologians; they were classicists and language arts teachers!

So how do we do this thing? How do we study great American literature and not be snared by aberrant cultural symbols and norms?

Theologian H. Richard Niebuhr posited five different relationships that the Christian has with culture (www.calvin.edu/academic/rit/webBook/chapter7/niebuhrTech.htm):

- Opposition
- Agreement
- Christ above culture
- Tension
- Reformation

The first two choices are the extremes. Opposition means that the Christian opposes all cultural relics as "worldly." Agreement takes the other extreme, where Christians finds their faith to be fundamentally compatible with the culture around them. Here, the internet is simply an extension of God's good creation, put here for us to develop and use as we wish.

The last three choices are somewhere between the extremes. The "Christ above culture" option was supported by medieval theologian Thomas Aquinas. Aquinas would read Mark Twain and see his books as a fine product of culture, but as such, it could never approach the sublime beauty of Christ. The tension option, advocated by Martin Luther, places the Christian in a tension between Christ and culture. We are in the world but not of it and must be careful not to estrange ourselves from the world, but at the same time not to embrace it either. In short, we are citizens of two worlds that are often at odds with each other. Applied to American literature, the great books may be read, and studied, but with care and guidance. Luther might find a fitting hermeneutic metaphor for a sermon from *The Adventures of Huckleberry Finn*, but he would not reference it in his theology.

The final option is the one the author embraces. I believe that the appropriate relationship between Christianity and culture is a reforming or transforming approach. Culture is a manifestation of God's good creation, an outgrowth of human creativity and community; unfortunately, though, sin deeply infects every part of the creation, including human culture; but we can redeem culture in the name of Christ. This redemption is a transformation of culture by seeking, enhancing, and celebrating the original good we find in culture while identifying the effects of sin (and working to reduce those effects). Frederick and Catherine, for instance, in *A Farewell to Arms*, love each other, and God is love. Unfortunately, their love is self-destructive because these two twentieth century characters do not obey the Word of God.

I believe you, my students, the most strategic generation in human history, can and will transform all future literature, all future world culture, by knowing and loving the World of God and knowing and understanding human culture. Someday, twenty or thirty years from now, future students will be reading your great novels, short stories, and poetry! The beautiful theism of Chiam Potok will be the rule and not the exception.

What does it mean to live in a society and culture that does not read the classics? It means we have no way to talk to one another. We no longer have common metaphors and motifs from which to share consensus. We wonder from one existential moment to another. Augustine and C. S. Lewis both dreaded that eventuality. It is up to you, young people, to be such competent, but Godly writers, that society cannot ignore, and then, you will resurrect the old and add to the expanding canon. This old man, and this tired culture, will know a spiritual revival that is the stuff of dreams and visions!

American literature, like all American culture, is an extension of God's good creation and thus has extraordinary potential. However, it also exhibits the deep effects of sin. Christians are thus called to transform culture in the name of Christ. This book attempts to take just that approach, demonstrating the intrinsic, creational good that can be found in human culture while recognizing the deep effects of sin, and suggesting ways to transform American culture in the name of Jesus Christ, so that His Kingdom come, His will be done, on earth as it is in Heaven!

Introduction to American Literature

American Literature is a rhetoric-level course. Two things are distinctive about rhetoric-level courses: they are content-driven and they presume higher-level thinking. In most cases, you are going to have to read in excess of 200 pages per chapter. Therefore, it is highly advisable that you begin reading the material during the summer prior to beginning this course.

In any event, you must read the whole book/literary work before the lesson begins. Sometimes this is no big deal (e.g., reading Phillis Wheatley's poetry). In other cases it will take you more than a week to read the assigned text (e.g., *The Scarlet Letter*, Nathaniel Hawthorne).

By now you should already know how to do basic literary criticism. If you are worried, don't be. You will review how to do literary analysis as the course progresses. Literary analysis questions are the most often asked questions and they fall under the three main types of questions in the text: critical thinking, biblical application, and enrichment.

Literature is defined in *Merriam Webster's Collegiate Dictionary* (10th ed., 1993) as "writings in prose or verse: especially having excellence of form or expression and expressing ideas of permanent or universal interest."

The person who examines, interprets, and analyzes literature is a critic. That is your job. A critic is a guide to the reader, not a prophet or a therapist. While it is the critic's right to express his preferences, and even his privilege to influence others, it is not his job to tell the reader what to like or not like. However, the critic is a helper, a guide helping the reader to better understand the author's intention and art. In fact, the critic is concerned about the structure, sound, and meaning of the literary piece. These structures are described as genres: *narrative prose, essays, poetry*, and *drama*.

God is raising a mighty generation! You will be the culture-creators of the next century. You are a special generation, a special people. My prayer for each student who reads this course is:

I kneel before the Father, from whom his whole family in heaven and on earth derives its name. I pray that out of his glorious riches he may strengthen you with power through his Spirit in your inner being, so that Christ may dwell in your hearts through faith. And I pray that you, being rooted and established in love, may have power, together with all the saints, to grasp how wide and long and high and deep is the love of Christ, and to know this love that surpasses knowledge — that you may be filled to the measure of all the fullness of God. Now to him who is able to do immeasurably more than all we ask or imagine, according to his power that is at work within us, to him be glory in the church and in Christ Jesus throughout all generations, for ever and ever! Amen (Eph. 3:14–21).

Worldview Formation

First Thoughts From the beginning, America was an evangelical Christian nation — it built its universities to train Christian leaders, for it earnestly sought to be governed by and have its culture created by evangelical Christians. The now rapid retreat from that sacred beginning is perhaps the key to understanding the American experience.

Chapter Learning Objectives In chapter 1 we examine worldviews and grasp the import of being in a culture war. For the Christian believer, there is no middle ground anymore. We are in a war. This chapter examines seven worldviews and gives clues on how we can discern these worldviews in culture. You will learn to articulate your own worldview as you evaluate the veracity of other worldviews.

As a result of this chapter study you will be able to . . .

1. Compare several worldviews.

2. Compare the worldviews of John Smith and William Bradford.

3. Discuss if Old Testament law should have literal application to today's society.

4. Discern the worldviews of several television commercials.

Weekly Essay Options: Begin on page 274 of the Teacher Guide.

Reading ahead: *A Treatise Concerning Religious Affections*, by Jonathan Edwards, and poems by Anne Bradstreet.

Everyone Has a Worldview

The word "worldview" comes from the German word "weltanschauung," which is literally "world perception." One's worldview is formed early on by the values and principles of family and friends. It can be shaped further by peers, by personal experiences or observations, by social-religious organizations, as well as by the culture and media. Everyone has a worldview that reflects his or her personal bias in regard to the world based on both facts and personal opinion.

Throughout this course and your educational career you will be challenged to analyze the world-views of many writers. You will be asked to articulate and defend your own worldview against all sorts of assaults. William Bradford, for instance, has a worldview that is radically different from many writers you have read and hopefully similar to yours. What is Bradford's worldview? His worldview is obviously Christian theistic. For now, though, it is important that you pause and examine several worldviews that you will encounter in literature and the arts. You will then need to articulate your own worldview.

Developing a worldview: Consider how each of the following areas influences your personal belief system:

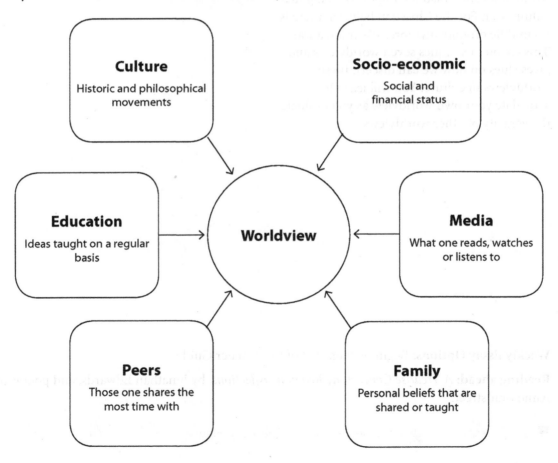

- Warm-up: Who is your favorite author and what do you think formed his or her worldview?
- Student should complete Concept Builder 1-A.
- Students should review the required reading(s) before the assigned chapter begins.
- Teachers shall assign the required essay. The rest of the essays can be outlined, answered with shorter answers, discussed, or skipped.

CONCEPT BUILDER 1-A
My Worldview

Outline a worldview for yourself.

Authority — Is the Bible important to you? Do you obey God and other authorities — your parents — even when doing so is uncomfortable?	
Pleasure — What do you really enjoy doing? Does it please God?	
Fate — What/who really determines your life? Chance? Circumstances? God?	
Justice — What are the consequences of our actions? Is there some sort of judgment? Do bad people suffer? Why do good people suffer?	

Worldviews Review

From the time of Aristotle and Plato a panoply of worldviews evolved into four main epochs.

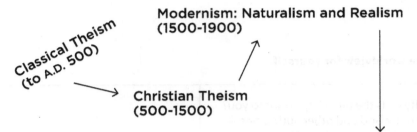

The following are characteristics of each epoch:

Classical Theism	Pernicious gods involved in human affairs
Christian Theism	Loving God involved in human affairs
Modernism	Faith in science
Post-Modernism	Faith in experience; suspicious of science

The four epochs above manifested seven basic worldviews. The worldviews are best discerned through works of art and of literature. The worldview of an artist/writer is a reflection of how the author expresses his views on essential issues like God, man, and morality.

Theism: Christian theism advances a worldview that there is an omnipotent God who has authored an inspired, authoritative work called the Bible, upon whose precepts mankind should base its society.

Deism: Deism advances a worldview that accepts the notion that there is an authoritative, inspired source from which mankind should base its society (i.e., the Bible). Likewise, the deist is certain that there was once an omnipotent God. However, once the world was created, that same omnipotent God chose to absent Himself from His creation. The world, then, is like a clock. It was once created by an intelligent process. However, now the Creator is absent, leaving mankind on its own to figure out how the clock works and go on living.

Romanticism: A natural companion to deism was rationalism. Rationalism (e.g., John Locke's philosophy) invited the deist to see mankind as a "chalkboard" on which was written experience that ultimately created a personality. Thus, rationalists/deists were fond of speaking of "unalienable right" or "common sense." The romantic (in America the romantic would be called "the transcendentalist") took issue with deism and theism. To the romantic, nature was god. Nature — an undefined indigenous, omnipotent presence — was very good. Original sin was man's separation from nature. In fact, the degree to which mankind returned to nature would determine his goodness and effectiveness. Thus, a man like Henry David Thoreau lived a year on Walden Pond so that he could find his God. In *The Deerslayer*, by James Fenimore Cooper, the protagonist is safe while he is on a lake separated from evil mankind. Only when he participates in human society is he in trouble. The romantic was naturally suspicious of theism because theism appeared to be dogmatic and close-minded. The romantics had confessions, but they had no dogma. Deism also bothered the romantics. Romanticism emphasized the subjective; deism emphasized the objective. In the romantic novel *Frankenstein*, the deist/rationalist Dr. Frankenstein creates a monster. Dr. Frankenstein, with disastrous results, turns his back on the subjective and tries to use science to create life.

Naturalism: Naturalism was inclined to agree with romanticism's criticism of theism and deism, but did not believe in a benevolent nature. In fact, nature, to the naturalist, was malevolent, mischievous, and unpredictable. Mankind, as it were, lost control of the universe and the person who had control did not really care much for his creation. Theism, of course, was absurd. How could any sane person who experienced World War I believe in a loving, living God? Deism was equally wrong. God was not absent — he was present in an unpredictable, at times evil, way. Romanticism was on the right track, but terribly naive. God and His creation were certainly not "good" in any sense of the word. Nature was evil. Naturalism embraced a concept of fate similar to that held by the Greeks. In Homer's *The Iliad*, for instance, the characters were subject to uncontrolled fate and pernicious gods and goddesses who inflicted terrible and good things on mankind with no apparent design or reason. No, to the naturalist, God was at best absent or wimpish; at worst, He was malevolent.

Realism: Realism was philosophically akin to naturalism. In a sense, naturalism was a natural companion to realism. Realism was different from naturalism in degree, not in substance. Realism argued that if people were honest they would admit that God was not present at all. If there was anything worth embracing, it was reality. Realism advanced an in-your-face view of life. Realists prided themselves in "telling it like it is." They entered the cosmic arena and let the chips fall where they may. They shared the same criticisms of views that the naturalists held.

Absurdism: Absurdism certainly believed that realism was on track. Where realism erred, however, was its propensity to see meaning in life. Mind you, the meaning was tied to things one could see and feel — not in things that were abstract or immutable — but the realist still sought some meaning in this life. The absurdist abandoned all hope of finding meaning in life and embraced a sort of nihilism. The absurdist was convinced that everything was meaningless and absurd. The subjectivity of a romantic was appealing to the absurd. However, even that implied that something was transcendent — a desire — and the absurdist would have nothing to do with that. Billy Pilgrim, a protagonist in one of the absurdist Kurt Vonnegut Jr.'s novels, became "unhinged from time" and "wandered around in the cosmos. Things without meaning happened to him whose life had no meaning. Everything was absurd.

Existentialism: Existentialism stepped outside the debate of meaning altogether. Existentialists argued that the quest was futile. The only thing that mattered was subjective feeling. "Experience" was a god at whose feet the existentialist worshiped. Romanticism was on the right track in that it invited mankind to explore subjectivity. Where it erred was when it refused to give up the deity. Naturalism was an anomaly. It was too busy arguing with the cosmos to see that reality was in human desire not in providence. The degree to which mankind was to discover and experience these desires determined the degree to which people participated in the divine.

Assignments

- Warm-up: Pretend a four-year-old family member has just watched a cartoon with too much violence. He/she is very sad. What do you say to him/her?
- Student should complete Concept Builder 1-B.
- Student should review reading(s) from next chapter.
- Student should outline essay due at the end of the week.
- Per teacher instructions, students may answer orally, in a group setting, the essays that are not assigned as formal essays.

CONCEPT BUILDER 1-B
Family Worldview

Encourage your family to write a joint worldview statement. Here is an example of the author's family worldview statement.

The Stobaugh Family Worldview Statement

We are called to live radical Christian lives as if we belong to God and not to ourselves (Gal. 2:20). Therefore, we will seek the Lord with all our heart — knowing He will be found. We will have a heart for the lost. He has given us the ministry of reconciliation; indeed, our family is an image of this reconciliation (Rom. 8; 2 Cor. 5). We will be His ambassadors. He has given us a family to raise and people to influence for Him. We want to be world changers. The job(s) that God has called us to do is requiring all we have and it is worthy of our best and total efforts.

In summary, henceforth the Stobaughs shall make decisions based on this mission statement — not on circumstances. Every new job or activity must further this mission statement or be rejected.

My Family Worldview Statement

General Statements:

Specific Statements:

Our Jobs (or Callings):

Summary:

Culture Wars: Part One

The following is a summary of early worldview philosophies:

Greek Mythology		The Greeks introduced the idea that the universe was orderly, that man's senses were valid, and, as a consequence, that man's proper purpose was to live his own life to the fullest.
The Phythagoreans	530 B.C.	Phythagoras was the first philosopher to require some standard of behavior from his followers. One can imagine what a novel and important step this was — that a religion would require a commitment from its adherents.
Ionian School	500 B.C.	The Ionian fascination with the physical world anticipated later discussions in Western philosophy.
The Eleatic School	500 B.C.	The Eleatic School argued that reality was indivisible and endless.
The Pluralists	500 B.C.	With no outside force in place, by chance the universe evolved from chaos to structure, and vice versa, in an eternal cycle.
The Sophists	500 B.C.	Ethical rules needed to be followed only when it was to one's practical advantage to do so. Goodness, morality, and ethics were a reflection of culture rather than vice versa.
Socrates	469–399 B.C.	For the first time, the importance of human language was advanced by a philosopher. The intellectual basis of virtue was stressed, identifying virtue with wisdom.
Plato	428 B.C.–?	"Love," to Plato, was a "form" from which virtue flowed.
Aristotle	350 B.C.–?	Aristotle was the first agnostic. Aristotle argued that reality lay in empirical, measurable knowledge. Aristotle, for the first time, discussed the gods as if they were quantified entities. He spoke about them as if they were not present.
Cynicism	350 B.C.	For the first time, philosophers began to talk about the individual in earnest, as if he were a subject to be studied.
Skepticism	300 B.C.	Skepticism maintained that human beings could know nothing of the real nature of things, and that consequently the wise person would give up trying to know anything.
Epicurianism	300 B.C.	The aim of human life, Epicurus claimed, was to achieve maximum pleasure with the least effort and risk.
Stoicism	300 B.C.	Stoicism celebrated the human spirit and it became the measuring rod against which all social and religious institutions were measured.
Neoplatonism	A.D. 50	Neoplatonism dared to speak of a religious experience as a philosophical phenomenon.
Augustine	A.D. 354–430	Augustine effectively articulated a theology and worldview for the Church as it journeyed into the inhospitable, post-Christian, barbarian era.
Scholasticism	A.D. 50	Scholasticism, with varying degrees of success, attempted to use natural human reason — in particular, the philosophy and science of Aristotle — to understand the metaphysical content of Christian revelation.

- Warm-up: Some artists claim that obscenity is necessary to the "artistic effect." Is there such a thing as "necessary obscenity"?
- Students should complete Concept Builder 1-C.
- Students should write rough drafts of assigned essay.
- The teacher may correct rough drafts.

CONCEPT BUILDER 1-C
Values

Worldviews are about values. Rate the following items: 1 equals "do not value at all"; 5 equals "value a whole lot."

Value	Myself	My Parents	My Grandparents
Psychology			
Money			
The Lawrence Welk Show			
Winning sports teams			
Snow days			
Opinions of friends			
Church/temple/other religious events			
Vacation			
A rock/hip hop/rap concert			
Watching a ballet			
Visiting relatives			
Reading good books			
Watching television			
Doing chores/jobs			
Easter			
Being honest			
Elves			

Culture Wars: Part Two

The following is a summary of more modern worldview philosophies:

Erasmus	1466–1536	Erasmus, for the first time, discussed things like happiness as being centered in the self or personhood of the man or woman. Happiness was based on some narcissist notions of self-love.
Michel de Montaigne	1533–1592	Montaigne re-introduced Greek skepticism to Western culture.
Frances Bacon	1561–1626	Bacon advanced vigorously the idea that reasoning must triumph over theology.
Thomas Hobbes	1588–1679	Hobbes was one of the first modern Western thinkers to provide a secular justification for political power.
Rene Descartes	1596–1650	After Descartes, mankind replaced God as the center of the universe in the minds of many. This was an ominous moment in Western culture.
Benedictus de Spinoza	1732–1677	Spinoza argued that human morality arose from self-interest.
John Locke	1632–1704	Locke believed in reasoning and common sense, rather than in metaphysics.
G. W. Leibniz	1646–1716	Leibniz believed in a God who created a world separate from His sovereignty.
George Berkeley	1685–1753	Berkeley called "intuition" the voice of God to mankind.
Davie Hume	1711–1726	Hume, for the first time in Western history, seriously suggested that there was no necessary connection between cause and effect.
Immanuel Kant	1724–1804	Kant argued that reality was experience. If one could not experience something with his senses, then it was not real.
Jean Jacques Rousseau	1712–1778	Rousseau advocated one of the first "back-to-nature" movements.
William Godwin	1756–1836	The notion that there were individual rights, or a codex of governing laws, was anathema to Godwin.
Soren Kierkegaard	1813–1855	Kiergegaard explained life in terms of logical necessity; a means of avoiding choice and responsibility.
G.W.F. Hegel	1770–1831	Truth had no application if there were not opposites warring for its reality.

Karl Marx	1818–1883	To the Hegelian Marx, Christianity was a fairy tale created to placate weak people.
Pierre Joseph Proudhon	1809–1865	Proudhon instituted the last serious philosophical attempt to undermine the human will as a determining factor in human decision-making.
Arthur Schopenhauer	1788–1860	The human will, with all its chauvinism and narcissism, was the most powerful human impulse.
Herbert Spencer	1820–1903	Spencer argued that in biological sciences and in the social sciences the fittest and the strongest survived.
Frederich Nietzsche	1844–1890	Nietzsche believed that the collapse of the religious impulse left a huge vacuum. The history of modern times is in great part the history of how that vacuum is filled.
Martin Heidegger	1889–1976	The meaning of the world must be discovered outside human experience.
Jean Paul Sartre	1905–1980	People exist in a world of their own making.
Simone De Beauvoir	1906–1986	Beauvoir was an advocate of "free love" and completely rejected the biblical understanding of marriage, which she saw as an oppressive institution.
John Dewey	1859–1952	Truth to Dewey was a reflection of circumstances and contingencies.
Bertrand Russell	1872–1970	If an actual event could not be quantified or repeated, then it was not real.
John Stuart Mill	1806–1873	To Mill, the individual and his needs were paramount.
Max Weber	1864–1920	The notion that God was pleased with hard work and frugal living assured a healthy maturation of society.
Ludwig Wittgenstein	1889–1951	If a person could not speak it, it was not real.
Richard Rorty	1931–2007	Truth to Rorty was what we all agree is truth, and what we agree is truth is more a reflection of circumstances than it is any absolute or objective reality outside mankind's experience.
Alfred North Whitehead	1861–1947	The agnostic Whitehead believed in God — if a decidedly anemic God.
Jacques Derrida	1930–2004	Derrida argued that most of us merely play language games. Every utterance is a move in a language game.
Jean Baudrillard	1929–2007	Reality to Baudrillard was not necessarily defined by human language: it was defined by the public media.
Jurgen Habermas	1929–	Habermas has resurrected the works of Plato and other metaphysicists and has taken philosophy away from language and communication and has taken it back to a discussion of rationality.
Viktor E. Frankl	1905–1997	Man was now the result of a purposeless and materialistic process that did not have him in mind.

- Warm-up: Is it possible for Christians to lose the culture war? How?
- Student should complete Concept Builder 1-D.
- Student will re-write corrected copy of essay due tomorrow.

CONCEPT BUILDER 1-D
Movies

America obtains most of its worldviews from movies. Check the worldviews represented in the following popular movies. There will be multiple correct answers.

Movie	Theism	Deism	Romanticism	Naturalism	Realism	Extentlalism	Absurdism
Bambi							
Titantic							
Toy Story							
Lion King							
The Sound of Music							
The Incredibles							

Worldview Review

Recreate this chart with your responses on a seperate sheet of paper, define the basic influences that develop your personal worldview:

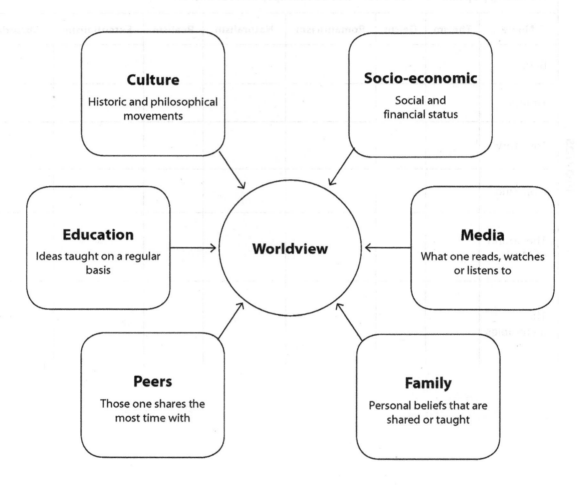

Determine if these sources influence you in positive or negative ways.

Based on the worldview chart, develop your own system to determine the worldview of the notions and beliefs you come across each day through various media and personal interactions. Remember, everyone has a worldview by which they interpret the world.

Assignments

- Warm-up: Describe one of the worldviews in your own words
- Student should complete Concept Builder 1-E.
- Essay is due. Students should take the chapter 1 test.

CONCEPT BUILDER 1-E
Books

The following books are very popular in American high schools. Check the worldviews represented in the following popular titles. There will be multiple correct answers.

Movie	Theism	Deism	Romanticism	Naturalism	Realism	Extentlalism	Absurdism
Romeo and Juliet							
Johnny Tremain							
Walden							
Call of the Wild							
Poems by Robert Frost							
The Book of Job (Bible)							

Chapter 2

The New Land to 1750:

Puritanism & Native American Voices

First Thoughts

Puritanism was a religious reform movement in the late 16th and 17th centuries that sought to "purify" the Church of England of remnants of Roman Catholicism. A radical form of Puritanism was Separatism, embraced by the Pilgrims. Puritans became noted in the 17th century for a spirit of moral and religious earnestness that affected their whole way of life, and they sought to make their lifestyle the pattern for the whole new world. Their culture, art and literature, then, reflect this earnestness and the reader will experience anew the vitality and pathos of a people mostly misunderstood.

Author Worldview Watch

William Bradford was a strong Christian, whose orthodox faith, Christian theism, was only rivaled by his extensive knowledge of Greek history and philosophy. Bradford, Cotton Mather, Anne Bradstreet built this great nation and we all owe them a debt of gratitude. The Native Americans whom they encountered were stanch polytheists, but soon many responded to the Gospel and American literature began.

Chapter Learning Objectives

In chapter 2 we will look more closely at the writings of William Bradford and Edward Taylor. We will look at Mourt's Relations, the Mayflower Compact, and a portion of a speech by John Winthrop. Next, we will examine Native American literature, including Creation Narratives and a portion of the Iroquois Constitution. We will be amazed again at the beginnings that so richly blessed our great nation.

As a result of this chapter study you will be able to . . .

1. Understand what William Bradford's view of nature was.

2. Compare and contrast Edward Taylor's poetry with British metaphysical poetry.

3. Define and discover allusions in William Bradford's *Of Plimoth Plantation.*

4. Compare and contrast Native American views of mankind with biblical views

Weekly Essay Options: Begin on page 274 of the Teacher Guide.

Reading ahead: No readings are necessary for chapter 2. Students should review Jonathan Edwards, *A Treatise Concerning Religious Affections* (Philadelphia, PA: Printed for Mathew Carey, 1794) for chapter 3.

 History connections: *American History* chapter 2, "Slavery and Religious Freedom."

Background

The Puritan Separatists, incorrectly called *Pilgrims* by later generations, were members of a religious sect called *Puritans*. They separated from the Church of England and thus were called *Separatist Puritans*. Other Puritans — who settled in the Boston area — sought to *purify* the church, not to *withdraw* from it. They were merely called Puritans. The Separatists included those who settled at Plymouth, Massachusetts in 1620. The Puritans settled in Boston in 1630.

The Plymouth settlers included both religious saints — the Separatist Puritans — and secular adventurers. The Puritans as well as the Separatist Puritans, then, were fervently religious people with a firm belief in God's omnipotence and in His abiding love. In this section we will look at several examples of Puritan literature. Most of us think of Puritans as colorless, unhappy, stuffy white-collared, black-coated, frowning saints. Nothing could be further from the truth. They were fun-loving, active people whose love of life was surpassed only by their love of God. Actually, the Puritan civilization was a successful marriage between cultural sonority and Christian devotion.

Puritanism, a movement arising within the Church of England in the latter part of the 16th century, sought to carry the reformation of that church beyond the point the early Anglican or Church of England had reached. The Church of England was attempting to establish a middle course between Roman Catholicism and the ideas of the Protestant reformers. This was unacceptable to a growing number of Puritan reformers, who wanted the Church of England to reject Anglicanism and embrace Calvinism. The term "Puritanism" was also used in a broader sense to refer to attitudes and values considered characteristic of these radical reformers. Thus, the Separatists in the 16th century, the Quakers in the 17th century, and Nonconformists after the Restoration were called Puritans, although they were no longer part of the established church. For our purposes, though, we will refer to the Puritans in two ways: Puritans and Pilgrims.

Like the Puritan Separatists, the Puritans of Boston in 1630 arrived in Massachusetts Bay. They had sailed to America to worship God freely. The Puritans did not desire to separate themselves from the Church of England but, rather, hoped to reform it. Nonetheless, the notions of freedom and equality, so precious to later New England patriots, were completely foreign to Puritan leaders. The leaders of the Massachusetts Bay enterprise never intended their colony to be a bastion of freedom and tolerance in the New World; rather, they intended it to be a "City on a Hill," a model of Christian felicity and enthusiasm.

"City Upon a Hill," a speech by Massachusetts Bay's first governor, John Winthrop, in 1630 is a remarkable testimony to the spiritual roots of our country.

Now the onely way to avoyde this ship-wracke and to provide for our posterity is to followe the Counsell of Micah, to doe Justly, to love mercy, to walke humbly with our

John Calvin believed that salvation was accomplished by the almighty power of the triune God. The Father chose a people, the Son died for them, the Holy Spirit makes Christ's death effective by bringing the elect to faith and repentance, thereby causing them willingly to obey the gospel. The entire process (election, redemption, regeneration) was the work of God and was by grace alone. Thus God, not man, determined who would be the recipients of the gift of salvation.

God, for this end, wee must be knitt together in this worke as one man, wee must entertaine each other in brotherly Affeccion, wee must be willing to abridge our selves of our superfluities, for the supply of others necessities, wee must uphold a familiar Commerce together in all meekenes, gentlenes, patience and liberallity, wee must delight in eache other, make others Condicions our owne rejoyce together, mourne together, labour, and suffer together, allwayes haveing before our eyes our Commission and Community in the worke, our Community as members of the same body, soe shall wee keepe the unitie of the spirit in the bond of peace, the Lord will be our God and delight to dwell among us, as his owne people and will commaund a blessing upon us in all our wayes, soe that wee shall see much more of his wisdome power goodnes and truthe then formerly wee have beene acquainted with, wee shall finde that the God of Israell is among us, when tenn of us shall be able to resist a thousand of our enemies, when hee shall make us a prayse and glory, that men shall say of succeeding plantacions: the lord make it like that of New England: for wee must Consider that wee shall be as a Citty upon a Hill, the eies of all people are uppon us; soe that if wee shall deale falsely with our god in this worke wee have undertaken and soe cause him to withdrawe his present help from us, wee shall be made a story and a byword through the world, wee shall open the mouthes of enemies to speake evill of the wayes of god and all professours for Gods sake; wee shall shame the faces of many of gods worthy servants, and cause theire prayers to be turned into Cursses upon us till wee be consumed out of the good land whether wee are going: And to shutt upp this discourse with that exhortacion of Moses that faithfull servant of the Lord in his last farewell to Israell Deut. 30. Beloved there is now sett before us life, and good, deathe and evill in that wee are

"Embarkation of the Pilgrims," by Robert Walter Weir (c1857, US-PD). William Bradford is depicted at center, kneeling in the background, symbolically behind Gov. John Carver (holding hat) whom Bradford would succeed.

Commaunded this day to love the Lord our God, and to love one another to walke in his wayes and to keepe his Commaundements and his Ordinance, and his lawes, and the Articles of our Covenant with him that wee may live and be multiplyed, and that the Lord our God may blesse us in the land whether wee goe to possesse it: But if our heartes shall turne away soe that wee will not obey, but shall be seduced and worshipp other Gods our pleasures, and proffitts, and serve them, it is propounded unto us this day, wee shall surely perishe out of the good Land whether wee passe over this vast Sea to possesse it;

Therefore lett us choose life,

that wee, and our Seede,

may live; by obeyeing his voyce,

and cleaveing to him,

for hee is our life, and our prosperity (theroadupward.com/archives/1889).

Assignments

- Warm-up: When you hear the word "Puritan" what do you think?

- Student should complete Concept Builder 2-A.

- Students should review the required reading(s) *before* the assigned chapter begins.

- Teachers may want to discuss assigned reading(s) with students.

- Teachers shall assign the required essay. The rest of the essays can be outlined, answered with shorter answers, discussed, or skipped.

- Students will review all readings for chapter 2.

CONCEPT BUILDER 2-A

Read the excerpt of *History of Plimoth Plantation* by William Bradford, then answer the following questions.

1	What is the narrative technique? What are advantages and disadvantages of using this narrative technique?
2	Who is the speaker and what can you surmise about his character?
3	Predict what will happen when the Pilgrims land on Cape Cod.
4	What is the setting and is the setting important?
5	How does Bradford present the Native Americans?
6	How reliable or credible is this narrator? Defend your answer.

The History of Plimoth Plantation
William Bradford

William Bradford went with his separatist English friends (called *Pilgrims*) for an 11-year stay in Holland. Later the pilgrims returned to England. In 1620 he lead the historic Pilgrim group when it sailed from England to settle at Plymouth. William Bradford's *The History of Plimoth Plantation* is best termed a chronicle, a non-fictional literary genre showing a factual record of events in chronological order.

The following is a copy of chapter 9, *The History of Plimoth Plantation* (www.gutenberg.org/catalog/world/readfile?fk_files=1538426).

September 6 (1620). These troubles being blown over, and now all being compact together in one ship, they put to sea again with a prosperous wind, which continued divers days together, which was some encouragement unto them; yet according to the usual manner many were afflicted with sea sickness. And I may not omit here a special work of God's providence. There was a proud and very profane young man, one of the sea-men, of a lusty, able body, which made him the more haughty; he would always be condemning the poor people in their sickness, and cursing them daily with grievous execrations, and did not let to tell them, that he hoped to help to cast half of them overboard before they came to their journey's end, and to make merry with what they had; and if he were by any gently reproved, he would curse and swear most bitterly. But it pleased God before they came half seas over, to smite this young man with a grievous disease, of which he died in a desperate manner, and so was himself the first that was thrown overboard. Thus his curses light on his own head; and it was an astonishment to all his fellows, for they noted it to be the just hand of God upon him.

After they had enjoyed fair winds and weather for a season, they were encountered many times with cross winds, and met with many fierce storms, with which the ship was shroudly shaken, and her upper works made very leaky; and one of the main beams in the mid ships was bowed and cracked, which put them in some fear that the ship could not be able to perform the voyage. So some of the chief of the company, perceiving the mariners to fear the sufficiency of the ship, as appeared by their mutterings, they entered into serious consultation with the master and other officers of the ship, to consider in time of the danger; and rather to return then to cast themselves into a desperate and inevitable peril. And truly there was great distraction and difference of opinion among the mariners themselves; fain would they do what could be done for their wages sake (being now half the seas over), and on the other hand they were loath to hazard their lives too desperately.

But in examining of all opinions, the master and others affirmed they knew the ship to be strong and firm under water; and for the buckling of the main beam, there was a great iron screw the passengers brought out of Holland, which would raise the beam into his place; the which being done, the carpenter and master affirmed that with a post put under it, set firm in the lower deck, and other-ways bound, he would make it sufficient. And as for the decks and upper works they would caulk them as well as they could, and though with the working of the ship they would not long keep staunch, yet there would otherwise be no great danger, if they did not over-press her with sails. So they committed themselves to the will of God, and resolved to proceed. In sundry of these storms the winds were so fierce, and the seas so high, as they could not bear a knot of sail, but were forced to hull, for divers days together. And in one of them, as they thus lay at hull, in a mighty storm, a lusty young man (called John Howland) coming upon some occasion above the gratings, was, with a seele of the ship thrown into the sea; but it pleased God that he caught hold of the topsail halyards, which hung overboard, and ran out at length; yet he held his hold (though he was sundry fathoms under water) till he was hauled up by the same rope to the brim of the water, and then with a boat hook and other means got into the ship again, and his life saved; and though he was something ill with it, yet he lived many years after, and became a profitable member both in church and commonwealth. In all this voyage their died but one of the passengers, which was William Butten, a youth, servant to Samuel Fuller, when they drew near the coast. But to omit other things (that I may be brief), after long beating at sea they fell with that land which is called Cape Cod; the which being made and certainly known to be it, they were not a little joyful. After some deliberation had amongst themselves and with the master of the ship, they tacked about and resolved to stand for the southward (the wind and weather being fair) to find some place about Hudson's River for their habitation.

But after they had sailed that course about half a day, they fell amongst dangerous shoals and roaring breakers, and they were so far entangled therewith as they conceived themselves in great danger; and the wind shrinking upon them withal, they resolved to bear up again for the Cape, and thought themselves happy to get out of those dangers before night overtook them, as by God's providence they did. And the next day they got into the Cape-harbor where they rid in safety. A word or two by the way of this cape; it was thus first named by Captain Gosnold and his company, Anno. 1602, and after by Captain Smith was called Cape James; but it retains the former name amongst seamen. Also that point which first showed these dangerous shoals unto them, they called Point Care, and Tucker's Terror; but the French and Dutch to this day call it Malabar, by reason of those perilous shoals, and the losses they have suffered there.

Being thus arrived in a good harbor and brought safe to land, they fell upon their knees and blessed the God of heaven, who had brought them over the vast and furious ocean, and delivered them from all the perils and miseries thereof, again to set their feet on the firm and stable earth, their proper element. And no marvel if they were thus joyful, seeing wise Seneca was so affected with sailing a few miles on the coast of his own Italy; as he affirmed, that he had rather remain twenty years on his way by land, then pass by sea to any place in a short time; so tedious and dreadful was the same unto him.

But here I cannot but stay and make a pause, and stand half amazed at this poor people's present condition; and so I think will the reader too, when he well considers the same. Being thus passed the vast ocean, and a sea of troubles before in their preparation (as may be remembered by that which went before), they had now no friends to welcome them, nor inns to entertain or refresh their weatherbeaten bodies, no houses or much less towns to repair to, to seek for succor. It is recorded in scripture as a mercy to the apostle and his shipwrecked company, that the barbarians showed no small kindness in refreshing them, but these savage barbarians, when they met with them (as after will appear) were readier to fill their sides full of arrows then otherwise. And for the season it was winter, and they that know the winters of that country know them to be sharp and violent and subject to cruel and fierce storms, dangerous to travel to known places, much more to search an unknown coast. Besides, what could they see but a hideous and desolate wilderness, full of wild beasts and wild men? and what multitudes there might be of them they knew not. Neither could they, as it were, go up to the top of Pigsah, to view from this wilderness a more goodly country to feed their hopes; for which way soever they turned their eyes (save upward to the heavens) they could have little solace or content in respect of any outward objects. For summer being done, all things stand upon them with a weatherbeaten face; and the whole country, full of woods and thickets, represented a wild and savage hew. If they looked behind them, there was the mighty ocean which they had passed, and was now as a main bar and gulf to separate them from all the civil parts of the world. If it be said they had a ship to succor them, it is true; but what heard they daily from the master and company? But that with speed they should look out a place with their shallop, where they would be at some near distance; for the season was such as he would not stir from thence till a safe harbor was discovered by them where they would be, and he might go without danger; and that victuals consumed apace, but he must and would keep sufficient for themselves and their return. Yea, it was muttered by some, that if they got not a place in time, they would turn them and their goods ashore and leave them. Let it also be considered what weak hopes of supply and succor they left behind them, that might bear up their minds in this sad condition and trials they were under; and they could not but be very small. It is true, indeed, the affections and love of their brethren at Leyden was cordial and entire towards them, but they had little power to help them, or themselves; and how the case stood between them and the merchants at their coming away, hath already been declared. What could now sustain them but the spirit of God and his grace?

May not and ought not the children of these fathers rightly say: "Our fathers were Englishmen which came over this great ocean, and were ready to perish in this wilderness; but they cried unto the Lord, and he heard their voice, and looked on their adversity, etc. Let them therefore praise the Lord, because he is good, and his mercies endure forever. Yea, let them which have been redeemed of the Lord, show how he hath delivered them from the hand of the oppressor. When they wandered in the desert wilderness out of the way, and found no city to dwell in, both hungry, and thirsty, their soul was overwhelmed in them. Let them confess before the Lord his loving kindness, and his wonderful works before the sons of men.

Mourt's Relation was written by Edward Winslow, although many scholars argue that William Bradford collaborated. Written between November 1620 and November 1621, it describes in detail what happened to the Pilgrims. It is the only extant version of the first "Thanksgiving" that exists. Why is it called *Mourt's Relation*? *Mourt's Relation* was first published in London in 1622, presumably by George Morton (hence the title, *Mourt's Relation,* www.histarch.uiuc.edu/plymouth/mourt1.html).

Wednesday, the sixth of September, the winds coming east north east, a fine small gale, we loosed from Plymouth, having been kindly entertained and courteously used by divers friends there dwelling, and after many difficulties in boisterous storms, at length, by God's providence, upon the ninth of November following, by break of the day we espied land which was deemed to be Cape Cod, and so afterward it proved. And the appearance of it much comforted us, especially seeing so goodly a land, and wooded to the brink of the sea. It caused us to rejoice together, and praise God that had given us once again to see land. And thus we made our course south south west, purposing to go to a river ten leagues to the south of the Cape, but at night the wind being contrary, we put round again for the bay of Cape Cod; and upon the 11th of November we came to an anchor in the bay, which is a good harbor and pleasant bay, circled round, except in the entrance which is about four miles over from land to land, compassed about to the very sea with oaks, pines, juniper, sassafras, and other sweet wood; it is a harbor wherein a thousand sail of ships may safely ride: there we relieved ourselves with wood and water, and refreshed our people, which our shallop was fitted to coast the bay, to search for a habitation; there was the greatest store of fowl that ever we saw.

And every day we saw whales playing hard by us, of which in that place, if we had instruments and means to take them, we might have made a very rich return, which to our great grief we wanted. Our master and his mate, and others experienced in fishing, professed we might have made three or four thousand pounds worth of oil; they preferred it before Greenland whale-fishing, and purpose the next winter to fish for whale here. For cod we assayed, but found none, there is good store, no doubt, in their season. Neither got we any fish all the time we lay there, but some few little ones on the shore. We found great mussels, and very fat and full of sea-pearl, but we could not eat them, for they made us all sick that did eat, as well sailors as passengers; they caused to cast and scour, but they were soon well again.

The bay is so round and circling, that before we could come to anchor we went round all the points of the compass. We could not come near the shore by three quarters of an English mile, because of shallow water, which was a great prejudice to us, for our people going on shore were forced to wade a bow shot or two in going a-land, which caused many to get colds and coughs, for it was nigh times freezing cold weather.

This day before we came to harbor, observing some not well affected to unity and concord, but gave some appearance of faction, it was thought good there should be an association and agreement that we should combine together in one body, and to submit to such government and governors as we should by common consent agree to make and choose, and set our hands to this that follows word for word.

Assignments

- Warm-up: Pretend that you are part of an expedition to Mars. What similarities do you find to Bradford's diary?

- Student should complete Concept Builder 2-B.

- Student should review reading(s) from next chapter.

- Student should outline essays due at the end of the week.

- Per teacher instructions, students may answer orally, in a group setting, some of the essays that are not assigned as the formal essay.

CONCEPT BUILDER 2-B
Allusions

An allusion is a brief, often indirect reference to a person, place, event, or artistic work which the author assumes the reader will recognize. Find two allusions in *Of Plimoth Plantation* and give its description.

It is recorded in Scripture as a mercy to the Apostle and his shipwrecked company, that the barbarians showed them no small kindness in refreshing them, but these savage barbarians, when they met with them (as after will appear) were readier to fill their sides full of arrows than otherwise.

This is a comparison of the Pilgrim landing at Cape Cod and first encounter with Native Amerians to Paul's shipwreck on Malta.

In Love with God

Edward Taylor (1642–1729) was a New England Puritan's Puritan. Taylor was a colleague of the famous Increase Mather. American critic Donald Stanford says, "Taylor seems to have been endowed with most of those qualities usually connoted by the word puritan. He was learned, grave, severe, stubborn, and stiff-necked. He was very, very pious. But his piety was sincere. It was fed by a long continuous spiritual experience arising, so he felt, from a mystical communion with Christ. The reality and depth of this experience is amply witnessed by his poetry" (Donald E. Stanford, *The Poems of Edward Taylor*, unc press, xxiii).

It was his custom to write a poem ("Meditation") before each Lord's Supper. These poems are wonderful examples of spiritual experience and devotion. Some readers are embarrassed by Taylor's raw intimacy with our Lord!

Meditation 1

What Love is this of thine, that Cannot bee

In thine Infinity, O Lord, Confinde,

Unless it in thy very Person see,

Infinity, and Finity Conjoyn'd?

What hath thy Godhead, as not satisfide

Marri'de our Manhood, making it its Bride?

Oh, Matchless Love! filling Heaven to the brim!

O're running it: all running o're beside

This World! Nay Overflowing Hell; wherein

For thine Elect, there rose a mighty Tide!

That there our Veans might through thy Person bleed,

To quench those flames, that else would on us feed.

www.puritansermons.com/poetry/taylor7.htm

I can clearly remember a day when as a young graduate student at Harvard University in the mid-1970s, surrounded by ivy-covered brick walls, slightly east from Sevier Hall, I stood in Harvard Yard looking at a statue of John Harvard and wondered what had gone wrong. All around me was nihilism and chaos, intellectual pretension and mendacity. Where was the beautiful simplicity and intellectual integrity of the Puritan John Harvard who had founded Harvard College in 1636? Then, to my wonder and surprise, I heard an old praise song. "We are one in the Spirit, we are one in the Lord. . . ." It was coming from the Dunster House, which apparently not only had the best breakfast in the yard (i.e., Harvard Yard), but also had a thriving Christian fellowship. Yes, God was very much alive at Harvard University. These saints were the spiritual children of John Harvard, the very reason he founded this august institution.

- Warm-up: Write a letter to God.

- Student should complete Concept Builder 2-C.

- Students should write rough draft of assigned essay.

- The teacher may correct rough draft.

CONCEPT BUILDER 2-C
MAKING GENERALIZATIONS

Generalizations are broad statements about a subject that are inferred from a number of facts and observations. For example "Snowfall will generate many auto accidents" is a generalizaiton that will have to be supported by facts and observations. Give two other facts/observations that lead you to these generalizations.

OF PLIMOTH PLANTATION

Fact/Observation	The weather is harsh and bitter.
Fact/Observation	
Fact/Observation	

↓

Generalization: The Pilgrims are facing a terrible winter in the new land.

Native American Voices

It would be a mistake to think of Native American peoples as being one people, one nation. In fact, dozens of Native American tribes lived along the eastern seaboard and warred against one another.

The main Native American tribe in the Virginia area in the early 17th century was the Lenape Powhatan Tribe. By the time the English colonists had arrived, the chief of the Powhatans, Chief Powhatan, ruled a formidable 30-tribe confederacy. He allegedly controlled 128 villages with about 9,000 inhabitants. Powhatan initially opposed the English settlement at Jamestown. According to legend, he changed his policy in 1607 when he released the captured Smith. In April 1614, Pocahontas, Powhatan's daughter, married the planter John Rolfe, and afterward Powhatan negotiated a peace agreement with his son-in-law's people.

Peace reigned until after Powhatan died in 1618. In 1622 a great war broke out between the English settlers and the Powhatan Confederacy. Initially the Powhatan Confederation very nearly destroyed the Jamestown settlement. In the long term, however, the war destroyed the Confederacy as a viable entity.

The main Native American tribe that the Pilgrims (i.e., Separatist Puritans) encountered, were the Wampanoag. In 1600 the Wampanoag probably were as many as 12,000 with 40 villages divided roughly between 8,000 on the mainland and another 4,000 on the offshore islands of Martha's Vineyard and Nantucket. However, epidemics swept across New England between 1614 and 1620 and devastated the Wampanoag. Thus, when the Pilgrims landed in 1620, fewer than 2,000 Wampanoag had survived.

The following story exemplifies most Native American creation legends (www.livinginthelightms.com/navahocreation.html). Contrast this legend with the biblical account of creation in Genesis chapters 1 and 2.

Navajo Creation Legend

These stories were told to Sandoval, Hastin Tlo'tsi hee, by his grandmother, Esdzan Hosh kige. Her ancestor was Esdzan at a', the medicine woman who had the Calendar Stone in her keeping. Here are the stories of the Four Worlds that had no sun, and of the Fifth, the world we live in, which some call the Changeable World (www.livinginthelightms.com/navahocreation.html).

The First World, Ni'hodilqil, was black as black wool. It had four corners, and over these appeared four clouds. These four clouds contained within themselves the elements of the First World. They were in color, black, white, blue, and yellow.

The Black Cloud represented the Female Being or Substance. For as a child sleeps when being nursed, so life slept in the darkness of the Female Being. The White Cloud represented the Male Being or Substance. He was the Dawn, the Light-Which-Awakens, of the First World.

In the East, at the place where the Black Cloud and the White Cloud met, First Man, Atse'hastqin was formed; and with him was formed the white corn, perfect in shape, with kernels covering the whole ear. Dolionot i'ni is the name of this first seed corn, and it is also the name of the place where the Black Cloud and the White Cloud met.

The First World was small in size, a floating island in mist or water. On it there grew one tree, a pine tree, which was later brought to the present world for firewood.

Man was not, however, in his present form. The conception was of a male and a female being who were to become man and woman. The creatures of the First World are thought of as the Mist People; they had no definite form, but were to change to men, beasts, birds, and reptiles of this world.

Now on the western side of the First World, in a place that later was to become the Land of Sunset, there appeared the Blue Cloud, and opposite it there appeared the Yellow Cloud. Where they came together First Woman was formed, and with her the yellow corn. This ear of corn was also perfect. With First Woman there came the white shell and the turquoise and the yucca.

First Man stood on the eastern side of the First World. He represented the Dawn and was the Life Giver. First Woman stood opposite in the West. She represented Darkness and Death.

First Man burned a crystal for a fire. The crystal belonged to the male and was the symbol of the mind and of clear seeing. When First Man burned it, it was the mind's awakening. First Woman burned her turquoise for a fire. They saw each other's lights in the distance. When the Black Cloud and the White Cloud rose higher in the sky First Map. set out to find the turquoise light. He went twice without success, and again a third time; then he broke a forked branch from his tree, and, looking through the fork, he marked the place where the light burned. And the fourth time he walked to it and found smoke coming from a home.

"Here is the home I could not find," First Man said.

First Woman answered: "Oh, it is you. I saw you walking around and I wondered why you did not come."

Again the same thing happened when the Blue Cloud and the Yellow Cloud rose higher in the sky. First Woman saw a light and she went out to find it. Three times she was unsuccessful, but the fourth time she saw the smoke and she found the home of First Man.

"I wondered what this thing could be," she said.

"I saw you walking and I wondered why you did not come to me," First Man answered.

First Woman saw that First Man had a crystal for a fire, and she saw that it was stronger than her turquoise fire. And as she was thinking, First Man spoke to her. "Why do you not come with your fire and we will live together." The woman agreed to this. So instead of the man going to the woman, as is the custom now, the woman went to the man.

About this time there came another person, the Great-Coyote-Who-Was-Formed-in-the-Water, and he was in the form of a male being. He told the two that he had been hatched from an egg. He knew all that was under the water and all that was in the skies. First Man placed this person ahead of himself in all things. The three began to plan what was to come to pass; and while they were thus occupied another being came to them. He also had the form of a man, but he wore a hairy coat, lined with white fur, that fell to his knees and was belted in at the waist. His name was Atse'hashke, First Angry or Coyote. He said to the three: "You believe that you were the first persons. You are mistaken. I was living when you were formed."

Then four beings came together. They were yellow in color and were called the tsts'na, or wasp people. They knew the secret of shooting evil and could harm others. They were very powerful.

This made eight people.

Four more beings came. They were small in size and wore red shirts and had little black eyes. They were the naazo'zi or spider ants. They knew how to sting, and were a great people.

After these came a whole crowd of beings. Dark colored they were, with thick lips and dark, protruding eyes. They were the wolazhi'ni, the black ants. They also knew the secret of shooting evil and were powerful; but they killed each other steadily.

By this time there were many people. Then came a multitude of little creatures. They were peaceful and harmless, but the odor from them was unpleasant. They were called the wolazhi'ni nlchu nigi, meaning that which emits an odor.

And after the wasps and the different ant people there came the beetles, dragonflies, bat people, the Spider Man and Woman, and the Salt Man and Woman, and others that rightfully had no definite form but were among those people who peopled the First World. And this world, being small in size, became crowded, and the people quarreled and fought among themselves, and in all ways made living very unhappy.

Because of the strife in the First World, First Man, First Woman, the Great-Coyote-Who-Was-Formed-in-the-Water, and the Coyote called First

Angry, followed by all the others, climbed up from the World of Darkness and Dampness to the Second or Blue World.

They found a number of people already living there: blue birds, blue hawks, blue jays, blue herons, and all the blue-feathered beings. The powerful swallow people lived there also, and these people made the Second World unpleasant for those who had come from the First World. There was fighting and killing.

The First Four found an opening in the World of Blue Haze; and they climbed through this and led the people up into the Third or Yellow world.

The bluebird was the first to reach the Third or Yellow World. After him came the First Four and all the others.

A great river crossed this land from north to south. It was the Female River. There was another river crossing it from east to West, it was the Male River. This Male River flowed through the Female River and on; and the name of this place is tqo alna'osdli, the Crossing of the waters.

There were six mountains in the Third World. In the East was Sis na' jin, the Standing Black Sash. Its ceremonial name is Yolgai'dzil, the Dawn or White Shell Mountain. In the South stood Tso'dzil, the Great Mountain, also called Mountain Tongue. Its ceremonial name is Yodolt i'zhi dzil, the Blue Bead or Turquoise Mountain. In the West stood Dook'oslid, and the meaning of this name is forgotten. Its ceremonial name is Dichi'li dzil, the Abalone Shell Mountain. In the North stood Debe'ntsa, Many Sheep Mountain. Its ceremonial name is Bash'zhini dzil, Obsidian Mountain. Then there was Dzil na'odili, the Upper Mountain. It was very sacred; and its name means also the Center Place, and the people moved around it. Its ceremonial name is Ntl'is dzil, Precious Stone or Banded Rock Mountain. There was still another mountain called Chol'i'i or Dzil na'odili choli, and it was also a sacred mountain.

There was no sun in this land, only the two rivers and the six mountains. And these rivers and mountains were not in their present form, but rather the substance of mountains and rivers as were First Man, First Woman, and the others.

Now beyond Sis na' jin, in the east, there lived the Turquoise Hermaphrodite, Ashton nutli. He was also known as the Turquoise Boy. And near this person grew the male reed. Beyond, still farther in the east, there lived a people called the Hadahuneya'nigi, the Mirage or Agate People. Still farther in the east there lived twelve beings called the Naaskiddi. And beyond the home of these beings there lived four others — the Holy Man, the Holy Woman, the Holy Boy, and the Holy Girl.

In the West there lived the White Shell Hermaphrodite or Girl, and with her was the big female reed which grew at the water's edge. It had no tassel. Beyond her in the West there lived another stone people called the Hadahunes'tqin, the Ground Heat People. Still farther on there lived another twelve beings, but these were all females. And again, in the Far West, there lived four Holy Ones.

Within this land there lived the Kisa'ni, the ancients of the Pueblo People. On the six mountains there lived the Cave Dwellers or Great Swallow People. On the mountains lived also the light and dark squirrels, chipmunks, mice, rats, the turkey people, the deer and cat people, the spider people, and the lizards and snakes. The beaver people lived along the rivers, and the frogs and turtles and all the underwater people in the water. So far all the people were similar. They had no definite form, but they had been given different names because of different characteristics.

Now the plan was to plant.

First Man called the people together. He brought forth the white corn which had been formed with him. First Woman brought the yellow corn. They laid the perfect ears side by side; then they asked one person from among the many to come and help them. The Turkey stepped forward. They asked him where he had come from, and he said that he had come from the Gray Mountain. He danced back and forth four times, then he shook his feather coat and there dropped from his clothing four kernels of corn, one gray, one blue, one black, and one red. Another person was asked to help in the plan of the planting. The Big Snake came forward. He likewise brought forth four seeds, the pumpkin, the watermelon, the cantaloupe, and the muskmelon. His plants all crawl on the ground.

They planted the seeds, and their harvest was great.

After the harvest the Turquoise Boy from the East came and visited First Woman. When First Man returned to his home he found his wife with this boy. First Woman told her husband that Ashon nutli' was of her flesh and not of his flesh. She said that she had used her own fire, the turquoise, and had ground her own yellow corn into meal. This corn she had planted and cared for herself.

Now at that time there were four chiefs: Big Snake, Mountain Lion, Otter, and Bear. And it was the custom when the black cloud rose in the morning for First Man to come out of his dwelling and speak to the people. After First Man had spoken the four chiefs told them what they should do that day. They also spoke of the past and of the future. But after First Man found his wife with another he would not come out to speak to the people. The black cloud rose higher, but First Man would not leave his dwelling; neither would he eat or drink. No one spoke to the people for days. All during this time First Man remained silent, and would not touch food or water. Four times the white cloud rose. Then the four chiefs went to First Man and demanded to know why he would not speak to the people. The chiefs asked this question three times, and a fourth, before First Man would answer them.

He told them to bring him an emetic. This he took and purified himself. First Man then asked them to send the hermaphrodite to him. When he came First Man asked him if the metate and brush were his. He said that they were. First Man asked him if he could cook and prepare food like a woman, if he could weave, and brush the hair. And when he had assured First Man that he could do all manner of woman's work, First Man said: "Go and prepare food and bring it to me." After he had eaten, First Man told the four chiefs what he had seen, and what his wife had said.

At this time the Great-Coyote-Who-Was-Formed-in-the-Water came to First Man and told him to cross the river. They made a big raft and crossed at the place where the Male River followed through the Female River. And all the male beings left the female beings on the river bank; and as they rowed across the river they looked back and saw that First Woman and the female beings were laughing. They were also behaving very wickedly.

In the beginning the women did not mind being alone. They cleared and planted a small field. On the other side of the river First Man and the chiefs hunted and planted their seeds. They had a good harvest. Nadle ground the corn and cooked the food. Four seasons passed. The men continued to have plenty and were happy; but the women became lazy, and only weeds grew on their land. The women wanted fresh meat. Some of them tried to join the men and were drowned in the river...

...When First Man learned of this he warned his men that they would all be killed. He told them that they were indulging in a dangerous practice. Then the second chief spoke: he said that life was hard and that it was a pity to see women drowned. He asked why they should not bring the women across the river and all live together again.

"Now we can see for ourselves what comes from our wrong doing," he said. "We will know how to act in the future." The three other chiefs of the animals agreed with him, so First Man told them to go and bring the women.

After the women had been brought over the river First Man spoke: "We must be purified," he said. "Everyone must bathe. The men must dry themselves with white corn meal, and the women, with yellow."

This they did, living apart for days. After the fourth day First Woman came and threw her right arm around her husband. She spoke to the others and said that she could see her mistakes, but with her husband's help she would henceforth lead a good life. Then all the male and female beings came and lived with each other again.

The people moved to different parts of the land. Some time passed; then First Woman became troubled by the monotony of life. She made a plan. She went to Atse'hashke, the Coyote called First Angry, and giving him the rainbow she said: "I have suffered greatly in the past. I have suffered from want of meat and corn and clothing. Many of my maidens have died. I have suffered many things. Take the rainbow and go to the place where the rivers cross. Bring me the two pretty children of Tqo holt sodi, the Water Buffalo, a boy and a girl.

The Coyote agreed to do this. He walked over the rainbow. He entered the home of the Water Buffalo and stole the two children; and these he hid in his big skin coat with the white fur lining. And when he returned he refused to take off his coat, but pulled it around himself and looked very wise. After this happened the people saw white light in the East and in the South and West and North. One of the deer people ran to the East, and returning, said that the white light was a great sheet of water. The sparrow hawk flew to the South, the great hawk to the West, and the kingfisher to the North. They returned and said that a flood was coming. The kingfisher said that the water was greater in the North, and that it was near.

The flood was coming and the Earth was sinking. And all this happened because the Coyote had stolen the two children of the Water Buffalo, and only First Woman and the Coyote knew the truth.

When First Man learned of the coming of the water he sent word to all the people, and he told them to come to the mountain called Sis na'jin. He told them to bring with them all of the seeds of the plants used for food. All living beings were to gather on the top of Sis na'jin. First Man traveled to the six sacred mountains, and, gathering earth from them, he put it in his medicine bag.

The water rose steadily.

When all the people were halfway up Sis na' jin, First Man discovered that he had forgotten his medicine bag. Now this bag contained not only the earth from the six sacred mountains, but his magic, the medicine he used to call the rain down upon the earth and to make things grow. He could not live without his medicine bag, and he wished to jump into the rising water; but the others begged him not to do this. They went to the kingfisher and asked him to dive into the water and recover the bag. This the bird did. When First Man had his medicine bag again in his possession he breathed on it four times and thanked his people.

When they had all arrived it was found that the Turquoise Boy had brought with him the big Male Reed; and the White Shell Girl had brought with her the big Female Reed. Another person brought poison ivy; and another, cotton, which was later used for cloth. This person was the spider. First Man had

with him his spruce tree which he planted on the top of Sis na'jin. He used his fox medicine to make it grow; but the spruce tree began to send out branches and to taper at the top, so First Man planted the big Male Reed. All the people blew on it, and it grew and grow until it reached the canopy of the sky. They tried to blow inside the reed, but it was solid. They asked the woodpecker to drill out the hard heart. Soon they were able to peek through the opening, but they had to blow and blow before it was large enough to climb through. They climbed up inside the big male reed, and after them the water continued to rise.

When the people reached the Fourth World they saw that it was not a very large place. Some say that it was called the White World; but not all medicine men agree that this is so.

The last person to crawl through the reed was the turkey from Gray Mountain. His feather coat was flecked with foam, for after him came the water. And with the water came the female Water Buffalo who pushed her head through the opening in the reed. She had a great quantity of curly hair which floated on the water, and she had two horns, half black and half yellow. From the tips of the horns the lightning flashed.

First Man asked the Water Buffalo why she had come and why she had sent the flood. She said nothing. Then the Coyote drew the two babies from his coat and said that it was, perhaps, because of them.

The Turquoise Boy took a basket and filled it with turquoise. On top of the turquoise he placed the blue pollen, tha'di'thee do tlij, from the blue flowers, and the yellow pollen from the corn; and on top of these he placed the pollen from the water flags, tquel aqa'di din; and. again on top of these he placed the crystal, which is river pollen. This basket he gave to the Coyote who put it between the horns of the Water Buffalo. The Còyote said that with this sacred offering he would give back the male child. He said that the male child would be known as the Black Cloud or Male Rain, and that he would bring the thunder and lightning. The female child he would keep. She would be known as the Blue, Yellow, and White Clouds or Female Rain. She would be the gentle rain that would moisten the earth and. help them to live. So he kept the female child, and he placed the male child on the sacred basket between the horns of the Water Buffalo. And the Water Buffalo disappeared, and the waters with her.

After the water sank there appeared another person. They did not know him, and they asked him where he had come from. He told them that he was the badger, nahashch'id, and that he had been formed where the Yellow Cloud had touched the Earth. Afterward this Yellow Cloud turned out to be a sunbeam. First Man was not satisfied with the Fourth World. It was a small barren land; and the great water had soaked the earth and made the sowing of seeds impossible. He planted the big Female Reed and it grew up to the vaulted roof of this Fourth World. First Man sent the newcomer, the badger, up inside the reed, but before he reached the upper world water began to drip, so he returned and said that he was frightened.

At this time there came another strange being. First Man asked him where he had been formed, and he told him that he had come from the Earth itself. This was the locust. He said that it was now his turn to do something, and he offered to climb up the reed.

The locust made a headband of a little reed, and on his forehead he crossed two arrows. These arrows were dressed with yellow tail feathers. With this sacred headdress and the help of all the Holy Beings the locust climbed up to the Fifth World. He dug his way through the reed as he digs in the earth now. He then pushed through mud until he came to water. When he emerged he saw a black water bird swimming toward him. He had arrows crossed on the back of his head and big eyes.

The bird said: "What are you doing here? This is not your country." And continuing, he told the locust that unless he could make magic be would not allow him to remain.

The black water bird drew an arrow from back of his head, and shoving it into his mouth drew it out his nether extremity. He inserted it underneath his body and drew it out of his mouth.

"That is nothing," said the locust. He took the arrows from his headband and pulled them both ways through his body, between his shell and his heart. The bird believed that the locust possessed great medicine, and he swam away to the East, taking the water with him.

Then came the blue water bird from the South, and the yellow water bird from the West, and the white water bird from the North, and everything happened as before. The locust performed the magic with his arrows; and when the last water bird had gone he found himself sitting on land.

The locust returned to the lower world and told the people that the beings above had strong medicine, and that he had had great difficulty getting the best of them.

Now two dark clouds and two white clouds rose, and this meant that two nights and two days had passed, for there was still no sun. First Man again sent the badger to the upper world, and he returned covered with mud, terrible mud. First Man gathered chips of turquoise which he offered to the five Chiefs of the Winds who lived in the uppermost world of all. They were pleased with the gift, and they sent down the winds and dried the Fifth World.

First Man and his people saw four dark clouds and four white clouds pass, and then they sent the badger up the reed. This time when the badger returned he said that he had come out on solid earth. So First Man and First Woman led the people to the Fifth World, which some call the Many Colored Earth and some the Changeable Earth. They emerged through a lake surrounded by four mountains. The water bubbles in this lake when anyone goes near.

Now after all the people had emerged from the lower worlds First Man and First Woman dressed the Mountain Lion with yellow, black, white, and grayish corn and placed him on one side. They dressed the Wolf with white tail feathers and placed him on the other side. They divided the people into two groups. The first group was told to choose whichever chief they wished. They made their choice, and, although they thought they had chosen the Mountain Lion, they found that they had taken the Wolf for their chief. The Mountain Lion was the chief for the other side. And these people who had the Mountain Lion for their chief turned out to be the people of the Earth. They were to plant seeds and harvest corn. The followers of the Wolf chief became the animals and birds; they turned into all the creatures that fly and crawl and run and swim.

And after all the beings were divided, and each had his own form, they went their ways.

This is the story of the Four Dark Worlds and the Fifth, the World we live in. Some medicine men tell us that there are two worlds above us, the first is the World of the Spirits of Living Things, the second is the Place of Melting into One.

Assignments

- Warm-up: Compare the above creation legend with Genesis 1–2.
- Student should complete Concept Builder 2-D.
- Student will re-write corrected copies of essay due tomorrow.

CONCEPT BUILDER 2-D
RHYME SCHEME

Circle the words that jump out at you. Give the rhyme scheme (this is a repeated sound at the end of each verse) for the first four lines of the second poem. What sounds are repeated?

"THE SONG OF THE SKY LOOM"
O our Mother the Earth, O our Father the Sky,

. . . weave for us a garment of brightness;
May the warp be the white light of morning,
May the weft be the red light of evening,
May the border be the standing rainbow.
May the fringes be the falling rain= metaphor comparison to a human garment.
That we may walk fittingly where birds sing,
That we may walk fittingly where grass is green,
O our Mother the Earth, O our father the Sky!

HUNTING SONG (Navajo)
Comes the deer to my singing,
Comes the deer to my song,
Comes the deer to my singing.
He, the blackbird, he am I,
Bird beloved of the wild deer.
Comes the deer to my singing.
From the Mountain Black,
From the summit,
Down the trail, coming, coming now,
Comes the deer to my singing.
Through the blossoms,
Through the flowers, coming, coming now,
Comes the deer to my singing.
Through the flower dew-drops,
Coming, coming now,
Comes the deer to my singing.

Through the pollen, flower pollen,
Coming, coming now,
Comes the deer to my singing.
Starting with his left fore-foot,
Stamping, turns the frightened deer,
Comes the deer to my singing.
Quarry mine, blessed am I
In the luck of the chase.
Comes the deer to my singing.
Comes the deer to my singing,
Comes the deer to my song,
Comes the deer to my singing.

The First Constitution in North America

Iroquois Confederacy Constitution

Background Another important eastern Native American representation was the Iroquois Confederacy. The Iroquois was founded in the 16th century in what is now central New York State. The original confederacy consisted of five tribes — the Mohawk, Onondaga, Cayuga, Oneida, and Seneca — and was known as the Five Nations, or the League of Five Nations. Sometime between 1715 and 1722, however, the Tuscaroras, an Iroquoian tribe originally of North Carolina, which had migrated to New York, was formally admitted to the confederacy, and the name of the league was changed to the Six Nations, or the League of Six Nations. At least 150 years before the American Colonists wrote their constitution, the Iroquois nation had a constitution. The first section of that lengthy constitution is presented below (www.constitution.org/iroquois.htm).

The Great Binding Law, Gaywnashagowa

1. I am Dekanawidah and with the Five Nations' Confederate Lords I plant the Tree of Great Peace. I plant it in your territory, Adodarhoh, and the Onondaga Nation, in the territory of you who are Firekeepers.

   I name the tree the Tree of the Great Long Leaves. Under the shade of this Tree of the Great Peace we spread the soft white feathery down of the globe thistle as seats for you, Adodarhoh, and your cousin Lords.

   We place you upon those seats, spread soft with the feathery down of the globe thistle, there beneath the shade of the spreading branches of the Tree of Peace. There shall you sit and watch the Council Fire of the Confederacy of the Five Nations, and all the affairs of the Five Nations shall be transacted at this place before you, Adodarhoh, and your cousin Lords, by the Confederate Lords of the Five Nations.

2. Roots have spread out from the Tree of the Great Peace, one to the north, one to the east, one to the south and one to the west. The name of these roots is The Great White Roots and their nature is Peace and Strength.

   If any man or any nation outside the Five Nations shall obey the laws of the Great Peace and make known their disposition to the Lords of the Confederacy, they may trace the Roots to the Tree and if their minds are clean and they are obedient and promise to obey the wishes of the Confederate Council, they shall be welcomed to take shelter beneath the Tree of the Long Leaves.

   We place at the top of the Tree of the Long Leaves an Eagle who is able to see afar. If he sees in the distance any evil approaching or any danger threatening he will at once warn the people of the Confederacy.

3. To you Adodarhoh, the Onondaga cousin Lords, I and the other Confederate Lords have entrusted the caretaking and the watching of the Five Nations Council Fire.

   When there is any business to be transacted and the Confederate Council is not in session, a messenger shall be dispatched either to Adodarhoh, Hononwirehtonh or Skanawatih, Fire Keepers, or to their War Chiefs with a full statement of the case desired to be considered.

Then shall Adodarhoh call his cousin (associate) Lords together and consider whether or not the case is of sufficient importance to demand the attention of the Confederate Council. If so, Adodarhoh shall dispatch messengers to summon all the Confederate Lords to assemble beneath the Tree of the Long Leaves.

When the Lords are assembled the Council Fire shall be kindled, but not with chestnut wood, and Adodarhoh shall formally open the Council.

Then shall Adodarhoh and his cousin Lords, the Fire Keepers, announce the subject for discussion.

The Smoke of the Confederate Council Fire shall ever ascend and pierce the sky so that other nations who may be allies may see the Council Fire of the Great Peace.

Adodarhoh and his cousin Lords are entrusted with the Keeping of the Council Fire.

4. You, Adodarhoh, and your thirteen cousin Lords, shall faithfully keep the space about the Council Fire clean and you shall allow neither dust nor dirt to accumulate. I lay a Long Wing before you as a broom. As a weapon against a crawling creature I lay a staff with you so that you may thrust it away from the Council Fire. If you fail to cast it out then call the rest of the United Lords to your aid.

5. The Council of the Mohawk shall be divided into three parties as follows: Tekarihoken, Ayonhwhathah and Shadekariwade are the first party; Sharenhowaneh, Deyoenhegwenh and Oghrenghrehgowah are the second party, and Dehennakrineh, Aghstawenserenthah and Shoskoharowaneh are the third party. The third party is to listen only to the discussion of the first and second parties and if an error is made or the proceeding is irregular they are to call attention to it, and when the case is right and properly decided by the two parties they shall confirm the decision of the two parties and refer the case to the Seneca Lords for their decision. When the Seneca Lords have decided in accord with the Mohawk Lords, the case or question shall be referred to the Cayuga and Oneida Lords on the opposite side of the house.

6. I, Dekanawidah, appoint the Mohawk Lords the heads and the leaders of the Five Nations Confederacy. The Mohawk Lords are the foundation of the Great Peace and it shall, therefore, be against the Great Binding Law to pass measures in the Confederate Council after the Mohawk Lords have protested against them.

No council of the Confederate Lords shall be legal unless all the Mohawk Lords are present.

7. Whenever the Confederate Lords shall assemble for the purpose of holding a council, the Onondaga Lords shall open it by expressing their gratitude to their cousin Lords and greeting them, and they shall make an address and offer thanks to the earth where men dwell, to the streams of water, the pools, the springs and the lakes, to the maize and the fruits, to the medicinal herbs and trees, to the forest trees for their usefulness, to the animals that serve as food and give their pelts for clothing, to the great winds and the lesser winds, to the Thunderers, to the Sun, the mighty warrior, to the moon, to the messengers of the Creator who reveal his wishes and to the Great Creator who dwells in the heavens above, who gives all the things useful to men, and who is the source and the ruler of health and life.

Then shall the Onondaga Lords declare the council open.

The council shall not sit after darkness has set in.

8. The Firekeepers shall formally open and close all councils of the Confederate Lords, and they shall pass upon all matters deliberated upon by the two sides and render their decision.

Every Onondaga Lord (or his deputy) must be present at every Confederate Council and must agree with the majority without unwarrantable dissent, so that a unanimous decision may be rendered.

If Adodarhoh or any of his cousin Lords are absent from a Confederate Council, any other Firekeeper may open and close the Council, but the Firekeepers present may not give any decisions, unless the matter is of small importance.

9. All the business of the Five Nations Confederate Council shall be conducted by the two combined bodies of Confederate Lords. First the question shall be passed upon by the Mohawk and Seneca Lords, then it shall be discussed and passed by the Oneida and Cayuga Lords. Their decisions shall then be referred to the Onondaga Lords, (Fire Keepers) for final judgement.

    The same process shall obtain when a question is brought before the council by an individual or a War Chief.

10. In all cases the procedure must be as follows: when the Mohawk and Seneca Lords have unanimously agreed upon a question, they shall report their decision to the Cayuga and Oneida Lords who shall deliberate upon the question and report a unanimous decision to the Mohawk Lords. The Mohawk Lords will then report the standing of the case to the Firekeepers, who shall render a decision as they see fit in case of a disagreement by the two bodies, or confirm the decisions of the two bodies if they are identical. The Fire Keepers shall then report their decision to the Mohawk Lords who shall announce it to the open council.

11. If through any misunderstanding or obstinacy on the part of the Fire Keepers, they render a decision at variance with that of the Two Sides, the Two Sides shall reconsider the matter and if their decisions are jointly the same as before they shall report to the Fire Keepers who are then compelled to confirm their joint decision.

12. When a case comes before the Onondaga Lords (Fire Keepers) for discussion and decsion, Adodarho shall introduce the matter to his comrade Lords who shall then discuss it in their two bodies. Every Onondaga Lord except Honon-wiretonh shall deliberate and he shall listen only. When a unanimous decision shall have been reached by the two bodies of Fire Keepers, Adodarho shall notify Hononwiretonh of the fact when he shall confirm it. He shall refuse to confirm a decision if it is not unanimously agreed upon by both sides of the Fire Keepers.

13. No Lord shall ask a question of the body of Confederate Lords when they are discussing a case, question or proposition. He may only deliberate in a low tone with the separate body of which he is a member.

14. When the Council of the Five Nation Lords shall convene they shall appoint a speaker for the day. He shall be a Lord of either the Mohawk, Onondaga or Seneca Nation.

    The next day the Council shall appoint another speaker, but the first speaker may be reappointed if there is no objection, but a speaker's term shall not be regarded more than for the day.

Large group of Iroquois Native Americans. Photograph by William Alexander Drennan, c1914 (LOC-PD-US)..

15. No individual or foreign nation interested in a case, question or proposition shall have any voice in the Confederate Council except to answer a question put to him or them by the speaker for the Lords.

16. If the conditions which shall arise at any future time call for an addition to or change of this law, the case shall be carefully considered and if a new beam seems necessary or beneficial, the proposed change shall be voted upon and if adopted it shall be called, "Added to the Rafters."

Assignments

- Warm-up: Compare the Iroquois Constitution with the U.S. Constitution.
- Student should complete Concept Builder 2-E.
- Essay is due. Students should take the chapter 2 test.

CONCEPT BUILDER 2-E
Native American Views

Based on the assigned readings, rate how Native Americans would feel about a statement and then rate how you would feel: 1 is not true at all; 5 is true all the time.

Statement	Native American	Myself
A person should be brave all the time.		
A person can lie if it advances his purposes.		
Love your enemies.		
If one works hard enough, one will succeed.		
A person should not make hasty decisions.		
Be careful what you wish — it just might come true!		
The good guys always win.		
Bad things happen to good people.		
Women and men are equal in all ways.		
Friendship is important.		
Do what is right, whether if feels good or not.		
Do unto others as you would have them do unto you.		
Kill or be killed.		
Change your mind if it suits your purposes.		
Children are to be seen, not heard.		
Traditions are important.		
Animals are as important as humans.		

Chapter 3

The New Land to 1750:
Puritanism

First Thoughts When I was 12 years old I received a diary for Christmas and for the next two years I recorded my most private thoughts. It is amusing to me today to think about what I thought was important 47 years ago and what I think is important today. We will glimpse into the mind of the great evangelist Jonathan Edwards and his daughter, Esther. We will also explore the private thoughts of Anne Bradstreet, homeschool mom extraordinaire who was arguably the greatest poet of the 17th century.

Author Worldview Watch One can imagine the surprise when monotone Calvinist preacher Jonathan Edwards delivered his "Sinners in the Hands of an Angry God" and evoked a revivalistic fervor of unprecedented proportions. Yet, it is perhaps not so strange, this great man of God who loved his God first and then his family. The American world was transformed by this shy, spider-loving husband/father/pastor.

Chapter Learning Objectives In chapter 3 we read primary source sermons from Jonathan Edwards, a diary entry from his daughter, and a short essay by Cotton Mather. You will write your own worldview and learn about Puritan worldviews in this chapter. You will also read *A Treatise Concerning Religious Affections*, by Jonathan Edwards, and "Diary Entries," by Esther Edwards, and poems by Anne Bradstreet.

As a result of this chapter study you will be able to . . .

1. Compare and contrast the image we see of Jonathan Edwards through his sermon and the way Esther his daughter saw him.

2. Describe Edwards' religious affections and explain how they are evidences of true religion.

3. Find scriptural evidence that commands you to forgive those who have wronged you.

4. Summarize what Edwards says about the youth of his town in this passage from "A Faithful Narrative of the Surprising Work of God."

5. Write a worldview for yourself.

Weekly Essay Options: Begin on page 274 of the Teacher Guide.

Reading ahead: *The Autobiography of Benjamin Franklin* by Benjamin Franklin.

45

A Treatise Concerning Religious Affections
Jonathan Edwards

PART I. CONCERNING THE NATURE OF THE AFFECTIONS AND THEIR IMPORTANCE IN RELIGION.

First Peter 1:8: Whom having not seen, ye love; in whom, though now ye see him not, yet believing, ye rejoice with joy unspeakable and full of glory.

In these words, the apostle represents the state of the minds of the Christians he wrote to, under the persecutions they were then the subjects of. These persecutions are what he has respect to, in the two preceding verses, when he speaks of the trial of their faith, and of their being in heaviness through manifold temptations.

Such trials are of threefold benefit to true religion. Hereby the truth of it is manifested, and it appears to be indeed true religion; they, above all other things, have a tendency to distinguish between true religion and false, and to cause the difference between them evidently to appear. Hence they are called by the name of trials, in the verse nextly preceding the text, and in innumerable other places; they try the faith and religion of professors, of what sort it is, as apparent gold is tried in the fire, and manifested, whether it be true gold or no. And the faith of true Christians being thus tried and proved to be true, is "found to praise, and honor, and glory," as in that preceding verse.

And then, these trials are of further benefit to true religion; they not only manifest the truth of it, but they make its genuine beauty and amiableness remarkably to appear. True virtue never appears so lovely, as when it is most oppressed; and the divine excellency of real Christianity, is never exhibited with such advantage, as when under the greatest trials: then it is that true faith appears much more precious than gold! And upon this account is "found to praise, and honor, and glory."

And again, another benefit that such trials are of to true religion, is, that they purify and increase it. They not only manifest it to be true, but also tend to refine it, and deliver it from those mixtures of that which is false, which encumber and impede it; that nothing may be left but that which is true. They tend to cause the amiableness of true religion to appear to the best advantage, as was before observed; and not only so, but they tend to increase its beauty, by establishing and confirming it, and making it more lively and vigorous, and purifying it from those things that obscured its luster and glory. As gold that is tried in the fire, is purged from its alloy, and all remainders of dross, and comes forth more solid and beautiful; so true faith being tried as gold is tried in the fire, becomes more precious, and thus also is "found unto praise, and honor, and glory." The apostle seems to have respect to each of these benefits, that persecutions are of to true religion, in the verse preceding the text.

And, in the text, the apostle observes how true religion operated in the Christians he wrote to, under their persecutions, whereby these benefits of persecution appeared in them; or what manner of operation of true religion, in them, it was, whereby their religion, under persecution, was manifested to be true religion, and eminently appeared in the genuine beauty and amiableness of true religion, and also appeared to be increased and purified, and so was like to be "found unto praise, and honor, and glory, at the appearing of Jesus Christ." And there were two kinds of operation, or exercise of true religion, in them, under their sufferings, that the apostle takes notice of in the text, wherein these benefits appeared.

1. Love to Christ: "Whom having not yet seen, ye love." The world was ready to wonder, what strange principle it was, that influenced them to expose themselves to so great sufferings, to forsake the things that were seen, and renounce all that was dear and pleasant, which was the object of sense. They seemed to the men of the world about them, as though they were beside themselves, and to act as though they hated themselves; there was nothing in their view, that could induce them thus to suffer, and support them under, and carry them through such trials. But although there was nothing that was seen, nothing that the world saw, or that the Christians themselves ever saw with their bodily eyes, that thus influenced and supported them, yet they had a supernatural principle of love to something unseen; they loved Jesus Christ, for they saw him spiritually whom the world saw not, and whom they themselves had never seen with bodily eyes.

2. Joy in Christ. Though their outward sufferings were very grievous, yet their inward spiritual joys were greater than their sufferings; and these supported them, and enabled them to suffer with cheerfulness.

There are two things which the apostle takes notice of in the text concerning this joy.

1. The manner in which it rises, the way in which Christ, though unseen, is the foundation of it, viz., by faith; which is the evidence of things not seen: "In whom, though now ye see him not, yet believing, ye rejoice."

2. The nature of this joy; "unspeakable and full of glory." Unspeakable in the kind of it; very different from worldly joys, and carnal delights; of a vastly more pure, sublime, and heavenly nature, being something supernatural, and truly divine, and so ineffably excellent; the sublimity and exquisite

sweetness of which, there were no words to set forth. Unspeakable also in degree; it pleasing God to give them this holy joy, with a liberal hand, and in large measure, in their state of persecution.

Their joy was full of glory. Although the joy was unspeakable, and no words were sufficient to describe it, yet something might be said of it, and no words more fit to represent its excellency than these, that it was full of glory; or, as it is in the original, glorified joy. In rejoicing with this joy, their minds were filled, as it were, with a glorious brightness, and their natures exalted and perfected. It was a most worthy, noble rejoicing, that did not corrupt and debase the mind, as many carnal joys do; but did greatly beautify and dignify it; it was a prelibation of the joy of heaven, that raised their minds to a degree of heavenly blessedness; it filled their minds with the light of God's glory, and made themselves to shine with some communication of that glory.

Hence the proposition or doctrine, that I would raise from these words, is this: True religion, in great part, consists in holy affections.

We see that the apostle, in observing and remarking the operations and exercises of religion in these Christians he wrote to, wherein their religion appeared to be true and of the right kind, when it had its greatest trial of what sort it was, being tried by persecution as gold is tried in the fire, and when their religion not only proved true, but was most pure, and cleansed from its dross and mixtures of that which was not true, and when religion appeared in them most in its genuine excellency and native beauty, and was found to praise, and honor, and glory; he singles out the religious affections of love and joy, that were then in exercise in them: these are the exercises of religion he takes notice of wherein their religion did thus appear true and pure, and in its proper glory. Here, I would (1) show what is intended by the affections, and (2) observe some things which make it evident, that a great part of true religion lies in the affections.

- Warm-up: John Winthrop, first governor of the Puritan Massachusetts Bay Colony, in his book *A Modell of Christian Charity* (1630) wrote: The Lord will make our name a praise and glory, so that men shall say of succeeding plantations: The Lord make it like that of New England. For we must consider that we shall be like a City upon a Hill; the eyes of all people are on us. What does Winthrop mean "a City upon a Hill?" Does this statement seem a little presumptuous on his part?

- Students should complete Concept Builder 3-A.

- Students review the required reading(s) *before* the assigned chapter begins.

- Teachers may want to discuss assigned reading(s) with students.

- Teachers shall assign the required essay. The rest of the essays can be outlined, answered with shorter answers, discussed, or skipped.

- Students will review all readings for chapter 3.

CONCEPT BUILDER 3-A
Active Reading

1 Peter 1:8: Whom having not seen, ye love; in whom, though now ye see him not, yet believing, ye rejoice with joy unspeakable and full of glory.

In these words, the apostle represents the state of the minds of the Christians he wrote to, under the persecutions they were then the subjects of. These persecutions are what he has respect to, in the two preceding verses, when he speaks of the trial of their faith, and of their being in heaviness through manifold temptations.

Such trials are of threefold benefit to true religion. Hereby the truth of it is manifested, and it appears to be indeed true religion; they, above all other things, have a tendency to distinguish between true religion and false, and to cause the difference between them evidently to appear. Hence they are called by the name of trials, in the verse nextly preceding the text, and in innumerable other places; they try the faith and religion of professors, of what sort it is, as apparent gold is tried in the fire, and manifested, whether it be true gold or no. And the faith of true Christians being thus tried and proved to be true, is "found to praise, and honor, and glory," as in that preceding verse.

And then, these trials are of further benefit to true religion; they not only manifest the truth of it, but they make its genuine beauty and amiableness remarkably to appear. True virtue never appears so lovely, as when it is most oppressed; and the divine excellency of real Christianity, is never exhibited with such advantage, as when under the greatest trials: then it is that true faith appears much more precious than gold! And upon this account is "found to praise, and honor, and glory."

And again, another benefit that such trials are to true religion, is, that they purify and increase it. They not only manifest it to be true, but also tend to refine it, and deliver it from those mixtures of that which is false, which encumber and impede it; that nothing may be left but that which is true. They tend to cause the amiableness of true religion to appear to the best advantage, as was before observed; and not only so, but they tend to increase its beauty, by establishing and confirming it, and making it more lively and vigorous, and purifying it from those things that obscured its luster and glory. As gold that is tried in the fire, is purged from its alloy, and all remainders of dross, and comes forth more solid and beautiful; so true faith being tried as gold is tried in the fire, becomes more precious, and thus also is "found unto praise, and honor, and glory." The apostle seems to have respect to each of these benefits, that persecutions are of to true religion, in the verse preceding the text (www.ccel.org/ccel/edwards/affections.html).

1. What does Edwards mean when he says "religious affections?"

2. How do trials benefit true religion?

3. Do you know someone who is like Jonathan Edwards?

Sinners in the Hands of an Angry God

Read Jonathan Edwards' sermon entitled "Sinners in the Hands of an Angry God." A portion of the sermon is included below. It is interesting that Jonathan Edwards delivered his sermon from a written manuscript with no emotion at all! But Edwards was more than a great preacher. He was a devoted husband and beloved dad. His family adored him. He loved Mrs. Edwards so much that every afternoon he and his wife would enjoy long horseback rides. Every night he would read stories to his children. In fact, he was such a dedicated father that he was ultimately fired from his church. They were bothered that he did not visit his congregation more. Think about it: the most famous evangelist of the 18th century fired because he did not visit old Sally Jones or Mary Smith!

The use of this awful subject may be of awakening unconverted persons in this congregation. This that you have heard is the case of every one of you that are out of Christ. That world of mercy, that lake of burning brimstone, is extended abroad under you. There is the dreadful pit of the glowing flames of the wrath of god; there is hell's wide gaping mouth opn; and you have nothing to stand upon, nor any thing to take hold of. There is nothing between you and hell but the air; it is only the power and mere pleasure of God that holds you up.

You probably are not sensible of this; you find you are kept out of hell but do not see the hand of God in it; but look at other things, as the good state of your bodily constitution, your care of your own life, and the means you use for your own preservation. But indeed these things are nothing; if God should withdraw His hand, they would avail no more to keep you from falling than the thin air to hold up a person that is suspended in it.

Your wickedness makes you, as it were, heavy as lead and to tend downwards with great weight and pressure towards hell; and if God should let you go, you would immediately sink and swiftly descend and plunge into the bottomless gulf, and your healthy constitution, and your care and prudence, and best contrivance, and all your righteousness, would have no more influence to uphold you and keep you out of hell, than a spider's web would have to stop a falling rock. Were it not that so is the sovereign pleasure of God, the earth would not bear you one moment; for you are a burden to it; the creation groans with you; the creature is made subject to the bondage of your corruption, not willingly; the sun does not willingly shine upon you to give you light to serve sin and Satan; the earth does not willingly yield her increase to satisfy your lusts; nor is it willingly a stage for your wickedness to be acted upon; the air does not willingly serve you for breath to maintain the flame of life in your vitals while you spend your life in the service of God's enemies (Jonathan Edwards, "Sinners in the Hands of an Angry God" sermon, 1741, www.ccel.org/ccel/edwards/sermons.sinners.html).

- Warm-up: Puritans effectively combined sound scholarship and profound spirituality. They led American society in education and science for a century. They founded most of the universities in New England. Some modern evangelical scholars lament that this combination has been lost. Professor Mark Noll, former professor at Wheaton College, now a professor at Harvard University, argues that "the scandal of the evangelical mind is that there is not much of an evangelical mind." Noll is speaking of a comprehensive ability to think theologically across a broad spectrum of life (e.g., politics, arts, culture, and economics). Evangelicals, he argues, have a propensity for shallow analysis of complex cultural issues (Mark A. Noll, *The Scandal of the Evangelical Mind*, Grand Rapids, MI: Eerdmans Publishing Company, 1994). This is a view held by other scholars as well. David F. Wells says, "Surely the God who is rendered 'weightless' by modern culture (especially evangelical Christians) is quite different from the living God" (David F. Wells, *God in the Wasteland: The Reality of Truth in a World of Fading Dreams*, Grand Rapids, MI: Eerdmans, 1994). Do you agree with Noll and Wells? Is there hope that born-again Christians again will regain the high ground in culture and thought?

- Student *should* complete Concept Builder 3-B.

- Student *should* review reading(s) from next chapter.

- Student should outline essays. due at the end of the week.

- Per teacher instructions, students may answer orally, in a group setting, some of the essays that are not assigned as formal essays.

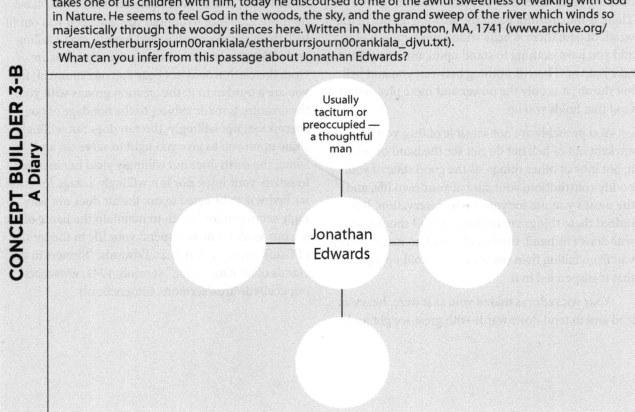

CONCEPT BUILDER 3-B
A Diary

Read the following diary entry from Jonathan Edward's daughter Esther.

Though father is usually taciturn or preoccupied, my mother will call these large words, even when he takes one of us children with him, today he discoursed to me of the awful sweetness of walking with God in Nature. He seems to feel God in the woods, the sky, and the grand sweep of the river which winds so majestically through the woody silences here. Written in Northhampton, MA, 1741 (www.archive.org/stream/estherburrsjourn00rankiala/estherburrsjourn00rankiala_djvu.txt).

What can you infer from this passage about Jonathan Edwards?

Usually taciturn or preoccupied — a thoughtful man

Jonathan Edwards

Upon the Burning of Our House
Anne Bradstreet

Anne Bradstreet was born in England, married a Puritan believer, immigrated to America, and wrote some of the most engaging poetry of the 17th century. On a ship named the *Arabella*, Anne and her husband brought their Puritan faith to America. After

> A homeschooling mom of eight, Bradstreet found time to write poetry. She wrote: "Diverse children have their different natures; some are like flesh which nothing but salt will keep from putrefaction; some again like tender fruits that are best preserved with sugar: those parents are wise that can fit their nurture according to their Nature."

short stays in Salem, Charlestown, and Newtown (now Cambridge), they settled in Ipswich, outside Boston, in what was then the frontier. There, Anne homeschooled eight children and wrote many of the poems that were eventually published in *The Tenth Muse* (Anne Bradstreet, *The Tenth Muse*, London: Stephen Bowtell, 1650) after her brother-in-law took her manuscript back with him to England and had it printed without her knowledge. The Bradstreets moved to Andover, Massachusetts, in the mid-1640s, where Anne lived until her death in 1672. Remarkably, Bradstreet wrote many poems, full of literary techniques and Christian flavor, raised eight children, and helped create a new nation. As today's younger generation is called to create a new civilization, they would all do well to look closely at Bradstreet's life. There is little doubt that Anne's work was extremely difficult and exhausting. Anne's full-time job was homemaking. She had to cook meals, make clothing, and doctor her family on top of cleaning, making household goods to use and to sell, taking care of the family's animals, maintaining a fire, and even tending to the kitchen gardens. The house she maintained was a thatch-roofed structure with a dirt floor. Colonial women were often married by the age of 13 or 14. Marriage was mostly for economic benefits, not romantic situations. In the case of Anne, evidence suggests that she deeply loved her husband and saw her union as a way to be more effective for the Kingdom.

In silent night when rest I took,
For sorrow near I did not look,
I waken'd was with thund'ring noise
And piteous shrieks of dreadful voice.
That fearful sound of fire and fire,
Let no man know is my desire.

I, starting up, the light did spy,
And to my God my heart did cry
To strengthen me in my distress
And not to leave me succorless.
Then coming out beheld a space,
The flame consume my dwelling place.

And, when I could no longer look,
I blest his name
That gave and took,
That laid my good now in the dust:
Yea so it was, and so 'twas just.
It was his own: it was not mine;
Far be it that I should repine.

He might of all justly bereft,
But yet sufficient for us left.
When by the ruins oft I past,
My sorrowing eyes aside did cast,
And here and there the places spy

Where oft I sat, and long did lie.
Here stood that trunk,
And there that chest;
There lay that store I counted best:
My pleasant things in ashes lie,
And them behold no more shall I.
Under thy roof no guest shall sit,
Nor at thy table eat a bit. . . .

Then straight I gin my heart to chide,
And did thy wealth on earth abide?
Didst fix thy hope on mould'ring dust,
The arm of flesh dist make thy trust?
Raise up thy thoughts above the sky
That dunghill mists away may fly.

Thou has an house on high erect,
Fram'd by that mighty Architect,
With glory richly furnished,
Stands permanent tho' this be fled.
It's purchased, and paid for too
By him who hath enough to do.

A prize so vast as is unknown,
Yet, by his gift, is made thine own.
There's wealth enough, I need no more;
Farewell my pelf, farewell my store.
The world no longer let me love,
My hope and treasure lies above.

Assignments

- Warm-up: Compare "Eleanor Rigby" by Paul McCartney and John Lennon (available online) with Anne Bradstreet's "Upon the Burning of Our House." Identify differences in theme, tone, plot, and use of figurative language.
- Student should complete Concept Builder 3-C.
- Student should write rough drafts of all assigned essays.
- The teacher may correct rough drafts.

CONCEPT BUILDER 3-C My Diary	Keep a diary of what happens to you today.
	My devotional passage:
	My favorite activity today:
	What God taught me today:
	What is a mistake I made today:
	What is the best thing that happened today:
	What goals do I have for tomorrow:

No Book to Ban

Perhaps no group of people in history have been so maligned and ridiculed as the Puritans. Yet, in truth, these stalwart people created a nation in a wilderness and inspire this author still.

To be "puritanical" is to be "close-minded" and "intolerant." Yet, today, in our hedonist world, I long for a little order and control.

I was reading an essay by Neil Postman, author of *Amusing Ourselves to Death* (New York: Penguin Books, 2006). He reminds us that 1984 came and went and Orwell's nightmare did not occur. The roots of liberal democracy had held.

But we had forgotten that alongside Orwell's dark vision there was another equally chilling apocalyptic vision: Aldous Huxley's *Brave New World* (Garden City, NY: Doubleday, Doran & Co., Inc., 1932). Contrary to common belief, Huxley and Orwell did not prophesy the same thing. Orwell warns that we will be overcome by an externally imposed oppression — Big Brother. But in Huxley's vision, no Big Brother is required to deprive people of their autonomy, maturity, and history. As he saw it, people will come to love their oppression, to adore the technologies that undo their capacities to think.

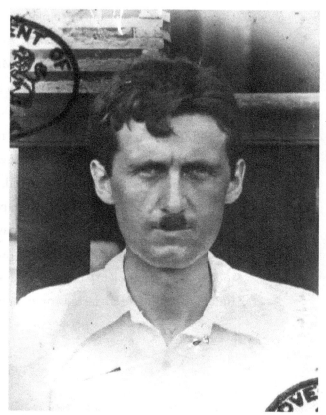

A passport photo showing George Orwell during his time in Burma. Photographer and date unknown (PD-US).

What Orwell feared were those who would ban books. What Huxley feared was that there would be no reason to ban a book, for there would be no one who wanted to read one. Orwell feared those who would deprive us of information. Huxley feared those who would give us so much that we would be reduced to passivity and egoism. Orwell feared that the truth would be concealed from us. Huxley feared the truth would be drowned in a sea of neglect. Orwell feared we would become a captive to ubiquitous culture. Huxley feared we would become a trivial culture. As Huxley remarked in his sequel *Brave New World Revisited* (Aldous Huxley, *Brave New World Revisited*, New York: Harper, 1958), the civil libertarians who are ever on the alert to oppose tyranny "failed to take into account man's almost infinite appetite for distractions" (Aldous Huxley, *Brave New World Revisited* (New York: Harper, 1958). In Orwell's 1984, Huxley added, people are controlled by inflicting pain. In *Brave New World*, they are controlled by inflicting pleasure. In short, Orwell feared that what we hate will ruin us. Huxley feared that what we love will ruin us.

Assignments

- Warm-up: Modern Americans accuse the Puritans of being colorless and legalistic. Typically, to be "Puritan" means "to hide one's feelings." Yet, to read Anne Bradstreet, one is struck by the power of Puritan emotion! She never hesitated to share her heart with her reader.

> To My Dear And Loving Husband
>
> If ever two were one, then surely we.
>
> If ever man were lov'd by wife, then thee.
>
> If ever wife was happy in a man,
>
> Compare with me, ye women, if you can.
>
> I prize thy love more than whole Mines of gold
>
> Or all the riches that the East doth hold.
>
> My love is such that Rivers cannot quench,
>
> Nor ought but love from thee give recompense.
>
> Thy love is such I can no way repay.
>
> The heavens reward thee manifold, I pray.
>
> Then while we live, in love let's so persevere
>
> That when we live no more, we may live ever.

  Do you think the Puritans were stiff, tyrannical, unfeeling people?

- Student should complete Concept Builder 3-D

- Student will re-write corrected copies of essays due tomorrow.

Get involved with the poem. Mark it up!

- What words should be accented?
- Consider the title of the poem carefully. Is it a correct title?
- Read through the poem, several times if you can, both silently and aloud. What does it sound like? What does it mean?
- What is the poem's basic situation? What is going on in it?
- What figurative language is used? Is the language in the poem abstract or concrete? How is this appropriate to the poem's subject?

Mark up the following poem.

"Upon the Burning of Our House"
By Anne Bradstreet

In silent night when rest I took,
For sorrow near I did not look,
I waken'd was with thund'ring noise
And piteous shrieks of dreadful voice.
That fearful sound of fire and fire,
Let no man know is my desire.

I, starting up, the light did spy,
And to my God my heart did cry
To strengthen me in my distress
And not to leave me succorless.
Then coming out beheld a space,
The flame consume my dwelling place.

And, when I could no longer look,
I blest his name
That gave and took,
That laid my good now in the dust:
Yea so it was, and so 'twas just.
It was his own: it was not mine;
Far be it that I should repine.

He might of all justly bereft,
But yet sufficient for us left.
When by the ruins oft I past,
My sorrowing eyes aside did cast,
And here and there the places spy
Where oft I sat, and long did lie.

Here stood that trunk,
And there that chest;
There lay that store I counted best:
My pleasant things in ashes lie,
And them behold no more shall I.
Under thy roof no guest shall sit,
Nor at thy table eat a bit. . .

Then straight I gin my heart to chide,
And did thy wealth on earth abide?
Didst fix thy hope on mould'ring dust,
The arm of flesh dist make thy trust?
Raise up thy thoughts above the sky
That dunghill mists away may fly.
Thou has an house on high erect,
Fram'd by that mighty Architect,
With glory richly furnished,
Stands permanent tho' this be fled.
It's purchased, and paid for too
By him who hath enough to do.

A prize so vast as is unknown,
Yet, by his gift, is made thine own.
There's wealth enough, I need no more;
Farewell my pelf, farewell my store.
The world no longer let me love,
My hope and treasure lies above.

CONCEPT BUILDER 3-D
A DIARY

"A Good School"
Cotton Mather

A Good School deserves to be call'd, the very Salt of the Town, that hath it: And the Pastors of every Town are under peculiar obligations to make this a part of their Pastoral Care, That they may have a Good School, in their Neighbourhood.

A woeful putrefaction threatens the Rising Generation; Barbarous Ignorance, and the unavoidable consequence of it, Outrageous Wickedness will make the Rising Generation Loathsome, if it have not Schools to preserve it.

But Schools, wherein the Youth may by able Masters be Taught the Things that are necessary to qualify them for future Serviceableness, and have their Manners therewithal well-formed under a Laudable Discipline, and be over and above Well-Catechised in the principles of Religion, Those would be a Glory of our Land, and the preservatives of all other Glory. . . .

When the Reformation began in Europe an hundred and fourscore years ago, to Erect Schools everywhere was one principal concern of the Glorious and Heroic Reformers; and it was a common thing even for Little Villages of Twenty or Thirty Families, in the midst of all their Charges, and their Dangers, to maintain one of them.

The Colonies of New England were planted on the Design of pursuing that Holy Reformation; and now the Devil cannot give a greater Blow to the Reformation among us, than by causing Schools to Languish under Discouragements.

If our General Courts decline to contrive and provide Laws for the Support of Schools; or if particular Towns Employ their Wits, for Cheats to Elude the wholesome Laws; little do they consider how much they expose themselves to that Rebuke of God,

Often remembered for his role in the Salem witch trials, Cotton Mather was a socially and politically influential New England Puritan minister, prolific author and pamphleteer. Mather was named after his maternal grandfather, John Cotton. A huge influence throughout Mather's career was Robert Boyle.

Thou hast destroyed thyself, O New England. . . .

And the first Instance of their Barbarity will be, that they will be undone for want of men, but not see and own what it was that undid them. You will therefore pardon my Freedom with you, if I Address you, in the words of Luther:

"If ever there be any Considerable Blow given to the Devil's Kingdom, it must be, by Youth Excellently Educated. It is a serious Thing, a weighty Thing, and a thing that hath much of the Interest of Christ, and of Christianity in it, that Youth be well-trained up, and that Schools, and School-Masters be maintained. Learning is an unwelcome guest to the Devil, and therefore he would fain starve it out."

But the Freedom with which this Address is made unto you, is not so great as the Fervour that has animated it. My Fathers and Brethren, If you have any Love to God and Christ and Posterity; let. (Godly) Schools be more Encouraged (www.spurgeon.org/~phil/mather/edkids.htm).

Assignments

- Warm-up: Do you agree or disagree with Puritan Cotton Mather's rendition of what a good school is?

- Student should complete Concept Builder 3-E.

- Essays are due. Students should take the chapter 3 test.

Write a prose (writing in its normal continuous form, without the rhythmic or visual line structure of poetry) description of a sunset.

Write a poetry description of a sunset.

Draw a picture of a sunset

Chapter 4

1750–1800 (Part 1):
The Revolutionary Period

First Thoughts Benjamin Franklin is one of the enigmatic figures in American colonial history. He lived through two kings and saw two American governments formed. He lived through one world war and one revolution. He helped write the U.S. Constitution. He was a statesman, but was he a Christian believer? His personal behavior would suggest otherwise but what does his *Autobiography* say?

Author Worldview Watch Ben Franklin is an enigma. While there is clear evidence that Franklin grew up in a Calvinist home, and perhaps made an early commitment to Christ, his *Autobiography* degenerates into a lukewarm Christian theism at best, or a cold deism at worst. The truth is, the intelligent and capable the genius Benjamin Franklin was a giant in the intellectual world but in the world view universe, Franklin was confused and conflicted.

Chapter Learning Objectives In chapter 4 we examine the fascinating life of Benjamin Franklin by looking at several of his literary creations. You will analyze *The Autobiography of Benjamin Franklin*.

As a result of this chapter study you will be able to . . .

1. Evaluate Ben Franklin's faith journey.
2. Discuss if the autobiography was a "rags to riches" story or was it a self-serving, egotistical story of a man's self-absorption.

Weekly Essay Options: Begin on page 274 of the Teacher Guide.

Reading ahead: poems by Phillis Wheatley; *Speech in the Virginia Convention*, Patrick Henry; *The Declaration of Independence*, Thomas Jefferson; *Letter to Her Daughter from the New White House*, Abigail Adams.

The Autobiography of Benjamin Franklin
Benjamin Franklin

Speaking to his "Dear Son," Benjamin Franklin began what is one of the most famous autobiographies in world history. At the age of 62, Franklin wrote his reminiscences for the benefit of his son William Franklin (1731–1813). The book was composed in sections, the first part dealing with Franklin's first 24 years. He finished this in 1771. Then, with the end of the American Revolution, he resumed his writing again in 1783. He finished it in 1789. Ironically, though, the *Autobiography* covers his life only until 1757. There is no mention, for instance, of the American Revolution. Nonetheless, full of anecdotes and wisdom, *The Autobiography of Benjamin Franklin* remains a timeless classic.

Benjamin Franklin. Located at the white House in Washington, D.C. Oil on canvas by David Martin, c1767 (PD-US).

Assignments

- Warm-up: Did Benjamin Franklin create his era or did his era create Benjamin Franklin?
- Students should complete Concept Builder 4-A.
- Students review the required reading(s) *before* the assigned chapter begins.
- Teachers may want to discuss assigned reading(s) with students.
- Teachers shall assign the required essay. The rest of the essays can be outlined, answered with shorter answers, discussed, or skipped.
- Students will review all readings for chapter 4.

DEAR SON: I have ever had pleasure in obtaining any little anecdotes of my ancestors. You may remember the inquiries I made among the remains of my relations when you were with me in England, and the journey I undertook for that purpose. Imagining it may be equally agreeable to you to know the circumstances of my life, many of which you are yet unacquainted with, and expecting the enjoyment of a week's uninterrupted leisure in my present country retirement, I sit down to write them for you. To which I have besides some other inducements. Having emerged from the poverty and obscurity in which I was born and bred, to a state of affluence and some degree of reputation in the world, and having gone so far through life with a considerable share of felicity, the conducing means I made use of, which with the blessing of God so well succeeded, my posterity may like to know, as they may find some of them suitable to their own situations, and therefore fit to be imitated.

That felicity, when I reflected on it, has induced me sometimes to say, that were it offered to my choice, I should have no objection to a repetition of the same life from its beginning, only asking the advantages authors have in a second edition to correct some faults of the first. So I might, besides correcting the faults, change some sinister accidents and events of it for others more favorable. But though this were denied, I should still accept the offer. Since such a repetition is not to be expected, the next thing most like living one's life over again seems to be a recollection of that life, and to make that recollection as durable as possible by putting it down in writing.

Hereby, too, I shall indulge the inclination so natural in old men, to be talking of themselves and their own past actions; and I shall indulge it without being tiresome to others, who, through respect to age, might conceive themselves obliged to give me a hearing, since this may be read or not as any one pleases. And, lastly (I may as well confess it, since my denial of it will be believed by nobody), perhaps I shall a good deal gratify my own vanity. Indeed, I scarce ever heard or saw the introductory words, "Without vanity I may say," &c., but some vain thing immediately followed. Most people dislike vanity in others, whatever share they have of it themselves; but I give it fair quarter wherever I meet with it, being persuaded that it is often productive of good to the possessor, and to others that are within his sphere of action; and therefore, in many cases, it would not be altogether absurd if a man were to thank God for his vanity among the other comforts of life.

And now I speak of thanking God, I desire with all humility to acknowledge that I owe the mentioned happiness of my past life to His kind providence, which lead me to the means I used and gave them success. My belief of this induces me to hope, though I must not presume, that the same goodness will still be exercised toward me, in continuing that happiness, or enabling me to bear a fatal reverse, which I may experience as others have done: the complexion of my future fortune being known to Him only in whose power it is to bless to us even our afflictions (www.earlyamerica.com/lives/franklin).

1.	Did Franklin write this autobiography only for his son? How do you know?
2.	What does Franklin say about growing old?
3.	If this was the only reference you possessed about Franklin's faith, would you say that he was a believer?

The Pennsylvania Gazette
Benjamin Franklin

The Pennsylvania Gazette was one of the United States' most prominent newspapers from 1728, before the time period of the American Revolution, until 1815. It was first published by Samuel Keimer. On October 2, 1729, Benjamin Franklin and Hugh Meredith bought the paper. Some of the most famous issues included an editorial. On August 6, 1741, Franklin published an editorial about the recently deceased Andrew Hamilton, a lawyer and public figure in Philadelphia who had been a friend. The editorial praised the man highly and showed Franklin had held the man in high esteem. In 1752, Franklin published a third-person account of his pioneering kite experiment in the *Pennsylvania Gazette,* without mentioning that he himself had performed it.

Philadelphia, Oct. 19. 1752

As frequent mention is made in the newspapers from Europe, of the success of the Philadelphia experiment for drawing the electric fire from clouds by means of pointed rods of iron erected on high buildings, etc, it may be agreeable to inform the curious that the same experiment has succeeded in Philadelphia, tho' made in a different and more easy manner, which is as follows:

Make a small cross of two light strips of cedar, the arms so long as to reach to the four corners of a large thin silk handkerchief when extended; tie the corners of the handkerchief to the extremities of the cross, so you have the body of a kite; which being properly accommodated with a tail, loop, and string, will rise in the air, like those made of paper; but this being of silk is fitter to bear the wind and wet of a thunder gust without tearing. To the top of the upright stick of the cross is to be fixed a very sharp pointed wire, rising a foot or more above the wood. To the end of the twine, next the hand, is to be ty'd a silk ribbon, and where the silk and twine join, a key may be fastened. This kite is to be raised when a thunder gust appears to be coming on, and the person who holds the string must stand within a door, or window, or under some cover, so that the silk ribbon may not be wet; and care must be taken that the twine does not touch the frame of the door or window. As soon as any of the thunder clouds come over the kite, the pointed wire will draw the electric fire from them, and the kite, with all the twine, will be electrified, and the loose filaments of the twine will stand out every way, and be attracted by an approaching finger. And when the rain has wet the kite and twine, so that it can conduct the electric fire freely, you will find it stream out plentifully from the key on the approach of your knuckle. At this key the phial may be charged; and from electric fire thus obtained, spirits may be kindled, and all the other electric experiments be performed, which are usually done by the help of a rubbed glass globe or tube; and thereby the sameness of the electric matter with that of lightning compleatly demonstrated.

—B.F.

Assignments

- Warm-up: Write an editorial to your local newspaper explaining how you feel about an issue.
- Student should complete Concept Builder 4-B.
- Student should review reading(s) from next chapter.
- Student should outline essay due at the end of the week.
- Per teacher instructions, students may answer orally, in a group setting, some of the essays that are not assigned as the formal essay.

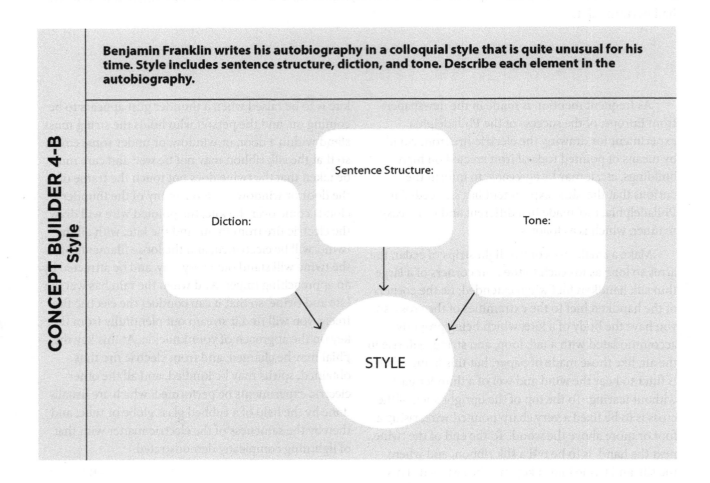

CONCEPT BUILDER 4-B
Style

Benjamin Franklin writes his autobiography in a colloquial style that is quite unusual for his time. Style includes sentence structure, diction, and tone. Describe each element in the autobiography.

Sentence Structure:

Diction:

Tone:

STYLE

Political Cartoons

"Join, or Die" is a well-known political cartoon, created by Benjamin Franklin and first published in the *Pennsylvania Gazette* on May 9, 1754. The original publication by the *Gazette* is the earliest known pictorial representation of colonial union. It is a woodcut showing a snake severed into eighths, with each segment labeled with the initials of an American colony or region. New England was represented as one segment and Delaware and Georgia were omitted completely. Thus, it has 8 segments of snake rather than the traditional 13 colonies. During that era, there was a superstition that a snake that had been cut into pieces would come back to life if the pieces were put together before sunset.

Assignments

- Warm-up: What message is Franklin conveying in this political cartoon?
- Student should complete Concept Builder 4-C.
- Student should write rough drafts of all assigned essays.
- The teacher may correct rough drafts.

CONCEPT BUILDER 4-C — My Autobiography		
If you were writing your autobiography, who would be the five most influential people in your life? Why?		
My Autobiography		
Person(s)	Why	

Collected Edition of Experiments and Observations on Electricity Made at Philadelphia in America

Originally published as a series of pamphlets in 1751, the first collected edition of *Experiments and Observations on Electricity Made at Philadelphia in America* by Benjamin Franklin was the fourth publication of his seminal experiments concerning electricity. Franklin did not claim to be the authority on electricity, but wished to use his pamphlets to entice other scientists, mostly French scientists, to collaborate with him in further studies.

Assignments

- Warm-up: Describe in detail how your parent/guardian cooks spaghetti.
- Student should complete Concept Builder 4-D.
- Student will re-write corrected copies of essay due tomorrow.

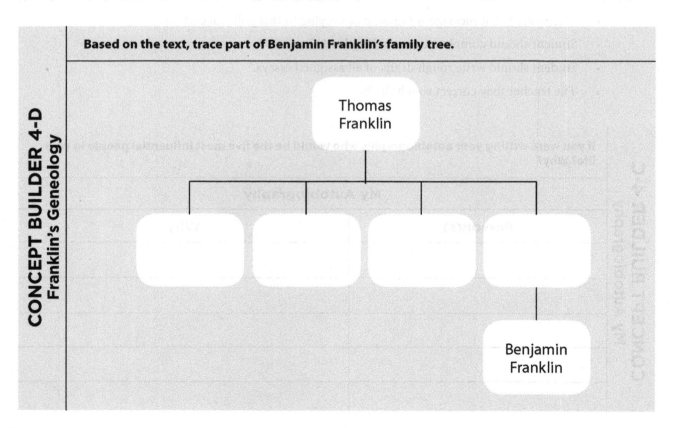

CONCEPT BUILDER 4-D
Franklin's Geneology

Based on the text, trace part of Benjamin Franklin's family tree.

Thomas Franklin

Benjamin Franklin

LESSON 5

Poor Richard's Almanac

Poor Richard's Almanac was a yearly almanac published by Benjamin Franklin, who adopted the pseudonym of "Poor Richard." The publication appeared continually from 1732 to 1758. It was a best seller and print runs reached 10,000 per year.

1. A child thinks 20 shillings and 20 years can scarce ever be spent.

2. A cold April, the barn will fill.

3. A countryman between two lawyers, is like a fish between two cats.

4. Act uprightly, and despise calumny; dirt may stick to a mud wall, but not to polish'd marble.

5. A cypher and humility make the other figures and virtues of tenfold value.

6. A false friend and a shadow attend only while the sun shines.

7. A father's a treasure ; a brother's a comfort; a friend is both.

8. A fat kitchen, a lean will.

9. A fine genius in his own country, is like gold in the mine.

10. A flatterer never seems absurd : The flatter'd always takes his word.

11. After three days men grow weary of a wench, a guest, and weather rainy.

12. After crosses and losses men grow humbler and wiser.

13. A full belly is the mother of all evil.

14. A full belly makes a dull brain.

15. A good example is the best sermon.

16. A good lawyer, a bad neighbor.

17. A good man is seldom uneasy, an ill one never easy.

18. A house without woman and firelight is like a body without soul or sprite.

19. A lean award is better than a fat judgment.

20. A learned blockhead is a greater blockhead than an ignorant one.

21. A lie stands on one leg, truth on two.

22. A life of leisure, and a life of laziness are two things.

23. A light purse is a heavy curse.

24. A little house well fill'd, a little field well till'd, and a little wife well will'd, are great riches.

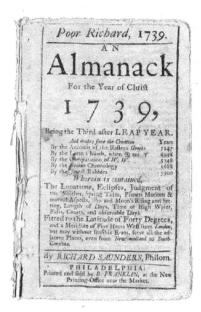

25. All blood is alike ancient.

26. All mankind are beholden to him that is kind to the good.

27. All things are cheap to the saving, dear to the wasteful.

28. All things are easy to industry, all things difficult to sloth.

archive.org/details/poorrichardsalma00franrich.

Assignments

- Warm-up: In a short essay give five wise things that life has taught you.
- Student should complete Concept Builder 4-E.
- Essays are due. Students should take the chapter 4 test.

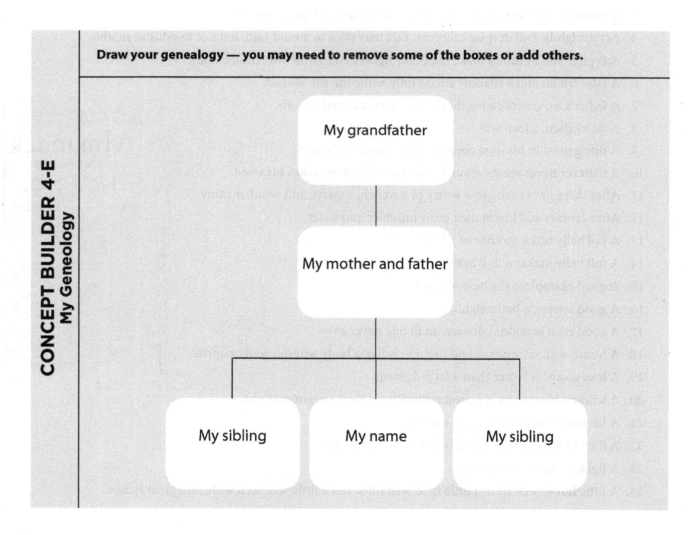

CONCEPT BUILDER 4-E
My Geneology

Draw your genealogy — you may need to remove some of the boxes or add others.

My grandfather

My mother and father

My sibling | My name | My sibling

Chapter 5

1750–1800 (Part 2):
The Revolutionary Period

First Thoughts

In 1994 my neighbor, Joe Black, held a family-centered rally to celebrate Christian values and American patriotism. This rally included family friendly picnics, craft exhibits, and patriotic lectures. To top the evening off, there was a bonfire — a cross burning. Joe Black was the Grand Wizard of the Somerset County, Pennsylvania, Ku Klux Klan. An ad posted on a local restaurant, Jim and Jimmies, stated, "(The Ku Klux Klan is here) . . . to protect the weak, the innocent, and the defenseless from the indignities . . . of the lawless; to relieve the injured and oppressed; to succor the suffering and unfortunate, and especially the widows and orphans of Confederate soldiers." How could we digress so far from the godly vision of the Puritans and founding fathers?

Author Worldview Watch

During the revolutionary era there were Christian giants, James Madison among them. Patrick Henry wrote many private letters about his faith in Christ. However, many patriots were deists, including Thomas Jefferson. However, readers should be careful not to judge too harshly. One would have preferred a more pristine statement of Christian faith. There is no doubt, however, that the slave and great poet Philis Wheatley was a Christian theist. Her poetry is full of Christian/biblical metaphors.

Chapter Learning Objectives

In chapter 5 we visit Phillis Wheatley and as we do that we look again at the horrible reality that was antebellum, chattel slavery. Next, we look at Patrick Henry's iconic or patriotic — you choose — speech rallying the Virginia House of Burgesses to rebel against England. Then we look at Thomas Jefferson's Declaration of Independence that was, quite literally, rebellion. We finish with a gentle look into the mind and the life of an extraordinary American colonial woman. You will read and analyze poems by Phillis Wheatley, *Speech in the Virginia Convention* by Patrick Henry, *The Declaration of Independence* by Thomas Jefferson, and *Letter to Her Daughter from the New White House* by Abigail Adams.

As a result of this chapter study you will be able to . . .

1. Write a descriptive essay about colonial women.

2. Evaluate when rebellion is appropriate.

Weekly Essay Options: Begin on page 274 of the Teacher Guide.

Reading ahead: Students should read 18th- and 19th-century poetry and the 19th-century short story "The Devil and Tom Walker," by Washington Irving.

Phillis Wheatley
Part One

Background Born in 1753 in Africa, seven-year-old Phillis Wheatley was kidnapped and sold to a prosperous Boston family, the Wheatleys. While nothing could soften the horrors of slavery, the Wheatley family was very kind to her. They valued her sharp mind and taught her grammar and writing. It is clear that the Wheatley family were born-again Christians. Therefore, it is not surprising that Phillis Wheatley committed her life to Christ and came to know the Bible well. At the same time, three English Christian poets — Milton, Pope, and Gray — touched her deeply and exerted a strong influence on her verse. She became a sensation in Boston in the 1760s when her poem on the death of the great evangelist George Whitefield was circulated.

Phillis Wheatley was one of the earliest African–American evangelists. She argued that all men and women, regardless of race or class, were in need of salvation. To students at Harvard College, she wrote:

> Students, to you 'tis given to scan the heights
>
> Above, to traverse the ethereal space,
>
> And mark the systems of revolving worlds.
>
> Still more, ye sons of science ye receive
>
> The blissful news by messengers from heav'n,
>
> How Jesus blood for your redemption flows.
>
> See Him with hands outstretched upon the cross;
>
> Immense compassion in His bosom glows;
>
> He hears revilers, nor resents their scorn:
>
> What matchless mercy in the Son of God!
>
> When the whole human race by sin had fall'n,
>
> He deigned to die that they might rise again,
>
> And share with in the sublimist skies,
>
> Life without death, and glory without end.
>
> Improve your privileges while they stay,
>
> Ye pupils, and each hour redeem, that bears
>
> Or good or bad report of you to heav'n.
>
> Let sin, that baneful evil to the soul,
>
> By you be shunned, nor once remit your guard;
>
> Suppress the deadly serpent in its egg.
>
> Ye blooming plants of human race divine,
>
> An Ethiop tells you 'tis your greatest foe;
>
> Its transient sweetness turns to endless pain,
>
> And immense perdition sinks the soul.

By the time Phillis Wheatley wrote her poetry, slavery had existed in the American colonies for more than 160 years. In fact, the institution of slavery had existed in Western Civilization since biblical times, but the first slaves came to the Western Hemisphere in the early 1500s. However, not until 20 African slaves were brought to Jamestown, Virginia, in 1619, was slavery present in America. In fact, is it not altogether clear if the first African slaves were brought as indentured servants (to be released in seven years) or chattel slavery (never to be released). Nevertheless, it quickly became a moot point. A series of complex colonial laws made sure that Africans and their descendants were to remain in slavery for perpetuity. What came first, racism or slavery? It is hard to say, but racism was not institutionalized in America until white Americans created a language to describe American people groups. When in 1619 the first African American came to the Jamestown colony, that language was already present. Europeans from the 1200s to the early 1500s used terms such as "Negro" to refer to persons with dark-colored skin. Initially, these terms were used not to denigrate a "race" or caste, nor were they used in a genealogical sense. They were used to designate a different physical attribute. Later, "Negro" and "Mulatto" gained a negative connotation.

As white Americans learned to name minorities, a system of control arose, resulting in racism. Racism, with all its stereotyping components, evolved into the deprecating form in which it exists today. The historian David R. Roediger argues, "The idea of race, then, emerges from the ways that social meaning becomes attached to physical differences. White Europeans gave such meaning an inherent, God-given origin, and (white) Americans kept up the tradition." (Ethan Bronner, "Inventing the Notion of Race," in *The New York Times*, January 10, 1998).

Assignments

- Warm-up: How do differences tend to divide people rather than unite them? How might this be changed in order to show God's grace to everyone?

- Student should complete Concept Builder 5-A.

- Students review the required reading(s) before the assigned chapter begins.

- Teachers may want to discuss assigned reading(s) with students.

- Teachers shall assign the required essay. The rest of the essays can be outlined, answered with shorter answers, discussed, or skipped.

- Students will review all readings for chapter 5.

CONCEPT BUILDER 5-A
Paraphrase

A paraphrase is a prose rewriting of a poem in your own words. Paraphrase the following poem by Phillis Wheatley.

On Being Brought from Africa to America

'Twas mercy brought me from my Pagan land,
Taught my benighted soul to understand
That there's a God, that there's a Saviour too:
Once I redemption neither fought nor knew,
Some view our sable race with scornful eye,
"Their colour is a diabolic dye."
Remember, Christians, Negroes, black as Cain,
May be refin'd, and join th' angelic train.

Phillis Wheatley
Part Two

Most slaves were taken from West Africa. There is little doubt that Phillis Wheatley came from this area. The historian Benjamin Quarles described these West African people groups:

> Of the varied Old World people that entered America, none came with as wide a geographical area as the blacks. The vast majority came from the West Coast of Africa, a 3000-mile stretch extending from the Senegal River . . . . to Angola . . . These groups shared no common language . . . Indeed, there are more than 200 distinct languages in present day Nigeria alone. There was no such thing as the "African personality" since the varied groups differed as much in their way of life as in the physical characteristics they exhibited . . . Whatever the type of society, the different groups of Africans all operated under well-organized social systems . . . African societies before the coming of the Europeans were not backward and changeless. . . . (Benjamin Quarles, Black Abolitionists, New York: Oxford University Press, 1969, p. 74).

Quarles also described slave trading and the middle passage. Normally, European settlers established forts on the edge of the jungle. The Africans, wishing to obtain the trade goods, would capture young men and women and take them to the fort. The terror is unimaginable! African young people were stolen from their families and were never seen again. The slaves were kept in makeshift prisons or warehouses until their proprietor had enough to justify a shipment — about 250.

One of the most awful parts of slavery was the middle passage. Imagine being stolen from everything familiar, from everyone you love. Placed in a dark prison — perhaps raped and abused — then, chained side-to-side, naked, with hundreds of strangers of all ages and sexes inside the dark insides of a ship. Imagine lying in your own waste for six weeks. Hear the cries of anguish and death. Smell the results of human sin! Phillis Wheatley experienced this middle passage and yet there seems to be no invectiveness in her writing.

The South Atlantic trade network involved several international routes. The best known of the triangular trades included the transportation of manufactured goods from Europe to Africa, where they were traded for slaves. Slaves were then transported across the Atlantic — the infamous middle passage — primarily to Brazil and the Caribbean, where they were sold. It was not uncommon for up to one-eighth of the human cargo to die. Dead slaves were thrown overboard and schools of sharks followed the slave ships. But profits were so vast that the loss was considered to be incidental. Often the slaves would stay in the West Indies for several weeks while they were acclimated to their new North American home.

The final leg of this triangular trade brought tropical products to Europe. In another variation, manufactured goods from colonial America were taken to West Africa; slaves were carried to the Caribbean and Southern colonies; and sugar, molasses, and other goods were returned to the home ports.

A basic step toward successful slave management was to implant in the slaves an identity of personal inferiority. They had to keep their places, to understand that bondage was their natural status. Thus, from the beginning, Africans understood that their resistance to white domination was a question of identity survival. Indeed, resistance seemed to be the only way to survive in the face of profound white systemic racism. It was from this root that later separatism ideology sprang.

However, Africans began to resist even before they were out of sight of Africa. Resistance became a way of life. Whether it was in the colonial South Carolina Stono Rebellion or in the Brer Rabbit stories, or in everyday work in the cotton fields, African Americans resisted. Slaves defiantly cut off the roots of the plants with their hoes, just under the ground so no one noticed. Slaves used work stoppages, self-injuries, and, especially in the first few weeks of bondage, suicide to resist white enslavement. African Americans were resisting so vigorously that at times it seemed like a white minority was under siege.

One of the most clever ways the African Americans resisted the whites was by their maintenance of a rich culture. This pattern of behavior continued into the 20th century. Number and size of African American communities affected the degree and nature of resistance, but resistance existed. A chasm grew between whites and African Americans that politics, religion, and economics would never bridge. This chasm, real or imagined, became an indelible part of the American ethos.

African American slaves stayed aloof from the dominant culture, which was especially true in their religious life. Many African American church leaders resisted assimilation into church institutions in which whites participated. It was a fundamental way that African Americans showed their defiance. In fact, the early civil rights movement, to many observers, appeared to be a religious protest movement more than a political protest movement.

Assignments

- Warm-up: Some critics — especially of African American descent — have been critical of Phillis Wheatley. While they respect her achievements and writing ability, they wish that she had used her talents to lead a slave revolt or to perform a Harriet Tubman-like role, at least not to extol the whites. She seemed too willing to accept her station in life. Do you agree?

- Students should complete Concept Builder 5-B.

- Student should review reading(s) from the next chapter.

- Student should outline essay due at the end of the week

- Per teacher instructions, students may answer orally, in a group setting, some of the essays that are not assigned as formal essays. Students will review all readings for chapter 4.

In the Declaration of Independence, Thomas Jefferson sought to persuade his audience to a position. He used special words, some words that had double meanings: a denotation and a connotation. A denotation is the actual, dictionary definition of a word. The connotation is an emotional association with the word. For example, scatterbrained means the same as absentminded, but the former has a much more negative connotation. Give the denotation and connotation of the words that are in bold below. Add one more word that you found in the document.

When in the Course of human events, it becomes necessary for one people to dissolve the political bands which have connected them with another, and to assume among the powers of the earth, the separate and equal station to which the Laws of Nature and of Nature's God entitle them, a decent respect to the opinions of mankind requires that they should declare the causes which impel them to the separation.

We hold these truths to be self-evident, that all men are created equal, that they are endowed by their Creator with certain unalienable Rights, that among these are Life, Liberty and the pursuit of Happiness. — That to secure these rights, Governments are instituted among Men, deriving their just powers from the consent of the governed, — That whenever any Form of Government becomes destructive of these ends, it is the Right of the People to alter or to abolish it, and to institute new Government, laying its foundation on such principles and organizing its powers in such form, as to them shall seem most likely to effect their Safety and Happiness. Prudence, indeed, will dictate that Governments long established should not be changed for light and transient causes; and accordingly all experience hath shewn, that mankind are more disposed to suffer, while evils are sufferable, than to right themselves by abolishing the forms to which they are accustomed. But when a long train of abuses and usurpations, pursuing invariably the same Object evinces a design to reduce them under absolute Despotism, it is their right, it is their duty, to throw off such Government, and to provide new Guards for their future security. — Such has been the patient sufferance of these Colonies; and such is now the necessity which constrains them to alter their former Systems of Government. The history of the present King of Great Britain [George III] is a history of repeated injuries and usurpations, all having in direct object the establishment of an absolute Tyranny over these States. To prove this, let Facts be submitted to a candid world (www.archives.gov/exhibits/charters/decloration.html).

Word	Denotation	Connotation
Dissolve	To cause to disappear	To completely remove with malice
Destructive	To destroy completely	
Dictator	Total authority held by a leader	

Give Me Liberty or Give Me Death

A speech delivered by Patrick Henry on March 23, 1775.

No man thinks more highly than I do of the patriotism, as well as abilities, of the very worthy gentlemen who have just addressed the House. But different men often see the same subject in different lights; and, therefore, I hope it will not be thought disrespectful to those gentlemen if, entertaining as I do opinions of a character very opposite to theirs, I shall speak forth my sentiments freely and without reserve. This is no time for ceremony. The questing before the House is one of awful moment to this country. For my own part, I consider it as nothing less than a question of freedom or slavery; and in proportion to the magnitude of the subject ought to be the freedom of the debate. It is only in this way that we can hope to arrive at truth, and fulfill the great responsibility which we hold to God and our country. Should I keep back my opinions at such a time, through fear of giving offense, I should consider myself as guilty of treason towards my country, and of an act of disloyalty toward the Majesty of Heaven, which I revere above all earthly kings.

Mr. President, it is natural to man to indulge in the illusions of hope. We are apt to shut our eyes against a painful truth, and listen to the song of that siren till she transforms us into beasts. Is this the part of wise men, engaged in a great and arduous struggle for liberty? Are we disposed to be of the number of those who, having eyes, see not, and, having ears, hear not, the things which so nearly concern their temporal salvation? For my part, whatever anguish of spirit it may cost, I am willing to know the whole truth; to know the worst, and to provide for it.

I have but one lamp by which my feet are guided, and that is the lamp of experience. I know of no way of judging of the future but by the past. And judging by the past, I wish to know what there has been in the conduct of the British ministry for the last ten years to justify those hopes with which gentlemen have been pleased to solace themselves and the House. Is it that insidious smile with which our petition has been lately received? Trust it not, sir; it will prove a snare to your feet. Suffer not yourselves to be betrayed with a kiss. Ask yourselves how this gracious reception of our petition comports with those warlike preparations which cover our waters and darken our land. Are fleets and armies necessary to a work of love and reconciliation? Have we shown ourselves so unwilling to be reconciled that force must be called in to win back our love? Let us not deceive ourselves, sir. These are the implements of war and subjugation; the last arguments to which kings resort. I ask gentlemen, sir, what means this martial array, if its purpose be not to force us to submission? Can gentlemen assign any other possible motive for it? Has Great Britain any enemy, in this quarter of the world, to call for all this accumulation of navies and armies? No, sir, she has none. They are meant for us: they can be meant for no other. They are sent over to bind and rivet upon us those chains which the British ministry have been so long forging. And what have we to oppose to them? Shall we try argument? Sir, we have been trying that for the last ten years. Have we anything new to offer upon the subject? Nothing. We have held the subject up in every light of which it is capable; but it has been all in vain. Shall we resort to entreaty and humble supplication? What terms shall we find which have not been already exhausted? Let us not, I beseech you, sir, deceive ourselves. Sir, we have done everything that could be done to avert the storm which is now coming on. We have petitioned; we have remonstrated; we have supplicated; we have prostrated ourselves before the throne, and have implored its interposition to arrest the tyrannical hands of the ministry and Parliament. Our petitions have been slighted; our remonstrances have produced additional violence and insult; our supplications have been disregarded; and we have been spurned, with contempt, from the foot of the throne! In vain, after these things, may we indulge the fond hope of peace and reconciliation. There is no longer any room for hope. If we wish to be free — if we mean to preserve inviolate those inestimable privileges for which we have been so long contending — if we mean not basely to abandon the noble struggle in which we have been so long engaged, and which we have pledged ourselves never to abandon until the glorious object of our contest shall be obtained — we must fight! I repeat it, sir, we must fight! An appeal to arms and to the God of hosts is all that is left us!

They tell us, sir, that we are weak; unable to cope with so formidable an adversary. But when shall we be stronger? Will it be the next week, or the next year? Will it be when we are totally disarmed, and when a British guard shall be stationed in every house? Shall we gather strength but irresolution and inaction? Shall we acquire the means of effectual resistance by lying supinely on our backs and hugging the delusive phantom of hope, until our enemies shall have bound us hand and foot? Sir, we are not weak if we make a proper use of those means which the God of nature hath placed in our power. The millions of people, armed in the holy cause of liberty, and in such a country as that which we possess, are invincible by any force which our enemy can send against us. Besides, sir, we shall not fight our battles alone. There is a just God who presides over the destinies of nations, and who will raise up friends to fight our battles for us. The battle, sir, is not to the strong alone; it is to the vigilant, the active, the brave. Besides, sir, we have no election. If we

Patrick Henry Before the Virginia House of Burgesses by Peter F. Rothermel, 1851 (PD-Art).

were base enough to desire it, it is now too late to retire from the contest. There is no retreat but in submission and slavery! Our chains are forged! Their clanking may be heard on the plains of Boston! The war is inevitable — and let it come! I repeat it, sir, let it come.

It is in vain, sir, to extenuate the matter. Gentlemen may cry, Peace, Peace — but there is no peace. The war is actually begun! The next gale that sweeps from the north will bring to our ears the clash of resounding arms! Our brethren are already in the field! Why stand we here idle? What is it that gentlemen wish? What would they have? Is life so dear, or peace so sweet, as to be purchased at the price of chains and slavery? Forbid it, Almighty God! I know not what course others may take; but as for me, give me liberty or give me death!

Assignments

- Warm-up: What rhetorical devices does Henry employ to persuade his audience?

- Students should complete Concept Builder 5-C.

- Students should write rough drafts of assigned essay.

- The teacher may correct rough drafts.

- Per teacher instructions, students may answer orally, in a group setting, some of the essays that are not assigned as formal essays. Students will review all readings for chapter 5.

CONCEPT BUILDER 5-C
Identifying Persuasive Techniques

Speech makers can resort to several techniques in order to persuade a reader to accept his position. Identify several of the following in Patrick Henry's speech, "Give me Liberty or Give me Death."

Persuasive Technique	Textual Example
Either-or Fallacy Henry suggests an either-or situation when the whole situation is more complicated.	They are sent over to bind and rivet upon us those chains which the British ministry have been so long forging. And what have we to oppose to them? Shall we try argument? Sir, we have been trying that for the last ten years. Have we anything new to offer upon the subject? Nothing.
Overgeneralization and Stereotype Henry evokes stereotypes, or preconceived impressions about people, places, or things.	
Loaded Words Henry uses words loaded with emotional connotations.	

The Declaration of Independence of the Thirteen Colonies

July 4, 1776 When in the Course of human events, it becomes necessary for one people to dissolve the political bands which have connected them with another, and to assume among the powers of the earth, the separate and equal station to which the Laws of Nature and of Nature's God entitle them, a decent respect to the opinions of mankind requires that they should declare the causes which impel them to the separation.

We hold these truths to be self-evident, that all men are created equal, that they are endowed by their Creator with certain unalienable Rights, that among these are Life, Liberty and the pursuit of Happiness. — That to secure these rights, Governments are instituted among Men, deriving their just powers from the consent of the governed — That whenever any Form of Government becomes destructive of these ends, it is the Right of the People to alter or to abolish it, and to institute new Government, laying its foundation on such principles and organizing its powers in such form, as to them shall seem most likely to effect their Safety and Happiness. Prudence, indeed, will dictate that Governments long established should not be changed for light and transient causes; and accordingly all experience hath shewn, that mankind are more disposed to suffer, while evils are sufferable, than to right themselves by abolishing the forms to which they are accustomed. But when a long train of abuses and usurpations, pursuing invariably the same Object evinces a design to reduce them under absolute Despotism, it is their right, it is their duty, to throw off such Government, and to provide new Guards for their future security. — Such has been the patient sufferance of these Colonies; and such is now the necessity which constrains them to alter their former Systems of Government. The history of the present King of Great Britain [George III] is a history of repeated injuries and usurpations, all having in direct object the establishment of an absolute Tyranny over these States. To prove this, let Facts be submitted to a candid world.

He has refused his Assent to Laws, the most wholesome and necessary for the public good.

He has forbidden his Governors to pass Laws of immediate and pressing importance, unless suspended in their operation till his Assent should be obtained; and when so suspended, he has utterly neglected to attend to them.

He has refused to pass other Laws for the accommodation of large districts of people, unless those people would relinquish the right of Representation in the Legislature, a right inestimable to them and formidable to tyrants only.

He has called together legislative bodies at places unusual, uncomfortable, and distant from the depository of their public Records, for the sole purpose of fatiguing them into compliance with his measures.

He has dissolved Representative Houses repeatedly, for opposing with manly firmness his invasions on the rights of the people.

He has refused for a long time, after such dissolutions, to cause others to be elected; whereby the Legislative powers, incapable of Annihilation, have returned to the People at large for their exercise; the State remaining in the mean time exposed to all the dangers of invasion from without, and convulsions within.

He has endeavoured to prevent the population of these States; for that purpose obstructing the Laws for Naturalization of Foreigners; refusing to pass others to encourage their migrations hither, and raising the conditions of new Appropriations of Lands.

He has obstructed the Administration of Justice, by refusing his Assent to Laws for establishing Judiciary powers.

He has made Judges dependent on his Will alone, for the tenure of their offices, and the amount and payment of their salaries.

He has erected a multitude of New Offices, and sent hither swarms of Officers to harass our people, and eat out their substance.

He has kept among us, in times of peace, Standing Armies without the consent of our legislatures.

He has affected to render the Military independent of and superior to the Civil power.

He has combined with others to subject us to a jurisdiction foreign to our constitution and unacknowledged by our laws; giving his Assent to their Acts of pretended Legislation:

For Quartering large bodies of armed troops among us:

For protecting them, by a mock Trial, from punishment for any Murders which they should commit on the Inhabitants of these States:

For cutting off our Trade with all parts of the world:

For imposing Taxes on us without our Consent:

For depriving us, in many cases, of the benefits of Trial by Jury:

For transporting us beyond Seas to be tried for pretended offences:

For abolishing the free System of English Laws in a neighbouring Province, establishing therein an Arbitrary government, and enlarging its Boundaries so as to render it at once an example and fit instrument for introducing the same absolute rule into these Colonies:

For taking away our Charters, abolishing our most valuable Laws, and altering fundamentally the Forms of our Governments:

For suspending our own Legislatures, and declaring themselves invested with power to legislate for us in all cases whatsoever.

He has abdicated Government here, by declaring us out of his Protection and waging War against us.

He has plundered our seas, ravaged our Coasts, burnt our towns, and destroyed the lives of our people.

He is at this time transporting large Armies of foreign Mercenaries to compleat the works of death, desolation and tyranny, already begun with circumstances of Cruelty and perfidy scarcely paralleled in the most barbarous ages, and totally unworthy the Head of a civilized nation.

He has constrained our fellow Citizens taken Captive on the high Seas to bear Arms against their Country, to become the executioners of their friends and Brethren, or to fall themselves by their Hands.

He has excited domestic insurrections amongst us, and has endeavoured to bring on the inhabitants of our frontiers, the merciless Indian Savages, whose known rule of warfare, is an undistinguished destruction of all ages, sexes and conditions.

In every stage of these Oppressions We have Petitioned for Redress in the most humble terms: Our repeated Petitions have been answered only by repeated injury. A Prince whose character is thus marked by every act which may define a Tyrant, is unfit to be the ruler of a free people.

Nor have We been wanting in attentions to our British brethren. We have warned them from time to time of attempts by their legislature to extend an unwarrantable jurisdiction over us. We have reminded them of the circumstances of our emigration and settlement here. We have appealed to their native justice and magnanimity, and we have conjured them by the ties of our common kindred to disavow these usurpations, which, would inevitably interrupt our connections and correspondence. They too have been deaf to the voice of justice and of consanguinity. We must, therefore, acquiesce in the necessity, which denounces our Separation, and hold them, as we hold the rest of mankind, Enemies in War, in Peace Friends.

We, therefore, the Representatives of the united States of America, in General Congress, Assembled, appealing to the Supreme Judge of the world for the rectitude of our intentions, do, in the Name, and by the Authority of the good People of these Colonies, solemnly publish and declare, That these United Colonies are, and of Right ought to be Free and Independent States; that they are Absolved from all Allegiance to the British Crown, and that all political connection between them and the State of Great Britain, is and ought to be totally dissolved; and that as Free and Independent States, they have full Power to levy War, conclude Peace, contract Alliances, establish Commerce, and to do all other Acts and Things which Independent States may of right do. And for the support of this Declaration, with a firm reliance on the protection of divine Providence, we mutually pledge to each other our Lives, our Fortunes and our sacred Honor.

Assignments

- Warm-up: Did the Americans exaggerate a tad bit in this "declaration of independence"?
- Students should complete Concept Builder 5-D.
- Student will re-write corrected copy of essay due tomorrow.

CONCEPT BUILDER 5-D Active Readng		Read the "Give Me Liberty or Give Me Death" speech in the text by Patrick Henry then answer the following questions.
	1	Why did the British government send their navy to the American colonies?
	2	Why does Henry use rhetorical questions (questions with no expectation of a response, whose answers are often obvious)?
	3	Based on this speech, what sort of man would you say Patrick Henry is?
	4	Would you like to be debating an opposite position?

Letter to Her Daughter
Abigail Adams

Abigail Adams, wife of the second president of the United States, watched the first battle of the American Revolution from her front porch and lived to see the nation secure under a new president. In 1800 she wrote the following letter to her daughter from the White House:

Washington, November 21, 1800

My Dear Child,

I arrived here on Sunday last, and without meeting with any accident worth noticing, except losing ourselves when we left Baltimore, and going eight or nine miles on the Frederick road, by which means we were obliged to go the other eight through woods, where we wandered two hours without finding a guide or the path. Fortunately, a straggling black came up with us, and we engaged him as a guide to extricate us out of our difficulty. But woods are all you see from Baltimore until you reach the city, which is only so in name. Here and there is a small cot, without a glass window, interspersed amongst the forests, through which you travel miles without seeing any human being. In the city there are buildings enough, if they were compact and finished, to accommodate Congress and those attached to it: but as they are, and scattered as they are, I see no great comfort for them. The river, which runs up to Alexandria, is in full view of my window, and I see the vessels as they pass and repass. The house is upon a grand and superb scale, requiring about thirty servants to attend and keep the apartments in proper order, and perform the ordinary business of the house and stables: an establishment very well proportioned to the President's salary. The light in the apartments from the kitchen to parlours and chambers, is a tax indeed; daily agues, is another very cheering comfort. To assist us in this great castle, and render less attendance necessary, bells are wholly wanting, not one single one being hung through the whole house, and promises are all you can obtain. This is so great an inconvenience, that I know not what to do, or how to do. The ladies from Georgetown and in the city have many of them visited me. Yesterday I returned fifteen visits — but such a place as Georgetown appears — why our Milton is beautiful. But no comparisons — if they will put me up some bells, and let me have wood enough to keep fires, I design to be pleased. I could content myself almost anywhere three months; but surrounded with forest, can you believe that wood is not to be had, because people cannot be found to cut and cart it? Briesler entered into a contract with a man to supply him with wood; a small part, a few cords only, has he been able to get. Most of that was expended to dry the walls of the house before we came in, and yesterday the man told him it was impossible for him to procure it to be cut and carted. He has had recourse to coals; but we cannot get grates made and set. We have indeed come into a new country.

You must keep all this to yourself, and when asked how I like it, say that I write you the situation is beautiful, which is true. The house is made habitable, but there is not a single apartment finished, and all withinside, except the plastering, has been done since Briesler came. We have not the least fence-yard, or other convenience, without, and the great unfinished audience room I make a drying-room of, to hang up the clothes in. The principal stairs are not up, and will not be this winter. Six chambers are made comfortable; two are occupied by the President and Mr. Shaw; two lower rooms, one for a common parlor and one for a levee room. Upstairs there is the oval room, which is designed for the drafting-room, and has the crimson furniture in it. It is a very handsome room now, but when completed, wilt be beautiful. If the twelve years, in which this place has been considered as the future seat of government, had been improved, as they would have been if in New England, very many of the present inconveniences would have been removed. It is a beautiful spot, capable of every improvement, and the more I view it, the more I am delighted with it. Since I sat down to write, I have been called down to a servant from Mount Vernon, with a billet from Major Custis, and a haunch of venison, and a kind, congratulatory letter from Mrs. Lewis, upon my arrival in the city, with Mrs. Washington's love, inviting me to Mount Vernon, where, health permitting, I will go, before I leave this place. Two articles are much distressed for: the one is bells, but the more important one is wood. Yet you cannot see wood for the trees. No arrangement has been made, but by promises never performed, to supply the newcomers with fuel. Of the promises, Briesler had received his full share. He had procured nine cords of wood: between six and seven of that was kindly burnt up to dry the walls of the house, which ought to have been done by the commissioners, but which, if left to them, would have remained undone to this day. Congress poured in, but shiver, shiver. No wood-cutters nor carters to be had at any rate. We are now indebted to a Pennsylvania waggon to bring us, through the first clerk in the Treasury Office, one cord and a half of wood, which is all we have for this house, where twelve fires are constantly required and where, we are told, the roads will soon be so bad that it cannot be drawn. Briesler procured two hundred bushels of coal, or we must have suffered. This is the situation of almost every other person. The public officers have sent to Philadelphia for wood cutters and wagons.

The vessel which has my clothes and other matters is not arrived. The ladies are impatient for a drawing-room: I have no looking-glasses, but dwarfs, for this house; not a twentieth part lamps enough to light it. Many things were stolen, many are broken by the removal; amongst the number, my tea-china is more than half missing. Georgetown affords nothing. My rooms are very pleasant and warm, whilst the doors of the hall are closed.

You can scarce believe that here, in this wilderness-city, I should find myself so occupied as it is. My visitors — some of them come three or four miles. The return of one of them is the work of one day. Most of the ladies reside in Georgetown, or in scattered parts of the city, at two and three miles' distance. We have all been very well as yet; if we can by any means get wood, we shall not let our fires go out, but it is at a price indeed; from four dollars it has risen to nine. Some say it will fall, but there must be more industry than is to be found here to bring half enough to the market for the consumption of the inhabitants.

Assignments

- Warm-up: Describe a friend or acquaintance who is free–spirited and describe how he/she feels without any apologies.
- Students should complete Concept Builder 5-E.
- Essays are due. Students should take the chapter 5 test.

CONCEPT BUILDER 5-E		Read Abigail Adams' *Letter To Her Daughter* in the textbook, answer the following questions.
	1	How would you describe Abigail Adams' feelings toward her new house (the White House) in Washington DC?
	2	What tongue-in-cheek comment is Abigail Adams making about Congress?

Chapter 6

1800–1840: National Period (Part 1):

A Growing Nation

First Thoughts The first 50 years of our nation's social history were some of the most volatile in our entire history. Transportation, industry, education, social reform — all took leaps forward. As radical as these changes were, the changes in worldview were doubly radical. In one generation, America moved from orthodox Christian theism to pagan romanticism/transcendentalism. But our worldview journey was just beginning!

Author Worldview Watch William Cullen Bryant and Washington Irving were nascent (early) romantics, which means, they embraced some of former Christian theistic symbols, and Judeo-Christian morality, but flirted with early nature-loving idolatry. At least deism is dead!

Chapter Learning Objectives In chapter 6 we read poetry by William Cullen Bryant and two selections by Washington Irving. We observe the early movement away from Puritan theism toward transcendental romanticism. You will analyze "Thanatopsis," by William Cullen Bryant and the short stories "The Devil and Tom Walker" and "The Legend of Sleepy Hollow," by Washington Irving.

As a result of this chapter study you will be able to . . .

1. Offer several examples of figurative language and discuss how Bryant uses them to advance the purposes of his poem.

2. Offer evidence of irony in the conclusion of "The Devil and Tom Walker."

3. Define hyperbole and discuss its use in "The Devil and Tom Walker."

4. Examine themes in "The Devil and Tom Walker."

5. Create a modern version of "The Devil and Tom Walker." Your short story should be about five to ten pages.

Weekly Essay Options: Begin on page 274 of the Teacher Guide.

Reading ahead: Students should review the poem "The Raven" and the short stories "Fall of the House of Usher" and "The Tell Tale Heart" both by Edgar Allan Poe.

81

Real Change

In 1800, for the first time in history, an elected government replaced an entirely different ideological party. Granted, there were no political parties as we know them today in 1800. Nonetheless, it is remarkable and a credit to the American civilization that two candidates could vigorously debate issues and remain friends and colleagues after one is elected.

If unity prevailed nationally, disunity grew among the states. Namely, there was the growing struggle over slavery expansion. As long as the United States was confined to the eastern seaboard and southern and northern states had approximately the same representation in Congress, slavery was only a moral issue. With the acquisition of the Louisiana Purchase that all changed. The Missouri Compromise of 1820 tried to answer the problem of slavery expansion by stating that slavery was to be confined to the area south of the Missouri border (which was a slave state). Of course, the problem was not solved, only postponed.

The real changes in America, however, from 1800–1840 (and beyond) were in the social realm. This era was a time of the extension of the American nation and, above all, of the American ethos. The advent of steam travel and railroad transportation profoundly changed American life. A trip from Philadelphia to Pittsburgh (both in the same state) for instance, could take two months in 1820. By 1835 it would take two days!

At the same time, steamboats replaced rafts on the Mississippi and sharply reduced the price of Mississippi commerce. The Erie Canal, the most successful private project constructed during the era, enabled efficient western grain producers to ship their produce east and therefore encouraged western expansion.

Assignments

- Warm-up: In your lifetime, describe an election where the people elected someone much different from the incumbent.
- Student should complete Concept Builder 6-A.
- Students review the required reading(s) *before* the assigned chapter begins.
- Teachers may want to discuss assigned reading(s) with students.
- Teachers shall assign the required essay. The rest of the essays can be outlined, answered with shorter answers, discussed, or skipped.
- Students will review all readings for chapter 6.

Read excerpt from *The Devil and Tom Walker* **by Washington Irving**

A few miles from Boston, in Massachusetts, there is a deep inlet winding several miles into the interior of the country from Charles Bay, and terminating in a thickly wooded swamp, or morass. On one side of this inlet is a beautiful dark grove; on the opposite side the land rises abruptly from the water's edge, into a high ridge on which grow a few scattered oaks of great age and immense size. Under one of these gigantic trees, according to old stories, there was a great amount of treasure buried by Kidd the pirate. The inlet allowed a facility to bring the money in a boat secretly and at night to the very foot of the hill. The elevation of the place permitted a good look out to be kept that no one was at hand, while the remarkable trees formed good landmarks by which the place might easily be found again. The old stories add, moreover, that the devil presided at the hiding of the money, and took it under his guardianship; but this, it is well known, he always does with buried treasure, particularly when it has been ill gotten. Be that as it may, Kidd never returned to recover his wealth; being shortly after seized at Boston, sent out to England, and there hanged for a pirate.

About the year 1727, just at the time when earthquakes were prevalent in New England, and shook many tall sinners down upon their knees, there lived near this place a meagre miserly fellow of the name of Tom Walker. He had a wife as miserly as himself; they were so miserly that they even conspired to cheat each other. Whatever the woman could lay hands on she hid away: a hen could not cackle but she was on the alert to secure the new-laid egg. Her husband was continually prying about to detect her secret hoards, and many and fierce were the conflicts that took place about what ought to have been common property. They lived in a forlorn looking house, that stood alone and had an air of starvation. A few straggling savin trees, emblems of sterility, grew near it; no smoke ever curled from its chimney; no traveller stopped at its door. A miserable horse, whose ribs were as articulate as the bars of a gridiron, stalked about a field where a thin carpet of moss, scarcely covering the ragged beds of pudding stone, tantalized and balked his hunger; and sometimes he would lean his head over the fence, look piteously at the passer by, and seem to petition deliverance from this land of famine. The house and its inmates had altogether a bad name. Tom's wife was a tall termagant, fierce of temper, loud of tongue, and strong of arm. Her voice was often heard in wordy warfare with her husband; and his face sometimes showed signs that their conflicts were not confined to words (classiclit.about.com/od/devilandtomwalker/a/aa_deviltomwalker.html).

1	Why does Irving begin his short story by discussing the setting rather than introducing any characters?
2	Both Tom Walker and his wife are "type characters" or archetypes. What sort of archetypes are they?

William Cullen Bryant

William Cullen Bryant (1794–1878) was born in Massachusetts in a rural area. The rural motif was to dominate most of his poetry. He was a child prodigy. When he was only 17 he wrote his most famous poem, "Thanatopsis."

Thanatopsis

To him who in the love of Nature holds
Communion with her visible forms, she speaks
A various language; for his gayer hours
She has a voice of gladness, and a smile
And eloquence of beauty, and she glides
Into his darker musings, with a mild
And healing sympathy, that steals away
Their sharpness, ere he is aware. When thoughts
Of the last bitter hour come like a blight
Over thy spirit, and sad images
Of the stern agony, and shroud, and pall,
And breathless darkness, and the narrow house,
Make thee to shudder, and grow sick at heart; —
Go forth, under the open sky, and list
To Nature's teachings, while from all around —
Earth and her waters, and the depths of air —
Comes a still voice — Yet a few days, and thee
The all-beholding sun shall see no more
In all his course; nor yet in the cold ground,
Where thy pale form was laid, with many tears,
Nor in the embrace of ocean, shall exist
Thy image. Earth, that nourished thee, shall claim
Thy growth, to be resolved to earth again,
And, lost each human trace, surrendering up
Thine individual being, shalt thou go
To mix forever with the elements,
To be a brother to the insensible rock
And to the sluggish clod, which the rude swain

Turns with his share, and treads upon. The oak
Shall send his roots abroad, and pierce thy mould.

Yet not to thine eternal resting-place
Shalt thou retire alone, nor couldst thou wish
Couch more magnificent. Thou shalt lie down
With patriarchs of the infant world — with kings,
The powerful of the earth — the wise, the good,
Fair forms, and hoary seers of ages past,
All in one mighty sepulchre. The hills
Rock-ribbed and ancient as the sun — the vales
Stretching in pensive quietness between;
The venerable woods — rivers that move
In majesty, and the complaining brooks
That make the meadows green; and, poured round all
Old Ocean"s gray and melancholy waste —
Are but the solemn decorations all
Of the great tomb of man. The golden sun,
The planets, all the infinite host of heaven,
Are shining on the sad abodes of death,
Through the still lapse of ages. All that tread
The globe are but a handful to the tribes
That slumber in its bosom. — Take the wings
Of morning, pierce the Barcan wilderness,
Or lose thyself in the continuous woods
Where rolls the Oregon, and hears no sound,
Save his own dashings — yet the dead are there:
And millions in those solitudes, since first
The flight of years began, have laid them down

In their last sleep — the dead reign there alone.
So shalt thou rest, and what if thou withdraw
In silence from the living, and no friend
60 Take note of thy departure? All that breathe
Will share thy destiny. The gay will laugh
When thou art gone, the solemn brood of care
Plod on, and each one as before will chase
His favorite phantom; yet all these shall leave
Their mirth and their employments, and shall come
And make their bed with thee. As the long train
Of ages glide away, the sons of men,
The youth in life's green spring, and he who goes
In the full strength of years, matron and maid,

The speechless babe, and the gray-headed man —
Shall one by one be gathered to thy side,
By those, who in their turn shall follow them.

So live, that when thy summons comes to join
The innumerable caravan, which moves
To that mysterious realm, where each shall take
His chamber in the silent halls of death,
Thou go not, like the quarry-slave at night,
Scourged to his dungeon, but, sustained and soothed
By an unfaltering trust, approach thy grave,
Like one who wraps the drapery of his couch
About him, and lies down to pleasant dreams

Assignments

- Warm-up: Bryant was worried that some of his Christian readers would be offended by "Thanatopsis." Did he have reason to worry?

- Students should complete Concept Builder 6-B.

- Student should review reading(s) from the next chapter.

- Student should outline essay due at the end of the week.

- Per teacher instructions, students may answer orally, in a group setting, some of the essays that are not assigned as formal essays.

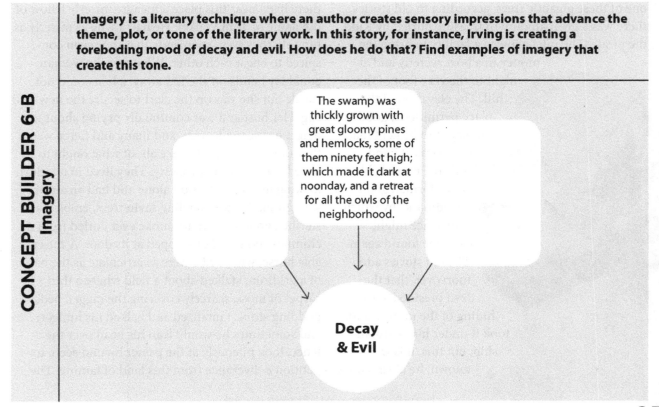

CONCEPT BUILDER 6-B
Imagery

Imagery is a literary technique where an author creates sensory impressions that advance the theme, plot, or tone of the literary work. In this story, for instance, Irving is creating a foreboding mood of decay and evil. How does he do that? Find examples of imagery that create this tone.

The swamp was thickly grown with great gloomy pines and hemlocks, some of them ninety feet high; which made it dark at noonday, and a retreat for all the owls of the neighborhood.

Decay & Evil

Washington Irving

Irving was one of the first really popular American writers. A prolific if mediocre writer, Irving was read by people all over the world. He was the John Grisham of his day! Irving (1783–1859) is remembered today for having written *Rip Van Winkle* and *The Legend of Sleepy Hollow*. In these stories, as well as in *Knickerbocker's History of New York*, Irving celebrated the folkways of New York's Dutch settlers. The following is one of Irving's most famous short stories:

The Devil and Tom Walker

A few miles from Boston, in Massachusetts, there is a deep inlet winding several miles into the interior of the country from Charles Bay, and terminating in a thickly wooded swamp, or morass. On one side of this inlet is a beautiful dark grove; on the opposite side the land rises abruptly from the water's edge, into a high ridge on which grow a few scattered oaks of great age and immense size. Under one of these gigantic trees, according to old stories, there was a great amount of treasure buried by Kidd the pirate. The inlet allowed a facility to bring the money in a boat secretly and at night to the very foot of the hill. The elevation of the place permitted a good look out to be kept that no one was at hand, while the remarkable trees formed good landmarks by which the place might easily be found again. The old stories add, moreover, that the devil presided at the hiding of the money, and took it under his guardianship; but this, it is well known, he always does

with buried treasure, particularly when it has been ill gotten. Be that as it may, Kidd never returned to recover his wealth; being shortly after seized at Boston, sent out to England, and there hanged for a pirate.

About the year 1727, just at the time when earthquakes were prevalent in New England, and shook many tall sinners down upon their knees, there lived near this place a meagre miserly fellow of the name of Tom Walker. He had a wife as miserly as himself; they were so miserly that they even conspired to cheat each other. Whatever the woman could lay hands on she hid away: a hen could not cackle but she was on the alert to secure the new-laid egg. Her husband was continually prying about to detect her secret hoards, and many and fierce were the conflicts that took place about what ought to have been common property. They lived in a forlorn looking house, that stood alone and had an air of starvation. A few straggling savin trees, emblems of sterility, grew near it; no smoke ever curled from its chimney; no traveller stopped at its door. A miserable horse, whose ribs were as articulate as the bars of a gridiron, stalked about a field where a thin carpet of moss, scarcely covering the ragged beds of pudding stone, tantalized and balked his hunger; and sometimes he would lean his head over the fence, look piteously at the passer by, and seem to petition deliverance from this land of famine. The

Bust of Washington Irving in Brooklyn, New York.
Photo by Jim.henderson, 2010 (CC0 1.0).

house and its inmates had altogether a bad name. Tom's wife was a tall termagant, fierce of temper, loud of tongue, and strong of arm. Her voice was often heard in wordy warfare with her husband; and his face sometimes showed signs that their conflicts were not confined to words. No one ventured, however, to interfere between them; the lonely wayfarer shrunk within himself at the horrid clamour and clapper clawing; eyed the den of discord askance, and hurried on his way, rejoicing, if a bachelor, in his celibacy.

One day that Tom Walker had been to a distant part of the neighbourhood, he took what he considered a short cut homewards through the swamp. Like most short cuts, it was an ill chosen route. The swamp was thickly grown with great gloomy pines and hemlocks, some of them ninety feet high; which made it dark at noonday, and a retreat for all the owls of the neighborhood. It was full of pits and quagmires, partly covered with weeds and mosses; where the green surface often betrayed the traveler into a gulf of black smothering mud; there were also dark and stagnant pools, the abodes of the tadpole, the bullfrog, and the water snake, and where trunks of pines and hemlocks lay half drowned, half rotting, looking like alligators, sleeping in the mire.

Tom had long been picking his way cautiously through this treacherous forest; stepping from tuft to tuft of rushes and roots which afforded precarious footholds among deep sloughs; or pacing carefully, like a cat, along the prostrate trunks of trees; startled now and then by the sudden screaming of the bittern, or the quacking of a wild duck, rising on the wing from some solitary pool. At length he arrived at a piece of firm ground, which ran out like a peninsula into the deep bosom of the swamp. It had been one of the strong holds of the Indians during their wars with the first colonists. Here they had thrown up a kind of fort which they had looked upon as almost impregnable, and had used as a place of refuge for their squaws and children. Nothing remained of the Indian fort but a few embankments gradually sinking to the level of the surrounding earth, and already overgrown in part by oaks and other forest trees, the foliage of which formed a contrast to the dark pines and hemlocks of the swamp.

It was late in the dusk of evening that Tom Walker reached the old fort, and he paused there for a while to rest himself. Any one but he would have felt unwilling to linger in this lonely melancholy place, for the common people had a bad opinion of it from the stories handed down from the time of the Indian wars; when it was asserted that the savages held incantations here and made sacrifices to the evil spirit. Tom Walker, however, was not a man to be troubled with any fears of the kind.

He reposed himself for some time on the trunk of a fallen hemlock, listening to the boding cry of the tree toad, and delving with his walking staff into a mound of black mold at his feet. As he turned up the soil unconsciously, his staff struck against something hard. He raked it out of the vegetable mold, and lo! a cloven skull with an Indian tomahawk buried deep in it, lay before him. The rust on the weapon showed the time that had elapsed since this death blow had been given. It was a dreary memento of the fierce struggle that had taken place in this last foothold of the Indian warriors.

"Humph!" said Tom Walker, as he gave the skull a kick to shake the dirt from it.

"Let that skull alone!" said a gruff voice.

Tom lifted up his eyes and beheld a great black man, seated directly opposite him on the stump of a tree. He was exceedingly surprised, having neither seen nor heard any one approach, and he was still more perplexed on observing, as well as the gathering gloom would permit, that the stranger was neither Negro nor Indian. It is true, he was dressed in a rude, half Indian garb, and had a red belt or sash swathed round his body, but his face was neither black nor copper color, but swarthy and dingy and begrimed with soot, as if he had been accustomed to toil among fires and forges. He had a shock of coarse black hair, that stood out from his head in all directions; and bore an axe on his shoulder.

He scowled for a moment at Tom with a pair of great red eyes.

"What are you doing in my grounds?" said the black man, with a hoarse growling voice.

"Your grounds?" said Tom, with a sneer; "no more your grounds than mine: they belong to Deacon Peabody."

"Deacon Peabody be d——d," said the stranger, "as I flatter myself he will be, if he does not look more to his own sins and less to his neighbour's. Look yonder, and see how Deacon Peabody is faring."

Tom looked in the direction that the stranger pointed, and beheld one of the great trees, fair and flourishing without, but rotten at the core, and saw that it had been nearly hewn through, so that the first high wind was likely to below it down. On the bark of the tree was scored the name of Deacon Peabody. He now looked round and found most of the tall trees marked with the name of some great men of the colony, and all more or less scored by the axe. The one on which he had been seated, and which had evidently just been hewn down, bore the name of Crowninshield; and he recollected a mighty rich man of that name, who made a vulgar display of wealth, which it was whispered he had acquired by buccaneering.

"He's just ready for burning!" said the black man, with a growl of triumph. "You see I am likely to have a good stock of firewood for winter."

"But what right have you," said Tom, "to cut down Deacon Peabody's timber?"

"The right of prior claim," said the other. "This woodland belonged to me long before one of your white faced race put foot upon the soil."

"And pray, who are you, if I may be so bold?" said Tom.

"Oh, I go by various names. I am the Wild Huntsman in some countries; the Black Miner in others. In this neighborhood I am known by the name of the Black Woodsman. I am he to whom the red men devoted this spot, and now and then roasted a white man by way of sweet smelling sacrifice. Since the red men have been exterminated by you white savages, I amuse myself by presiding at the persecutions of Quakers and Anabaptists; I am the great patron and prompter of slave dealers, and the grand master of the Salem witches."

"The upshot of all which is, that, if I mistake not," said Tom, sturdily, "you are he commonly called Old Scratch."

"The same at your service!" replied the black man, with a half civil nod.

Such was the opening of this interview, according to the old story, though it has almost too familiar an air to be credited. One would think that to meet with such a singular personage in this wild lonely place, would have shaken any man's nerves: but Tom was a hard—minded fellow, not easily daunted, and he had lived so long with a termagant wife, that he did not even fear the devil.

It is said that after this commencement, they had a long and earnest conversation together, as Tom returned homewards. The black man told him of great sums of money which had been buried by Kidd the pirate, under the oak trees on the high ridge not far from the morass. All these were under his command and protected by his power, so that none could find them but such as propitiated his favor. These he offered to place within Tom Walker's reach, having conceived an especial kindness for him: but they were to be had only on certain conditions. What these conditions were, may easily be surmised, though Tom never disclosed them publicly. They must have been very hard, for he required time to think of them, and he was not a man to stick at trifles where money was in view. When they had reached the edge of the swamp the stranger paused.

"What proof have I that all you have been telling me is true?" said Tom.

"There is my signature," said the black man, pressing his finger on Tom's forehead. So saying, he turned off among the thickets of the swamp, and seemed, as Tom said, to go down, down, down, into the earth, until nothing but his head and shoulders could be seen, and so on until he totally disappeared.

When Tom reached home he found the black print of a finger burnt, as it were, into his forehead, which nothing could obliterate.

The first news his wife had to tell him was the sudden death of Absalom Crowninshield the rich buccaneer. It was announced in the papers with the usual flourish, that "a great man had fallen in Israel."

Tom recollected the tree which his black friend had just hewn down, and which was ready for burning. "Let the freebooter roast," said Tom, "who cares!" He now felt convinced that all he had heard and seen was no illusion.

He was not prone to let his wife into his confidence; but as this was an uneasy secret, he willingly shared it with her. All her avarice was awakened at the mention of hidden gold, and she urged her husband to comply with the black man's terms and secure what would make them wealthy for life. However Tom might have felt disposed to sell himself to the devil, he was determined not to do so to oblige his wife; so he flatly refused out of the mere spirit of contradiction. … At length she determined to drive the bargain on her own account, and if she succeeded, to keep all the gain to herself.

Being of the same fearless temper as her husband, she set off for the old Indian fort towards the close of a summer's day. She was many hours absent. When she came back she was reserved and sullen in her replies. She spoke something of a black man whom she had met about twilight, hewing at the root of a tall tree. He was sulky, however, and would not come to terms; she was to go again with a propitiatory offering, but what it was she forbore to say.

The next evening she set off again for the swamp, with her apron heavily laden. Tom waited and waited for her, but in vain: midnight came, but she did not make her appearance; morning, noon, night returned, but still she did not come. Tom now grew uneasy for her safety; especially as he found she had carried off in her apron the silver teapot and spoons and every portable article of value. Another night elapsed, another morning came; but no wife. In a word, she was never heard of more.

What was her real fate nobody knows, in consequence of so many pretending to know. It is one of those facts that have become confounded by a variety of historians. Some asserted that she lost her way among the tangled mazes of the swamp and sunk into some pit or slough; others, more uncharitable, hinted that she had eloped with the household booty, and made off to some other province; while others assert that the tempter had decoyed her into a dismal quagmire on top of which her hat was found lying. In confirmation of this, it was said a great black man with an axe on his shoulder was seen late that very evening coming out of the swamp, carrying a bundle tied in a check apron, with an air of surly triumph.

The most current and probable story, however, observes that Tom Walker grew so anxious about the fate of his wife and his property that he sat out at length to seek them both at the Indian fort. During a long summer's afternoon he searched about the gloomy place, but no wife was to be seen. He called her name repeatedly, but she was no where to be heard. The bittern alone responded to his voice, as he flew screaming by; or the bull frog croaked dolefully from a neighboring pool. At length, it is said, just in the brown hour of twilight, when the owls began to hoot and the bats to flit about, his attention was attracted by the clamor of carrion crows that were hovering about a cypress tree. He looked and beheld a bundle tied in a check apron and hanging in the branches of the tree; with a great vulture perched hard by, as if keeping watch upon it. He leaped with joy, for he recognized his wife's apron, and supposed it to contain the household valuables.

"Let us get hold of the property," said he, consolingly to himself, "and we will endeavor to do without the woman."

As he scrambled up the tree the vulture spread its wide wings, and sailed off screaming into the deep shadows of the forest. Tom seized the check apron, but, woeful sight! found nothing but a heart and liver tied up in it.

Such, according to the most authentic old story, was all that was to be found of Tom's wife. She had probably attempted to deal with the black man as she had been accustomed to deal with her husband; but though a female scold is generally considered a match for the devil, yet in this instance she appears to have had the worst of it. She must have died game however; for it is said Tom noticed many prints of cloven feet deeply stamped about the tree, and several handful of hair, that looked as if they had been plucked from the coarse black shock of the woodsman.

Tom knew his wife's prowess by experience. He shrugged his shoulders as he looked at the signs of a fierce clapper clawing. "Egad," said he to himself, "Old Scratch must have had a tough time of it!"

Tom consoled himself for the loss of his property with the loss of his wife; for he was a man of fortitude. He even felt something like gratitude towards the black woodsman, who he considered had done him a kindness. He sought, therefore, to cultivate a farther acquaintance with him, but for some time without success; the old black legs played shy, for whatever people may think, he is not always to be had for calling for; he knows how to play his cards when pretty sure of his game.

At length, it is said, when delay had whetted Tom's eagerness to the quick, and prepared him to agree to any thing rather than not gain the promised treasure, he met the black man one evening in his usual woodman dress, with his axe on his shoulder, sauntering along the edge of the swamp, and humming a tune. He affected to receive Tom's advance with great indifference, made brief replies, and went on humming his tune.

By degrees, however, Tom brought him to business, and they began to haggle about the terms on which the former was to have the pirate's treasure. There was one condition which need not be mentioned, being generally understood in all cases where the devil grants favors; but there were others about which, though of less importance, he was inflexibly obstinate. He insisted that the money found through his means should be employed in his service. He proposed, therefore, that Tom should employ it in the black traffic; that is to say, that he should fit out a slave ship. This, however, Tom resolutely refused; he was bad enough in all conscience; but the devil himself could not tempt him to turn slave dealer.

Finding Tom so squeamish on this point, he did not insist upon it, but proposed instead that he should turn usurer; the devil being extremely anxious for the increase of usurers, looking upon them as his peculiar people.

To this no objections were made, for it was just to Tom's taste.

"You shall open a broker's shop in Boston next month," said the black man.

"I'll do it tomorrow, if you wish," said Tom Walker.

"You shall lend money at two per cent a month."

"Egad, I'll charge four!" replied Tom Walker.

"You shall extort bonds, foreclose mortgages, drive the merchant to bankruptcy —"

"I'll drive him to the d——l," cried Tom Walker, eagerly.

"You are the usurer for my money!" said the black legs, with delight. "When will you want the rhino?"

"This very night."

"Done!" said the devil.

"Done!" said Tom Walker. So they shook hands, and struck a bargain.

A few days' time saw Tom Walker seated behind his desk in a counting house in Boston. His reputation for a ready moneyed man, who would lend money out for a good consideration, soon spread abroad. Every body remembers the days of Governor Belcher, when money was particularly scarce. It was a time of paper credit. The country had been deluged with government bills; the famous Land Bank had been established; there had been a rage for speculating; the people had run mad with schemes for new settlements; for building cities in the wilderness; land jobbers went about with maps of grants, and townships, and Eldorados, lying nobody knew where, but which every body was ready to purchase. In a word, the great speculating fever which breaks out every now and then in the country, had raged to an alarming degree, and every body was dreaming of making sudden fortunes from nothing. As usual the fever had subsided; the dream had gone off, and the imaginary fortunes with it; the patients were left in doleful plight, and the whole country resounded with the consequent cry of "hard times."

At this propitious time of public distress did Tom Walker set up as a usurer in Boston. His door was soon thronged by customers. The needy and the adventurous; the gambling speculator; the dreaming land jobber; the thriftless tradesman; the merchant with cracked credit; in short, every one driven to raise money by desperate means and desperate sacrifices, hurried to Tom Walker.

Thus Tom was the universal friend of the needy, and he acted like a "friend in need;" that is to say, he always exacted good pay and good security. In proportion to the distress of the applicant was the hardness of his terms. He accumulated bonds and mortgages; gradually squeezed his customers closer and closer; and sent them at length, dry as a sponge from his door.

In this way he made money hand over hand; became a rich and mighty man, and exalted his cocked hat upon change. He built himself, as usual, a vast house, out of ostentation; but left the greater part of it unfinished and unfurnished out of parsimony. He even set up a carriage in the fullness of his vain glory, though he nearly starved the horses which drew it; and as the ungreased wheels groaned and screeched on the axle trees, you would have thought you heard the souls of the poor debtors he was squeezing.

As Tom waxed old, however, he grew thoughtful. Having secured the good things of this world, he began to feel anxious about those of the next. He thought with regret on the bargain he had made with his black friend, and set his wits to work to cheat him out of the conditions. He became, therefore, all of a sudden, a violent church goer. He prayed loudly and strenuously as if heaven were to be taken by force of lungs. Indeed, one might always tell when he had sinned most during the week, by the clamor of his Sunday devotion. The quiet Christians who had been modestly and steadfastly traveling Zionward, were struck with self reproach at seeing themselves so suddenly outstripped in their career by this new—made convert. Tom was as rigid in religious, as in money matters; he was a stern supervisor and censurer of his neighbors, and seemed to think every sin entered up to their account became a credit on his own side of the page. He even talked of the expediency of reviving the persecution of Quakers and Anabaptists. In a word, Tom's zeal became as notorious as his riches.

Still, in spite of all this strenuous attention to forms, Tom had a lurking dread that the devil, after all, would have his due. That he might not be taken unawares, therefore, it is said he always carried a small bible in his coat pocket. He had also a great folio bible on his counting house desk, and would frequently be found reading it when people called on business; on such occasions he would lay his green spectacles on the book, to mark the place, while he turned round to drive some usurious bargain.

Some say that Tom grew a little crack brained in his old days, and that fancying his end approaching, he had his horse new shod, saddled and bridled, and buried with his feet uppermost; because he supposed that at the last day the world would be turned upside down; in which case he should find his horse standing ready for mounting, and he was determined at the worst to give his old friend a run for it. This, however, is probably a mere old wives fable. If he really did take such a precaution it was totally superfluous; at least so says the authentic old legend which closes his story in the following manner.

On one hot afternoon in the dog days, just as a terrible black thundergust was coming up, Tom sat in his counting house in his white linen cap and India silk morning gown. He was on the point of foreclosing a mortgage, by which he would complete the ruin of an unlucky land speculator for whom he had professed the greatest friendship. The poor land jobber begged him to grant a few months indulgence. Tom had grown testy and irritated and refused another day.

"My family will be ruined and brought upon the parish," said the land jobber.

"Charity begins at home," replied Tom, "I must take care of myself in these hard times."

"You have made so much money out of me," said the speculator.

Tom lost his patience and his piety — "The devil take me," said he, "if I have made a farthing!"

Just then there were three loud knocks at the street door. He stepped out to see who was there. A black man was holding a black horse which neighed and stamped with impatience.

"Tom, you're come for!" said the black fellow, gruffly. Tom shrunk back, but too late. He had left his little bible at the bottom of his coat pocket, and his big bible on the desk buried under the mortgage he was about to foreclose: never was sinner taken more unawares. The black man whisked him like a child astride the horse and away he galloped in the midst of a thunder storm. The clerks stuck their pens behind their ears and stared after him from the windows. Away went Tom Walker, dashing down the streets; his white cap bobbing up and down; his morning gown fluttering in the wind, and his steed striking fire out of the pavement at every bound. When the clerks turned to look for the black man he had disappeared.

Tom Walker never returned to foreclose the mortgage. A countryman who lived on the borders of the swamp, reported that in the height of the thunder gust he had heard a great clattering of hoofs and a howling along the road, and that when he ran to the window he just caught sight of a figure, such as I have described, on a horse that galloped like mad across the fields, over the hills and down into the black hemlock swamp towards the old Indian fort; and that shortly after a thunderbolt fell in that direction which seemed to set the whole forest in a blaze.

The good people of Boston shook their heads and shrugged their shoulders, but had been so much accustomed to witches and goblins and tricks of the devil in all kinds of shapes from the first settlement of the colony, that they were not so much horror struck as might have been expected. Trustees were appointed to take charge of Tom's effects. There was nothing, however, to administer upon. On searching his coffers all his bonds and mortgages were found reduced to cinders. In place of gold and silver his iron chest was filled with chips and shavings; two skeletons lay in his stable instead of his half starved horses, and the very next day his great house took fire and was burnt to the ground.

Such was the end of Tom Walker and his ill gotten wealth. Let all griping money brokers lay this story to heart. The truth of it is not to be doubted. The very hole under the oak trees, from whence he dug Kidd's money is to be seen to this day; and the neighboring swamp and old Indian fort is often haunted in stormy nights by a figure on horseback, in a morning gown and white cap, which is doubtless the troubled spirit of the usurer. In fact, the story has resolved itself into a proverb, and is the origin of that popular saying, prevalent throughout New England, of "The Devil and Tom Walker."

Assignments

- Warm-up: Some Christian critics are offended by Washington Irving. They claim he trivializes the supernatural. What do you think?
- Students should complete Concept Builder 6-C.
- Students should write rough draft of assigned essay.
- The teacher may correct rough drafts.

CONCEPT BUILDER 6-C
Symbolism

A symbol is a literary technique where the author represents something with something entirely different. For instance, explain what the great tree scored (carved) with the name of Deacon Peabody "rotten at the core" means.

The tree is fair and flourishing without, but rotten to the core.

=

The Legend of Sleepy Hollow

A pleasing land of drowsy head it was,
Of dreams that wave before the half-shut eye;
And of gay castles in the clouds that pass,
Forever flushing round a summer sky.

— Castle of Indolence.

In the bosom of one of those spacious coves which indent the eastern shore of the Hudson, at that broad expansion of the river denominated by the ancient Dutch navigators the Tappan Zee, and where they always prudently shortened sail and implored the protection of St. Nicholas when they crossed, there lies a small market town or rural port, which by some is called Greensburgh, but which is more generally and properly known by the name of Tarry Town. This name was given, we are told, in former days, by the good housewives of the adjacent country, from the inveterate propensity of their husbands to linger about the village tavern on market days. Be that as it may, I do not vouch for the fact, but merely advert to it, for the sake of being precise and authentic. Not far from this village, perhaps about two miles, there is a little valley or rather lap of land among high hills, which is one of the quietest places in the whole world. A small brook glides through it, with just murmur enough to lull one to repose; and the occasional whistle of a quail or tapping of a woodpecker is almost the only sound that ever breaks in upon the uniform tranquility.

I recollect that, when a stripling, my first exploit in squirrel shooting was in a grove of tall walnut trees that shades one side of the valley. I had wandered into it at noontime, when all nature is peculiarly quiet, and was startled by the roar of my own gun, as it broke the Sabbath stillness around and was prolonged and reverberated by the angry echoes. If ever I should wish for a retreat whither I might steal from the world and its distractions, and dream quietly away the remnant of a troubled life, I know of none more promising than this little valley.

From the listless repose of the place, and the peculiar character of its inhabitants, who are descendants from the original Dutch settlers, this sequestered glen has long been known by the name of Sleepy Hollow, and its rustic lads are called the Sleepy Hollow Boys throughout all the neighboring country. A drowsy, dreamy influence seems to hang over the land, and to pervade the very atmosphere. Some say that the place was bewitched by a High German doctor, during the early days of the settlement; others, that an old Indian chief, the prophet or wizard of his tribe, held his powwows there before the country was discovered by Master Hendrick Hudson. Certain it is, the place still continues under the sway of some witching power, that holds a spell over the minds of the good people, causing them to walk in a continual reverie. They are given to all kinds of marvelous beliefs; are subject to trances and visions, and frequently see strange sights, and hear music and voices in the air. The whole neighborhood abounds with local tales, haunted spots, and twilight superstitions; stars shoot and meteors glare oftener across the valley than in any other part of the country, and the nightmare, with her whole ninefold, seems to make it the favorite scene of her gambols.

The dominant spirit, however, that haunts this enchanted region, and seems to be commander-in-chief of all the powers of the air, is the apparition of a figure on horseback, without a head. It is said by some to be the ghost of a Hessian trooper, whose head had been carried away by a cannonball, in some nameless battle during the Revolutionary War, and who is ever and anon seen by the country folk hurrying along in the gloom of night, as if on the wings of the wind. His haunts are not confined to the valley, but extend at times to the adjacent roads, and especially to the vicinity of a church at no great distance. Indeed, certain of the most authentic historians of those parts, who have been careful in collecting and collating the floating facts concerning this specter, allege that the body of the trooper having been buried in the churchyard, the ghost rides forth to the scene of battle in nightly quest of his head, and that the rushing speed with which he sometimes passes along the Hollow, like a midnight blast, is owing to his being belated, and in a hurry to get back to the churchyard before daybreak.

The Headless Horseman Pursuing Ichabod Crane located at the Smithsonian American Art Museum by John Quidor, 1858 (PD-Art).

Such is the general purport of this legendary superstition, which has furnished materials for many a wild story in that region of shadows; and the specter is known at all the country firesides, by the name of the Headless Horseman of Sleepy Hollow.

It is remarkable that the visionary propensity I have mentioned is not confined to the native inhabitants of the valley, but is unconsciously imbibed by every one who resides there for a time. However wide awake they may have been before they entered that sleepy region, they are sure, in a little time, to inhale the witching influence of the air, and begin to grow imaginative, to dream dreams, and see apparitions.

I mention this peaceful spot with all possible laud for it is in such little retired Dutch valleys, found here and there embosomed in the great State of New York, that population, manners, and customs remain fixed, while the great torrent of migration and improvement, which is making such incessant changes in other parts of this restless country,

sweeps by them unobserved. They are like those little nooks of still water, which border a rapid stream, where we may see the straw and bubble riding quietly at anchor, or slowly revolving in their mimic harbor, undisturbed by the rush of the passing current. Though many years have elapsed since I trod the drowsy shades of Sleepy Hollow, yet I question whether I should not still find the same trees and the same families vegetating in its sheltered bosom.

In this byplace of nature there abode, in a remote period of American history, that is to say, some thirty years since, a worthy wight of the name of Ichabod Crane, who sojourned, or, as he expressed it, "tarried," in Sleepy Hollow, for the purpose of instructing the children of the vicinity. He was a native of Connecticut, a State which supplies the Union with pioneers for the mind as well as for the forest, and sends forth yearly its legions of frontier woodmen and country schoolmasters. The cognomen of Crane was not inapplicable to his person. He was tall, but exceedingly lank, with narrow shoulders, long arms and legs, hands that dangled a mile out of his sleeves, feet that might have served for shovels, and his whole frame most loosely hung together. His head was small, and flat at top, with huge ears, large green glassy eyes, and a long snipe nose, so that it looked like a weathercock perched upon his spindle neck to tell which way the wind blew. To see him striding along the profile of a hill on a windy day, with his clothes bagging and fluttering about him, one might have mistaken him for the genius of famine descending upon the earth, or some scarecrow eloped from a cornfield.

His schoolhouse was a low building of one large room, rudely constructed of logs; the windows partly glazed, and partly patched with leaves of old copybooks. It was most ingeniously secured at vacant hours, by a withe twisted in the handle of the door, and stakes set against the window shutters; so that though a thief might get in with perfect ease, he would find some embarrassment in getting out, — an idea most probably borrowed by the architect, Yost Van Houten, from the mystery of an eelpot. The schoolhouse stood in a rather lonely but pleasant situation, just at the foot of a woody hill, with a brook running close by, and a formidable birchtree growing at one end of it. From hence the low murmur of his pupils' voices, conning over their Chapters, might be heard in a drowsy summer's day, like the hum of a beehive; interrupted now and then by the authoritative voice of the master, in the tone of menace or command, or, peradventure, by the appalling sound of the birch, as he urged some tardy loiterer along the flowery path of knowledge. Truth to say, he was a conscientious man, and ever bore in mind the golden maxim, "Spare the rod and spoil the child." Ichabod Crane's scholars certainly were not spoiled.

I would not have it imagined, however, that he was one of those cruel potentates of the school who joy in the smart of their subjects; on the contrary, he administered justice with discrimination rather than severity; taking the burden off the backs of the weak, and laying it on those of the strong. Your mere puny stripling, that winced at the least flourish of the rod, was passed by with indulgence; but the claims of justice were satisfied by inflicting a double portion on some little tough wrong headed, broadskirted Dutch urchin, who sulked and swelled and grew dogged and sullen beneath the birch. All this he called "doing his duty by their parents;" and he never inflicted a chastisement without following it by the assurance, so consolatory to the smarting urchin,

that "he would remember it and thank him for it the longest day he had to live."

When school hours were over, he was even the companion and playmate of the larger boys; and on holiday afternoons would convoy some of the smaller ones home, who happened to have pretty sisters, or good housewives for mothers, noted for the comforts of the cupboard. Indeed, it behooved him to keep on good terms with his pupils. The revenue arising from his school was small, and would have been scarcely sufficient to furnish him with daily bread, for he was a huge feeder, and, though lank, had the dilating powers of an anaconda; but to help out his maintenance, he was, according to country custom in those parts, boarded and lodged at the houses of the farmers whose children he instructed. With these he lived successively a week at a time, thus going the rounds of the neighborhood, with all his worldly effects tied up in a cotton handkerchief.

That all this might not be too onerous on the purses of his rustic patrons, who are apt to considered the costs of schooling a grievous burden, and schoolmasters as mere drones he had various ways of rendering himself both useful and agreeable. He assisted the farmers occasionally in the lighter labors of their farms, helped to make hay, mended the fences, took the horses to water, drove the cows from pasture, and cut wood for the winter fire. He laid aside, too, all the dominant dignity and absolute sway with which he lorded it in his little empire, the school, and became wonderfully gentle and ingratiating. He found favor in the eyes of the mothers by petting the children, particularly the youngest; and like the lion bold, which whilom so magnanimously the lamb did hold, he would sit with a child on one knee, and rock a cradle with his foot for whole hours together.

In addition to his other vocations, he was the singing master of the neighborhood, and picked up many bright shillings by instructing the young folks in psalmody. It was a matter of no little vanity to him on Sundays, to take his station in front of the church gallery, with a band of chosen singers; where, in his own mind, he completely carried away the palm from the parson. Certain it is, his voice resounded far above all the rest of the congregation; and there are peculiar quavers still to be heard in that church, and which may even be heard half a mile off, quite to the opposite side of the millpond, on a still Sunday morning, which are said to be legitimately descended from the nose of Ichabod Crane. Thus, by divers little makeshifts, in that ingenious way which is commonly denominated "by hook and by crook," the worthy pedagogue got on tolerably enough, and was thought, by all who understood nothing of the labor of headwork, to have a wonderfully easy life of it.

The schoolmaster is generally a man of some importance in the female circle of a rural neighborhood; being considered a kind of idle, gentlemanlike personage, of vastly superior taste and accomplishments to the rough country swains, and, indeed, inferior in learning only to the parson. His appearance, therefore, is apt to occasion some little stir at the tea table of a farmhouse, and the addition of a supernumerary dish of cakes or sweetmeats, or, peradventure, the parade of a silver teapot. Our man of letters, therefore, was peculiarly happy in the smiles of all the country damsels. How he would figure among them in the churchyard, between services on Sundays; gathering grapes for them from the wild vines that overran the surrounding trees; reciting for their amusement all the epitaphs on the tombstones; or sauntering, with a whole bevy of them, along the banks of the adjacent millpond; while the more bashful country bumpkins hung sheepishly back, envying his superior elegance and address.

From his half-itinerant life, also, he was a kind of traveling gazette, carrying the whole budget of local gossip from house to house, so that his appearance was always greeted with satisfaction. He was, moreover, esteemed by the women as a man of great erudition, for he had read several books quite through, and was a perfect master of Cotton Mather's "History of New England Witchcraft," in which, by the way, he most firmly and potently believed.

He was, in fact, an odd mixture of small shrewdness and simple credulity. His appetite for the marvelous, and his powers of digesting it, were equally extraordinary; and both had been increased by his residence in this spellbound region. No tale was too gross or monstrous for his capacious swallow. It was often his delight, after his school was dismissed in the afternoon, to stretch himself on the rich bed of clover bordering the little brook that whimpered by his schoolhouse, and there con over old Mather's direful tales, until the gathering dusk of evening made the printed page a mere mist before his eyes. Then, as he wended his way by swamp and stream and awful woodland, to the farmhouse where he happened to be quartered, every sound of nature, at that witching hour, fluttered his excited imagination, the moan of the whippoorwill from the hillside, the boding cry of the tree toad, that harbinger of storm, the dreary hooting of the screech owl, to the sudden rustling in the thicket of birds frightened from their roost. The fireflies, too, which sparkled most vividly in the darkest places, now and then startled him, as one of uncommon brightness would stream across his path; and if, by chance, a huge blockhead of a beetle came winging his blundering flight against him, the poor varlet was ready to give up the ghost, with the idea that he was struck with a witch's token. His only resource on such occasions, either to drown thought or drive away evil spirits, was to sing psalm tunes and the good people of Sleepy Hollow, as they sat by their doors of an evening, were often filled with awe at hearing his nasal melody, "in linked sweetness long drawn out," floating from the distant hill, or along the dusky road.

Another of his sources of fearful pleasure was to pass long winter evenings with the old Dutch wives, as they sat spinning by the fire, with a row of apples roasting and spluttering along the hearth, and listen to their marvelous tales of ghosts and goblins, and haunted fields, and haunted brooks, and haunted bridges, and haunted houses, and particularly of the headless horseman, or Galloping Hessian of the Hollow, as they sometimes called him. He would delight them equally by his anecdotes of witchcraft, and of the direful omens and portentous sights and sounds in the air, which prevailed in the earlier times of Connecticut; and would frighten them woefully with speculations upon comets and shooting stars; and with the alarming fact that the world did absolutely turn round, and that they were half the time topsy-turvy!

But if there was a pleasure in all this, while snugly cuddling in the chimney corner of a chamber that was all of a ruddy glow from the crackling wood fire, and where, of course, no specter dared to show its face, it was dearly purchased by the terrors of his subsequent walk homewards. What fearful shapes and shadows beset his path, amidst the dim and ghastly glare of a snowy night! With what wistful look did he eye every trembling ray of light streaming across the waste fields from some distant window! How often was he appalled by some shrub covered with snow, which, like a sheeted specter, beset his very path! How often did he shrink with curdling awe at the sound of his own steps on the frosty crust beneath his feet; and dread to look over his shoulder, lest he should behold some uncouth being tramping close behind him! and how often was he thrown into complete dismay by some rushing blast, howling among the trees, in the idea that it was the Galloping Hessian on one of his nightly scourings!

All these, however, were mere terrors of the night, phantoms of the mind that walk in darkness; and though he had seen many specters in his time, and been more than once beset by Satan in divers shapes, in his lonely perambulations, yet daylight put an end to all these evils; and he would have passed a pleasant life of it, in despite of the Devil and all his works, if his path had not been crossed by a being that causes more perplexity to mortal man than ghosts, goblins, and the whole race of witches put together, and that was—a woman.

Among the musical disciples who assembled, one evening in each week, to receive his instructions in psalmody, was Katrina Van Tassel, the daughter and only child of a substantial Dutch farmer. She was a booming lass of fresh eighteen; plump as a partridge; ripe and melting and rosy cheeked as one of her father's peaches, and universally famed, not merely for her beauty, but her vast expectations. She was withal a little of a coquette, as might be perceived even in her dress, which was a mixture of ancient and modern fashions, as most suited to set of her charms. She wore the ornaments of pure yellow gold, which her great, great, grandmother had brought over from Saar dam; the tempting stomacher of the olden time, and withal a provokingly short petticoat, to display the prettiest foot and ankle in the country round.

Ichahod Crane had a soft and foolish heart towards the sex; and it is not to be wondered at, that so tempting a morsel soon found favor in his eyes, more especially after he had visited her in her paternal mansion. Old Baltus Van Tassel was a perfect picture of a thriving, contented, liberal-hearted farmer. He seldom, it is true, sent either his eyes or his thoughts beyond the boundaries of his own farm; but within those everything was snug, happy and well conditioned. He was satisfied with his wealth, but not proud of it; and piqued himself upon the hearty abundance, rather than the style in which he lived. His stronghold was situated on the banks of the Hudson, in one of those green, sheltered, fertile nooks in which the Dutch farmers are so fond of nestling. A great elm tree spread its broad branches over it, at the foot of which bubbled up a spring of the softest and sweetest water, in a little well formed of a barrel; and then stole sparkling away through the grass, to a neighboring brook, that babbled along among alders and dwarf willows. Hard by the farmhouse was a vast barn, that might have served for a church; every window and crevice of which seemed bursting forth with the treasures of the farm; the flail was busily resounding within it from morning to night; swallows and martins skimmed twittering about the eaves; an rows of pigeons, some with one eye turned up, as if watching the weather, some with their heads under their wings or buried in their bosoms, and others swelling, and cooing, and bowing about their dames, were enjoying the sunshine on the roof. Sleek unwieldy porkers were grunting in the repose and abundance of their pens, from whence sallied forth, now and then, troops of sucking pigs, as if to snuff the air. A stately squadron of snowy geese were riding in an adjoining pond, convoying whole fleets of ducks; regiments of turkeys were gobbling through the farmyard, and Guinea fowls fretting about it, like ill-tempered housewives, with their peevish, discontented cry. Before the barn door strutted the gallant cock, that pattern of a husband, a warrior and a fine gentleman, clapping his burnished wings and crowing in the pride and gladness of his heart, — sometimes tearing up the earth with his feet, and then generously calling his ever-hungry family of wives and children to enjoy the rich morsel which he had discovered.

The pedagogue's mouth watered as he looked upon this sumptuous promise of luxurious winter fare. In his devouring mind's eye, he pictured to himself every roasting pig running about with a pudding in his belly, and an apple in his mouth; the pigeons were snugly put to bed in a comfortable pie, and tucked in with a coverlet of crust; the geese were swimming in their own gravy; and the ducks pairing cosily in dishes, like snug married couples, with a decent competency of onion sauce. In the porkers he saw carved out the future sleek side of bacon, and juicy relishing ham; not a turkey but he beheld daintily trussed up, with its gizzard under its wing, and, peradventure, a necklace of savory sausages; and even bright chanticleer himself lay sprawling on his back, in a side dish, with uplifted claws, as if craving that quarter which his chivalrous spirit disdained to ask while living.

As the enraptured Ichabod fancied all this, and as he rolled his great green eyes over the fat meadow lands, the rich fields of wheat, of rye, of buckwheat, and Indian corn, and the orchards burdened with ruddy fruit, which surrounded the warm tenement of Van Tassel, his heart yearned after the damsel who was to inherit these domains, and his imagination expanded with the idea, how they might be readily turned into cash, and the money invested in immense tracts of wild land, and shingle palaces in the wilderness. Nay, his busy fancy already realized his hopes, and presented to him the blooming Katrina, with a whole family of children, mounted on the top of a wagon loaded with household trumpery, with pots and kettles dangling beneath; and he beheld himself bestriding a pacing mare, with a colt at her heels, setting out for Kentucky, Tennessee, — or the Lord knows where!

When he entered the house, the conquest of his heart was complete. It was one of those spacious farmhouses, with high-ridged but lowly sloping roofs, built in the style handed down from the first Dutch settlers; the low projecting eaves forming a piazza along the front, capable of being closed up in bad weather. Under this were hung flails, harness, various utensils of husbandry, and nets for fishing in the neighboring river. Benches were built along the sides for summer use; and a great spinning—wheel at one end, and a churn at the other, showed the various uses to which this important porch might be devoted. From this piazza the wondering Ichabod entered the hall, which formed the center of the mansion, and the place of usual residence. Here rows of resplendent pewter, ranged on a long dresser, dazzled his eyes. In one corner stood a huge bag of wool, ready to be spun; in another, a quantity of linsey-woolsey just from the loom; ears of Indian corn, and strings of dried apples and peaches, hung in gay festoons along the walls, mingled with the gaud of red peppers; and a door left ajar gave him a peep into the best parlor, where the claw-footed chairs and dark mahogany tables shone like mirrors; andirons, with their accompanying shovel and tongs, glistened from their covert of asparagus tops; mock oranges and conch shells decorated the mantelpiece; strings of various-colored birds eggs were suspended above it; a great ostrich egg was hung from the center of the room, and a corner cupboard, knowingly left open, displayed immense treasures of old silver and well-mended china.

From the moment Ichabod laid his eyes upon these regions of delight, the peace of his mind was at an end, and his only study was how to gain the affections of the peerless daughter of Van Tassel. In this enterprise, however, he had more real difficulties than generally fell to the lot of a knight — errant of yore, who seldom had anything but giants, enchanters, fiery dragons, and such like easily conquered adversaries, to contend with and had to make his way merely through gates of iron and brass, and walls of adamant to the castle keep, where the lady of his heart was confined; all which he achieved as easily as a man would carve his way to the center of a Christmas pie; and then the lady gave him her hand as a matter of course. Ichabod, on the contrary, had to win his way to the heart of a country coquette, beset with a labyrinth of whims and caprices, which were forever presenting new difficulties and impediments; and he had to encounter a host of fearful adversaries of real flesh and blood, the numerous rustic admirers, who beset every portal to her heart, keeping a watchful and angry eye upon each other, but ready to fly out in the common cause against any new competitor.

Among these, the most formidable was a burly, roaring, roistering blade, of the name of Abraham, or, according to the Dutch abbreviation, Brom Van Brunt, the hero of the country round which rang with his feats of strength and hardihood. He was broad-shouldered and double-jointed, with short curly black hair, and a bluff but not unpleasant countenance, having a mingled air of fun and arrogance From his Herculean frame and great powers of limb he had received the nickname of Brom Bones, by which he was universally known. He was famed for great knowledge and skill in horsemanship, being as dexterous on horseback as a Tartar. He was foremost at all races and cock fights; and, with the ascendancy which bodily strength always acquires in rustic life, was the umpire in all disputes, setting his hat on one side, and giving his decisions with an air and tone that admitted of no gainsay or appeal. He was always ready for either a fight or a frolic; but had more mischief than ill-will in his composition; and with all his overbearing roughness, there was a strong dash of waggish good humor at bottom. He had three or four boon companions, who regarded him as their model, and at the head of whom he scoured the country, attending every scene of feud or merriment for miles round. In cold weather he was distinguished by a fur cap, surmounted with a flaunting fox's tail; and when the folks at a country gathering descried this well-known crest at a distance, whisking about among a squad of hard riders, they always stood by for a squall. Sometimes his crew would be heard dashing along past the farmhouses at midnight, with whoop and halloo, like a troop of Don Cossacks; and the old dames, startled out of their sleep, would listen for a moment till the hurry-scurry had clattered by, and then exclaim, "Ay, there goes Brom Bones and his gang!" The neighbors looked upon him with a mixture of awe, admiration, and good will; and, when any madcap prank or rustic brawl occurred in the vicinity, always shook their heads, and warranted Brom Bones was at the bottom of it.

This rantipole hero had for some time singled out the blooming Katrina for the object of his uncouth gallantries, and though his amorous toyings were something like the gentle caresses and endearments of a bear, yet it was whispered that she did not altogether discourage his hopes. Certain it is, his advances were signals for rival candidates to retire, who felt no inclination to cross a lion in his amours; insomuch, that when his horse was seen tied to Van Tassel's paling, on a Sunday night, a sure sign that his master was courting, or, as it is termed, "sparking," within, all other suitors passed by in despair, and carried the war into other quarters.

Such was the formidable rival with whom Ichabod Crane had to contend, and, considering, all things, a stouter man than he would have shrunk from the competition, and a wiser man would have despaired. He had, however, a happy mixture of pliability and perseverance in his nature; he was in form and spirit like a supple-jack yielding, but tough; though he bent, he never broke; and though he bowed beneath the slightest pressure, yet, the moment it was away — jerk! — he was as erect, and carried his head as high as ever.

To have taken the field openly against his rival would have been madness; for he was not a man to be thwarted in his amours, any more than that stormy lover, Achilles. Ichabod, therefore, made his advances in a quiet and gently insinuating manner. Under cover of his character of singing master, he made frequent visits at the farmhouse; not that he had anything to apprehend from the meddlesome interference of parents, which is so often a stumbling block in the path of lovers. Balt Van Tassel was an easy indulgent soul; he loved his daughter better even than his pipe, and, like a reasonable man and an excellent father, let her have her way in everything. His notable little wife, too, had enough to do to attend to her housekeeping and manage her poultry; for, as she sagely observed, ducks and geese are foolish things, and must be looked after, but girls can take care of themselves. Thus, while the busy dame bustled about the house, or plied her spinning wheel at one end of the piazza, honest Balt would sit smoking his evening pipe at the other, watching the achievements of a little wooden warrior, who, armed with a sword in each hand, was most valiantly fighting the wind on the pinnacle of the barn. In the mean time, Ichabod would carry on his suit with the daughter by the side of the spring under the great elm, or sauntering along in the twilight, that hour so favorable to the lover's eloquence.

I profess not to know how women's hearts are wooed and won. To me they have always been matters of riddle and admiration. Some seem to have but one vulnerable point, or door of access; while others have a thousand avenues, and may be captured in a thousand different ways. It is a great triumph of skill to gain the former, but a still greater proof of generalship to maintain possession of the latter, for man must battle for his fortress at every door and window. He who wins a thousand common hearts is therefore entitled to some renown; but he who keeps undisputed sway over the heart of a coquette is indeed a hero. Certain it is, this was not the case with the redoubtable Brom Bones; and from the moment Ichabod Crane made his advances, the interests of the former evidently declined: his horse was no longer seen tied to the palings on Sunday nights, and a deadly feud gradually arose between him and the preceptor of Sleepy Hollow.

Brom, who had a degree of rough chivalry in his nature, would fain have carried matters to open warfare and have settled their pretensions to the lady, according to the mode of those most concise and simple reasoners, the knights — errant of yore, — by single combat; but Ichabod was too conscious of the superior might of his adversary to enter the lists against him; he had overheard a boast of Bones, that he would "double the schoolmaster up, and lay him on a shelf of his own schoolhouse;" and he was too wary to give him an opportunity. There was something extremely provoking, in this obstinately pacific system; it left Brom no alternative but to draw upon the funds of rustic waggery in his disposition, and to play off boorish practical jokes upon his rival. Ichabod became the object of whimsical persecution to Bones and his gang of rough riders. They harried his hitherto peaceful domains, smoked out his singing—school by stopping up the chimney, broke into the schoolhouse at night, in spite of its formidable fastenings of withe and window stakes, and turned everything topsy turvy, so that the poor schoolmaster began to think all the witches in the country held their meetings there. But what was still more annoying, Brom took all Opportunities of turning him into ridicule in presence of his mistress, and had a scoundrel dog whom he taught to whine in the most ludicrous manner, and introduced as a rival of Ichabod's, to instruct her in psalmody.

In this way matters went on for some time, without producing any material effect on the relative situations of the contending powers. On a fine autumnal afternoon, Ichabod, in pensive mood, sat enthroned on the lofty stool from whence he usually watched all the concerns of his little literary realm. In his hand he swayed a ferule, that scepter of despotic power; the birch of justice reposed on three nails behind the throne, a constant terror to evil doers, while on the desk before him might be seen sundry contraband articles and prohibited weapons, detected upon the persons of idle urchins, such as half-munched apples, popguns, whirligigs, fly-cages, and whole legions of rampant little paper gamecocks. Apparently there had been some appalling act of justice recently inflicted, for his scholars were all busily intent upon their books, or slyly whispering behind them with one eye kept upon the master; and a kind of buzzing stillness reigned throughout the schoolroom. It was suddenly interrupted by the appearance of a Negro in tow — cloth jacket and trousers, a round-crowned fragment of a hat, like the cap of Mercury, and mounted on the back of a ragged, wild, half-broken colt, which he managed with a rope by way of halter. He came clattering up to the school-door with an invitation to Ichabod to attend a merry-making or "quilting frolic," to be held that evening at Mynheer Van Tassel's; and having delivered his message with that air of importance and effort at fine language which a negro is apt to display on petty embassies of the kind, he dashed over the brook, and was seen scampering, away up the Hollow, full of the importance and hurry of his mission.

All was now bustle and hubbub in the late quiet schoolroom. The scholars were hurried through their Chapters without stopping at trifles; those who were nimble skipped over half with impunity, and those who were tardy had a smart application now and then in the rear, to quicken their speed or help them over a tall word. Books were flung aside without being put away on the shelves, inkstands were overturned, benches thrown down, and the whole school was turned loose an hour before the usual time, bursting forth like a legion of young imps, yelping and racketing about the green in joy at their early emancipation.

The gallant Ichabod now spent at least an extra half hour at his toilet, brushing and furbishing up his best, and indeed only suit of rusty black, and arranging his locks by a bit of broken looking glass that hung up in the schoolhouse. That he might make his appearance before his mistress in the true style of a cavalier, he borrowed a horse from the farmer with whom he was domiciliated, a choleric old Dutchman of the name of Hans Van Ripper, and, thus gallantly mounted, issued forth like a knight — errant in quest of adventures. But it is meet I should, in the true spirit of romantic story, give some account of the looks and equipments of my hero and his steed. The animal he bestrode was a broken-down plow-horse, that had outlived almost everything but its viciousness. He was gaunt and shagged, with a ewe neck, and a head like a hammer; his rusty mane and tail were tangled and knotted with burs; one eye had lost its pupil, and was glaring and spectral, but the other had the gleam of a genuine devil in it. Still he must have had fire and mettle in his day, if we may judge from the name he bore of Gunpowder. He had, in fact, been a favorite steed of his master's, the choleric Van Ripper, who was a furious rider, and had infused, very probably, some of his own spirit into the animal; for, old and broken-down as he looked, there was more of the lurking devil in him than in any young filly in the country.

Ichabod was a suitable figure for such a steed. He rode with short stirrups, which brought his knees nearly up to the pommel of the saddle; his sharp elbows stuck out like grasshoppers'; he carried his whip perpendicularly in his hand, like a scepter, and as his horse jogged on, the motion of his arms was not unlike the flapping of a pair of wings. A small wool hat rested on the top of his nose, for so his scanty strip of forehead might be called, and the skirts of his black coat fluttered out almost to the horses tail. Such was the appearance of Ichabod and his steed as they shambled out of the gate of Hans Van Ripper, and it was altogether such an apparition as is seldom to be met with in broad daylight.

It was, as I have said, a fine autumnal day; the sky was clear and serene, and nature wore that rich and golden livery which we always associate with the idea of abundance. The forests had put on their sober brown and yellow, while some trees of the tenderer kind had been nipped by the frosts into brilliant dyes of orange, purple, and scarlet. Streaming files of wild ducks began to make their appearance high in the air; the bark of the squirrel might be heard from the groves of beech and hickory nuts, and the pensive whistle of the quail at intervals from the neighboring stubble field.

The small birds were taking their farewell banquets. In the fullness of their revelry, they fluttered, chirping and frolicking from bush to bush, and tree to tree, capricious from the very profusion and variety around them. There was the honest cockrobin, the favorite game of stripling sportsmen, with its loud querulous note; and the twittering blackbirds flying in sable clouds, and the golden-winged woodpecker with his crimson crest, his broad black gorget, and splendid plumage; and the cedar-bird, with its red tipped wings and yellow-tipt tail and its little monteiro cap of feathers; and the blue jay, that noisy coxcomb, in his gay light blue coat and white underclothes, screaming and chattering, nodding and bobbing and bowing, and pretending to be on good terms with every songster of the grove.

As Ichabod jogged slowly on his way, his eye, ever open to every symptom of culinary abundance, ranged with delight over the treasures of jolly autumn. On all sides he beheld vast store of apples: some hanging in oppressive opulence on the trees; some gathered into baskets and barrels for the market; others heaped up in rich piles for the cider press. Farther on he beheld great fields of Indian corn, with its golden ears peeping from their leafy coverts, and holding out the promise of cakes and hasty pudding; and the yellow pumpkins lying beneath them, turning up their fair round bellies to the sun, and giving ample prospects of the most luxurious of pies; and anon he passed the fragrant buckwheat fields breathing the odor of the beehive, and as he beheld them, soft anticipations stole over his mind of dainty slapjacks, well buttered, and garnished with honey or treacle, by the delicate little dimpled hand of Katrina Van Tassel.

Thus feeding his mind with many sweet thoughts and "sugared suppositions," he journeyed along the sides of a range of hills which look out upon some of the goodliest scenes of the mighty Hudson. The sun gradually wheeled his broad disk down in the west. The wide bosom of the Tappan Zee lay motionless and glassy, excepting that here and there a gentle undulation waved and prolonged the blue shallow of the distant mountain. A few amber clouds floated in the sky, without a breath of air to move them. The horizon was of a fine golden tint, changing gradually into a pure apple green, and from that into the deep blue of the mid-heaven. A slanting ray lingered on the woody crests of the precipices that overhung some parts of the river, giving greater depth to the dark gray and purple of their rocky sides. A sloop was loitering in the distance, dropping slowly down with the tide, her sail hanging uselessly against the mast; and as the reflection of the sky gleamed along the still water, it seemed as if the vessel was suspended in the air.

It was toward evening that Ichabod arrived at the castle of the Heer Van Tassel, which he found thronged with the pride and flower of the adjacent country Old farmers, a spare leathern-faced race, in homespun coats and breeches, blue stockings, huge shoes, and magnificent pewter buckles. Their brisk, withered little dames, in close crimped caps, long waisted short-gowns, homespun petticoats, with scissors and pincushions, and gay calico pockets hanging on the outside. Buxom lasses, almost as antiquated as their mothers, excepting where a straw hat, a fine ribbon, or perhaps a white frock, gave symptoms of city innovation. The sons, in short square-skirted coats, with rows of stupendous brass buttons, and their hair generally queued in the fashion of the times, especially if they could procure an eelskin for the purpose, it being esteemed throughout the country as a potent nourisher and strengthener of the hair.

Brom Bones, however, was the hero of the scene, having come to the gathering on his favorite steed Daredevil, a creature, like himself, full of mettle and mischief, and which no one but himself could manage. He was, in fact, noted for preferring vicious animals, given to all kinds of tricks which kept the rider in constant risk of his neck, for he held a tractable, well-broken horse as unworthy of a lad of spirit.

Fain would I pause to dwell upon the world of charms that burst upon the enraptured gaze of my hero, as he entered the state parlor of Van Tassel's mansion. Not those of the bevy of buxom lasses, with their luxurious display of red and white; but the ample charms of a genuine Dutch country tea table, in the sumptuous time of autumn. Such heaped up platters of cakes of various and almost indescribable kinds, known only to experienced Dutch house-wives! There was the doughty doughnut, the tender olykoek, and the crisp and crumbling cruller; sweet cakes and short cakes, ginger cakes and honey cakes, and the whole family of cakes. And then there were apple pies, and peach pies, and pumpkin pies; besides slices of ham and smoked beef; and more-over delectable dishes of preserved plums, and peaches, and pears, and quinces; not to mention broiled shad and roasted chickens; together with bowls of milk and cream, all mingled higgledy-pig-glely, pretty much as I have enumerated them, with the motherly teapot sending up its clouds of vapor from the midst — Heaven bless the mark! I want breath and time to discuss this banquet as it deserves, and am too eager to get on with my story. Happily, Ichabod Crane was not in so great a hurry as his historian, but did ample justice to every dainty.

He was a kind and thankful creature, whose heart dilated in proportion as his skin was filled with good cheer, and whose spirits rose with eating, as some men's do with drink. He could not help, too, rolling his large eyes round him as he ate, and chuckling with the possibility that he might one day be lord of all this scene of almost unimaginable luxury and splendor. Then, he thought, how soon he 'd turn his back upon the old schoolhouse; snap his fingers in the face of Hans Van Ripper, and every other niggardly patron, and kick any itinerant pedagogue out of doors that should dare to call him comrade!

Old Baltus Van Tassel moved about among his guests with a face dilated with content and good humor, round and jolly as the harvest moon. His hospitable attentions were brief, but expressive, being confined to a shake of the hand, a slap on the shoulder, a loud laugh, and a pressing invitation to "fall to, and help themselves."

And now the sound of the music from the common room, or hall, summoned to the dance. The musician was an old gray-headed negro, who had been the itinerant orchestra of the neighbor-hood for more than half a century. His instrument was as old and battered as himself. The greater part of the time he scraped on two or three strings, accompanying every movement of the bow with a motion of the head; bowing almost to the ground, and stamping with his foot whenever a fresh couple were to start.

Ichabod prided himself upon his dancing as much as upon his vocal powers. Not a limb, not a fibre about him was idle; and to have seen his loosely hung frame in full motion, and clattering about the room, you would have thought St. Vitus himself, that blessed patron of the dance, was figuring before you in person. He was the admiration of all the Negroes; who, having gathered, of all ages and sizes, from the farm and the neighborhood, stood forming a pyramid of shining black faces at every door and window; gazing with delight at the scene; rolling their white eyeballs, and showing grinning rows of ivory from ear to ear. How could the flogger of urchins be otherwise than animated and joyous? the lady of his heart was his partner in the dance, and smiling graciously in reply to all his amorous oglings; while Brom Bones, sorely smitten with love and jealousy, sat brooding by himself in one corner.

When the dance was at an end, Ichabod was attracted to a knot of the sager folks, who, with Old Van Tassel, sat smoking at one end of the piazza, gossiping over former times, and drawing out long stories about the war.

This neighborhood, at the time of which I am speaking, was one of those highly favored places which abound with chronicle and great men. The British and American line had run near it during the war; it had, therefore, been the scene of marauding and infested with refugees, cowboys, and all kinds of border chivalry. Just sufficient time had elapsed to enable each storyteller to dress up his tale with a little becoming fiction, and, in the indistinctness of his recollection, to make himself the hero of every exploit.

There was the story of Doffue Martling, a large bluebearded Dutchman, who had nearly taken a British frigate with an old iron nine-pounder from a mud breastwork, only that his gun burst at the sixth discharge. And there was an old gentleman who shall be nameless, being too rich a mynheer to be lightly mentioned, who, in the battle of White Plains, being an excellent master of defense, parried a musketball with a small sword, insomuch that he absolutely felt it whiz round the blade, and glance off at the hilt; in proof of which he was ready at any time to show the sword, with the hilt a little bent. There were several more that had been equally great in the field, not one of whom but was persuaded that he had a considerable hand in bringing the war to a happy termination.

But all these were nothing to the tales of ghosts and apparitions that succeeded. The neighborhood is rich in legendary treasures of the kind. Local tales and superstitions thrive best in these sheltered, long settled retreats; but are trampled under foot by the shifting throng that forms the population of most of our country places. Besides, there is no encouragement for ghosts in most of our villages, for they have scarcely had time to finish their first nap and turn themselves in their graves, before their surviving friends have traveled away from the neighborhood; so that when they turn out at night to walk their rounds, they have no acquaintance left to call upon. This is perhaps the reason why we so seldom hear of ghosts except in our long-established Dutch communities.

The immediate cause, however, of the prevalence of supernatural stories in these parts, was doubtless owing to the vicinity of Sleepy Hollow. There was a contagion in the very air that blew from that haunted region; it breathed forth an atmosphere of dreams and fancies infecting all the land. Several of the Sleepy Hollow people were present at Van Tassel's, and, as usual, were doling out their wild and wonderful legends. Many dismal tales were told about funeral trains, and mourning cries and wailings heard and seen about the great tree where the unfortunate Major Andre was taken, and which stood in the neighborhood. Some mention was made also of the woman in white, that haunted the dark glen at Raven Rock, and was often heard to shriek on winter nights before a storm, having perished there in the snow. The chief part of the stories, however, turned upon the favorite spectre of Sleepy Hollow, the Headless Horseman, who had been heard several times of late, patrolling the country; and, it was said, tethered his horse nightly among the graves in the churchyard.

The sequestered situation of this church seems always to have made it a favorite haunt of troubled spirits. It stands on a knoll, surrounded by locust, trees and lofty elms, from among which its decent, whitewashed walls shine modestly forth, like Christian purity beaming through the shades of retirement. A gentle slope descends from it to a silver sheet of water, bordered by high trees, between which, peeps may be caught at the blue hills of the Hudson. To look upon its grass-grown yard, where the sunbeams seem to sleep so quietly, one would think that there at least the dead might rest in peace. On one side of the church extends a wide woody dell, along which raves a large brook among broken rocks and trunks of fallen trees. Over a deep black part of the stream, not far from the church, was formerly thrown a wooden bridge; the road that led to it, and the bridge itself, were thickly shaded by overhanging trees, which cast a gloom about it, even in the daytime; but occasioned a fearful darkness at night. Such was one of the favorite haunts of the Headless Horseman, and the place where he was most frequently encountered. The tale was told of old Brouwer, a most heretical disbeliever in ghosts, how he met the Horseman returning from his foray into Sleepy Hollow, and was obliged to get up behind him; how they galloped over bush and brake, over hill and swamp, until they reached the bridge; when the Horseman suddenly turned into a skeleton, threw old Brouwer into the brook, and sprang away over the treetops with a clap of thunder.

This story was immediately matched by a thrice marvelous adventure of Brom Bones, who made light of the Galloping Hessian as an arrant jockey. He affirmed that on returning one night from the neighboring village of Sing Sing, he had been overtaken by this midnight trooper; that he had offered to race with him for a bowl of punch, and should have won it too, for Daredevil beat the goblin horse all hollow, but just as they came to the church bridge, the Hessian bolted, and vanished in a flash of fire.

All these tales, told in that drowsy undertone with which men talk in the dark, the countenances of the listeners only now and then receiving a casual gleam from the glare of a pipe, sank deep in the mind of Ichabod. He repaid them in kind with large extracts from his invaluable author, Cotton Mather, and added many marvelous events that had taken place in his native State of Connecticut, and fearful sights which he had seen in his nightly walks about Sleepy Hollow.

The revel now gradually broke up. The old farmers gathered together their families in their wagons, and were heard for some time rattling along the hollow roads, and over the distant hills. Some of the damsels mounted on pillions behind their favorite swains, and their lighthearted laughter, mingling with the clatter of hoofs, echoed along the silent woodlands, sounding fainter and fainter, until they gradually died away, and the late scene of noise and frolic was all silent and deserted. Ichabod only lingered behind, according to the custom of country lovers, to have a tete-a-tete with the heiress; fully convinced that he was now on the high road to success. What passed at this interview I will not pretend to say, for in fact I do not know. Something, however, I fear me, must have gone wrong, for he certainly sallied forth, after no very great interval, with an air quite desolate and chapfallen. Oh, these women! These women! Could that girl have been playing off any of her coquettish tricks? Was her encouragement of the poor pedagogue all a mere sham to secure her conquest of his rival? Heaven only knows, not I! Let it suffice to say, Ichabod stole forth with the air of one who had been sacking a henroost, rather than a fair lady's heart. Without looking to the right or left to notice the scene of rural wealth, on which he had so often gloated, he went straight to the stable, and with several hearty cuffs and kicks roused his steed most uncourteously from the comfortable quarters in which he was soundly sleeping, dreaming of mountains of corn and oats, and whole valleys of timothy and clover.

It was the very witching time of night that Ichabod, heavy hearted and crestfallen, pursued his travels homewards, along the sides of the lofty hills which rise above Tarry Town, and which he had traversed so cheerily in the afternoon. The hour was as dismal as himself. Far below him the Tappan Zee spread its dusky and indistinct waste of waters, with here and there the tall mast of a sloop, riding quietly at anchor under the land. In the dead hush of midnight, he could even hear the barking of the watchdog from the opposite shore of the Hudson; but it was so vague and faint as only to give an idea of his distance from this faithful companion of man. Now and then, too, the long-drawn crowing of a cock, accidentally awakened, would sound far, far off, from some farmhouse away among the hills — but it was like a dreaming sound in his ear. No signs of life occurred near him, but occasionally the melancholy chirp of a cricket, or perhaps the guttural twang of a bullfrog from a neighboring marsh, as if sleeping uncomfortably and turning suddenly in his bed.

All the stories of ghosts and goblins that he had heard in the afternoon now came crowding upon his recollection. The night grew darker and darker; the stars seemed to sink deeper in the sky, and driving clouds occasionally hid them from his sight. He had never felt so lonely and dismal. He was, moreover, approaching the very place where many of the scenes of the ghost stories had been laid. In the center of the road stood an enormous tulip tree, which towered like a giant above all the other trees of the neighborhood, and formed a kind of landmark. Its limbs were gnarled and fantastic, large enough to form trunks for ordinary trees, twisting down almost to the earth, and rising again into the air. It was connected with the tragical story of the unfortunate Andre, who had been taken prisoner hard by; and was universally known by the name of Major Andre's tree. The common people regarded it with a mixture of respect and superstition, partly out of sympathy for the fate of its ill-starred namesake, and partly from the tales of strange sights, and doleful lamentations, told concerning it.

As Ichabod approached this fearful tree, he began to whistle; he thought his whistle was answered; it was but a blast sweeping sharply through the dry branches. As he approached a little nearer, he thought he saw something white, hanging in the midst of the tree: he paused, and ceased whistling but, on looking more narrowly, perceived that it was a place where the tree had been scathed by lightning, and the white wood laid bare. Suddenly he heard a groan — his teeth chattered, and his knees smote against the saddle: it was but the rubbing of one huge bough upon another, as they were swayed about by the breeze. He passed the tree in safety, but new perils lay before him.

About two hundred yards from the tree, a small brook crossed the road, and ran into a marshy and thickly wooded glen, known by the name of Wiley's Swamp. A few rough logs, laid side by side, served for a bridge over this stream. On that side of the road where the brook entered the wood, a group of oaks and chestnuts, matted thick with wild grapevines, threw a cavernous gloom over it. To pass this bridge was the severest trial. It was at this identical spot that the unfortunate Andre was captured, and under the covert of those chestnuts and vines were the sturdy yeomen concealed who surprised him. This has ever since been considered a haunted stream, and fearful are the feelings of the schoolboy who has to pass it alone after dark.

As he approached the stream, his heart began to thump he summoned up, however, all his resolution, gave his horse half a score of kicks in the ribs, and attempted to dash briskly across the bridge; but instead of starting forward, the perverse old animal made a lateral movement, and ran broadside against the fence. Ichabod, whose fears increased with the delay, jerked the reins on the other side, and kicked lustily with the contrary foot: it was all in vain; his steed started, it is true, but it was only to plunge to the opposite side of the road into a thicket of brambles and alder bushes. The schoolmaster now bestowed both whip and heel upon the starveling ribs of old Gunpowder, who dashed forward, snuffling and snorting, but came to a stand just by the bridge, with a suddenness that had nearly sent his rider sprawling over his head. Just at this moment a plashy tramp by the side of the bridge caught the sensitive ear of Ichabod. In the dark shadow of the grove, on the margin of the brook, he beheld something huge, misshapen and towering. It stirred not, but seemed gathered up in the gloom, like some gigantic monster ready to spring upon the traveller.

The hair of the affrighted pedagogue rose upon his head with terror. What was to be done? To turn and fly was now too late; and besides, what chance was there of escaping ghost or goblin, if such it was, which could ride upon the wings of the wind?

Summoning up, therefore, a show of courage, he demanded in stammering accents, "Who are you?" He received no reply. He repeated his demand in a still more agitated voice. Still there was no answer. Once more he cudgelled the sides of the inflexible Gunpowder, and, shutting his eyes, broke forth with involuntary fervor into a psalm tune. Just then the shadowy object of alarm put itself in motion, and with a scramble and a bound stood at once in the middle of the road. Though the night was dark and dismal, yet the form of the unknown might now in some degree be ascertained. He appeared to be a horseman of large dimensions, and mounted on a black horse of powerful frame. He made no offer of molestation or sociability, but kept aloof on one side of the road, jogging along on the blind side of old Gunpowder, who had now got over his fright and waywardness.

Ichabod, who had no relish for this strange midnight companion, and bethought himself of the adventure of Brom Bones with the Galloping Hessian, now quickened his steed in hopes of leaving him behind. The stranger, however, quickened his horse to an equal pace. Ichabod pulled up, and fell into a walk, thinking to lag behind — the other did the same. His heart began to sink within him; he endeavored to resume his psalm tune, but his parched tongue clove to the roof of his mouth, and he could not utter a stave. There was something in the moody and dogged silence of this pertinacious companion that was mysterious and appalling. It was soon fearfully accounted for. On mounting a rising ground, which brought the figure of his fellow traveler in relief against the sky, gigantic in height, and muffled in a cloak, Ichabod was horror — struck on perceiving that he was headless! But his horror was still more increased on observing that the head, which should have rested on his shoulders, was carried before him on the pommel of his saddle! His terror rose to desperation; he rained a shower of kicks and blows upon Gunpowder, hoping by a sudden movement to give his companion the slip; but the specter started full jump with him. Away, then, they dashed through thick and thin; stones flying and sparks flashing at every bound. Ichabod's flimsy garments fluttered in the air, as he stretched

his long lank body away over his horse's head, in the eagerness of his flight.

They had now reached the road which turns off to Sleepy Hollow; but Gunpowder, who seemed possessed with a demon, instead of keeping up it, made an opposite turn, and plunged headlong down hill to the left. This road leads through a sandy hollow shaded by trees for about a quarter of a mile, where it crosses the bridge famous in goblin story; and just beyond swells the green knoll on which stands the whitewashed church.

As yet the panic of the steed had given his unskillful rider an apparent advantage in the chase, but just as he had got half way through the hollow, the girths of the saddle gave way, and he felt it slipping from under him. He seized it by the pommel, and endeavored to hold it firm, but in vain; and had just time to save himself by clasping old Gunpowder round the neck, when the saddle fell to the earth, and he heard it trampled under foot by his pursuer. For a moment the terror of Hans Van Ripper's wrath passed across his mind, for it was his Sunday saddle; but this was no time for petty fears; the goblin was hard on his haunches; and (unskillful rider that he was!) he had much ado to maintain his seat; sometimes slipping on one side, sometimes on another, and sometimes jolted on the high ridge of his horse's backbone, with a violence that he verily feared would cleave him asunder.

An opening, in the trees now cheered him with the hopes that the church bridge was at hand. The wavering reflection of a silver star in the bosom of the brook told him that he was not mistaken. He saw the walls of the church dimly glaring under the trees beyond. He recollected the place where Brom Bones' ghostly competitor had disappeared. "If I can but reach that bridge," thought Ichabod, "I am safe." Just then he heard the black steed panting and blowing close behind him; he even fancied that he felt his hot breath. Another convulsive kick in the ribs, and old Gunpowder sprang upon the bridge; he thundered over the resounding planks; he gained the opposite side; and now Ichabod cast a look behind to see if his pursuer should vanish, according to rule, in a flash of fire and brimstone. Just then he saw the goblin rising in his stirrups, and in the very act of hurling his head at him. Ichabod endeavored to dodge the horrible missile, but too late. It encountered his cranium with a tremendous crash — he was tumbled headlong into the dust, and Gunpowder, the black steed, and the goblin rider, passed by like a whirlwind.

The next morning the old horse was found without his saddle, and with the bridle under his feet, soberly cropping the grass at his master's gate. Ichabod did not make his appearance at breakfast; dinnerhour came, but no Ichabod. The boys assembled at the schoolhouse, and strolled idly about the banks of the brook; but no schoolmaster. Hans Van Ripper now began to feel some uneasiness about the fate of poor Ichabod, and his saddle. An inquiry was set on foot, and after diligent investigation they came upon his traces. In one part of the road leading to the church was found the saddle trampled in the dirt; the tracks of horses' hoofs deeply dented in the road, and evidently at furious speed, were traced to the bridge, beyond which, on the bank of a broad part of the brook, where the water ran deep and black, was found the hat of the unfortunate Ichabod, and close beside it a shattered pumpkin.

The brook was searched, but the body of the schoolmaster was not to be discovered. Hans Van Ripper as executor of his estate, examined the bundle which contained all his worldly effects. They consisted of two shirts and a half; two stocks for the neck; a pair or two of worsted stockings; an old pair of corduroy small clothes; a rusty razor; a book of psalm tunes full of dog's ears; and a broken pitchpipe. As to the books and furniture of the schoolhouse, they belonged to the community, excepting Cotton Mather's History of Witchcraft, a New England Almanac, and book of dreams and fortunetelling; in which last was a sheet of foolscap much scribbled and blotted in several fruitless attempts to make a copy of verses in honor of the heiress of Van Tassel. These magic books and the poetic scrawl were forthwith consigned to the flames by Hans Van Ripper; who, from that time forward, determined to send his children no more to school; observing that he never knew any good come of this same reading and writing. Whatever money the schoolmaster possessed, and he had received his quarter's pay but a day or two before, he must have

had about his person at the time of his disappearance.

The mysterious event caused much speculation at the church on the following Sunday. Knots of gazers and gossips were collected in the churchyard, at the bridge, and at the spot where the hat and pumpkin had been found. The stories of Brouwer, of Bones, and a whole budget of others were called to mind; and when they had diligently considered them all, and compared them with the symptoms of the present case, they shook their heads, and came to the conclusion chat Ichabod had been carried off by the Galloping Hessian. As he was a bachelor, and in nobody's debt, nobody troubled his head any more about him; the school was removed to a different quarter of the Hollow, and another pedagogue reigned in his stead.

It is true, an old farmer, who had been down to New York on a visit several years after, and from whom this account of the ghostly adventure was received, brought home the intelligence that Ichabod Crane was still alive; that he had left the neighborhood partly through fear of the goblin and Hans Van Ripper, and partly in mortification at having been suddenly dismissed by the heiress; that he had changed his quarters to a distant part of the country; had kept school and studied law at the same time; had been admitted to the bar; turned politician; electioneered; written for the newspapers; and finally had been made a justice of the ten pound court. Brom Bones, too, who, shortly after his rival's disappearance conducted the blooming Katrina in triumph to the altar, was observed to look exceedingly knowing whenever the story of Ichabod was related, and always burst into a hearty laugh at the mention of the pumpkin; which led some to suspect that he knew more about the matter than he chose to tell.

The old country wives, however, who are the best judges of these matters, maintain to this day that Ichabod was spirited away by supernatural means; and it is a favorite story often told about the neighborhood round the winter evening fire. The bridge became more than ever an object of superstitious awe; and that may be the reason why the road has been altered of late years, so as to approach the church by the border of the millpond. The school-house being deserted soon fell to decay, and was reported to be haunted by the ghost of the unfortunate pedagogue and the ploughboy, loitering homeward of a still summer evening, has often fancied his voice at a distance, chanting a melancholy psalm tune among the tranquil solitudes of Sleepy Hollow.

Assignments

- Warm-up: Compare "Sleepy Hollow" with "The Devil and Tom Walker."
- Students should complete Concept Builder 6-D.
- Student will re-write corrected copies of essay due tomorrow.

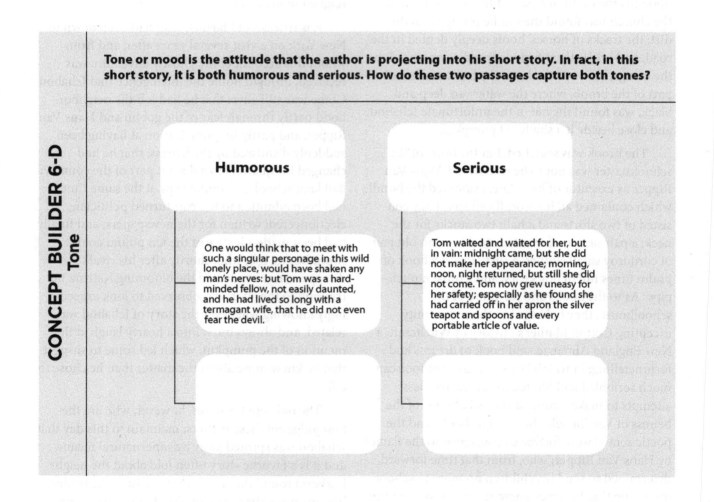

CONCEPT BUILDER 6-D
Tone

Tone or mood is the attitude that the author is projecting into his short story. In fact, in this short story, it is both humorous and serious. How do these two passages capture both tones?

Humorous

One would think that to meet with such a singular personage in this wild lonely place, would have shaken any man's nerves: but Tom was a hard-minded fellow, not easily daunted, and he had lived so long with a termagant wife, that he did not even fear the devil.

Serious

Tom waited and waited for her, but in vain: midnight came, but she did not make her appearance; morning, noon, night returned, but still she did not come. Tom now grew uneasy for her safety; especially as he found she had carried off in her apron the silver teapot and spoons and every portable article of value.

Moral Man and Immoral Society

For the first eight years of my schooling, I stood in front of an ancient oak tree in front of my family home on South Highway, McGehee, Arkansas, and caught a big yellow school bus to McGehee Elementary School. My buddies, Craig Towles and Pip Runyan, wickedly violated school bus riding etiquette and abandoned their boring bus stop two doors down and joined me so that we could secretly deposit acorns, AKA pretend "soldiers," in the middle of the road to be squashed by speeding autos, AKA pretend German Panzer Tanks. The old oak tree liberally deposited brave acorn Wehrmacht African Korps recruits on the crab grass carpet that my grandmother had futilely tried to replace with St. Augustine grass.

We made the most of the oak's generousness. Those little buggers made a wonderful chartreuse stain on the already steaming South Highway concrete crown. This was innocent enough — no one would miss a few acorns from a stupid oak tree — but before long, you guessed it, we — more precisely Pip — who was always full of errant but terribly interesting pretend scenarios — that boy always worried Craig and me — suggested that we abandon the acorns and start throwing grenades, AKA rocks, at passing cars. (Pip will deny this, of course, but you must corroborate this story with Craig.) We finally hit (blew up) a few Tiger Tanks and got into big trouble (were captured by the enemy — the Gestapo — and were thoroughly punished — our parents beat the crap out of us).

The truth is Jimmy, Craig, or Pip alone would not do such a depraved thing (well maybe Pip would do it — he tortured frogs, too). In a group together, however, such a thing not only was plausible, it was downright desirable. Jimmy, Craig, and Pip did things Jimmy or Craig or Pip would never do alone.

In a crowd we did things we would not do as individuals.

A Christian theologian named Reinhold Neibuhr said as much in a book he wrote called *Moral Man and Immoral Society*. Niebuhr insisted that public politics is concerned with correcting, balancing as it were, the sinfulness of human nature, that is, the self-centeredness of individuals and groups. But he understood that while little boys and political despots might behave nicely if they are alone, in groups they became monsters. He suggested that moral men became immoral men when they were together in a social group (Reinhold Neibuhr, *Moral Man and Immoral Society*, New York, London: C. Scribner's Sons, 1932).

Niebuhr fervently hoped that a person would experience redemption and thereby redeem his society by a Hegelian, reductionist struggle with sinfulness. Hegel said, in short, that folks changed as they struggled with life. Hegel hoped that people came through a struggle, hard times, as better people. Just like my mother hoped that my whipping for throwing the rocks with Craig and Pip would cause me to be a better person, too. In my case, the mental dissonance, combined with physical pain, worked! I have never thrown rocks at cars since then. I still relieve myself outside behind another oak tree once in a while — another terrible thing that Pip and Craig taught me to do and my fussy mother told me not to do — but, hey, I live on a farm! But I have never again thrown rocks at cars.

Niebuhr advanced the thesis that what the individual is able to achieve singly cannot be a possibility for social groups. He believed that Jimmy Stobaugh would be a good boy alone but inevitably, without a doubt, once he was with Craig and Pip or his other buddies he would indulge in sinfulness. It was inevitable. Thus, Niebuhr believed in moral individuals and immoral societies or groups. He called it "the herd mentality."

In other words, Niebuhr correctly saw the immorality of systems in society (e.g., social welfare) and its futile attempts to ameliorate individuals and their needs through systemic interventions. In other words, Niebuhr was not naïve — he knew that systems and cultures change and individual hearts change. But it was much harder to convince a group to change than an individual.

Niebuhr warned that one should try to change individual hearts first, but, in a last resort, power could and should be used to stop societies from harming its members and then other societies.

Once, Craig and I were melting down Mr. Chilcoat's discarded tar shingles to make spears. We were full of bad ideas, but they always exhibited élan and ingenuity. We carefully placed the tar shingles in empty, discarded metal pork and bean cans sitting in a roaring fire. Once the tar was bubbling we placed old broom handles in the mixture and, once the broom handles were removed, and the tar somewhat cooled, we placed stone heads — carefully chiseled as surrogate Indian spear heads — into the warm tar. Thus, we created an alligator-killing weapon that we used to kill pretend reptiles in Mrs. Beck's water garden.

My dad, observing our behavior, and, furthermore, discerning the obvious dangers of placing boiling tar and eight-year-old boys in the same vicinity, prophetically warned, "Jimmy, stop or you will burn yourself badly."

Well, he was right. Within the next hour I spilled burning tar on my right hand causing painful third-degree burns. I spent the rest of the day in Dr. Parker's waiting room. Even looking at lovely Jane Parker, Dr. Parker's oldest daughter, my first heart-throb, only to be replaced by perennial goddess Jamie Fraser the following year, could not mitigate the pain. It was a Sunday afternoon and Jane had accompanied her dad to his office, which was normally closed. I longingly lobbied for curative sympathy from this exquisite beauty, but Jane, always the pragmatist, simply thought I was stupid and resented that her dad had to waste his time on such a dope.

The thing is, I always wondered, why didn't my dad STOP me from burning Mr. Chilcoat's roof shingles and, more pointedly, from burning to the third degree his accident-prone, stupid middle son's hand? What if I had killed myself or something? I imagined Dad saying, "Well Jimmy's dead — I told him it was going to happen." Or "Well, now what am I going to do — there is no one to take the trash out in the morning!" My dad would have been sorry, I was convinced, if the fates of burning tar had snatched me from this world.

Or worse, what if I hurt Craig — something I was always doing. Poor Craig, more times than not, got hurt more often by my dim-witted choices than I did. Craig got four stitches in his chin the next year when I caught his face with an army surplus shovel as we dug foxholes to escape the inevitable Japanese Banzai charge that would be visited on us at Guadalcanal. Didn't Dad at least want to protect poor Craig? It would have been pretty embarrassing to tell Mom and Mrs. Towles, "Sorry to tell you — Jimmy and Craig were killed while making tar spears to kill pretend alligators in Mrs. Beck's water garden." Pathetic parenting.

I once asked Dad, and Dad, with an iconic grin, responded, "Jimmy, even at age eight, you manifested an obduracy that I could not overcome. In the presence of Craig, in order to maintain your pride, I knew you would never listen to me. You needed to experience the consequences of your actions before you would stop the action."

Especially as I look down right now, as I type and I look at my scarred right hand, I realize my sagacious father was right. Dad's point was that individuals may be sincere in their understanding about several issues; in fact, they may be right about some issues. But they are wrong, too, and when that group gains political hegemony it can lose focus and direction and can do immoral things — like throwing rocks at cars — and stupid things — like making tar spears.

Individuals can be moral in purpose and in actions. But combining a bunch of individuals into a coercive group can cause the group to become immoral. For example, Adolf Hitler's rise to power was initially a pretty good thing for Germany. However, as he gained power, the good was replaced by the bad. This may not be inevitable, but it happens so often that we should be cautious in giving so much power to groups. As an interesting sidebar, Niebuhr is directly contradicting the liberal Dewey who applauded the notion that the community, or larger society, created the greater good.

The answer to this apparent contradiction is, of course, the gospel. Societies and groups change as individuals change. Niebuhr stressed the role of the Holy Spirit (what he calls the "religious imagination"). In a sense, the group remained moral because the individuals in that society answer to a "higher power," not to the coercion of the group or to the agenda of the group. Dietrich Bonheoffer, a German World War II martyr, for example, was perhaps the most patriotic of Germans because he loved his God and his country enough to obey God and His Word above all persons. This was the only way, Bonheoffer understood, that his nation could be moral and right before the God he served. Unfortunately, he was a lone voice in the wilderness!

We live today in a world that is full of the tyranny of the majority. The world tells us to relax, be happy and do what is right in our own eyes. We do things as a group we would never do as individuals. But judgment comes not to groups but to individuals!

The truth, then, is that change — real change — is a "God" thing. Only God can really change persons. And as He changes persons and families, then He will change communities and nations.

Assignments

- Warm up: Critic Harold Bloom in *The Western Canon* laments the propensity for other critics to discuss worldview in literary works. He argues that suggesting that literary works have a worldview cheapens their artistic value (Harold Bloom, *The Western Canon*, New York: Harcourt Brace, 1994). Is it possible to read literature as if it does not have a worldview?

- Students should complete Concept Builder 6-E.

- Essays are due. Students should take the chapter 6 test.

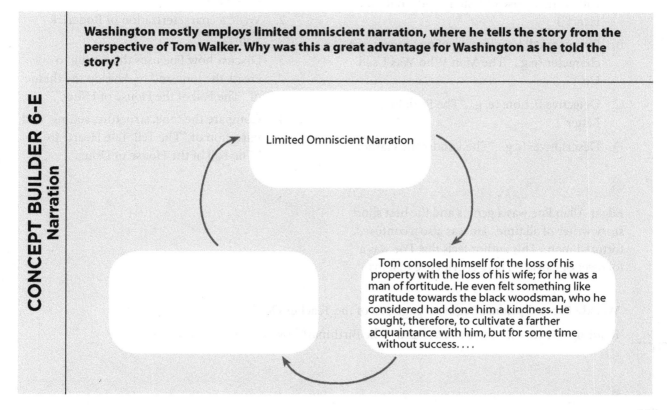

CONCEPT BUILDER 6-E
Narration

Washington mostly employs limited omniscient narration, where he tells the story from the perspective of Tom Walker. Why was this a great advantage for Washington as he told the story?

Limited Omniscient Narration

Tom consoled himself for the loss of his property with the loss of his wife; for he was a man of fortitude. He even felt something like gratitude towards the black woodsman, who he considered had done him a kindness. He sought, therefore, to cultivate a farther acquaintance with him, but for some time without success....

Chapter 7

1800–1840: National Period (Part 2):
A Growing Nation

First Thoughts Christian teacher Thomas Merton, in an essay entitled "A Devout Meditation in Memory of Adolf Eichmann (a Nazi Leader Who Implemented the Holocaust)," challenges modern man to rethink sanity. "One of the most disturbing facts," Merton begins, "that came out in the Eichmann trial was that a psychiatrist examined him and pronounced him perfectly sane." The fact is, given our world, we can no longer assume that because a person is "sane" or "adjusted" he/she is okay. Edgar Allan Poe was a romantic eccentric. He was a disturbed man, but his short stories were some of the best ever written. Poe wrote four types of short stories:

A. Strange: use of the supernatural; symbolic fantasies of the human condition (e. g., "The Fall of the House of Usher" and "Tell-Tale Heart")

B. Exaggerated: heightening of one aspect of a character (e.g., "The Man Who Was Used Up")

C. Detective fiction: (e. g., "The Purloined Letter")

D. Descriptive: (e.g., "The Landscape Garden")

Author Worldview Watch

Edgar Allan Poe was a genius and the best short story writer of all time. He was also a confused, tortured man. This author feels that Poe was a follower of Christ. There is evidence that his adopted family took him to Bible-believing churches and that he might have embraced Christ as savior. On the other hand, Poe explored the supernatural in ways that were new to Americans and may have put him in harm's way spiritually.

Chapter Learning Objectives In chapter 7 we focus entirely on the writings of Edgar Allan Poe. You will analyze the poem "The Raven," and the short stories "Fall of the House of Usher" and "The Tell-Tale Heart," all by Edgar Allan Poe.

As a result of this chapter study you will be able to . . .

1. Explore the way Poe uses figurative language.

2. Write a characterization of Roderick Usher.

3. Discuss how Poe uses the setting to create the tone and to develop the theme of "The Fall of the House of Usher."

4. Compare the tone, structure, setting, and narration of "The Tell-Tale Heart" to "The Fall of the House of Usher."

Weekly Essay Options: Begin on page 274 of the Teacher Guide.

Reading ahead: *The Scarlet Letter* and "The Birthmark" by Nathaniel Hawthorne.

Edgar Allan Poe

Edgar Allan Poe, the greatest American short story writer, invented the modern detective story. His poetry, too, was extraordinary. In fact, Poe was perhaps the first and greatest poet America produced. In Poe's poems, like his tales, his characters were tortured by nameless fears and longings. Today, Poe is acclaimed as one of America's greatest writers, but in his own unhappy lifetime he knew little but failure. Struggling with ill health, and later drug and alcohol addiction, Poe was a broken man. The untimely death of his young wife was the last straw. It broke his heart and perhaps drove him mad.

Assignments

- Warm-up: Considering the dreary tone and non-Christian content of his writings, why should Christians read anything by Edgar Allan Poe?

- Student should complete Concept Builder 7-A.

- Students review the required reading(s) *before* the assigned chapter begins.

- Teachers may want to discuss assigned reading(s) with students.

- Teachers shall assign the required essay. The rest of the essays can be outlined, answered with shorter answers, discussed, or skipped.

- Students will review all readings for chapter 7.

CONCEPT BUILDER 7-A
Setting

Clearly the setting is critical to any literary work. It sets the tone, develops the plot, and reinforces the theme. What elements would you include if creating a poem or a story like Poe himself?

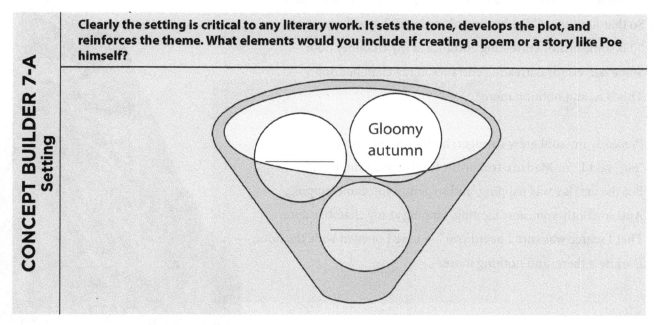

Gloomy autumn

THE RAVEN
Edgar Allan Poe

Once upon a midnight dreary, while I pondered, weak and weary,
Over many a quaint and curious volume of forgotten <u>lore</u>, *Knowledge*
While I nodded, nearly napping, suddenly there came a tapping,
As of some one gently rapping, rapping at my chamber door.
"'Tis some visitor," I muttered, "tapping at my chamber door —
Only this, and nothing more."

Ah, distinctly I remember it was in the bleak December,
And each separate dying ember wrought its ghost upon the floor.
Eagerly I wished the morrow; vainly I had sought to borrow
From my books surcease of sorrow — sorrow for the lost Lenore —
For the rare and radiant maiden whom the angels name Lenore —
Nameless here for evermore.

And the silken sad uncertain rustling of each purple curtain
Thrilled me — filled me with fantastic terrors never felt before;
So that now, to still the beating of my heart, I stood repeating,
"'Tis some visitor entreating entrance at my chamber door —
Some late visitor entreating entrance at my chamber door; —
This it is, and nothing more."

Presently my soul grew stronger; hesitating then no longer,
"Sir," said I, "or Madam, truly your forgiveness I implore;
But the fact is I was napping, and so gently you came rapping,
And so faintly you came tapping, tapping at my chamber door,
That I scarce was sure I heard you" — here I opened wide the door; —
Darkness there, and nothing more.

Deep into that darkness peering, long I stood there wondering, fearing,

Doubting, dreaming dreams no mortals ever dared to dream before;

But the silence was unbroken, and the stillness gave no token,

And the only word there spoken was the whispered word, "Lenore!"

This I whispered, and an echo murmured back the word, "Lenore!" —

Merely this, and nothing more.

Back into the chamber turning, all my soul within me burning,

Soon again I heard a tapping somewhat louder than before.

"Surely," said I, "surely that is something at my window lattice:

Let me see, then, what the threat is, and this mystery explore —

Let my heart be still a moment and this mystery explore; —

'Tis the wind and nothing more."

Open here I flung the shutter, when, with many a flirt and flutter,

In there stepped a stately raven of the saintly days of yore;

Not the least obeisance made he; not a minute stopped or stayed he;

But, with mien of lord or lady, perched above my chamber door —

Perched upon a bust of Pallas just above my chamber door —

Perched, and sat, and nothing more.

Then this ebony bird beguiling my sad fancy into smiling,

By the grave and stern decorum of the countenance it wore.

"Though thy crest be shorn and shaven, thou," I said, "art sure no craven,

Ghastly grim and ancient raven wandering from the Nightly shore —

Tell me what thy lordly name is on the Night's Plutonian shore!"

Quoth the Raven, "Nevermore."

Much I marvelled this ungainly fowl to hear discourse so plainly,

Though its answer little meaning — little relevancy bore;

For we cannot help agreeing that no living human being

Ever yet was blest with seeing bird above his chamber door —

Bird or beast upon the sculptured bust above his chamber door,

With such name as "Nevermore."

But the raven, sitting lonely on the placid bust, spoke only
That one word, as if his soul in that one word he did outpour.
Nothing further then he uttered — not a feather then he fluttered —
Till I scarcely more than muttered, "other friends have flown before —
On the morrow he will leave me, as my hopes have flown before."
Then the bird said, "Nevermore."

Startled at the stillness broken by reply so aptly spoken,
"Doubtless," said I, "what it utters is its only stock and store,
Caught from some unhappy master whom unmerciful Disaster
Followed fast and followed faster till his songs one burden bore —
Till the dirges of his Hope that melancholy burden bore
Of 'Never — nevermore.'"

But the Raven still beguiling all my fancy into smiling,
Straight I wheeled a cushioned seat in front of bird, and bust and door;
Then upon the velvet sinking, I betook myself to linking
Fancy unto fancy, thinking what this ominous bird of yore —
What this grim, ungainly, ghastly, gaunt and ominous bird of yore
Meant in croaking "Nevermore."

This I sat engaged in guessing, but no syllable expressing
To the fowl whose fiery eyes now burned into my bosom's core;
This and more I sat divining, with my head at ease reclining
On the cushion's velvet lining that the lamplight gloated o'er,
But whose velvet violet lining with the lamplight gloating o'er,
She shall press, ah, nevermore!

Then methought the air grew denser, perfumed from an unseen censer
Swung by Seraphim whose footfalls tinkled on the tufted floor.
"Wretch," I cried, "thy God hath lent thee — by these angels he hath sent thee
Respite — respite and nepenthe, from thy memories of Lenore!
Quaff, oh quaff this kind nepenthe and forget this lost Lenore!"
Quoth the Raven, "Nevermore."

"Prophet!" said I, "thing of evil! — prophet still, if bird or devil! —

Whether Tempter sent, or whether tempest tossed thee here ashore,

Desolate yet all undaunted, on this desert land enchanted —

On this home by horror haunted — tell me truly, I implore —

Is there — is there balm in Gilead? — tell me — tell me, I implore!"

Quoth the Raven, "Nevermore."

"Prophet!" said I, "thing of evil — prophet still, if bird or devil!

By that Heaven that bends above us — by that God we both adore —

Tell this soul with sorrow laden if, within the distant Aidenn,

It shall clasp a sainted maiden whom the angels name Lenore —

Clasp a rare and radiant maiden whom the angels name Lenore."

Quoth the Raven, "Nevermore."

"Be that word our sign in parting, bird or fiend," I shrieked upstarting —

"Get thee back into the tempest and the Night's Plutonian shore!

Leave no black plume as a token of that lie thy soul hath spoken!

Leave my loneliness unbroken! — quit the bust above my door!

Take thy beak from out my heart, and take thy form from off my door!"

Quoth the Raven, "Nevermore."

And the Raven, never flitting, still is sitting, still is sitting

On the pallid bust of Pallas just above my chamber door;

And his eyes have all the seeming of a demon's that is dreaming,

And the lamplight o'er him streaming throws his shadow on the floor;

And my soul from out that shadow that lies floating on the floor

Shall be lifted — nevermore!

"I had gone so far as the conception of a Raven — the bird of ill omen — monotonously repeating the one word, "Nevermore," at the conclusion of each stanza, in a poem of melancholy tone, and in length about one hundred lines. Now, never losing sight of the object supremeness, or perfection, at all points, I asked myself — "Of all melancholy topics, what, according to the universal understanding of mankind, is the most melancholy?" Death — was the obvious reply. "And when," I said, "is the most melancholy of topics most poetical?" From what I have already explained at some length, the answer, here also, is obvious — "When it most closely allies itself to beauty: the death, then, of a beautiful woman is, unquestionably, the most poetical topic in the world — and equally is it beyond doubt that the lips best suited for such a topic are those of a bereaved lover."

From Edgar Allan Poe's "The Philosophy of Composition," first published in *Graham's Magazine*, April 1846.

Assignments

- Warm-up: How would you describe the tone of "The Raven"?

- Students should complete Concept Builder 7-B.

- Student should review reading(s) from the next chapter.

- Student should outline essays due at the end of the week.

- Per teacher instructions, students may answer orally, in a group setting, some of the essays that are not assigned as formal essays.

Illustration for Edgar Allan Poe's "The Raven". Accompanies the phrase "And my soul from out that shadow that lies floating on the floor/Shall be lifted--nevermore!" Image by Gustave Doré, 1884 (PD-US).

CONCEPT BUILDER 7-B Active Reading		Read the first four stanzas of "The Raven" and answer the following questions:
	1	Find two examples of alliteration (repetition of consonant sounds). What effect does this have on readers?
	2	What can you surmise about the speaker's state of mind by the raven's entrance into the room?
	3	What effect does this have on readers?

An Essay, "Edgar Allan Poe" by James Russell Lowell

THE situation of American literature is anomalous. It has no centre, or, if it have, it is like that of the sphere of Hermes. It is divided into many systems, each revolving round its several suns, and often presenting to the rest only the faint glimmer of a milk-and-water way. Our capital city, unlike London or Paris, is not a great central heart from which life and vigor radiate to the extremities, but resembles more an isolated umbilicus stuck down as near as may be to the centre of the land, and seeming rather to tell a legend of former usefulness than to serve any present need. Boston, New York, Philadelphia, each has its literature almost more distinct than those of the different dialects of Germany; and the Young Queen of the West has also one of her own, of which some articulate rumor barely has reached us dwellers by the Atlantic.

Perhaps there is no task more difficult than the just criticism of contemporary literature. It is even more grateful to give praise where it is needed than where it is deserved, and friendship so often seduces the iron stylus of justice into a vague flourish, that she writes what seems rather like an epitaph than a criticism. Yet if praise be given as an alms, we could not drop so poisonous a one into any man's hat. The critic's ink may suffer equally from too large an infusion of nutgalls or of sugar. But it is easier to be generous than to be just, and we might readily put faith in that fabulous direction to the hiding place of truth, did we judge from the amount of water which we usually find mixed with it.

Remarkable experiences are usually confined to the inner life of imaginative men, but Mr. Poe's biography displays a vicissitude and peculiarity of interest such as is rarely met with. The offspring of a romantic marriage, and left an orphan at an early

James Russell Lowell. Photographer unknown, c1855 (LOC, PD-Art).

age, he was adopted by Mr. Allan, a wealthy Virginian, whose barren marriage-bed seemed the warranty of a large estate to the young poet.

Having received a classical education in England, he returned home and entered the University of Virginia, where, after an extravagant course, followed by reformation at the last extremity, he was graduated with the highest honors of his class. Then came a boyish attempt to join the fortunes of the insurgent Greeks, which ended at St. Petersburg, where he got into difficulties through want of a passport, from which he was rescued by the American consul and sent home. He now entered the military academy at West Point, from which he obtained a dismissal on hearing of the birth of a son to his adopted father, by a second marriage, an event which cut off his expectations as an heir. The death of Mr. Allan, in whose will his name was not mentioned, soon after relieved him of all doubt in this regard, and he committed himself at once to authorship for a support. Previously to this, however, he had published (in 1827) a small volume of poems, which soon ran through three editions, and excited high expectations of its author's future distinction in the minds of many competent judges.

That no certain augury can be drawn from a poet's earliest lispings there are instances enough to prove. Shakespeare's first poems, though brimful of vigor and youth and picturesqueness, give but a very faint promise of the directness, condensation and overflowing moral of his maturer works. Perhaps, however, Shakespeare is hardly a case in point, his "Venus and Adonis" having been published, we believe, in his twenty-sixth year. Milton's Latin verses show tenderness, a fine eye for nature, and a delicate appreciation of classic models, but give no hint of the author of a new style in poetry. Pope's youthful pieces have all the sing-song, wholly unrelieved by the glittering malignity and eloquent irreligion of his later productions. Collins' callow namby-pamby died and gave no sign of the vigorous and original genius which he afterward displayed. We have never thought that the world lost more in the "marvellous boy," Chatterton, than a very ingenious imitator of obscure and antiquated dulness. Where he becomes original (as it is called), the interest of ingenuity ceases and he becomes stupid. Kirke White's promises were indorsed by the respectable name of Mr. Southey, but surely with no authority from Apollo. They have the merit of a traditional piety, which to our mind, if uttered at all, had been less objectionable in the retired closet of a diary, and in the sober raiment of prose. They do not clutch hold of the memory with the drowning pertinacity of Watts; neither have they the interest of his occasional

simple, lucky beauty. Burns having fortunately been rescued by his humble station from the contaminating society of the "Best models," wrote well and naturally from the first. Had he been unfortunate enough to have had an educated taste, we should have had a series of poems from which, as from his letters, we could sift here and there a kernel from the mass of chaff. Coleridge's youthful efforts give no promise whatever of that poetical genius which produced at once the wildest, tenderest, most original and most purely imaginative poems of modern times. Byron's "Hours of Idleness" would never find a reader except from an intrepid and indefatigable curiosity. In Wordsworth's first preludings there is but a dim foreboding of the creator of an era. From Southey's early poems, a safer augury might have been drawn. They show the patient investigator, the close student of history, and the unwearied explorer of the beauties of predecessors, but they give no assurances of a man who should add aught to stock of household words, or to the rarer and more sacred delights of the fireside or the arbor. The earliest specimens of Shelley's poetic mind already, also, give tokens of that ethereal sublimation in which the spirit seems to soar above the regions of words, but leaves its body, the verse, to be entombed, without hope of resurrection, in a mass of them. Cowley is generally instanced as a wonder of precocity. But his early insipidities show only a capacity for rhyming and for the metrical arrangement of certain conventional combinations of words, a capacity wholly dependent on a delicate physical organization, and an unhappy memory. An early poem is only remarkable when it displays an effort of reason, and the rudest verses in which we can trace some conception of the ends of poetry, are worth all the miracles of smooth juvenile versification. A school-boy, one would say, might acquire the regular see-saw of Pope merely by an association with the motion of the play-ground tilt.

Mr. Poe's early productions show that he could see through the verse to the spirit beneath, and that he already had a feeling that all the life and grace of the one must depend on and be modulated by the will of the other. We call them the most remarkable boyish poems that we have ever read. We know of none that can compare with them for maturity of purpose, and a nice understanding of the effects of language and metre. Such pieces are only valuable when they display what we can only express by the contradictory phrase of innate experience. We copy one of the shorter poems, written when the author was only fourteen. There is a little dimness in the filling up, but the grace and symmetry of the outline are such as few poets ever attain. There is a smack of ambrosia about it.

TO HELEN

Helen, thy beauty is to me
Like those Nicean barks of yore,
That gently, o'er a perfumed sea,
The weary, way-worn wanderer bore
To his own native shore.

On desperate seas long wont to roam,
Thy hyacinth hair, thy classic face,
Thy Naiad airs have brought me home
To the glory that was Greece
And the grandeur that was Rome.

Lo! in yon brilliant window-niche
How statue-like I see thee stand!
The agate lamp within thy hand,
Ah! Psyche, from the regions which
Are Holy Land!

It is the tendency of the young poet that impresses us. Here is no "withering scorn," no heart "blighted" ere it has safely got into its teens, none of the drawing-room sansculottism which Byron had brought into vogue. All is limpid and serene, with a pleasant dash of the Greek Helicon in it. The melody of the whole, too, is remarkable. It is not of that kind which can be demonstrated arithmetically upon the tips of the fingers. It is of that finer sort which the inner ear alone can estimate. It seems simple, like a Greek column, because of its perfection. In a poem named "Ligeia," under which title he intended to personify the music of nature, our boy-poet gives us the following exquisite picture:

Ligeia! Ligeia!
My beautiful one,
Whose harshest idea
Will to melody run,
Say, is it thy will,
On the breezes to toss,
Or, capriciously still,
Like the lone albatross,
Incumbent on night,
As she on the air,
To keep watch with delight
On the harmony there?

John Neal, himself a man of genius, and whose lyre has been too long capriciously silent, appreciated the high merit of these and similar passages, and drew a proud horoscope for their author.

Mr. Poe had that indescribable something which men have agreed to call genius. No man could ever tell us precisely what it is, and yet there is none who is not inevitably aware of its presence and its power. Let talent writhe and contort itself as it may, it has no such magnetism. Larger of bone and sinew it may be, but the wings are wanting. Talent sticks fast to earth, and its most perfect works have still one foot of clay. Genius claims kindred with the very workings of Nature herself, so that a sunset shall seem like a quotation from Dante, and if Shakespeare be read in the very presence of the sea itself, his verses shall but seem nobler for the sublime criticism of ocean. Talent may make friends for itself, but only genius can give to its creations the divine power of winning love and veneration. Enthusiasm cannot cling to what itself is unenthusiastic, nor will he ever have disciples who has not himself impulsive zeal enough to be a disciple. Great wits are allied to madness only inasmuch as they are possessed and carried away by their demon, While talent keeps him, as Paracelsus did, securely prisoned in the pommel of his sword. To the eye of genius, the veil of the spiritual world is ever rent asunder that it may perceive the ministers of good and evil who throng continually around it. No man of mere talent ever flung his inkstand at the devil.

When we say that Mr. Poe had genius, we do not mean to say that he has produced evidence of the highest. But to say that he possesses it at all is to say that he needs only zeal, industry, and a reverence for the trust reposed in him, to achieve the proudest triumphs and the greenest laurels. If we may believe the Longinuses; and Aristotles of our newspapers, we have quite too many geniuses of the loftiest order to render a place among them at all desirable, whether for its hardness of attainment or its seclusion. The highest peak of our Parnassus is, according to these gentlemen, by far the most thickly settled portion of the country, a circumstance which must make it an uncomfortable residence for individuals of a poetical temperament, if love of solitude be, as immemorial tradition asserts, a necessary part of their idiosyncrasy.

Mr. Poe has two of the prime qualities of genius, a faculty of vigorous yet minute analysis, and a wonderful fecundity of imagination. The first of these faculties is as needful to the artist in words, as a knowledge of anatomy is to the artist in colors or in stone. This enables him to conceive truly, to maintain a proper relation of parts, and to draw a correct outline, while the second groups, fills up and colors. Both of these Mr. Poe has displayed with singular distinctness in his prose works, the last predominating in his earlier tales, and the first in his later ones. In judging of the merit of an author, and assigning him his particular niche, we have a right to regard him from our own point of view, and to measure him by our own standard. But, in estimating the amount of power displayed in his works, we must be governed by his own design, and placing them by the side of his own ideal, find how much is wanting. We differ from Mr. Poe in his opinions of the objects of art. He esteems that object to be the creation of Beauty, and perhaps it is only in the definition of that word that we disagree with him. But in what we shall say of his writings, we shall take his own standard as our guide. The temple of the god of song is equally accessible from every side, and there is room enough in it for all who bring offerings, or seek in oracle.

In his tales, Mr. Poe has chosen to exhibit his power chiefly in that dim region which stretches from the very utmost limits of the probable into the weird confines of superstition and unreality. He combines in a very remarkable manner two faculties which are seldom found united; a power of influencing the mind of the reader by the impalpable shadows of mystery, and a minuteness of detail which does not leave a pin or a button unnoticed. Both are, in truth, the natural results of the predominating quality of his mind, to which we have before alluded, analysis. It is this which distinguishes the artist. His mind at once reaches forward to the effect to be produced. Having resolved to bring about certain emotions in the reader, he makes all subordinate parts tend strictly to the common centre. Even his mystery is mathematical to his own mind. To him X is a known quantity all along. In any picture that he paints he understands the chemical properties of all his colors. However vague some of his figures may seem, however formless the shadows, to him the outline is as clear and distinct as that of a geometrical diagram. For this reason Mr. Poe has no sympathy with Mysticism. The Mystic dwells in the mystery, is enveloped with it; it colors all his thoughts; it affects his optic nerve especially, and the commonest things get a rainbow edging from it. Mr. Poe, on the other hand, is a spectator ab extra. He analyzes, he dissects, he watches for such it practically is to him, with wheels and cogs and piston-rods, all working to produce a certain end.

This analyzing tendency of his mind balances the poetical, and by giving him the patience to be minute, enables him to throw a wonderful reality into his most unreal fancies. A monomania he paints with great power. He loves to dissect one of these cancers of the mind, and to trace all the subtle ramifications of its roots. In raising images of horror, also, he has strange success, conveying to us sometimes by a dusky hint some terrible doubt which is the secret of all horror. He leaves to imagination the task of finishing the picture, a task to which only she is competent.

Besides the merit of conception, Mr. Poe's writings have also that of form.

His style is highly finished, graceful and truly classical. It would be hard to find a living author who had displayed such varied powers. As an example of his style we would refer to one of his tales, "The House of Usher," in the first volume of his "Tales of the Grotesque and Arabesque." It has a singular charm for us, and we think that no one could read it without being strongly moved by its serene and sombre beauty. Had its author written nothing else, it would alone have been enough to stamp him as a man of genius, and the master of a classic style. In this tale occurs, perhaps, the most beautiful of his poems.

The great masters of imagination have seldom resorted to the vague and the unreal as sources of effect. They have not used dread and horror alone, but only in combination with other qualities, as means of subjugating the fancies of their readers. The loftiest muse has ever a household and fireside charm about her. Mr. Poe's secret lies mainly in the skill with which he has employed the strange fascination of mystery and terror. In this his success is so great and striking as to deserve the name of art, not artifice. We cannot call his materials the noblest or purest, but we must concede to him the highest merit of construction.

As a critic, Mr. Poe was aesthetically deficient. Unerring in his analysis of dictions, metres and plots, he seemed wanting in the faculty of perceiving the profounder ethics of art. His criticisms are, however, distinguished for scientific precision and coherence of logic. They have the exactness, and at the same time, the coldness of mathematical demonstrations. Yet they stand in strikingly refreshing contrast with the vague generalisms and sharp personalities of the day. If deficient in warmth, they are also without the heat of partisanship. They are especially valuable as illustrating the great truth, too generally overlooked, that analytic power is a subordinate quality of the critic.

On the whole, it may be considered certain that Mr. Poe has attained an individual eminence in our literature which he will keep. He has given proof of power and originality. He has done that which could only be done once with success or safety, and the imitation or repetition of which would produce weariness (www.gutenberg.org/).

Assignments

- Warm-up: Compare "Sleepy Hollow" with "The Devil and Tom Walker."
- Students should complete Concept Builder 7-C.
- Student will re-write corrected copies of essay due tomorrow.

CONCEPT BUILDER 7-C

Respond to the essay about Edgar Allan Poe by James Russell Lowell. Discuss points of agreement and thoughts you disagree with.

Agree	Disagree

The Fall of the House of Usher
Edgar Allan Poe

During the whole of a dull, dark, and soundless day in the autumn of the year, when the clouds hung oppressively low in the heavens, had been passing alone, on horseback, through a singularly dreary tract of country; and at length found myself, as the shades of the evening drew on, within view of the melancholy House of Usher. I know not how it was — but, with the first glimpse of the building, a sense of insufferable gloom pervaded my spirit. I say insufferable; for the feeling was unrelieved by any of that half-pleasurable, because poetic, sentiment, with which the mind usually receives even the sternest natural images of the desolate or terrible. I looked upon the scene before me — upon the mere house, and the simple landscape features of the domain — upon the bleak walls — upon the vacant eye-like windows — upon a few rank sedges — and upon a few white trunks of decayed trees — with an utter depression of soul which I can compare to no earthly sensation more properly than to the after-dream of the reveler upon opium — the bitter lapse into everyday life — the hideous dropping off of the veil. There was an iciness, a sinking, a sickening of the heart — an unredeemed dreariness of thought which no goading of the imagination could torture into aught of the sublime. What was it — I paused to think — what was it that so unnerved me in the contemplation of the House of Usher? It was a mystery all insoluble; nor could I grapple with the shadowy fancies that crowded upon me as I pondered. I was forced to fall back upon the unsatisfactory conclusion, that while, beyond doubt, there are combinations of very simple natural objects which have the power of thus affecting us, still the analysis of this power lies among considerations beyond our depth.

It was possible, I reflected, that a mere different arrangement of the particulars of the scene, of the details of the picture, would be sufficient to modify, or perhaps to annihilate its capacity for sorrowful impression; and, acting upon this idea, I reined my horse to the precipitous brink of a black and lurid tarn that lay in unruffled luster by the dwelling, and gazed down — but with a shudder even more thrilling than before — upon the remodeled and inverted images of the gray sedge, and the ghastly tree-stems, and the vacant and eye-like windows.

Nevertheless, in this mansion of gloom I now proposed to myself a sojourn of some weeks. Its proprietor, Roderick Usher, had been one of my boon companions in boyhood; but many years had elapsed since our last meeting. A letter, however, had lately reached me in a distant part of the country — a letter from him — which, in its wildly importunate nature, had admitted of no other than a personal reply. The MS. gave evidence of nervous agitation. The writer spoke of acute bodily illness — of a mental disorder which oppressed him — and of an earnest desire to see me, as his best, and indeed his only personal friend, with a view of attempting, by the cheerfulness of my society, some alleviation of his malady. It was the manner in which all this, and much more, was said — it the apparent heart that went with his request — which allowed me no room for hesitation; and I accordingly obeyed forthwith what I still considered a very singular summons.

Although, as boys, we had been even intimate associates, yet I really knew little of my friend. His reserve had been always excessive and habitual. I was aware, however, that his very ancient family had

Illustration from *The Fall of the House of Usher* by Aubrey Beardsley, 1894 (PD-Art).

been noted, time out of mind, for a peculiar sensibility of temperament, displaying itself, through long ages, in many works of exalted art, and manifested, of late, in repeated deeds of munificent yet unobtrusive charity, as well as in a passionate devotion to the intricacies, perhaps even more than to the orthodox and easily recognizable beauties, of musical science. I had learned, too, the very remarkable fact, that the stem of the Usher race, all time-honored as it was, had put forth, at no period, any enduring branch; in other words, that the entire family lay in the direct line of descent, and had always, with very trifling and very temporary variation, so lain. It was this deficiency, I considered, while running over in thought the perfect keeping of the character of the premises with the accredited character of the people, and while speculating upon the possible influence which the one, in the long lapse of centuries, might have exercised upon the other — it was this deficiency, perhaps, of collateral issue, and the consequent undeviating transmission, from sire to son, of the patrimony with the name, which had, at length, so identified the two as to merge the original title of the estate in the quaint and equivocal appellation of the "House of Usher" — an appellation which seemed to include, in the minds of the peasantry who used it, both the family and the family mansion.

I have said that the sole effect of my somewhat childish experiment — that of looking down within the tarn — had been to deepen the first singular impression. There can be no doubt that the consciousness of the rapid increase of my superstition — for why should I not so term it? — served mainly to accelerate the increase itself. Such, I have long known, is the paradoxical law of all sentiments having terror as a basis. And it might have been for this reason only, that, when I again uplifted my eyes to the house itself, from its image in the pool, there grew in my mind a strange fancy — a fancy so ridiculous, indeed, that I but mention it to show the vivid force of the sensations which oppressed me. I had so worked upon my imagination as really to believe that about the whole mansion and domain there hung an atmosphere peculiar to themselves and their immediate vicinity — an atmosphere which had no affinity with the air of heaven, but which had reeked up from the decayed trees, and the gray wall, and the silent tarn — a pestilent and

mystic vapor, dull, sluggish, faintly discernible, and leaden-hued. Shaking off from my spirit what must have been a dream, I scanned more narrowly the real aspect of the building. Its principal feature seemed to be that of an excessive antiquity. The discoloration of ages had been great. Minute fungi overspread the whole exterior, hanging in a fine tangled web-work from the eaves. Yet all this was apart from any extraordinary dilapidation. No portion of the masonry had fallen; and there appeared to be a wild inconsistency between its still perfect adaptation of parts, and the crumbling condition of the individual stones. In this there was much that reminded me of the specious totality of old wood-work which has rotted for long years in some neglected vault, with no disturbance from the breath of the external air. Beyond this indication of extensive decay, however, the fabric gave little token of instability. Perhaps the eye of a scrutinizing observer might have discovered a barely perceptible fissure, which, extending from the roof of the building in front, made its way down the wall in a zigzag direction, until it became lost in the sullen waters of the tarn.

Noticing these things, I rode over a short causeway to the house. A servant in waiting took my horse, and I entered the Gothic archway of the hall. A valet, of stealthy step, thence conducted me, in silence, through many dark and intricate passages in my progress to the studio of his master. Much that I encountered on the way contributed, I know not how, to heighten the vague sentiments of which I have already spoken. While the objects around me — while the carvings of the ceilings, the somber tapestries of the walls, the ebon blackness of the floors, and the phantasmagoric armorial trophies which rattled as I strode, were but matters to which, or to such as which, I had been accustomed from my infancy — while I hesitated not to acknowledge how familiar was all this — I still wondered to find how unfamiliar were the fancies which ordinary images were stirring up. On one of the staircases, I met the physician of the family. His countenance, I thought, wore a mingled expression of low cunning and perplexity. He accosted me with trepidation and passed on. The valet now threw open a door and ushered me into the presence of his master. The room in which I found myself was very large and lofty. The windows were long, narrow, and pointed, and at so vast a distance from the black oaken floor as to be altogether inaccessible from within. Feeble gleams of encrimsoned light made their way through the trellised panes, and served to render sufficiently distinct the more prominent objects around the eye, however, struggled in vain to reach the remoter angles of the chamber, or the recesses of the vaulted and fretted ceiling. Dark draperies hung upon the walls. The general furniture was profuse, comfortless, antique, and tattered. Many books and musical instruments lay scattered about, but failed to give any vitality to the scene. I felt that I breathed an atmosphere of sorrow. An air of stern, deep, and irredeemable gloom hung over and pervaded all.

Upon my entrance, Usher arose from a sofa on which he had been lying at full length, and greeted me with a vivacious warmth which had much in it, I at first thought, of an overdone cordiality — of the constrained effort of the ennui man of the world. A glance, however, at his countenance, convinced me of his perfect sincerity. We sat down; and for some moments, while he spoke not, I gazed upon him with a feeling half of pity, half of awe. Surely, man had never before so terribly altered, in so brief a period, as had Roderick Usher! It was with difficulty that I could bring myself to admit the identity of the wan being before me with the companion of my early boyhood. Yet the character of his face had been at all times remarkable. A cadaverousness of complexion; an eye large, liquid, and luminous beyond comparison; lips somewhat thin and very pallid, but of a surpassingly beautiful curve; a nose of a delicate Hebrew model, but with a breadth of nostril unusual in similar formations; a finely molded chin, speaking, in its want of prominence, of a want of moral energy; hair of a more than web-like softness and tenuity; these features, with an inordinate expansion above the regions of the temple, made up altogether a countenance not easily to be forgotten. And now in the mere exaggeration of the prevailing character of these features, and of the expression they were wont to convey, lay so much of change that I doubted to whom I spoke. The now ghastly pallor of the skin, and the now miraculous luster of the eve, above all things startled and even awed me. The silken hair, too, had been suffered to grow all unheeded, and as, in its wild gossamer texture, it floated rather than fell about the face, I could not, even with effort, connect its Arabesque expression with any idea of simple humanity.

In the manner of my friend I was at once struck with an incoherence — an inconsistency; and I soon found this to arise from a series of feeble and futile struggles to overcome an habitual trepidancy — an excessive nervous agitation. For something of this nature I had indeed been prepared, no less by his letter, than by reminiscences of certain boyish traits, and by conclusions deduced from his peculiar physical conformation and temperament. His action was alternately vivacious and sullen. His voice varied rapidly from a tremulous indecision (when the animal spirits seemed utterly in abeyance) to that species of energetic concision — that abrupt, weighty, unhurried, and hollow-sounding enunciation — that leaden, self-balanced and perfectly modulated guttural utterance, which may be observed in the lost drunkard, or the irreclaimable eater of opium, during the periods of his most intense excitement.

It was thus that he spoke of the object of my visit, of his earnest desire to see me, and of the solace he expected me to afford him. He entered, at some length, into what he conceived to be the nature of his malady. It was, he said, a constitutional and a family evil, and one for which he despaired to find a remedy — a mere nervous affection, he immediately added, which would undoubtedly soon pass off. It displayed itself in a host of unnatural sensations. Some of these, as he detailed them, interested and bewildered me; although, perhaps, the terms, and the general manner of the narration had their weight. He suffered much from a morbid acuteness of the senses; the most insipid food was alone endurable; he could wear only garments of certain texture; the odors of all flowers were oppressive; his eyes were tortured by even a faint light; and there were but peculiar sounds, and these from stringed instruments, which did not inspire him with horror. To an anomalous species of terror I found him a bounden slave. "I shall perish," said he, "I must perish in this deplorable folly. Thus, thus, and not otherwise, shall I be lost. I dread the events of the future, not in themselves, but in their results. I shudder at the thought of any, even the most trivial, incident, which may operate upon this intolerable agitation of soul. I have, indeed, no abhorrence of danger, except in its absolute effect

— in terror. In this unnerved — in this pitiable condition — I feel that the period will sooner or later arrive when I must abandon life and reason together, in some struggle with the grim phantasm, FEAR." I learned, moreover, at intervals, and through broken and equivocal hints, another singular feature of his mental condition. He was enchained by certain superstitious impressions in regard to the dwelling which he tenanted, and whence, for many years, he had never ventured forth — in regard to an influence whose supposititious force was conveyed in terms too shadowy here to be re-stated — an influence which some peculiarities in the mere form and substance of his family mansion, had, by dint of long sufferance, he said, obtained over his spirit-an effect which the physique of the gray walls and turrets, and of the dim tarn into which they all looked down, had, at length, brought about upon the morale of his existence.

He admitted, however, although with hesitation, that much of the peculiar gloom which thus afflicted him could be traced to a more natural and far more palpable origin — to the severe and long-continued illness — indeed to the evidently approaching dissolution-of a tenderly beloved sister — his sole companion for long years — his last and only relative on earth. "Her decease," he said, with a bitterness which I can never forget, "would leave him (him the hopeless and the frail) the last of the ancient race of the Ushers." While he spoke, the lady Madeline (for so was she called) passed slowly through a remote portion of the apartment, and, without having noticed my presence, disappeared. I regarded her with an utter astonishment not unmingled with dread — and yet I found it impossible to account for such feelings. A sensation of stupor oppressed me, as my eyes followed her retreating steps. When a door, at length, closed upon her, my glance sought instinctively and eagerly the countenance of the brother—but he had buried his face in his hands, and I could only perceive that a far more than ordinary wanness had overspread the emaciated fingers through which trickled many passionate tears. The disease of the lady Madeline had long baffled the skill of her physicians. A settled apathy, a gradual wasting away of the person, and frequent although transient affections of a partially catalepti-cal character, were the unusual diagnosis. Hitherto she had steadily borne up against the pressure of her malady, and had not betaken herself finally to bed; but, on the closing in of the evening of my arrival at the house, she succumbed (as her brother told me at night with inexpressible agitation) to the prostrating power of the destroyer; and I learned that the glimpse I had obtained of her person would thus probably be the last I should obtain — that the lady, at least while living, would be seen by me no more.

For several days ensuing, her name was unmentioned by either Usher or myself: and during this period I was busied in earnest endeavors to alleviate the melancholy of my friend. We painted and read together; or I listened, as if in a dream, to the wild improvisations of his speaking guitar. And thus, as a closer and still intimacy admitted me more unreservedly into the recesses of his spirit, the more bitterly did I perceive the futility of all attempt at cheering a mind from which darkness, as if an inherent positive quality, poured forth upon all objects of the moral and physical universe, in one unceasing radiation of gloom.

I shall ever bear about me a memory of the many solemn hours I thus spent alone with the master of the House of Usher. Yet I should fail in any attempt to convey an idea of the exact character of the studies, or of the occupations, in which he involved me, or led me the way. An excited and highly distempered ideality threw a sulphurous luster over all. His long improvised dirges will ring forever in my ears. Among other things, I hold painfully in mind a certain singular perversion and amplification of the wild air of the last waltz of Von Weber. From the paintings over which his elaborate fancy brooded, and which grew, touch by touch, into vaguenesses at which I shuddered the more thrillingly, because I shuddered knowing not why; from these paintings (vivid as their images now are before me) I would in vain endeavor to educe more than a small portion which should lie within the compass of merely written words. By the utter simplicity, by the nakedness of his designs, he arrested and over-awed attention. If ever mortal painted an idea, that mortal was Roderick Usher. For me at least — in the circumstances then surrounding me — there arose out of the pure abstractions which the hypochon-driac contrived to throw upon his canvas, an intensity of intolerable awe, no shadow of which felt

I ever yet in the contemplation of the certainly glowing yet too concrete reveries of Fuseli.

One of the phantasmagoric conceptions of my friend, partaking not so rigidly of the spirit of abstraction, may be shadowed forth, although feebly, in words. A small picture presented the interior of an immensely long and rectangular vault or tunnel, with low walls, smooth, white, and without interruption or device. Certain accessory points of the design served well to convey the idea that this excavation lay at a exceeding depth below the surface of the earth. No outlet was observed in any portion of its vast extent, and no torch, or other artificial source of light was discernible; yet a flood of intense rays rolled throughout, and bathed the whole in a ghastly and inappropriate splendor.

I have just spoken of that morbid condition of the auditory nerve which rendered all music intolerable to the sufferer, with the exception of certain effects of stringed instruments. It was, perhaps, the narrow limits to which he thus confined himself upon the guitar, which gave birth, in great measure, to the fantastic character of his performances. But the fervid facility of his impromptus could not be so accounted for. They must have been, and were, in the notes, as well as in the words of his wild fantasias (for he not unfrequently accompanied himself with rhymed verbal improvisations), the result of that intense mental collectedness and concentration to which I have previously alluded as observable only in particular moments of the highest artificial excitement. The words of one of these rhapsodies I have easily remembered. I was, perhaps, the more forcibly impressed with it, as he gave it, because, in the under or mystic current of its meaning, I fancied that I perceived, and for the first time, a full consciousness on the part of Usher, of the tottering of his lofty reason upon her throne. The verses, which were entitled "The Haunted Palace," ran very nearly, if not accurately, thus:

I.

In the greenest of our valleys,
By good angels tenanted,
Once fair and stately palace —
Radiant palace — reared its head.

In the monarch Thought's dominion —
It stood there!
Never seraph spread a pinion
Over fabric half so fair.

II.

Banners yellow, glorious, golden,
On its roof did float and flow;
(This — all this — was in the olden
Time long ago)
And every gentle air that dallied,
In that sweet day,
Along the ramparts plumed and pallid,
A winged odor went away.

III.

Wanderers in that happy valley
Through two luminous windows saw
Spirits moving musically
To a lute's well-tuned law,
Round about a throne, where sitting
(Porphyrogene!)
In state his glory well befitting,
The ruler of the realm was seen.

IV.

And all with pearl and ruby glowing
Was the fair palace door,
Through which came flowing, flowing, flowing
And sparkling evermore,
A troop of Echoes whose sweet duty
Was but to sing,
In voices of surpassing beauty,
The wit and wisdom of their king.

V.

But evil things, in robes of sorrow,
Assailed the monarch's high estate;
(Ah, let us mourn, for never morrow
Shall dawn upon him, desolate!)

And, round about his home, the glory

That blushed and bloomed

Is but a dim-remembered story

Of the old time entombed.

VI.

And travelers now within that valley,

Through the red-litten windows, see

Vast forms that move fantastically

To a discordant melody;

While, like a rapid ghastly river,

Through the pale door,

A hideous throng rush out forever,

And laugh — but smile no more.

I well remember that suggestions arising from this ballad led us into a train of thought wherein there became manifest an opinion of Usher's which I mention not so much on account of its novelty, (for other men have thought thus,) as on account of the pertinacity with which he maintained it. This opinion, in its general form, was that of the sentience of all vegetable things. But, in his disordered fancy the idea had assumed a more daring character, and trespassed, under certain conditions, upon the kingdom of inorganization. I lack words to express the full extent, or the earnest abandon of his persuasion. The belief, however, was connected (as I have previously hinted) with the gray stones of the home of his forefathers. The conditions of the sentience had been here, he imagined, fulfilled in the method of collocation of these stones — in the order of their arrangement, as well as in that of the many fungi which overspread them, and of the decayed trees which stood around — above all, in the long undisturbed endurance of this arrangement, and in its reduplication in the still waters of the tarn. Its evidence — the evidence of the sentience — was to be seen, he said, (and I here started as he spoke,) in the gradual yet certain condensation of an atmosphere of their own about the waters and the walls. The result was discoverable, he added, in that silent, yet importunate and terrible influence which for centuries had molded the destinies of his family, and which made him what I now saw him — what he

was. Such opinions need no comment, and I will make none.

Our books — the books which, for years, had formed no small portion of the mental existence of the invalid — were, as might be supposed, in strict keeping with this character of phantasm. We pored together over such works as the Ververt et Chartreuse of Gresset; the Belphegor of Machiavelli; the Heaven and Hell of Swedenborg; the Subterranean Voyage of Nicholas Klimm by Holberg; the Chiromancy of Robert Flud, of Jean D'Indagine, and of De la Chambre; the Journey into the Blue Distance of Tieck; and the City of the Sun of Campanella. One favorite volume was a small octavo edition of the Directorium Inquisitorum, by the Dominican Eymeric de Gironne; and there were passages in Pomponius Mela, about the old African Satyrs over which Usher would sit dreaming for hours. His chief delight, however, was found in the perusal of an exceedingly rare and curious book in quarto Gothic — the manual of a forgotten church — the Vigilae Mortuorum secundum Chorum Ecclesiae Maguntinae. I could not help thinking of the wild ritual of this work, and of its probable influence upon the hypochondriac, when, one evening, having informed me abruptly that the lady Madeline was no more, he stated his intention of preserving her corpse for a fortnight, (previously to its final interment,) in one of the numerous vaults within the main walls of the building. The worldly reason, however, assigned for this singular proceeding, was one which I did not feel at liberty to dispute. The brother had been led to his resolution (so he told me) by consideration of the unusual character of the malady of the deceased, of certain obtrusive and eager inquiries on the part of her medical men, and of the remote and exposed situation of the burial-ground of the family. I will not deny that when I called to mind the sinister countenance of the person whom I met upon the stair case, on the day of my arrival at the house, I had no desire to oppose what I regarded as at best but a harmless, and by no means an unnatural, precaution. At the request of Usher, I personally aided him in the arrangements for the temporary entombment. The body having been encoffined, we two alone bore it to its rest. The vault in which we placed it (and which had been so long unopened that our torches, half smothered in its oppressive atmosphere, gave us little opportunity for investigation) was small, damp, and entirely without means of admission for light; lying, at great depth, immediately beneath that portion of the building in which was my own sleeping apartment. It had been used, apparently, in remote feudal times, for the worst purposes of a donjon-keep, and, in later days, as a place of deposit for powder, or some other highly combustible substance, as a portion of its floor, and the whole interior of a long archway through which we reached it, were carefully sheathed with copper. The door, of massive iron, had been, also, similarly protected. Its immense weight caused an unusually sharp grating sound, as it moved upon its hinges.

Having deposited our mournful burden upon tressels within this region of horror, we partially turned aside the yet unscrewed lid of the coffin, and looked upon the face of the tenant. A striking similitude between the brother and sister now first arrested my attention; and Usher, divining, perhaps, my thoughts, murmured out some few words from which I learned that the deceased and himself had been twins, and that sympathies of a scarcely intelligible nature had always existed between them. Our glances, however, rested not long upon the dead — for we could not regard her unawed. The disease which had thus entombed the lady in the maturity of youth, had left, as usual in all maladies of a strictly cataleptical character, the mockery of a faint blush upon the bosom and the face, and that suspiciously lingering smile upon the lip which is so terrible in death. We replaced and screwed down the lid, and, having secured the door of iron, made our way, with toll, into the scarcely less gloomy apartments of the upper portion of the house.

And now, some days of bitter grief having elapsed, an observable change came over the features of the mental disorder of my friend. His ordinary manner had vanished. His ordinary occupations were neglected or forgotten. He roamed from chamber to chamber with hurried, unequal, and objectless step. The pallor of his countenance had assumed, if possible, a more ghastly hue — but the luminousness of his eye had utterly gone out. The once occasional huskiness of his tone was heard no more; and a tremulous quaver, as if of extreme terror, habitually characterized his utterance. There were

times, indeed, when I thought his unceasingly agitated mind was laboring with some oppressive secret, to divulge which he struggled for the necessary outrage. At times, again, I was obliged to resolve all into the mere inexplicable vagaries of madness, for I beheld him gazing upon vacancy for long hours, in an attitude of the profoundest attention, as if listening to some imaginary sound. It was no wonder that his condition terrified-that it infected me. I felt creeping upon me, by slow yet certain degrees, the wild influences of his own fantastic yet impressive superstitions. It was, especially, upon retiring to bed late in the night of the seventh or eighth day after the placing of the lady Madeline within the donjon, that I experienced the full power of such feelings.

Sleep came not near my couch — while the hours waned and waned away. I struggled to reason off the nervousness which had dominion over me. I endeavored to believe that much, if not all of what I felt, was due to the bewildering influence of the gloomy furniture of the room — of the dark and tattered draperies, which, tortured into motion by the breath of a rising tempest, swayed fitfully to and fro upon the walls, and rustled uneasily about the decorations of the bed. But my efforts were fruitless. An irrepressible tremor gradually pervaded my frame; and, at length, there sat upon my very heart an incubus of utterly causeless alarm. Shaking this off with a gasp and a struggle, I uplifted myself upon the pillows, and, peering earnestly within the intense darkness of the chamber, hearkened — I know not why, except that an instinctive spirit prompted me — to certain low and indefinite sounds which came, through the pauses of the storm, at long intervals, I knew not whence. Overpowered by an intense sentiment of horror, unaccountable yet unendurable, I threw on my clothes with haste (for I felt that I should sleep no more during the night), and endeavored to arouse myself from the pitiable condition into which I had fallen, by pacing rapidly to and fro through the apartment.

I had taken but few turns in this manner, when a light step on an adjoining staircase arrested my attention. I presently recognized it as that of Usher. In an instant afterward he rapped, with a gentle touch, at my door, and entered, bearing a lamp. His countenance was, as usual, cadaverously wan — but, moreover, there was a species of mad hilarity in his eyes — an evidently restrained hysteria in his whole demeanor. His air appalled me — but anything was preferable to the solitude which I had so long endured, and I even welcomed his presence as a relief.

"And you have not seen it?" he said abruptly, after having stared about him for some moments in silence — "you have not then seen it? — but, stay! you shall." Thus speaking, and having carefully shaded his lamp, he hurried to one of the casements, and threw it freely open to the storm.

The impetuous fury of the entering gust nearly lifted us from our feet. It was, indeed, a tempestuous yet sternly beautiful night, and one wildly singular in its terror and its beauty. A whirlwind had apparently collected its force in our vicinity; for there were frequent and violent alterations in the direction of the wind; and the exceeding density of the clouds (which hung so low as to press upon the turrets of the house) did not prevent our perceiving the life-like velocity with which they flew careering from all points against each other, without passing away into the distance. I say that even their exceeding density did not prevent our perceiving this — yet we had no glimpse of the moon or stars — nor was there any flashing forth of the lightning. But the under surfaces of the huge masses of agitated vapor, as well as all terrestrial objects immediately around us, were glowing in the unnatural light of a faintly luminous and distinctly visible gaseous exhalation which hung about and enshrouded the mansion.

"You must not — you shall not behold this!" said I, shudderingly, to Usher, as I led him, with a gentle violence, from the window to a seat. "These appearances, which bewilder you, are merely electrical phenomena not uncommon — or it may be that they have their ghastly origin in the rank miasma of the tarn. Let us close this casement; the air is chilling and dangerous to your frame. Here is one of your favorite romances. I will read, and you shall listen; and so we will pass away this terrible night together."

The antique volume which I had taken up was the "Mad Trist" of Sir Launcelot Canning; but I had called it a favorite of Usher's more in sad jest than in earnest; for, in truth, there is little in its uncouth and unimaginative prolixity which could have had interest for the lofty and spiritual ideality of my friend. It was, however, the only book immediately at hand; and I indulged a vague hope that the excitement which now agitated the hypochondriac, might find relief (for the history of mental disorder is full of similar anomalies) even in the extremeness of the folly which I should read. Could I have judged, indeed, by the wild over-strained air of vivacity with which he hearkened, or apparently hearkened, to the words of the tale, I might well have congratulated myself upon the success of my design. I had arrived at that well-known portion of the story where Ethelred, the hero of the Trist, having sought in vain for peaceable admission into the dwelling of the hermit, proceeds to make good an entrance by force. Here, it will be remembered, the words of the narrative run thus: "And Ethelred, who was by nature of a doughty heart, and who was now mighty withal, on account of the powerfulness of the wine which he had drunken, waited no longer to hold parley with the hermit, who, in sooth, was of an obstinate and maliceful turn, but, feeling the rain upon his shoulders, and fearing the rising of the tempest, uplifted his mace outright, and, with blows, made quickly room in the plankings of the door for his gauntleted hand; and now pulling there-with sturdily, he so cracked, and ripped, and tore all asunder, that the noise of the dry and hollow-sounding wood alarmed and reverberated throughout the forest.

At the termination of this sentence I started, and for a moment, paused; for it appeared to me (although I at once concluded that my excited fancy had deceived me) — it appeared to me that, from some very remote portion of the mansion, there came, indistinctly, to my ears, what might have been, in its exact similarity of character, the echo (but a stifled and dull one certainly) of the very cracking and ripping sound which Sir Launcelot had so particularly described.

It was, beyond doubt, the coincidence alone which had arrested my attention; for, amid the rattling of the sashes of the casements, and the ordinary commingled noises of the still increasing storm, the sound, in itself, had nothing, surely, which should have interested or disturbed me. I continued the story:

"But the good champion Ethelred, now entering within the door, was sore enraged and amazed to perceive no signal of the maliceful hermit; but, in the stead thereof, a dragon of a scaly and prodigious demeanor, and of a fiery tongue, which sate in guard before a palace of gold, with a floor of silver; and upon the wall there hung a shield of shining brass with this legend enwritten — Who entereth herein, a conqueror hath bin; Who slayeth the dragon, the shield he shall win; And Ethelred uplifted his mace, and struck upon the head of the dragon, which fell before him, and gave up his pasty breath, with a shriek so horrid and harsh, and withal so piercing, that Ethelred had fain to close his ears with his hands against the dreadful noise of it, the like whereof was never before heard."

Here again I paused abruptly, and now with a feeling of wild amazement — for there could be no doubt whatever that, in this instance, I did actually hear (although from what direction it proceeded I found it impossible to say) a low and apparently distant, but harsh, protracted, and most unusual screaming or grating sound — the exact counterpart of what my fancy had already conjured up for the dragon's unnatural shriek as described by the romancer.

Oppressed, as I certainly was, upon the occurrence of the second and most extraordinary coincidence, by a thousand conflicting sensations, in which wonder and extreme terror were predominant, I still retained sufficient presence of mind to avoid exciting, by any observation, the sensitive nervousness of my companion. I was by no means certain that he had noticed the sounds in question; although, assuredly, a strange alteration had, during the last few minutes, taken place in his demeanor. From a position fronting my own, he had gradually brought round his chair, so as to sit with his face to the door of the chamber; and thus I could but partially perceive his features, although I saw that his lips trembled as if he were murmuring inaudibly. His head had dropped upon his breast — yet I knew that he was not asleep, from the wide and rigid opening of the eye as I caught a glance of it in profile. The motion of his body, too, was at variance with this idea — for he rocked from side to side with a gentle yet constant and uniform sway. Having rapidly taken notice of all this, I resumed the narrative of Sir Launcelot, which thus proceeded: "And now, the champion, having escaped from the terrible fury of the dragon, bethinking himself of the brazen shield, and of the breaking up of the enchantment which was upon it, removed the carcass from out of the way before him, and approached valorously over the silver pavement of the castle to where the shield was upon the wall; which in sooth tarried not for his full coming, but fell down at his feet upon the silver floor, with a mighty great and terrible ringing sound."

No sooner had these syllables passed my lips, than — as if a shield of brass had indeed, at the moment, fallen heavily upon a floor of silver became aware of a distinct, hollow, metallic, and clangorous, yet apparently muffled reverberation. Completely unnerved, I leaped to my feet; but the measured rocking movement of Usher was undisturbed. I rushed to the chair in which he sat. His eyes were bent fixedly before him, and throughout his whole countenance there reigned a stony rigidity. But, as I placed my hand upon his shoulder, there came a strong shudder over his whole person; a sickly smile quivered about his lips; and I saw that he spoke in a low, hurried, and gibbering murmur, as if unconscious of my presence. Bending closely over him, I at length drank in the hideous import of his words.

"Not hear it? — yes, I hear it, and have heard it. Long — long — long — many minutes, many hours, many days, have I heard it — yet I dared not — oh, pity me, miserable wretch that I am! — I dared not — I dared not speak! We have put her living in the tomb! Said I not that my senses were acute? I now tell you that I heard her first feeble movements in the hollow coffin. I heard them — many, many days ago — yet I dared not — I dared not speak! And now — to-night — Ethelred — ha! ha! — the breaking of the hermit's door, and the death-cry of the dragon, and the clangor of the shield! — say, rather, the rending of her coffin, and the grating of the iron hinges of her prison, and her struggles within the coppered archway of the vault! Oh whither shall I fly? Will she not be here anon? Is she not hurrying to upbraid me for my haste? Have I not heard her footstep on the stair? Do I not distinguish that heavy and horrible beating of her heart? MADMAN!" here he sprang furiously to his feet, and shrieked out his syllables, as if in the effort he were giving up his soul — "MADMAN! I TELL YOU THAT SHE NOW STANDS WITHOUT THE DOOR!"

As if in the superhuman energy of his utterance there had been found the potency of a spell — the huge antique panels to which the speaker pointed, threw slowly back, upon the instant, ponderous and ebony jaws. It was the work of the rushing gust — but then without those doors there DID stand the lofty and enshrouded figure of the lady Madeline of Usher. There was blood upon her white robes, and the evidence of some bitter struggle upon every portion of her emaciated frame. For a moment she remained trembling and reeling to and fro upon the threshold, then, with a low moaning cry, fell heavily inward upon the person of her brother, and in her violent and now final death-agonies, bore him to the floor a corpse, and a victim to the terrors he had anticipated.

From that chamber, and from that mansion, I fled aghast. The storm was still abroad in all its wrath as I found myself crossing the old causeway. Suddenly there shot along the path a wild light, and I turned to see whence a gleam so unusual could have issued; for the vast house and its shadows were alone behind me. The radiance was that of the full, setting, and blood-red moon which now shone vividly through that once barely-discernible fissure of which I have before spoken as extending from the roof of the building, in a zigzag direction, to the base. While I gazed, this fissure rapidly widened — there came a fierce breath of the whirlwind — the entire orb of the satellite burst at once upon my sight — my brain reeled as I saw the mighty walls rushing asunder — there was a long tumultuous shouting sound like the voice of a thousand waters — and the deep and dank tarn at my feet closed sullenly and silently over the fragments of the "HOUSE OF USHER."

Assignments

- Warm-up: Is this story a horror story or a romantic (as in "worldview") story?
- Students should complete Concept Builder 7-D.
- Student will re-write corrected copies of essay due tomorrow.

CONCEPT BUILDER 7-D Active Reading		Read "The Fall of the House of Usher" by Edgar Allan Poe in the text then answer the following questions.
	1	The narrative technique is limited omniscient. Poe chooses to tell the story from a neutral observer — someone not involved in the story. Why is this a good idea?
	2	Even from the first few words of this short story, what would you say the tone is?
	3	What will happen at the end of this short story? Why do you feel that way?
	4	Foreshadowing is a warning of something to follow. What does the phrase "barely perceptible fissure" foreshadow?

The Tell-Tale Heart
Edgar Allan Poe

TRUE! nervous, very, very dreadfully nervous I had been and am; but why WILL you say that I am mad? The disease had sharpened my senses, not destroyed, not dulled them. Above all was the sense of hearing acute. I heard all things in the heaven and in the earth. I heard many things in hell. How then am I mad? Hearken! and observe how healthily, how calmly, I can tell you the whole story.

It is impossible to say how first the idea entered my brain, but, once conceived, it haunted me day and night. Object there was none. Passion there was none. I loved the old man. He had never wronged me. He had never given me insult. For his gold I had no desire. I think it was his eye! Yes, it was this! One of his eyes resembled that of a vulture — a pale blue eye with a film over it. Whenever it fell upon me my blood ran cold, and so by degrees, very gradually, I made up my mind to take the life of the old man, and thus rid myself of the eye for ever.

Now this is the point. You fancy me mad. Madmen know nothing. But you should have seen me. You should have seen how wisely I proceeded — with what caution — with what foresight, with what dissimulation, I went to work! I was never kinder to the old man than during the whole week before I killed him. And every night about midnight I turned the latch of his door and opened it oh, so gently! And then, when I had made an opening sufficient for my head, I put in a dark lantern all closed, closed so that no light shone out, and then I thrust in my head. Oh, you would have laughed to see how cunningly I thrust it in! I moved it slowly, very, very slowly, so that I might not disturb the old man's sleep. It took me an hour to place my whole head within the opening so far that I could see him as he lay upon his bed. Ha! would a madman have been so wise as this? And then when my head was well in the room I undid the lantern cautiously — oh, so cautiously — cautiously (for the hinges creaked), I undid it just so much that a single thin ray fell upon the vulture eye. And this I did for seven long nights, every night just at midnight, but I found the eye always closed, and so it was impossible to do the work, for it was not the old man who vexed me but his Evil Eye. And every morning, when the day broke, I went boldly into the chamber and spoke courageously to him, calling him by name in a hearty tone, and inquiring how he had passed the night. So you see he would have been a very profound old man, indeed, to suspect that every night, just at twelve, I looked in upon him while he slept.

Upon the eighth night I was more than usually cautious in opening the door. A watch's minute hand moves more quickly than did mine. Never before that night had I felt the extent of my own powers, of my sagacity. I could scarcely contain my feelings of triumph. To think that there I was opening the door little by little, and he not even to dream of my secret deeds or thoughts. I fairly chuckled at the idea, and perhaps he heard me, for he moved on the bed suddenly as if startled. Now you may think that I drew back — but no. His room was as black as pitch with the thick darkness (for the shutters were close fastened through fear of robbers), and so I knew that he could not see the opening of the door, and I kept pushing it on steadily, steadily.

I had my head in, and was about to open the lantern, when my thumb slipped upon the tin fastening, and the old man sprang up in the bed, crying out, "Who's there?"

I kept quite still and said nothing. For a whole hour I did not move a muscle, and in the meantime I did not hear him lie down. He was still sitting up in the bed, listening; just as I have done night after night hearkening to the death watches in the wall.

Presently, I heard a slight groan, and I knew it was the groan of mortal terror. It was not a groan of pain or of grief — oh, no! It was the low stifled sound that arises from the bottom of the soul when overcharged with awe. I knew the sound well. Many a night, just at midnight, when all the world slept, it has welled up from my own bosom, deepening, with its dreadful echo, the terrors that distracted me. I say I knew it well. I knew what the old man felt, and pitied him although I chuckled at heart. I knew that he had been lying awake ever since the first slight noise when he had turned in the bed. His fears had been ever since growing upon him. He had been trying to fancy them causeless, but could not. He had been saying to himself, "It is nothing but the wind in the chimney, it is only a mouse crossing the floor," or, "It is merely a cricket which has made a single chirp." Yes he has been trying to comfort himself with these suppositions ; but he had found all in vain. ALL IN VAIN, because Death in approaching him had stalked with his black shadow before him and enveloped the victim. And it was the mournful influence of the unperceived shadow that caused him to feel, although he neither saw nor heard, to feel the presence of my head within the room.

When I had waited a long time very patiently without hearing him lie down, I resolved to open a little — a very, very little crevice in the lantern. So I opened it — you cannot imagine how stealthily, stealthily — until at length a single dim ray like the thread of the spider shot out from the crevice and fell upon the vulture eye.

It was open, wide, wide open, and I grew furious as I gazed upon it. I saw it with perfect distinctness — all a dull blue with a hideous veil over it that chilled the very marrow in my bones, but I could see nothing else of the old man's face or person, for I had directed the ray as if by instinct precisely upon the … spot.

And now have I not told you that what you mistake for madness is but over-acuteness of the senses? now, I say, there came to my ears a low, dull,

Illustration of "The Tell-Tale Heart" by Harry Clarke. Printed in Edgar Allan Poe's *Tales of Mystery and Imagination,* c1919 (PD-US).

quick sound, such as a watch makes when enveloped in cotton. I knew that sound well too. It was the beating of the old man's heart. It increased my fury as the beating of a drum stimulates the soldier into courage.

But even yet I refrained and kept still. I scarcely breathed. I held the lantern motionless. I tried how steadily I could maintain the ray upon the eye. Meantime the hellish tattoo of the heart increased. It grew quicker and quicker, and louder and louder, every instant. The old man's terror must have been extreme! It grew louder, I say, louder every moment! — do you mark me well? I have told you that I am nervous: so I am. And now at the dead hour of the night, amid the dreadful silence of that old house, so strange a noise as this excited me to uncontrollable terror. Yet, for some minutes longer I refrained and stood still. But the beating grew louder, louder! I thought the heart must burst. And now a new anxiety seized me — the sound would be heard by a neighbour! The old man's hour had come! With a loud yell, I threw open the lantern and leaped into the room. He shrieked once — once only. In an instant I dragged him to the floor, and pulled the heavy bed over him. I then smiled gaily, to find the deed so far done. But for many minutes the heart beat on with a muffled sound. This, however, did not vex me; it would not be heard through the wall. At length it ceased. The old man was dead. I removed the bed and examined the corpse. Yes, he was stone, stone dead. I placed my hand upon the heart and held it there many minutes. There was no pulsation. He was stone dead. His eye would trouble me no more.

If still you think me mad, you will think so no longer when I describe the wise precautions I took for the concealment of the body. The night waned, and I worked hastily, but in silence.

I took up three planks from the flooring of the chamber, and deposited all between the scantlings. I then replaced the boards so cleverly so cunningly, that no human eye — not even his — could have detected anything wrong. There was nothing to wash out — no stain of any kind — no blood-spot whatever. I had been too wary for that.

When I had made an end of these labors, it was four o'clock — still dark as midnight. As the bell sounded the hour, there came a knocking at the street door. I went down to open it with a light heart, for what had I now to fear? There entered three men, who introduced themselves, with perfect suavity, as officers of the police. A shriek had been heard by a neighbour during the night; suspicion of foul play had been aroused; information had been lodged at the police office, and they (the officers) had been deputed to search the premises.

I smiled, — for what had I to fear? I bade the gentlemen welcome. The shriek, I said, was my own in a dream. The old man, I mentioned, was absent in the country. I took my visitors all over the house. I bade them search — search well. I led them, at length, to his chamber. I showed them his treasures, secure, undisturbed. In the enthusiasm of my confidence, I brought chairs into the room, and desired them here to rest from their fatigues, while I myself, in the wild audacity of my perfect triumph,

Poe spent the last few years of his life in this small cottage in the Bronx, New York. Photo by Zoirusha, 2007 (PD-US).

placed my own seat upon the very spot beneath which reposed the corpse of the victim.

The officers were satisfied. My MANNER had convinced them. I was singularly at ease. They sat and while I answered cheerily, they chatted of familiar things. But, ere long, I felt myself getting pale and wished them gone. My head ached, and I fancied a ringing in my ears; but still they sat, and still chatted. The ringing became more distinct: I talked more freely to get rid of the feeling: but it continued and gained definitiveness — until, at length, I found that the noise was NOT within my ears.

No doubt I now grew VERY pale; but I talked more fluently, and with a heightened voice. Yet the sound increased — and what could I do? It was A LOW, DULL, QUICK SOUND — MUCH SUCH A SOUND AS A WATCH MAKES WHEN ENVELOPED IN COTTON. I gasped for breath, and yet the officers heard it not. I talked more quickly, more vehemently but the noise steadily increased. I arose and argued about trifles, in a high key and with violent gesticulations; but the noise steadily increased. Why WOULD they not be gone? I paced the floor to and fro with heavy strides, as if excited to fury by the observations of the men, but the noise steadily increased. O God! what COULD I do? I foamed — I raved — I swore! I swung the chair upon which I had been sitting, and grated it upon the boards, but the noise arose over all and continually increased. It grew louder — louder — louder! And still the men chatted pleasantly, and smiled. Was it possible they heard not? Almighty God! — no, no? They heard! — they suspected! — they KNEW! — they were making a mockery of my horror! — this I thought, and this I think. But anything was better than this agony! Anything was more tolerable than this derision! I could bear those hypocritical smiles no longer! I felt that I must scream or die! — and now — again — hark! louder! louder! louder! LOUDER! —

"Villains!" I shrieked, "dissemble no more! I admit the deed! — tear up the planks! — here, here! — it is the beating of his hideous heart!"

Assignments

- Warm-up: Can you believe the narrator of this short story? Why or why not?
- Students should complete Concept Builder 7-E.
- Essays are due. Students should take the chapter 7 test.

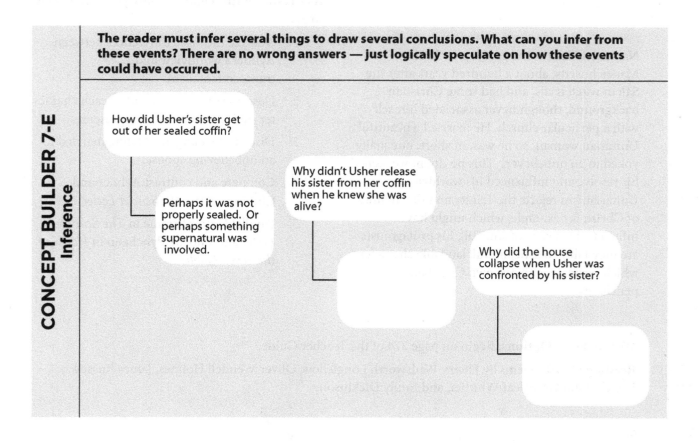

CONCEPT BUILDER 7-E
Inference

The reader must infer several things to draw several conclusions. What can you infer from these events? There are no wrong answers — just logically speculate on how these events could have occurred.

How did Usher's sister get out of her sealed coffin?

Perhaps it was not properly sealed. Or perhaps something supernatural was involved.

Why didn't Usher release his sister from her coffin when he knew she was alive?

Why did the house collapse when Usher was confronted by his sister?

Chapter 8

1840–1855 (Part 1):

Romanticism:
New England Renaissance

First Thoughts Romanticism is a literary and artistic movement that arose in the middle of the 19th century. Romanticism as a worldview was a reaction to the perceived rigidity of Puritanism on one hand, and to the chauvinistic elements of rationalism on the other. Romanticism, and the American version called transcendentalism, placed the individual center stage and celebrated human emotion, intuition, subjectivity, and freedom. Romanticism naturally, then, preferred an unsoiled nature to human civilization.

Author Worldview Watch
Nathaniel Hawthorne grew up in Salem, Massachusetts, about a hundred years after the Salem witch trials, and had some Christian background, though never associated himself with a particular church. He married a beautiful Unitarian woman, so he was, in short, unequally yoked to an unbeliever! This no doubt weakened his resolve and influenced his worldview. Unitarianism rejects the Trinity and the divinity of Christ, for example, which might have influenced his view of sin. Still, his protagonists are inevitably theistic, moral, laudable characters which resonate with our own Christian penchants.

Chapter Learning Objectives In chapter 8 we encounter romanticism in a big way. We examine the writings of Nathaniel Hawthorne and reflect on the importance of morality, or its absence, in society. We will also explore a short story that more or less is a cautionary tale about the excesses of science. You will analyze *The Scarlet Letter* and "The Birthmark," by Nathaniel Hawthorne.

As a result of this chapter study you will be able to . . .

1. Analyze the basic differences between Aylmer's worldview and transcendentalism.

2. Describe the moral qualities each character in *The Scarlet Letter* represent.

3. Discuss the dangers of being married to an unbelieving spouse.

4. Compare and contrast Aylmer and Chillingworth (*The Scarlet Letter*).

5. Parallel Hester Prynne in *The Scarlet Letter* and Phoebe Pyncheon in *House of the Seven Gables*.

Weekly Essay Options: Begin on page 274 of the Teacher Guide.

Reading ahead: poems by Henry Wadsworth Longfellow, Oliver Wendell Holmes, James Russell Lowell, John Greenleaf Whittier, and Emily Dickinson.

 History connections: *American History* chapter 8, "Nationalism."

"The Birthmark"
Nathaniel Hawthorne

After an initial period of anonymity during his so-called solitary years from 1825 to 1837, and a time of very little literary success, Nathaniel Hawthorne finally achieved a reputation as a gifted author. His short story "The Birthmark" was one of the best fruits from this time. Some critics described Hawthorne as writing a "dense spiritual autobiography" when he wrote stories like "The Birthmark." See if you agree.

In the latter part of the last century, there lived a man of science — an eminent proficient in every branch of natural philosophy — who, not long before our story opens, had made experience of a spiritual affinity, more attractive than any chemical one. He had left his laboratory to the care of an assistant, cleared his fine countenance from the furnace smoke, washed the stain of acids from his fingers, and persuaded a beautiful woman to become his wife. In those days, when the comparatively recent discovery of electricity, and other kindred mysteries of nature, seemed to open paths into the region of miracle, it was not unusual for the love of science to rival the love of woman, in its depth and absorbing energy. The higher intellect, the imagination, the spirit, and even the heart, might all find their congenial aliment in pursuits which, as some of their ardent votaries believed, would ascend from one step of powerful intelligence to another, until the philosopher should lay his hand on the secret of creative force, and perhaps make new worlds for himself. We know not whether Aylmer possessed this degree of faith in man's ultimate control over nature. He had devoted himself, however, too unreservedly to scientific studies, ever to be weaned from them by any second passion. His love for his young wife might prove the stronger of the two; but it could only be by intertwining itself with his love of science, and uniting the strength of the latter to its own.

Such an union accordingly took place, and was attended with truly remarkable consequences, and a deeply impressive moral. One day, very soon after their marriage, Aylmer sat gazing at his wife, with a trouble in his countenance that grew stronger, until he spoke.

"Georgiana," said he, "has it never occurred to you that the mark upon your cheek might be removed?"

"No, indeed," said she, smiling; but perceiving the seriousness of his manner, she blushed deeply. "To tell you the truth, it has been so often called a charm, that I was simple enough to imagine it might be so."

"Ah, upon another face, perhaps it might," replied her husband. "But never on yours! No, dearest Georgiana, you came so nearly perfect from the hand of Nature, that this slightest possible defect — which we hesitate whether to term a defect or a beauty — shocks me, as being the visible mark of earthly imperfection."

"Shocks you, my husband!" cried Georgiana, deeply hurt; at first reddening with momentary anger, but then bursting into tears. "Then why did you take me from my mother's side? You cannot love what shocks you!"

To explain this conversation, it must be mentioned, that, in the center of Georgiana's left cheek, there was a singular mark, deeply interwoven, as it were, with the texture and substance of her face. In the usual state of her complexion — a healthy, though delicate bloom — the mark wore a tint of deeper crimson, which imperfectly defined its shape amid the surrounding rosiness. When she blushed, it gradually became more indistinct, and finally vanished amid the triumphant rush of blood, that bathed the whole cheek with its brilliant glow. But, if any shifting emotion caused her to turn pale, there was the mark again, a crimson stain upon the snow, in what Aylmer sometimes deemed an almost fearful distinctness. Its shape bore not a little similarity to the human hand, though of the smallest pigmy size. Georgiana's lovers were wont to say, that some fairy, at her birth hour, had laid her tiny hand upon the infant's cheek, and left this impress there, in token of the magic endowments that were to give her such sway over all hearts. Many a desperate swain would have risked life for the privilege of pressing his lips to the mysterious hand. It must not be concealed, however, that the impression wrought by this fairy sign manual varied exceedingly, according to the difference of temperament in the beholders. Some fastidious persons — but they were exclusively of her own sex — affirmed that the Bloody Hand, as they chose to call it, quite destroyed the effect of Georgiana's beauty, and rendered her countenance even hideous. But it would be as reasonable to say, that one of those small blue stains, which sometimes occur in the purest statuary marble, would convert the Eve of Powers to a monster. Masculine observers, if the birthmark did not heighten their admiration, contented themselves with wishing it away, that the world might possess one living specimen of ideal loveliness, without the semblance of a flaw. After his marriage—for he thought little or nothing of the matter before — Aylmer discovered that this was the case with himself.

Had she been less beautiful — if Envy's self could have found aught else to sneer at — he might have felt his affection heightened by the prettiness of this mimic hand, now vaguely portrayed, now lost, now stealing forth again, and glimmering to and fro with every pulse of emotion that throbbed within her heart. But, seeing her otherwise so perfect, he found this one defect grow more and more intolerable, with every moment of their united lives. It was the fatal flaw of humanity, which Nature, in one shape or another, stamps ineffaceably on all her productions, either to imply that they are temporary and finite, or that their perfection must be wrought by toil and pain. The Crimson Hand expressed the ineludible gripe, in which mortality clutches the highest and purest of earthly mold, degrading them into kindred with the lowest, and even with the very brutes, like whom their visible frames return to dust. In this manner, selecting it as the symbol of his wife's liability to sin, sorrow, decay, and death, Aylmer's somber imagination was not long in rendering the birthmark a frightful object, causing him more trouble and horror than ever Georgiana's beauty, whether of soul or sense, had given him delight.

At all the seasons which should have been their happiest, he invariably, and without intending it — nay, in spite of a purpose to the contrary — reverted to this one disastrous topic. Trifling as it at first appeared, it so connected itself with innumerable trains of thought, and modes of feeling, that it became the central point of all. With the morning twilight, Aylmer opened his eyes upon his wife's face, and recognized the symbol of imperfection; and when they sat together at the evening hearth, his eyes wandered stealthily to her cheek, and beheld, flickering with the blaze of the wood fire, the spectral Hand that wrote mortality where he would fain have worshiped. Georgiana soon learned to shudder at his gaze. It needed but a glance, with the peculiar expression that his face often wore, to change the roses of her cheek into a deathlike paleness, amid which the Crimson Hand was brought strongly out, like a bas relief of ruby on the whitest marble.

Late, one night, when the lights were growing dim, so as hardly to betray the stain on the poor wife's cheek, she herself, for the first time, voluntarily took up the subject.

"Do you remember, my dear Aylmer," said she, with a feeble attempt at a smile, "have you any recollection of a dream, last night, about this odious Hand?"

"None! None whatever!" replied Aylmer, starting; but then he added in a dry, cold tone, affected for the sake of concealing the real depth of his emotion: "I might well dream of it; for, before I fell asleep, it had taken a pretty firm hold of my fancy."

"And you did dream of it," continued Georgiana, hastily; for she dreaded lest a gush of tears should interrupt what she had to say. "A terrible dream! I wonder that you can forget it. Is it possible to forget this one expression? 'It is in her heart now; we must have it out!' Reflect, my husband; for by all means I would have you recall that dream."

The mind is in a sad state, when Sleep cannot confine her specters within the dim region of her sway, but suffers them to break forth, affrighting this actual life with secrets that perchance belong to a deeper one. Aylmer now remembered his dream. He had fancied himself, with his servant Aminadab, attempting an operation for the removal of the birthmark. But the deeper went the knife, the deeper sank the Hand, until at length its tiny grasp appeared to have caught hold of Georgiana's heart; whence, however, her husband was inexorably resolved to cut or wrench it away.

When the dream had shaped itself perfectly in his memory, Aylmer sat in his wife's presence with a guilty feeling. Truth often finds its way to the mind close muffled in robes of sleep, and then speaks with uncompromising directness of matters in regard to which we practice an unconscious self-deception, during our waking moments. Until now, he had not been aware of the tyrannizing influence acquired by one idea over his mind, and of the lengths which he might find in his heart to go, for the sake of giving himself peace.

"Aylmer," resumed Georgiana, solemnly, "I know not what may be the cost to both of us, to rid me of this fatal birthmark. Perhaps its removal may cause cureless deformity. Or, it may be, the stain goes as deep as life itself. Again, do we know that there is a possibility, on any terms, of unclasping the firm gripe of this little Hand, which was laid upon me before I came into the world?"

"Dearest Georgiana, I have spent much thought upon the subject," hastily interrupted Aylmer. "I am convinced of the perfect practicability of its removal."

"If there be the remotest possibility of it," continued Georgiana, "let the attempt be made, at whatever risk. Danger is nothing to me; for life, while this hateful mark makes me the object of your horror and disgust — life is a burthen which I would fling down with joy. Either remove this dreadful Hand, or take my wretched life! You have deep science! All the world bears witness of it. You have achieved great wonders! Cannot you remove this little, little mark, which I cover with the tips of two small fingers! Is this beyond your power, for the sake of your own peace, and to save your poor wife from madness?"

"Noblest, dearest, tenderest wife!" cried Aylmer, rapturously. "Doubt not my power. I have already given this matter the deepest thought — thought which might almost have enlightened me to create a being less perfect than yourself. Georgiana, you have led me deeper than ever into the heart of science. I feel myself fully competent to render this dear cheek as faultless as its fellow; and then, most beloved, what will be my triumph, when I shall have corrected what Nature left imperfect, in her fairest work!" …

"It is resolved, then," said Georgiana, faintly smiling. "And, Aylmer, spare me not, though you should find the birthmark take refuge in my heart at last."

Her husband tenderly kissed her cheek — her right cheek — not that which bore the impress of the Crimson Hand.

The next day, Aylmer apprized his wife of a plan that he had formed, whereby he might have opportunity for the intense thought and constant watchfulness which the proposed operation would require; while Georgiana, likewise, would enjoy the perfect repose essential to its success. They were to seclude themselves in the extensive apartments occupied by Aylmer as a laboratory, and where, during his toilsome youth, he had made discoveries in the elemental powers of Nature, that had roused the admiration of all the learned societies in Europe. Seated calmly in this laboratory, the pale philosopher had investigated the secrets of the highest cloud-region, and of the profoundest mines; he had satisfied himself of the causes that kindled and kept alive the fires of the volcano; and had explained the mystery of fountains, and how it is that they gush forth, some so bright and pure, and others with such rich medicinal virtues, from the dark bosom of the earth. Here, too, at an earlier period, he had studied the wonders of the human frame, and attempted to fathom the very process by which Nature assimilates all her precious influences from earth and air, and from the spiritual world, to create and foster Man, her masterpiece. …

As he led her over the threshold of the laboratory, Georgiana was cold and tremulous. Aylmer looked cheerfully into her face, with intent to reassure her, but was so startled with the intense glow of the birthmark upon the whiteness of her cheek, that he could not restrain a strong convulsive shudder. His wife fainted.

"Aminadab! Aminadab!" shouted Aylmer, stamping violently on the floor.

Forthwith, there issued from an inner apartment a man of low stature, but bulky frame, with shaggy hair hanging about his visage, which was grimed with the vapors of the furnace. This personage had been Aylmer's under-worker during his whole scientific career, and was admirably fitted for that office by his great mechanical readiness, and the skill with which, while incapable of comprehending a single principle, he executed all the practical details of his master's experiments. With his vast strength, his shaggy hair, his smoky aspect, and the indescribable earthiness that encrusted him, he seemed to represent man's physical nature; while Aylmer's slender figure, and pale, intellectual face, were no less apt a type of the spiritual element.

"Throw open the door of the boudoir, Aminadab," said Aylmer, "and burn a pastille."

"Yes, master," answered Aminadab, looking intently at the lifeless form of Georgiana; and then he muttered to himself: "If she were my wife, I'd never part with that birthmark."

When Georgiana recovered consciousness, she found herself breathing an atmosphere of penetrating fragrance, the gentle potency of which had recalled her from her deathlike faintness. The scene around her looked like enchantment. Aylmer had converted those smoky, dingy, somber rooms, where he had spent his brightest years in recondite pursuits, into a series of beautiful apartments, not unfit to be the secluded abode of a lovely woman. The walls were hung with gorgeous curtains, which imparted the combination of grandeur and grace, that no other species of adornment can achieve; and

as they fell from the ceiling to the floor, their rich and ponderous folds, concealing all angles and straight lines, appeared to shut in the scene from infinite space. For aught Georgiana knew, it might be a pavilion among the clouds. And Aylmer, excluding the sunshine, which would have interfered with his chemical processes, had supplied its place with perfumed lamps, emitting flames of various hue, but all uniting in a soft, empurpled radiance. He now knelt by his wife's side, watching her earnestly, but without alarm; for he was confident in his science, and felt that he could draw a magic circle round her, within which no evil might intrude.

"Where am I? Ah, I remember!" said Georgiana, faintly; and she placed her hand over her cheek, to hide the terrible mark from her husband's eyes.

"Fear not, dearest!" exclaimed he. "Do not shrink from me! Believe me, Georgiana, I even rejoice in this single imperfection, since it will be such a rapture to remove it."

"Oh, spare me!" sadly replied his wife. "Pray do not look at it again. I never can forget that convulsive shudder."

In order to soothe Georgiana, and, as it were, to release her mind from the burden of actual things, Aylmer now put in practice some of the light and playful secrets which science had taught him among its profounder lore. Airy figures, absolutely bodiless ideas, and forms of unsubstantial beauty, came and danced before her, imprinting their momentary footsteps on beams of light. Though she had some indistinct idea of the method of these optical phenomena, still the illusion was almost perfect enough to warrant the belief that her husband possessed sway over the spiritual world. Then again, when she felt a wish to look forth from her seclusion, immediately, as if her thoughts were answered, the procession of external existence flitted across a screen. The scenery and the figures of actual life were perfectly represented, but with that bewitching, yet indescribable difference, which always makes a picture, an image, or a shadow, so much more attractive than the original. When wearied of this, Aylmer bade her cast her eyes upon a vessel, containing a quantity of earth. She did so, with little interest at first, but was soon startled to perceive the germ of a plant, shooting upward from the soil. Then came the slender stalk; the leaves gradually unfolded themselves; and amid them was a perfect and lovely flower.

"It is magical!" cried Georgiana, "I dare not touch it."

"Nay, pluck it," answered Aylmer, "pluck it, and inhale its brief perfume while you may. The flower will wither in a few moments, and leave nothing save its brown seed-vessels but thence may be perpetuated a race as ephemeral as itself."

But Georgiana had no sooner touched the flower than the whole plant suffered a blight, its leaves turning coal-black, as if by the agency of fire.

"There was too powerful a stimulus," said Aylmer thoughtfully.

To make up for this abortive experiment, he proposed to take her portrait by a scientific process of his own invention. It was to be effected by rays of light striking upon a polished plate of metal. Georgiana assented — but, on looking at the result, was affrighted to find the features of the portrait blurred and indefinable; while the minute figure of a hand appeared where the cheek should have been. Aylmer snatched the metallic plate, and threw it into a jar of corrosive acid.

Soon, however, he forgot these mortifying failures. In the intervals of study and chemical experiment, he came to her, flushed and exhausted, but seemed invigorated by her presence, and spoke in glowing language of the resources of his art. He gave a history of the long dynasty of the Alchemists, who spent so many ages in a quest of the universal solvent, by which the Golden Principle might be elicited from all things vile and base. Aylmer appeared to believe, that, by the plainest scientific logic, it was altogether within the limits of possibility to discover this long-sought medium; but, he added, a philosopher who should go deep enough to acquire the power, would attain too lofty a wisdom to stoop to the exercise of it. Not less singular were his opinions in regard to the Elixir Vitae. He more than intimated, that it was at his option to concoct a liquid that should prolong life for years — perhaps interminably — but that it would produce a discord in nature, which all the world, and chiefly the quaffer of the immortal nostrum, would find cause to curse.

"Aylmer, are you in earnest?" asked Georgiana, looking at him with amazement and fear. "It is terrible to possess such power, or even to dream of possessing it.

"Oh, do not tremble, my love!" said her husband. "I would not wrong either you or myself, by working such inharmonious effects upon our lives. But I would have you consider how trifling, in comparison, is the skill requisite to remove this little Hand."

At the mention of the birthmark, Georgiana, as usual, shrank, as if a red-hot iron had touched her cheek.

Again Aylmer applied himself to his labors. She could hear his voice in the distant furnace-room, giving directions to Aminadab, whose harsh, uncouth, misshapen tones were audible in response, more like the grunt or growl of a brute than human speech. After hours of absence, Aylmer reappeared, and proposed that she should now examine his cabinet of chemical products, and natural treasures of the earth. Among the former, he showed her a small vial, in which, he remarked, was contained a gentle yet most powerful fragrance, capable of impregnating all the breezes that blow across a kingdom. They were of inestimable value, the contents of that little vial; and, as he said so, he threw some of the perfume into the air, and filled the room with piercing and invigorating delight.

"And what is this?" asked Georgiana, pointing to a small crystal globe, containing a gold-colored liquid. "It is so beautiful to the eye, that I could imagine it the Elixir of Life."

"In one sense it is," replied Aylmer, "or rather the Elixir of Immortality. It is the most precious poison that ever was concocted in this world. By its aid, I could apportion the lifetime of any mortal at whom you might point your finger. The strength of the dose would determine whether he were to linger out years, or drop dead in the midst of a breath. No king, on his guarded throne, could keep his life, if I, in my private station, should deem that the welfare of millions justified me in depriving him of it."

"Why do you keep such a terrific drug?" inquired Georgiana in horror.

"Do not mistrust me, dearest!" said her husband, smiling. "Its virtuous potency is yet greater than its harmful one. But, see! Here is a powerful cosmetic. With a few drops of this, in a vase of water, freckles may be washed away as easily as the hands are cleansed. A stronger infusion would take the blood out of the cheek, and leave the rosiest beauty a pale ghost."

"Is it with this lotion that you intend to bathe my cheek?" asked Georgiana, anxiously.

"Oh, no!" hastily replied her husband, "this is merely superficial. Your case demands a remedy that shall go deeper."

In his interviews with Georgiana, Aylmer generally made minute inquiries as to her sensations, and whether the confinement of the rooms, and the temperature of the atmosphere, agreed with her. These questions had such a particular drift, that Georgiana began to conjecture that she was already subjected to certain physical influences, either breathed in with the fragrant air, or taken with her food. She fancied, likewise — but it might be alto-gether fancy — that there was a stirring up of her system: a strange, indefinite sensation creeping through her veins, and tingling, half-painfully, half-pleasurably, at her heart. Still, whenever she dared to look into the mirror, there she beheld herself, pale as a white rose, and with the crimson birthmark stamped upon her cheek. Not even Aylmer now hated it so much as she.

To dispel the tedium of the hours which her husband found it necessary to devote to the processes of combination and analysis, Georgiana turned over the volumes of his scientific library. In many dark old tomes, she met with chapters full of romance and poetry. They were the works of the philosophers of the middle ages, such as Albertus Magnus, Cornelius Agrippa, Paracelsus, and the famous friar who created the prophetic Brazen Head. All these antique natural-ists stood in advance of their centuries, yet were imbued with some of their credulity, and therefore were believed, and perhaps imagined themselves, to have acquired from the investigation of nature a power above nature, and from physics a sway over the spiritual world. Hardly less curious and imaginative were the early volumes of the Transactions of the Royal Society, in which the members, knowing little of the limits of natural possibility, were continually recording wonders, or proposing methods whereby

wonders might be wrought.

But, to Georgiana, the most engrossing volume was a large folio from her husband's own hand, in which he had recorded every experiment of his scientific career, with its original aim, the methods adopted for its development, and its final success or failure, with the circumstances to which either event was attributable. The book, in truth, was both the history and emblem of his ardent, ambitious, imaginative, yet practical and laborious, life. He handled physical details, as if there were nothing beyond them; yet spiritualized them all, and redeemed himself from materialism, by his strong and eager aspiration toward the infinite. In his grasp, the veriest clod of earth assumed a soul. Georgiana, as she read, reverenced Aylmer, and loved him more profoundly than ever, but with a less entire depen-dence on his judgment than heretofore. Much as he had accomplished, she could not but observe that his most splendid successes were almost invariably failures, if compared with the ideal at which he aimed. His brightest diamonds were the merest pebbles, and felt to be so by himself, in comparison with the inestimable gems which lay hidden beyond his reach. The volume, rich with achievements that had won renown for its author, was yet as melan-choly a record as ever mortal hand had penned. It was the sad confession, and continual exemplifica-tion, of the short-comings of the composite man — the spirit burthened with clay and working in matter; and of the despair that assails the higher nature, at finding itself so miserably thwarted by the earthly part. Perhaps every man of genius, in what-ever sphere, might recognize the image of his own experience in Aylmer's journal.

So deeply did these reflections affect Georgiana, that she laid her face upon the open volume, and burst into tears. In this situation she was found by her husband.

"It is dangerous to read in a sorcerer's books," said he, with a smile, though his countenance was uneasy and displeased. "Georgiana, there are pages in that volume, which I can scarcely glance over and keep my senses. Take heed lest it prove as detrimen-tal to you!"

"It has made me worship you more than ever," said she.

"Ah! wait for this one success," rejoined he, "then worship me if you will. I shall deem myself hardly unworthy of it. But, come! I have sought you for the luxury of your voice. Sing to me, dearest!"

So she poured out the liquid music of her voice to quench the thirst of his spirit. He then took his leave, with a boyish exuberance of gaiety, assuring her that her seclusion would endure but a little longer, and that the result was already certain. Scarcely had he departed, when Georgiana felt irresistibly impelled to follow him. She had forgotten to inform Aylmer of a symptom, which, for two or three hours past, had begun to excite her attention. It was a sensation in the fatal birthmark, not painful, but which induced a restlessness throughout her system. Hastening after her husband, she intruded, for the first time, into the laboratory.

The first thing that struck her eye was the furnace, that hot and feverish worker, with the intense glow of its fire, which, by the quantities of soot clustered above it, seemed to have been burning for ages. There was a distilling apparatus in full operation. Around the room were retorts, tubes, cylinders, crucibles, and other apparatus of chemical research. An electrical machine stood ready for immediate use. The atmosphere felt oppressively close, and was tainted with gaseous odors, which had been tormented forth by the processes of science. The severe and homely simplicity of the apartment, with its naked walls and brick pavement, looked strange, accustomed as Georgiana had become to the fantastic elegance of her boudoir. But what chiefly, indeed almost solely, drew her attention, was the aspect of Aylmer himself.

He was pale as death, anxious, and absorbed, and hung over the furnace as if it depended upon his utmost watchfulness whether the liquid, which it was distilling, should be the draught of immortal happiness or misery. How different from the san-guine and joyous mien that he had assumed for Georgiana's encouragement!

"Carefully now, Aminadab! Carefully, thou human machine! Carefully, thou man of clay!" muttered Aylmer, more to himself than his assistant. "Now, if there be a thought too much or too little, it is all over!"

"Hoh! Hoh!" mumbled Aminadab. "Look, master, look!"

Aylmer raised his eyes hastily, and at first reddened, then grew paler than ever, on beholding Georgiana. He rushed towards her, and seized her arm with a gripe that left the print of his fingers upon it.

"Why do you come hither? Have you no trust in your husband?" cried he impetuously. "Would you throw the blight of that fatal birthmark over my labors? It is not well done. Go, prying woman, go!"

"Nay, Aylmer," said Georgiana, with the firm-ness of which she possessed no stinted endowment, "it is not you that have a right to complain. You mistrust your wife! You have concealed the anxiety with which you watch the development of this experiment. Think not so unworthily of me, my husband! Tell me all the risk we run and fear not that I shall shrink, for my share in it is far less than your own!"

"No, no, Georgiana!" said Aylmer impatiently, "it must not be."

"I submit," replied she calmly. "And, Aylmer, I shall quaff whatever drought you bring me; but it will be on the same principle that would induce me to take a dose of poison, if offered by your hand."

"My noble wife," said Aylmer, deeply moved, "I knew not the height and depth of your nature, until now. Nothing shall be concealed. Know, then, that this Crimson Hand, superficial as it seems, has clutched its grasp into your being, with a strength of which I had no previous conception. I have already administered agents powerful enough to do aught except to change your entire physical system. Only one thing remains to be tried. If that fail us, we are ruined!"

"Why did you hesitate to tell me this?" asked she.

"Because, Georgiana," said Aylmer, in a low voice, "there is danger!"

"Danger? There is but one danger — that this horrible stigma shall be left upon my cheek!" cried Georgiana. "Remove it! Remove it! Whatever be the cost, or we shall both go mad!"

"Heaven knows, your words are too true," said

Aylmer, sadly. "And now, dearest, return to your boudoir. In a little while, all will be tested."

He conducted her back, and took leave of her with a solemn tenderness, which spoke far more than his words how much was now at stake. After his departure, Georgiana became wrapped in musings. She considered the character of Aylmer, and did it completer justice than at any previous moment. Her heart exulted, while it trembled, at his honorable love, so pure and lofty that it would accept nothing less than perfection, nor miserably make itself contented with an earthlier nature than he had dreamed of. She felt how much more precious was such a sentiment, than that meaner kind which would have borne with the imperfection for her sake, and have been guilty of treason to holy love, by degrading its perfect idea to the level of the actual. And, with her whole spirit, she prayed, that, for a single moment, she might satisfy his highest and deepest conception. Longer than one moment, she well knew, it could not be; for his spirit was ever on the march — ever ascending — and each instant required something that was beyond the scope of the instant before.

The sound of her husband's footsteps aroused her. He bore a crystal goblet, containing a liquor colorless as water, but bright enough to be the drought of immortality. Aylmer was pale; but it seemed rather the consequence of a highly wrought state of mind, and tension of spirit, than of fear or doubt.

"The concoction of the drought has been perfect," said he, in answer to Georgiana's look. "Unless all my science have deceived me, it cannot fail."

"Save on your account, my dearest Aylmer," observed his wife, "I might wish to put off this birthmark of mortality by relinquishing mortality itself, in preference to any other mode. Life is but a sad possession to those who have attained precisely the degree of moral advancement at which I stand. Were I weaker and blinder, it might be happiness. Were I stronger, it might be endured hopefully. But, being what I find myself, methinks I am of all mortals the most fit to die."

"You are fit for heaven without tasting death!" replied her husband. "But why do we speak of dying? The drought cannot fail. Behold its effect upon this plant!"

On the window-seat there stood a geranium, diseased with yellow blotches, which had overspread all its leaves. Aylmer poured a small quantity of the liquid upon the soil in which it grew. In a little time, when the roots of the plant had taken up the moisture, the unsightly blotches began to be extinguished in a living verdure.

"There needed no proof," said Georgiana, quietly. "Give me the goblet. I joyfully stake all upon your word."

"Drink, then, thou lofty creature!" exclaimed Aylmer, with fervid admiration. "There is no taint of imperfection on thy spirit. Thy sensible frame, too, shall soon be all perfect!"

She quaffed the liquid, and returned the goblet to his hand.

"It is grateful," said she, with a placid smile. "Methinks it is like water from a heavenly fountain; for it contains I know not what of unobtrusive fragrance and deliciousness. It allays a feverish thirst, that had parched me for many days. Now, dearest, let me sleep. My earthly senses are closing over my spirit, like the leaves around the heart of a rose, at sunset."

She spoke the last words with a gentle reluctance, as if it required almost more energy than she could command to pronounce the faint and lingering syllables. Scarcely had they loitered through her lips, ere she was lost in slumber. Aylmer sat by her side, watching her aspect with the emotions proper to a man, the whole value of whose existence was involved in the process now to be tested. Mingled with this mood, however, was the philosophic investigation, characteristic of the man of science. Not the minutest symptom escaped him. A heightened flush of the cheek, a slight irregularity of breath, a quiver of the eyelid, a hardly perceptible tremor through the frame — such were the details which, as the moments passed, he wrote down in his folio volume. Intense thought had set its stamp upon every previous page of that volume; but the thoughts of years were all concentrated upon the last.

While thus employed, he failed not to gaze often at the fatal Hand, and not without a shudder. Yet once, by a strange and unaccountable impulse, he pressed it with his lips. His spirit recoiled, however, in the very act, and Georgiana, out of the midst of her deep sleep, moved uneasily and murmured, as if in remonstrance. Again, Aylmer resumed his watch. Nor was it without avail. The Crimson Hand, which at first had been strongly visible upon the marble paleness of Georgiana's cheek now grew more faintly outlined. She remained not less pale than ever; but the birthmark, with every breath that came and went, lost somewhat of its former distinctness. Its presence had been awful; its departure was more awful still. Watch the stain of the rainbow fading out of the sky; and you will know how that mysterious symbol passed away.

"By Heaven, it is well-nigh gone!" said Aylmer to himself, in almost irrepressible ecstasy. "I can scarcely trace it now. Success! Success! And now it is like the faintest rose-color. The slightest flush of blood across her cheek would overcome it. But she is so pale!"

He drew aside the window-curtain, and suffered the light of natural day to fall into the room, and rest upon her cheek. At the same time, he heard a gross, hoarse chuckle, which he had long known as his servant Aminadab's expression of delight.

"Ah, clod! Ah, earthly mass!" cried Aylmer, laughing in a sort of frenzy. "You have served me well! Master and Spirit — Earth and Heaven — have both done their part in this! Laugh, thing of the senses! You have earned the right to laugh."

These exclamations broke Georgiana's sleep. She slowly unclosed her eyes, and gazed into the mirror, which her husband had arranged for that purpose. A faint smile flitted over her lips, when she recognized how barely perceptible was now that Crimson Hand, which had once blazed forth with such disastrous brilliancy as to scare away all their happiness. But then her eyes sought Aylmer's face, with a trouble and anxiety that he could by no means account for.

"My poor Aylmer!" murmured she.

"Poor? Nay, richest! Happiest! Most favored!" exclaimed he. "My peerless bride, it is successful! You are perfect!"

"My poor Aylmer!" she repeated, with a more than human tenderness. "You have aimed loftily! You have done nobly! Do not repent, that, with so high and pure a feeling, you have rejected the best the earth could offer. Aylmer — dearest Aylmer, I am dying!"

Alas, it was too true! The fatal Hand had grappled with the mystery of life, and was the bond by which an angelic spirit kept itself in union with a mortal frame. As the last crimson tint of the birthmark — that sole token of human imperfection — faded from her cheek, the parting breath of the now perfect woman passed into the atmosphere, and her soul, lingering a moment near her husband, took its heavenward flight. Then a hoarse, chuckling laugh was heard again! Thus ever does the gross Fatality of Earth exult in its invariable triumph over the immortal essence, which, in this dim sphere of half-development, demands the completeness of a higher state. Yet, had Aylmer reached a profounder wisdom, he need not thus have flung away the happiness, which would have woven his mortal life of the self-same texture with the celestial. The momentary circumstance was too strong for him; he failed to look beyond the shadowy scope of Time, and living once for all in Eternity, to find the perfect Future in the present.

Assignments

- Warm-up: A tautology is a way of saying the same thing twice. Natural selection predicts that the fittest organisms will produce the most offspring, and it defines the fittest organisms as the ones that produce the most offspring! Can you find other tautologies in modern science?

- Student should complete Concept Builder 8-A.

- Students review the required reading(s) *before* the assigned chapter begins.

- Teachers may want to discuss assigned reading(s) with students.

- Teachers shall assign the required essay. The rest of the essays can be outlined, answered with shorter answers, discussed, or skipped.

CONCEPT BUILDER 8-A Active Reading		
		Read "The Birthmark" by Nathaniel Hawthorne in the text, then answer the following questions.
	1	The narrative technique is limited omniscient. What advantages does this offer the author?
	2	Contrast Georgiana and Alymer.
	3	How do you predict this story will end?
	4	Why does the author capitalize Nature?
	5	Georgiana warns her husband that it may be a big mistake to remove her birthmark. Why?

Romanticism/Transcendentalism

Romanticism is a worldview in philosophy and literature that argued for a higher reality than that found in tactile experience or in a higher kind of knowledge than that achieved by human reason. Romanticism celebrated the subjective and the unusual. For our purposes, transcendentalism was an American version of romanticism.

Elements of Romanticism	Frontier is a vast expanse; it represents freedom, innocence, and opportunity.
Writing Techniques	1. Appeals to imagination; use of the "willing suspension of disbelief" 2. Stress on emotion and imagination rather than reason; optimism, geniality 3. Subjectivity: in form and meaning 4. Prefers the remote setting in time and space 5. Prefers the exotic and improbable plots 6. Prefers aberrant characterization 7. Form rises out of content, non-formal 8. Prefers individualized, subjective writing

Transcendentalism as an artistic and intellectual movement was localized in New England. Thus, this period is called the New England Renaissance.

Assignments

- Warm-up: When you see the word "romanticism" what comes to mind?
- Students should complete Concept Builder 8-B.
- Student should review reading(s) from the next chapter.
- Student should outline essays due at the end of the week
- Per teacher instructions, students may answer orally, in a group setting, some of the essays that are not assigned as formal essays.

Read *The Scarlet Letter* (Chapter Two) by Nathaniel Hawthorne then answer the following questions.

1	Have you made a bad choice and been publicly punished? How did it feel?
2	What contemporary actress would best fit the role of Hester Prynne?
3	How do the people react to Hester Prynne? What does that tell you about what they think about her?
4	Hawthorne employs an omniscient point of view. What is that and why does he use it?
5	Based upon the way that this community is handling Hester's crime, how do you think they would react to a businessman who wanted to open a bar?

The Scarlett Letter
Nathaniel Hawthorne

Background *The Scarlet Letter* is based on a true incident. In 1697, the Rev. John Cotton, pastor of a Plymouth, Massachusetts, church, was fired from his job for committing adultery. Nearly 150 years later Hawthorne wrote a similar story. This novel, however, represents both a literary milestone and a worldview milestone. First, *The Scarlet Letter* is perhaps the best American romantic novel ever written. Secondly, this is the final American novel, many believe, that has a moral vision. In short, *The Scarlet Letter* is the last American Christian theistic novel of superior quality that was to appear for 150 years. In *The Scarlet Letter*, Hawthorne unapologetically presents a character who takes responsibility for her sin and, as a result, is extolled and admired by her community. Hester Prynne and Arthur Dimmesdale are correctly punished by God for their sin. They grow stronger — not weaker — for their felicity and fidelity. This is one of the last critically acclaimed American novels where this occurs. By contrast, Hawthorne's contemporary, Herman Melville, wrote *Billy Budd* where the protagonist, Billy Budd, is "redeemed" by some sort of self-actualization. The preacher in *Billy Budd* is a wimpish, amoral character who, on the last night of Billy Budd's life, abandoned his attempt to lead Billy Budd to a saving relationship with Christ because Billy Budd appeared to be saved already by his good works. On the other hand, Arthur Dimmesdale, the pastor in *The Scarlet Letter*, sinned grievously but, at the end of the novel, was nonetheless "redeemed" by honest confession of sin. He may be the last American literary character who is.

About the Author Born in Salem, Massachusetts, in 1804, Hawthorne later graduated from Bowdoin College, in Brunswick, Maine. Nathaniel Hawthorne wrote *The Scarlet Letter*, a historical romance of 17th-century Boston, as one reliving his own historical past. Hawthorne's first relative came to Salem in 1630 "a soldier, legislator, judge, and Puritan." The next ancestor was a Salem witch trial judge. Hawthorne's father was a sea captain who died when his only son was four. Hawthorne, in this and later books, explored his own past. Hester Prynne, Chillingworth, and Dimmesdale are truly contemporary characters. The Scarlet Letter remains as modern, as dramatic, as passionate, and as moving as if it were written yesterday.

Other Notable Works

Twice-Told Tales (1837)

The House of the Seven Gables (1851)

Suggested Vocabulary Words As you read the assigned prose, poetry, and novels, keep vocabulary cards. On one side put the word you do not know. On the other side put the definition of the word and a sentence with the word used in it. Read 35–50 pages per night (or 200 pages per week). At the same time, create 3x5 vocabulary cards. You should use five new words in each essay

Statue of Nathaniel Hawthorne in Salem, Massachusetts by sculptor Bela Pratt (PD-US).

you write. The following are vocabulary words in *The Scarlet Letter*. Find more.

Chapter II: ignominy

Chapter III: heterogeneous, iniquity

Chapter VIII: imperious

Chapter XII: dauntless, forlorn, odious, efficacious

Chapter XIII: expiation, scurrilous

Chapter XIX: misanthropy

Chapter XX: effluence, choleric

Chapter XXI: vicissitude

Assignments

- Warm-up: A recent television commercial argued, "Doesn't everyone deserve a second chance?" Do you agree with this statement? Does this book offend your sense of justice?
- Students should complete Concept Builder 8-C.
- Students should write rough drafts of assigned essay.
- The teacher may correct rough drafts.

CONCEPT BUILDER 8-C Romanticism	Hawthorne is writing in a romantic style. Romanticism exhibits the following writing styles:	
	1	Appeals to imagination; use of the "willing suspension of disbelief."
	2	Stress on emotion and imagination rather than reason; optimism, geniality.
	3	Subjectivity: in form and meaning.
	4	Prefers the remote setting in time and space.
	5	Prefers the exotic and improbable plots.
	6	Prefers aberrant characterization.
	7	Form rises out of content, non-formal.
	8	Prefers individualized, subjective writing.
	Find at least four of these elements in *The Scarlet Letter*.	
	1	
	2	
	3	
	4	

What Critics Said about Hawthorne

Hawthorne was morally, in an appreciative degree, a chip off the old block. His forefathers crossed the Atlantic for conscience sake, and it was the idea of the urgent conscience that haunted the imagination of their so-called degenerate successor. The Puritan strain in his blood ran clear — there are passages in his diaries, kept during his residence in Europe, which might almost have been written by the grimmest of the old Salem worthies.

—Henry James, 1879 (*Nathaniel Hawthorne, 1804–1864. The Scarlet Letter & Rappaccini's Daughter.* "The Harvard Classics Shelf of Fiction." 1917. I. By Henry James, Bartleby.com).

"The Custom House" throws light on a theme in *The Scarlet Letter* which is easily overlooked amid the ethical concerns of the book. Every character, in effect, re-enacts "The Custom House" scene in which Hawthorne himself contemplated the letter, so that the entire "romance" becomes a kind of exposition on the nature of symbolic perception. Hawthorne's subject is not only the meaning of adultery but also meaning in general; not only what the focal symbol means but also how it gains significance.

—Charles Feidelson Jr. (*Symbolism and American Literature*, 1953).

Above all it is Hester Prynne whose passion and beauty dominate every other person, and color each event. Hawthorne has conceived her as he has conceived his scene, in the full strength of his feeling for ancient New England. He is the Homer of that New England, and Hester is its most heroic creature. Tall, with dark and abundant hair and deep black eyes, a rich complexion that makes modern women (says Hawthorne) pale and thin by comparison, and a dignity that throws into low relief the "delicate, evanescent, and indescribable grace" by which gentility in girls has since come to be known, from the very first — and we believe it — she is said to cast a spell over those who behold her

—Mark Van Doren (*Hawthorne*, 1949).

Assignments

- Warm-up: *The Scarlet Letter* was a critical success but not a best seller. In American society today, so structured around entertainment, one wonders if Hawthorne could find a publisher. In his book *Amusing Ourselves to Death*, Neil Postman argues that television is transforming our culture into one vast arena for show business. TV is the highest order of abstract thinking and consistently undermines critical thinking (Postman, *Amusing Ourselves to Death*, p. 80, 41). The message has become the medium. What do you think?

- Students should complete Concept Builder 8-D.

- Student will re-write corrected copies of essay due tomorrow.

Foils are characters whose primary, if not sole purpose, is to develop the protagonist (main character), in this case Hester Prynne. Discuss how each foil develops Hester Prynne.

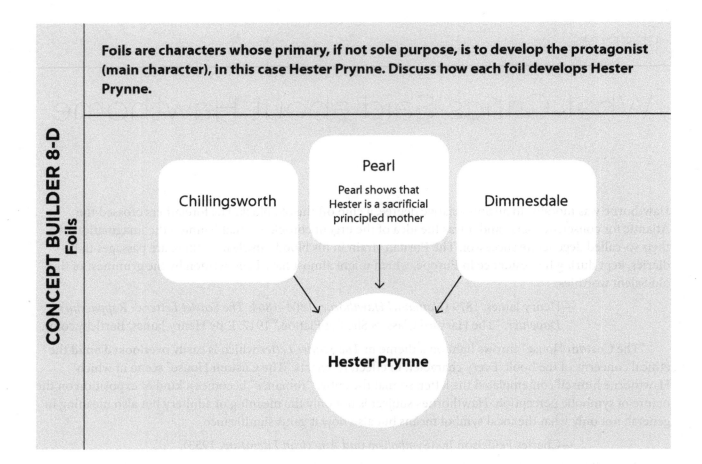

Chillingsworth

Pearl

Pearl shows that Hester is a sacrificial principled mother

Dimmesdale

Hester Prynne

Essay

In *The Scarlet Letter*, chapter 18, a crisis has arisen. Dimmesdale has just discovered that his boarder, Dr. Chillingworth, is actually the husband of Hester Prynne and a diabolical, evil man, committed to destroying Dimmesdale. But, in the face of his lover, and good friend, Hester Prynne, there is hope and joy. Hester is undeterred by the exigencies of life — she has lived isolated from human company for eight years. She has grown closer to her God and more secure in her consciousness.

But Hester Prynne, with a mind of native courage and activity, and for so long a period not merely estranged, but outlawed, from society, had habituated herself to such latitude of speculation as was altogether foreign to the clergyman. She had wandered, without rule or guidance, in a moral wilderness; as vast, as intricate and shadowy, as the untamed forest, amid the gloom of which they were now holding a colloquy that was to decide their fate. Her intellect and heart had their home, as it were, in desert places, where she roamed as freely as the wild Indian in his woods. For years past she had looked from this estranged point of view at human institutions, and whatever priests or legislators had established; criticizing all with hardly more reverence than the Indian would feel for the clerical band, the judicial robe, the pillory, the gallows, the fireside, or the church. The tendency of her fate and fortunes had been to set her free. The scarlet letter was her passport into regions where other women dared not tread. Shame, Despair, Solitude! These had been her teachers — stern and wild ones — and they had made her strong, but taught her much amiss.

She "had habituated herself to such latitude of speculation as was altogether foreign to the clergyman." Do you know any saints like this? A man or a woman of such strength and character that he or she can be trusted with anything? That person is a great friend.

Life had made Hester strong but not bitter.

I propose that these are the very best friends to have. Friends whose "tendency of her fate and fortunes has been to set her free."

The protagonist in *A Separate Peace*, by John Knowles is having a conversation with a good friend, a friend who is injured. The injured friend shares some incredible things about life with the protagonist. The protagonist argues with his injured friend and asks him, "How do you know this thing to be true?"

"How do I know it is true?" the friend retorts. "I know it is true because I have suffered."

I thank God for the hard times that He gives me and for friends to walk through them with me. I thank God for the people I know who have "passports to regions" I have never been but am sure some day I shall surely go (www.sparknotes.com/nofear/lit/the-scarlet-letter/chapter-18/).

Assignments

- Warm-up: Share how a hard time in your life has made you a better person.
- Students should complete Concept Builder 8-E.
- Essays are due. Students should take the chapter 8 test.

A.   Contrast the way Hester's community handles her adultery and the way Jesus dealt with the adulterous woman who was brought to Him (John 8).

B.   Also, contrast the way Hester handled her sin and the way the adulterous woman handled her sin.

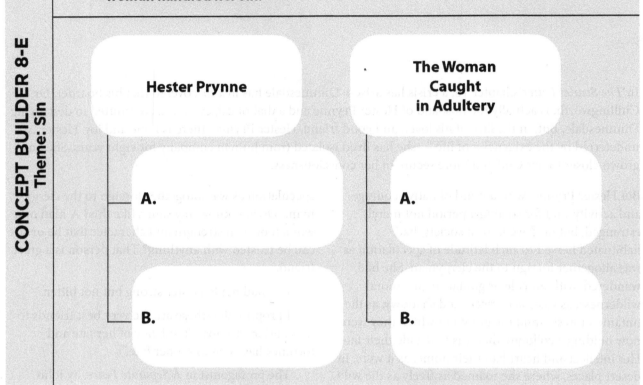

Chapter 9

1840–1855 (Part 2):

Romanticism: New England Renaissance

First Thoughts American poetry by many estimations was inferior to European poetry, especially English poetry. America had no Wordsworth, Byron, Shelley, or Keats. But then there was Dickinson. She was something different. She lived during the Second Great Awakening (Charles Finney, et al.). Many of her family members and friends were converted. They shared Christ with Dickinson. She resisted their advances. Either her deep religious skepticism, or her own curiosity, drove her to flirt with new metaphysics, precursors of what would be called modernism. Dickinson, at the end of her life, pulled completely away from the safe motifs of Christianity, and embraced a sort of agnosticism. Her poetry expressed both her ambiguity about Christianity and her guilt over her inability to join in the religious revivalism that gripped her family and friends. This tension was to color almost all the fabric of antebellum America.

Author Worldview Watch Longfellow, Holmes, et al., were all mediocre romantic poets (but the best we had to offer) in a literary world that was dominated by Wordsworth and Shelley (in England). Their metaphysics was as muddled as their writing was ordinary! Not so with Emily Dickinson

who presents somewhat of a problem. She apparently grew up in a Christian home and, at least when she was young, went to Church. However, later in life she becomes modern and cynical. However, that in no way diminishes the quality of her work — which was iconic and brilliant.

Chapter Learning Objectives In chapter 9 we will examine the poetry of the best early 19th-century poets. These include Longfellow, Lowell, Whittier, and Dickinson. You will analyze poems by Henry Wadsworth Longfellow, Oliver Wendell Holmes, James Russell Lowell, John Greenleaf Whittier, and Emily Dickinson.

As a result of this chapter study you will be able to . . .

1. Find examples of romanticism in poems by Longfellow, Bryant, Lowell, and Whittier.

2. Explain what is so modern about Dickinson's poetry.

Weekly Essay Options: Begin on page 274 of the Teacher Guide.

Reading ahead: Poems by Ralph Waldo Emerson.

Henry Wadsworth Longfellow

Probably the best loved of American poets is Henry Wadsworth Longfellow. Many of his lines are as familiar to us as rhymes from Mother Goose or the words of nursery songs learned in early childhood. Longfellow wrote on archetype themes that appeal to all kinds of people. His poems are easily understood and full of rhyme and meter. Above all, though, Longfellow wrote with optimism and hope uncharacteristic of the post-Civil War.

Paul Revere's Ride

Listen my children and you shall hear
Of the midnight ride of Paul Revere,
On the eighteenth of April, in Seventy-five;
Hardly a man is now alive
Who remembers that famous day and year.

He said to his friend, "If the British march
By land or sea from the town tonight,
Hang a lantern aloft in the belfry arch
Of the North Church tower as a signal light,
One if by land, and two if by sea;
And I on the opposite shore will be,
Ready to ride and spread the alarm
Through every Middlesex village and farm,
For the country folk to be up and to arm."

Then he said "Goodnight!" and with muffled oar
Silently rowed to the Charlestown shore,
Just as the moon rose over the bay,
Where swinging wide at her moorings lay

The Somerset, British man of war;
A phantom ship, with each mast and spar
Across the moon like a prison bar,
And a huge black hulk, that was magnified
By its own reflection in the tide.

Meanwhile, his friend through alley and street
Wanders and watches, with eager ears,
Till in the silence around him he hears
The muster of men at the barrack door,
The sound of arms, and the tramp of feet,
And the measured tread of the grenadiers,
Marching down to their boats on the shore.

Then he climbed the tower of the Old North Church,
By the wooden stairs, with stealthy tread,
To the belfry chamber overhead,
And startled the pigeons from their perch
On the sombre rafters, that round him made
Masses and moving shapes of shade,

By the trembling ladder, steep and tall,
To the highest window in the wall,
Where he paused to listen and look down
A moment on the roofs of the town
And the moonlight flowing over all.

Beneath, in the churchyard, lay the dead,
In their night encampment on the hill,
Wrapped in silence so deep and still
That he could hear, like a sentinel's tread,
The watchful nightwind, as it went
Creeping along from tent to tent,
And seeming to whisper, "All is well!"
A moment only he feels the spell
Of the place and the hour, and the secret dread
Of the lonely belfry and the dead;
For suddenly all his thoughts are bent
On a shadowy something far away,
Where the river widens to meet the bay,
A line of black that bends and floats
On the rising tide like a bridge of boats.

Meanwhile, impatient to mount and ride,
Booted and spurred, with a heavy stride
On the opposite shore walked Paul Revere.
Now he patted his horse's side,
Now he gazed at the landscape far and near,
Then, impetuous, stamped the earth,
And turned and tightened his saddle girth;
But mostly he watched with eager search
The belfry tower of the Old North Church,
As it rose above the graves on the hill,
Lonely and spectral and sombre and still.
And lo! as he looks, on the belfry's height
A glimmer, and then a gleam of light!

He springs to the saddle, the bridle he turns,
But lingers and gazes, till full on his sight
A second lamp in the belfry burns.

A hurry of hoofs in a village street,
A shape in the moonlight, a bulk in the dark,
And beneath, from the pebbles, in passing, a spark
Struck out by a steed flying fearless and fleet;
That was all! And yet, through the gloom and the light,
The fate of a nation was riding that night;
And the spark struck out by that steed, in his flight,
Kindled the land into flame with its heat.
He has left the village and mounted the steep,
And beneath him, tranquil and broad and deep,
Is the Mystic, meeting the ocean tides;
And under the alders that skirt its edge,
Now soft on the sand, now loud on the ledge,
Is heard the tramp of his steed as he rides.

It was twelve by the village clock
When he crossed the bridge into Medford town.
He heard the crowing of the cock,
And the barking of the farmer's dog,
And felt the damp of the river fog,
That rises after the sun goes down.

It was one by the village clock,
When he galloped into Lexington.
He saw the gilded weathercock
Swim in the moonlight as he passed,
And the meetinghouse windows, black and bare,
Gaze at him with a spectral glare,
As if they already stood aghast
At the bloody work they would look upon.

It was two by the village clock,
When he came to the bridge in Concord town.
He heard the bleating of the flock,
And the twitter of birds among the trees,
And felt the breath of the morning breeze
Blowing over the meadow brown.
And one was safe and asleep in his bed
Who at the bridge would be first to fall,
Who that day would be lying dead,
Pierced by a British musket ball.

You know the rest. In the books you have read
How the British Regulars fired and fled,
How the farmers gave them ball for ball,
From behind each fence and farmyard wall,
Chasing the redcoats down the lane,
Then crossing the fields to emerge again
Under the trees at the turn of the road,
And only pausing to fire and load.

So through the night rode Paul Revere;
And so through the night went his cry of alarm
To every Middlesex village and farm,
A cry of defiance, and not of fear,
A voice in the darkness, a knock at the door,
And a word that shall echo for evermore!
For, borne on the nightwind of the Past,
Through all our history, to the last,
In the hour of darkness and peril and need,
The people will waken and listen to hear
The hurrying hoof—beats of that steed,
And the midnight message of Paul Revere.

Assignments

- Warm-up: Longfellow was popular among ordinary people, but mostly criticized by scholars. People loved the very thing that critics disliked: the predictable narrative enclosed in tiresome rhymes. Agree or disagree with the critics.
- Students should complete Concept Builder 9-A.
- Students review the required reading(s) *before* the assigned chapter begins.
- Teachers may want to discuss assigned reading(s) with students.
- Teachers shall assign the required essay. The rest of the essays can be outlined, answered with shorter answers, discussed, or skipped.
- Students will review all readings for chapter 9.

"A Psalm of Life"
Henry Wadsworth Longfellow

What the Heart of the Young Man
Said to the Psalmist.

Tell me not, in mournful numbers,
Life is but an empty dream!
For the soul is dead that slumbers,
And things are not what they seem.
Life is real! Life is earnest!
And the grave is not its goal;
Dust thou art, to dust returnest,
Was not spoken of the soul.
Not enjoyment, and not sorrow,
Is our destined end or way;
But to act, that each tomorrow
Find us farther than today.
Art is long, and Time is fleeting,
And our hearts, though stout and brave,
Still, like muffled drums, are beating
Funeral marches to the grave.
In the world's broad field of battle,
In the bivouac of Life,
Be not dumb, driven cattle!
Be a hero in the strife!
Trust no Future, howe'er pleasant!
Let the dead Past bury its dead!
Act, act in the living Present!
Heart within, and God o'erhead!
Lives of great men all remind us
We can make our lives sublime,
And, departing, leave behind us
Footprints on the sands of time;
Footprints, that perhaps another,
Sailing o'er life's solemn main,
A forlorn and shipwrecked brother,
Seeing, shall take heart again.
Let us, then, be up and doing,
With a heart for any fate;
Still achieving, still pursuing,
Learn to labor and to wait.

Longfellow writes this poem in first person. Who is the speaker? Who is the audience?

Paraphrase this stanza.

What is the central metaphor that Longfellow employs? What is his point?

Oliver Wendell Holmes

Oliver Wendell Holmes (1809–1894) was born in Cambridge, Massachusetts, August 29, 1809, and educated at Harvard College. After graduation, he entered the Law School, but soon gave up law for medicine. From 1847 to 1882 he was a professor of anatomy and physiology in the Harvard Medical School. He died in Boston, October 7, 1894. However, Holmes's reputation as a scientist was overshadowed by his reputation as a poet.

The Chambered Nautilus

THIS is the ship of pearl, which, poets feign,

Sails the unshadowed main,

The venturous bark that flings

On the sweet summer wind its purpled wings

In gulfs enchanted, where the siren sings,

And coral reefs lie bare,

Where the cold sea-maids rise to sun their streaming hair.

Its webs of living gauze no more unfurl;

Wrecked is the ship of pearl!

And every chambered cell,

Where its dim dreaming life was wont to dwell,

As the frail tenant shaped his growing shell,

Before thee lies revealed,

Its irised ceiling rent, its sunless crypt unsealed!

Year after year beheld the silent toil

That spread his lustrous coil;

Still, as the spiral grew,

He left the past year's dwelling for the new,

Stole with soft step its shining archway through,

Built up its idle door,

Stretched in his last-found home, and knew the old no more.

Thanks for the heavenly message brought by thee,

Child of the wandering sea,

Cast from her lap, forlorn!

From thy dead lips a clearer note is born

Than ever Triton blew from wreathèèd horn!

While on mine ear it rings,

Through the deep caves of thought I hear a voice that sings:

Build thee more stately mansions, O my soul,

As the swift seasons roll!

Leave thy low-vaulted past!

Let each new temple, nobler than the last,

Shut thee from heaven with a dome more vast,

Till thou at length art free,

Leaving thine outgrown shell by life's unresting sea!

The Last Leaf

I SAW him once before,
As he passed by the door;
And again
The pavement stones resound,
As he totters o'er the ground
With his cane.

They say that in his prime,
Ere the pruning-knife of Time
Cut him down,
Not a better man was found
By the Crier on his round
Through the town.

But now he walks the streets,
And he looks at all he meets
Sad and wan;
And shakes his feeble head,
That it seems as if he said,
"They are gone."

The mossy marbles rest
On the lips that he has prest
In their bloom;
And the names he loved to hear
Have been carved for many a year
On the tomb.

My grandmamma has said
Poor old lady, she is dead
Long ago
That he had a Roman nose,
And his cheek was like a rose
In the snow.

But now his nose is thin,
And it rests upon his chin
Like a staff;
And a crook is in his back,
And a melancholy crack
In his laugh.

I know it is a sin
For me to sit and grin
At him here;
But the old three-cornered hat,
And the breeches and all that,
Are so queer!

And if I should live to be
The last leaf upon the tree
In the spring,
Let them smile, as I do now,
At the old forsaken bough
Where I cling.

Assignments

- Warm-up: Who is " The Last Leaf" describing?
- Students should complete Concept Builder 9-B.
- Student should review reading(s) from the next chapter.
- Student should outline essay due at the end of the week.
- Per teacher instructions, students may answer orally, in a group setting, some of the essays that are not assigned as formal essays.

In "A Psalm of Life" Longfellow makes assumptions about Christianity that are untrue. Examine these quotes and discuss what assumptions he is making.

Quotes	False Assumptions
Tell me not, in mournful numbers, Life is but an empty dream!	
Life is real! Life is earnest! And the grave is not its goal; Dust thou art, to dust returnest, Was not spoken of the soul.	
Trust no Future, howe'er pleasant! Let the dead Past bury its dead! Act, act in the living Present! Heart within, and God o'erhead!	

James Russell Lowell

James Russell Lowell (1819–1891) was born at Cambridge, Massachusetts, the son of a Unitarian minister. Educated at Harvard College, he tried the law, but soon gave it up for literature. In 1857 he became the first editor of the *Atlantic Monthly*, and after 1864 he collaborated with Charles Eliot Norton in the editorship of the *North American Review*.

Selections from the Bigalow Papers

What Mr. Robinson Thinks

GUVENER B. is a sensible man;

He stays to his home an' looks arter his folks;

He draws his furrer ez straight ez he can,

An' into nobody's tater-patch pokes;

But John P.

Robinson he

Sez he wunt vote fer Guvener B.

My! aint it terrible? Wut shall we du?

We can't never choose him o' course, thet's flat;

Guess we shall hev to come round, (don't you?)

An' go in fer thunder an' guns, an' all that;

Fer John P.

Robinson he

Sez he wunt vote fer Guvener B.

Gineral C. is a dreffle smart man;

He's ben on all sides thet give places or pelf;

But consistency still wuz a part of his plan,

He's been true to one party, an' thet is himself;

So John P.

Robinson he

Sez he shall vote fer Gineral C.

Gineral C. he goes in fer the war;

He don't vally principle morn'n an old cud;

Wut did God make us raytional creeturs fer,

But glory an' gunpowder, plunder an' blood?

So John P.

Robinson he

Sez he shall vote fer Gineral C.

We were gittin' on nicely up here to our village,

With good old idees o' wut's right an' wut aint,

We kind o' thought Christ went agin war an' pillage,

An' thet eppyletts worn't the best mark of a saint;

But John P.

Robinson he

Sez this kind o' thing's an exploded idee.

The side of our country must ollers be took,

An' Presidunt Polk, you know, he is our country.

An' the angel thet writes all our sins in a book

Puts the debit to him, an' to us the per contry;

An' John P.

Robinson he

Sez this is his view o' the thing to a T.

Parson Wilbur he calls all these argimunts lies;

Sez they're nothin, on airth but jest fee, faw, fum:
An' thet all this big talk of our destinies
Is half on it ign'ance, an' t'other half rum;
But John P.
Robinson he
Sez it aint no sech thing; an', of course, so must we.
Parson Wilbur sez he never heerd in his life
Thet th' Apostles rigged out in their swaller-tail coats,
An' marched round in front of a drum an' a fife,
To git some on 'em office, an' some on 'em votes;

But John P.
Robinson he
Sez they didn't know everythin' down in Judee.
Wal, it's a marcy we've gut folks to tell us
The rights an' the wrongs o' these matters, I vow,
God sends country lawyers, an' other wise fellers,
To start the world's team wen it gits in a slough;
Fer John P.
Robinson he
Sez the world'll go right, ef he hollers out Gee!

Assignments

- Warm-up: Give an example of satire in "The Biglow Papers" and discuss its purpose.
- Students should complete Concept Builder 9-C.
- Students should write rough drafts of assigned essay.
- The teacher may correct rough drafts.

CONCEPT BUILDER 9-C
Theme

In "The Chambered Nautilus" Oliver Wendell Holmes uses the image of a sea urchin to talk about life.

Year after year beheld the silent toil
That spread his lustrous coil;
Still, as the spiral grew,
He left the past year's dwelling for the new,
Stole with soft step its shining archway through,
Built up its idle door,
Stretched in his last-found home, and knew the old no more.

Re-read the end of the poem and reflect on what theme (core meaning) Holmes is trying to communicate.

Leave thy low-vaulted past!

Let each new temple, nobler than the last,

Shut thee from heaven with a dome more vast,

Till thou at length art free,

Leaving thine outgrown shell by life's unresting sea!

John Greenleaf Whittier

John Greenleaf Whittier (1807–1892) was also a New Englander who was also an abolitionist.

The Barefoot Boy

Blessings on thee, little man,
Barefoot boy, with cheek of tan!
With thy turned-up pantaloons,
And thy merry whistled tunes;
With thy red lip, redder still
Kissed by strawberries on the hill;
With the sunshine on thy face,
Through thy torn brim's jaunty grace;
From my heart I give thee joy, —
I was once a barefoot boy!
Prince thou art, — the grown-up man
Only is republican.
Let the million-dollared ride!
Barefoot, trudging at his side,
Thou hast more than he can buy
In the reach of ear and eye, —
Outward sunshine, inward joy:
Blessings on thee, barefoot boy!

Oh for boyhood's painless play,
Sleep that wakes in laughing day,
Health that mocks the doctor's rules,
Knowledge never learned of schools,
Of the wild bee's morning chase,
Of the wild-flower's time and place,

Flight of fowl and habitude
Of the tenants of the wood;
How the tortoise bears his shell,
How the woodchuck digs his cell,
And the ground-mole sinks his well;
How the robin feeds her young,
How the oriole's nest is hung;
Where the whitest lilies blow,
Where the freshest berries grow,
Where the ground-nut trails its vine,
Where the wood-grape's clusters shine;
Of the black wasp's cunning way,
Mason of his walls of clay,
And the architectural plans
Of gray hornet artisans!
For, eschewing books and tasks,
Nature answers all he asks;
Hand in hand with her he walks,
Face to face with her he talks,
Part and parcel of her joy, —
Blessings on the barefoot boy!

Oh for boyhood's time of June,
Crowding years in one brief moon,
When all things I heard or saw,

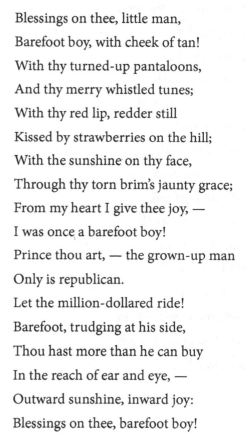

Me, their master, waited for.
I was rich in flowers and trees,
Humming-birds and honey-bees;
For my sport the squirrel played,
Plied the snouted mole his spade;
For my taste the blackberry cone
Purpled over hedge and stone;
Laughed the brook for my delight
Through the day and through the night,
Whispering at the garden wall,
Talked with me from fall to fall;
Mine the sand-rimmed pickerel pond,
Mine the walnut slopes beyond,
Mine, on bending orchard trees,
Apples of Hesperides!
Still as my horizon grew,
Larger grew my riches too;
All the world I saw or knew
Seemed a complex Chinese toy,
Fashioned for a barefoot boy!
Oh for festal dainties spread,
Like my bowl of milk and bread;
Pewter spoon and bowl of wood,
On the door-stone, gray and rude!
O'er me, like a regal tent,
Cloudy-ribbed, the sunset bent,
Purple-curtained, fringed with gold,
Looped in many a wind-swung fold;

While for music came the play
Of the pied frogs' orchestra;
And, to light the noisy choir,
Lit the fly his lamp of fire.
I was monarch: pomp and joy
Waited on the barefoot boy!

Cheerily, then, my little man,
Live and laugh, as boyhood can!
Though the flinty slopes be hard,
Stubble-speared the new-mown sward,
Every morn shall lead thee through
Fresh baptisms of the dew;
Every evening from thy feet
Shall the cool wind kiss the heat:
All too soon these feet must hide
In the prison cells of pride,
Lose the freedom of the sod,
Like a colt's for work be shod,
Made to treat the mills of toil,
Up and down in ceaseless moil:
Happy if their track be found
Never on forbidden ground;
Happy if they sink not in
Quick and treacherous sands of sin.
Ah! that thou couldst know thy joy,
Ere it passes, barefoot boy!

Assignments

- Warm-up: There is a theme of mutability in "The Barefoot Boy." Define what mutability is and find an example.
- Students should complete Concept Builder 9-D.
- Student will re-write corrected copies of essays due tomorrow.

Style is the technique authors use to communicate their truths. Emily Dickinson, discussed in lesson 5, liked to use quatrains, or stanzas of four lines, that, to her, repeated the songs she heard in church. She also wrote in free verse (lines that do not rhyme). Finally, she freely violated grammar rules. In the following poem find examples of each element.

I'm Nobody! Who Are You?
I'm nobody! Who are you?

Are you nobody, too?
Then there's a pair of us — don't tell!
They'd banish us, you know.
How dreary to be somebody!
How public, like a frog
To tell your name the livelong day
To an admiring bog!

1	Quatrains	
2	Free verse	
3	Violated grammar rules	

Emily Dickinson

Emily Dickinson, the "belle of Amherst," is almost as famous for her mysteriously secluded life as for her poetry, which ranks her with Walt Whitman as one of the most gifted poets in modern American literature. In fact, she and Whitman introduced "realism in poetry." She never married, and after age 30 she became a recluse. Some scholars believe that this was her response to the narrow literary establishment of her time, which expected female writers to limit their subjects to home life and romance. Dickinson, on the other hand, preferred images of real life.

Of Dickinson's 1,700-plus poems, only 10 were published in her lifetime, and those without her permission. After her death, however, her sister found and published the body of her work. Dickinson wrote from a romantic worldview in a decidedly modern way.

Emancipation

No rack can torture me,

My soul's at liberty

Behind this mortal bone

There knits a bolder one

You cannot prick with saw, Nor rend with scymitar.

Two bodies therefore be;

Bind one, and one will flee.

The eagle of his nest

No easier divest

And gain the sky,

Than mayest thou,

Except thyself may be

Thine enemy;

Captivity is consciousness,

So's liberty.

I'm Nobody! Who Are You?

I'm nobody! Who are you?

Are you nobody, too?

Then there 's a pair of us — don't tell!

They 'd banish us, you know.

How dreary to be somebody!

How public, like a frog

To tell your name the livelong day

To an admiring bog!

Assignments

- Warm-up: Dickinson was a very private person. Do you think she would have written on different subjects if she knew that you — the public — would be reading her poetry?

- Students should complete Concept Builder 9-E.

- Essays are due. Students should take the chapter 9 test.

Now it is your turn! Using Dickinson's style, write four-line poems describing these topics:

Fun	
Love	
Family	

Chapter 10

1840–1855 (Part 3):

Romanticism: New England Renaissance

First Thoughts Born in 1803, Ralph Waldo Emerson began his working life as a Unitarian preacher. Early widowhood plunged him into a crisis of faith (already weakened by Unitarian universalism), and he resigned his ministry in 1832. He abandoned any semblance of theism. In nature alone he found his comfort and direction. But Emerson had an ambivalent viewpoint toward nature. He loved and respected nature, but to Emerson, nature was all-powerful and reverent. Emerson's faith ultimately strayed into pantheistic nature worship. Pantheism argues that God is alive everywhere — in animate and inanimate objects alike. There is nothing new under the sun! Likenesses of Emerson's pantheism were very common in the Bible. In the Old Testament, worship of Baal (attacked by Elijah) was very similar to Emerson's transcendentalism. Such a thing was coming again to America in the 1830s.

Author Worldview Watch Ralph Waldo Emerson was a failure at farming and at pastoring. Unitarianism was a haven for his injured soul but this cold, leprous faith offers little succor to the heart. Perhaps it was this passion, a sort of apostasy that empowered his human centered but romantic directed poetry and prose.

Chapter Learning Objectives In chapter 10 we look more closely at Ralph Waldo Emerson's writing that goes far beyond romanticism and into pantheistic or universalism worship. Students will analyze poems by Ralph Waldo Emerson.

As a result of this chapter study you will be able to . . .

1. Identify the worldview in "The Snowstorm."

2. Find instances in the Bible where nature is controlled by God.

3. Give several evidences of transcendentalism from these poems. Compare the poetry of Ralph Waldo Emerson with that of another New England poet, Anne Bradstreet.

Weekly Essay Options: Begin on page 274 of the Teacher Guide.

Reading ahead: *Walden*, by Henry David Thoreau

History connections: *American History* chapter 10, "Age of Reform."

Ralph Waldo Emerson

Ralph Waldo Emerson represents well the transition from puritanism to transcendentalism. Though closely related to European romanticism, transcendentalism was a philosophical movement that had a peculiarly American flavor. Both celebrated individualism and subjectivity. Both argued that the intuition was more important than stated fact. Two of the most famous European romantics were Goethe and Beethoven. Two of the most famous American transcendentalists were Emerson and Thoreau, with optimism and hope uncharacteristic of the post-Civil War.

My Garden

If I could put my woods in song
And tell what's there enjoyed,
All men would to my gardens throng,
And leave the cities void.

In my plot no tulips blow,--
Snow-loving pines and oaks instead;
And rank the savage maples grow
From Spring's faint flush to Autumn red.

My garden is a forest ledge
Which older forests bound;
The banks slope down to the blue lake-edge,
Then plunge to depths profound.

Here once the Deluge ploughed,
Laid the terraces, one by one;
Ebbing later whence it flowed,
They bleach and dry in the sun.

The sowers made haste to depart,--
The wind and the birds which sowed it;
Not for fame, nor by rules of art,
Planted these, and tempests flowed it.

Waters that wash my garden-side

Play not in Nature's lawful web,
They heed not moon or solar tide,--
Five years elapse from flood to ebb.

…

Keen ears can catch a syllable,
As if one spake to another,
In the hemlocks tall, untamable,
And what the whispering grasses smother.

…

Canst thou copy in verse one chime
Of the wood-bell's peal and cry,
Write in a book the morning's prime,
Or match with words that tender sky?

Wonderful verse of the gods,
Of one import, of varied tone;
They chant the bliss of their abodes
To man imprisoned in his own.

Ever the words of the gods resound;
But the porches of man's ear
Seldom in this low life's round
Are unsealed, that he may hear.

Wandering voices in the air
And murmurs in the wold
Speak what I cannot declare,
Yet cannot all withhold.

When the shadow fell on the lake,
The whirlwind in ripples wrote
Air-bells of fortune that shine and break,
And omens above thought.

But the meanings cleave to the lake,
Cannot be carried in book or urn;
Go thy ways now, come later back,
On waves and hedges still they burn.

These the fates of men forecast,
Of better men than live to-day;
If who can read them comes at last
He will spell in the sculpture, 'Stay.'

- Warm-up: : Research transcendentalism and the effect it had on American thought.
- Students should complete Concept Builder 10-A.
- Students review the required reading(s) *before* the assigned chapter begins.
- Teachers may want to discuss assigned reading(s) with students.
- Teachers shall assign the required essay. The rest of the essays can be outlined, answered with shorter answers, discussed, or skipped.
- Students will review all readings for chapter 10.

CONCEPT BUILDER 10-A
Active Reading

"The Snowstorm"
Ralph Waldo Emerson

Announced by all the trumpets of the sky,
Arrives the snow, and, driving o'er the fields,
Seems nowhere to alight: the whited air
Hides hills and woods, the river, and the heaven,
And veils the farmhouse at the garden's end.
The sled and traveler stopped, the courier's feet
Delayed, all friends shut out, the housemates sit
Around the radiant fireplace, enclosed
In a tumultuous privacy of storm.

Come see the north wind's masonry.
Out of an unseen quarry evermore
Furnished with tile, the fierce artificer
Curves his white bastions with projected roof
Round every windward stake, or tree, or door.
Speeding, the myriad-handed, his wild work
So fanciful, so savage, nought cares he
For number or proportion. Mockingly,
On coop or kennel he hangs Parian wreaths;

A swanlike form invests the hidden thorn;
Fills up the farmer's lane from wall to wall,
Maugre the farmer's sighs; and at the gate
A tapering turret overtops the work.
And when his hours are numbered, and the world
Is all his own, retiring, as he were not,
Leaves, when the sun appears, astonished Art
To mimic in slow structures, stone by stone,
Built in an age, the mad wind's night-work,
The frolic architecture of the snow.

Who/what is coming?

What sort of things will the snowstorm do?

Who is the architect of the snow?

What sort of creature is he?

"Day"
Ralph Waldo Emerson

DAUGHTERS of Time, the hypocritic Days,
Muffled and dumb like barefoot dervishes,
And marching single in an endless file,
Bring diadems and fagots in their hands.
To each they offer gifts after his will,
Bread, kingdoms, stars, and sky that holds them all.
I, in my pleached garden, watched the pomp,
Forgot my morning wishes, hastily
Took a few herbs and apples, and the Day
Turned and departed silent. I, too late,
Under her solemn fillet saw the scorn.

Assignments

- Warm-up: In Emerson's poem "Day," why is the day scornful? Write an essay explaining at whom the scorn is directed.

- Students should complete Concept Builder 10-B.

- Student should review reading(s) from the next chapter.

- Student should outline essay due at the end of the week.

- Per teacher instructions, students may answer orally, in a group setting, some of the essays that are not assigned as formal essays.

Emerson makes frequent use of figurative language. He compares one idea and another that is quite different. He, and other poets, use four degrees or stages of subtlety in putting image/comparisons together:

1	Simple comparisons, "the man was as hungry as a horse."
2	Comparisons where the poet states that two things are like one another, but the reader must discover for how they are alike. "The pool at evening is like a darkened mirror," is this sort of comparison.
3	Comparisons that drop the word that indicates that the two are only like each or, not the same as each other. For example, "Love is a many–splendored thing."
4	The subtlest but most effective comparison is a comparison that is only implied, not stated. For example, Shakespeare describes ambition as a horse, and Macbeth is the rider. "I have no spur / To prick the sides of my intent, but only / Vaulting ambition, which overleaps itself? And falls on the other [side].

Match the above descriptions with the following examples.

___ A	Daughters of Time, the hypocritic Days / Muffled and dumb like barefoot dervishes, And marching single in an endless file.
___ B	Is all his own, retiring, as he were not, Leaves, when the sun appears, astonished Art To mimic in slow structures, stone by stone, Built in an age, the mad wind's night-work, The frolic architecture of the snow.
___ C	Why thou wert there, O rival of the rose! I never thought to ask, I never knew: But, in my simple ignorance, suppose The self-same Power that brought me there brought you.
___ D	Announced by all the trumpets of the sky, Arrives the snow, and, driving o'er the fields, Seems nowhere to alight: the whited air Hides hills and woods, the river, and the heaven, And veils the farm-house at the garden's end.

"The Rhodora"
Ralph Waldo Emerson

The Rhodora

In May, when sea-winds pierced our solitudes,
I found the fresh Rhodora in the woods,
Spreading its leafless blooms in a damp nook,
To please the desert and the sluggish brook.
The purple petals, fallen in the pool,

Made the black water with their beauty gay;
Here might the red-bird come his plumes to cool,
And court the flower that cheapens his array.
Rhodora! if the sages ask thee why
This charm is wasted on the earth and sky,
Tell them, dear, that if eyes were made for seeing,
Then Beauty is its own excuse for being:

Why thou wert there, O rival of the rose!
I never thought to ask, I never knew:
But, in my simple ignorance, suppose
The self-same Power that brought me there brought you.

Fable

The mountain and the squirrel
Had a quarrel,
And the former called the latter "Little Prig."
Bun replied,
"You are doubtless very big;
But all sorts of things and weather
Must be taken in together,
To make up a year
And a sphere.
And I think it no disgrace
To occupy my place.
If I'm not so large as you,
You are not so small as I,
And not half so spry.
I'll not deny you make
A very pretty squirrel track;
Talents differ; all is well and wisely put;
If I cannot carry forests on my back,
Neither can you crack a nut."

- Warm-up: Based on "The Rhodora," what is Emerson's idea of a god? Emerson could not accept the idea that God is separate from man and nature; in other words, Emerson was not a Christian believer. Yet, in his own way, he was a deeply religious person. How is this revealed in the last four lines of the poem? Using the poems above, and other Emerson writings, show how Emerson was "religious."
- Students should complete Concept Builder 10-C.
- Students should write rough drafts of all assigned essays.
- The teacher may correct rough drafts.

CONCEPT BUILDER 10-C
Making Comparisons

Effective comparisons:
- **are fresh, new comparisons, not clichés!**
- **are specific — not vague comparisons**
- **are within the experience of your reader**

Now it is your turn. Using these guidelines, write some phrases that compare to how the following words feel.

Loneliness	Loneliness is a cold, icy morning in the middle of December. A day full of bleak, sterile cold — unadorned by pleasant, hopeful snowfall.
Hope	
Tentativeness	

What Critics Say

Matthew Arnold, in an address on Emerson delivered in Boston, gave an excellent estimate of the rank we should accord to him in the great hierarchy of letters. Some perhaps will think that Arnold was unappreciative and cold, but dispassionate readers will be inclined to agree with his judgment of our great American.

After a review of the poetical works of Emerson the English critic draws his conclusions as follows:

"I do not then place Emerson among the great poets. But I go farther, and say that I do not place him among the great writers, the great men of letters. Who are the great men of letters? They are men like Cicero, Plato, Bacon, Pascal, Swift, Voltaire — writers with, in the first place, a genius and instinct for style. . . . Brilliant and powerful passages in a man's writings do not prove his possession of it. Emerson has passages of noble and pathetic eloquence; he has passages of shrewd and felicitous wit; he has crisp epigram; he has passages of exquisitely touched observation of nature. Yet he is not a great writer. . . . Carlyle formulates perfectly the defects of his friend's poetic and literary productions when he says: 'For me it is too ethereal, speculative, theoretic; I will have all things condense themselves, take shape and body, if they are to have my sympathy.'"

. . . Not with the Miltons and Grays, not with the Platos and Spinozas, not with the Swifts and Voltaires, not with the Montaignes and Addisons, can we rank Emerson. No man could see this clearer than Emerson himself. 'Alas, my friend,' he writes in reply to Carlyle, who had exhorted him to creative work, — 'Alas, my friend, I can do no such gay thing as you say. I do not belong to the poets, but only to a low department of literature, — the reporters; suburban men.' He deprecated his friend's praise;

praise 'generous to a fault' he calls it; praise 'generous to the shaming of me, — cold, fastidious, ebbing person that I am.'"

After all this unfavorable criticism Arnold begins to praise. Quoting passages from the *Essays*, he adds:

"This is tonic indeed! And let no one object that it is too general; that more practical, positive direction is what we want. . . . Yes, truly, his insight is admirable; his truth is precious. Yet the secret of his effect is not even in these; it is in his temper. It is in the hopeful, serene, beautiful temper wherewith these, in Emerson, are indissolubly united; in which they work and have their being. . . . One can scarcely overrate the importance of holding fast to happiness and hope. It gives to Emerson's work an invaluable virtue. As Wordsworth's poetry is, in my judgment, the most important done in verse, in our language, during the present century, so Emerson's Essays are, I think, the most important work done in prose. . . . But by his conviction that in the life of the spirit is happiness, and by his hope that this life of the spirit will come more and more to be sanely understood, and to prevail, and to work for happiness, — by this conviction and hope Emerson was great, and he will surely prove in the end to have been right in them. . . . You cannot prize him too much, nor heed him too diligently."

E.P. Whipple, the well-known American critic, wrote soon after Emerson's death:

"But 'sweetness and light' are precious and inspiring only so far as they express the essential sweetness of the disposition of the thinker, and the essential illuminating power of his intelligence. Emerson's greatness came from his character. Sweetness and light streamed from him because they were in him. In everything he thought, wrote, and did, we feel the presence of a personality as vigorous and brave as it was sweet, and the particular radical thought he at any time expressed derived its power to animate and illuminate other minds from the might of the manhood, which was felt to be within and behind it. To 'sweetness and light' he therefore added the prime quality of fearless manliness.

"If the force of Emerson's character was thus inextricably blended with the force of all his faculties of intellect and imagination, and the refinement of all his sentiments, we have still to account for the peculiarities of his genius, and to answer the question, why do we instinctively apply the epithet 'Emersonian' to every characteristic passage in his writings? We are told that he was the last in a long line of clergymen, his ancestors, and that the modern doctrine of heredity accounts for the impressive emphasis he laid on the moral sentiment; but that does not solve the puzzle why he unmistakably differed in his nature and genius from all other Emersons. An imaginary genealogical chart of descent connecting him with Confucius or Gautama would be more satisfactory.

"What distinguishes the Emerson was his exceptional genius and character, that something in him which separated him from all other Emersons, as it separated him from all other eminent men of letters, and impressed every intelligent reader with the feeling that he was not only 'original but aboriginal.' Some traits of his mind and character may be traced back to his ancestors, but what doctrine of heredity can give us the genesis of his genius? Indeed, the safest course to pursue is to quote his own words, and despairingly confess that it is the nature of genius 'to spring, like the rainbow daughter of Wonder, from the invisible, to abolish the past, and refuse all history'" (Ralph Waldo Emerson, *Essays*, New York: Charles E. Merrill, 1910), p. 11, www.gutenberg.org/files/16643/16643-h/16643-h.htm).

Assignments

- Warm-up: In what way is this statement by the transcendentalist/romantic Emerson about Jesus inconsistent with a Christian theistic worldview? "An immense progress in natural and religious knowledge has been made since his death. Yet in the 'Life of Christ' I have thought him a Christian Plato; so rich and great was his philosophy. Is it possible the intellect should be so inconsistent with itself? It is singular also that the bishop's morality should sometimes trip, as in his explanation of false witness."

- Students should complete Concept Builder 10-D.

- Students will re-write corrected copy of essay due tomorrow.

The last six lines of "The Snowstorm" contain a description of the events of the next morning. What is Emerson trying to say? What is his worldview? Which does the author consider the true artist? Support your conclusions with references from the poem.

The snowstorm is over. All creation is at rest. This scene evokes the same sobriety of the creation scene in Genesis 1. As God rested in Genesis 1, nature rests at the end of "The Snowstorm."

And when his hours are numbered, and the world
Is all his own, retiring, as he were not,
Leaves, when the sun appears, astonished Art
To mimic in slow structures, stone by stone,
Built in an age, the mad wind's night-work,
The frolic architecture of the snow.

Therefore,

Spiritual War

Ralph Waldo Emerson did much damage to Christianity. His universalism, incorporated into unitarianism/transcendentalism, drew many Christians away from the faith. Read the following texts from Emerson's essay "Nature" (1836). I have provided the lie that is clearly exhibited by the excerpts. Spiritual warfare is uncovering deceptions and speaking truth based on the Word of God. What Scriptures would you quote to refute the lies below?

The texts below are from "Nature" (1836):

The Lie	Direct revelation comes to man through nature.

The foregoing generations beheld God face to face; we, through their eyes. Why should not we also enjoy an original relation to the universe? Why should not we have . . . a religion by revelation to us, and not the history of theirs? Embosomed for a season in nature, whose floods of life stream around and through us, and invite us by the powers they supply, to action . . . ?

The Truth	Revelation comes to man through God; He has chosen to speak most definitively to us through the Word of God.

The Lie	"God" exists everywhere — but especially in Nature.

. One might think the atmosphere was made transparent with this design, to give man, in the heavenly bodies, the perpetual presence of the sublime. . . . If the stars should appear one night in a thousand years, how would men believe and adore; and preserve for many generations the remembrance of the City of God which had been shown! . . . But all natural objects make a kindred impression, when the mind is open to their influence. . . . Nature says, — he is my creature. . . .

The Truth	God is omniscient, but He is also omnipotent. He is not to be sentimentalized. He is to be worshiped. He is no man's creature!

The Lie	Nature unifies us all.

A leaf, a drop, a crystal, a moment of time is related to the whole, and partakes of the perfection of the whole. Each particle is a microcosm, and faithfully renders the likeness of the world. . . . So intimate is this Unity, that, it is easily seen, it lies under the undermost garment of nature, and betrays its source in the Universal Spirit. . . .

The Truth	Man is hopelessly lost without the Lord Jesus Christ. All have sinned, all are separated from God and one another without the miraculous intervention of God. Furthermore, man is separate from animals. He has a soul and was commanded by God in the Bible to rule over the other animals. Only man is created in the image of God.

Assignments

- Warm-up: At the same time that Emerson was writing his poetry, the well-attended revivals led by Charles Finney were being held in upstate New York. In fact, this revival had a greater impact than Emerson's essays and poetry on American society. Literature books rarely print a sermon by Charles Finney, even though many more people read his sermons and attended his revivals. Why?
- Students should complete Concept Builder 10-E.
- Essays are due. Students should take the chapter 10 test.

CONCEPT BUILDER 10-E
Transcendentalism

Transcendentalism was an American version of European romanticism, but transcendentalism had a decidedly religious tone. The following were elements of transcendentalism:	
1	There is an absence of an omnipotent God; nature was omniscient.
2	Nature is venerated, if not worshiped.
3	Subjectivity is celebrated — empiricism is suspect.
Match the above elements of transcendentalism with the following passages:	
____ A	Built in an age, the mad wind's night-work, The frolic architecture of the snow.
____ B	But, in my simple ignorance, suppose The self-same Power that brought me there brought you.
____ C	Tell them, dear, that if eyes were made for seeing, Then Beauty is its own excuse for being.

1840–1855 (Part 4):

Romanticism: New England Renaissance

First Thoughts

America experienced an unprecedented reform movement from 1840–1855. At the center of this movement were New Englanders, notably Ralph Waldo Emerson and Henry David Thoreau. *Walden Pond*, in particular, captured the imagination of an age, and along the way encouraged quite a lot of chicanery!

Author Worldview Watch

There is a Harvard Divinity School legend that Thoreau was lazy and charming--a fatal combination in the search for a productive Christian life but fared him well in the pretentious rarefied air of ante-bellum New England. Thoreau was sort of a theist, sort of a romantic, but mostly a sanguine, facile thinker who lived alone on a pond for a year but purported to have taken his clothes home to his mom to wash every weekend. With his belief that God is found in nature, Thoreau endures as one of America's romantic authors. However, the Christian theist knows that God is greater than any of His creation.

Chapter Learning Objectives

Chapter 11 develops Henry David Thoreau's *Walden* and revisits romanticism. You will analyze *Walden* by Henry David Thoreau.

As a result of this chapter study you will be able to . . .

1. Analyze the quote by Ezra Pound.

2. Evaluate Thoreau's views on death.

3. Explain why this book was so popular in the 1960s.

Weekly Essay Options: Begin on page 274 of the Teacher Guide.

Reading ahead: *Billy Budd*, by Herman Melville

Age of Reform

Antebellum America generated an extraordinary outpouring of literary creativity, unprecedented at that time, and not to be equaled until the hedonistic 1960s. American artists and writers abandoned their subservience to foreign models—particularly English models-- and created a distinctly American literature.

For example, Edgar Allan Poe (1809–1849) dominated the short story literary genre. Poe invented the short detective novel. At the same time he edited a highly respected literary journal.

Nathaniel Hawthorne (1804–1864) was to the novel what Poe was to poetry. Hawthorne was the Dostoevsky of his time. "In the depths of every human heart," Hawthorne wrote in an early tale, "there is a tomb and a dungeon, though the lights, the music, the revelry above may cause us to forget their existence, and the buried ones, or prisoners whom they hide." (www.digitalhistory.uh.edu/database/article_display.cfm?HHID=645). In his fiction, Hawthorne, more than any other early 19th-century American writer, challenged the larger society's faith in science, technology, progress, and humanity's essential goodness. His effort would be paralleled later by the English novelist Mary Shelley.

Herman Melville (1819–1891), author of *Moby Dick* (1851), possibly America's greatest romance, but certainly its longest, took American by storm.

Municipal ferry, named *Brooklyn*, City of New York, c1909 (LOC, PD-US).

Meanwhile, historian Steve Mintz writes, "In 1842, Ralph Waldo Emerson lectured in New York and called for a truly original American poet who could fashion verse out of 'the factory, the railroad, and the wharf.' Sitting in Emerson's audience was a 22-year-old New York printer and journalist named Walt Whitman (1819–1892). A carpenter's son with only five years of schooling, Whitman soon became Emerson's ideal of the Native American poet, with the publication of *Leaves of Grass* in 1855. "A mixture of Yankee transcendentalism and New York rowdyism," *Leaves of Grass* was, wrote Emerson, "the most extraordinary piece of wit & wisdom that America has yet contributed." Most reviewers,

Panoramic shot of New York City, 1900 (LOC, PD-US).

however, reacted scornfully to the book, deeming it "trashy, profane & obscene" for its sexual frankness. A sprawling portrait of America, encompassing every aspect of American life, from the steam-driven Brooklyn ferry to the use of ether in surgery, the volume opens not with the author's name but simply with his daguerreotype (a forerunner of the photograph). Unconventional in style--Whitman invented "free verse" rather than use conventionally rhymed or regularly metered verse--the volume stands out as a landmark in the history of American literature for its celebration of the diversity, the energy, and the expansiveness of pre–Civil War America." (www.digitalhistory.uh.edu/credits.cfm).

Fifth Ave. Hotel, c1888 (LOC, PD-US).

Assignments

- Warm-up: If you could join a reform movement, what would it be?
- Students should complete Concept Builder 11-A.
- Students review the required reading(s) *before* the assigned chapter begins.
- Teachers may want to discuss assigned reading(s) with students.
- Teachers shall assign the required essay. The rest of the essays can be outlined, answered with shorter answers, discussed, or skipped.
- Students will review all readings for chapter 11.

CONCEPT BUILDER 11-A Active Reading		
	Read Walden (Chapter Two) by Henry David Thoreau then answer the following questions.	
	1	What is Thoreau's remedy for the hustle and bustle of life?
	2	Why did Thoreau move into the woods?
	3	Thoreau loves hyperbole, or exaggeration. What is he exaggerating here?

Henry David Thoreau

Henry David Thoreau was born in 1817 to an ordinary family in Concord, Massachusetts, and lived most of his life in the Northeast. He was the third child of a small businessman named John Thoreau and his sanguine, talkative wife, Cynthia Dunbar Thoreau. His parents sent him in 1828 to Concord Academy where he impressed his teachers and so was permitted to prepare for college. Upon graduating from the academy, he entered Harvard in 1833. Graduating in the middle ranks of the class of 1837, he searched for a teaching job and secured one in Concord at his old grammar school. He was not successful at these jobs until he embraced the romanticism of his good friend Ralph Waldo Emerson and started writing verse. In 1845 the certifiable eccentric Henry David Thoreau leased some land owned by his friend and mentor Ralph Waldo Emerson on Walden Pond near Concord, Massachusetts, and lived in a cabin on it for two years, two months, and two days. While there, Thoreau wrote one of the most memorable, if egocentric, journal/novels in American literature.

Assignments

- Warm-up: Thoreau extols hard work while doing very little of it. Is he a sensitive observer of nature or a lazy over-educated snob hanging out doing nothing for a year?
- Students should complete Concept Builder 11-B.
- Student should review reading(s) from the next chapter.
- Student should outline essay due at the end of the week.
- Per teacher instructions, students may answer orally, in a group setting, some of the essays that are not assigned as formal essays.

CONCEPT BUILDER 11-B Observation		Examine the picture. ⟶
	1	Of what is it a picture?
	2	Look more closely. Compare it to a dissimilar object.
	3	Contrast the lines/veins of the leaf with the external texture.
	4	What is its purpose?
	5	How is this picture like life?

Student Essay

"As I turned to my hoeing again I was filled with an inexpressible confidence, and pursued my labor cheerfully with a calm trust in the future." Henry David Thoreau, a philosopher and proponent of the transcendental worldview, conducted the memorable experiment of living alone on the shores of Walden Pond in a cabin for two years, two months, and two days. From this experiment came Thoreau's famous novel, *Walden*. Thoreau's novel extols the benefits of labor done with one's own hands and the satisfaction that lies in this. However, Thoreau extols hard work while doing very little of it with his own hands. Is Thoreau a sensitive observer of nature or a lazy eccentric who spent a fruitless and slothful two years in the woods? Although Thoreau preached a passionate message in his *Walden*, he did not practice his beliefs, and was more indolent than hard-working.

Thoreau extols solitude and hard work as being the panacea to all ills in the human life. Although Thoreau lived at Walden Pond, he hardly forged his own living, his substance of livelihood being taken mostly from the town shops and grocers (www. suite101.com/content/the-littleknown-henry-david-thoreau-revealed-a64538). Thoreau's time, in fact, seems to have been mostly spent on observing the beauty of nature.

THIS IS A delicious evening, when the whole body is one sense, and imbibes delight through every pore. I go and come with a strange liberty in Nature, a part of herself. As I walk along the stony shore of the pond in my shirt-sleeves, though it is cool as well as cloudy and windy, and I see nothing special to attract me, all the elements are unusually congenial to me. The bullfrogs trump to usher in the night, and the note of the whip-poor-will is borne on the rippling wind from over the water. Sympathy with the fluttering alder and poplar leaves almost takes away my breath; yet, like the lake, my serenity is rippled but not ruffled.

While Thoreau makes a sensitive observant of the natural world around him, he would be better benefited by fulfilling the message of hard work and simplicity that is extolled in his *Walden*.

I Find it wholesome to be alone the greater part of the time. To be in company, even with the best, is soon wearisome and dissipating. I love to be alone. I never found the companion that was so companionable as solitude. We are for the most part more lonely when we go abroad among men than when we stay in our chambers. A man thinking or working is always alone, let him be where he will. Solitude is not measured by the miles of space that intervene between a man and his fellows.

This from the man who had dinner regularly with Emerson and his contemporaries, and walked into town every weekend to have his mother do his laundry!

Henry David Thoreau was content to sit back and criticize the world around him without changing the essence of his own daily habits. Although Thoreau preached a passionate message in his *Walden*, he did not back it up with his actions. Instead of being a sensitive observer of nature, he was a lazy and over-educated idealist who refused to back up his ideals with action.

(Alouette, age 14)

Assignments

- Warm-up: : Do you agree with this essay?
- Students should complete Concept Builder 11-C.
- Students should write rough drafts of assigned essay.
- The teacher may correct rough drafts.

CONCEPT BUILDER 11-C
Solitude

This is a delicious evening, when the whole body is one sense, and imbibes delight through every pore. I go and come with a strange liberty in Nature, a part of herself. As I walk along the stony shore of the pond in my shirt-sleeves, though it is cool as well as cloudy and windy, and I see nothing special to attract me, all the elements are unusually congenial to me. The bullfrogs trump to usher in the night, and the note of the whip-poor-will is borne on the rippling wind from over the water. Sympathy with the fluttering alder and poplar leaves almost takes away my breath; yet, like the lake, my serenity is rippled but not ruffled. These small waves raised by the evening wind are as remote from storm as the smooth reflecting surface. Though it is now dark, the wind still blows and roars in the wood, the waves still dash, and some creatures lull the rest with their notes. The repose is never complete. The wildest animals do not repose, but seek their prey now; the fox, and skunk, and rabbit, now roam the fields and woods without fear. They are Nature's watchmen— links which connect the days of animated life. . . . Men frequently say to me, "I should think you would feel lonesome down there, and want to be nearer to folks, rainy and snowy days and nights especially." I am tempted to reply to such — This whole earth which we inhabit is but a point in space. How far apart, think you, dwell the two most distant inhabitants of yonder star, the breadth of whose disk cannot be appreciated by our instruments? Why should I feel lonely? Is not our planet in the Milky Way? This which you put seems to me not to be the most important question. What sort of space is that which separates a man from his fellows and makes him solitary? I have found that no exertion of the legs can bring two minds much nearer to one another. What do we want most to dwell near to?

1	Of what is Thoreau a part?
2	Why doesn't Thoreau feel lonely?

Poems on Thoreau

Thoreau's Flute by Louisa May Alcott

We sighing said, "Our Pan is dead;
His pipe hangs mute beside the river
Around it wistful sunbeams quiver,
But Music's airy voice is fled.
Spring mourns as for untimely frost;
The bluebird chants a requiem;
The willow-blossom waits for him;
The Genius of the wood is lost."

Then from the flute, untouched by hands,
There came a low, harmonious breath:
"For such as he there is no death;
His life the eternal life commands;
Above man's aims his nature rose.
The wisdom of a just content
Made one small spot a continent
And tuned to poetry life's prose.

"Haunting the hills, the stream, the wild,
Swallow and aster, lake and pine,
To him grew human or divine,
Fit mates for this large-hearted child.
Such homage Nature ne'er forgets,
And yearly on the coverlid
'Neath which her darling lieth hid
Will write his name in violets.

"To him no vain regrets belong
Whose soul, that finer instrument,
Gave to the world no poor lament,
But wood-notes ever sweet and strong.
O lonely friend! he still will be
A potent presence, though unseen,
Steadfast, sagacious, and serene;
Seek not for him — he is with thee."

Thoreau by Amos Bronson Alcott

WHO nearer Nature's life would truly come
Must nearest come to him of whom I speak;
He all kinds knew, — the vocal and the dumb;
Masterful in genius was he, and unique,
Patient, sagacious, tender, frolicsome.
This Concord Pan would oft his whistle take,
And forth from wood and fen, field, hill, and lake,

Trooping around him in their several guise,
The shy inhabitants their haunts forsake:
Then he, like Æsop, man would satirize,
Hold up the image wild to clearest view
Of undiscerning manhood's puzzled eyes,
And mocking say, "Lo! mirrors here for you:
Be true as these, if ye would be more wise.

The Lake Isle of Innisfree by William Butler Yeats

I will arise and go now, and go to Innisfree,

And a small cabin build there, of clay and wattles made,

Nine bean-rows will I have there, a hive for the honey bee,

And live alone in the bee-loud glade.

And I shall have some peace there, for peace comes dropping slow,

Dropping from the veils of the morning to where the cricket sings;

There midnight's all aglimmer, and noon a purple glow,

And evening full of linnet's wings.

I will arise and go now, for always night and day,

I hear lake and water lapping with low sounds by the shore;

While I stand on the roadway, or on the pavements gray,

I hear it in the deep heart's core.

Assignments

- Warm-up: Write a short poem to Thoreau.
- Students should complete Concept Builder 11-D.
- Students will re-write corrected copies of essay due tomorrow.

I left the woods for as good a reason as I went there. Perhaps it seemed to me that I had several more lives to live, and could not spare any more time for that one. It is remarkable how easily and insensibly we fall into a particular route, and make a beaten track for ourselves. I had not lived there a week before my feet wore a path from my door to the pond-side; and though it is five or six years since I trod it, it is still quite distinct. It is true, I fear, that others may have fallen into it, and so helped to keep it open. The surface of the earth is soft and impressible by the feet of men; and so with the paths which the mind travels. How worn and dusty, then, must be the highways of the world, how deep the ruts of tradition and conformity! I did not wish to take a cabin passage, but rather to go before the mast and on the deck of the world, for there I could best see the moonlight amid the mountains. I do not wish to go below now.

I learned this, at least, by my experiment: that if one advances confidently in the direction of his dreams, and endeavors to live the life which he has imagined, he will meet with a success unexpected in common hours. He will put some things behind, will pass an invisible boundary; new, universal, and more liberal laws will begin to establish themselves around and within him; or the old laws be expanded, and interpreted in his favor in a more liberal sense, and he will live with the license of a higher order of beings. In proportion as he simplifies his life, the laws of the universe will appear less complex, and solitude will not be solitude, nor poverty poverty, nor weakness weakness. If you have built castles in the air, your work need not be lost; that is where they should be. Now put the foundations under them (Ibid).

Why did Thoreau leave Walden Pond and re-enter society?

Critics and Quotes

thoreau.eserver.org/walden00.html.

"The economical details and calculations in this book are more curious than useful; for the author's life in the woods was on too narrow a scale to find imitators. But . . . he says so many pithy and brilliant things, and offers so many piquant, and, we may add, so many just, comments on society as it is, that this book is well worth the reading, both for its actual contents and its suggestive capacity."

— A.P. Peabody,
North American Review, 1854

"Thoreau, very likely without quite knowing what he was up to, took man's relation to nature and man's dilemma in society and man's capacity for elevating his spirit and he beat all these matters together, in a wild free interval of self-justification and delight, and produced an original omelette from which people can draw nourishment in a hungry day."

— E.B. White,
The Yale Review, 1954

"Our problem today is that we have allowed the internal to become lost in the external. . . . So much of modern life can be summarized in that arresting dictum of the poet Thoreau: 'Improved means to an unimproved end.' "

— Martin Luther King Jr.,
Nobel Lecture, December 11, 1964

"In Walden, Thoreau . . . opens the inner frontier of self-discovery as no American book had up to this time. As deceptively modest as Thoreau's ascetic life, it is no less than a guide to living the classical ideal of the good life. Both poetry and philosophy, this long poetic essay challenges the reader to examine his or her life and live it authentically."

— Kathryn VanSpanckeren

"The best and most Romantic memoir an American has produced is Walden — though nobody calls it one. . . . What Thoreau has to overcome during his time in the woods is not a lapse in mental health. His great problem is to escape the mental health of his neighbors, their collection-plate opinions, their studious repetition of gossip. . . . There's not a note in the book of self-pity, or nostalgia. And why did he quit his cabin in the end? 'It seemed to me that I had several more lives to live.' "

— Benjamin Kunkel

Assignments

- Warm-up: Which quote most captures your feelings toward *Walden*? Why?
- Students should complete Concept Builder 11-E.
- Essays are due. Students should take the chapter 11 test.

Pretend that you are H.D. Thoreau and you have spent a six months on Walden Pond. Your parents, however, miss you and want you to return home. Write a letter explaining why you want to live alone on Walden Pond.

Dear Mom and Dad,

Chapter 12

1840–1855 (Part 5):

Romanticism: New England Renaissance

First Thoughts Perhaps the best characterization of Melville is found in the writings of his good friend Nathaniel Hawthorne. Hawthorne describes Melville in this way:

> We took a pretty long walk together, and sat down in a hollow among the sand hills. . . . Melville, as he always does, began to reason of Providence and futurity, and of everything that lies beyond human ken, and informed me that he had "pretty much made up his mind to be annihilated"; but still he does not seem to rest in that anticipation; and, I think, will never rest until he gets hold of a definite belief. . . . He can neither believe, nor be comfortable in his unbelief; and he is too honest and courageous not to try to do one or the other. . . . (Bartleby" and "The Custom-house" Joseph J. Moldenhauer, web. ku.edu/~zeke/bartleby/moldenha.htm).

He can neither believe, nor be comfortable in his unbelief. What a marvelous description of modern man.

Author Worldview Watch Herman Melville was a great author who tries to preserve the essence of Christianity without embracing its dogma. In other words, Melville articulated a sort of

modernism that presages the cynicism of later naturalism. Perhaps the best way to understand Melville is to understand the pathetic chaplain who met with Billy Budd the night before Budd was executed. The poor man was neither a lucid theologian nor a capable counselor. But despite his good intentions, it is impossible for Christians to adhere to both theism and romanticism, as Melville attempted to do.

Chapter Learning Objectives Chapter 12 analyzes *Billy Budd* and pays particular attention to Melville's view of God and Christianity. You will analyze the romantic/naturalist novel *Billy Budd*, by Herman Melville. Students should review "Oh Captain! My Captain!" by Walt Whitman; Negro spirituals; "The Gettysburg Address" by Abraham Lincoln; and "Surrender Speech" by Chief Joseph.

As a result of this chapter study you will be able to . . .

1. Discuss a modern tragedy.
2. Analyze Melville's view toward sin and depravity.
3. Understand how Melville creates his characters.
4. Compare Billy Budd to Christ.
5. Discuss Melville's views of salvation.

Weekly Essay Options: Begin on page 274 of the Teacher Guide.

 History connections: *American History* chapter 12, "Revivalism."

Billy Budd
Herman Melville

Background This extraordinary novel is a story of Billy Budd, a young man who is assailed by uncontrollable forces. This is a world where an omnipotent God is absent. Welcome to the New World!

About the Author Herman Melville, born on August 19, 1819, was part of a radically changing world. Within his lifetime, the population of the United States increased 400 percent. Travel from New York to Boston decreased from five days to eight hours. The generation that lived in the middle period of American history, in most respects, experienced more changes than any American generation — including our own. Melville's books struggle, then, to make sense of all these changes. Melville was a very talented writer. But in his heart, Melville was a sailor. He spent almost 20 years traveling the South Seas. Melville, in microcosm, represents the quintessential 19th-century American.

Other Notable Works

Typee (1846)

Moby Dick (1851)

Suggested Vocabulary Words

Chapter I: motley, retinue, genial, decorum

Chapter III: deference, appellation

Chapter VIII: felonious, comely

Chapter IX: clandestine

Chapter XV: immured

Assignments

- Warm-up: : In *Billy Budd* there are no women. Would it be a different story if all the main characters were women instead of men?
- Students should complete Concept Builder 12-A.
- Students review the required reading(s) *before* the assigned chapter begins.
- Teachers may want to discuss assigned reading(s) with students.
- Teachers shall assign the required essay. The rest of the essays can be outlined, answered with shorter answers, discussed, or skipped.
- Students will review all readings for chapter 12.

Read *Billy Budd* Chapter 25 by Herman Melville then answer the following questions.

1	Is the Chaplain able to minister to the condemned prisoner?
2	Why does Melville call Billy Budd the Handsome Sailor?
3	What sort of young man is Billy Budd?
4	In the final paragraph the author speaks directly to the reader (omniscient narration). Why?
5	What does this quote mean? "And this sailor-way of taking clerical discourse is not wholly unlike the way in which the pioneer of Christianity full of transcendent miracles was received long ago on tropic isles by any superior savage so called — a Tahitian say of Captain Cook's time or shortly after that time."

Poetry by Melville

America

I

Where the wings of a sunny Dome expand
I saw a Banner in gladsome air —
Starry, like Berenice's Hair —
Afloat in broadened bravery there;
With undulating long-drawn flow,
As rolled Brazilian billows go
Voluminously o'er the Line.
The Land reposed in peace below;
 The children in their glee
Were folded to the exulting heart
Of young Maternity.

II

Later, and it streamed in fight
When tempest mingled with the fray,
And over the spear-point of the shaft
 I saw the ambiguous lightning play.
Valor with Valor strove, and died:
Fierce was Despair, and cruel was Pride;
And the lorn Mother speechless stood,
Pale at the fury of her brood.

III

Yet later, and the silk did wind
 Her fair cold for;
Little availed the shining shroud,
 Though ruddy in hue, to cheer or warm

A watcher looked upon her low, and said —
She sleeps, but sleeps, she is not dead.
 But in that sleep contortion showed
The terror of the vision there —
 A silent vision unavowed,
Revealing earth's foundation bare,
 And Gorgon in her hidden place.
It was a thing of fear to see
 So foul a dream upon so fair a face,
And the dreamer lying in that starry shroud.

IV

But from the trance she sudden broke —
The trance, or death into promoted life;
At her feet a shivered yoke,
And in her aspect turned to heaven
 No trace of passion or of strife —
A clear calm look. It spake of pain,
But such as purifies from stain —
Sharp pangs that never come again —
 And triumph repressed by knowledge meet,
Power delicate, and hope grown wise,
 And youth matured for age's seat —
Law on her brow and empire in her eyes.
 So she, with graver air and lifted flag;
While the shadow, chased by light,
Fled along the far-brawn height,
 And left her on the crag (www.poets.com).

Assignments

- Warm-up: Melville (who was a transitional romantic) and contemporary romantic writers tried to embrace the best of both cosmological worlds. They believed in God, although they dilute His person and substance with natural science, but they also believe in human ingenuity and subjectivity. It was very hard to keep both of these worldview balls in the air at the same time. Compare Melville to Ahab (1 Kings), who also struggled to be a theist and a pagan — both at the same time.

- Students should complete Concept Builder 12-B.

- Student should review reading(s) from the next chapter.

- Student should outline essay due at the end of the week.

- Per teacher instructions, students may answer orally, in a group setting, some of the essays that are not assigned as formal essays.

Most readers see Billy Budd as a Christ-like figure. Compare the life of Christ to the life of Billy Budd.

Jesus Christ

Billy Budd

His enemies thought he was Illegitimate .

Billy was the illegitimate son of an English lord.

He was innocent in all things.

He was unjustly accused of a crime.

He labored into the night in the Garden of Gethsemane.

He was crucified for a crime he did not commit.

Critics and Quotes

From Barrons Booknotes, www. AOL.com

Following out the biblical parallels that have been suggested at crucial points throughout this story, if Billy is young Adam before the Fall, and Claggart is almost the devil incarnate, Vere is the Wise Father, terribly severe but righteous. No longer does Melville feel the fear and dislike of Jehovah that were oppressing him through Moby Dick and Pierre. He is no longer protesting against determined laws as being savagely inexorable. He has come to respect necessity. He can therefore treat a character like Vere's with full sympathy.

— F.O. Matthiessen,
American Renaissance

We may say that Billy Budd is a vision of man in society, a vision of man's moral quandary or his responsibility; but its meaning is more general than these, and that is why it haunts us. So haunted, I find the work not an essay on a moral issue but a form for embodying the feeling and idea of thinking about a moral issue, the experience of facing, or choosing, of being uneasy about one's choice, of trying to know. Not a conclusion like a sermon, Billy Budd is a vision of confronting what confronts us, of man thinking things out with all the attendant confusions and uncertainties.

— William York Tindall,
"The Ceremony of Innocence," 1956

Billy Budd is an intensely modern novel. It is concerned with the coming of a materialist, commercial civilization, rational and scientific, in which society grows ever more distant from the rich overflowing of human experience. Billy harks back to a more adventurous and youthful America which, with the frontier and the whaleship, was already passing in Melville's lifetime. Billy's type comes from "the time before steamships," the significant words with which the novel opens.

— Charles A. Reich,
"The Tragedy of Justice in Bully Budd," 1967

It may be argued that, while both Vere and Claggart possess intelligence, Vere uses his wisely and justly. But this argument collapses when it is perceived that Vere does not do what reason would suggest in so dubious a case, i.e., jail Billy until they reach land. The real point is, of course, that Vere does not act on reason and intelligence at all, but on fear; his intelligence, instead of being a guide, is a perverted instrument. Such scenes as the confusion of the officers and the doubt of the surgeon concerning Vere's sanity make sense only when regarded as putting into issue Vere's stature and ability.

— Phil Withim,
"Billy Budd: Testament of Resistance," 1959

- Warm-up: What biblical imagery do you see in *Billy Budd*?
- Students should complete Concept Builder 12-C.
- Students should write rough drafts of assigned essay.
- The teacher may correct rough drafts.

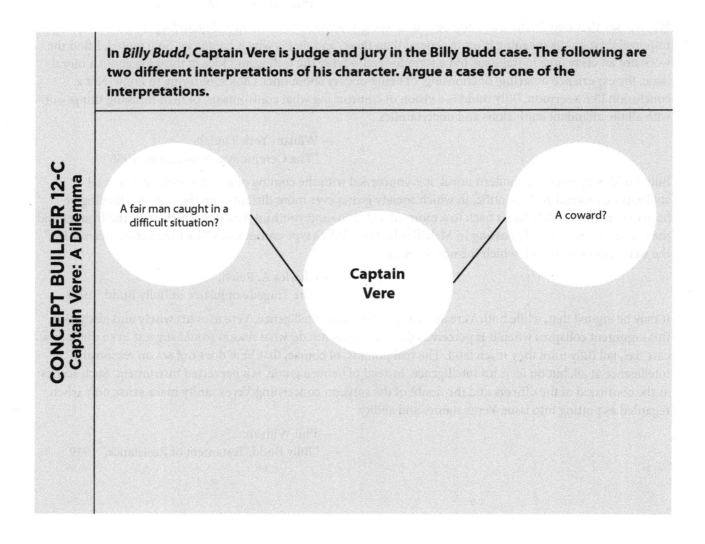

CONCEPT BUILDER 12-C
Captain Vere: A Dilemma

In *Billy Budd*, Captain Vere is judge and jury in the Billy Budd case. The following are two different interpretations of his character. Argue a case for one of the interpretations.

A fair man caught in a difficult situation?

Captain Vere

A coward?

Setting

Billy Budd occurs on a single ship, but its scope transcends time and geography. Life aboard the *Bellipotent* is a representation of life itself. The ocean isolates everyone from the rest of the world. Melville takes the conflict on board the British man-of-war *Bellipotent* and crafts it into an epic drama. It is a story of Billy Budd, but it is a larger drama between good and evil, between God and Satan. It is as much an epic drama as John Milton's *Paradise Lost*.

 Billy Budd is set in a time of war and mutiny, and these factors have a major impact on the story and on Captain Vere's decision to condemn Billy to death. During the last quarter of the 18th century, the British saw revolution sweep first through their American colonies and then, several years later, through France. This spawned the Napoleonic Wars and England, quite literally, was almost defeated. The action of *Billy Budd* unfolds against the backdrop of the Napoleonic Wars. And the war enters into the story in several ways. Britain was so desperate for sailors to man her large fleet at this time that it became legal for naval officers to board private ships and press into service whatever men they wanted into the British Navy. Billy Budd was forced to be a sailor on a British man-of-war. It was not by choice.

 Even more important to the atmosphere and action of *Billy Budd* are the two mutinies that occurred in the British Navy just months prior to the story. Though the mutinies were suppressed, one can

Man-of-war ship firing a salute. *The Cannon Shot*, painted by Willem van de Velde the Younger, c1680 (PD-US).

imagine the fear they caused throughout Britain. New legislation was passed in Britain to allow naval officers to deal swiftly and brutally with any new mutinous outbreak. These laws and this atmosphere of tension work against Billy when Claggart decides to go after him. And the consequences are fatal to Billy Budd.

- Warm-up: In *Billy Budd* the setting helps to reveal character and to shape events. Give evidence for this statement.

- Students should complete Concept Builder 12-D.

- Students will re-write corrected copies of essay due tomorrow.

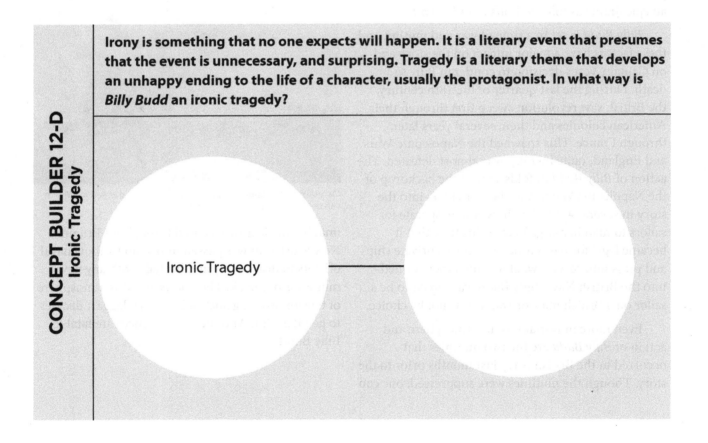

CONCEPT BUILDER 12-D
Ironic Tragedy

Irony is something that no one expects will happen. It is a literary event that presumes that the event is unnecessary, and surprising. Tragedy is a literary theme that develops an unhappy ending to the life of a character, usually the protagonist. In what way is *Billy Budd* an ironic tragedy?

Ironic Tragedy

I and My Chimney

I and my chimney, two grey-headed old smokers, reside in the country. We are, I may say, old settlers here; particularly my old chimney, which settles more and more every day.

Though I always say, *I and My Chimney*, as Cardinal Wolsey used to say, "I and My King," yet this egotistic way of speaking, wherein I take precedence of my chimney, is hereby borne out by the facts; in everything, except the above phrase, my chimney taking precedence of me.

Within thirty feet of the turf-sided road, my chimney — a huge, corpulent old Harry VIII of a chimney — rises full in front of me and all my possessions. Standing well up a hillside, my chimney, like Lord Rosse's monster telescope, swung vertical to hit the meridian moon, is the first object to greet the approaching traveler's eye, nor is it the last which the sun salutes. My chimney, too, is before me in receiving the first-fruits of the seasons. The snow is on its head ere on my hat; and every spring, as in a hollow beech tree, the first swallows build their nests in it.

But it is within doors that the pre-eminence of my chimney is most manifest. When in the rear room, set apart for that object, I stand to receive my guests (who, by the way call more, I suspect, to see my chimney than me) I then stand, not so much before, as, strictly speaking, behind my chimney, which is, indeed, the true host. Not that I demur. In the presence of my betters, I hope I know my place.

From this habitual precedence of my chimney over me, some even think that I have got into a sad rearward way altogether; in short, from standing behind my old-fashioned chimney so much, I have got to be quite behind the age too, as well as running behindhand in everything else. But to tell the truth, I never was a very forward old fellow, nor what my farming neighbors call a forehanded one. Indeed, those rumors about my behindhandedness are so far correct, that I have an odd sauntering way with me sometimes of going about with my hands behind my back. As for my belonging to the rear-guard in general, certain it is, I bring up the rear of my chimney— which, by the way, is this moment before me — and that, too, both in fancy and fact. In brief, my chimney is my superior; my superior, too, in that humbly bowing over with shovel and tongs, I much minister to it; yet never does it minister, or incline over to me; but, if anything, in its settlings, rather leans the other way.

My chimney is grand seignior here — the one great domineering object, not more of the landscape, than of the house; all the rest of which house, in each architectural arrangement, as may shortly appear, is, in the most marked manner, accommodated, not to my wants, but to my chimney's, which, among other things, has the center of the house to himself, leaving but the odd holes and corners to me.

But I and my chimney must explain; and as we are both rather obese, we may have to expatiate.

In those houses which are strictly double houses — that is, where the hall is in the middle — the fireplaces usually are on opposite sides; so that while one member of the household is warming himself at a fire built into a recess of the north wall, say another member, the former's own brother, perhaps, may be holding his feet to the blaze before a hearth in the south wall — the two thus fairly sitting back to back. Is this well? Be it put to any man who has a proper fraternal feeling. Has it not a sort of sulky appearance? But very probably this style of chimney building originated with some architect afflicted with a quarrelsome family.

Then again, almost every modern fireplace has its separate flue — separate throughout, from hearth to chimney-top. At least such an arrangement is deemed desirable. Does not this look egotistical, selfish? But still more, all these separate flues, instead of having independent masonry establishments of their own, or instead of being grouped together in one federal stock in the middle of the house— instead of this, I say, each flue is surreptitiously honey-combed into the walls; so that these last are here and there, or indeed almost anywhere, treacherously hollow, and, in consequence, more or less weak. Of course, the main reason of this style of chimney building is to economize room. In cities, where lots are sold by the inch, small space is to spare for a chimney constructed on magnanimous principles; and, as with most thin men, who are generally tall, so with such houses, what is lacking in breadth, must be made up in height. This remark holds true even with regard to many very stylish abodes, built by the most stylish of gentlemen. And yet, when that stylish gentleman, Louis le Grand of France, would build a palace for his lady, friend, Madame de Maintenon, he built it but one story high — in fact in the cottage style. But then, how uncommonly quadrangular, spacious, and broad — horizontal acres, not vertical ones. Such is the palace, which, in all its one-storied magnificence of Languedoc marble, in the garden of Versailles, still remains to this day. Any man can buy a square foot of land and plant a liberty-pole on it; but it takes a king to set apart whole acres for a grand triannon.

But nowadays it is different; and furthermore, what originated in a necessity has been mounted into a vaunt. In towns there is large rivalry in building tall houses. If one gentleman builds his house four stories high, and another gentleman comes next door and builds five stories high, then the former, not to be looked down upon that way, immediately sends for his architect and claps a fifth and a sixth story on top of his previous four. And, not till the gentleman has achieved his aspiration, not till he has stolen over the way by twilight and observed how his sixth story soars beyond his neighbor's fifth — not till then does he retire to his rest with satisfaction.

Such folks, it seems to me, need mountains for neighbors, to take this emulous conceit of soaring out of them.

If, considering that mine is a very wide house, and by no means lofty, aught in the above may appear like interested pleading, as if I did but fold myself about in the cloak of a general proposition, cunningly to tickle my individual vanity beneath it, such misconception must vanish upon my frankly conceding, that land adjoining my alder swamp was sold last month for ten dollars an acre, and thought a rash purchase at that; so that for wide houses hereabouts there is plenty of room, and cheap. Indeed so cheap — dirt cheap — is the soil, that our elms thrust out their roots in it, and hang their great boughs over it, in the most lavish and reckless way. Almost all our crops, too, are sown broadcast, even peas and turnips. A farmer among us, who should go about his twenty-acre field, poking his finger into it here and there, and dropping down a mustard seed, would be thought a penurious, narrow-minded husbandman. The dandelions in the river-meadows, and the forget-me-nots along the mountain roads, you see at once they are put to no economy in space. Some seasons, too, our rye comes up here and there a spear, sole and single like a church-spire. It doesn't care to crowd itself where it knows there is such a deal of room. The world is wide, the world is all before us, says the rye. Weeds, too, it is amazing how they spread. No such thing as arresting them — some of our pastures being a sort of Alsatia for the weeds. As for the grass, every spring it is like Kossuth's rising of what he calls the peoples. Mountains, too, a regular camp-meeting of them. For the same reason, the same all-sufficiency of room, our shadows march and countermarch, going through their various drills and masterly evolutions, like the old imperial guard on the Champs de Mars. As for the hills, especially where the roads cross them the supervisors of our various towns have given notice to all concerned, that they can come and dig them down and cart them off, and never a cent to pay, no more than for the privilege of picking blackberries. The stranger who is buried here, what liberal-hearted landed proprietor among us grudges him six feet of rocky pasture?

Nevertheless, cheap, after all, as our land is, and much as it is trodden under foot, I, for one, am proud of it for what it bears; and chiefly for its three great lions — the Great Oak, Ogg Mountain, and my chimney.

Most houses, here, are but one and a half stories high; few exceed two. That in which I and my chimney dwell, is in width nearly twice its height, from sill to eaves — which accounts for the magnitude of its main content — besides showing that in this house, as in this country at large, there is abundance of space, and to spare, for both of us.

The frame of the old house is of wood — which but the more sets forth the solidity of the chimney, which is of brick. And as the great wrought nails, binding the clapboards, are unknown in these degenerate days, so are the huge bricks in the chimney walls. The architect of the chimney must have had the pyramid of Cheops before him; for, after that famous structure, it seems modeled, only its rate of decrease towards the summit is considerably less, and it is truncated. From the exact middle of the mansion it soars from the cellar, right up through each successive floor, till, four feet square, it breaks water from the ridge-pole of the roof, like an anvil-headed whale, through the crest of a billow. Most people, though, liken it, in that part, to a razed observatory, masoned up.

The reason for its peculiar appearance above the roof touches upon rather delicate ground. How shall I reveal that, forasmuch as many years ago the original gable roof of the old house had become very leaky, a temporary proprietor hired a band of woodmen, with their huge, cross-cut saws, and went to sawing the old gable roof clean off. Off it went, with all its birds' nests, and dormer windows. It was replaced with a modern roof, more fit for a railway wood-house than an old country gentleman's abode. This operation — razeeing the structure some fifteen feet — was, in effect upon the chimney, something like the falling of the great spring tides. It left uncommon low water all about the chimney — to abate which appearance, the same person now proceeds to slice fifteen feet off the chimney itself, actually beheading my royal old chimney — a regicidal act, which, were it not for the palliating fact that he was a poulterer by trade, and, therefore, hardened to such neck-wringings, should send that former proprietor down to posterity in the same cart with Cromwell.

Owing to its pyramidal shape, the reduction of the chimney inordinately widened its razed summit. Inordinately, I say, but only in the estimation of such as have no eye to the picturesque. What care I, if, unaware that my chimney, as a free citizen of this free land, stands upon an independent basis of its own, people passing it, wonder how such a brick-kiln, as they call it, is supported upon mere joists and rafters? What care I? I will give a traveler a cup of switchel, if he want it; but am I bound to supply him with a sweet taste? Men of cultivated minds see, in my old house and chimney, a goodly old elephant-and-castle.

All feeling hearts will sympathize with me in what I am now about to add. The surgical operation, above referred to, necessarily brought into the open air a part of the chimney previously under cover, and intended to remain so, and, therefore, not built of what are called weather-bricks. In consequence, the chimney, though of a vigorous constitution, suffered not a little, from so naked an exposure; and, unable to acclimate itself, ere long began to fail — showing blotchy symptoms akin to those in measles. Whereupon travelers, passing my way, would wag their heads, laughing; "See that wax nose — how it melts off!" But what cared I? The same travelers would travel across the sea to view Kenilworth peeling away, and for a very good reason: that of all artists of the picturesque, decay wears the palm — I would say, the ivy. In fact, I've often thought that the proper place for my old chimney is ivied old England.

In vain my wife — with what probable ulterior intent will, ere long, appear — solemnly warned me, that unless something were done, and speedily, we should be burnt to the ground, owing to the holes crumbling through the aforesaid blotchy parts, where the chimney joined the roof. "Wife," said I, "far better that my house should bum down, than that my chimney should be pulled down, though but a few feet. They call it a wax nose; very good; not for me to tweak the nose of my superior." But at last the man who has a mortgage on the house dropped me a note, reminding me that, if my chimney was allowed to stand in that invalid condition, my policy of insurance would be void. This was a sort of hint not to be neglected. All the world over, the picturesque yields to the pocketesque. The mortgagor cared not, but the mortgagee did.

So another operation was performed. The wax nose was taken off, and a new one fitted on. Unfortunately for the expression — being put up by a squint-eyed mason, who, at the time, had a bad stitch in the same side — the new nose stands a little awry, in the same direction.

Of one thing, however, I am proud. The horizontal dimensions of the new part are unreduced.

Large as the chimney appears upon the roof, that is nothing to its spaciousness below. At its base in the cellar, it is precisely twelve feet square; and hence covers precisely one hundred and forty-four superficial feet. What an appropriation of terra firma for a chimney, and what a huge load for this earth! In fact, it was only because I and my chimney formed no part of his ancient burden, that that stout peddler, Atlas of old, was enabled to stand up so bravely under his pack. The dimensions given may, perhaps, seem fabulous. But, like those stones at Gilgal, which Joshua set up for a memorial of having passed over Jordan, does not my chimney remain, even unto this day?

Very often I go down into my cellar, and attentively survey that vast square of masonry. I stand long, and ponder over, and wonder at it. It has a druidical look, away down in the umbrageous cellar there whose numerous vaulted passages, and far glens of gloom, resemble the dark, damp depths of primeval woods. So strongly did this conceit steal over me, so deeply was I penetrated with wonder at the chimney, that one day — when I was a little out of my mind, I now think — getting a spade from the garden, I set to work, digging round the foundation, especially at the corners thereof, obscurely prompted by dreams of striking upon some old, earthen-worn memorial of that by-gone day, when, into all this gloom, the light of heaven entered, as the masons laid the foundation-stones, peradventure sweltering under an August sun, or pelted by a March storm.

Plying my blunted spade, how vexed was I by that ungracious interruption of a neighbor who, calling to see me upon some business, and being informed that I was below said I need not be troubled to come up, but he would go down to me; and so, without ceremony, and without my having been forewarned, suddenly discovered me, digging in my cellar.

"Gold digging, sir?"

"Nay, sir," answered I, starting, "I was merely — ahem! — merely — I say I was merely digging — round my chimney."

"Ah, loosening the soil, to make it grow. Your chimney, sir, you regard as too small, I suppose; needing further development, especially at the top?"

"Sir!" said I, throwing down the spade, "do not be personal. I and my chimney —"

"Personal?"

"Sir, I look upon this chimney less as a pile of masonry than as a personage. It is the king of the house. I am but a suffered and inferior subject."

In fact, I would permit no gibes to be cast at either myself or my chimney; and never again did my visitor refer to it in my hearing, without coupling some compliment with the mention. It well deserves a respectful consideration. There it stands, solitary and alone — not a council — of ten flues, but, like his sacred majesty of Russia, a unit of an autocrat.

Even to me, its dimensions, at times, seem incredible. It does not look so big — no, not even in the cellar. By the mere eye, its magnitude can be but imperfectly comprehended, because only one side can be received at one time; and said side can only present twelve feet, linear measure. But then, each other side also is twelve feet long; and the whole obviously forms a square and twelve times twelve is one hundred and forty-four. And so, an adequate conception of the magnitude of this chimney is only to be got at by a sort of process in the higher mathematics by a method somewhat akin to those whereby the surprising distances of fixed stars are computed.

It need hardly be said, that the walls of my house are entirely free from fireplaces. These all congregate in the middle — in the one grand central chimney, upon all four sides of which are hearths — two tiers of hearths — so that when, in the various chambers, my family and guests are warming themselves of a cold winter's night, just before retiring, then, though at the time they may not be thinking so, all their faces mutually look towards each other, yea, all their feet point to one center; and, when they go to sleep in their beds, they all sleep round one warm chimney, like so many Iroquois Indians, in the woods, round their one heap of embers. And just as the Indians' fire serves, not only to keep them comfortable, but also to keep off wolves, and other savage monsters, so my chimney, by its obvious smoke at top, keeps off prowling burglars from the towns — for what burglar or murderer would dare break into an abode from whose chimney issues such a continual smoke — betokening that if the inmates are not stirring, at least fires are, and in case of an alarm, candles may readily be lighted, to say nothing of muskets.

But stately as is the chimney — yea, grand high altar as it is, right worthy for the celebration of high mass before the Pope of Rome, and all his cardinals — yet what is there perfect in this world? Caius Julius Caesar, had he not been so inordinately great, they say that Brutus, Cassius, Antony, and the rest, had been greater. My chimney, were it not so mighty in its magnitude, my chambers had been larger. How often has my wife ruefully told me, that my chimney, like the English aristocracy, casts a contracting shade all round it. She avers that endless domestic inconveniences arise — more particularly from the chimney's stubborn central locality. The grand objection with her is, that it stands midway in the place where a fine entrance hall ought to be. In truth, there is no hall whatever to the house —nothing but a sort of square landing-place, as you enter from the wide front door. A roomy enough landing-place, I admit, but not attaining to the dignity of a hall. Now, as the front door is precisely in the middle of the front of the house, inwards it faces the chimney. In fact, the opposite wall of the landing-place is formed solely by the chimney; and hence-owing to the gradual tapering of the chimney — is a little less than twelve feet in width. Climbing the chimney in this part, is the principal staircase — which, by three abrupt turns, and three minor landing-places,

mounts to the second floor, where, over the front door, runs a sort of narrow gallery, something less than twelve feet long, leading to chambers on either hand. This gallery, of course, is railed; and so, looking down upon the stairs, and all those landing-places together, with the main one at bottom, resembles not a little a balcony for musicians, in some jolly old abode, in times Elizabethan. Shall I tell a weakness? I cherish the cobwebs there, and many a time arrest Biddy in the act of brushing them with her broom, and have many a quarrel with my wife and daughters about it.

Now the ceiling, so to speak, of the place where you enter the house, that ceiling is, in fact, the ceiling of the second floor, not the first. The two floors are made one here; so that ascending this turning stairs, you seem going up into a kind of soaring tower, or lighthouse. At the second landing, midway up the chimney, is a mysterious door, entering to a mysterious closet; and here I keep mysterious cordials, of a choice, mysterious flavor, made so by the constant nurturing and subtle ripening of the chimney's gentle heat, distilled through that warm mass of masonry. Better for wines is it than voyages to the Indias; my chimney itself a tropic. A chair by my chimney in a November day is as good for an invalid as a long season spent in Cuba. Often I think how grapes might ripen against my chimney. How my wife's geraniums bud there! Bud in December. Her eggs, too—can't keep them near the chimney, an account of the hatching. Ah, a warm heart has my chimney.

How often my wife was at me about that projected grand entrance-hall of hers, which was to be knocked clean through the chimney, from one end of the house to the other, and astonish all guests by its generous amplitude. "But, wife," said I, "the chimney — consider the chimney: if you demolish the foundation, what is to support the superstructure?" "Oh, that will rest on the second floor." The truth is, women know next to nothing about the realities of architecture. However, my wife still talked of running her entries and partitions. She spent many long nights elaborating her plans; in imagination building her boasted hall through the chimney, as though its high mightiness were a mere spear of sorrel-top. At last, I gently reminded her that, little as she might fancy it, the chimney was a fact — a sober, substantial fact, which, in all her plannings, it would be well to take into full consideration. But this was not of much avail.

And here, respectfully craving her permission, I must say a few words about this enterprising wife of mine. Though in years nearly old as myself, in spirit she is young as my little sorrel mare, Trigger, that threw me last fall. What is extraordinary, though she comes of a rheumatic family, she is straight as a pine, never has any aches; while for me with the sciatica, I am sometimes as crippled up as any old apple-tree. But she has not so much as a toothache. As for her hearing — let me enter the house in my dusty boots, and she away up in the attic. And for her sight — Biddy, the housemaid, tells other people's house-maids, that her mistress will spy a spot on the dresser straight through the pewter platter, put up on purpose to hide it. Her faculties are alert as her limbs and her senses. No danger of my spouse dying of torpor. The longest night in the year I've known her lie awake, planning her campaign for the morrow. She is a natural projector. The maxim, "Whatever is, is right," is not hers. Her maxim is, Whatever is, is wrong; and what is more, must be altered; and what is still more, must be altered right away. Dreadful maxim for the wife of a dozy old dreamer like me, who dote on seventh days as days of rest, and out of a sabbatical horror of industry, will, on a week day, go out of my road a quarter of a mile, to avoid the sight of a man at work.

That matches are made in heaven, may be, but my wife would have been just the wife for Peter the Great, or Peter the Piper. How she would have set in order that huge littered empire of the one, and with indefatigable painstaking picked the peck of pickled peppers for the other.

But the most wonderful thing is, my wife never thinks of her end. Her youthful incredulity, as to the plain theory, and still plainer fact of death, hardly seems Christian. Advanced in years, as she knows she must be, my wife seems to think that she is to teem on, and be inexhaustible forever. She doesn't believe in old age. At that strange promise in the plain of Mamre, my old wife, unlike old Abraham's, would not have jeeringly laughed within herself.

Judge how to me, who, sitting in the comfortable shadow of my chimney, smoking my comfortable pipe, with ashes not unwelcome at my feet, and ashes not unwelcome all but in my mouth; and who am thus in a comfortable sort of not unwelcome, though, indeed, ashy enough way, reminded of the ultimate exhaustion even of the most fiery life; judge how to me this unwarrantable vitality in my wife must come, sometimes, it is true, with a moral and a calm, but oftener with a breeze and a ruffle.

If the doctrine be true, that in wedlock contraries attract, by how cogent a fatality must I have been drawn to my wife! While spicily impatient of present and past, like a glass of ginger-beer she overflows with her schemes; and, with like energy as she puts down her foot, puts down her preserves and her pickles, and lives with them in a continual future; or ever full of expectations both from time and space, is ever restless for newspapers, and ravenous for letters. Content with the years that are gone, taking no thought for the morrow, and looking for no new thing from any person or quarter whatever, I have not a single scheme or expectation on earth, save in unequal resistance of the undue encroachment of hers.

Old myself, I take to oldness in things; for that cause mainly loving old Montague, and old cheese, and old wine; and eschewing young people, hot rolls, new books, and early potatoes and very fond of my old claw-footed chair, and old club-footed Deacon White, my neighbor, and that still nigher old neighbor, my betwisted old grape-vine, that of a summer evening leans in his elbow for cosy company at my window-sill, while I, within doors, lean over mine to meet his; and above all, high above all, am fond of my high-mantled old chimney. But she, out of the infatuate juvenility of hers, takes to nothing but newness; for that cause mainly, loving new cider in autumn, and in spring, as if she were own daughter of Nebuchadnezzar, fairly raving after all sorts of salads and spinages, and more particularly green cucumbers (though all the time nature rebukes such unsuitable young hankerings in so elderly a person, by never permitting such things to agree with her), and has an itch after recently discovered fine prospects (so no graveyard be in the background), and also after Sweden-borganism, and the Spirit Rapping philosophy, with other new views, alike in things natural and unnatural; and immortally hopeful, is forever making new flower-beds even on the north side of the house where the bleak mountain wind would scarce allow the wiry weed called hard-hack to gain a thorough footing; and on the road-side sets out mere pipe-stems of young elms; though there is no hope of any shade from them, except over the ruins of her great granddaughter's gravestones; and won't wear caps, but plaits her gray hair; and takes the Ladies' Magazine for the fashions; and always buys her new almanac a month before the new year; and rises at dawn; and to the warmest sunset turns a cold shoulder; and still goes on at odd hours with her new course of history, and her French, and her music; and likes a young company; and offers to ride young colts; and sets out young suckers in the orchard; and has a spite against my elbowed old grape-vine, and my club-footed old neighbor, and my claw-footed old chair, and above all, high above all, would fain persecute, until death, my high-mantled old chimney. By what perverse magic, I a thousand times think, does such a very autumnal old lady have such a very vernal young soul? When I would remonstrate at times, she spins round on me with, "Oh, don't you grumble, old man (she always calls me old man), it's I, young I, that keep you from stagnating." Well, I suppose it is so. Yea, after all, these things are well ordered. My wife, as one of her poor relations, good soul, intimates, is the salt of the earth, and none the less the salt of my sea, which otherwise were unwholesome. She is its monsoon, too, blowing a brisk gale over it, in the one steady direction of my chimney.

Not insensible of her superior energies, my wife has frequently made me propositions to take upon herself all the responsibilities of my affairs. She is desirous that, domestically, I should abdicate; that, renouncing further rule, like the venerable Charles V, I should retire into some sort of monastery. But indeed, the chimney excepted, I have little authority to lay down. By my wife's ingenious application of the principle that certain things belong of right to female jurisdiction, I find myself, through my easy compliances, insensibly stripped by degrees of one masculine prerogative after another. In a dream I go about my fields, a sort of lazy, happy-go-lucky,

good-for-nothing, loafing old Lear. Only by some sudden revelation am I reminded who is over me; as year before last, one day seeing in one corner of the premises fresh deposits of mysterious boards and timbers, the oddity of the incident at length begat serious meditation. "Wife," said I, "whose boards and timbers are those I see near the orchard there? Do you know anything about them, wife? Who put them there? You know I do not like the neighbors to use my land that way, they should ask permission first."

She regarded me with a pitying smile.

"Why, old man, don't you know I am building a new barn? Didn't you know that, old man?"

This is the poor old lady who was accusing me of tyrannizing over her.

To return now to the chimney. Upon being assured of the futility of her proposed hall, so long as the obstacle remained, for a time my wife was for a modified project. But I could never exactly comprehend it. As far as I could see through it, it seemed to involve the general idea of a sort of irregular archway, or elbowed tunnel, which was to penetrate the chimney at some convenient point under the staircase, and carefully avoiding dangerous contact with the fireplaces, and particularly steering clear of the great interior flue, was to conduct the enterprising traveler from the front door all the way into the dining-room in the remote rear of the mansion. Doubtless it was a bold stroke of genius, that plan of hers, and so was Nero's when he schemed his grand canal through the Isthmus of Corinth. Nor will I take oath, that, had her project been accomplished, then, by help of lights hung at judicious intervals through the tunnel, some Belzoni or other might have succeeded in future ages in penetrating through the masonry, and actually emerging into the dining-room, and once there, it would have been inhospitable treatment of such a traveler to have denied him a recruiting meal.

But my bustling wife did not restrict her objections, nor in the end confine her proposed alterations to the first floor. Her ambition was of the mounting order. She ascended with her schemes to the second floor, and so to the attic. Perhaps there was some small ground for her discontent with things as they were. The truth is, there was no regular passage-way up-stairs or down, unless we again except that little orchestra-gallery before mentioned. And all this was owing to the chimney, which my gamesome spouse seemed despitefully to regard as the bully of the house. On all its four sides, nearly all the chambers sidled up to the chimney for the benefit of a fireplace. The chimney would not go to them; they must needs go to it. The consequence was, almost every room, like a philosophical system, was in itself an entry, or passage-way to other rooms, and systems of rooms — a whole suite of entries, in fact. Going through the house, you seem to be forever going somewhere, and getting nowhere. It is like losing one's self in the woods; round and round the chimney you go, and if you arrive at all, it is just where you started, and so you begin again, and again get nowhere. Indeed — though I say it not in the way of faultfinding at all — never was there so labyrinthine an abode. Guests will tarry with me several weeks and every now and then, be anew astonished at some unforseen apartment.

The puzzling nature of the mansion, resulting from the chimney, is peculiarly noticeable in the dining-room, which has no less than nine doors, opening in all directions, and into all sorts of places. A stranger for the first time entering this dining-room, and naturally taking no special heed at which door he entered, will, upon rising to depart, commit the strangest blunders. Such, for instance, as opening the first door that comes handy, and finding himself stealing up-stairs by the back passage. Shutting that he will proceed to another, and be aghast at the cellar yawning at his feet. Trying a third, he surprises the housemaid at her work. In the end, no more relying on his own unaided efforts, he procures a trusty guide in some passing person, and in good time successfully emerges. Perhaps as curious a blunder as any, was that of a certain stylish young gentleman, a great exquisite, in whose judicious eyes my daughter Anna had found especial favor. He called upon the young lady one evening, and found her alone in the dining-room at her needlework. He stayed rather late; and after abundance of superfine discourse, all the while retaining his hat and cane, made his profuse adieus, and with repeated graceful bows proceeded to depart, after fashion of courtiers from the Queen, and by so doing, opening a door at

random, with one hand placed behind, very effectually succeeded in backing himself into a dark pantry, where be carefully shut himself up, wondering there was no light in the entry. After several strange noises as of a cat among the crockery, he reappeared through the same door, looking uncommonly crestfallen, and, with a deeply embarrassed air, requested my daughter to designate at which of the nine he should find exit. When the mischievous Anna told me the story, she said it was surprising how unaffected and matter-of-fact the young gentleman's manner was after his reappearance. He was more candid than ever, to be sure; having inadvertently thrust his white kids into an open drawer of Havana sugar, under the impression, probably, that being what they call "a sweet fellow," his route might possibly lie in that direction.

Another inconvenience resulting from the chimney is, the bewilderment of a guest in gaining his chamber, many strange doors lying between him and it. To direct him by finger-posts would look rather queer; and just as queer in him to be knocking at every door on his route, like London's city guest, the king, at Temple-Bar.

Now, of all these things and many, many more, my family continually complained. At last my wife came out with her sweeping proposition — in toto to abolish the chimney.

"What!" said I, "abolish the chimney? To take out the backbone of anything, wife, is a hazardous affair. Spines out of backs, and chimneys out of houses, are not to be taken like frosted lead pipes from the ground. Besides," added I, "the chimney is the one grand permanence of this abode. If undisturbed by innovators, then in future ages, when all the house shall have crumbled from it, this chimney will still survive — a Bunker Hill monument. No, no, wife, I can't abolish my backbone."

So said I then. But who is sure of himself, especially an old man, with both wife and daughters ever at his elbow and ear? In time, I was persuaded to think a little better of it; in short, to take the matter into preliminary consideration. At length it came to pass that a master-mason — a rough sort of architect — one Mr. Scribe, was summoned to a conference. I formally introduced him to my chimney. A previous introduction from my wife had introduced him to myself. He had been not a little employed by that lady, in preparing plans and estimates for some of her extensive operations in drainage. Having, with much ado, exhorted from my spouse the promise that she would leave us to an unmolested survey, I began by leading Mr. Scribe down to the root of the matter, in the cellar. Lamp in hand, I descended; for though up-stairs it was noon, below it was night.

We seemed in the pyramids; and I, with one hand holding my lamp over head, and with the other pointing out, in the obscurity, the hoar mass of the chimney, seemed some Arab guide, showing the cobwebbed mausoleum of the great god Apis.

"This is a most remarkable structure, sir," said the master-mason, after long contemplating it in silence, "a most remarkable structure, sir."

"Yes," said I complacently, "every one says so."

"But large as it appears above the roof, I would not have inferred the magnitude of this foundation, sir," eyeing it critically.

Then taking out his rule, he measured it.

"Twelve feet square; one hundred and forty-four square feet! Sir, this house would appear to have been built simply for the accommodation of your chimney."

"Yes, my chimney and me. Tell me candidly, now," I added, "would you have such a famous chimney abolished?"

"I wouldn't have it in a house of mine, sir, for a gift," was the reply. "It's a losing affair altogether, sir. Do you know, sir, that in retaining this chimney, you are losing, not only one hundred and forty-four square feet of good ground, but likewise a considerable interest upon a considerable principal?"

"How?"

Look, sir!" said he, taking a bit of red chalk from his pocket, and figuring against a whitewashed wall, "twenty times eight is so and so; then forty-two times thirty-nine is so and so — ain't it, sir? Well, add those together, and subtract this here, then that makes so and so," still chalking away.

To be brief, after no small ciphering, Mr. Scribe informed me that my chimney contained, I am ashamed to say how many thousand and odd valuable bricks.

"No more," said I fidgeting. "Pray now, let us have a look above."

In that upper zone we made two more circum-navigations for the first and second floors. That done, we stood together at the foot of the stairway by the front door; my hand upon the knob, and Mr. Scribe hat in hand.

"Well, sir," said he, a sort of feeling his way, and, to help himself, fumbling with his hat, "well, sir, I think it can be done."

"What, pray, Mr. Scribe; what can be done?"

"Your chimney, sir; it can without rashness be removed, I think."

"I will think of it, too, Mr. Scribe" said I, turning the knob and bowing him towards the open space without, "I will think of it, sir; it demands consideration; much obliged to ye; good morning, Mr. Scribe."

"It is all arranged, then," cried my wife with great glee, bursting from the nighest room.

"When will they begin?" demanded my daughter Julia.

"To-morrow?" asked Anna.

"Patience, patience, my dears," said I, "such a big chimney is not to be abolished in a minute."

Next morning it began again.

"You remember the chimney," said my wife. "Wife," said I, "it is never out of my house and never out of my mind."

"But when is Mr. Scribe to begin to pull it down?" asked Anna.

"Not to-day, Anna," said I.

"When, then?" demanded Julia, in alarm.

Now, if this chimney of mine was, for size, a sort of belfry, for ding-donging at me about it, my wife and daughters were a sort of bells, always chiming together, or taking up each other's melodies at every pause, my wife the key-clapper of all. A very sweet ringing, and pealing, and chiming, I confess; but then, the most silvery of bells may, sometimes, dismally toll, as well as merrily play. And as touching the subject in question, it became so now. Perceiving a strange relapse of opposition in me, wife and daughters began a soft and dirge-like, melancholy tolling over it.

At length my wife, getting much excited, declared to me, with pointed finger, that so long as that chimney stood, she should regard it as the monument of what she called my broken pledge. But finding this did not answer, the next day, she gave me to understand that either she or the chimney must quit the house.

Finding matters coming to such a pass, I and my pipe philosophized over them awhile, and finally concluded between us, that little as our hearts went with the plan, yet for peace' sake, I might write out the chimney's death-warrant, and, while my hand was in, scratch a note to Mr. Scribe.

Considering that I, and my chimney, and my pipe, from having been so much together, were three great cronies, the facility with which my pipe consented to a project so fatal to the goodliest of our trio; or rather, the way in which I and my pipe, in secret, conspired together, as it were, against our unsuspicious old comrade—this may seem rather strange, if not suggestive of sad reflections upon us two. But, indeed, we, sons of clay, that is my pipe and I, are no better than the rest. Far from us, indeed, to have volunteered the betrayal of our crony. We are of a peaceable nature, too. But that love of peace it was which made us false to a mutual friend, as soon as his cause demanded a vigorous vindication. But, I rejoice to add, that better and braver thoughts soon returned, as will now briefly be set forth.

To my note, Mr. Scribe replied in person.

Once more we made a survey, mainly now with a view to a pecuniary estimate.

"I will do it for five hundred dollars," said Mr. Scribe at last, again hat in hand.

"Very well, Mr. Scribe, I will think of it," replied I, again bowing him to the door.

Not unvexed by this, for the second time, unexpected response, again he withdrew, and from my wife, and daughters again burst the old exclamations.

The truth is, resolved how I would, at the last pinch I and my chimney could not be parted.

So Holofernes will have his way, never mind whose heart breaks for it" said my wife next morning, at breakfast, in that half-didactic, half-reproachful way of hers, which is harder to bear than her most energetic assault. Holofernes, too, is with her a pet name for any fell domestic despot. So, whenever, against her most ambitious innovations, those which saw me quite across the grain, I, as in the present instance, stand with however little steadfastness on the defense, she is sure to call me Holofernes, and ten to one takes the first opportunity to read aloud, with a suppressed emphasis, of an evening, the first newspaper paragraph about some tyrannic day-laborer, who, after being for many years the Caligula of his family, ends by beating his long-suffering spouse to death, with a garret door wrenched off its hinges, and then, pitching his little innocents out of the window, suicidally turns inward towards the broken wall scored with the butcher's and baker's bills, and so rushes headlong to his dreadful account.

Nevertheless, for a few days, not a little to my surprise, I heard no further reproaches. An intense calm pervaded my wife, but beneath which, as in the sea, there was no knowing what portentous movements might be going on. She frequently went abroad, and in a direction which I thought not unsuspicious; namely, in the direction of New Petra, a griffin-like house of wood and stucco, in the highest style of ornamental art, graced with four chimneys in the form of erect dragons spouting smoke from their nostrils; the elegant modern residence of Mr. Scribe, which he had built for the purpose of a standing advertisement, not more of his taste as an architect, than his solidity as a master-mason.

At last, smoking my pipe one morning, I heard a rap at the door, and my wife, with an air unusually quiet for her brought me a note. As I have no correspondents except Solomon, with whom in his sentiments, at least, I entirely correspond, the note occasioned me some little surprise, which was not dismissed upon reading the following:

NEW PETRA, April 1st. Sir — During my last examination of your chimney, possibly

you may have noted that I frequently applied my rule to it in a manner apparently unnecessary. Possibly, also, at the same time, you might have observed in me more or less of perplexity, to which, however, I refrained from giving any verbal expression. I now feel it obligatory upon me to inform you of what was then but a dim suspicion, and as such would have been unwise to give utterance to, but which now, from various subsequent calculations assuming no little probability, it may be important that you should not remain in further ignorance of. It is my solemn duty to warn you, sir, that there is architectural cause to conjecture that somewhere concealed in your chimney is a reserved space, hermetically closed, in short, a secret chamber, or rather closet. How long it has been there, it is for me impossible to say. What it contains is hid, with itself, in darkness. But probably a secret closet would not have been contrived except for some extraordinary object, whether for the concealment of treasure, or for what other purpose, may be left to those better acquainted with the history of the house to guess. But enough: in making this disclosure, sir, my conscience is eased. Whatever step you choose to take upon it, is of course a matter of indifference to me; though, I confess, as respects the character of the closet, I cannot but share in a natural curiosity. Trusting that you may be guided aright, in determining whether it is Christian-like knowingly to reside in a house, hidden in which is a secret closet, I remain, with much respect, Yours very humbly,
— HIRAM SCRIBE.

My first thought upon reading this note was, not of the alleged mystery of manner to which, at the outset, it alluded — for none such had I at all observed in the master-mason during his surveys — but of my late kinsman, Captain Julian Dacres, long a ship-master and merchant in the Indian trade, who, about thirty years ago, and at the ripe age of ninety, died a bachelor, and in this very house, which he had built. He was supposed to have retired into this country with a large fortune. But to the general surprise, after being at great cost in building himself this mansion, he settled down into a sedate, reserved and inexpensive old age, which by the neighbors was thought all the better for his heirs: but lo! upon opening the will, his property was found to consist but of the house and grounds, and some ten thousand dollars in stocks; but the place, being found heavily mortgaged, was in consequence sold. Gossip had its day, and left the grass quietly to creep over the captain's grave, where he still slumbers in a privacy as unmolested as if the billows of the Indian Ocean, instead of the billows of inland verdure, rolled over him. Still, I remembered long ago, hearing strange solutions whispered by the country people for the mystery involving his will, and, by reflex, himself; and that, too, as well in conscience as purse. But people who could circulate the report (which they did), that Captain Julian Dacres had, in his day, been a Borneo pirate, surely were not worthy of credence in their collateral notions. It is queer what wild whimsies of rumors will, like toadstools, spring up about any eccentric stranger, who settling down among a rustic population, keeps quietly to himself. With some, inoffensiveness would seem a prime cause of offense. But what chiefly had led me to scout at these rumors, particularly as referring to concealed treasure, was the circumstance, that the stranger (the same who razed the roof and the chimney) into whose hands the estate had passed on my kinsman's death, was of that sort of character, that had there been the least ground for those reports, he would speedily have tested them, by tearing down and rummaging the walls.

Nevertheless, the note of Mr. Scribe, so strangely recalling the memory of my kinsman, very naturally chimed in with what had been mysterious, or at least unexplained, about him; vague flashings of ingots united in my mind with vague gleamings of skulls. But the first cool thought soon dismissed such chimeras; and, with a calm smile, I turned towards my wife, who, meantime, had been sitting nearby, impatient enough, I dare say, to know who could have taken it into his head to write me a letter.

"Well, old man," said she, "who is it from, and what is it about?"

"Read it, wife," said I, handing it.

Read it she did, and then — such an explosion! I will not pretend to describe her emotions, or repeat her expressions. Enough that my daughters were quickly called in to share the excitement. Although they had never dreamed of such a revelation as Mr. Scribe's; yet upon the first suggestion they instinctively saw the extreme likelihood of it. In corroboration, they cited first my kinsman, and second, my chimney; alleging that the profound mystery involving the former, and the equally profound masonry involving the latter, though both acknowledged facts, were alike preposterous on any other supposition than the secret closet.

But all this time I was quietly thinking to myself: Could it be hidden from me that my credulity in this instance would operate very favorably to a certain plan of theirs? How to get to the secret closet, or how to have any certainty about it at all, without making such fell work with my chimney as to render its set destruction superfluous? That my wife wished to get rid of the chimney, it needed no reflection to show; and that Mr. Scribe, for all his pretended disinterestedness, was not opposed to pocketing five hundred dollars by the operation, seemed equally evident. That my wife had, in secret, laid heads together with Mr. Scribe, I at present refrain from affirming. But when I consider her enmity against my chimney, and the steadiness with which at the last she is wont to carry out her schemes, if by hook or crook she can, especially after having been once baffled, why, I scarcely knew at what step of hers to be surprised.

Of one thing only was I resolved, that I and my chimney should not budge.

In vain all protests. Next morning I went out into the road, where I had noticed a diabolical-looking old gander, that, for its doughty exploits in the way of scratching into forbidden enclosures, had been rewarded by its master with a portentous, four-pronged, wooden decoration, in the shape of a collar of the Order of the Garotte. This gander I cornered and rummaging out its stiffest quill, plucked it, took it home, and making a stiff pen, inscribed the following stiff note:

CHIMNEY SIDE, April 2. MR. SCRIBE Sir:
For your conjecture, we return you our joint thanks and compliments, and beg leave to assure you, that we shall remain, Very faithfully, The same, I AND MY CHIMNEY.

Of course, for this epistle we had to endure some pretty sharp raps. But having at last explicitly understood from me that Mr. Scribe's note had not altered my mind one jot, my wife, to move me, among other things said, that if she remembered aright, there was a statute placing the keeping in private of secret closets on the same unlawful footing with the keeping of gunpowder. But it had no effect.

A few days after, my spouse changed her key.

It was nearly midnight, and all were in bed but ourselves, who sat up, one in each chimney-corner; she, needles in hand, indefatigably knitting a sock; I, pipe in mouth, indolently weaving my vapors.

It was one of the first of the chill nights in autumn. There was a fire on the hearth, burning low. The air without was torpid and heavy; the wood, by an oversight, of the sort called soggy.

"Do look at the chimney," she began; "can't you see that something must be in it?"

"Yes, wife. Truly there is smoke in the chimney, as in Mr. Scribe's note."

"Smoke? Yes, indeed, and in my eyes, too. How you two wicked old sinners do smoke! — this wicked old chimney and you."

"Wife," said I, "I and my chimney like to have a quiet smoke together, it is true, but we don't like to be called names."

"Now, dear old man," said she, softening down, and a little shifting the subject, "when you think of that old kinsman of yours, you know there must be a secret closet in this chimney."

"Secret ash-hole, wife, why don't you have it? Yes, I dare say there is a secret ash-hole in the chimney; for where do all the ashes go to that drop down the queer hole yonder?"

"I know where they go to; I've been there almost as many times as the cat."

"What devil, wife, prompted you to crawl into the ash-hole? Don't you know that St. Dunstan's devil emerged from the ash-hole? You will get your death one of these days, exploring all about as you do. But supposing there be a secret closet, what then?"

"What then? why what should be in a secret closet but —"

"Dry bones, wife," broke in I with a puff, while the sociable old chimney broke in with another.

"There again! Oh, how this wretched old chimney smokes," wiping her eyes with her handkerchief. "I've no doubt the reason it smokes so is, because that secret closet interferes with the flue. Do see, too, how the jambs here keep settling; and it's down hill all the way from the door to this hearth. This horrid old chimney will fall on our heads yet; depend upon it, old man."

"Yes, wife, I do depend on it; yes indeed, I place every dependence on my chimney. As for its settling, I like it. I, too, am settling, you know, in my gait. I and my chimney are settling together, and shall keep settling, too, till, as in a great feather-bed, we shall both have settled away clean out of sight. But this secret oven; I mean, secret closet of yours, wife; where exactly do you suppose that secret closet is? "

"That is for Mr. Scribe to say."

"But suppose he cannot say exactly; what, then?"

"Why then he can prove, I am sure, that it must be somewhere or other in this horrid old chimney."

"And if he can't prove that; what, then?"

"Why then, old man," with a stately air, "I shall say little more about it."

"Agreed, wife," returned I, knocking my pipe-bowl against the jamb, "and now, to-morrow, I will for a third time send for Mr. Scribe. Wife, the sciatica takes me; be so good as to put this pipe on the mantel."

"If you get the step-ladder for me, I will. This shocking old chimney, this abominable old-fashioned old chimney's mantels are so high, I can't reach them."

No opportunity, however trivial, was overlooked for a subordinate fling at the pile.

Here, by way of introduction, it should be mentioned, that besides the fireplaces all round it, the chimney was, in the most haphazard way, excavated on each floor for certain curious out-of-the-way cupboards and closets, of all sorts and sizes, clinging here and there, like nests in the crotches of some old oak. On the second floor these closets were by far the most irregular and numerous. And yet this should hardly have been so, since the theory of the chimney was, that it pyramidically diminished as it ascended. The abridgment of its square on the roof was obvious enough; and it was supposed that the reduction must be methodically graduated from bottom to top.

"Mr. Scribe," said I when, the next day, with an eager aspect, that individual again came, "my object in sending for you this morning is, not to arrange for the demolition of my chimney, nor to have any particular conversation about it, but simply to allow you every reasonable facility for verifying, if you can, the conjecture communicated in your note."

Though in secret not a little crestfallen, it may be, by my phlegmatic reception, so different from what he had looked for; with much apparent alacrity he commenced the survey; throwing open the cupboards on the first floor, and peering into the closets on the second; measuring one within, and then comparing that measurement with the measurement without. Removing the fireboards, he would gaze up the flues. But no sign of the hidden work yet.

Now, on the second floor the rooms were the most rambling conceivable. They, as it were, dove-tailed into each other. They were of all shapes; not one mathematically square room among them all — a peculiarity which by the master-mason had not been unobserved. With a significant, not to say portentous expression, he took a circuit of the chimney, measuring the area of each room around it; then going down stairs, and out of doors, he measured the entire ground area; then compared the sum total of the areas of all the rooms on the second floor with the ground area; then, returning to me in no small excitement, announced that there was a difference of no less than two hundred and odd square feet — room enough, in all conscience, for a secret closet.

"But, Mr. Scribe," said I, stroking my chin, "have you allowed for the walls, both main and sectional? They take up some space, you know."

"Ah, I had forgotten that," tapping his forehead; "but," still ciphering on his paper, "that will not make up the deficiency."

"But, Mr. Scribe, have you allowed for the recesses of so many fireplaces on a floor, and for the fire-walls, and the flues; in short, Mr. Scribe, have you allowed for the legitimate chimney itself — some one hundred and forty-four square feet or thereabouts, Mr. Scribe?"

"How unaccountable. That slipped my mind, too."

"Did it, indeed, Mr. Scribe?"

He faltered a little, and burst forth with, "But we must now allow one hundred and forty-four square feet for the legitimate chimney. My position is, that within those undue limits the secret closet is contained."

I eyed him in silence a moment; then spoke: "Your survey is concluded, Mr. Scribe; be so good now as to lay your finger upon the exact part of the chimney wall where you believe this secret closet to be; or would a witch-hazel wand assist you, Mr. Scribe?"

"No, Sir, but a crowbar would," he, with temper, rejoined.

Here, now, thought I to myself, the cat leaps out of the bag. I looked at him with a calm glance, under which he seemed somewhat uneasy. More than ever now I suspected a plot. I remembered what my wife had said about abiding by the decision of Mr. Scribe. In a bland way, I resolved to buy up the decision of Mr. Scribe.

"Sir," said I, "really, I am much obliged to you for this survey. It has quite set my mind at rest. And no doubt you, too, Mr. Scribe, must feel much relieved. Sir," I added, "you have made three visits to the chimney. With a business man, time is money. Here are fifty dollars, Mr. Scribe. Nay, take it. You have earned it. Your opinion is worth it. And by the way," as he modestly received the money "have you any objections to give me a — a — little certificate — something, say, like a steamboat certificate, certifying that you, a competent surveyor, have surveyed my chimney, and found no reason to believe any unsoundness; in short, any — any secret closet in it. Would you be so kind, Mr. Scribe?"

"But, but, sir," stammered he with honest hesitation."

"Here, here are pen and paper," said I, with entire assurance.

Enough.

That evening I had the certificate framed and hung over the dining-room fireplace, trusting that the continual sight of it would forever put at rest at once the dreams and stratagems of my household.

But, no. Inveterately bent upon the extirpation of that noble old chimney, still to this day my wife goes about it, with my daughter Anna's geological hammer, tapping the wall all over, and then holding her ear against it, as I have seen the physicians of life insurance companies tap a man's chest, and then incline over for the echo. Sometimes of nights she almost frightens one, going about on this phantom errand, and still following the sepulchral response of the chimney, round and round, as if it were leading her to the threshold of the secret closet.

"How hollow it sounds," she will hollowly cry. "Yes, I declare," with an emphatic tap, "there is a secret closet here. Here, in this very spot. Hark! How hollow!"

"Psha! wife, of course it is hollow. Who ever heard of a solid chimney?" But nothing avails. And my daughters take after, not me, but their mother.

Sometimes all three abandon the theory of the secret closet and return to the genuine ground of attack — the unsightliness of so cumbrous a pile, with comments upon the great addition of room to be gained by its demolition, and the fine effect of the projected grand hall, and the convenience resulting from the collateral running in one direction and another of their various partitions. Not more ruthlessly did the Three Powers partition away poor Poland, than my wife and daughters would fain partition away my chimney.

But seeing that, despite all, I and my chimney still smoke our pipes, my wife reoccupies the ground of the secret closet, enlarging upon what wonders are there, and what a shame it is, not to seek it out and explore it.

"Wife," said I, upon one of these occasions, "why speak more of that secret closet, when there before you hangs contrary testimony of a master mason, elected by yourself to decide. Besides, even if there were a secret closet, secret it should remain, and secret it shall. Yes, wife, here for once I must say my say.

Infinite sad mischief has resulted from the profane bursting open of secret recesses. Though standing in the heart of this house, though hitherto we have all nestled about it, unsuspicious of aught hidden within, this chimney may or may not have a secret closet. But if it have, it is my kinsman's. To break into that wall, would be to break into his breast. And that wall-breaking wish of Momus I account the wish of a church-robbing gossip and knave. Yes, wife, a vile eavesdropping varlet was Momus."

"Moses? Mumps? Stuff with your mumps and Moses?"

The truth is, my wife, like all the rest of the world, cares not a fig for philosophical jabber. In dearth of other philosophical companionship, I and my chimney have to smoke and philosophize together. And sitting up so late as we do at it, a mighty smoke it is that we two smoky old philosophers make.

But my spouse, who likes the smoke of my tobacco as little as she does that of the soot, carries on her war against both. I live in continual dread lest, like the golden bowl, the pipes of me and my chimney shall yet be broken. To stay that mad project of my wife's, naught answers. Or, rather, she herself is incessantly answering, incessantly besetting me with her terrible alacrity for improvement, which is a softer name for destruction. Scarce a day I do not find her with her tape-measure, measuring for her grand hall, while Anna holds a yardstick on one side, and Julia looks approvingly on from the other. Mysterious intimations appear in the nearest village paper, signed "Claude," to the effect that a certain structure, standing on a certain hill, is a sad blemish to an otherwise lovely landscape. Anonymous letters arrive, threatening me with I know not what, unless I remove my chimney. Is it my wife, too, or who, that sets up the neighbors to badgering me on the same subject, and hinting to me that my chimney, like a huge elm, absorbs all moisture from my garden? At night, also, my wife will start as from sleep, professing to hear ghostly noises from the secret closet. Assailed on all sides, and in all ways, small peace have I and my chimney.

Were it not for the baggage, we would together pack up and remove from the country.

What narrow escapes have been ours! Once I found in a drawer a whole portfolio of plans and estimates. Another time, upon returning after a day's absence, I discovered my wife standing before the chimney in earnest conversation with a person whom I at once recognized as a meddlesome architectural reformer, who, because he had no gift for putting up anything was ever intent upon pulling them down; in various parts of the country having prevailed upon half-witted old folks to destroy their old-fashioned houses, particularly the chimneys.

But worst of all was, that time I unexpectedly returned at early morning from a visit to the city, and upon approaching the house, narrowly escaped three brickbats which fell, from high aloft, at my feet. Glancing up, what was my horror to see three savages, in blue jean overalls in the very act of commencing the long-threatened attack. Aye, indeed, thinking of those three brickbats, I and my chimney have had narrow escapes.

It is now some seven years since I have stirred from my home. My city friends all wonder why I don't come to see them, as in former times. They think I am getting sour and unsocial. Some say that I have become a sort of mossy old misanthrope, while all the time the fact is, I am simply standing guard over my mossy old chimney; for it is resolved between me and my chimney, that I and my chimney will never surrender.

Assignments

- Warm-up: Discuss how Melville is poking fun at his friend Ralph Waldo Emerson and other romantics in his essay "I and My Chimney."

- Students should complete Concept Builder 12-E.

- Essays are due. Students should take the chapter 12 test.

Billy Budd is a study of evil. As evil takes away life, Melville defines it in the personhood of Claggart. How is Claggart evil? Give three reasons.

An intelligent, malevolent villian

Claggart

Chapter 13

1855–1865 (Part 1):

Division, War, and Reconciliation

First Thoughts The Civil war was neither the fault of the North nor the South. Or rather, it was the fault of both! The combination of an expanding economy, a flood of immigrants, the second Great Awakening, Manifest Destiny, and the failure of the American political system brought the young republic to the brink of Civil War. Ultimately, though, the failure of nerve manifested by American political leaders thrust the nation into its bloodiest war in American history. No war quite captured the minds and hearts of Americans as this war did, and this is reflected in the literature of this nation.

Author Worldview Watch Walt Whitman, like his contemporary Emily Dickinson, was the first truly modern American poet, blending realism and transcendentalism into his writing. He wrapped up his theistic morality in blank verse and earthy metaphors. Some of his works are still considered overt in the sexuality they express. The Negro spirituals, however, are a rich metaphor of biblical metaphors and narratives.

Chapter Learning Objectives Chapter 13 examines the poetry of Walt Whitman, the first, thoroughly modern American poet. We also examine Negro spirituals and Abraham Lincoln's "Gettysburg Address." Finally, we read the poignant words of Chief Joseph. You will analyze "Oh Captain! My Captain!" by Walt Whitman, Negro Spirituals, "The Gettysburg Address" by Abraham Lincoln, and "Surrender Speech" by Chief Joseph.

As a result of this chapter study you will be able to . . .

1. Describe the metaphors that Whitman uses in "O Captain, My Captain."

2. Explain in what sense Whitman's poetry is modern and romantic.

3. Analyze in what ways Negro spirituals were a form of resistance to chattel slavery.

4. Analyze Geronimo's views on Americans.

Weekly Essay Options: Begin on page 274 of the Teacher Guide.

Reading ahead: *Narrative of the Life of Frederick Douglass* by Frederick Douglass.

The American Civil War

Background In 1858, Senator William H. Seward of New York examined the sources of the conflicts between the North and the South. Some people, said Seward, thought the sectional conflict was "accidental, unnecessary, the work of interested or fanatical agitators, and therefore ephemeral." But Seward believed that these people were wrong. The roots of the conflict went far deeper. "It is an irrepressible conflict," Seward said, "between opposing and enduring forces." (www.bartleby.com/268/9/16.html, www.digitalhistory.uh.edu/database/article_display.cfm?HHID=335).

By 1858, a growing number of Northerners were convinced that two fundamentally antagonistic societies had evolved in the nation, one dedicated to freedom, the other opposed. They had come to believe that their society was locked in a life and death struggle with a Southern society dominated by an aggressive slave power, which had seized control of the federal government and imperiled the liberties of free people. Declared the *New York Tribune*:

We are not one people. We are two peoples. We are a people for Freedom and a people for Slavery. Between the two, conflict is inevitable (chroniclingamerica.loc.gov/).

G. K. Chesterton wrote in his book *What I Saw in America* (1923):

Again, it is characteristic that while the modern English know nothing about Lee they do know something about Lincoln; and nearly all that they know is wrong. They know nothing of his Southern connections, nothing of his considerable Southern sympathy, nothing of the meaning of his moderation in face of the problem of slavery, now lightly treated as self-evident. Above all, they know nothing about the respect in which Lincoln was quite un-English, was indeed the very reverse of English; and can be understood better if we think of him as a Frenchman, since it seems so hard for some of us to believe that he was an American. I mean his lust for logic for its own sake, and the way he kept mathematical truths in his mind like the fixed stars. He was so far from being a merely practical man, impatient of academic abstractions, that he reviewed and reveled in academic abstractions, even while he could not apply them to practical life. He loved to repeat that slavery was intolerable while he tolerated it, and to prove that something ought to be done while it was impossible to do it. This was probably very bewildering to his brother-politicians; for politicians always whitewash what they do not destroy. But for all that this inconsistent consistency beat the politicians at their own game, and this abstracted logic proved the most practical of all. For when the chance did come to do something, there was no doubt about the thing to be done. The thunderbolt fell from the clear heights of heaven; it had not been tossed about and lost like a common missile in the market-place. The matter is worth mentioning, because it has a moral for a much larger modern question. A wise man's attitude towards industrial capitalism will be very like Lincoln's attitude towards slavery. That is, he will manage to endure capitalism; but he will not endure a defense of capitalism. He will recognize the value, not only of knowing what he is doing, but of knowing what he would like to do. He will recognize the importance of having a thing clearly labeled in his own mind as bad, long before the opportunity comes to abolish it. He may recognize the risk of even worse things in immediate abolition, as Lincoln did in abolitionism. He will not call all business men brutes, any more than Lincoln would call all planters demons; because he knows they are not. He will regard many alternatives to capitalism as crude and inhuman, as Lincoln regarded John Brown's raid; because they are. But he will clear his mind from cant about capitalism; he will have no doubt of what is the truth about Trusts and Trade Combines and the concentration of capital; and it is the truth that they endure under one of the ironic silences of heaven, over the pageants and the passing triumphs of hell.—p.226 (www.gutenberg.org files/27250/27250-h/27250-h. htm#What_is_America)

Assignments

- Warm-up: If you lived during the Civil War, on which side would you fight?
- Students should complete Concept Builder 13-A.
- Students review the required reading(s) *before* the assigned chapter begins.
- Teachers may want to discuss assigned reading(s) with students.
- Teachers shall assign the required essay. The rest of the essays can be outlined, answered with shorter answers, discussed, or skipped.
- Students will review all readings for chapter 13.

CONCEPT BUILDER 13-A
Active Reading

"I Hear America Sing"
Walt Whitman

In this most famous of Walt Whitman's poems, he captures the spirit and essence of America in the middle of the 19th Century.

I hear America singing, the varied carols I hear,
Those of mechanics, each one singing his as it should be blithe and strong,
The carpenter singing his as he measures his plank or beam,
The mason singing his as he makes ready for work, or leaves off work,
The boatman singing what belongs to him in his boat, the deck hand singing on the steamboat deck,
The shoemaker singing as he sits on his bench, the hatter singing as he stands,
The woodcutter's song, the ploughboy's on his way in the morning, or at noon intermission or at sundown,
The delicious singing of the mother, or of the young wife at work, or of the girl sewing or washing,
Each singing what belongs to him or her and to none else,
The day what belongs to the day — at night the party of young fellows, robust, friendly,
Singing with open mouths their strong melodious songs.

Draw a picture that captures the essence of the United States of America in the beginning of the 21st century.

Walt Whitman

Background Whitman was one of the first American poets to abandon most of the romanticism of earlier poetry and create a distinctly American idiom to address those he celebrated as the "American masses." Walt Whitman, and later Carl Sandburg, spoke for a nation. Whitman and Emily Dickinson were the first modern American poets.

O Captain! My Captain!

O CAPTAIN! my Captain! our fearful trip is done;

The ship has weather'd every rack, the prize we sought is won;

The port is near, the bells I hear, the people all exulting,

While follow eyes the steady keel, the vessel grim and daring:

But O heart! heart! heart!

O the bleeding drops of red,

Where on the deck my Captain lies,

Fallen cold and dead.

O Captain! my Captain! rise up and hear the bells;

Rise up — for you the flag is flung — for you the bugle trills;

For you bouquets and ribbon'd wreaths — for you the shores a-crowding;

For you they call, the swaying mass, their eager faces turning;

Here Captain! dear father!

This arm beneath your head;

It is some dream that on the deck,

You've fallen cold and dead.

My Captain does not answer, his lips are pale and still;

My father does not feel my arm, he has no pulse nor will;

The ship is anchor'd safe and sound, its voyage closed and done;

From fearful trip, the victor ship, comes in with object won;

Exult, O shores, and ring, O bells!

But I, with mournful tread,

Walk the deck my Captain lies,

Fallen cold and dead.

Assignments

- Warm-up: Write a poem about someone you were very close to who died.
- Students should complete Concept Builder 13-B.
- Student should review reading(s) from the next chapter.
- Student should outline essay due at the end of the week.
- Per teacher instructions, students may answer orally, in a group setting, some of the essays that are not assigned as formal essays.

CONCEPT BUILDER 13-B
Active Reading

Read "O Captain! My Captain!" by Walt Whitman in the text and then answer the following questions.

1	What is the central metaphor that Whitman is offering?
2	What is the crisis?
3	What effect does Whitman create by repeating this refrain throughout the poem?

The Walt Whitman House in Camden, NJ, where Walt Whitman spent the last years of his life. Photo by Midnightdreary, 2007 (PD-US).

Negro Spirituals

Spirituals were the sacred hymns of the African American slave community. They most often communicated a chapter and account from the Old Testament.

The most grievous historical metaphor for the African-American community is chattel slavery. It is the quintessential image of the apparent triumph of white racism in the American civilization. This unhappy time captures the African American heart as strongly as the Egyptian bondage motif captures the Old Testament community. Slavery presented African Americans with a disconcerting contradiction: legally they were defined as property; but, at the same time, they were called upon to act in sentient, articulate, and human ways.

The ultimate goal of many African peoples was preservation and promotion of community, not retribution and revenge. This community spirit of beneficence, forbearance, practical wisdom, improvisation, forgiveness, and justice was nurtured, preserved, and celebrated in the African American community — but only at great personal sacrifice. Therefore, African American resistance was a uniquely American phenomenon. This resulted from 300 years of historical oppression.

Deep River

Deep river,
My home is over Jordan.
Deep river, Lord,
I want to cross over into campground.
Lord, I want to cross over into campground.

Oh, don't you want to go,
To that gospel feast;
That Promised Land,

Where all is peace?
Walk into heaven, and take a seat,
And cast my crown at Jesus feet.

Lord, I want to cross over into campground.
Lord, I want to cross over into campground.
Lord, I want to cross over into campground.
Lord, I want to cross over into campground.

Roll Jordan, Roll

Roll, Jordan, roll.
Roll, Jordan, roll.
I wanter go to heav'n when I die,
To hear ol' Jordan roll.
O brethren,
Roll, Jordan, roll.
Roll, Jordan, roll.
I wanter go to heav'n when I die,
To hear ol' Jordan roll.

Oh, brothers you oughter been dere.
Yes, my Lord,
A-sittin' in the Kingdom,
To hear ol' Jordan roll.

Sing it over,
Oh, sinner you oughter been dere.
Yes my Lord,
A-sittin' in the Kingdom,
To hear ol' Jordan roll.

Swing Low, Sweet Chariot

Swing low, sweet chariot,
Coming for to carry me home.
Swing low, sweet chariot,
Coming for to carry me home.

I looked over Jordan, and I what did I see,
Coming for to carry me home?
A band of angels coming after me,
Coming for to carry me home.

If you get there before I do,
Coming for to carry me home.
Tell all my friends I coming too,
Coming for to carry me home.

I'm sometimes up, I'm sometimes down,
Coming for to carry me home.
But still my soul feels heavenly bound,
Coming for to carry me home.

Assignments

- Warm-up: Why were African American slaves so attracted to Christianity?
- Students should complete Concept Builder 13-C.
- Students should write rough drafts of assigned essay.
- The teacher may correct rough drafts.

CONCEPT BUILDER 13-C
Active Reading

Explain why each of the highlighted stanzas are examples of slave resistance.

When Israel was in Egypt's land
Let my people go　————————
Oppressed so hard they could not stand
Let my people go

Go down Moses
Way down in Egypt land
Tell old Pharaoh
Let my people go

Thus spoke the Lord
bold Moses said
Let my people go

If not I'll smite your first born dead
Let my people go　————————

No more in bondage shall they toil
Let my people go

Let them come out with Egypt's spoil
Let my people go

Abraham Lincoln

Sometimes great literature takes months, even years to create. Apparently, Lincoln wrote this most famous of small speeches while traveling on a train from Washington, DC, to Gettysburg, Pennsylvania. It was presented on November 19, 1863, to dedicate a cemetery interning Union war dead who fell at the Battle of Gettysburg, July 1–3, 1863.

Gettysburg Address

Fourscore and seven years ago our fathers brought forth on this continent a new nation, conceived in liberty and dedicated to the proposition that all men are created equal. Now we are engaged in a great civil war, testing whether that nation or any nation so conceived and so dedicated can long endure. We are met on a great battlefield of that war. We have come to dedicate a portion of that field as a final resting-place for those who here gave their lives that that nation might live. It is altogether fitting and proper that we should do this. But in a larger sense, we cannot dedicate, we cannot consecrate, we cannot hallow this ground. The brave men, living and dead who struggled here have consecrated it far above our poor power to add or detract. The world will little note nor long remember what we say here, but it can never forget what they did here. It is for us the living rather to be dedicated here to the unfinished work which they who fought here have thus far so nobly advanced. It is rather for us to be here dedicated to the great task remaining before us — that from these honored dead we take increased devotion to that cause for which they gave the last full measure of devotion — that we here highly resolve that these dead shall not have died in vain, that this nation under God shall have a new birth of freedom, and that government of the people, by the people, for the people shall not perish from the earth.

Assignments

- Warm-up: Why is this simple, short speech so effective
- Students should complete Concept Builder 13-D.
- Students will re-write corrected copies of essay due tomorrow.

If you were writing a poem celebrating yourself, or your family, what would you celebrate?

My soccer skills

Myself

Chief Joseph of the Nez Perce

Chief Joseph (1840?–1904) was chief of the Nez Perce and one of the leaders of Native American resistance to white assimilation and domination in the western United States. Following his father's example, Chief Joseph continued a policy of non-compliance to an 1863 treaty that confined the Nez Perce to a government reservation. In 1877, hostilities broke out. The Nez Perce were ordered to leave the Oregon territory and relocate to a reservation in Idaho. Joseph reluctantly agreed to the demand, but when a few of his men killed a group of whites, he decided to lead several hundred people on a march to find refuge in Canada. He defeated United States Army units that tried to stop him on the Big Hole River in Montana, but was stopped about 48 miles from the border where he presented the following speech.

I Will Fight No More Forever 1877

I will fight no more forever.

I am tired of fighting.

Our chiefs are killed.

Looking Glass is dead.

Toohulhulsote is dead.

The old men are all dead.

It is the young men who say no and yes.

He who led the young men is dead.

It is cold and we have no blankets.

The little children are freezing to death.

My people, some of them,

Have run away to the hills

And have no blankets, no food.

No one knows where they are

Perhaps they are freezing to death.

I want to have time to look for my children

And see how many of them I can find.

Maybe I shall find them among the dead.

Hear me, my chiefs, I am tired.

My heart is sad and sick.

From where the sun now stands

I will fight no more forever.

Assignments

- Warm-up: Write a letter to Chief Joseph explaining to him what has happened.
- Students should complete Concept Builder 13-E.
- Essays are due. Students should take the chapter 13 test.

Chief Joseph wrote that Whitman likes to use repetition and parallelism (related ideas). Find examples of repetition and parallelism in his poem, "I Will Fight No More Forever."

Repetition	Parallelism

Nez Perce Chief Joseph and his family in Leavenworth where they were exiled from 1877 to 1885. Photo by F. M. Sargent, c1880 (PD-US).

Chapter 14

1855–1865 (Part 2):

Division, War, and Reconciliation

First Thoughts Frederick Douglass, an ex-slave, through his biography gives an insightful narrative of what was the abominable institution of slavery, which itself was ended by the most deadly of American conflicts, the American Civil War. Douglass wrote, "Slavery does away with fathers, as it does away with families. Slavery has no use for either fathers or families, and its laws do not recognize their existence in the social arrangements of the plantation. . . . I assert most unhesitatingly, that the religion of the South — as I have observed it and proved it — is a mere covering for the most horrid crimes; a justifier of the most appalling barbarity; a sanctifier of the most hateful frauds; and a dark shelter, under which the darkest, foulest, grossest, and most infernal abominations fester and flourish. Were I again to be reduced to the condition of a slave, next to that calamity, I should regard the fact of being the slave of a religious slaveholder, the greatest that could befall me" (Frederick Douglass, *Narrative of the Life of Frederick Douglass*, chapters 3 and 18).

Author Worldview Watch Frederick Douglass is truly a great American. His profound faith drove his education and his education drove his acute sense of social justice. His narratives are full of inspiring biblical allusions to Christian virtue.

Chapter Learning Objectives In chapter 14 we examine one of the most important autobiographies in American literature: Narrative of the Life of Frederick Douglass by Frederick Douglass, who was born in slavery and died a free American.

As a result of this chapter study you will be able to . . .

1. Discuss the style and form of *Narrative of the Life of Frederick Douglass*.

2. Discuss Douglass's faith journey.

3. Consider if there are biblical reasons why two believers of different races should not be married.

4. Compare Phillis Wheatley and Frederick Douglass.

Weekly Essay Options: Begin on page 274 of the Teacher Guide.

Reading ahead: *The Adventures of Huckleberry Finn,* by Mark Twain.

Narrative of the Life of Frederick Douglass

Frederick Douglass

Frederick Douglass was born into slavery sometime in 1817 or 1818. Like many slaves, he was unsure of his exact date of birth. Douglass was separated from his mother, Harriet Bailey, soon after he was born. His father was most likely their white master, Captain Anthony. Captain Anthony was the clerk of a rich man named Colonel Lloyd. Lloyd owned hundreds of slaves. Life on any of Lloyd's plantations, like that on many Southern plantations, was brutal. In 1845, just seven years after his escape from slavery, the young Frederick Douglass published this powerful account of his life in bondage. Its original name was *Narrative of the life of Frederick Douglass*, an American Slave (1845). It was rewritten as *My Bondage and My Freedom* (1855) and then as *Life and Times of Frederick Douglass* (1881).

Frederick Douglass House, Washington, D.C., is preserved as a National Historic Site. Photo by Walter Smalling, 1977 (Library of Congress, Prints & Photographs Division, DC,WASH,166-12).

Assignments

- Warm-up: What does Douglass learn that is the key to freedom?
- Students should complete Concept Builder 14-A.
- Students review the required reading(s) *before* the assigned chapter begins.
- Teachers may want to discuss assigned reading(s) with students.
- Teachers shall assign the required essay. The rest of the essays can be outlined, answered with shorter answers, discussed, or skipped.
- Students will review all readings for chapter 14.

The Narrative of the Life of Frederick Douglass
by Frederick Douglass

I had left Master Thomas's house, and went to live with Mr. Covey, on the 1st of January, 1833. I was now, for the first time in my life, a field hand. In my new employment, I found myself even more awkward than a country boy appeared to be in a large city. I had been at my new home but one week before Mr. Covey gave me a very severe whipping, cutting my back, causing the blood to run, and raising ridges on my flesh as large as my little finger. The details of this affair are as follows: Mr. Covey sent me, very early in the morning of one of our coldest days in the month of January, to the woods, to get a load of wood. He gave me a team of unbroken oxen. He told me which was the in-hand ox, and which the off-hand one. He then tied the end of a large rope around the horns of the in-hand ox, and gave me the other end of it, and told me, if the oxen started to run, that I must hold on upon the rope. I had never driven oxen before, and of course I was very awkward. I, however, succeeded in getting to the edge of the woods with little difficulty; but I had got a very few rods into the woods, when the oxen took fright, and started full tilt, carrying the cart against trees, and over stumps, in the most frightful manner. I expected every moment that my brains would be dashed out against the trees. After running thus for a considerable distance, they finally upset the cart, dashing it with great force against a tree, and threw themselves into a dense thicket. How I escaped death, I do not know. There I was, entirely alone, in a thick wood, in a place new to me. My cart was upset and shattered, my oxen were entangled among the young trees, and there was none to help me. After a long spell of effort, I succeeded in getting my cart righted, my oxen disentangled, and again yoked to the cart. I now proceeded with my team to the place where I had, the day before, been chopping wood, and loaded my cart pretty heavily, thinking in this way to tame my oxen. I then proceeded on my way home. I had now consumed one half of the day. I got out of the woods safely, and now felt out of danger. I stopped my oxen to open the woods gate; and just as I did so, before I could get hold of my ox-rope, the oxen again started, rushed through the gate, catching it between the wheel and the body of the cart, tearing it to pieces, and coming within a few inches of crushing me against the gate-post. Thus twice, in one short day, I escaped death by the merest chance. On my return, I told Mr. Covey what had happened, and how it happened. He ordered me to return to the woods again immediately. I did so, and he followed on after me. Just as I got into the woods, he came up and told me to stop my cart, and that he would teach me how to trifle away my time, and break gates. He then went to a large gum-tree, and with his axe cut three large switches, and, after trimming them up neatly with his pocket knife, he ordered me to take off my clothes. I made him no answer, but stood with my clothes on. He repeated his order. I still made him no answer, nor did I move to strip myself. Upon this he rushed at me with the fierceness of a tiger, tore off my clothes, and lashed me till he had worn out his switches, cutting me so savagely as to leave the marks visible for a long time after. This whipping was the first of a number just like it, and for similar of offenses. . . . Mr. Covey's forte consisted in his power to deceive. His life was devoted to planning and perpetrating the grossest deceptions. Everything he possessed in the shape of learning or religion, he made conform to his disposition to deceive. He seemed to think himself equal to deceiving the Almighty. He would make a short prayer in the morning, and a long prayer at night; and, strange as it may seem, few men would at times appear more devotional.

Frederick Douglass, *The Narrative of the Life of Frederick Douglass* (New York: Penguin Classics, 1845), sunsite.berkeley.edu/Literature/Douglass/Auto-biography.

1	Is Douglass a credible witness? Can we rely on his remembrances as being accurate portrayals of slave life?
2	What will happen to Frederick Douglass when Mr. Cove discovers Douglass has wrecked his cart?

Civil War Poetry

www.civilwarpoetry.org/

ROBERT E. LEE by Julia Ward Howe (1819–1910)

A gallant foeman in the fight,
A brother when the fight was o'er,
The hand that led the host with might
The blessed torch of learning bore.

No shriek of shells nor roll of drums,
No challenge fierce, resounding far,

When reconciling Wisdom comes
To heal the cruel wounds of war.

Thought may the minds of men divide,
Love makes the heart of nations one,
And so, the soldier grave beside,
We honor thee, Virginia's son.

JACKSON'S FOOT-CAVALRY By Hard-Cracker

Day after day our way has been
O'er many a hill and hollow;
Through marsh and bog, by wood and glen —
Where "Stonewall" leads, we follow.
Through dust-clouds rising dim and thick,
Or smoke of battle o'er us,
Close to our leader we must "stick,"
As he trots on before us.

Now we're trotting up a hill,
Or fast behind it sinking;
Or jumping o'er some road-side rill,
Without a pause for drinking;
Now crowding on the narrow road
In thick and struggling masses;
Now skirmishing the fields so broad,
Or guarding mountain passes.

Our march is thirty miles a day,
And forty — now and then —

But that's not strange, you well may say,
For we are Jackson's men.
Before the sun gets up, we rise,
And eat our beef and dough,
And e'er the morn has left the skies,
We're off upon the "go."

With five days' rations of fresh meat,
(And no shirts) on our backs,
And "nary a leather" on our feet,
We're ever making tracks.
In this sad plight we dash ahead
From morn till late at night,
Or else are halted, well-nigh dead,
To charge the foe in fight.

Ah! then we throw aside our beef —
Our blankets follow suit;
The exchange, we know, is our relief —
We're sure to get the boot.

No wonder that the Yankees run,
And will not stop to fight;
For we've no need of sword or gun —
They cannot stand a sight.
Our long hair floating on the wind,
Like witches in Macbeth —
They know they dare not lag behind —
We'll have their — shoes, or death!

Young man! if truly you desire
To join our gallant band —
If "Jack's" the leader you admire,
Enlist in our command.
You'll meet the "Yanks" ere many a day.
If killed — why, what's the loss?
In Heaven you'll be proud to say,
I was one of "Jack's Foot Horse."

LINCOLN MONUMENT: WASHINGTON by Langston Hughes (1902–1967)

Let's go see Old Abe
Sitting in the marble and the moonlight,
Sitting lonely in the marble and the moonlight,
Quiet for ten thousand centuries, old Abe.
Quiet for a million, million years.
Quiet —

And yet a voice forever
Against the
Timeless walls
Of time —
Old Abe.

KILLED AT THE FORD by Henry Wadsworth Longfellow (1807–1882)

He is dead, the beautiful youth,
The heart of honor, the tongue of truth,
He, the life and light of us all,
Whose voice was blithe as a bugle-call,
Whom all eyes followed with one consent,
The cheer of whose laugh, and whose pleasant word,
Hushed all murmurs of discontent.

Only last night, as we rode along,
Down the dark of the mountain gap,
To visit the picket-guard at the ford,
Little dreaming of any mishap,
He was humming the words of some old song:
"Two red roses he had on his cap
And another he bore at the point of his sword."

Sudden and swift a whistling ball
Came out of a wood, and the voice was still;
Something I heard in the darkness fall,
And for a moment my blood grew chill;
I spoke in a whisper, as he who speaks

In a room where some one is lying dead;
But he made no answer to what I said.

We lifted him up to his saddle again,
And through the mire and the mist and the rain
Carried him back to the silent camp,
And laid him as if asleep on his bed;
And I saw by the light of the surgeon's lamp
Two white roses upon his cheeks,
And one, just over his heart, blood red!

And I saw in a vision how far and fleet
That fatal bullet went speeding forth,
Till it reached a town in the distant North,
Till it reached a house in a sunny street,
Till it reached a heart that ceased to beat
Without a murmur, without a cry;
And a bell was tolled in that far-off town,
For one who had passed from cross to crown,
And the neighbors wondered that she should die.

Assignments

- Warm-up: What is your favorite Civil War poem and why?
- Students should complete Concept Builder 14-B.
- Student should review reading(s) from the next chapter.
- Student should outline essay due at the end of the week.
- Per teacher instructions, students may answer orally, in a group setting, some of the essays that are not assigned as formal essays.

CONCEPT BUILDER 14-B
Factual vs. Subjective

Facts are uncontestable events that can be reliably related to the reader. Subjective statements are opinion, with room for interpretation. List at least one of the facts and subjective statements of the passage on 14-A, or use other passages in Douglass' autobiography.

Fact	Subjective Statement

Civil War Songs

THE BATTLE HYMN OF THE REPUBLIC

by Julia Ward Howe (1819–1910)

Mine eyes have seen the glory of the coming of the Lord;

He is trampling out the vintage where grapes of wrath are stored;

He hath loosed the fateful lightning of His terrible swift sword,

His truth is marching on.

CHORUS: Glory, glory, hallelujah! Glory, glory, hallelujah!

Glory, glory, hallelujah! His truth is marching on.

I have seen Him in the watchfires of a hundred circling camps;

They have builded Him an altar in the evening dews and damps;

I can read His righteous sentence by the dim and flaring lamps,

His day is marching on. — CHORUS

I have read a fiery gospel writ in burnished rows of steel:

"As ye deal with My contemners, so with you My Grace shall deal;

Let the Hero, born of woman, crush the serpent with his heel,

Since God is marching on." — CHORUS

He has sounded forth the trumpet that shall never call retreat;

He is sifting out the hearts of men before His Judgement Seat.

Oh! Be swift, my soul, to answer Him, be jubilant, my feet!

Our God is marching on. — CHORUS

In the beauty of the lilies Christ was born across the sea,

With a glory in his bosom that transfigures you and me;

As he died to make men holy, let us die to make men free,

While God is marching on. — CHORUS

WHEN THIS CRUEL WAR IS OVER by Charles Carroll Sawyer

Dearest Love, do you remember, when we last did meet,

How you told me that you loved me, kneeling at my feet?

Oh! How proud you stood before me, in your suit of blue,

When you vow'd to me and country, ever to be true.

CHORUS: Weeping, sad and lonely, hopes and fears how vain!

When this cruel war is over, praying that we meet again.

When the summer breeze is sighing, mournfully along,

Or when autumn leaves are falling, sadly breathes the song.

Oft in dreams I see thee lying on the battle plain,

Lonely, wounded, even dying, calling but in vain. — CHORUS

If amid the din of battle, nobly you should fall,

Far away from those who love you, none to hear you call —

Who would whisper words of comfort, who would soothe your pain? ·

Ah! The many cruel fancies, ever in my brain. — CHORUS

But our Country called you, Darling, angels cheer your way;

While our nation's sons are fighting, we can only pray.

Nobly strike for God and Liberty, let all nations see

How we loved the starry banner, emblem of the free. — CHORUS

DIXIE'S LAND by Daniel Decatur Emmett (1815–1904)

I wish I was in the land of cotton,

Old times there are not forgotten;

Look away! Look away! Look away, Dixie's Land!

In Dixie's Land where I was born in,

Early on one frosty morning,

Look away! Look away! Look away, Dixie's Land!

CHORUS: Then I wish I was in Dixie! Hooray! Hooray!

In Dixie's Land I'll take my stand, to live and die in Dixie!

Away! Away! Away down South in Dixie!

Away! Away! Away down South in Dixie!

Old Missus married "Will the Weaver";

William was a gay deceiver!

Look away! Look away! Look away, Dixie's Land!

But when he put his arm around her,

Smiled as fierce as a forty-pounder!

Look away! Look away! Look away, Dixie's Land! — CHORUS

His face was sharp as a butcher's cleaver;

But that did not seem to grieve her!

Look away! Look away! Look away, Dixie's Land!

Old Missus acted the foolish part

And died for a man that broke her heart!

Look away! Look away! Look away, Dixie's Land! — CHORUS

Now here's a health to the next old missus

And all the gals that want to kiss us!

Look away! Look away! Look away, Dixie's Land!

But if you want to drive away sorrow,

Come and hear this song tomorrow!

Look away! Look away! Look away, Dixie's Land! — CHORUS

There's buckwheat cakes and Injin batter,

Makes you fat or a little fatter!

Look away! Look away! Look away, Dixie's Land!

Then hoe it down and scratch your gravel,

To Dixie's Land I'm bound to travel!

Look away! Look away! Look away, Dixie's Land! — CHORUS

THE YELLOW ROSE OF TEXAS

There's a yellow rose in Texas
That I am going to see.
No other soldier knows her —
No soldier, only me.
She cried so when I left her,
It like to broke my heart,
And if I ever find her,
We never more shall part.

CHORUS: She's the sweetest rose of color
This soldier ever knew.
Her eyes are bright as diamonds,
They sparkle like the dew.
You may talk about your dearest May
And sing of Rosa Lee,
But the Yellow Rose of Texas
Beats the belles of Tennessee.

Where the Rio Grande is flowing
And the starry skies are bright,
She walks along the river
In the quiet summer night.

She thinks, if I remember,
When we parted long ago,
I promised to come back again
And not to leave her so. — CHORUS

Oh, now I'm going to find her,
For my heart is full of woe,
And we'll sing the song together
That we sang so long ago.
We'll play the banjo gaily,
And we'll sing the songs of yore,
And the Yellow Rose of Texas
Shall be mine forever more. — CHORUS

Oh, now I'm headed southward,
For my heart is full of woe.
I'm going back to Georgia
To find my Uncle Joe.
You may talk about your Beauregard
And sing of Bobby Lee,
But the gallant Hood of Texas,
He played hell in Tennessee! — CHORUS

Assignments

- Warm-up: Living a part of my life north of Vicksburg, Mississippi, less than 100 years after the American Civil War, I never heard the "Battle Hymn of the Republic" except on the radio and on television. Why? Was such a thing petty or patriotic?
- Students should complete Concept Builder 14-C.
- Students should write rough drafts of assigned essay.
- The teacher may correct rough drafts.

Long before daylight, I was called to go and rub, curry, and feed, the horses. I obeyed, and was glad to obey. But whilst thus engaged, whilst in the act of throwing down some blades from the loft, Mr. Covey entered the stable with a long rope; and just as I was half out of the loft, he caught hold of my legs, and was about tying me. As soon as I found what he was up to, I gave a sudden spring, and as I did so, he holding to my legs, I was brought sprawling on the stable floor. Mr. Covey seemed now to think he had me, and could do what he pleased; but at this moment — from whence came the spirit I don't know — I resolved to fight; and, suiting my action to the resolution, I seized Covey hard by the throat; and as I did so, I rose. He held on to me, and I to him. My resistance was so entirely unexpected that Covey seemed taken all aback. He trembled like a leaf. This gave me assurance, and I held him uneasy, causing the blood to run where I touched him with the ends of my fingers. Mr. Covey soon called out to Hughes for help. Hughes came, and, while Covey held me, attempted to tie my right hand. While he was in the act of doing so, I watched my chance, and gave him a heavy kick close under the ribs. This kick fairly sickened Hughes, so that he left me in the hands of Mr. Covey. This kick had the effect of not only weakening Hughes, but Covey also. When he saw Hughes bending over with pain, his courage quailed. He asked me if I meant to persist in my resistance. I told him I did, come what might; that he had used me like a brute for six months, and that I was determined to be used so no longer. With that, he strove to drag me to a stick that was lying just out of the stable door. He meant to knock me down. But just as he was leaning over to get the stick, I seized him with both hands by his collar, and brought him by a sudden snatch to the ground. By this time, Bill came. Covey called upon him for assistance. Bill wanted to know what he could do. Covey said, "Take hold of him, take hold of him!" Bill said his master hired him out to work, and not to help to whip me; so he left Covey and myself to fight our own battle out. We were at it for nearly two hours. Covey at length let me go, puffing and blowing at a great rate, saying that if I had not resisted, he would not have whipped me half so much. The truth was, that he had not whipped me at all. I considered him as getting entirely the worst end of the bargain; for he had drawn no blood from me, but I had from him. The whole six months afterwards, that I spent with Mr. Covey, he never laid the weight of his finger upon me in anger. He would occasionally say, he didn't want to get hold of me again. "No," thought I, "you need not; for you will come off worse than you did before."

This battle with Mr. Covey was the turning point in my career as a slave. It rekindled the few expiring embers of freedom, and revived within me a sense of my own manhood. It recalled the departed self-confidence, and inspired me again with a determination to be free. The gratification afforded by the triumph was a full compensation for whatever else might follow, even death itself. He only can understand the deep satisfaction which I experienced, who has himself repelled by force the bloody arm of slavery. I felt as I never felt before. It was a glorious resurrection, from the tomb of slavery, to the heaven of freedom. My long-crushed spirit rose, cowardice departed, bold defiance took its place; and I now resolved that, however long I might remain a slave in form, the day had passed forever when I could be a slave in fact. I did not hesitate to let it be known of me, that the white man who expected to succeed in whipping, must also succeed in killing me.

From this time I was never again what might be called fairly whipped, though I remained a slave four years afterwards. I had several fights, but was never whipped.

What does the protagonist learn about himself and Mr. Covey and how does this change him forever?

The Civil War
Shelby Foote

Shelby Foote (November 17, 1916–June 27, 2005) was an American historian and novelist who wrote *The Civil War: A Narrative*, a massive, three-volume history of the war, and in many ways the definitive historical work on the subject. Foote was born across the river from where I was born, Greenville, Mississippi, a thriving river town until the Mississippi River changed course and formed Lake Ferguson.

Shelby Foote called the American Civil War "the last romantic and the first modern war." Literary critic Peter S. Prescott wrote, "History and literature are rarely so thoroughly combined as here."

"I glory in Mississippi's star! But before I would see it dishonored I would tear it from its place, to be set on the perilous ridge of battle as a sign around which her bravest and best shall meet the harvest home of death."

— Jefferson Davis, speaking in November 1860

When a Virginian or a Carolinian spoke of his "country," he meant Virginia or Carolina. It was not so with Davis. Tennessee and Kentucky were as familiar to him as Mississippi; the whole south, as a region, formed his background; he was 30 before he knew a real home in any real sense of the word.

Davis was winning a position as a leader in the Senate, he had become the spokesman for southern nationalism, which in those days meant not independence but domination from within the Union. This movement had been given impetus by the Mexican War. Up till then the future of the country pointed north and west, but now the needle trembled and suddenly swung south. The treaty signed as Guadelupe Hidalgo brought into the Union a new southwestern domain, seemingly ripe for slavery and the southern way of life . . . here was room for expansion indeed, with more to follow; for the nationalists looked forward to taking what was left of Mexico . . . yet the North, so recently having learned the comfort of the saddle, had no intention of yielding the reins. The South would have to fight for this; and this the South was prepared to do, using States Rights for a spear and the Constitution for a shield . . . the North opposed this dream of southern expansion by opposing the extension of slavery, without which the new southwestern territory would be anything but southern.

"When the white man governs himself, that is self-government; but when he governs himself and also governs another man, that is more than self-government, that is despotism."

— Abraham Lincoln, speaking in October 1854

The Whigs had foundered, the Democrats had split on all those rocks. Like many men just know, Lincoln hardly knew where he stood along party lines . . . he was waiting and looking. And then he found the answer. It was 1856, a presidential election year. Out of the Nebraska crisis, two years before, the Republican Party had been born, a coalition of foundered Whigs and disaffected northern Democrats, largely abolitionist at the core.

"You people of the South don't know what you are doing. This country will be drenched in blood, and God only knows how it will end. It is folly, madness, a crime against civilization! You people speak so lightly of war; you don't know what you're talking about. War is a terrible thing! You mistake too, the people of the North. They are a peaceable people but an earnest people, and they will fight too. They are not going to let this country be destroyed without a mighty effort to save it. . . . Besides, where are your man and appliances of war to contend against them? The North can make a steam engine, locomotive or railway car, hardly a yard of cloth or a pair of shoes can you make. You are rushing into war with one of the most powerful, ingeniously mechanical people on earth — right at your doors. You are bound to fail. Only in your spirit and your determination are you prepared for war. In all else you are totally unprepared, with a bad cause to start with. At first you will make headway, but as your limited resources begin to fail, shut out from the markets of Europe as you will be, your cause will begin to wane. If your people will but stop and think, they must see that in the end you will surely fail."

— William Tecumseh Sherman, speaking in December 1860

Strategically the South would fight a defensive war, and to her accordingly would proceed all the advantages of the defensive: advantages which had been increasing in ratio to the improvements in modern weapons. A study of the map would show additional difficulties for the North, particularly in the theater lying between the two capitals, where the rivers ran east and west across the line of march, presenting a series of obstacles to the invader. In the West it would be otherwise; there the rivers ran north and south for the most part, broad highways for invasion; but few were looking westward in those days. The northern objective, announced early in the war by the man who would be her leading general, was "unconditional surrender." Against this stern demand, southern soldiers would fight in defense of their homes, with all the fervour and desperation accompanying such a position. The contrast, of course, would be as true on the home front as in the armies, together with additional knowledge on both sides that the North could stop fighting at any time, with no loss of independence or personal liberty: whereas the South would lose not only her national existence, but would have to submit, in the course of peace, to any terms the victor might exact under a government that would interpret, and even rewrite, the Constitution in whatever manner seemed most to its advantage. Under such conditions, given the American pride and the American love of liberty and self-government, it seemed certain that the South would fight would all her strength. Whether the North, driven by no such necessities, would exert herself to a similar extent in a war of conquest remained to be seen.

In Richmond, Jefferson Davis repeated, "All we ask is to be let alone," a remark which a Virginia private was to translate into combat terms when he told his captors, "I'm fighting because you're down here." Davis knew as well as Lincoln that after the balance sheet was struck, after the advantages of the preponderance of manpower and materiel had been weighed against the advantages of the strategical defensive, what would decide the contest was the people's will to resist, on the home front as well as on the field of battle (http://homepage.eircom.net/~odyssey/Quotes/History/Shelby_Foote.html).

Assignments

- Warm-up: What does Foote mean when he calls the American Civil War the last romantic and first modern war"?
- Students should complete Concept Builder 14-D.
- Student will re-write corrected copies of essay due tomorrow.

CONCEPT BUILDER 14-D
Character Profile

Circle words on the following figure that describe Frederick Douglass from your reading earlier in the week. Under what character heading (choleric, melancholic, sanguine, phlegmatic) does he lie? How does he change?

Frederick Douglass

Melancholic	**Choleric**
moody	touchy
anxious	restless
rigid	aggressive
sober	excitable
pessimistic	changeable
reserved	impulsive
unsociable	optimistic
quiet	active
Phlegmatic	**Sanguine**
passive	sociable
careful	outgoing
thoughtful	talkative
peaceful	responsive
controlled	easy-going
reliable	lively
even-tempered	carefree
calm	leadership

The Battle of Antietam

Harper's Weekly, October 4, 1862

The Internet closed down most magazines; however, during the Civil War *Harper's Weekly* sold thousands of copies of its magazine every week. This is a news correspondent account of the Battle of Antietam where 23,000 soldiers — more than all previous American wars combined — were killed, wounded, or missing after 12 hours of savage combat on September 17, 1862.

The battle began with the dawn. Morning found both armies just as they had slept, almost close enough to look into each other's eyes. The left of Meade's reserves and the right of Rickett's line became engaged at nearly the same moment, one with artillery, the other with infantry. A battery was almost immediately pushed forward beyond the central woods, over a plowed field, near the top of the slope where the corn-field began. On this open field, in the corn beyond, and in the woods, which stretched forward into the broad fields like a promontory into the ocean, were the hardest and deadliest struggles of the day.

For half an hour after the battle had grown to its full strength the line of fire swayed neither way. Hooker's men were fully up to their work. They saw their General every where in front, never away from the fire, and all the troops believed in their commander, and fought with a will. Two-thirds of them were the same men who, under M'Dowell, had broken at Manassas.

The half hour passed, the rebels began to give way a little, only a little, but at the first indication of a receding fire, Forward! was the word, and on went the line with a cheer and a rush. Back across the corn-field, leaving dead and wounded behind them, over the fence, and across the road, and then back again into the dark woods which closed around them, went the retreating rebels.

Meade and his Pennsylvanians followed hard and fast—followed til they came within easy range of the woods, among which they saw their beaten enemy disappearing—followed still, with another cheer, and flung themselves against the cover.

But out of those gloomy woods came suddenly and heavier terrible volleys—volleys which smote, and bent, and broke in a moment that eager front, and hurled them swiftly back for half the distance they had won. Not swiftly, nor in a panic, any further. Closing up their shattered lines, they came slowly away—a regiment where a brigade had been, hardly a brigade where a whole division had been, victorious. They had met from the woods the first volleys of musketry from fresh troops—had met them and returned them till their line had yielded and gone down before the weight of fire, and till their ammunition was exhausted.

In ten minutes the fortune of the day seemed to have changed—it was the rebels now who were advancing, pouring out of the woods in endless lines, sweeping through the corn-field from which their comrades had just fled. Hooker sent in his nearest brigade to meet them, but it could not do the work. He called for another. There was nothing close enough, unless he took it from his right. His right might be in danger if it was weakened, but his centre was already threatened with annihilation. Not hesitating one moment, he sent to Doubleday, "Give me your best brigade instantly."

The best brigade came down the hill to the right on the run, went through the timber in front through a storm of shot and bursting shell and crashing limbs, over the open field beyond, and straight into the corn-field, passing as they went the fragments of three brigades shattered by the rebel fire, and streaming to the rear. They passed by Hooker, whose eyes lighted as he saw these veteran troops led by a soldier whom he knew he could trust. "I think they will hold it," he said.

General Hartsuff took his troops very steadily, but now that they were under fire, not hurriedly, up the hill, from which the corn-field begins to descend, and formed them on the crest. Not a man who was not in full view—not one who bent before the storm. Firing at first in volleys, they fired them at will with wonderful rapidity and effect. The whole line crowned the hill and stood out darkly against the sky, but lighted and shrouded ever in flame and smoke. There were the Twelfth and Thirteenth Massachusetts, and another regiment which I can not remember—old troops all of them.

There for half an hour they held the ridge, unyielding in purpose, exhaustless in courage. There were gaps in the line, but in nowhere quailed. Their General was wounded badly early in the fight, but they fought on. Their supports did not come—they determine to win without them. They began to go down the hill and into the corn; they did not stop to think that their ammunition was nearly gone; they were there to win that field, and they won it. The rebel line for the second time fled through the corn and into the woods. I can not tell how few of Hartsuff's brigade were left when the work was done, but it was done. There was no more gallant, determined, heroic fighting in all this desperate day. General Hartsuff is very severely wounded, but I do not believe he counts his success too dearly purchased.

After describing the progress of the fight, the wounding of Hooker, the command devolving upon Sumner, the advance of Sedgwick, and finally the abandonment of the corn-field after a terrible struggle . . . (www.civilwarliterature.com/).

Assignments

- Warm-up: Young men, hardly more than boys, would attack impregnable positions with the expectation that they would die. Could you do that?

- Students should complete Concept Builder 14-E.

- Essays are due. Students should take the chapter 14 test.

CONCEPT BUILDER 14-E
Literature and History

The Narrative of the Life of Frederick Douglass **is a story of a real man in a real time in history when mankind enslaved each other. The picture below is a famous picture found in a North Carolina attic in 2010 of two slave children. Write a story describing what life is like for these two children.**

Chapter 15

1865–1915 (Part 1):
Realism, Naturalism, and the Frontier

First Thoughts "All modern American literature comes from one book by Mark Twain called *Huckleberry Finn*."

— Ernest Hemingway (classiclit.about. com/od/.../a/huckfinn_writer.htm)

He didn't mean that no Americans before Mark Twain had written anything worthy of being called literature. What he meant was that Twain had written the first truly American piece of literature. Twain was responsible for defining what would make American literature different from everybody else's literature. Twain was the first major writer to use real American speech to deal with themes and topics that were important to Americans, and to assume that the concerns of Americans were as worthy of serious treatment as European motifs. Twain, then, in a real way, was the 19th-century Durante degli Alighieri, who was bold enough to write the first major literary piece in his own, native language. Both books, by the way, were scandalous among their first audiences.

Author Worldview Watch The talented Mark Twain was the first enigmatic realist and in his memorable protagonist Huck Finn we see a marriage of morality and realism that will not last long. Though Twain believed in a "god," he disliked orthodox Christianity, disbelieved literal interpretations of the Bible, and had a misconstrued concept of sin. Still, the reader can find Christian truth in Adventures of Huckleberry Finn.

Chapter Learning Objectives In chapter 15 we begin our study of *The Adventures of Huckleberry Finn* by Mark Twain.

As a result of this chapter study you will be able to . . .

1. Compare Huckleberry Finn to the young Samuel of the Old Testament (1 Sam.1–3).

2. Explain how Twain develops the character Jim.

3. Contrast Huck in the beginning of the novel with the Huck who emerges at the end.

4. Explain what advantages and disadvantages does first-person narration present Twain.

5. Imagine the realist Huck joining the romantic/transcendalist Henry David Thoreau for a year on the edge of Walden Pond. What would be their points of agreement? Disagreement?

Weekly Essay Options: Begin on page 274 of the Teacher Guide.

 History connections: *American History* chapter 15, "Reconstruction."

The Adventures of Huckleberry Finn

Mark Twain

Background In the final paragraph of *The Adventures of Huckleberry Finn*, Huck says, ". . . so there ain't nothing more to write about, and I am rotten glad of it, because if I'd 'a' knowed what a trouble it was to make a book I wouldn't 'a' tackled it, and ain't a' going to no more." As you'll see when you've read the novel, the mock-sentiment is very much in character; but you can also read it as an expression of Mark Twain's relief at finishing the most difficult book he ever wrote. The book had taken him more than seven years to complete! At one point he was so frustrated with it that he considered burning what he'd written. Instead, he put it aside and worked on three other books that were published before *Huck Finn*. On one level, *Huckleberry Finn* is a hilarious adventure of a free-spirited young American doing what we all want to do: live in the woods and have no responsibilities. On another level, however, Twain is exploring the more despondent side of humanity. At the end of his life, Twain had to endure many unhappy tragedies. His wife died in 1904. In 1909 his youngest daughter died, leaving Twain a sick and unhappy man. As you read *Huckleberry Finn* see if you can identify both Mark Twains.

About the Author Samuel Langhorne Clemens, Mark Twain (1835–1910), was born in Florida, Missouri, but grew up on the Mississippi River in Hannibal, Missouri. He happily lived as a river pilot on the Mississippi River until the Civil War ended river traffic. In 1861, Twain moved west. It was in the West that he wrote "The Celebrated Jumping Frog of Calavaras County." Throughout his life Twain enjoyed entertaining Americans with his whimsical writings; but below the surface, Twain was a complicated, and, many felt, a bitter man. At the end of his life, Mark Twain said, "Everything human is pathetic. The secret source of humor itself is not joy but sorrow. There is no humor in heaven" (www.brainyquote.com/quotes/authors/m/mark_twain.html).

Other Notable Works

The Adventures of Tom Sawyer (1876)

Life on the Mississippi (1883)

A Connecticut Yankee in King Arthur's Court (1889)

A literary movement called realism began with the writings of Mark Twain. Realism is defined as the faithful representation in literature of the actual events of life. Realism grew out of a protest against romanticism — a literary movement that sentimentalized nature.

Suggested Vocabulary Words
Use these words in essays that you write this week.

Chapter V: temperance

Chapter IX: reticule

Chapter XVII: wince pensive

Chapter XX: degraded histrionic

Chapter XXV: obsequies

Chapter XXIX: ingenious

Mark Twain's boyhood home in Hannibal, Missouri.
Photo by Andrew Balet, 2006 (CC BY-SA 3.0).

Assignments

- Warm-up: Jim and Huck are ironically trying to escape from slavery by floating down the Mississippi River. Why is this escape ironic?

- Students should complete Concept Builder 15-A.

- Students review the required reading(s) before the assigned chapter begins.

- Teachers may want to discuss assigned reading(s) with students.

- Teachers shall assign the required essay. The rest of the essays can be outlined, answered with shorter answers, discussed, or skipped.

- Students will review all readings for chapter 15.

CONCEPT BUILDER 15-A Active Reading		
	Read *The Adventures of Huckleberry Finn*, chapter one, by Mark Twain then answer the following questions.	
	1	Twain is writing to an audience that does not have televisions or computers. Twain has to use language to paint a picture for his audience. Notice the descriptions that Twain uses. Write two here.
	2	How does Twain create humor in this passage?
	3	What is the narrative point of view? Why does Twain choose this narrative point of view?

Realism

Principles of Realism	1. Insistence upon the experienced commonplace 2. Character more important than plot 3. Attack upon romanticism and romantic writers 4. Morality is fluid not static. Situation ethics is the rule of the day. 5. Concept of realism as a realization of democracy
Identifying Characteristics of Realistic Writing	1. The purpose of writing is to instruct and to entertain. Realists were pragmatic, relativistic, democratic, and experimental. 2. The subject matter of realism is drawn from the common, the average, the non-extreme, the representative, the probable. 3. The morality of realism is intrinsic and relativistic. 4. Emphasis is placed upon scenic presentation, de-emphasizing authorial comment and evaluation. Realistic novels rarely use the omniscient point of view.
Realistic Characterization	Realists believe that humans control their destinies; characters act on their environment rather than simply reacting to it. Character is superior to circumstance.
The Use of Symbolism and Imagery	The realists generally reject the kind of symbolism suggested by Emerson when he said, "Every natural fact is a symbol of some spiritual fact" (www.brainyquote.com/quotes/authors/m/mark_twain.html).Their use of symbolism is controlled and limited; they depend more on the use of images.
Writing Techniques	1. Settings thoroughly familiar to the writer 2. Plots emphasizing the norm of daily experience 3. Ordinary characters, studied in depth 4. Complete authorial objectivity 5. A world truly reported

Assignments

- Warm-up: Give examples of realism in *Huckleberry Finn*.
- Students should complete Concept Builder 15-B.
- Students should review reading(s) from the next chapter.
- Students should outline essay due at the end of the week.
- Per teacher instructions, students may answer orally, in a group setting, some of the essays that are not assigned as formal essays.

CONCEPT BUILDER 15-B
Active Reading

Read *The Adventures of Huckleberry Finn*, chapter two, by Mark Twain and then answer the following questions.

1	How does Twain introduce Jim to the reader?
2	Tom Sawyer is a foil. How does Twain use Tom Sawyer to develop Huck?
3	How necessary is the vulgarity in this story?

Point of View

Point of view is the relationship of the narrator to the events of the story. *Huckleberry Finn* is told by the character Huck. Is he a credible reliable narrator?

It seems like he is. Huck uses ordinary words like you and I use and he does it through first person. This makes him personable; but it does not make him credible.

Questions about credibility are important. We see everything through Huck's eyes. We don't have a distant narrator telling the story; we do not have two or three narrators telling the story. We have no other perspective to compare this story to, except the perspective of Huck Finn.

Is Huck reliable? Huck is an uneducated 14-year-old boy living in a village in the 1840s. He has the knowledge, beliefs, and experiences of a 14-year-old illiterate boy. He is a prejudiced Southerner.

Huck Finn is an unreliable narrator — one who does not understand the full significance of the events he describes and comments on. Huck is not intentionally unreliable; his lack of education and experience makes him so. In fact, Huck's incredulity creates much of the humor in the novel.

This does not mean that Huck Finn is not a unique, extraordinary American fictional protagonist. In Huck, Twain creates a character who was very unlike himself and you and me, and he had Huck speak in a way that probably would have offended the ears of many people. In choosing Huck as his narrator, Twain was declaring a vow of divorce from formal, stiff literature. This was no helpless Oliver Twist. This was no pensive, insightful Jane Eyre. Huck was not a Frederick Usher whose life was complicated by the intrusion of the supernatural.

With Huck, Twain broke this mold and started something new.

Assignments

- Warm-up: What is your first impression of Huck? Why?
- Students should complete Concept Builder 15-C.
- Students should write rough drafts of assigned essay.
- The teacher may correct rough drafts.

A	Judge Thatcher
B	The Widow Douglas and Miss Watson
C	Jim
D	Aunt Polly
E	The duke and the dauphin
F	The Grangerfords
G	Tom Sawyer
H	The Wilks
I	Pap
J	Silas Phelps and Sally Phelps
K	Huck Finn

Place the correct letter in the blank.

___ 1	A family who befriend Huck and offer him a place to stay after a steamboat hits his raft. They are involved in a feud with another family, the Shepherdsons, which eventually gets many of them killed.
___ 2	The central character and storyteller in *The Adventures of Huckleberry Finn*.
___ 3	Huck's friend. He is creative, bossy, and loves to re-create crazy adventures found in novels.
___ 4	Two rich sisters who live together and adopt Huck.
___ 5	One of the sisters' slaves. He is superstitious, intelligent, practical, and often degraded by other characters in the novel.
___ 6	Family is made up of three sisters, who are rich, kind, and vulnerable.
___ 7	Tom Sawyer's aunt and uncle, whom Huck finds in his search for Jim after the con men sell him.
___ 8	Tom Sawyer's aunt and Sally Phelps's sister.
___ 9	Huck's father, the town's drunken bum. He is illiterate and beats Huck regularly, especially for going to school.
___ 10	Age 30, and age 70, are a couple of con men rescued by Huck and Jim as they are run out of a river town.
___ 11	A local magistrate, also cares for Huck and is responsible for the money Huck and Tom found in the book.

Characterization

Characterization is the technique a writer uses to help you become acquainted with a person, or character. There are basically four methods of characterization: physical appearance, speech and actions, attitudes of other characters toward the main character, and the main character's inner thoughts and feelings. Motivation is the combination of character traits that causes a character to act in a certain manner. In good writing, the reader can find valid reasons for the characters' behavior.

Huck is the son of the town drunkard, a perfect foil for the young Huck. He is a man who goes away for long stretches and beats his son when he's home. He is, in short, the penultimate opposite of Huck, his son.

Huck is perhaps the first post-modern character in American literature. Post-modernism celebrates the subjective and is post-structuralism. In other words, Huck's behavior is unpredictable. He is very thoughtful about his approach to problems and to challenges. Most importantly, though, he is very moral. But his morality is loosely what I call a "nostalgic Judeo-Christian" morality based mostly on the Golden Rule. In fact, it is a morality very close to the Golden Mean developed by Aristotle in his book on ethics, *Nicomachean Ethics*.

Huck Finn approaches traditional ideas and practices (e.g., slavery) in non-traditional ways that deviate from pre-established superstructural modes.

Huck has an ambivalent attitude toward himself. On the one hand, he keeps telling us that he knows he's "low-down" and "ornery," and that he is not at all "respectable." On the other hand, he is selfish. He almost always goes his own way, makes up his own mind, and lives by his own standards with no regard to others.

The realist, post-modern Huck, has romantic tendencies. He prefers living in the woods to being in a "sivilized" home. But, when push comes to shove, he does what he considers to be the "right" thing.

Assignments

- Warm-up: Huck is not a static character. As the novel progresses, he matures. What additional knowledge about the problems of life has Huck acquired by the time he gets to the Phelps' farm?

- Students should complete Concept Builder 15-D.

- Student will re-write corrected copies of essay due tomorrow.

Place these events in the right order:

____	Jim is recaptured and Tom and Huck have to explain what they've done. Tom, it turns out, knew all along that Miss Watson had set Jim free in her will, so everyone can now return home together. Huck, however, thinks he's had enough of civilization, and hints that he might take off for the Indian Territory instead of going back home.
____	He tells us about Miss Watson, the widow's sister, who is bent on teaching him manners and religion, and about Tom Sawyer, a boy Huck looks up to because of his wide reading and vivid imagination. He's also friendly with Jim, Miss Watson's black slave.
____	Jim is also hiding on the island, since he has run away from Miss Watson, who was about to sell him and separate him from his wife and children. They decide to escape together, and when they find a large raft, their journey along the Mississippi River begins.
____	Huck introduces himself as someone who appeared in an earlier book by Mark Twain, reminding us of what happened at the end of that story.
____	Huck's father returns and takes him away from the widow. When his father begins beating him too often, Huck runs away and makes it look as though he's been murdered. He hides out on a nearby island, intending to take off after his neighbors stop searching for his body.
____	By this time Jim has repaired the raft, and Huck rejoins him. They're soon joined by two men who are escaping the law and who claim to be a duke and the son of the king of France. Huck knows they're actually small-time con men, but he pretends to believe them.
____	After a couple of adventures on the river, their raft is hit by a steamboat, and Huck and Jim are separated. Huck goes ashore and finds himself at the home of the Grangerfords, who allow him to come and live with them. At first he admires these people for what he thinks is their class and good taste. But when he learns about the deaths caused by a feud with another family, he becomes disgusted with them.
____	True to his imaginative style, Tom devises a plan that is infinitely more complicated than it has to be. Eventually they actually pull it off and reach the raft without being caught. Tom, however, has been shot in the leg, and Jim refuses to leave until the wound has been treated.
____	The two crooks sell Jim to a farmer in one of the towns they're visiting. Huck learns about this and decides to free his friend. The farmer turns out to be Tom Sawyer's uncle, and through a misunderstanding he and his wife think Huck is Tom. When Tom himself arrives, Huck brings him up to date on what's happening. Tom pretends to be his own brother Sid, and the two boys set about to rescue Jim.
____	After watching these frauds bilk people of their money in two towns, Huck is forced to help them try to swindle an inheritance out of three girls who were recently orphaned. He goes along at first because he doesn't want them to turn Jim in, but eventually he decides that the thieves have gone too far. He invents a complicated plan to escape and to have them arrested.

Criticisms

Criticism quotes compiled from barronsbooknotes.com *The Adventures of Huckleberry Finn*

His fresh handling of the materials and techniques of backwoods story-tellers is the clearest example in our history of the adaptation of a folk art to serious literary uses.

— Henry Nash Smith, Mark Twain, 1963

Mark Twain, in short, who as a personality could not help but be a humorist, as a literary artist whose works were channeled by such currents, could not help but be an American humorist. His works are, in a sense, a summary of nineteenth-century native American humor.

— Walter Blair, Mark Twain and Huck Finn, 1960

The Adventures of Huckleberry Finn is a book, rare in our literature, which manages to suggest the lovely possibilities of life in America without neglecting its terrors.

— Leo Marx, "Mr. Eliot, Mr. Trilling, and Huckleberry Finn," 1953

The Adventures of Huckleberry Finn is one of those rare books which are at once acceptable to the intelligentsia and to that celebrated American phenomenon, the average citizen; it is a book which even anti-literary children read and enjoy. Even if the language of the book should eventually be lost or, worse still, replaced by convenient abridgements, the memory of Huck Finn would still survive among us like some old and indestructible god.

— James M. Cox, "Remarks on the Sad Initiation of Huckleberry Finn," 1955

Clemens was sole, incomparable, the Lincoln of our literature.

— William Dean Howells, in Mark Twain's Huckleberry Finn, 1959

I think he mainly misses fire. I think his life misses fire; he might have been something; but he never arrives.

— Walt Whitman in Mark Twain's Huckleberry Finn, 1959

All modern American literature comes from one book by Mark Twain called Huckleberry Finn. If you read it you must stop where Jim is stolen from the boys. That is the real end. The rest is just cheating. But it's the best book we've had. All American writing comes from that. There was nothing before. There has been nothing as good since.

— Ernest Hemingway, in Mark Twain's Huckleberry Finn, 1959

Huck Finn is alone: there is no more solitary character in fiction. The fact that he has a father only emphasizes his loneliness; and he views his father with a terrifying detachment. So we come to see Huck himself in the end as one of the permanent symbolic figures of fiction; not unworthy to take a place with *Ulysses, Faust, Don Quixote, Don Juan, Hamlet,* and other great discoveries that man has made about himself.

— T.S. Eliot, in Mark Twain's Huckleberry Finn, 1959

In one sense, *Huckleberry Finn* seems a circular book, ending as it began with a refused adoption and a projected flight; and certainly it has the effect of refusing the reader's imagination passage into the future. But there is a break-through in the last pages, especially in the terrible sentence which begins, "But I reckon I got to light out for the territory ahead of the rest. . . ." In these words, the end of childhood is clearly signaled; and we are forced to ask the question, which, duplicitously, the book refuses to answer: what will become of Huck if he persists in his refusal to return to the place where he has been before?

— Leslie A. Fiedler, Love and Death in the American Novel, 1982

(Barrons Booknotes free to AOL customers http://aol.com)

Steamboat on the Mississippi River

Assignments

- Warm-up: Why does Huck put a dead snake on Jim's blanket? What harm comes to Jim as a result of the incident? Huck feels regret. Have you done something that you regret?

- Students should complete Concept Builder 15-E.

- Essays are due. Students should take the chapter 15 test.

Twain tells his story in informal/slang English. Rewrite these passages in more formal English.

YOU don't know about me without you have read a book by the name of The Adventures of Tom Sawyer; but that ain't no matter. That book was made by Mr. Mark Twain, and he told the truth, mainly. There was things which he stretched, but mainly he told the truth. That is nothing. I never seen anybody but lied one time or another, without it was Aunt Polly, or the widow, or maybe Mary. Aunt Polly — Tom's Aunt Polly, she is — and Mary, and the Widow Douglas is all told about in that book, which is mostly a true book, with some stretchers, as I said before.

How Jim speaking. "Say, who is you? Whar is you? Dog my cats ef I didn' hear sumf'n. Well, I know what I's gwyne to do: I's gwyne to set down here and listen tell I hears it agin."
So he set down on the ground betwixt me and Tom. He leaned his back up against a tree, and stretched his legs out till one of them most touched one of mine. My nose begun to itch. It itched till the tears come into my eyes. But I dasn't scratch. Then it begun to itch on the inside. Next I got to itching underneath. I didn't know how I was going to set still. This miserableness went on as much as six or seven minutes; but it seemed a sight longer than that. I was itching in eleven different places now. I reckoned I couldn't stand it more'n a minute longer, but I set my teeth hard and got ready to try. Just then Jim begun to breathe heavy; next he begun to snore — and then I was pretty soon comfortable again.

Chapter 16

1865–1915 (Part 2):

Realism, Naturalism, and the Frontier

First Thoughts One of the reasons we classify some writers as great is that they permanently change the world in which they live. They alter the consciousness of the people they write for. They create a prototype for all writers who come after them. Mark Twain was such an author. He made Americans proud of their unique surroundings and their special heritage. Twain made it respectable to feature a hero who could barely read and write, whose language was peppered with vulgarity and figures of speech. Huck would be out of place in the living rooms of most of the readers of the novel but he lives on in all our hearts — anyone who has wanted to build a raft and escape on the river. Literary critic Frank Baldanza writes, "Huck Finn is an allegory about God and man. The Mississippi River is a force that provides both beauty and terror. Huck represents mankind's need to retreat (at least from time to time) from the real world and to take solace in the pleasures of religion" (Frank Baldanza, *Mark Twain*, 1961).

Chapter Learning Objectives In chapter 16 we continue our study of *The Adventures of Huckleberry Finn*, by Mark Twain. You will analyze *The Adventures of Huckleberry Finn*, Mark Twain.

As a result of this chapter study you will be able to . . .

1. Evaluate the effectiveness of the end of the novel.

2. Analyze Twain's handling of Christianity.

3. Describe what the goal of Huck's journey is.

4. Give at least one example of Twain's cynicism.

5. Describe when, if ever, civil disobedience is appropriate.

Weekly Essay Options: Begin on page 274 of the Teacher Guide.

 History connections: *American History* chapter 16, "Reconstruction: Primary Sources."

Jim

Jim, the slave, is perhaps the most "moral" person in the novel. He never lies. His affection and loyalty for Huck is genuine.

Jim is a slave owned by Miss Watson, the sister of the woman who's caring for Huck. He has a wife and small children, and the threat of being separated from them causes him to run away from his owner before she can sell him. Jim is a stereotypical, Southern version of a slave — illiterate, superstitious, childlike, and afraid of the supernatural, characteristics that are the subject of some of the humor in the book. But he's also gentle, sensitive, loyal, and capable of very profound, evocative feelings. In some scenes he seems more childish than Huck; in others, he's an adult for Huck to rely on. In fact, he is the most mature adult in the entire novel!

He is the perfect foil for Huck because he becomes Huck's conscience. Some critics even suggest that he is the protagonist himself. Jim is also the person who brings Huck to a series of important moral decisions. Huck develops what is very much like a fraternal love for this African-American man. Notwithstanding Uncle Tom, in Harriet Beecher Stowe's *Uncle Tom's Cabin*, this is the first time in literature that an American novelist creates a strong African-American character.

Assignments

- Warm-up: Is Jim a credible, reliable character?
- Students should complete Concept Builder 16-A.
- Students review the required reading(s) before the assigned chapter begins.
- Teachers may want to discuss assigned reading(s) with students.
- Teachers shall assign the required essay. The rest of the essays can be outlined, answered with shorter answers, discussed, or skipped.
- Students will review all readings for chapter 16.

CONCEPT BUILDER 16-A Active Reading		Read *The Adventures of Huckleberry Finn* chapter three by Mark Twain and then answer the following questions.
	1	Discuss Twain's views about religion.
	2	Huck is a realist; Tom is a romantic. Give an example to illustrate both worldviews.
	3	Why does Huck refer to a people group as the A-rabs? Does he mean any disrespect?

Tom Sawyer

Tom is a friend of Huck, a boy Huck admires for his wide reading, unbridled imagination, and flair. Tom is the Romantic. Tom is the "sophisticated" interpreter of reality. He has a lot of credibility with Huck. Less with Jim. Almost none with readers.

An expert at everything, Tom appoints himself leader of a gang dedicated to robbing and killing. Unlike Huck, Tom is a weaver of fantastic tales and grand schemes. Since most of his knowledge of the world comes from his reading of romantic novels, his life plots and schemes are redundant. He's amusing when he shows his imperfect understanding of what he has read, and when he gives literal meaning to things that existed only in the imagination of the people who wrote those books.

Whereas Huck Finn is acutely aware of the exigencies of the real world, Tom Sawyer never lives in the real world. Critic Frank Baldanza writes, "Huck is as ambivalent about Tom as he is about himself. On the one hand, Huck idolizes him. He sees Tom's wide reading and vivid imagination as qualities that set Tom far above himself, and he often mentions how Tom would have enjoyed some particularly difficult feat that he himself has just pulled off. On the other hand, Huck has little patience with fantasies, including Tom's. Huck is interested in the concrete, the here-and-now, and he doesn't have the faith necessary to engage in fantasies. He often becomes annoyed with Tom's daydreams, but he always goes along because he believes that Tom is one of his betters" (Frank Baldanza, *Mark Twain*, 1961).

Assignments

- Warm-up: Why is Tom Sawyer an antagonist, or close to it, in this novel?
- Students should complete Concept Builder 16-B.
- Students should review reading(s) from the next chapter.
- Students should outline essay due at the end of the week.
- Per teacher instructions, students may answer orally, in a group setting, some of the essays that are not assigned as formal essays.

CONCEPT BUILDER 16-B Active Reading		Read *The Adventures of Huckleberry Finn*, chapters four and five, by Mark Twain and then answer the following questions.
	1	Why does Huck give away his money?
	2	Why does Twain introduce Huck's father at this time? What do you think will happen?

Form and Structure

The structure of a literary piece is the way an author places his literary elements to tell his story. Normally, author choices in structure are most evident in the plot. Does the author use a flashback and a frame story? Is there one climax or multiple climaxes? Is there one continuous plot — like *A Tale of Two Cities* — or are there multiple episodes and plot strains — like *Huckleberry Finn.*

Along that line, many critics were disappointed with the last quarter of the book — the section in which Tom Sawyer puts Jim and Huck through his meaningless "adventure" rituals. Until that point, the book has a fairly purposeful structure; and then, some people say, it wanders off into another story that has little to do with everything that went before.

Twain divides his novel into three sections. In the first section, Huck introduces himself, Tom, and Jim. He gives us a lot of background information about what he thinks and how he's different from the people he knows. And we learn more about him by contrasting foils in his life — Tom Sawyer, Pap, and Miss Watson. The second — and longest — section has Huck running away from civilization and Jim running away from slavery. They do this together. The second section is the part where Jim and Huck develop a friendship and Huck matures considerably.

In the final section, Huck is back in civilization. In the Arkansas feuding section this return is quite sobering. Jim becomes little more than a stage prop, and Huck is an observer, as Tom once again steals center stage. This final structural section bothers a lot of critics.

The structure of *Huckleberry Finn* is the weakest part of this novel.

Assignments

- Warm-up: Pretend you are Mark Twain's editor and you are going to publish a second edition. What changes in structure would you suggest?
- Students should complete Concept Builder 16-C.
- Students should write rough drafts of assigned essay.
- The teacher may correct rough drafts.

CONCEPT BUILDER 16-C
Exaggerations/Similes

Create similes (exaggerations):

I am as hungry as a _____.

I am as tall as a _____.

I am as quiet as a _____.

I am sleeping like a _____.

The mountain is as wide as a _____.

My school work is as difficult as a _____.

Time is moving as slowly as a _____.

Morning comes as quickly as _____.

Vacation seems as far away as _____.

The cool water felt like _____.

Student Essay:

Cynicism in *Huckleberry Finn*

Diogenes of Sinope's life was the quintessential paradigm of the Greek philosophical movement known as Cynicism. From his example, in which, "he strove to destroy social conventions" ("Cynic." *Encyclopedia Britannica.* 15th ed. Print), the modern word 'cynicism' was born. This contempt for social conventions, or cynicism, can be seen in Mark Twain's novel, *Huckleberry Finn,* where the characters violate the present-day legal and social norms regarding slavery.

Early on in his journey down the Mississippi river, Huckleberry Finn begins to experience misgivings about assisting Jim, his companion who is a runaway slave, in his escape. Indeed, so strong is the social code which has been ingrained into Finn, that he contemplates turning Jim in. Though Finn feels, "easy, and happy, and light as a feather right off" (Twain, Mark. *Adventures of Huckleberry Finn.* New York: Dover Publications, Inc., 1994. Print.), his conscience soon starts to nag him, and he gives up on his plan. Twain shows us that Huck's actions, while violating social conventions, are nevertheless commendable:

> "Then I thought a minute, and says to myself, hold on,—suppose you'd a done right and give Jim up, would you feel better than what you do now? No, says I, I'd feel bad… Well then, says I, what's the use in you learning to do right…?" (Twain 69)

Slavery was a volatile issue in Twain's time—it indirectly sparked the Civil War—and the social mandate was a policy of immediately turning in runaway slaves. Twain's violation of this mandate is an expression of cynicism.

Not only does Twain transgress legal standards, he also departs from social convention. After telling a lie to Jim, Huck is rebuked:

> "En all you wuz thinkin 'bout wuz how you could make a fool uv ole Jim wid a lie. Dat truck dah is *trash*, en trash is what people is dat puts dirt on de head er de fren's en makes 'em ashamed." (Twain 65)

This rebuke is not without its effect, and Huck proceeds to apologize to Jim, a slave—something unheard of in the antebellum south. Despite the stigma of this act, Twain again shows that a violation of social norms is acceptable. In the early 19th century southern United States, a white would never apologize for anything to a slave—his piece of property. However, Twain contradicts social norms by implying that Huck's *avant garde* apology to Jim was commendable.

In his *tour-de-force, Huckleberry Finn,* Mark Twain uses cynicism by expressing contempt for both the legal standards and social conventions of the antebellum South. Not only do his characters, like Diogenes of Sinope, "strive to destroy social conventions" (Cynic), their non-conformism is commended.(Daniel)

Assignments

- Warm-up: Give at least one definition of cynicism in Mark Twain's novel *Huckleberry Finn*.
- Students should complete Concept Builder 16-D.
- Student will re-write corrected copies of essay due tomorrow.

CONCEPT BUILDER 16-D **Vernacular**	**Vernacular language is neither slang nor informal. It is merely the way people would normally speak (but not write). Write these phrases in your own words:**	
	1	You are a very sophisticated young man!
	2	I like the beautiful young lady.
	3	The day was not very good.
	4	I did not have a good time at the party.
	5	It has been a perfect day!
	6	This is an important event!
	7	The football team is the very best team I know.

The Celebrated Jumping Frog of Calaveras County

Mark Twain

In compliance with the request of a friend of mine, who wrote me from the East, I called on good-natured, garrulous old Simon Wheeler, and inquired after my friend's friend, Leonidas W. Smiley, as requested to do, and I hereunto append the result. I have a lurking suspicion that Leonidas W. Smiley is a myth; that my friend never knew such a personage; and that he only conjectured that, if I asked old Wheeler about him, it would remind him of his infamous Jim Smiley, and he would go to work and bore me nearly to death with some infernal reminiscence of him as long and tedious as it should be useless to me. If that was the design, it certainly succeeded.

I found Simon Wheeler dozing comfortably by the barroom stove of the old, dilapidated tavern in the ancient mining camp of Angel's, and I noticed that he was fat and bald-headed, and had an expression of winning gentleness and simplicity upon his tranquil countenance. He roused up and gave me good-day. I told him a friend of mine had commissioned me to make some inquiries about a cherished companion of his boyhood named Leonidas W. Smiley — Rev. Leonidas W. Smiley, young minister of the Gospel, who he had heard was at one time a resident of Angel's Camp. I added that, if Mr. Wheeler could tell me anything about this Rev. Leonidas W. Smiley, I would feel under many obligations to him.

Simon Wheeler backed me into a corner and blockaded me there with his chair, and then sat me down and reeled off the monotonous narrative which follows this paragraph. He never smiled, he never frowned, he never changed his voice from the gentle-flowing key to which he tuned the initial sentence, he never betrayed the slightest suspicion of enthusiasm; but all through the interminable narrative there ran a vein of impressive earnestness and sincerity, which showed me plainly that, so far from his imagining that there was anything ridiculous or funny about his story, he regarded it as a really important matter, and admired its two heroes as men of transcendent genius in finesse. I let him go on in his own way, and never interrupted him once.

"Rev. Leonidas W. H'm, Reverend — well, there was a feller here once by the name of Jim Smiley, in the winter of '49 — or maybe it was the spring of '50 — I don't recollect exactly, somehow, though what makes me think it was one or the other is because I remember the big flume wasn't finished when he first came to the camp; but anyway, he was the curiousest man about always betting on anything that turned up you ever see, if he could get anybody to bet on the other side; and if he couldn't, he'd change sides. Any way that suited the other man would suit him — any way just so's he got a bet, he was satisfied. But still he was lucky, uncommon lucky; he most always come out winner. He was always ready and laying for a chance; there couldn't be no solit'ry thing mentioned but that feller'd offer to bet on it, and take any side you please, as I was just telling you. If there was a horse race, you'd find him flush, or you'd find him busted at the end of it; if there was a dogfight, he'd bet on it; if there was a cat-fight, he'd bet on it; if there was a chicken-fight, he'd bet on it; why, if there was two birds setting on a fence, he would bet you which one would fly first; or if there was a camp meeting, he would be there reg'lar, to bet on Parson Walker, which he judged to be the best exhorter about here, and so he was, too, and a good man. If he even seen a straddlebug start to go anywheres, he would bet you how long it would take him to get wherever he was going to, and if you took him up, he would foller that straddlebug to Mexico but what he would find out where he was bound for and how long he was on the road. Lots of the boys here has seen that Smiley, and can tell you about him. Why, it never made no difference to him — he would bet on anything — the dangdest feller. Parson Walker's wife laid very sick once, for a good while, and it seemed as if they warn't going to save her; but one morning he come in, and Smiley asked how she was, and he said she was considerable better — thank the Lord for his inf'nit mercy — and coming on so smart that, with the blessing of Prov'dence, she'd get well yet; and Smiley, before he thought, says, "Well, I'll risk two-and-a-half that she don't, anyway."

Thish-yer Smiley had a mare — the boys called her the fifteen-minute nag, but that was only in fun, you know, because, of course, she was faster than that — and he used to win money on that horse, for all she was so slow and always had the asthma, or the distemper, or the consumption, or something of that kind. They used to give her two or three hundred yards start, and then pass her under way; but always at the fag end of the race she'd get excited and desperate-like, and come cavorting and straddling up, and scattering her legs around limber, sometimes in the air, and sometimes out to one side amongst the fences, and kicking up m-o-r-e dust, and raising m-o-r-e racket with her coughing and sneezing and blowing her nose — and always fetch up at the stand just about a neck ahead, as near as you could cipher it down.

And he had a little small bull pup, that to look at him you'd think he wan't worth a cent, but to set around and look ornery, and lay for a chance to steal something. But as soon as money was up on him, he was a different dog; his underjaw'd begin to stick out like the fo-castle of a steamboat, and his teeth would uncover, and shine savage like the furnaces. And a dog might tackle him, and bullyrag him, and bite him, and throw him over his shoulder two or three times, and Andrew Jackson — which was the name of the pup — Andrew Jackson would never let on but what he was satisfied, and hadn't expected nothing else — and the bets being doubled and doubled on the other side all the time, till the money was all up; and then all of a sudden he would grab that other dog jest by the j'int of his hind leg and freeze to it — not chaw, you understand, but only jest grip and hang on till they throwed up the sponge, if it was a year. Smiley always come out winner on that pup, till he harnessed a dog once that didn't have no hind legs, because they'd been sawed off by a circular saw, and when the thing had gone along far enough, and the money was all up, and he come to make a snatch for his pet holt, he saw in a minute how he'd been imposed on, and how the other dog had him in the door, so to speak, and he 'peared surprised, and then he looked sorter dis-couraged-like, and didn't try no more to win the fight, and so he got shucked out bad. He give Smiley a look, as much as to say his heart was broke, and it was his fault for putting up a dog that hadn't no hind legs for him to take holt of, which was his main dependence in a fight, and then he limped off a piece and laid down and died. It was a good pup, was that Andrew Jackson, and would have made a name for hisself if he'd lived, for the stuff was in him, and he had genius — I know it, because he hadn't had no opportunities to speak of, and it don't stand to reason that a dog could make such a fight as he could under them circumstances, if he hadn't no talent. It always makes me feel sorry when I think of that last fight of his'n, and the way it turned out.

Well, thish-yer Smiley had rat-tarriers, and chicken cocks, and tomcats, and all them kind of things, till you couldn't rest, and you couldn't fetch nothing for him to bet on but he'd match you. He ketched a frog one day, and took him home, and said he cal'klated to edercate him; and so he never done nothing for three months but set in his back yard and learn that frog to jump. And you bet you he did learn him too. He'd give him a little punch behind, and the next minute you'd see that frog whirling in the air like a doughnut — see him turn one summer-set, or may be a couple, if he got a good start, and come down flatfooted and all right, like a cat. He got him up so in the matter of catching flies, and kept him in practice so constant, that he'd nail a fly every time as far as he could see him. Smiley said all a frog wanted was education, and he could do most anything — and I believe him. Why, I've seen him set Dan'l Webster down here on this floor — Dan'l Webster was the name of the frog — and sing out, "Flies, Dan'l, flies!" and quicker'n you could wink, he'd spring straight up, and snake a fly off'n the counter there, and flop down on the floor again as solid as a gob of mud, and fall to scratching the side of his head with his hind foot as indifferent as if he hadn't no idea he'd been doin' any more'n any frog might do. You never see a frog so modest and straightfor'ard as he was, for all he was so gifted. And when it came to fair and square jumping on a dead level, he could get over more ground at one straddle than any animal of his breed you ever see. Jumping on a dead level was his strong suit, you understand; and when it come to that, Smiley would ante up money on him as long as he had a red. Smiley was monstrous proud of his frog, and well he might be, for fellers that had traveled and been everywheres, all said he laid over any frog that ever they see.

Well, Smiley kept the beast in a little lattice box, and he used to fetch him downtown sometimes and lay for a bet. One day a feller — a stranger in the camp, he was — come across him with his box, and says:

"What might it be that you've got in the box?"

And Smiley says, sorter indifferent like, "It might be a parrot, or it might be a canary, maybe, but it an't — it's only just a frog."

And the feller took it, and looked at it careful, and turned it round this way and that, and says, "H'm — so 'tis. Well, what's he good for?"

"Well," Smiley says, easy and careless, "he's good enough for one thing, I should judge — he can outjump ary frog in Calaveras county."

The feller took the box again, and took another long, particular look, and give it back to Smiley, and says, very deliberate, "Well, I don't see no p'ints about that frog that's any better'n any other frog."

"Maybe you don't," Smiley says. "Maybe you understand frogs, and maybe you don't understand 'em; maybe you've had experience, and maybe you an't only a amature, as it were. Anyways, I've got my opinion, and I'll risk forty dollars that he can out-jump any frog in Calaveras county."

And the feller studied a minute, and then says, kinder sad like, "Well, I'm only a stranger here, and I an't got no frog; but if I had a frog, I'd bet you."

And then Smiley says, "That's all right — that's all right — if you'll hold my box a minute, I'll go and get you a frog." And so the feller took the box, and put up his forty dollars along with Smiley's and set down to wait.

So he set there a good while thinking and thinking to hisself, and then he got the frog out and prized his mouth open and took a teaspoon and filled him full of quail shot — filled him pretty near up to his chin — and set him on the floor. Smiley he went to the swamp and slopped around in the mud for a long time, and finally he ketched a frog, and fetched him in, and give him to this feller, and says:

"Now, if you're ready, set him alongside of Dan'l, with his fore-paws just even with Dan'l and I'll give the word." Then he says, "one — two — three — jump!" and him and the feller touched up the frogs from behind, and the new frog hopped off, but Dan'l give a heave, and hysted up his shoulders — so — like a French-man, but it wan't no use — he couldn't budge; he was planted as solid as an anvil, and he couldn't no more stir than if he was anchored out. Smiley was a good deal surprised, and he was disgusted too, but he didn't have no idea what the matter was, of course.

The feller took the money and started away; and when he was going out at the door, he sorter jerked his thumb over his shoulders — this way — at Dan'l, and says again, very deliberate, "Well, I don't see no p'ints about that frog that's any better'n any other frog."

Smiley he stood scratching his head and looking down at Dan'l a long time, and at last he says, "I do wonder what in the nation that frog throw'd off for — I wonder if there an't something the matter with him — he 'pears to look might baggy, somehow." And he ketched Dan'l by the nap of the neck, and lifted him up and says, "Why, blame my cats, if he don't weigh five pound!" and turned him upside down, and he belched out a double handful of shot. And then he see how it was, and he was the maddest man — he set the frog down and took out after that feller, but he never ketched him. And —

(Here Simon Wheeler heard his name called from the front yard, and got up to see what was wanted.) And turning to me as he moved away, he said: "Just set where you are, stranger, and rest easy — I an't going to be gone a second."

But, by your leave, I did not think that a continuation of the history of the enterprising vagabond Jim Smiley would be likely to afford me much information concerning the Rev. Leonidas W. Smiley, and so I started away.

At the door I met the sociable Wheeler returning, and he buttonholed me and recommenced:

Well, thish-yer Smiley had a yaller one-eyed cow that didn't have no tail, only jest a short stump like a bannanner, and —"

However, lacking both time and inclination, I did not wait to hear about the afflicted cow, but took my leave.

Assignments

- Warm-up: Compare the tone of the following short story with the tone in *Huck Finn.*
- Students should complete Concept Builder 16-E.
- Essays are due. Students should take the chapter 16 test.

The story presents a dichotomy between the cultural expressions of the east and west coasts of the United States back in 1865.

How can an author create humor by presenting a story from two or more differing viewpoints or perspectives, such as age, economic status, or regional vocabulary?

Irony is a humorous aspect of the story of the jumping frog, with a gambler having the tables turned on him. Write a short synopsis for a story where irony plays a major role in how the main character's life is impacted.

Chapter 17

1865–1915 (Part 3):
Realism, Naturalism, and the Frontier

First Thoughts "Let a thing become a tradition and it becomes half a lie," Crane said. He never created a Hester Prynne who gave her life to absolute truth or to a Huck Finn who had affectionate tolerance toward differing opinions. Crane's world was cynical and very dangerous. His world was full of opportunistic "demons" who sought to do him in.

The moribundity expressed by Crane becomes a recurring theme in American literature. Gone is the God of the Puritans and even the God whom Hester Prynne so faithfully served. The great-great-grandchildren of Anne Bradstreet doubted God really loved them at all. "Fate" was the true power that determined their future.

Author Worldview Watch Stephen Crane is proof positive that the energizing faith of the Puritans is dead in American literature. The Christlike Arthur Dimmesdale is replaced by the whinny naturalist Henry Fleming who discards all semblance of idealism for cold, cynical realism. The god he believes in doesn't care about him one iota and, therefore, his heroism is a sublime act of cynicism, some would say, cowardice.

Crane marked the beginning of naturalism in American literature, which replaced God with ideas like social Darwinism.

Chapter Learning Objectives In chapter 17 we will study naturalism and assess its effect on American culture. We will use Stephen Crane's *The Red Badge of Courage* as a vehicle to that end.

As a result of this chapter study you will be able to . . .

1. Define maturity. How was Henry more mature at the end of the novel than he was at the beginning?

2. Find examples of hopelessness in modern movies, television programs, and music and explain why, as Christian believers, we should reject this pessimism.

3. Discuss why we can know Crane personally had never been in a battle.

Weekly Essay Options: Begin on page 274 of the Teacher Guide.

Reading ahead: Students should review "Outcasts of Poker Flat" by Bret Harte; "The Story of an Hour" by Kate Chopin; "Luke Havergal" and "Credo" by Edwin Arlington Robinson; and "Lucinda Matlock" by Edgar Lee Masters (chapter 19).

273

The Red Badge of Courage
Stephen Crane

Background This impressive novel is one of the few unchallenged classics of modern American literature. Stephen Crane's immense talent is everywhere evident in his great work. This is not to say, though, that Crane's vision is correct. No, Crane's novel is full of naturalism — a germinating and menacing worldview still spreading across America. The naturalistic stories and novels of Stephen Crane truly mark the maturation of modernity. Major revealing features of *modernity* are an unrestrained, individual freedom — the goal of which is to liberate one from all restrictions, constraints, traditions, and all social patterning — all of which are *ipso facto* presumed to be dehumanizing. Modernity has contempt for other viewpoints. Ironically, in its nihilistic pursuit of tolerance it becomes intolerant! Modernity is reductionist naturalism. *What does the word "reductionist" mean?* Yes, Crane's works are wholly modern in both philosophy and technique. While remnants of romanticism may be found in the poems of Dickinson and Whitman, and some in Melville, none remains in Crane. At one point Henry faces death and "he had been to touch the great death, and found that, after all, it was but the great death. He was a man." The man Crane and his contemporaries create is not the man created in the image of God, the man who is precious and vital, but a man in a mob, a man who has no future. Crane offers his reader no salvation, no hope. Crane only validates the *now, the sensory touch, the empirical.*

Since the fall of the Berlin Wall, by the way, many historians argue that we are in a *post-modern era.* Now, many Americans are suspicious of science and any authority. This viewpoint has as a central credo: "Anything goes if I believe it sincerely." Stephen Crane brought us well along on this slippery trail.

This is a summary, then, of how history has unfolded in the last six centuries:

In the scheme of things, *The Red Badge of Courage* and naturalism ushered in a new philosophical era. It was one of the genuinely new cultural revolutions in American history. It was not to be the last.

About the Author Stephen Crane's life was full of tragedy. Born into a pastor's family, his beloved father died when he was 8 years old. Crane himself was 28 when he died of tuberculosis. Never popular in his lifetime, Crane lived in virtual poverty. In his two-plus decades, Crane wrote some of the best American literature of all time.

Other Notable Works

Maggie: A Girl of the Streets (1893)

Suggested Vocabulary Words

Chapter I: hilarious

Chapter III: impregnable

Chapter III: impetus, perambulating

Chapter VI: imprecations, querulous

Chapter IX: trepidation

Chapter X: perfunctory

Chapter XIX: petulantly, deprecating

Chapter XXI: temerity

Chapter XXIV: imperious, expletive, stentorian

Assignments

- Warm-up: What is your first response to Henry Fleming?

- Students should complete Concept Builder 17-A.

- Students review the required reading(s) before the assigned chapter begins.

- Teachers may want to discuss assigned reading(s) with students.

- Teachers shall assign the required essay. The rest of the essays can be outlined, answered with shorter answers, discussed, or skipped.

- Students will review all readings for chapter 17.

CONCEPT BUILDER 17-A **Active Reading**		**Read *Red Badge of Courage*, chapter one, by Stephen Crane, and then answer the following questions.**
	1	Why would the naturalistic Crane start with a picture of a foggy morning?
	2	What is the narrative point of view? Why does Crane choose this approach?
	3	Describe Henry Fleming at the beginning of the book. Is he more like Tom Sawyer or Huck Finn?
	4	Why does Fleming enlist?
	5	What is the emerging central internal conflict in Fleming's life?
	6	What is an example of foreshadowing?
	7	Clearly Fleming is the protagonist. Discuss how Crane uses a couple of foils.
	8	Do you think the Youth will run from the battle?

America 1860–1900

The U.S. Civil War (1861–1865) between the industrial North and the agricultural, slave-owning South was a turning point in American history. The innocent optimism of the young nation gave way, after the war, to a period of exhaustion. Reconstruction grew out of this fatigue — it was as if the American political system was not going to try to solve its problems. Before the war, idealists and romantics championed human rights, especially the abolition of slavery; after the war, Americans increasingly idealized progress and the self-made man. Ralph Waldo Emerson and Henry David Thoreau remained as icons of inevitable American progress. However, many philosophical changes were in the air. This was the era of the millionaire manufacturer and the speculator robber barons and trust busters, when Darwinian evolution and the "survival of the fittest" seemed to sanction the sometimes unethical methods of the successful business tycoon. Naturalism grew naturally out of the fertile ground of social Darwinism. This so-called "Gilded Age," a term coined by Mark Twain, was an age of thoughtless excess.

Business boomed after the war. The new inter-continental rail system, inaugurated in 1869, and the transcontinental telegraph, which began operating in 1861, gave industry access to materials, markets, and communications. The constant influx of immigrants provided a seemingly endless supply of inexpensive labor as well. More than 23 million foreigners — German, Scandinavian, and Irish in the early years, and increasingly Central and Southern Europeans thereafter — flowed into the United States between 1860 and 1910. American business interests imported Asian contract laborers on the West Coast. This created tensions that remain in America even today. In 1860, most Americans lived on farms or in small villages, but by 1919 half the population was concentrated in about 12 cities. Problems of urbanization and industrialization appeared. From 1860 to 1914, the United States changed from a small, young, agricultural country to a huge, modern, industrial nation.

America, however, was full of problems. The differences among people groups were immense and growing larger. It was to this world that men like Stephen Crane wrote. He attacked social problems. American literature openly discussed significant social problems. Previously, American fiction was entertaining and didactic, but not evaluative. Characteristic American novels of the period were Stephen Crane's *Maggie: A Girl of the Streets*, Jack London's *Martin Eden*, and, later, Theodore Dreiser's *An American Tragedy* depict the damage of economic forces and alienation of the vulnerable individual. Survivors, like Twain's Huck Finn, Humphrey Vanderveyden in London's *The Sea-Wolf*, Hemingway's Frederick Henry in *A Farewell to Arms*, and Dreiser's *Sister Carrie*, endure through inner strength and, above all, individuality. No longer is there a hint in American literature that there is a loving, caring God. The world that Anne Bradstreet knew is dead.

Assignments

- Warm-up: What would it be like to be a young person in post-Civil War America?

- Students should complete Concept Builder 17-B.

- Students should review reading(s) from the next chapter.

- Students should outline essay due at the end of the week.

- Per teacher instructions, students may answer orally, in a group setting, some of the essays that are not assigned as formal essays.

	Read *Red Badge of Courage*, chapter two, by Stephen Crane, and then answer the following questions.
1	*In regard to his companions his mind wavered between two opinions, according to his mood. Sometimes he inclined to believing them all heroes. In fact, he usually admired in secret the superior development of the higher qualities in others. He could conceive of men going very insignificantly about the world bearing a load of courage unseen, and although he had known many of his comrades through boyhood, he began to fear that his judgment of them had been blind. Then, in other moments, he flouted these theories, and assured him that his fellows were all privately wondering and quaking.* Paraphrase (put into your own words) this paragraph.
2	Given the author's naturalistic worldview, why is cowardice an irrelevant human motivation?
3	As Fleming debates whether or not he is a coward, within the mind of Henry Fleming the author develops one theme. What is this theme?
4	Why does Crane continue to refer to Fleming as the youth (and not by his proper name)?
5	Metaphors are comparisons between two dissimilar objects. Circle two metaphors.
6	What allure does home have to Henry Fleming?
7	What attitude does the author have toward the loud soldier?
8	*The Red Badge of Courage* is a story of how Henry Fleming changes. The questions before the reader are "How does he change?" or "He changes from what to what?"

CONCEPT BUILDER 17-B
Active Reading

More Background

The Red Badge of Courage is a story of an inexperienced "youth" undergoing his first experience of battle, his rite of passage. "The youth" in the novel, Henry Fleming, makes a journey of self-discovery, full of internal and external conflict. But what he learns and whether he learns from his experiences is a point that is still debated. Does he gain bravery? Or does he become a cynic?

In writing *The Red Badge of Courage* nearly 30 years after the Civil War ended, Crane referred to stories of actual battles written in popular magazines. Fleming, then, is more a creation of *Harper's Weekly* than real battle experience. He is a compilation of characters that Crane has harvested from secondary sources. He is, in other words, one of the first media-created actors in American literary history.

His creation is much like *The Monkees* in the 1960s. In an attempt to create a legitimate American version of a rock and roll group to compete with the English Beatles, American promoters gathered complete strangers and formed a singing group. To accelerate their rise to fame, the promoters created a television show *The Monkees* that was one of the most popular weekly evening shows in America. The Monkees group was an illusion. A creation of the media.

So was Henry Fleming. No American who fought in the Civil War would have exhibited such

Action photo of The Monkees from a full page ad for their third record album. From left: Mickey Dolenz, Davy Jones, Mike Nesmith, Peter Tork, 1967 (PD-US).

cynical, modernist, naturalistic behavior.

Crane would have his readers believe that battle is an initiation into manhood. War, to Fleming, was an experience of initiation, or growing up, in which he moves from innocence, to familiarity, to wisdom, to bravery. In fact, Fleming moves from romanticism to naturalism, from naiveté to cynicism. In constructing *The Red Badge of Courage*, Crane drew on a predictable pattern followed in Civil War memoirs and novels of initiation. But what Crane created was not an ordinary Civil War story. Crane wrote about late 19th-century America — a nation that was tortured with demons of social Darwinism and naturalism.

Assignments

- Warm-up: Craft an argument against slavery.
- Students should complete Concept Builder 17-C.
- Student should write rough drafts of assigned essay.

Match the following characters with their descriptions.

A	The Loud Man, Wilson
B	The Tall Man, Jim Conklin
C	Henry Fleming
D	The Tattered Man
E	The Colonel
F	The General
G	Henry's Mother

___ 1	New York state farm boy who enlists in the Union Army in the belief that war is a glorious adventure. The protagonist.
___ 2	Soldier who befriends Fleming. He suffers fatal wounds during the battle that Henry ran from and thus pricks Henry's conscience.
___ 3	Braggart who is really cowed by the prospect of war. After his first battle, he transforms into a different man: quiet, kind, brave. He becomes Henry Fleming's friend and captures the enemy flag while Henry fights at his side.
___ 4	Soldier who mistakes young Fleming for a wounded soldier and dogs Fleming with questions about the location of his wound.
___ 5	The lieutenant officer who harasses Henry at first, even beating him with a sword, in order to turn him into a soldier. Later, he praises Henry for his battlefield exploits.
___ 6	Officer who upbraids Henry's regiment for stopping short of victory during a battle.
___ 7	She opposes Henry's enlistment but accepts his decision to volunteer.

Literary Moves

Some think that the *The Red Badge of Courage* does not have a plot at all. They claim it is a bunch of disjointed scenes, more like a stream of consciousness than an organized story.

The language in *The Red Badge of Courage* is very important but also very unusual. The way things are described is very simply the way Henry Fleming sees them. The plot, theme, tone, and even the setting, is revealed through the mind and eyes of Fleming.

Therefore, instead of rising and falling action, Fleming is changing his perceptions. Fleming's changing perceptions are the book's main action. Crane uses two styles in *The Red Badge of Courage*. One is the straightforward realism of the dialogue. Most of the characters in the book talk in colloquial language, and their speech is reproduced accurately, dropping final g's and d's and using words like yer for your.

Robert Stallman in his "Introduction" to *The Red Badge of Courage* writes, "The book's other style is also realistic, but it is a special kind of realism. Crane usually does not tell us what a thing "really" was, but rather what it looked like to an observer, usually Henry Fleming. In the opening lines of the book, for example, the landscape didn't really change from brown to green, but the rising sun made the fields look green rather than brown. In the same way, campfires across the rivers are dragons, the marching army is a serpent; a line of guns are Indian chiefs at a powwow, because they look that way to Henry. Instead of giving us details about the characters, Crane simply gives us an impression of them — 'the loud soldier,' 'the youth,' 'the tall soldier.' It is like a line drawing rather than an oil painting. Crane writes in short sentences and paragraphs, and generally uses simple vocabulary. He usually turns to fancy words only when he is making fun of a character's pretensions."

Assignments

- Warm-up: Some critics have called the *The Red Badge of Courage* a nearly plotless novel. Many of the most important events occur inside Henry's head. In addition, the action does not rise steadily to a climax. Fleming has a series of crises and then reflection periods after the crises. This is not a normal plot: rising action, climax, resolution. Do you like books like this?

- Students should complete Concept Builder 17-D.

- Student will re-write corrected copies of essay due tomorrow.

No doubt the setting is critical to Stephen Crane's *Red Badge of Courage*. What is the setting? Move from general to specific details.

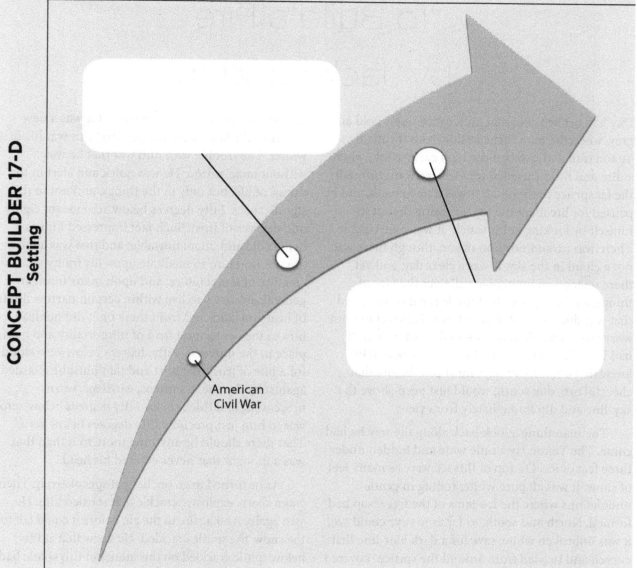

American
Civil War

To Build a Fire
by Jack London

Day had broken cold and grey, exceedingly cold and grey, when the man turned aside from the main Yukon trail and climbed the high earth-bank, where a dim and little-travelled trail led eastward through the fat spruce timberland. It was a steep bank, and he paused for breath at the top, excusing the act to himself by looking at his watch. It was nine o'clock. There was no sun nor hint of sun, though there was not a cloud in the sky. It was a clear day, and yet there seemed an intangible pall over the face of things, a subtle gloom that made the day dark, and that was due to the absence of sun. This fact did not worry the man. He was used to the lack of sun. It had been days since he had seen the sun, and he knew that a few more days must pass before that cheerful orb, due south, would just peep above the sky-line and dip immediately from view.

The man flung a look back along the way he had come. The Yukon lay a mile wide and hidden under three feet of ice. On top of this ice were as many feet of snow. It was all pure white, rolling in gentle undulations where the ice-jams of the freeze-up had formed. North and south, as far as his eye could see, it was unbroken white, save for a dark hair-line that curved and twisted from around the spruce- covered island to the south, and that curved and twisted away into the north, where it disappeared behind another spruce-covered island. This dark hair-line was the trail — the main trail — that led south five hundred miles to the Chilcoot Pass, Dyea, and salt water; and that led north seventy miles to Dawson, and still on to the north a thousand miles to Nulato, and finally to St. Michael on Bering Sea, a thousand miles and half a thousand more.

But all this — the mysterious, far-reaching hairline trail, the absence of sun from the sky, the tremendous cold, and the strangeness and weirdness of it all — made no impression on the man. It was not because he was long used to it. He was a new-comer in the land, a chechaquo, and this was his first winter. The trouble with him was that he was without imagination. He was quick and alert in the things of life, but only in the things, and not in the significances. Fifty degrees below zero meant eighty odd degrees of frost. Such fact impressed him as being cold and uncomfortable, and that was all. It did not lead him to meditate upon his frailty as a creature of temperature, and upon man's frailty in general, able only to live within certain narrow limits of heat and cold; and from there on it did not lead him to the conjectural field of immortality and man's place in the universe. Fifty degrees below zero stood for a bite of frost that hurt and that must be guarded against by the use of mittens, ear-flaps, warm moccasins, and thick socks. Fifty degrees below zero was to him just precisely fifty degrees below zero. That there should be anything more to it than that was a thought that never entered his head.

As he turned to go on, he spat speculatively. There was a sharp, explosive crackle that startled him. He spat again. And again, in the air, before it could fall to the snow, the spittle crackled. He knew that at fifty below spittle crackled on the snow, but this spittle had crackled in the air. Undoubtedly it was colder than fifty below — how much colder he did not know. But the temperature did not matter. He was bound for the old claim on the left fork of Henderson Creek, where the boys were already. They had come over across the divide from the Indian Creek country, while he had come the roundabout way to take a look at the possibilities of getting out logs in the spring from the islands in the Yukon. He would be in to camp by six o'clock; a bit after dark, it was true, but the boys would be there, a fire would be going, and a hot supper would be ready. As for lunch, he pressed his hand against the protruding bundle under his jacket. It was also under his shirt, wrapped up in a handkerchief and lying against the naked skin. It was the only way to keep the biscuits from freezing. He smiled agreeably to himself as he thought of those biscuits, each cut open and sopped in bacon grease, and each enclosing a generous slice of fried bacon.

He plunged in among the big spruce trees. The trail was faint. A foot of snow had fallen since the last sled had passed over, and he was glad he was without a sled, travelling light. In fact, he carried nothing but the lunch wrapped in the handkerchief. He was surprised, however, at the cold. It certainly was cold, he concluded, as he rubbed his numbed nose and cheek-bones with his mittened hand. He was a warm-whiskered man, but the hair on his face did not protect the high cheek-bones and the eager nose that thrust itself aggressively into the frosty air.

At the man's heels trotted a dog, a big native husky, the proper wolf-dog, grey-coated and without any visible or temperamental difference from its brother, the wild wolf. The animal was depressed by the tremendous cold. It knew that it was no time for travelling. Its instinct told it a truer tale than was told to the man by the man's judgment. In reality, it was not merely colder than fifty below zero; it was colder than sixty below, than seventy below. It was seventy-five below zero. Since the freezing-point is thirty-two above zero, it meant that one hundred and seven degrees of frost obtained. The dog did not know anything about thermometers. Possibly in its brain there was no sharp consciousness of a condition of very cold such as was in the man's brain. But the brute had its instinct. It experienced a vague but menacing apprehension that subdued it and made it slink along at the man's heels, and that made it question eagerly every unwonted movement of the man as if expecting him to go into camp or to seek shelter somewhere and build a fire. The dog had learned fire, and it wanted fire, or else to burrow under the snow and cuddle its warmth away from the air.

The frozen moisture of its breathing had settled on its fur in a fine powder of frost, and especially were its jowls, muzzle, and eyelashes whitened by its crystalled breath. The man's red beard and moustache were likewise frosted, but more solidly, the deposit taking the form of ice and increasing with every warm, moist breath he exhaled. Also, the man was chewing tobacco, and the muzzle of ice held his lips so rigidly that he was unable to clear his chin when he expelled the juice. The result was that a crystal beard of the colour and solidity of amber was increasing its length on his chin. If he fell down it would shatter itself, like glass, into brittle fragments. But he did not mind the appendage. It was the penalty all tobacco-chewers paid in that country, and he had been out before in two cold snaps. They had not been so cold as this, he knew, but by the spirit thermometer at Sixty Mile he knew they had been registered at fifty below and at fifty-five.

He held on through the level stretch of woods for several miles…and dropped down a bank to the frozen bed of a small stream. This was Henderson Creek, and he knew he was ten miles from the forks. He looked at his watch. It was ten o'clock. He was making four miles an hour, and he calculated that he would arrive at the forks at half-past twelve. He decided to celebrate that event by eating his lunch there.

The dog dropped in again at his heels, with a tail drooping discouragement, as the man swung along the creek-bed. The furrow of the old sled-trail was plainly visible, but a dozen inches of snow covered the marks of the last runners. In a month no man had come up or down that silent creek. The man held steadily on. He was not much given to thinking, and just then particularly he had nothing to think about save that he would eat lunch at the forks and that at six o'clock he would be in camp with the boys. There was nobody to talk to and, had there been, speech would have been impossible because of the ice-muzzle on his mouth. So he continued monotonously to chew tobacco and to increase the length of his amber beard.

Once in a while the thought reiterated itself that it was very cold and that he had never experienced such cold. As he walked along he rubbed his cheek-bones and nose with the back of his mittened hand. He did this automatically, now and again changing hands. But rub as he would, the instant he stopped his cheek-bones went numb, and the following instant the end of his nose went numb. He was sure to frost his cheeks; he knew that, and experienced a pang of regret that he had not devised a nose-strap of the sort Bud wore in cold snaps. Such a strap passed across the cheeks, as well, and saved them. But it didn't matter much, after all. What were frosted cheeks? A bit painful, that was all; they were never serious.

Empty as the man's mind was of thoughts, he was keenly observant, and he noticed the changes in the creek, the curves and bends and timber-jams, and always he sharply noted where he placed his feet. Once, coming around a bend, he shied abruptly, like a startled horse, curved away from the place where he had been walking, and retreated several paces back along the trail. The creek he knew was frozen clear to the bottom — no creek could contain water in that arctic winter — but he knew also that there were springs that bubbled out from the hillsides and ran along under the snow and on top the ice of the creek. He knew that the coldest snaps never froze these springs, and he knew likewise their danger. They were traps. They hid pools of water under the snow that might be three inches deep, or three feet. Sometimes a skin of ice half an inch thick covered them, and in turn was covered by the snow. Sometimes there were alternate layers of water and ice-skin, so that when one broke through he kept on breaking through for a while, sometimes wetting himself to the waist.

That was why he had shied in such panic. He had felt the give under his feet and heard the crackle of a snow-hidden ice-skin. And to get his feet wet in such a temperature meant trouble and danger. At the very least it meant delay, for he would be forced to stop and build a fire, and under its protection to bare his feet while he dried his socks and moccasins. He stood and studied the creek-bed and its banks, and decided that the flow of water came from the right. He reflected awhile, rubbing his nose and cheeks, then skirted to the left, stepping gingerly and testing the footing for each step. Once clear of the danger, he took a fresh chew of tobacco and swung along at his four-mile gait.

In the course of the next two hours he came upon several similar traps. Usually the snow above the hidden pools had a sunken, candied appearance that advertised the danger. Once again, however, he had a close call; and once, suspecting danger, he compelled the dog to go on in front. The dog did not want to go. It hung back until the man shoved it forward, and then it went quickly across the white, unbroken surface. Suddenly it broke through, floundered to one side, and got away to firmer footing. It had wet its forefeet and legs, and almost immediately the water that clung to it turned to ice. It made quick efforts to lick the ice off its legs, then

dropped down in the snow and began to bite out the ice that had formed between the toes. This was a matter of instinct. To permit the ice to remain would mean sore feet. It did not know this. It merely obeyed the mysterious prompting that arose from the deep crypts of its being. But the man knew, having achieved a judgment on the subject, and he removed the mitten from his right hand and helped tear out the ice- particles. He did not expose his fingers more than a minute, and was astonished at the swift numbness that smote them. It certainly was cold. He pulled on the mitten hastily, and beat the hand savagely across his chest.

At twelve o'clock the day was at its brightest. Yet the sun was too far south on its winter journey to clear the horizon. The bulge of the earth intervened between it and Henderson Creek, where the man walked under a clear sky at noon and cast no shadow. At half-past twelve, to the minute, he arrived at the forks of the creek. He was pleased at the speed he had made. If he kept it up, he would certainly be with the boys by six. He unbuttoned his jacket and shirt and drew forth his lunch. The action consumed no more than a quarter of a minute, yet in that brief moment the numbness laid hold of the exposed fingers. He did not put the mitten on, but, instead, struck the fingers a dozen sharp smashes against his leg. Then he sat down on a snow-covered log to eat. The sting that followed upon the striking of his fingers against his leg ceased so quickly that he was startled, he had had no chance to take a bite of biscuit. He struck the fingers repeatedly and returned them to the mitten, baring the other hand for the purpose of eating. He tried to take a mouthful, but the ice-muzzle pre-vented. He had forgotten to build a fire and thaw out. He chuckled at his foolishness, and as he chuckled he noted the numbness creeping into the exposed fingers. Also, he noted that the stinging which had first come to his toes when he sat down was already passing away. He wondered whether the toes were warm or numbed. He moved them inside the moccasins and decided that they were numbed.

He pulled the mitten on hurriedly and stood up. He was a bit frightened. He stamped up and down until the stinging returned into the feet. It certainly was cold, was his thought. That man from Sulphur Creek had spoken the truth when telling how cold it sometimes got in the country. And he had laughed at him at the time! That showed one must not be too sure of things. There was no mistake about it, it was cold. He strode up and down, stamping his feet and threshing his arms, until reassured by the returning warmth. Then he got out matches and proceeded to make a fire. From the undergrowth, where high water of the previous spring had lodged a supply of seasoned twigs, he got his firewood. Working carefully from a small beginning, he soon had a roaring fire, over which he thawed the ice from his face and in the protection of which he ate his biscuits. For the moment the cold of space was outwitted. The dog took satisfaction in the fire, stretching out close enough for warmth and far enough away to escape being singed.

When the man had finished, he filled his pipe and took his comfortable time over a smoke. Then he pulled on his mittens, settled the ear-flaps of his cap firmly about his ears, and took the creek trail up the left fork. The dog was disappointed and yearned back toward the fire. This man did not know cold. Possibly all the generations of his ancestry had been ignorant of cold, of real cold, of cold one hundred and seven degrees below freezing-point. But the dog knew; all its ancestry knew, and it had inherited the knowledge. And it knew that it was not good to walk abroad in such fearful cold. It was the time to lie snug in a hole in the snow and wait for a curtain of cloud to be drawn across the face of outer space whence this cold came. On the other hand, there was keen intimacy between the dog and the man. The one was the toil-slave of the other, and the only caresses it had ever received were the caresses of the whip-lash and of harsh and menacing throat-sounds that threatened the whip-lash. So the dog made no effort to communicate its apprehension to the man. It was not concerned in the welfare of the man; it was for its own sake that it yearned back toward the fire. But the man whistled, and spoke to it with the sound of whip-lashes, and the dog swung in at the man's heels and followed after.

The man took a chew of tobacco and proceeded to start a new amber beard. Also, his moist breath quickly powdered with white his moustache, eyebrows, and lashes. There did not seem to be so many springs on the left fork of the Henderson, and for half an hour the man saw no signs of any. And then it happened. At a place where there were no signs, where the soft, unbroken snow seemed to advertise solidity beneath, the man broke through. It was not deep. He wetted himself half-way to the knees before he floundered out to the firm crust.

He was angry, and cursed his luck aloud. He had hoped to get into camp with the boys at six o'clock, and this would delay him an hour, for he would have to build a fire and dry out his foot-gear. This was imperative at that low temperature — he knew that much; and he turned aside to the bank, which he climbed. On top, tangled in the underbrush about the trunks of several small spruce trees, was a high-water deposit of dry firewood — sticks and twigs principally, but also larger portions of seasoned branches and fine, dry, last-year's grasses. He threw down several large pieces on top of the snow. This served for a foundation and prevented the young flame from drowning itself in the snow it otherwise would melt. The flame he got by touching a match to a small shred of birch-bark that he took from his pocket. This burned even more readily than paper. Placing it on the foundation, he fed the young flame with wisps of dry grass and with the tiniest dry twigs.

He worked slowly and carefully, keenly aware of his danger. Gradually, as the flame grew stronger, he increased the size of the twigs with which he fed it. He squatted in the snow, pulling the twigs out from their entanglement in the brush and feeding directly to the flame. He knew there must be no failure. When it is seventy-five below zero, a man must not fail in his first attempt to build a fire — that is, if his feet are wet. If his feet are dry, and he fails, he can run along the trail for half a mile and restore his circulation. But the circulation of wet and freezing feet cannot be restored by running when it is seventy-five below. No matter how fast he runs, the wet feet will freeze the harder.

All this the man knew. The old-timer on Sulphur Creek had told him about it the previous fall, and now he was appreciating the advice. Already all sensation had gone out of his feet. To build the fire he had been forced to remove his mittens, and the fingers had quickly gone numb. His pace of four miles an hour had kept his heart pumping blood to the surface of his body and to all the extremities. But the instant he stopped, the action of the pump eased down. The cold of space smote the unprotected tip of the planet, and he, being on that unprotected tip, received the full force of the blow. The blood of his body recoiled before it. The blood was alive, like the dog, and like the dog it wanted to hide away and cover itself up from the fearful cold. So long as he walked four miles an hour, he pumped that blood, willy-nilly, to the surface; but now it ebbed away and sank down into the recesses of his body. The extremities were the first to feel its absence. His wet feet froze the faster, and his exposed fingers numbed the faster, though they had not yet begun to freeze. Nose and cheeks were already freezing, while the skin of all his body chilled as it lost its blood.

But he was safe. Toes and nose and cheeks would be only touched by the frost, for the fire was beginning to burn with strength. He was feeding it with twigs the size of his finger. In another minute he would be able to feed it with branches the size of his wrist, and then he could remove his wet foot-gear, and, while it dried, he could keep his naked feet warm by the fire, rubbing them at first, of course, with snow. The fire was a success. He was safe. He remembered the advice of the old-timer on Sulphur Creek, and smiled. The old-timer had been very serious in laying down the law that no man must travel alone in the Klondike after fifty below. Well, here he was; he had had the accident; he was alone; and he had saved himself. Those old-timers were rather womanish, some of them, he thought. All a man had to do was to keep his head, and he was all right. Any man who was a man could travel alone. But it was surprising, the rapidity with which his cheeks and nose were freezing. And he had not thought his fingers could go lifeless in so short a time. Lifeless they were, for he could scarcely make them move together to grip a twig, and they seemed remote from his body and from him. When he touched a twig, he had to look and see whether or not he had hold of it. The wires were pretty well down between him and his finger-ends.

All of which counted for little. There was the fire, snapping and crackling and promising life with every dancing flame. He started to untie his moccasins. They were coated with ice; the thick German socks were like sheaths of iron half-way to the knees; and the mocassin strings were like rods of steel all twisted and knotted as by some conflagration. For a moment he tugged with his numbed fingers, then, realizing the folly of it, he drew his sheath-knife.

But before he could cut the strings, it happened. It was his own fault or, rather, his mistake. He should not have built the fire under the spruce tree. He should have built it in the open. But it had been easier to pull the twigs from the brush and drop them directly on the fire. Now the tree under which he had done this carried a weight of snow on its boughs. No wind had blown for weeks, and each bough was fully freighted. Each time he had pulled a twig he had communicated a slight agitation to the tree — an imperceptible agitation, so far as he was concerned, but an agitation sufficient to bring about the disaster. High up in the tree one bough capsized its load of snow. This fell on the boughs beneath, capsizing them. This process continued, spreading out and involving the whole tree. It grew like an avalanche, and it descended without warning upon the man and the fire, and the fire was blotted out! Where it had burned was a mantle of fresh and disordered snow.

The man was shocked. It was as though he had just heard his own sentence of death. For a moment he sat and stared at the spot where the fire had been. Then he grew very calm. Perhaps the old-timer on Sulphur Creek was right. If he had only had a trail-mate he would have been in no danger now. The trail-mate could have built the fire. Well, it was up to him to build the fire over again, and this second time there must be no failure. Even if he succeeded, he would most likely lose some toes. His feet must be badly frozen by now, and there would be some time before the second fire was ready.

Such were his thoughts, but he did not sit and think them. He was busy all the time they were passing through his mind, he made a new foundation for a fire, this time in the open; where no treacherous tree could blot it out. Next, he gathered dry grasses and tiny twigs from the high-water flotsam. He could not bring his fingers together to pull them out, but he was able to gather them by the handful. In this way he got many rotten twigs and bits of green moss that were undesirable, but it was the best he could do. He worked methodically, even collecting an armful of the larger branches to be used later when the fire gathered strength. And all the while the dog sat and watched him, a certain yearning wistfulness in its eyes, for it looked upon him as the fire-provider, and the fire was slow in coming.

When all was ready, the man reached in his pocket for a second piece of birch-bark. He knew the bark was there, and, though he could not feel it with his fingers, he could hear its crisp rustling as he fumbled for it. Try as he would, he could not clutch hold of it. And all the time, in his consciousness, was the knowledge that each instant his feet were freezing. This thought tended to put him in a panic, but he fought against it and kept calm. He pulled on his mittens with his teeth, and threshed his arms back and forth, beating his hands with all his might against his sides. He did this sitting down, and he stood up to do it; and all the while the dog sat in the snow, its wolf-brush of a tail curled around warmly over its forefeet, its sharp wolf-ears pricked forward intently as it watched the man. And the man as he beat and threshed with his arms and hands, felt a great surge of envy as he regarded the creature that was warm and secure in its natural covering.

After a time he was aware of the first far-away signals of sensation in his beaten fingers. The faint tingling grew stronger till it evolved into a stinging ache that was excruciating, but which the man hailed with satisfaction. He stripped the mitten from his right hand and fetched forth the birch-bark. The exposed fingers were quickly going numb again. Next he brought out his bunch of sulphur matches. But the tremendous cold had already driven the life out of his fingers. In his effort to separate one match from the others, the whole bunch fell in the snow. He tried to pick it out of the snow, but failed. The dead fingers could neither touch nor clutch. He was very careful. He drove the thought of his freezing feet; and nose, and cheeks, out of his mind, devoting his whole soul to the matches. He watched, using the sense of vision in place of that of touch, and when he saw his fingers on each side the bunch, he closed them — that is, he willed to close them, for the wires were drawn, and the fingers did not obey. He pulled the mitten on the right hand, and beat it fiercely against his knee. Then, with both mittened hands, he scooped the bunch of matches, along with much snow, into his lap. Yet he was no better off.

After some manipulation he managed to get the bunch between the heels of his mittened hands. In this fashion he carried it to his mouth. The ice crackled and snapped when by a violent effort he opened his mouth. He drew the lower jaw in, curled the upper lip out of the way, and scraped the bunch with his upper teeth in order to separate a match. He succeeded in getting one, which he dropped on his lap. He was no better off. He could not pick it up. Then he devised a way. He picked it up in his teeth and scratched it on his leg. Twenty times he scratched before he succeeded in lighting it. As it flamed he held it with his teeth to the birch-bark. But the burning brimstone went up his nostrils and into his lungs, causing him to cough spasmodically. The match fell into the snow and went out.

The old-timer on Sulphur Creek was right, he thought in the moment of controlled despair that ensued: after fifty below, a man should travel with a partner. He beat his hands, but failed in exciting any sensation. Suddenly he bared both hands, removing the mittens with his teeth. He caught the whole bunch between the heels of his hands. His arm-muscles not being frozen enabled him to press the hand-heels tightly against the matches. Then he scratched the bunch along his leg. It flared into flame, seventy sulphur matches at once! There was no wind to blow them out. He kept his head to one side to escape the strangling fumes, and held the blazing bunch to the birch-bark. As he so held it, he became aware of sensation in his hand. His flesh was burning. He could smell it. Deep down below the surface he could feel it. The sensation developed into pain that grew acute. And still he endured it, holding the flame of the matches clumsily to the bark that would not light readily because his own burning hands were in the way, absorbing most of the flame.

At last, when he could endure no more, he jerked his hands apart. The blazing matches fell sizzling into the snow, but the birch-bark was alight. He began laying dry grasses and the tiniest twigs on the flame. He could not pick and choose, for he had to lift the fuel between the heels of his hands. Small pieces of rotten wood and green moss clung to the twigs, and he bit them off as well as he could with his teeth. He cherished the flame carefully and awkwardly. It meant life, and it must not perish. The withdrawal of blood from the surface of his body now made him begin to shiver, and he grew more awkward. A large piece of green moss fell squarely on the little fire. He tried to poke it out with his fingers, but his shivering frame made him poke too far, and he disrupted the nucleus of the little fire, the burning grasses and tiny twigs separating and scattering. He tried to poke them together again, but in spite of the tenseness of the effort, his shivering got away with him, and the twigs were hopelessly scattered. Each twig gushed a puff of smoke and went out. The fire-provider had failed. As he looked apathetically about him, his eyes chanced on the dog, sitting across the ruins of the fire from him, in the snow, making restless, hunching movements, slightly lifting one forefoot and then the other, shifting its weight back and forth on them with wistful eagerness.

The sight of the dog put a wild idea into his head. He remembered the tale of the man, caught in a blizzard, who killed a steer and crawled inside the carcass, and so was saved. He would kill the dog and bury his hands in the warm body until the numbness went out of them. Then he could build another fire. He spoke to the dog, calling it to him; but in his voice was a strange note of fear that frightened the animal, who had never known the man to speak in such way before. Something was the matter, and its suspicious nature sensed danger — it knew not what danger but somewhere, somehow, in its brain arose an apprehension of the man. It flattened its ears down at the sound of the man's voice, and its restless, hunching movements and the liftings and shiftings of its forefeet became more pronounced but it would not come to the man. He got on his hands and knees and crawled toward the dog. This unusual posture again excited suspicion, and the animal sidled mincingly away.

The man sat up in the snow for a moment and struggled for calmness. Then he pulled on his mittens, by means of his teeth, and got upon his feet. He glanced down at first in order to assure himself that he was really standing up, for the absence of sensation in his feet left him unrelated to the earth. His erect position in itself started to drive the webs of suspicion from the dog's mind; and when he spoke peremptorily, with the sound of whip-lashes in his voice, the dog rendered its customary allegiance and came to him. As it came within reaching distance, the man lost his control. His arms flashed out to the dog, and he experienced genuine surprise when he discovered that his hands could not clutch, that there was neither bend nor feeling in the fingers. He had forgotten for the moment that they were frozen and that they were freezing more and more. All this happened quickly, and before the animal

could get away, he encircled its body with his arms. He sat down in the snow, and in this fashion held the dog, while it snarled and whined and struggled.

But it was all he could do, hold its body encircled in his arms and sit there. He realized that he could not kill the dog. There was no way to do it. With his helpless hands he could neither draw nor hold his sheath-knife nor throttle the animal. He released it, and it plunged wildly away, with tail between its legs, and still snarling. It halted forty feet away and surveyed him curiously, with ears sharply pricked forward. The man looked down at his hands in order to locate them, and found them hanging on the ends of his arms. It struck him as curious that one should have to use his eyes in order to find out where his hands were. He began threshing his arms back and forth, beating the mittened hands against his sides. He did this for five minutes, violently, and his heart pumped enough blood up to the surface to put a stop to his shivering. But no sensation was aroused in the hands. He had an impression that they hung like weights on the ends of his arms, but when he tried to run the impression down, he could not find it.

A certain fear of death, dull and oppressive, came to him. This fear quickly became poignant as he realized that it was no longer a mere matter of freezing his fingers and toes, or of losing his hands and feet, but that it was a matter of life and death with the chances against him. This threw him into a panic, and he turned and ran up the creek-bed along the old, dim trail. The dog joined in behind and kept up with him. He ran blindly, without intention, in fear such as he had never known in his life. Slowly, as he ploughed and floundered through the snow, he began to see things again — the banks of the creek, the old timber-jams, the leafless aspens, and the sky. The running made him feel better. He did not shiver. Maybe, if he ran on, his feet would thaw out; and, anyway, if he ran far enough, he would reach camp and the boys. Without doubt he would lose some fingers and toes and some of his face; but the boys would take care of him, and save the rest of him when he got there. And at the same time there was another thought in his mind that said he would never get to the camp and the boys; that it was too many miles away, that the freezing had too great a start on him, and that he would soon be stiff and dead. This thought he kept in the background and refused to consider. Sometimes it pushed itself forward and demanded to be heard, but he thrust it back and strove to think of other things.

It struck him as curious that he could run at all on feet so frozen that he could not feel them when they struck the earth and took the weight of his body. He seemed to himself to skim along above the surface and to have no connection with the earth. Somewhere he had once seen a winged Mercury, and he wondered if Mercury felt as he felt when skimming over the earth.

His theory of running until he reached camp and the boys had one flaw in it: he lacked the endurance. Several times he stumbled, and finally he tottered, crumpled up, and fell. When he tried to rise, he failed. He must sit and rest, he decided, and next time he would merely walk and keep on going. As he sat and regained his breath, he noted that he was feeling quite warm and comfortable. He was not shivering, and it even seemed that a warm glow had come to his chest and trunk. And yet, when he touched his nose or cheeks, there was no sensation. Running would not thaw them out. Nor would it thaw out his hands and feet. Then the thought came to him that the frozen portions of his body must be extending. He tried to keep this thought down, to forget it, to think of something else; he was aware of the panicky feeling that it caused, and he was afraid of the panic. But the thought asserted itself, and persisted, until it produced a vision of his body totally frozen. This was too much, and he made another wild run along the trail. Once he slowed down to a walk, but the thought of the freezing extending itself made him run again.

And all the time the dog ran with him, at his heels. When he fell down a second time, it curled its tail over its forefeet and sat in front of him facing him curiously eager and intent. The warmth and security of the animal angered him, and he cursed it till it flattened down its ears appeasingly. This time the shivering came more quickly upon the man. He was losing in his battle with the frost. It was creeping into his body from all sides. The thought of it drove him on, but he ran no more than a hundred feet, when he staggered and pitched headlong. It was his last panic. When he had recovered his breath and control, he sat up and entertained in his mind the conception of meeting death with dignity. However, the conception did not come to him in such terms. His idea of it was that he had been making a fool of himself, running around like a chicken with its head cut off — such was the simile that occurred to him. Well, he was bound to freeze anyway, and he might as well take it decently. With this new-found peace of mind came the first glimmerings of drowsiness. A good idea, he thought, to sleep off to death. It was like taking an anaesthetic. Freezing was not so bad as people thought. There were lots worse ways to die.

He pictured the boys finding his body next day. Suddenly he found himself with them, coming along the trail and looking for himself. And, still with them, he came around a turn in the trail and found himself lying in the snow. He did not belong with himself any more, for even then he was out of himself, standing with the boys and looking at himself in the snow. It certainly was cold, was his thought. When he got back to the States he could tell the folks what real cold was. He drifted on from this to a vision of the old-timer on Sulphur Creek. He could see him quite clearly, warm and comfortable, and smoking a pipe.

"You were right, old hoss; you were right," the man mumbled to the old-timer of Sulphur Creek.

Then the man drowsed off into what seemed to him the most comfortable and satisfying sleep he had ever known. The dog sat facing him and waiting. The brief day drew to a close in a long, slow twilight. There were no signs of a fire to be made, and, besides, never in the dog's experience had it known a man to sit like that in the snow and make no fire. As the twilight drew on, its eager yearning for the fire mastered it, and with a great lifting and shifting of forefeet, it whined softly, then flattened its ears down in anticipation of being chidden by the man. But the man remained silent. Later, the dog whined loudly. And still later it crept close to the man and caught the scent of <u>death</u>. This made the animal bristle and back away. A little longer it delayed, howling under the stars that leaped and danced and shone brightly in the cold sky. Then it turned and trotted up the trail in the direction of the camp it knew, where were the other food-providers and fire-providers.

- Warm-up: Compare and contrast Stephen Crane's view of death with Jack London's view of death in this short story. They are both naturalist writers.

- Students should complete Concept Builder 17-E.

- Essays are due. Students should take the chapter 17 test.

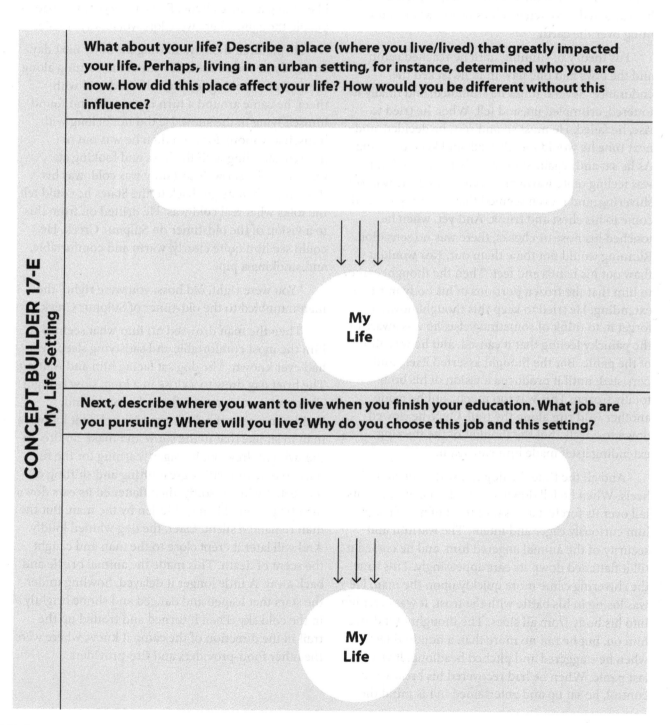

CONCEPT BUILDER 17-E
My Life Setting

What about your life? Describe a place (where you live/lived) that greatly impacted your life. Perhaps, living in an urban setting, for instance, determined who you are now. How did this place affect your life? How would you be different without this influence?

My Life

Next, describe where you want to live when you finish your education. What job are you pursuing? Where will you live? Why do you choose this job and this setting?

My Life

Chapter 18

1865–1915 (Part 4):

Realism, Naturalism, and the Frontier

First Thoughts Einstein was horrified that social scientists took his theory about the quantum nature of light, a description of molecular motion, and the special theory of relativity and created a social theory called relativism (www.bartleby.com/Albert Einstein, *Relativity: The Special and General Theory*, New York, 2000 Chapter VII). Relativism argued that persons should make decisions based upon the "relative worth" of that decision based on circumstances. In other words, a person was free to do what was relatively beneficial to one's situation, regardless of the consequences to others. This self-centeredness engenders desperate sadness in protagonists. Henry Fleming belongs more to the 21st century than to the middle of the 19th. He is a man who has become disconnected from his ethical moorings. He is totally, completely, alone. He worships in a forest chapel that is nothing that Emerson would recognize. Nor would William Bradford. Fleming, although he did not know it, had moved beyond Hemingway, beyond Faulkner, all the way to Albert Camus (existentialism) and he finds himself numb to any metaphysical joy that other characters once knew. He is no Hester Prynne who enjoys the company of her town and her lover. She has the joy of experiencing repentance and therefore redemption. Poor Fleming, like most protagonists in American literature post-1875, is lost, lonely, and desperately sad.

Chapter Learning Objectives In chapter 18 we will finish analyzing *The Red Badge of Courage*, paying particular attention to specific literary terms in passages.

As a result of this chapter study you will be able to . . .

1. Discuss the plot.

2. Analyze Crane's tone and writing style.

3. Contrast the naturalist view with some of the earlier romantic writers (e.g., Hawthorne).

4. Discuss what evidence of naturalism can be found in American culture today.

Weekly Essay Options: Begin on page 274 of the Teacher Guide.

Reading ahead: "Outcasts of Poker Flat" by Bret Harte; "The Story of an Hour" by Kate Chopin; "Luke Havergal" and "Credo" by Edwin Arlington Robinson; "Lucinda Matlock" by Edgar Lee Masters.

291

Imagery from
The Red Badge of Courage

Chapter 2

The next morning the youth discovered that his tall comrade had been the fast-flying messenger of a mistake. There was much scoffing at the latter by those who had yesterday been firm adherents of his views, and there was even a little sneering by men who had never believed the rumor. The tall one fought with a man from Chatfield Corners and beat him severely.

The youth felt, however, that his problem was in no wise lifted from him. There was, on the contrary, an irritating prolongation. The tale had created in him a great concern for himself. Now, with the newborn question in his mind, he was compelled to sink back into his old place as part of a blue demonstration.

For days he made ceaseless calculations, but they were all wondrously unsatisfactory. He found that he could establish nothing. He finally concluded that the only way to prove himself was to go into the blaze, and then figuratively to watch his legs to discover their merits and faults. He reluctantly admitted that he could not sit still and with a mental slate and pencil derive an answer. To gain it, he must have blaze, blood, and danger, even as a chemist requires this, that, and the other. So he fretted for an opportunity.

Meanwhile, he continually tried to measure himself by his comrades. The tall soldier, for one, gave him some assurance. This man's serene uncon-cern dealt him a measure of confidence, for he had known him since childhood, and from his intimate knowledge he did not see how he could be capable of anything that was beyond him, the youth. Still, he thought that his comrade might be mistaken about himself. Or, on the other hand, he might be a man heretofore doomed to peace and obscurity, but, in reality, made to shine in war.

The youth would have liked to have discovered another who suspected himself. A sympathetic comparison of mental notes would have been a joy to him.

He occasionally tried to fathom a comrade with seductive sentences. He looked about to find men in the proper mood. All attempts failed to bring forth any statement which looked in any way like a confession to those doubts which he privately acknowledged in himself. He was afraid to make an open declaration of his concern, because he dreaded to place some unscrupulous confidant upon the high plane of the unconfessed from which elevation he could be derided.

In regard to his companions his mind wavered between two opinions, according to his mood. Sometimes he inclined to believing them all heroes. In fact, he usually admired in secret the superior development of the higher qualities in others. He could conceive of men going very insignificantly about the world bearing a load of courage unseen, and although he had known many of his comrades through boyhood, he began to fear that his judgment of them had been blind. Then, in other moments, he flouted these theories, and assured him that his fellows were all privately wondering and quaking.

His emotions made him feel strange in the presence of men who talked excitedly of a prospec-tive battle as of a drama they were about to witness, with nothing but eagerness and curiosity apparent in their faces. It was often that he suspected them to be liars.

In his great anxiety his heart was continually clamoring at what he considered the intolerable slowness of the generals. They seemed content to perch tranquilly on the river bank, and leave him bowed down by the weight of a great problem. He wanted it settled forthwith. He could not long bear such a load, he said. Sometimes his anger at the commanders reached an acute stage, and he grumbled about the camp like a veteran.

One morning, however, he found himself in the ranks of his prepared regiment. The men were whispering speculations and recounting the old rumors. In the gloom before the break of the day their uniforms glowed a deep purple hue. From across the river the red eyes were still peering. In the eastern sky there was a yellow patch like a rug laid for the feet of the coming sun; and against it, black and patternlike, loomed the gigantic figure of the colonel on a gigantic horse.

From off in the darkness came the trampling of feet. The youth could occasionally see dark shadows that moved like monsters. The regiment stood at rest for what seemed a long time. The youth grew impatient. It was unendurable the way these affairs were managed. He wondered how long they were to be kept waiting.

As he looked all about him and pondered upon the mystic gloom, he began to believe that at any moment the ominous distance might be aflare, and the rolling crashes of an engagement come to his ears. Staring once at the red eyes across the river, he conceived them to be growing larger, as the orbs of a row of dragons advancing. He turned toward the colonel and saw him lift his gigantic arm and calmly stroke his mustache.

At last he heard from along the road at the foot of the hill the clatter of a horse's galloping hoofs. It must be the coming of orders. He bent forward, scarce breathing. The exciting clickety-click, as it grew louder and louder, seemed to be beating upon his soul. Presently a horseman with jangling equipment drew rein before the colonel of the regiment. The two held a short, sharp-worded conversation. The men in the foremost ranks craned their necks.

As the horseman wheeled his animal and galloped away he turned to shout over his shoulder, "Don't forget that box of cigars!" The colonel mumbled in reply. The youth wondered what a box of cigars had to do with war.

A moment later the regiment went swinging off into the darkness. It was now like one of those moving monsters wending with many feet. The air was heavy, and cold with dew. A mass of wet grass, marched upon, rustled like silk.

There was an occasional flash and glimmer of steel from the backs of all these huge crawling reptiles. From the road came creakings and grumblings as some surly guns were dragged away.

The men stumbled along still muttering speculations. There was a subdued debate. Once a man fell down, and as he reached for his rifle a comrade, unseeing, trod upon his hand. He of the injured fingers swore bitterly, and aloud. A low, tittering laugh went among his fellows.

Presently they passed into a roadway and marched forward with easy strides. A dark regiment moved before them, and from behind also came the tinkle of equipments on the bodies of marching men.

The rushing yellow of the developing day went on behind their backs. When the sunrays at last struck full and mellowingly upon the earth, the youth saw that the landscape was streaked with two long, thin, black columns which disappeared on the brow of a hill in front and rearward vanished in a wood. They were like two serpents crawling from the cavern of the night.

The river was not in view. The tall soldier burst into praises of what he thought to be his powers of perception.

Some of the tall one's companions cried with emphasis that they, too, had evolved the same thing, and they congratulated themselves upon it. But there were others who said that the tall one's plan was not the true one at all. They persisted with other theories. There was a vigorous discussion.

The youth took no part in them. As he walked along in careless line he was engaged with his own eternal debate. He could not hinder himself from dwelling upon it. He was despondent and sullen, and threw shifting glances about him. He looked ahead, often expecting to hear from the advance the rattle of firing.

But the long serpents crawled slowly from hill to hill without bluster of smoke. A dun-colored cloud of dust floated away to the right. The sky overhead was of a fairy blue.

The youth studied the faces of his companions, ever on the watch to detect kindred emotions. He suffered disappointment. Some ardor of the air which was causing the veteran commands to move with glee — almost with song — had infected the new regiment. The men began to speak of victory as of a thing they knew. Also, the tall soldier received his vindication. They were certainly going to come around in behind the enemy. They expressed commiseration for that part of the army which had been left upon the river bank, felicitating themselves upon being a part of a blasting host.

The youth, considering himself as separated from the others, was saddened by the blithe and merry speeches that went from rank to rank. The company wags all made their best endeavors. The regiment tramped to the tune of laughter.

The blatant soldier often convulsed whole files by his biting sarcasms aimed at the tall one.

And it was not long before all the men seemed to forget their mission. Whole brigades grinned in unison, and regiments laughed.

A rather fat soldier attempted to pilfer a horse from a dooryard. He planned to load his knapsack upon it. He was escaping with his prize when a young girl rushed from the house and grabbed the animal's mane. There followed a wrangle. The young girl, with pink cheeks and shining eyes, stood like a dauntless statue.

The observant regiment, standing at rest in the roadway, whooped at once, and entered whole-souled upon the side of the maiden. The men became so engrossed in this affair that they entirely ceased to remember their own large war. They jeered the piratical private, and called attention to various defects in his personal appearance; and they were wildly enthusiastic in support of the young girl.

To her, from some distance, came bold advice. "Hit him with a stick."

There were crows and catcalls showered upon him when he retreated without the horse. The regiment rejoiced at his downfall. Loud and vociferous congratulations were showered upon the maiden, who stood panting and regarding the troops with defiance.

At nightfall the column broke into regimental pieces, and the fragments went into the fields to camp. Tents sprang up like strange plants. Camp fires, like red, peculiar blossoms, dotted the night.

The youth kept from intercourse with his companions as much as circumstances would allow him. In the evening he wandered a few paces into the gloom. From this little distance the many fires, with the black forms of men passing to and fro before the crimson rays, made weird and satanic effects.

He lay down in the grass. The blades pressed tenderly against his cheek. The moon had been lighted and was hung in a treetop. The liquid stillness of the night enveloping him made him feel vast pity for himself. There was a caress in the soft winds; and the whole mood of the darkness, he thought, was one of sympathy for himself in his distress.

He wished, without reserve, that he was at home again making the endless rounds from the house to the barn, from the barn to the fields, from the fields to the barn, from the barn to the house. He remembered he had so often cursed the brindle cow and her mates, and had sometimes flung milking stools. But, from his present point of view, there was a halo of happiness about each of their heads, and he would have sacrificed all the brass buttons on the continent to have been enabled to return to them. He told himself that he was not formed for a soldier. And he mused seriously upon the radical differences between himself and those men who were dodging implike around the fires.

As he mused thus he heard the rustle of grass, and, upon turning his head, discovered the loud soldier. He called out, "Oh, Wilson!"

The latter approached and looked down. "Why, hello, Henry; is it you? What are you doing here?"

"Oh, thinking," said the youth.

The other sat down and carefully lighted his pipe. "You're getting blue my boy. You're looking thundering peek-ed. What the dickens is wrong with you?"

"Oh, nothing," said the youth.

The loud soldier launched then into the subject of the anticipated fight. "Oh, we've got 'em now!" As he spoke his boyish face was wreathed in a gleeful smile, and his voice had an exultant ring. "We've got 'em now. At last, by the eternal thunders, we'll like 'em good!"

"If the truth was known," he added, more soberly, "they've licked US about every clip up to now; but this time — this time — we'll lick 'em good!"

"I thought you was objecting to this march a little while ago," said the youth coldly.

"Oh, it wasn't that," explained the other. "I don't mind marching, if there's going to be fighting at the end of it. What I hate is this getting moved here and moved there, with no good coming of it, as far as I can see, excepting sore feet and … short rations."

"Well, Jim Conklin says we'll get plenty of fighting this time."

"He's right for once, I guess, though I can't see how it come. This time we're in for a big battle, and we've got the best end of it, certain sure. Gee rod! how we will thump 'em!"

He arose and began to pace to and fro excitedly. The thrill of his enthusiasm made him walk with an elastic step. He was sprightly, vigorous, fiery in his belief in success. He looked into the future with clear proud eye, and he swore with the air of an old soldier.

The youth watched him for a moment in silence. When he finally spoke his voice was as bitter as dregs. "Oh, you're going to do great things, I s'pose!"

The loud soldier blew a thoughtful cloud of smoke from his pipe. "Oh, I don't know," he remarked with dignity; "I don't know. I s'pose I'll do as well as the rest. I'm going to try like thunder." He evidently complimented himself upon the modesty of this statement.

"How do you know you won't run when the time comes?" asked the youth.

"Run?" said the loud one; "run? — of course not!" He laughed.

"Well," continued the youth, "lots of good-a-'nough men have thought they was going to do great things before the fight, but when the time come they skedaddled."

"Oh, that's all true, I s'pose," replied the other; "but I'm not going to skedaddle. The man that bets on my running will lose his money, that's all." He nodded confidently.

"Oh, shucks!" said the youth. "You ain't the bravest man in the world, are you?"

"No, I ain't," exclaimed the loud soldier indignantly; "and I didn't say I was the bravest man in the world, neither. I said I was going to do my share of fighting — that's what I said. And I am, too. Who are you, anyhow? You talk as if you thought you was Napoleon Bonaparte." He glared at the youth for a moment, and then strode away.

The youth called in a savage voice after his comrade: "Well, you needn't git mad about it!" But the other continued on his way and made no reply.

He felt alone in space when his injured comrade had disappeared. His failure to discover any mite of resemblance in their viewpoints made him more miserable than before. No one seemed to be wrestling with such a terrific personal problem. He was a mental outcast.

He went slowly to his tent and stretched himself on a blanket by the side of the snoring tall soldier. In the darkness he saw visions of a thousand-tongued fear that would babble at his back and cause him to flee, while others were going coolly about their country's business. He admitted that he would not be able to cope with this monster. He felt that every nerve in his body would be an ear to hear the voices, while other men would remain stolid and deaf.

And as he sweated with the pain of these thoughts, he could hear low, serene sentences. "I'll bid five." "Make it six." "Seven." "Seven goes."

He stared at the red, shivering reflection of a fire on the white wall of his tent until, exhausted and ill from the monotony of his suffering, he fell asleep.

Assignments

- Warm-up: The style is closely related point of view. In passage after passage, we experience Henry's impressions of his surroundings. For example, to Henry, the campfires of the enemy across the river look like the "red eyes" of a "row of dragons." In other cases, the images suggest the author's attitude. For example, as Henry's regiment marches through the woods and fields, the narrator says, "They were going to look at war, the red animal." At times the novel almost seems surreal! Find one other instance of this writing style.

- Students should complete Concept Builder 18-A.

- Students review the required reading(s) before the assigned chapter begins.

- Teachers may want to discuss assigned reading(s) with students.

- Teachers shall assign the required essay. The rest of the essays can be outlined, answered with shorter answers, discussed, or skipped.

- Students will review all readings for chapter 18.

CONCEPT BUILDER 18-A Active Reading		Read *Red Badge of Courage,* chapter three, by Stephen Crane, and then answer the following questions.
	1	The author continues to present the army itself as a living creature — earlier in chapter I he referred to it as a sleeping serpent. In this section he continues to personify the army. "The army sat down to think." Why does he do this?
	2	What is the setting? Is it hostile? Friendly?
	3	Find examples of religious language. In what way is this battle scene a religious scene?

Religious Imagery

Chapter 9

The youth fell back in the procession until the tattered soldier was not in sight. Then he started to walk on with the others.

But he was amid wounds. The mob of men was bleeding. Because of the tattered soldier's question he now felt that his shame could be viewed. He was continually casting sidelong glances to see if the men were contemplating the letters of guilt he felt burned into his brow.

At times he regarded the wounded soldiers in an envious way. He conceived persons with torn bodies to be peculiarly happy. He wished that he, too, had a wound, a red badge of courage.

The spectral soldier was at his side like a stalking reproach. The man's eyes were still fixed in a stare into the unknown. His gray, appalling face had attracted attention in the crowd, and men, slowing to his dreary pace, were walking with him. They were discussing his plight, questioning him and giving him advice. In a dogged way he repelled them, signing to them to go on and leave him alone. The shadows of his face were deepening and his tight lips seemed holding in check the moan of great despair. There could be seen a certain stiffness in the movements of his body, as if he were taking infinite care not to arouse the passion of his wounds. As he went on, he seemed always looking for a place, like one who goes to choose a grave.

Something in the gesture of the man as he waved the bloody and pitying soldiers away made the youth start as if bitten. He yelled in horror. Tottering forward he laid a quivering hand upon the man's arm. As the latter slowly turned his waxlike features toward him the youth screamed:

"Jim Conklin!"

The tall soldier made a little commonplace smile. "Hello, Henry," he said.

The youth swayed on his legs and glared strangely. He stuttered and stammered. "Oh, Jim — oh, Jim — oh, Jim —"

The tall soldier held out his gory hand. There was a curious red and black combination of new blood and old blood upon it. "Where yeh been, Henry?" he asked. He continued in a monotonous voice, "I thought mebbe yeh got keeled over. There 's been thunder t' pay t'-day. I was worryin' about it a good deal."

The youth still lamented. "Oh, Jim — oh, Jim — oh, Jim —"

"Yeh know," said the tall soldier, "I was out there." He made a careful gesture. "An', Lord, what a circus! An', b'jiminey, I got shot — I got shot. Yes, b'jiminey, I got shot." He reiterated this fact in a bewildered way, as if he did not know how it came about.

The youth put forth anxious arms to assist him, but the tall soldier went firmly as if propelled. Since the youth's arrival as a guardian for his friend, the other wounded men had ceased to display much interest. They occupied themselves again in dragging their own tragedies toward the rear.

Suddenly, as the two friends marched on, the tall soldier seemed to be overcome by a tremor. His face turned to a semblance of gray paste. He clutched the youth's arm and looked all about him, as if dreading to be overheard. Then he began to speak in a shaking whisper:

"I tell yeh what I'm 'fraid of, Henry — I'll tell yeh what I'm 'fraid of. I 'm 'fraid I 'll fall down — an' them yeh know — them artillery wagons — they like as not 'll run over me. That 's what I 'm 'fraid of."

The youth cried out to him hysterically: "I 'll take care of yeh, Jim! I 'll take care of yeh!"

"Sure — will yeh, Henry?" the tall soldier beseeched.

"Yes — yes — I tell yeh — I'll take care of yeh, Jim!" protested the youth. He could not speak accurately because of the gulpings in his throat.

But the tall soldier continued to beg in a lowly way. He now hung babelike to the youth's arm. His eyes rolled in the wildness of his terror. "I was allus a good friend t' yeh, wa'n't I, Henry? I 've allus been a pretty good feller, ain't I? An' it ain't much t' ask, is it? Jest t' pull me along outer th' road? I'd do it fer you, wouldn't I, Henry?"

He paused in piteous anxiety to await his friend's reply.

The youth had reached an anguish where the sobs scorched him. He strove to express his loyalty, but he could only make fantastic gestures.

However, the tall soldier seemed suddenly to forget all those fears. He became again the grim, stalking specter of a soldier. He went stonily forward. The youth wished his friend to lean upon him, but the other always shook his head and strangely protested. "No — no — no — leave me be — leave me be."

His look was fixed again upon the unknown. He moved with mysterious purpose, and all of the youth's offers he brushed aside. "No — no — leave me be — leave me be."

The youth had to follow.

Presently the latter heard a voice talking softly near his shoulder. Turning he saw that it belonged to the tattered soldier. "Ye'd better take 'im outa th' road, pardner. There's a batt'ry comin' helitywhoop down th' road an' he 'll git runned over. He 's a goner anyhow in about five minutes — yeh kin see that. Ye 'd better take 'im outa th' road. Where th' blazes does hi git his stren'th from?"

...

He ran forward presently and grasped the tall soldier by the arm. "Jim! Jim!" he coaxed, "come with me."

The tall soldier weakly tried to wrench himself free. "Huh," he said vacantly. He stared at the youth for a moment. At last he spoke as if dimly comprehending. "Oh! Inteh th' fields? Oh!"

He started blindly through the grass.

The youth turned once to look at the lashing riders and jouncing guns of the battery. He was startled from this view by a shrill outcry from the tattered man.

"He's runnin'!"

Turning his head swiftly, the youth saw his friend running in a staggering and stumbling way toward a little clump of bushes. His heart seemed to wrench itself almost free from his body at this sight. He made a noise of pain. He and the tattered man began a pursuit. There was a singular race.

When he overtook the tall soldier he began to plead with all the words he could find. "Jim — Jim — what are you doing — what makes you do this way — you'll hurt yerself."

The same purpose was in the tall soldier's face. He protested in a dulled way, keeping his eyes fastened on the mystic place of his intentions. "No — no — don't tech me — leave me be — leave me be."

The youth, aghast and filled with wonder at the tall soldier, began quaveringly to question him. "Where yeh goin', Jim? What you thinking about? Where you going? Tell me, won't you, Jim?"

The tall soldier faced about as upon relentless pursuers. In his eyes there was a great appeal. "Leave me be, can't yeh? Leave me be for a minnit."

The youth recoiled. "Why, Jim," he said, in a dazed way, "what 's the matter with you?"

The tall soldier turned and, lurching dangerously, went on. The youth and the tattered soldier followed, sneaking as if whipped, feeling unable to face the stricken man if he should again confront

them. They began to have thoughts of a solemn ceremony. There was something rite-like in these movements of the doomed soldier. And there was a resemblance in him to a devotee of a mad religion, blood-sucking, muscle-wrenching, bone-crushing. They were awed and afraid. They hung back lest he have at command a dreadful weapon.

At last, they saw him stop and stand motionless. Hastening up, they perceived that his face wore an expression telling that he had at last found the place for which he had struggled. His spare figure was erect; his bloody hands were quietly at his side. He was waiting with patience for something that he had come to meet. He was at the rendezvous. They paused and stood, expectant.

There was a silence.

Finally, the chest of the doomed soldier began to heave with a strained motion. It increased in violence until it was as if an animal was within and was kicking and tumbling furiously to be free.

This spectacle of gradual strangulation made the youth writhe, and once as his friend rolled his eyes, he saw something in them that made him sink wailing to the ground. He raised his voice in a last supreme call.

"Jim — Jim — Jim — "

The tall soldier opened his lips and spoke. He made a gesture. "Leave me be — don't tech me — leave me be — "

There was another silence while he waited.

Suddenly his form stiffened and straightened. Then it was shaken by a prolonged ague. He stared into space. To the two watchers there was a curious and profound dignity in the firm lines of his awful face.

He was invaded by a creeping strangeness that slowly enveloped him. For a moment the tremor of his legs caused him to dance a sort of hideous hornpipe. His arms beat wildly about his head in expression of implike enthusiasm.

His tall figure stretched itself to its full height. There was a slight rending sound. Then it began to swing forward, slow and straight, in the manner of a falling tree. A swift muscular contortion made the left shoulder strike the ground first.

The body seemed to bounce a little way from the earth. …

The youth had watched, spellbound, this ceremony at the place of meeting. His face had been twisted into an expression of every agony he had imagined for his friend.

He now sprang to his feet and, going closer, gazed upon the pastelike face. The mouth was open and the teeth showed in a laugh.

As the flap of the blue jacket fell away from the body, he could see that the side looked as if it had been chewed by wolves.

The youth turned, with sudden, livid rage, toward the battlefield. He shook his fist. He seemed about to deliver a philippic.

…

The red sun was pasted in the sky like a wafer.

Assignments

- Warm-up: "The red sun was pasted in the sky like a wafer." This sentence, which appears at the end of chapter 9, contains probably the most famous image in *The Red Badge of Courage*. The image is a topic of much debate. Some critics believe that Crane is making a comparison between the red sun and a communion wafer. In the Christian sacrament of communion, participants recognize the death and sacrifice of Christ by receiving both bread and wine as symbols of Christ's body. Readers who accept this interpretation of Crane's image also see Jim Conklin as a Christ-like figure who helps to redeem, or save, Henry. They point to his initials and to other elements of Christian imagery that occur in chapter 9 as justification for this interpretation. What effect does Jim Conklin have on Henry Fleming?

- Students should complete Concept Builder 18-B.

- Student should review reading(s) from the next chapter.

- Student should outline essay due at the end of the week.

- Per teacher instructions, students may answer orally, in a group setting, some of the essays that are not assigned as formal essays.

CONCEPT BUILDER 18-B
Style

The style of a literary work is the way that an author writes. Consider the writing style that Stephen Crane uses. Find examples of the following writing styles.

Style Technique	Passage
Sound and color effects	
Use of dialect in the dialoque	
Unusual word combinations	
Imagery	
Variety of sentence length	
Development of irony	

Violence in Literature

Chapter 18

The ragged line had respite for some minutes, but during its pause the struggle in the forest became magnified until the trees seemed to quiver from the firing and the ground to shake from the rushing of men. The voices of the cannon were mingled in a long and interminable row. It seemed difficult to live in such an atmosphere. The chests of the men strained for a bit of freshness, and their throats craved water.

There was one shot through the body, who raised a cry of bitter lamentation when came this lull. Perhaps he had been calling out during the fighting also, but at that time no one had heard him. But now the men turned at the woeful complaints of him upon the ground.

"Who is it? Who is it?"

"Its Jimmie Rogers. Jimmie Rogers."

When their eyes first encountered him there was a sudden halt, as if they feared to go near. He was thrashing about in the grass, twisting his shuddering body into many strange postures. He was screaming loudly. This instant's hesitation seemed to fill him with a tremendous, fantastic contempt...

The youth's friend had a geographical illusion concerning a stream, and he obtained permission to go for some water. Immediately canteens were showered upon him. "Fill mine, will yeh?" "Bring me some, too." "And me, too." He departed, ladened. The youth went with his friend, feeling a desire to throw his heated body into the stream and, soaking there, drink quarts.

They made a hurried search for the supposed stream, but did not find it. "No water here," said the youth. They turned without delay and began to retrace their steps.

From their position as they again faced toward the place of the fighting, they could of comprehend a greater amount of the battle than when their visions had been blurred by the hurling smoke of the line. They could see dark stretches winding along the land, and on one cleared space there was a row of guns making gray clouds, which were filled with large flashes of orange-colored flame. Over some foliage they could see the roof of a house. One window, glowing a deep murder red, shone squarely through the leaves. From the edifice a tall leaning tower of smoke went far into the sky.

Looking over their own troops, they saw mixed masses slowly getting into regular form. The sunlight made twinkling points of the bright steel. To the rear there was a glimpse of a distant roadway as it curved over a slope. It was crowded with retreating infantry. From all the interwoven forest arose the smoke and bluster of the battle. The air was always occupied by a blaring.

Near where they stood shells were flip-flapping and hooting. Occasional bullets buzzed in the air and spanged into tree trunks. Wounded men and other stragglers were slinking through the woods.

Looking down an aisle of the grove, the youth and his companion saw a jangling general and his staff almost ride upon a wounded man, who was crawling on his hands and knees. The general reined strongly at his charger's opened and foamy mouth and guided it with dexterous horsemanship past the man. The latter scrambled in wild and torturing haste. His strength evidently failed him as he reached a place of safety. One of his arms suddenly weakened, and he fell, sliding over upon his back. He lay stretched out, breathing gently.

A moment later the small, creaking cavalcade was directly in front of the two soldiers. Another officer, riding with the skillful abandon of a cowboy, galloped his horse to a position directly before the general. The two unnoticed foot soldiers made a little show of going on, but they lingered near in the desire to overhear the conversation. Perhaps, they thought, some great inner historical things would be said.

The general, whom the boys knew as the commander of their division, looked at the other officer and spoke coolly, as if he were criticising his clothes. "Th' enemy's formin' over there for another charge," he said. "It'll be directed against Whiterside, an' I fear they'll break through unless we work like thunder t' stop them."

The other swore at his restive horse, and then cleared his throat. He made a gesture toward his cap. "It'll be hell t' pay stoppin' them," he said shortly.

"I presume so," remarked the general. Then he began to talk rapidly and in a lower tone. He frequently illustrated his words with a pointing finger. The two infantrymen could hear nothing until finally he asked: "What troops can you spare?"

The officer who rode like a cowboy reflected for an instant. "Well," he said, "I had to order in th' 12th to help th' 76th, an' I haven't really got any. But there's th' 304th. They fight like a lot 'a mule drivers. I can spare them best of any."

The youth and his friend exchanged glances of astonishment.

The general spoke sharply. "Get 'em ready, then. I'll watch developments from here, an' send you word when t' start them. It'll happen in five minutes."

As the other officer tossed his fingers toward his cap and wheeling his horse, started away, the general called out to him in a sober voice: "I don't believe many of your mule drivers will get back."

The other shouted something in reply. He smiled.

With scared faces, the youth and his companion hurried back to the line.

These happenings had occupied an incredibly short time, yet the youth felt that in them he had been made aged. New eyes were given to him. And the most startling thing was to learn suddenly that he was very insignificant. The officer spoke of the regiment as if he referred to a broom. Some part of the woods needed sweeping, perhaps, and he merely indicated a broom in a tone properly indifferent to its fate. It was war, no doubt, but it appeared strange.

As the two boys approached the line, the lieutenant perceived them and swelled with wrath. "Fleming — Wilson — how long does it take yeh to git water, anyhow — where yeh been to."

But his oration ceased as he saw their eyes, which were large with great tales. "We're goin' t' charge — we're goin' t' charge!" cried the youth's friend, hastening with his news.

…

A little group of soldiers surrounded the two youths. "Are we, sure 'nough? Well, I'll be derned! Charge? What fer? What at? Wilson, you're lyin'."

"I hope to die," said the youth, pitching his tones to the key of angry remonstrance. "Sure as shooting, I tell you."

And his friend spoke in re-enforcement. "Not by a blame sight, he ain't lyin'. We heard 'em talkin'."

They caught sight of two mounted figures a short distance from them. One was the colonel of the regiment and the other was the officer who had received orders from the commander of the division. They were gesticulating at each other. The soldier, pointing at them, interpreted the scene.

One man had a final objection: "How could yeh hear 'em talkin'?" But the men, for a large part, nodded, admitting that previously the two friends had spoken truth.

They settled back into reposeful attitudes with airs of having accepted the matter. And they mused upon it, with a hundred varieties of expression. It was an engrossing thing to think about. Many tightened their belts carefully and hitched at their trousers.

A moment later the officers began to bustle among the men, pushing them into a more compact mass and into a better alignment. They chased those that straggled and fumed at a few men who seemed to show by their attitudes that they had decided to remain at that spot. They were like critical shepherds, struggling with sheep.

Presently, the regiment seemed to draw itself up and heave a deep breath. None of the men's faces were mirrors of large thoughts. The soldiers were bended and stooped like sprinters before a signal. Many pairs of glinting eyes peered from the grimy faces toward the curtains of the deeper woods. They seemed to be engaged in deep calculations of time and distance.

They were surrounded by the noises of the monstrous altercation between the two armies. The world was fully interested in other matters. Apparently, the regiment had its small affair to itself.

The youth, turning, shot a quick, inquiring glance at his friend. The latter returned to him the same manner of look. They were the only ones who possessed an inner knowledge. "Mule drivers … don't believe many will get back." It was an ironical secret. Still, they saw no hesitation in each other's faces, and they nodded a mute and unprotesting assent when a shaggy man near them said in a meek voice: "We'll git swallowed."

Assignments

- Warm-up: The descriptions of the deaths of Jim Conklin and Jimmie Rogers seem tame to us. We see worse every time we watch the news on TV. But death had never before been described this realistically in an American novel. Not ever! Readers were shocked and disturbed by this chapter.

- Students should complete Concept Builder 18-C.

- Students should write rough drafts of assigned essay.

- The teacher may correct rough drafts.

CONCEPT BUILDER 18-C
Theme: Maturity

Pre-eminently, the major theme of this novel is maturity. The author chooses to develop this theme through the character. Using internal conflict, the author uses the protagonist internal conflict to develop his theme. Trace the development of this theme through the following plot incidences.

Dreams of glory: *naivete*

Army camp life: *learning to wait*

Flight and contact with Conklin:

Wild charge against the enemy:

Maturity: *victory in battle*

The Final Chapter

Chapter 24

The roarings that had stretched in a long line of sound across the face of the forest began to grow intermittent and weaker. The stentorian speeches of the artillery continued in some distant encounter, but the crashes of the musketry had almost ceased. The youth and his friend of a sudden looked up, feeling a deadened form of distress at the waning of these noises, which had become a part of life. They could see changes going on among the troops. There were marchings this way and that way. A battery wheeled leisurely. On the crest of a small hill was the thick gleam of many departing muskets.

The youth arose. "Well, what now, I wonder?" he said. By his tone he seemed to be preparing to resent some new monstrosity in the way of dins and smashes. He shaded his eyes with his grimy hand and gazed over the field.

His friend also arose and stared. "I bet we're goin' t' git along out of this an' back over th' river," said he.

"Well, I swan!" said the youth.

They waited, watching. Within a little while the regiment received orders to retrace its way. The men got up grunting from the grass, regretting the soft repose. They jerked their stiffened legs, and stretched their arms over their heads. One man swore as he rubbed his eyes. They all groaned … They had as many objections to this change as they would have had to a proposal for a new battle.

They trampled slowly back over the field across which they had run in a mad scamper.

The regiment marched until it had joined its fellows. The reformed brigade, in column, aimed through a wood at the road. Directly they were in a mass of dust-covered troops, and were trudging along in a way parallel to the enemy's lines as these had been defined by the previous turmoil.

They passed within view of a stolid white house, and saw in front of it groups of their comrades lying in wait behind a neat breastwork. A row of guns were booming at a distant enemy. Shells thrown in reply were raising clouds of dust and splinters. Horsemen dashed along the line of intrenchments.

At this point of its march the division curved away from the field and went winding off in the direction of the river. When the significance of this movement had impressed itself upon the youth he turned his head and looked over his shoulder toward the trampled and debris-strewed ground. He breathed a breath of new satisfaction. He finally nudged his friend. "Well, it's all over," he said to him.

His friend gazed backward. "… it is," he assented. They mused.

For a time the youth was obliged to reflect in a puzzled and uncertain way. His mind was undergoing a subtle change. It took moments for it to cast off its battleful ways and resume its accustomed course of thought. Gradually his brain emerged from the clogged clouds, and at last he was enabled to more closely comprehend himself and circumstance.

He understood then that the existence of shot and countershot was in the past. He had dwelt in a land of strange, squalling upheavals and had come forth. He had been where there was red of blood and black of passion, and he was escaped. His first thoughts were given to rejoicings at this fact.

Later he began to study his deeds, his failures, and his achievements. Thus, fresh from scenes where many of his usual machines of reflection had been idle, from where he had proceeded sheeplike, he struggled to marshal all his acts.

At last they marched before him clearly. From this present view point he was enabled to look upon them in spectator fashion and criticise them with some correctness, for his new condition had already defeated certain sympathies.

Regarding his procession of memory he felt gleeful and unregretting, for in it his public deeds were paraded in great and shining prominence. Those performances which had been witnessed by his fellows marched now in wide purple and gold, having various deflections. They went gayly with music. It was pleasure to watch these things. He spent delightful minutes viewing the gilded images of memory.

He saw that he was good. He recalled with a thrill of joy the respectful comments of his fellows upon his conduct.

Nevertheless, the ghost of his flight from the first engagement appeared to him and danced. There were small shoutings in his brain about these matters. For a moment he blushed, and the light of his soul flickered with shame.

A specter of reproach came to him. There loomed the dogging memory of the tattered soldier--he who, gored by bullets and faint of blood, had fretted concerning an imagined wound in another; he who had loaned his last of strength and intellect for the tall soldier; he who, blind with weariness and pain, had been deserted in the field.

For an instant a wretched chill of sweat was upon him at the thought that he might be detected in the thing. As he stood persistently before his vision, he gave vent to a cry of sharp irritation and agony.

His friend turned. "What's the matter, Henry?" he demanded. The youth's reply was an outburst of crimson oaths.

As he marched along the little branch-hung roadway among his prattling companions this vision of cruelty brooded over him. It clung near him always and darkened his view of these deeds in purple and gold. Whichever way his thoughts turned they were followed by the somber phantom of the desertion in the fields. He looked stealthily at his companions, feeling sure that they must discern in his face evidences of this pursuit. But they were plodding in ragged array, discussing with quick tongues the accomplishments of the late battle.

"Oh, if a man should come up an' ask me, I'd say we got a dum good lickin'."

"Lickin' — in yer eye! We ain't licked, sonny. We're goin' down here aways, swing aroun', an' come in behint 'em."

"Oh, hush, with your comin' in behint 'em. I've seen all 'a that I wanta. Don't tell me about comin' in behint--"

"Bill Smithers, he ses he'd rather been in ten hundred battles than been in that … hospital. He ses they got shootin' in th' nighttime, an' shells dropped plum among 'em in th' hospital. He ses sech hollerin' he never see."

"Hasbrouck? He's th' best off'cer in this here reg'ment. He's a whale."

"Didn't I tell yeh we'd come aroun' in behint 'em? Didn't I tell yeh so? We — "

"Oh, shet yeh mouth!"

For a time this pursuing recollection of the tattered man took all elation from the youth's veins. He saw his vivid error, and he was afraid that it would stand before him all his life. He took no share in the chatter of his comrades, nor did he look at them or know them, save when he felt sudden suspicion that they were seeing his thoughts and scrutinizing each detail of the scene with the tattered soldier.

Yet gradually he mustered force to put the sin at a distance. And at last his eyes seemed to open to some new ways. He found that he could look back upon the brass and bombast of his earlier gospels and see them truly. He was gleeful when he discovered that he now despised them.

With this conviction came a store of assurance. He felt a quiet manhood, nonassertive but of sturdy and strong blood. He knew that he would no more quail before his guides wherever they should point. He had been to touch the great death, and found that, after all, it was but the great death. He was a man.

So it came to pass that as he trudged from the place of blood and wrath his soul changed. He came from hot plowshares to prospects of clover tranquilly, and it was as if hot plowshares were not. Scars faded as flowers.

It rained. The procession of weary soldiers became a bedraggled train, despondent and muttering, marching with churning effort in a trough of liquid brown mud under a low, wretched sky. Yet the youth smiled, for he saw that the world was a world for him, though many discovered it to be made of oaths and walking sticks. He had rid himself of the red sickness of battle. The sultry nightmare was in the past. He had been an animal blistered and sweating in the heat and pain of war. He turned now with a lover's thirst to images of tranquil skies, fresh meadows, cool brooks — an existence of soft and eternal peace.

Over the river a golden ray of sun came through the hosts of leaden rain clouds.

Assignments

- Warm-up: In chapter 9 Henry encounters the tattered man when, fleeing from his regiment, he falls in with a group of wounded soldiers. The tattered man appears to be simple and innocent. When we first meet him he is listening to a sergeant with such awe that the sergeant begins to laugh at him. The tattered man is almost pathetically eager to make friends with Henry. We meet him again in this final chapter. What is his purpose?

- Students should complete Concept Builder 18-D.

- Student will re-write corrected copies of essays due tomorrow.

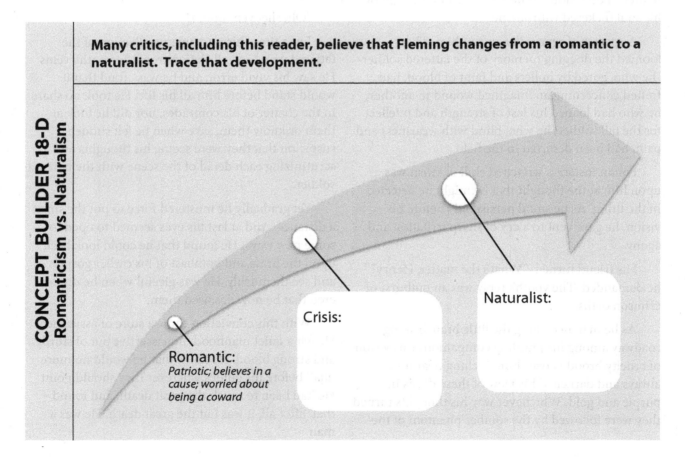

CONCEPT BUILDER 18-D
Romanticism vs. Naturalism

Many critics, including this reader, believe that Fleming changes from a romantic to a naturalist. Trace that development.

Naturalist:

Crisis:

Romantic:
Patriotic; believes in a cause; worried about being a coward

Blue Hotel

The Palace Hotel at Fort Romper was painted a light blue, a shade that is on the legs of a kind of heron, causing the bird to declare its position against any background. The Palace Hotel, then, was always screaming and howling in a way that made the dazzling winter landscape of Nebraska seem only a gray swampish hush. It stood alone on the prairie, and when the snow was falling the town two hundred yards away was not visible. But when the traveler alighted at the railway station he was obliged to pass the Palace Hotel before he could come upon the company of low clapboard houses which composed Fort Romper, and it was not to be thought that any traveler could pass the Palace Hotel without looking at it. Pat Scully, the proprietor, had proved himself a master of strategy when he chose his paints. It is true that on clear days, when the great trans-continental expresses, long lines of swaying Pullmans, swept through Fort Romper, passengers were overcome at the sight, and the cult that knows the brown-reds and the subdivisions of the dark greens of the East expressed shame, pity, horror, in a laugh. But to the citizens of this prairie town, and to the people who would naturally stop there, Pat Scully had performed a feat. With this opulence and splendor, these creeds, classes, egotisms, that streamed through Romper on the rails day after day, they had no color in common.

As if the displayed delights of such a blue hotel were not sufficiently enticing, it was Scully's habit to go every morning and evening to meet the leisurely trains that stopped at Romper and work his seductions upon any man that he might see wavering, gripsack in hand.

One morning, when a snow-crusted engine dragged its long string of freight cars and its one passenger coach to the station, Scully performed the marvel of catching three men. One was a shaky and quick-eyed Swede, with a great shining cheap valise; one was a tall bronzed cowboy, who was on his way to a ranch near the Dakota line; one was a little silent man from the East, who didn't look it, and didn't announce it. Scully practically made them prisoners. He was so nimble and merry and kindly that each probably felt it would be the height of brutality to try to escape. They trudged off over the creaking board sidewalks in the wake of the eager little Irishman.

He wore a heavy fur cap squeezed tightly down on his head. It caused his two red ears to stick out stiffly, as if they were made of tin. At last, Scully, elaborately, with boisterous hospitality, conducted them through the portals of the blue hotel. The room which they entered was small. It seemed to be merely a proper temple for an enormous stove, which, in the center, was humming with godlike violence. At various points on its surface the iron had become luminous and glowed yellow from the heat. Beside the stove Scully's son Johnnie was playing High-Five with an old farmer who had whiskers both gray and sandy. They were quarreling. Frequently the old farmer turned his face toward a box of sawdust- colored brown from tobacco juice-that was behind the stove, and spat with an air of great impatience and irritation. With a loud flourish of words Scully destroyed the game of cards, and bustled his son upstairs with part of the baggage of the new guests. He himself conducted them to three basins of the coldest water in the world. The cowboy and the Easterner burnished themselves fiery red with this water, until it seemed to be some kind of a metal polish. The Swede, however, merely dipped his fingers gingerly and with trepidation. It was notable that throughout this series of small ceremonies the three travelers were made to feel that Scully was very benevolent. He was conferring great favors upon them. He handed the towel from one to the other with an air of philanthropic impulse.

Afterward they went to the first room, and, sitting about the stove, listened to Scully's officious clamor at his daughters, who were preparing the midday meal. They reflected in the silence of experienced men who tread carefully amid new people. Nevertheless, the old farmer, stationary, invincible in his chair near the warmest part of the stove, turned his face from the sawdust box frequently and addressed a glowing commonplace to the strangers. Usually he was answered in short but adequate sentences by either the cowboy or the Easterner. The Swede said nothing. He seemed to be occupied in making furtive estimates of each man in the room. One might have thought that he had the sense of silly suspicion which comes to guilt. He resembled a badly frightened man.

Later, at dinner, he spoke a little, addressing his conversation entirely to Scully. He volunteered that he had come from New York, where for ten years he had worked as a tailor. These facts seem to strike Scull as fascinating, and afterward he volunteered that he had lived at Romper for fourteen years. The Swede asked about the crops and the price of labor. He seemed barely to listen to Scales extended replies. His eyes continued to rove from man to man.

Finally, with a laugh and a wink, he said that some of these Western Communities were very dangerous; and after his statement he straightened his legs under the table, tilted his head, and laughed again, loudly. It was plain that the demonstration had no meaning to the others. They looked at him wondering and in silence.

As the men trooped heavily back into the front room, the two little windows presented views of a turmoiling sea of snow. The huge arms of the wind were making attempts — mighty, circular, futile to embrace the flakes as they sped. A gate-post like a still man with a blanched face stood aghast amid this profligate fury. In a hearty voice Scully announced the presence of a blizzard. The guests of the blue hotel, lighting their pipes, assented with grunts of lazy masculine contentment. No island of the sea could be exempt in the degree of this little room with its humming stove. Johnnie, son of Scully, in a tone which defined his opinion of his ability as a card-player, challenged the old farmer of both gray and sandy whiskers to a game of High-Five. The farmer agreed with a contemptuous and bitter scoff. They sat close to the stove, and squared their knees under a wide board. The cowboy and the Easterner watched the game with interest. The Swede remained near the window, aloof, but with a countenance that showed signs of an inexplicable excitement.

The play of Johnnie and the gray-beard was suddenly ended by another quarrel. The old man arose while casting a look of heated scorn at his adversary. He slowly buttoned his coat, and then stalked with fabulous dignity from the room. In the discreet silence of all other men the Swede laughed. His laughter rang somehow childishly. Men by this time had begun to look at him askance, as if they wished to inquire what ailed him.

A new game was formed jocosely. The cowboy volunteered to become the partner of Johnnie, and them all then turned to ask the Swede to throw in his lot with the little Easterner. He asked some questions about the game, and learning that it wore many names, and that he had played it when it was under an alias, he accepted the invitation. He strode toward the men nervously, as if he expected to be assaulted. Finally, seated, he gazed from face to face and laughed shrilly. This laugh was so strange that the Easterner looked up quickly, the cowboy sat intent and with his mouth open, and Johnnie paused, holding the cards with still fingers. Afterward there was a short silence. Then Johnnie said: "Well, let's get at it. Come on now!" They pulled their chairs forward until their knees were bunched under the board. They began to play, and their interest in the game caused the others to forget the manner of the Swede.

The cowboy was a board-whacker. Each time that he held superior cards he whanged them, one by one, with exceeding force, down upon the improvised table, and took the tricks with a glowing air of prowess and pride that sent thrills of indignation into the hearts of his opponents. A game with a board-whacker in it is sure to become intense. The countenances of the Easterner and the Swede were miserable whenever the cowboy thundered down his aces and kings, while Johnnie, his eyes gleaming with joy, chuckled and chuckled. Because of the absorbing play none considered the strange ways of the Swede. They paid strict heed to the game. Finally, during a lull caused by a new deal, the Swede suddenly addressed Johnnie: "I suppose there have been a good many men killed in this room." The jaws of the others dropped and they looked at him. "What … are you talking about?" said Johnnie. The Swede laughed again his blatant laugh, full of a kind of false courage and defiance. "Oh, you know what I mean all right," he answered.

"I'm a liar if I do!" Johnnie protested. The card was halted, and the men stared at the Swede. Johnnie evidently felt that as the son of the proprietor he should make a direct inquiry. "Now, what might you be drivin' at, mister?" he asked. The Swede winked at him. It was a wink full of cunning. His fingers shook on the edge of the board. "Oh, maybe you think I have been to nowheres. Maybe you think I'm a tenderfoot?"

"I don't know nothin' about you," answered Johnnie, "… All I got to say is that I don't know what you're driving at. There hain't never been nobody killed in this room." The cowboy, who had been steadily gazing at the Swede, then spoke. "What's wrong with you, mister?"

Apparently it seemed to the Swede that he was formidably menaced. He shivered and turned white near the corners of his mouth. He sent an appealing glance in the direction of the little Easterner. During these moments he did not forget to wear his air of advanced pot-valor.

"They say they don't know what I mean," he remarked mockingly to the Easterner.

The latter answered after prolonged and cautious reflection. "I don't understand you," he said, impassively.

The Swede made a movement then which announced that he thought he had encountered treachery from the only quarter where he had expected sympathy if not help. "Oh, I see you are all against me. I see —" The cowboy was in a state of deep stupefaction. "Say," he cried, as he tumbled the deck violently down upon the board. "Say, what are you gittin' at, hey?"

The Swede sprang up with the celerity of a man escaping from a snake on the floor. "I don't want to fight!" he shouted. "I don't want to fight!"

The cowboy stretched his long legs indolently and deliberately. His hands were in his pockets. He spat into the sawdust box. …

The Swede backed rapidly toward a corner of the room. His hands were out protectingly in front of his chest, but he was making an obvious struggle to control his fright. "Gentlemen," he quavered, "I suppose I am going to be killed before I can leave this house! I suppose I am going to be killed before I can leave this house." In his eyes was the dying swan look. Through the windows could be seen the snow turning blue in the shadow of dusk. The wind tore at the house and some loose thing beat regularly against the clapboard like a spirit tapping.

A door opened, and Scully himself entered. He paused in surprise as he noted the tragic attitude of the Swede. Then he said: "What's the matter here?"

The Swede answered him swiftly and eagerly: "These men are going to kill me."

"Kill you!" ejaculated Scully. "Kill you! What are you talkin'?"

The Swede made the gesture of a martyr.

Scully wheeled sternly upon his son. "What is this, Johnnie?"

The lad had grown sullen. … "I can't make no sense to it." He began to shuffle the cards, fluttering them together with an angry snap. "He says a good many men have been killed in this room, or something like that. And he says he's goin' to be killed here too. I don't know what ails him. He's crazy, I shouldn't wonder."

Scully then looked for explanation to the cowboy, but the cowboy simply shrugged his shoulders.

"Kill you?" said Scully again to the Swede. "Kill you? Man, you're off your nut."

"Oh, I know," burst out the Swede. "I know what will happen. Yes, I'm crazy — yes. Yes, of course, I'm crazy — yes. But I know one thing —" There was a sort of sweat of misery and terror upon his face. "I know I won't get out of here alive."

The cowboy drew a deep breath, as if his mind was passing into the last stages of dissolution. "Well, I'm dog-goned," he whispered to himself.

Scully wheeled suddenly and faced his son. "You've been troublin' this man!"

Johnnie's voice was loud with its burden of grievance. "Why, …, I ain't done nothin' to 'im."

The Swede broke in. "Gentlemen, do not disturb yourselves. I will leave this house. I will go 'way because —" He accused them dramatically with his glance. "Because I do not want to be killed."

Scully was furious with his son. "Will you tell me what is the matter, you young divil? What's the matter, anyhow? Speak out!"

"Blame it," cried Johnnie in despair, "don't I tell you I don't know. He — he says we want to kill him, and that's all I know. I can't tell what ails him."

The Swede continued to repeat: "Never mind, Mr. Scully, never mind. I will leave this house. I will go away, because I do not wish to be killed. Yes, of course, I am crazy — yes. But I know one thing! I will go away. I will leave this house. Never mind, Mr. Scully, never mind. I will go away."

"You will not go 'way," said Scully. "You will not go 'way until I hear the reason of this business. If anybody has troubled you I will take care of him. This is my house. You are under my roof, and I will not allow any peaceable man to be troubled here." He cast a terrible eye upon Johnnie, the cowboy, and the Easterner.

"Never mind, Mr. Scully; never mind. I will go 'way. I do not wish to be killed." The Swede moved toward the door, which opened upon the stairs. It was evidently his intention to go at once for his baggage.

"No, no," shouted Scully peremptorily; but the whitefaced man slid by him and disappeared. "Now," said Scully severely, "what does this mane?"

Johnnie and the cowboy cried together: "Why, we didn't do nothin' to 'im!"

Scully's eyes were cold. "No," he said, "you didn't?"

Johnnie swore a deep oath. "Why, this is the wildest loon I ever see. We didn't do nothin' at all. We were jest sittin' here playin' cards and he —" The father suddenly spoke to the Easterner. "Mr. Blanc," he asked, "what has these boys been doin'?"

The Easterner reflected again. "I didn't see anything wrong at all," he said at last slowly.

Scully began to howl. "But what does it mane?" He stared ferociously at his son. "I have a mind to lather you for this, me boy."

Johnnie was frantic. "Well, what have I done?" he bawled at his father.

"I think you are tongue-tied," said Scully finally to his son, the cowboy and the Easterner, and at the end of this scornful sentence he left the room.

Upstairs the Swede was swiftly fastening the straps of his great valise. Once his back happened to be half-turned toward the door, and hearing a noise there, he wheeled and sprang up, uttering a loud cry. Scully's wrinkled visage showed grimly in the light of the small lamp he carried. This yellow effulgence, streaming upward, colored only his prominent features, and left his eyes, for instance, in mysterious shadow. He resembled a murderer.

"Man, man!" he exclaimed, "have you gone daffy?"

"Oh, no! Oh, no!" rejoined the other. "There are people in this world who know pretty nearly as much as you do — understand?" For a moment they stood gazing at each other. Upon the Swede's deathly pale cheeks were two spots brightly crimson and sharply edged, as if they had been carefully painted. Scully placed the light on the table and sat himself on the edge of the bed. He spoke ruminatively. "By cracky, I never heard of such a thing in my life. It's a complete muddle. I can't for the soul of me think how you ever got this idea into your head." Presently he lifted his eyes and asked: "And did you sure think they were going to kill you?" The Swede scanned the old man as if he wished to see into his mind. "I did," he said at last. He obviously suspected that this answer might precipitate an outbreak. As he pulled on a strap his whole arm shook, the elbow wavering like a bit of paper.

Scully banged his hand impressively on the foot-board of the bed. "Why, man, we're goin' to have a line of ilictric street-cars in this town next spring."

"'A line of electric street-cars,'" repeated the Swede stupidly.

"And," said Scully, "there's a new railroad goin' to be built down from Broken Arm to here. Not to mention the four churches and the smashin' big brick schoolhouse. Then there's the big factory, too. Why, in two years Romper'll be a met-tro-pol-is."

Having finished the preparation of his baggage, the Swede straightened himself. "Mr. Scully," he said with sudden hardihood, "how much do I owe you?"

"You don't owe me anythin'," said the old man angrily. "Yes, I do," retorted the Swede. He took seventy-five cents from his pocket and tendered it to Scully; but the latter snapped his fingers in disdainful refusal. However, it happened that they both stood gazing in a strange fashion at three silver pieces in the Swede's open palm.

"I'll not take your money," said Scully at last. "Not after what's been goin' on here." Then a plan seemed to strike him. "Here," he cried, picking up his lamp and moving toward the door. "Here! Come with me a minute."

"No," said the Swede in overwhelming alarm.

"Yes," urged the old man. "Come on! I want you to come and see a picter — just across the hall — in my room."

The Swede must have concluded that his hour was come. His jaw dropped and his teeth showed like a dead man's. He ultimately followed

Scully across the corridor, but he had the step of one hung in chains.

Scully flashed the light high on the wall of his own chamber. There was revealed a ridiculous photograph of a little girl. She was leaning against a balustrade of gorgeous decoration, and the formidable bang to her hair was prominent. The figure was as graceful as an upright sled-stake, and, withal,

it was of the hue of lead. "There," said Scully tenderly. "That's the picter of my little girl that died. Her name was Carrie. She had the purtiest hair you ever saw! I was that fond of her, she —" Turning then he saw that the Swede was not contemplating the picture at all, but, instead, was keeping keen watch on the gloom in the rear.

"Look, man!" shouted Scully heartily. "That's the picter of my little gal that died. Her name was Carrie. And then here's the picter of my oldest boy, Michael. He's a lawyer in Lincoln an' doin' well. I gave that boy a grand eddycation, and I'm glad for it now. He's a fine boy. Look at 'im now. Ain't he bold as blazes, him there in Lincoln, an honored an' respicted gintleman. An honored an' respicted gintleman," concluded Scully with a flourish. And so saying, he smote the Swede jovially on the back.

The Swede faintly smiled.

"Now," said the old man, "there's only one more thing." He dropped suddenly to the floor and thrust his head beneath the bed. The Swede could hear his muffled voice. "I'd keep it under me piller if it wasn't for that boy Johnnie. Then there's the old woman — where is it now? I never put it twice in the same place. Ah, now come out with you!"

Presently he backed clumsily from under the bed, dragging with him an old coat rolled into a bundle. "I've fetched him" he muttered. Kneeling on the floor he unrolled the coat and extracted from its heart a large yellow-brown whisky bottle.

His first maneuver was to hold the bottle up to the light.

Reassured, apparently, that nobody had been tampering with it, he thrust it with a generous movement toward the Swede.

The weak-kneed Swede was about to eagerly clutch this element of strength, but he suddenly jerked his hand away and cast a look of horror upon Scully.

"Drink," said the old man affectionately. He had arisen to his feet, and now stood facing the Swede.

There was a silence. Then again Scully said: "Drink!"

The Swede laughed wildly. He grabbed the bottle, put it to his mouth, and as his lips curled absurdly around the opening and his throat worked, he kept his glance burning with hatred upon the old man's face.

After the departure of Scully the three men, with the card-board still upon their knees, preserved for a long time an astounded silence. Then Johnnie said: "That's the dod-dangest Swede I ever see."

"He ain't no Swede," said the cowboy scornfully.

"Well, what is he then?" cried Johnnie. "What is he then?"

"It's my opinion," replied the cowboy deliberately, "he's some kind of a Dutchman." It was a venerable custom of the country to entitle as Swedes all light-haired men who spoke with a heavy tongue. In consequence the idea of the cowboy was not without its daring. "Yes, sir," he repeated. "It's my opinion this feller is some kind of a Dutchman."

"Well, he says he's a Swede, anyhow," muttered Johnnie sulkily. He turned to the Easterner: "What do you think, Mr. Blanc?"

"Oh, I don't know," replied the Easterner.

"Well, what do you think makes him act that way?" asked the cowboy.

"Why, he's frightened!" The Easterner knocked his pipe against a rim of the stove. "He's clear frightened out of his boots."

"What at?" cried Johnnie and cowboy together.

The Easterner reflected over his answer.

"What at?" cried the others again.

"Oh, I don't know, but it seems to me this man has been reading dime-novels, and he thinks he's right out in the middle of it- the shootin' and stabbin' and all."

"But," said the cowboy, deeply scandalized, "this ain't Wyoming, ner none of them places. This is Nebrasker."

"Yes," added Johnnie, "an' why don't he wait till he gits out West?"

The traveled Easterner laughed. "It isn't different there even- not in these days. ..."

Johnnie and the cowboy mused long.

"It's awful funny," remarked Johnnie at last.

"Yes," said the cowboy. "This is a queer game. I hope we don't git snowed in, because then we'd have to stand this here man bein' around with us all the time. That wouldn't be no good."

"I wish pop would throw him out," said Johnnie.

Presently they heard a loud stamping on the stairs, accompanied by ringing jokes in the voice of old Scully, and laughter, evidently from the Swede. The men around the stove stared vacantly at each other. "Gosh," said the cowboy. The door flew open, and old Scully, flushed and anecdotal, came into the room. He was jabbering at the Swede, who followed him, laughing bravely. It was the entry of two roysterers from a banquet hall.

"Come now," said Scully sharply to the three seated men, "move up and give us a chance at the stove." The cowboy and the Easterner obediently sidled their chairs to make room for the newcomers. Johnnie, however, simply arranged himself in a more indolent attitude, and then remained motionless.

"Come! Git over, there," said Scully.

"Plenty of room on the other side of the stove," said Johnnie.

"Do you think we want to sit in the draught?" roared the father.

But the Swede here interposed with a grandeur of confidence. "No, no. Let the boy sit where he likes," he cried in a bullying voice to the father. "All right! All right!" said Scully deferentially. The cowboy and the Easterner exchanged glances of wonder.

The five chairs were formed in a crescent about one side of the stove. The Swede began to talk; he talked arrogantly, profanely, angrily. Johnnie, the cowboy and the Easterner maintained a morose silence, while old Scully appeared to be receptive and eager, breaking in constantly with sympathetic ejaculations.

Finally the Swede announced that he was thirsty. He moved in his chair, and said that he would go for a drink of water.

"I'll git it for you," cried Scully at once.

"No," said the Swede contemptuously. "I'll get it for myself." He arose and stalked with the air of an owner off into the executive parts of the hotel.

As soon as the Swede was out of hearing Scully sprang to his feet and whispered intensely to the others. "Upstairs he thought I was tryin' to poison 'im."

"Say," said Johnnie, "this makes me sick. Why don't you throw 'im out in the snow?"

"Why, he's all right now," declared Scully. "It was only that he was from the East and he thought this was a tough place. That's all. He's all right now."

The cowboy looked with admiration upon the Easterner. "You were straight," he said, "You were on to that there Dutchman."

"Well," said Johnnie to his father, "he may be all right now, but I don't see it. Other time he was scared, and now he's too fresh."

Scully's speech was always a combination of Irish brogue and idiom, Western twang and idiom, and scraps of curiously formal diction taken from the story-books and newspapers. He now hurled a strange mass of language at the head of his son. "What do I keep? What do I keep? What do I keep?" he demanded in a voice of thunder. He slapped his knee impressively, to indicate that he himself was going to make reply, and that all should heed. "I keep a hotel," he shouted. "A hotel, do you mind? A guest under my roof has sacred privileges. He is to be intimidated by none. Not one word shall he hear that would prijudice him in favor of goin' away. I'll not have it. There's no place in this here town where they can say they iver took in a guest of mine because he was afraid to stay here." He wheeled suddenly upon the cowboy and the Easterner. "Am I right?"

"Yes, Mr. Scully," said the cowboy, "I think you're right."

"Yes, Mr. Scully," said the Easterner, "I think you're right."

At six-o'clock supper, the Swede fizzed like a firewheel. He sometimes seemed on the point of bursting into riotous song, and in all his madness he was encouraged by old Scully. The Easterner was incased in reserve; the cowboy sat in wide-mouthed amazement, forgetting to eat, while Johnnie wrathily demolished great plates of food. The daughters of the house when they were obliged to replenish the biscuits approached as warily as Indians, and, having succeeded in their purposes, fled with ill-concealed trepidation. The Swede domineered the whole feast, and he gave it the appearance of a cruel bacchanal. He seemed to have grown suddenly taller; he gazed, brutally disdainful, into every face. His voice rang through the room. Once when he jabbed out harpoon-fashion with his fork to pinion a biscuit the weapon nearly impaled the hand of the Easterner which had been stretched quietly out for the same biscuit. After supper, as the men filed toward the other room, the Swede smote Scully ruthlessly on the shoulder. "Well, old boy, that was a good square meal." Johnnie looked hopefully at his father; he knew that shoulder was tender from an old fall; and indeed it appeared for a moment as if Scully was going to flame out over the matter, but in the end he smiled a sickly smile and remained silent. The others understood from his manner that he was admitting his responsibility for the Swede's new viewpoint.

Johnnie, however, addressed his parent in an aside. "Why don't you license somebody to kick you downstairs?" Scully scowled darkly by way of reply.

When they were gathered about the stove, the Swede insisted on another game of High-Five. Scully gently deprecated the plan at first, but the Swede turned a wolfish glare upon him. The old man subsided, and the Swede canvassed the others. In his tone there was always a great threat. The cowboy and the Easterner both remarked indifferently that they would play. Scully said that he would presently have to go to meet the 6.58 train, and so the Swede turned menacingly upon Johnnie. For a moment their glances crossed like blades, and then Johnnie smiled and said: "Yes, I'll play."

They formed a square with the little board on their knees. The Easterner and the Swede were again partners. As the play went on, it was noticeable that the cowboy was not board-whacking as usual. Meanwhile, Scully, near the lamp, had put on his spectacles and, with an appearance curiously like an old priest, was reading a newspaper. In time he went out to meet the 6:58 train, and, despite his precautions, a gust of polar wind whirled into the room as he opened the door. Besides scattering the cards, it chilled the players to the marrow. The Swede cursed frightfully. When Scully returned, his entrance disturbed a cozy and friendly scene. The Swede again cursed. But presently they were once more intent, their heads bent forward and their hands moving swiftly. The Swede had adopted the fashion of board-whacking.

Scully took up his paper and for a long time remained immersed in matters which were extraordinarily remote from him. The lamp burned badly, and once he stopped to adjust the wick. The newspaper as he turned from page to page rustled with a slow and comfortable sound. Then suddenly he heard three terrible words: "You are cheatin'!"

Such scenes often prove that there can be little of dramatic import in environment. Any room can present a tragic front; any room can be comic. This little den was now hideous as a torture-chamber. The new faces of the men themselves had changed it upon the instant. The Swede held a huge fist in front of Johnnie's face, while the latter looked steadily over it into the blazing orbs of his accuser. The Easterner had grown pallid; the cowboy's jaw had dropped in that expression of bovine amazement which was one of his important mannerisms. After the three words, the first sound in the room was made by Scully's paper as it floated forgotten to his feet. His spectacles had also fallen from his nose, but by a clutch he had saved them in air. His hand, grasping the spectacles, now remained poised awkwardly and near his shoulder. He stared at the card-players.

Probably the silence was while a second elapsed. Then, if the floor had been suddenly twitched out from under the men they could not have moved quicker. The five had projected themselves headlong toward a common point. It happened that Johnnie in rising to hurl himself upon the Swede had stumbled slightly because of his curiously instinctive care for the cards and the board. The loss of the moment allowed time for the arrival of Scully, and also allowed the cowboy time to give the Swede a great push which sent him staggering back. The men found tongue together, and hoarse shouts or rage, appeal or fear burst from every throat. The cowboy

pushed and jostled feverishly at the Swede, and the Easterner and Scully clung wildly to Johnnie; but, through the smoky air, above the swaying bodies of the peace-compellers, the eyes of the two warriors ever sought each other in glances of challenge that were at once hot and steely.

Of course the board had been overturned, and now the whole company of cards was scattered over the floor, where the boots of the men trampled the fat and painted kings and queens as they gazed with their silly eyes at the war that was waging above them.

Scully's voice was dominating the yells. "Stop now! Stop, I say! Stop, now —"

Johnnie, as he struggled to burst through the rank formed by Scully and the Easterner, was crying: "Well, he says I cheated! He says I cheated! I won't allow no man to say I cheated! If he says I cheated, he's a —!"

The cowboy was telling the Swede: "Quit, now! Quit, d'ye hear —" The screams of the Swede never ceased. "He did cheat! I saw him! I saw him —" As for the Easterner, he was importuning in a voice that was not heeded. "Wait a moment, can't you? Oh, wait a moment. What's the good of a fight over a game of cards? Wait a moment —" In this tumult no complete sentences were clear. "Cheat" — "Quit" — "He says" — These fragments pierced the uproar and rang out sharply. It was remarkable that whereas Scully undoubtedly made the most noise, he was the least heard of any of the riotous band.

Then suddenly there was a great cessation. It was as if each man had paused for breath, and although the room was still lighted with the anger of men, it could be seen that there was no danger of immediate conflict, and at once Johnnie, shouldering his ways forward, almost succeeded in confronting the Swede. "What did you say I cheated for? What did you say I cheated for? I don't cheat and I won't let no man say I do!"

The Swede said: "I saw you! I saw you!"

"Well," cried Johnnie, "I'll fight any man what says I cheat!"

"No, you won't," said the cowboy. "Not here."

"Ah, be still, can't you?" said Scully, coming between them.

The quiet was sufficient to allow the Easterner's voice to be heard.

He was repeating: "Oh, wait a moment, can't you? What's the good of a fight over a game of cards? Wait a moment."

Johnnie, his red face appearing above his father's shoulder, hailed the Swede again. "Did you say I cheated?"

The Swede showed his teeth. "Yes."

"Then," said Johnnie, "we must fight."

"Yes, fight," roared the Swede. He was like a demoniac. "Yes, fight! I'll show you what kind of a man I am! I'll show you who you want to fight! Maybe you think I can't fight! Maybe you think I can't! I'll show you, you skin, you card-sharp! Yes, you cheated! You cheated! You cheated!"

"Well, let's git at it, then, mister," said Johnnie coolly.

The cowboy's brow was beaded with sweat from his efforts in intercepting all sorts of raids. He turned in despair to Scully. "What are you goin' to do now?"

A change had come over the Celtic visage of the old man. He now seemed all eagerness; his eyes glowed. "We'll let them fight," he answered stalwartly. "I can't put up with it any longer. I've stood this … Swede till I'm sick. We'll let them fight."

The men prepared to go out of doors. The Easterner was so nervous that he had great difficulty in getting his arms into the sleeves of his new leather-coat. As the cowboy drew his fur-cap down over his ears his hands trembled. In fact, Johnnie and old Scully were the only ones who displayed no agitation. These preliminaries were conducted without words.

Scully threw open the door. "Well, come on," he said. Instantly a terrific wind caused the flame of the lamp to struggle at its wick, while a puff of black smoke sprang from the chimney-top. The stove was in midcurrent of the blast, and its voice swelled to equal the roar of the storm. Some of the scarred and bedabbled cards were caught up from the floor and dashed helplessly against the further wall. The men lowered their heads and plunged into the tempest as into a sea.

No snow was falling, but great whirls and clouds of flakes, swept up from the ground by the frantic winds, were streaming southward with the speed of bullets. The covered land was blue with the sheen of an unearthly satin, and there was no other hue save where at the low black railway station, which seemed incredibly distant, one light gleamed like a tiny jewel. As the men floundered into a thigh-deep drift, it was known that the Swede was bawling out something. Scully went to him, put a hand on his shoulder and projected an ear.

"What's that you say?" he shouted.

"I say," bawled the Swede again, "I won't stand much show against this gang. I know you'll all pitch on me."

Scully smote him reproachfully on the arm. "Tut, man," he yelled. The wind tore the words from Scully's lips and scattered them far a-lee. "You are all a gang of —" boomed the Swede, but the storm also seized the remainder of this sentence. Immediately turning their backs upon the wind, the men had swung around a corner to the sheltered side of the hotel. It was the function of the little house to preserve here, amid this great devastation of snow, an irregular V-shape of heavily-incrusted grass, which crackled beneath the feet. One could imagine the great drifts piled against the windward side. When the party reached the comparative peace of this spot it was found that the Swede was still bellowing.

"Oh, I know what kind of a thing this is! I know you'll all pitch on me. I can't lick you all!"

Scully turned upon him panther-fashion. "You'll not have to whip all of us. You'll have to whip my son Johnnie. An' the man what troubles you durin' that time will have me to dale with."

The arrangements were swiftly made. The two men faced each other, obedient to the harsh commands of Scully, whose face, in the subtly luminous gloom, could be seen set in the austere impersonal lines that are pictured on the countenances of the Roman veterans. The Easterner's teeth were chattering, and he was hopping up and down like a mechanical toy. The cowboy stood rock-like.

The contestants had not stripped off any clothing. Each was in his ordinary attire. Their fists were up, and they eyed each other in a calm that had the elements of leonine cruelty in it.

During this pause, the Easterner's mind, like a film, took lasting impressions of three men- the iron-nerved master of the ceremony; the Swede, pale, motionless, terrible; and Johnnie, serene yet ferocious, brutish yet heroic. The entire prelude had in it a tragedy greater than the tragedy of action, and this aspect was accentuated by the long mellow cry of the blizzard, as it sped the tumbling and wailing flakes into the black abyss of the south.

"Now!" said Scully.

The two combatants leaped forward and crashed together like bullocks. There was heard the cushioned sound of blows, and of a curse squeezing out from between the tight teeth of one.

As for the spectators, the Easterner's pent-up breath exploded from him with a pop of relief, absolute relief from the tension of the preliminaries. The cowboy bounded into the air with a yowl. Scully was immovable as from supreme amazement and fear at the fury of the fight which he himself had permitted and arranged.

For a time the encounter in the darkness was such a perplexity of flying arms that it presented no more detail than would a swiftly-revolving wheel. Occasionally a face, as if illumined by a flash of light, would shine out, ghastly and marked with pink spots. A moment later, the men might have been known as shadows, if it were not for the involuntary utterance of oaths that came from them in whispers.

Suddenly a holocaust of warlike desire caught the cowboy, and he bolted forward with the speed of a broncho. "Go it, Johnnie; go it! Kill him! Kill him!"

Scully confronted him. "Kape back," he said; and by his glance the cowboy could tell that this man was Johnnie's father.

To the Easterner there was a monotony of unchangeable fighting that was an abomination. This confused mingling was eternal to his sense, which was concentrated in a longing for the end, the priceless end. Once the fighters lurched near him, and as he scrambled hastily backward, he heard them breathe like men on the rack.

"Kill him, Johnnie! Kill him! Kill him! Kill him!" The cowboy's face was contorted like one of those agony masks in museums.

"Keep still," said Scully icily.

Then there was a sudden loud grunt, incomplete, cut short, and Johnnie's body swung away from the Swede and fell with sickening heaviness to the grass. The cowboy was barely in time to prevent the mad Swede from flinging himself upon his prone adversary. "No, you don't," said the cowboy, interposing an arm. "Wait a second."

Scully was at his son's side. "Johnnie! Johnnie, me boy?" His voice had a quality of melancholy tenderness. "Johnnie? Can you go on with it?" He looked anxiously down into the bloody pulpy face of his son.

There was a moment of silence, and then Johnnie answered in his ordinary voice: "Yes, I — it — yes."

Assisted by his father he struggled to his feet. "Wait a bit now till you git your wind," said the old man.

A few paces away the cowboy was lecturing the Swede. "No, you don't!

Wait a second!"

The Easterner was plucking at Scully's sleeve. "Oh, this is enough," he pleaded. "This is enough! Let it go as it stands. This is enough!"

"Bill," said Scully, "git out of the road." The cowboy stepped aside. "Now." The combatants were actuated by a new caution as they advanced toward collision. They glared at each other, and then the Swede aimed a lightning blow that carried with it his entire weight. Johnnie was evidently half-stupid from weakness, but he miraculously dodged, and his fist sent the over-balanced Swede sprawling.

The cowboy, Scully and the Easterner burst into a cheer that was like a chorus of triumphant soldiery, but before its conclusion the Swede had scuffled agilely to his feet and come in berserk abandon at his foe. There was another perplexity of flying arms, and Johnnie's body again swung away and fell, even as a bundle might fall from a roof. The Swede instantly staggered to a little wind-waved tree and leaned upon it, breathing like an engine, while his savage and flame-lit eyes roamed from face to face as the men bent over Johnnie. There was a splendor of isolation in his situation at this time which the Easterner felt once when, lifting his eyes from the man on the ground, he beheld that mysterious and lonely figure, waiting. "Are you any good yet, Johnnie?" asked Scully in a broken voice.

The son gasped and opened his eyes languidly. After a moment he answered: "No — I ain't — any good — anymore." Then, from shame and bodily ill, he began to weep, the tears furrowing down through the bloodstains on his face. "He was too — too — too heavy for me."

Scully straightened and addressed the waiting figure. "Stranger," he said, evenly, "it's all up with our side." Then his voice changed into that vibrant huskiness which is commonly the tone of the most simple and deadly announcements. "Johnnie is whipped."

Without replying, the victor moved off on the route to the front door of the hotel.

The cowboy was formulating new and unspellable blasphemies. The Easterner was startled to find that they were out in a wind that seemed to come direct from the shadowed arctic floes. He heard again the wail of the snow as it was flung to its grave in the south. He knew now that all this time the cold had been sinking into him deeper and deeper, and he wondered that he had not perished. He felt indifferent to the condition of the vanquished man.

"Johnnie, can you walk?" asked Scully.

"Did I hurt — hurt him any?" asked the son.

"Can you walk, boy? Can you walk?"

Johnnie's voice was suddenly strong. There was a robust impatience in it. "I asked you whether I hurt him any!"

"Yes, yes, Johnnie," answered the cowboy consolingly, "he's hurt a good deal."

They raised him from the ground, and as soon as he was on his feet he went tottering off, rebuffing all attempts at assistance. When the party rounded the corner they were fairly blinded by the pelting of the snow. It burned their faces like fire. The cowboy carried Johnnie through the drift to the door. As

they entered some cards again rose from the floor and beat against the wall.

The Easterner rushed to the stove. He was so profoundly chilled that he almost dared to embrace the glowing iron. The Swede was not in the room. Johnnie sank into a chair, and folding his arms on his knees, buried his face in them. Scully, warming one foot and then the other at the rim of the stove, muttered to himself with Celtic mournfulness. The cowboy had removed his fur-cap, and with a dazed and rueful air he was now running one hand through his tousled locks. From overhead they could hear the creaking of boards, as the Swede tramped here and there in his room.

The sad quiet was broken by the sudden flinging open of a door that led toward the kitchen. It was instantly followed by an inrush of women. They precipitated themselves upon Johnnie amid a chorus of lamentation. Before they carried their prey off to the kitchen, there to be bathed and harangued with a mixture of sympathy and abuse which is a feat of their sex, the mother straightened herself and fixed old Scully with an eye of stern reproach. "Shame be upon you, Patrick Scully!" she cried, "Your own son, too. Shame be upon you!"

"There, now! Be quiet, now!" said the old man weakly.

"Shame be upon you, Patrick Scully!" The girls rallying to this slogan, sniffed disdainfully in the direction of those trembling accomplices, the cowboy and the Easterner. Presently they bore Johnnie away, and left the three men to dismal reflection.

"I'd like to fight this here Dutchman myself," said the cowboy, breaking a long silence.

Scully wagged his head sadly. "No, that wouldn't do. It wouldn't be right. It wouldn't be right."

"Well, why wouldn't it?" argued the cowboy. "I don't see no harm in it."

"No," answered Scully with mournful heroism. "It wouldn't be right. It was Johnnie's fight, and now we mustn't whip the man just because he whipped Johnnie."

"Yes, that's true enough," said the cowboy; "but- he better not get fresh with me, because I couldn't stand no more of it."

"You'll not say a word to him," commanded Scully, and even then they heard the tread of the Swede on the stairs. His entrance was made theatric. He swept the door back with a bang and swaggered to the middle of the room. No one looked at him. "Well," he cried, insolently, at Scully, "I s'pose you'll tell me now how much I owe you?"

The old man remained stolid. "You don't owe me nothin'."

"Huh!" said the Swede, "huh! Don't owe 'im nothin'."

The cowboy addressed the Swede. "Stranger, I don't see how you come to be so gay around here."

Old Scully was instantly alert. "Stop!" he shouted, holding his hand forth, fingers upward. "Bill, you shut up!"

The cowboy spat carelessly into the sawdust box. "I didn't say a word, did I?" he asked.

"Mr. Scully," called the Swede, "how much do I owe you?" It was seen that he was attired for departure, and that he had his valise in his hand.

"You don't owe me nothin'," repeated Scully in his same imperturbable way.

"Huh!" said the Swede. "I guess you're right. I guess if it was any way at all, you'd owe me somethin'. That's what I guess." He turned to the cowboy, "'Kill him! Kill him! Kill him!'" he mimicked, and then guffawed victoriously. "'Kill him!'" He was convulsed with ironical humor.

But he might have been jeering the dead. The three men were immovable and silent, staring with glassy eyes at the stove.

The Swede opened the door and passed into the storm, giving one derisive glance backward at the still group.

As soon as the door was closed, Scully and the cowboy leaped to their feet and began to curse. They trampled to and fro, waving their arms and smashing into the air with their fists. "Oh, but that was a hard minute! Him there leerin' and scoffin'! One bang at his nose was worth forty dollars to me that minute! How did you stand it, Bill?"

"How did I stand it?" cried the cowboy in a quivering voice. "How did I stand it? Oh!"

The old man burst into sudden brogue. "I'd loike to take that Swade," he wailed, " and hould 'im down on a shtone flure and bate 'im to a jelly wid a shtick!"

The cowboy groaned in sympathy. "I'd like to git him by the neck and ha-ammer him" — he brought his hand down on a chair with a noise like a pistol-shot — "hammer that there Dutchman until he couldn't tell himself from a dead coyote!"

"I'd bate 'im until he —"

"I'd show him some things —"

And then together they raised a yearning fanatic cry. "Oh-o-oh! if

we only could —"

"Yes!"

"Yes!"

"And then I'd —"

"O-o-oh!"

The Swede, tightly gripping his valise, tacked across the face of the storm as if he carried sails. He was following a line of little naked gasping trees, which he knew must mark the way of the road. His face, fresh from the pounding of Johnnie's fists, felt more pleasure than pain in the wind and the driving snow. A number of square shapes loomed upon him finally, and he knew them as the houses of the main body of the town. He found a street and made travel along it, leaning heavily upon the wind whenever, at a corner, a terrific blast caught him.

He might have been in a deserted village. We picture the world as thick with conquering and elate humanity, but here, with the bugles of the tempest pealing, it was hard to imagine a peopled earth. One viewed the existence of man then as a marvel, and conceded a glamour of wonder to these lice which were caused to cling to a whirling, fire-smote, ice-locked, disease-stricken, space-lost bulb. The conceit of man was explained by this storm to be the very engine of life. One was a coxcomb not to die in it. However, the Swede found a saloon.

In front of it an indomitable red light was burning, and the snowflakes were made blood-color as they flew through the circumscribed territory of the lamp's shining. The Swede pushed open the door of the saloon and entered. A sanded expanse was before him, and at the end of it four men sat about a table drinking. Down one side of the room extended a radiant bar, and its guardian was leaning upon his elbows listening to the talk of the men at the table. The Swede dropped his valise upon the floor, and, smiling fraternally upon the barkeeper, said: "Gimme some whisky, will you?" The man placed a bottle, a whisky-glass, and glass of ice-thick water upon the bar. The Swede poured himself an abnormal portion of whisky and drank it in three gulps. "Pretty bad night," remarked the bartender indifferently. He was making the pretension of blindness, which is usually a distinction of his class; but it could have been seen that he was furtively studying the half-erased blood-stains on the face of the Swede. "Bad night," he said again.

"Oh, it's good enough for me," replied the Swede, hardily, as he poured himself some more whisky. The barkeeper took his coin and maneuvered it through its reception by the highly-nickeled cash-machine. A bell rang; a card labeled "20 cts." had appeared.

"No," continued the Swede, "this isn't too bad weather. It's good enough for me."

"So?" murmured the barkeeper languidly.

The copious drams made the Swede's eyes swim, and he breathed a trifle heavier. "Yes, I like this weather. I like it. It suits me." It was apparently his design to impart a deep significance to these words.

"So?" murmured the bartender again. He turned to gaze dreamily at the scroll-like birds and bird-like scrolls which had been drawn with soap upon the mirrors back of the bar.

"Well, I guess I'll take another drink," said the Swede presently.

"Have something?"

"No, thanks; I'm not drinkin'," answered the bartender. Afterward he asked: "How did you hurt your face?"

The Swede immediately began to boast loudly. "Why, in a fight. I thumped the soul out of a man down here at Scully's hotel."

The interest of the four men at the table was at last aroused.

"Who was it?" said one.

"Johnnie Scully," blustered the Swede. "Son of the man what runs it. He will be pretty near dead for some weeks, I can tell you. I made a nice thing of him, I did. He couldn't get up. They carried him in the house. Have a drink?"

Instantly the men in some subtle way incased themselves in reserve. "No, thanks," said one. The group was of curious formation. Two were prominent local business men; one was the district-attorney; and one was a professional gambler of the kind known as "square." But a scrutiny of the group would not have enabled an observer to pick the gambler from the men of more reputable pursuits. He was, in fact, a man so delicate in manner, when among people of fair class, and so judicious in his choice of victims, that in the strictly masculine part of the town's life he had come to be explicitly trusted and admired. People called him a thoroughbred. The fear and contempt with which his craft was regarded was undoubtedly the reason that his quiet dignity shone conspicuous above the quiet dignity of men who might be merely hatters, billiard-markers or grocery clerks. Beyond an occasional unwary traveler, who came by rail, this gambler was supposed to prey solely upon reckless and senile farmers, who, when flush with good crops, drove into town in all the pride and confidence of an absolutely invulnerable stupidity. Hearing at times in circuitous fashion of the despoilment of such a farmer, the important men of Romper invariably laughed in contempt of the victim, and if they thought of the wolf at all, it was with a kind of pride at the knowledge that he would never dare think of attacking their wisdom and courage. Besides, it was popular that this gambler had a real wife, and two real children in a neat cottage in a suburb, where he led an exemplary home life, and when any one even suggested a discrepancy in his character, the crowd immediately vociferated descriptions of this virtuous family circle. Then men who led exemplary home lives, and men who did not lead exemplary home lives, all subsided in a bunch, remarking that there was nothing more to be said.

However, when a restriction was placed upon him — as, for instance, when a strong clique of members of the new Pollywog Club refused to permit him, even as a spectator, to appear in the rooms of the organization — the candor and gentleness with which he accepted the judgment disarmed many of his foes and made his friends more desperately partisan. He invariably distinguished between himself and a respectable Romper man so quickly and frankly that his manner actually appeared to be a continual broadcast compliment.

And one must not forget to declare the fundamental fact of his entire position in Romper. It is irrefutable that in all affairs outside of his business, in all matters that occur eternally and commonly between man and man, this thieving card-player was so generous, so just, so moral, that, in a contest, he could have put to flight the consciences of nine-tenths of the citizens of Romper.

And so it happened that he was seated in this saloon with the two prominent local merchants and the district-attorney.

The Swede continued to drink raw whisky, meanwhile babbling at the barkeeper and trying to induce him to indulge in potations. "Come on. Have a drink. Come on. What — no? Well, have a little one then. …, I've whipped a man to-night, and I want to celebrate. I whipped him good, too. Gentlemen," the Swede cried to the men at the table, "have a drink?"

"Ssh!" said the barkeeper.

The group at the table, although furtively attentive, had been pretending to be deep in talk, but now a man lifted his eyes toward the Swede and said shortly: "Thanks. We don't want any more." At this reply the Swede ruffled out his chest like a rooster. "Well," he exploded, "it seems I can't get anybody to drink with me in this town. Seems so, don't it? Well!"

"Ssh!" said the barkeeper.

"Say," snarled the Swede, "don't you try to shut me up. I won't have it. I'm a gentleman, and I want people to drink with me. And I want 'em to drink with me now. Now — do you understand?" He rapped the bar with his knuckles.

Years of experience had calloused the bartender. He merely grew sulky. "I hear you," he answered.

"Well," cried the Swede, "listen hard then. See those men over there? Well, they're going to drink with me, and don't you forget it. Now you watch."

"Hi!" yelled the barkeeper, "this won't do!"

"Why won't it?" demanded the Swede. He stalked over to the table, and by chance laid his hand upon the shoulder of the gambler. "How about this?" he asked, wrathfully. "I asked you to drink with me."

The gambler simply twisted his head and spoke over his shoulder. "My friend, I don't know you."

…

"Now, my boy," advised the gambler kindly, "take your hand off my shoulder and go 'way and mind your own business." He was a little slim man, and it seemed strange to hear him use this tone of heroic patronage to the burly Swede. The other men at the table said nothing.

"What? You won't drink with me, you little dude! I'll make you then! I'll make you!" The Swede had grasped the gambler frenziedly at the throat, and was dragging him from his chair. The other men sprang up. The barkeeper dashed around the corner of his bar. There was a great tumult, and then was seen a long blade in the hand of the gambler. It shot forward, and a human body, this citadel of virtue, wisdom, power, was pierced as easily as if it had been a melon. The Swede fell with a cry of supreme astonishment. The prominent merchants and the district-attorney must have at once tumbled out of the place backward. The bartender found himself hanging limply to the arm of a chair and gazing into the eyes of a murderer. "Henry," said the latter, as he wiped his knife on one of the towels that hung beneath the bar-rail, "you tell 'em where to find me. I'll be home, waiting for 'em." Then he vanished. A moment afterward the barkeeper was in the street dinning through the storm for help, and, moreover, companionship.

The corpse of the Swede, alone in the saloon, had its eyes fixed upon a dreadful legend that dwelt a-top of the cash-machine. "This registers the amount of your purchase."

Months later, the cowboy was frying pork over the stove of a little ranch near the Dakota line, when there was a quick thud of hoofs outside, and, presently, the Easterner entered with the letters and the papers. "Well," said the Easterner at once, "the chap that killed the Swede has got three years. Wasn't much, was it?"

"He has? Three years?" The cowboy poised his pan of pork, while he ruminated upon the news. "Three years. That ain't much."

"No. It was a light sentence," replied the Easterner as he unbuckled his spurs. "Seems there was a good deal of sympathy for him in Romper."

"If the bartender had been any good," observed the cowboy thoughtfully, "he would have gone in and cracked that there Dutchman on the head with a bottle in the beginnin' of it and stopped all this here murderin'."

"Yes, a thousand things might have happened," said the Easterner tartly.

The cowboy returned his pan of pork to the fire, but his philosophy continued. "It's funny, ain't it? If he hadn't said Johnnie was cheatin' he'd be alive this minute. He was an awful fool. Game played for fun, too. Not for money. I believe he was crazy."

"I feel sorry for that gambler," said the Easterner.

"Oh, so do I," said the cowboy. "He don't deserve none of it for killin' who he did."

"The Swede might not have been killed if everything had been square."

...

With these arguments the cowboy browbeat the Easterner and reduced him to rage. "You're a fool!" cried the Easterner viciously. "... Now let me tell you one thing. Let me tell you something. Listen! Johnnie was cheating!"

"Johnnie," said the cowboy blankly. There was a minute of silence, and then he said robustly: "Why, no. The game was only for fun."

"Fun or not," said the Easterner, "Johnnie was cheating. I saw him. I know it. I saw him. And I refused to stand up and be a man. I let the Swede fight it out alone. And you — you were simply puffing around the place and wanting to fight. And then old Scully himself! We are all in it! This poor gambler isn't even a noun. He is kind of an adverb. Every sin is the result of a collaboration. We, five of us, have collaborated in the murder of this Swede. Usually there are from a dozen to forty women really involved in every murder, but in this case it seems to be only five men — you, I, Johnnie, old Scully, and that fool of an unfortunate gambler came merely as a culmination, the apex of a human movement, and gets all the punishment."

The cowboy, injured and rebellious, cried out blindly into this fog of mysterious theory. "Well, I didn't do anythin', did I?"

Assignments

- Warm-up: Read the short story by Crane entitled "Blue Hotel" (1898) and find naturalistic themes.
- Students should complete Concept Builder 18-E.
- Essays are due. Students should take the chapter 18 test.

The style of a literary work is the way that an author writes. Consider the writing style that Stephen Crane uses. Find examples of the following writing styles.

Literary Element	*The Red Badge of Courage*	Fact
Character development	The protagonist changes from a romantic to a naturalist.	The protagonist is killed. His romanticism was killed by the naturalism of the Wild West.
Internal conflict		
External conflict		
Uses of foils		

Chapter 19

1865–1915 (Part 5):

Realism, Naturalism, and the Frontier

First Thoughts Crane was not the only naturalist author. Not by a long shot. In fact, naturalism became the worldview of choice of most high culture. The term "high culture" was coined by English essayist Matthew Arnold. Arnold defined culture as "the disinterested endeavour after man's perfection" and most famously wrote that having culture meant to "know the best that has been said and thought in the world" (Matthew Arnold 1869 of *Culture and Anarchy*, preface). Arnold saw high culture as a force for moral and political good. The term is contrasted with popular culture or mass culture and also with traditional cultures. High culture, that culture that is producing most American thought and literature, since at least 1875, has captured American culture.

Author Worldview Watch Chopin, Harte, et al., are new songs of the same genre. Now, in hopeless abandon, American readers are inundated with poor lost souls who have lost their way in a nihilistic universe. Why is it in a nation that was founded on biblical principles, we could have evolved to this level? While the despotic regimes of Russia are feasting on robust, rich Christian characters — Sonya for instance in *Crime and Punishment* — Americans are presented with the paltry offerings of the naturalists.

Chapter Learning Objectives In chapter 19 we will analyze authors who wrote from 1850 to 1900. You will analyze "Outcasts of Poker Flat" by Bret Harte; "The Story of an Hour" by Kate Chopin; "Luke Havergal" and "Credo" by Edwin Arlington Robinson; "Lucinda Matlock" by Edgar Lee Masters.

As a result of this chapter study you will be able to . . .

1. Understand how Bret Harte creates humor.

2. Describe the joy that killed Mrs. Mallard.

3. Explain what Lucinda Matlock means when she says, "It takes life to love Life."

4. Compare Mrs. Mallard to Lucinda Matlock.

Weekly Essay Options: Begin on page 274 of the Teacher Guide.

Reading ahead: *Ethan Frome* by Edith Wharton

 History connections: *American History* chapter 19, "The Gilded Age: Problems."

Bret Harte

Bret Harte (1836–1902), American writer, is best known for his short stories set in the American West. In 1868 Harte became editor of the *Overland Monthly*, which published many of his best-known stories, including "The Outcasts of Poker Flat" (1869). Despite the fact that these stories shocked many readers, these works have come to be regarded as classics of American regional literature and were noted for their descriptions of the mining camps and towns of California in the middle 19th century.

The Outcasts of Poker Flat

As Mr. John Oakhurst, gambler, stepped into the main street of Poker Flat on the morning of the twenty-third of November, 1850, he was conscious of a change in its moral atmosphere since the preceding night. Two or three men, conversing earnestly together, ceased as he approached, and exchanged significant glances. There was a Sabbath lull in the air which, in a settlement unused to Sabbath influences, looked ominous.

Mr. Oakhurst's calm, handsome face betrayed small concern in these indications. Whether he was conscious of any predisposing cause was another question. "I reckon they're after somebody," he reflected; "likely it's me." He returned to his pocket the handkerchief with which he had been whipping away the red dust of Poker Flat from his neat boots, and quietly discharged his mind of any further conjecture.

In point of fact, Poker Flat was "after somebody." It had lately suffered the loss of several thousand dollars, two valuable horses, and a prominent citizen. It was experiencing a spasm of virtuous reaction, quite as lawless and ungovernable as any of the acts that had provoked it. A secret committee had determined to rid the town of all improper persons. This was done permanently in regard of two men who were then hanging from the boughs of a sycamore in the gulch, and temporarily in the banishment of certain other objectionable characters. I regret to say that some of these were ladies. It is but due to the sex, however, to state that their impropriety was professional, and it was only in such easily established standards of evil that Poker Flat ventured to sit in judgment.

Mr. Oakhurst was right in supposing that he was included in this category. A few of the committee had urged hanging him as a possible example, and a sure method of reimbursing themselves from his pockets of the sums he had won from them. "It's agin justice," said Jim Wheeler, "to let this yer young man from Roaring Camp — an entire stranger — carry away our money." But a crude sentiment of equity residing in the breasts of those who had been fortunate enough to win from Mr. Oakhurst overruled this narrower local prejudice.

Mr. Oakhurst received his sentence with philosophic calmness, none the less coolly that he was aware of the hesitation of his judges. He was too much of a gambler not to accept Fate. With him life was at best an uncertain game, and he recognized the usual percentage in favor of the dealer.

A body of armed men accompanied the deported wickedness of Poker Flat to the outskirts of the settlement. Besides Mr. Oakhurst, who was known to be a coolly desperate man, and for whose intimidation the armed escort was intended, the expatriated party consisted of a young woman familiarly known as the "Duchess"; another, who had won the title of "Mother Shipton"; and "Uncle Billy," a suspected sluice-robber and confirmed drunkard. The cavalcade provoked no comments from the spectators, nor was any word uttered by the escort. Only, when the gulch which marked the uttermost limit of Poker Flat was reached, the leader spoke briefly and to the point. The exiles were forbidden to return at the peril of their lives.

As the escort disappeared, their pent-up feelings found vent in a few hysterical tears from the Duchess, some bad language from Mother Shipton, and a Parthian volley of expletives from Uncle Billy. The philosophic Oakhurst alone remained silent. He listened calmly to Mother Shipton's desire to cut somebody's heart out, to the repeated statements of the Duchess that she would die in the road, and to the alarming oaths that seemed to be bumped out of Uncle Billy as he rode forward. With the easy good humor characteristic of his class, he insisted upon exchanging his own riding horse, "Five Spot," for the sorry mule which the Duchess rode. But even this act did not draw the party into any closer sympathy. The young woman readjusted her somewhat draggled plumes with a feeble, faded coquetry; Mother Shipton eyed the possessor of "Five Spot" with malevolence, and Uncle Billy included the whole party in one sweeping anathema.

The road to Sandy Bar — a camp that, not having as yet experienced the regenerating influences of Poker Flat, consequently seemed to offer some invitation to the emigrants — lay over a steep mountain range. It was distant a day's severe travel. In that advanced season, the party soon passed out of the moist, temperate regions of the foothills into the dry, cold, bracing air of the Sierras. The trail was narrow and difficult. At noon the Duchess, rolling out of her saddle upon the ground, declared her intention of going no farther, and the party halted.

The spot was singularly wild and impressive. A wooded amphitheater, surrounded on three sides by precipitous cliffs of naked granite, sloped gently toward the crest of another precipice that overlooked the valley. It was, undoubtedly, the most suitable spot for a camp, had camping been advisable. But Mr. Oakhurst knew that scarcely half the journey to

Sandy Bar was accomplished, and the party were not equipped or provisioned for delay. This fact he pointed out to his companions curtly, with a philosophic commentary on the folly of "throwing up their hand before the game was played out." But they were furnished with liquor, which in this emergency stood them in place of food, fuel, rest, and prescience. In spite of his remonstrances, it was not long before they were more or less under its influence. Uncle Billy passed rapidly from a bellicose state into one of stupor, the Duchess became maudlin, and Mother Shipton snored. Mr. Oakhurst alone remained erect, leaning against a rock, calmly surveying them.

Mr. Oakhurst did not drink. It interfered with a profession which required coolness, impassiveness, and presence of mind, and, in his own language, he "couldn't afford it." As he gazed at his recumbent fellow exiles, the loneliness begotten of his pariah trade, his habits of life, his very vices, for the first time seriously oppressed him. He bestirred himself in dusting his black clothes, washing his hands and face, and other acts characteristic of his studiously neat habits, and for a moment forgot his annoyance. The thought of deserting his weaker and more pitiable companions never perhaps occurred to him. Yet he could not help feeling the want of that excitement which, singularly enough, was most conducive to that calm equanimity for which he was notorious. He looked at the gloomy walls that rose a thousand feet sheer above the circling pines around him; at the sky, ominously clouded; at the valley below, already deepening into shadow. And, doing so, suddenly he heard his own name called.

A horseman slowly ascended the trail. In the fresh, open face of the newcomer Mr. Oakhurst recognized Tom Simson, otherwise known as the "Innocent" of Sandy Bar. He had met him some months before over a "little game," and had, with perfect equanimity, won the entire fortune — amounting to some forty dollars — of that guileless youth. After the game was finished, Mr. Oakhurst drew the youthful speculator behind the door and thus addressed him: "Tommy, you're a good little man, but you can't gamble worth a cent. Don't try it over again." He then handed him his money back, pushed him gently from the room, and so made a devoted slave of Tom Simson.

There was a remembrance of this in his boyish and enthusiastic greeting of Mr. Oakhurst. He had started, he said, to go to Poker Flat to seek his fortune. "Alone?" No, not exactly alone; in fact (a giggle), he had run away with Piney Woods. Didn't Mr. Oakhurst remember Piney? She that used to wait on the table at the Temperance House? They had been engaged a long time, but old Jake Woods had objected, and so they had run away, and were going to Poker Flat to be married, and here they were. And they were tired out, and how lucky it was they had found a place to camp and company. All this the Innocent delivered rapidly, while Piney, a stout, comely damsel of fifteen, emerged from behind the pine tree, where she had been blushing unseen, and rode to the side of her lover.

Mr. Oakhurst seldom troubled himself with sentiment, still less with propriety; but he had a vague idea that the situation was not fortunate. He retained, however, his presence of mind sufficiently to kick Uncle Billy, who was about to say something, and Uncle Billy was sober enough to recognize in Mr. Oakhurst's kick a superior power that would not bear trifling. He then endeavored to dissuade Tom Simson from delaying further, but in vain. He even pointed out the fact that there was no provision, nor means of making a camp. But, unluckily, the Innocent met this objection by assuring the party that he was provided with an extra mule loaded with provisions and by the discovery of a rude attempt at a log house near the trail. "Piney can stay with Mrs. Oakhurst," said the Innocent, pointing to the Duchess, "and I can shift for myself."

Nothing but Mr. Oakhurst's admonishing foot saved Uncle Billy from bursting into a roar of laughter. As it was, he felt compelled to retire up the canyon until he could recover his gravity. There he confided the joke to the tall pine trees, with many slaps of his leg, contortions of his face, and the usual profanity. But when he returned to the party, he found them seated by a fire — for the air had grown strangely chill and the sky overcast — in apparently amicable conversation. Piney was actually talking in an impulsive, girlish fashion to the Duchess, who was listening with an interest and animation she had not shown for many days. The Innocent was holding forth, apparently with equal effect, to Mr. Oakhurst and Mother Shipton, who was actually relaxing into amiability. "Is this yer a picnic?" said Uncle Billy with inward scorn as he surveyed the sylvan group, the glancing firelight, and the tethered animals in the foreground. Suddenly an idea mingled with the alcoholic fumes that disturbed his brain. It was apparently of a jocular nature, for he felt impelled to slap his leg again and cram his fist into his mouth.

As the shadows crept slowly up the mountain, a slight breeze rocked the tops of the pine trees, and moaned through their long and gloomy aisles. The ruined cabin, patched and covered with pine boughs, was set apart for the ladies. As the lovers parted, they unaffectedly exchanged a kiss, so honest and sincere that it might have been heard above the swaying pines. The frail Duchess and the malevolent Mother Shipton were probably too stunned to remark upon this last evidence of simplicity, and so turned without a word to the hut. The fire was replenished, the men lay down before the door, and in a few minutes were asleep.

Mr. Oakhurst was a light sleeper. Toward morning he awoke benumbed and cold. As he stirred the dying fire, the wind, which was now blowing strongly, brought to his cheek that which caused the blood to leave it — snow!

He started to his feet with the intention of awakening the sleepers, for there was no time to lose. But turning to where Uncle Billy had been lying, he found him gone. A suspicion leaped to his brain and a curse to his lips. He ran to the spot where the mules had been tethered; they were no longer there. The tracks were already rapidly disappearing in the snow.

The momentary excitement brought Mr. Oakhurst back to the fire with his usual calm. He did not waken the sleepers. The Innocent slumbered peacefully, with a smile on his good-humored, freckled face; the virgin Piney slept beside her frailer sisters as sweetly as though attended by celestial guardians; and Mr. Oakhurst, drawing his blanket over his shoulders, stroked his mustaches and waited for the dawn. It came slowly in a whirling mist of snowflakes that dazzled and confused the eye. What could be seen of the landscape appeared magically changed. He looked over the valley, and summed up the present and future in two words — "snowed in!"

A careful inventory of the provisions, which, fortunately for the party, had been stored within the hut and so escaped the felonious fingers of Uncle Billy, disclosed the fact that with care and prudence they might last ten days longer. "That is," said Mr. Oakhurst, sotto voce to the Innocent, "if you're willing to board us. If you ain't — and perhaps you'd better not — you can wait till Uncle Billy gets back with provisions." For some occult reason, Mr. Oakhurst could not bring himself to disclose Uncle Billy's rascality, and so offered the hypothesis that he had wandered from the camp and had accidentally stampeded the animals. He dropped a warning to the Duchess and Mother Shipton, who of course knew the facts of their associate's defection. "They'll find out the truth about us all when they find out anything," he added, significantly, "and there's no good frightening them now."

Simson not only put all his worldly store at the disposal of Mr. Oakhurst, but seemed to enjoy the prospect of their enforced seclusion. "We'll have a good camp for a week, and then the snow'll melt, and we'll all go back together." The cheerful gaiety of the young man, and Mr. Oakhurst's calm, infected the others. The Innocent with the aid of pine boughs extemporized a thatch for the roofless cabin, and the Duchess directed Piney in the rearrangement of the interior with a taste and tact that opened the blue eyes of that provincial maiden to their fullest extent. "I reckon now you're used to fine things at Poker Flat," said Piney. The Duchess turned away sharply to conceal something that reddened her cheeks through its professional tint, and Mother Shipton requested Piney not to "chatter." But when Mr. Oakhurst returned from a weary search for the trail, he heard the sound of happy laughter echoed from the rocks. He stopped in some alarm, and his thoughts first naturally reverted to the whisky, which he had prudently cached. "And yet it don't somehow sound like whisky," said the gambler. It was not until he caught sight of the blazing fire through the still-blinding storm and the group around it that he settled to the conviction that it was "square fun."

Whether Mr. Oakhurst had cached his cards with the whisky as something debarred the free access of the community, I cannot say. It was certain that, in Mother Shipton's words, he "didn't say cards once" during that evening. Haply the time was beguiled by an accordion, produced somewhat ostentatiously by

Tom Simson from his pack. Notwithstanding some difficulties attending the manipulation of this instrument, Piney Woods managed to pluck several reluctant melodies from its keys, to an accompaniment by the Innocent on a pair of bone castanets. But the crowning festivity of the evening was reached in a rude camp-meeting hymn, which the lovers, joining hands, sang with great earnestness and vociferation. I fear that a certain defiant tone and Covenanter's swing to its chorus, rather than any devotional quality, caused it speedily to infect the others, who at last joined in the refrain:

"I'm proud to live in the service of the Lord,
And I'm bound to die in His army."

The pines rocked, the storm eddied and whirled above the miserable group, and the flames of their altar leaped heavenward as if in token of the vow.

At midnight the storm abated, the rolling clouds parted, and the stars glittered keenly above the sleeping camp. Mr. Oakhurst, whose professional habits had enabled him to live on the smallest possible amount of sleep, in dividing the watch with Tom Simson somehow managed to take upon himself the greater part of that duty. He excused himself to the Innocent by saying that he had "often been a week without sleep." "Doing what?" asked Tom. "Poker!" replied Oakhurst, sententiously; "when a man gets a streak of luck he don't get tired. The luck gives in first. Luck," continued the gambler, reflectively, "is a mighty queer thing. All you know about it for certain is that it's bound to change. And it's finding out when it's going to change that makes you. We've had a streak of bad luck since we left Poker Flat — you come along, and slap you get into it, too. If you can hold your cards right along you're all right. For," added the gambler, with cheerful irrelevance,

"I'm proud to live in the service of the Lord,
And I'm bound to die in His army."

The third day came, and the sun, looking through the white-curtained valley, saw the outcasts divide their slowly decreasing store of provisions for the morning meal. It was one of the peculiarities of that mountain climate that its rays diffused a kindly warmth over the wintry landscape, as if in regretful commiseration of the past. But it revealed drift on drift of snow piled high around the hut — a hopeless, uncharted, trackless sea of white lying below the rocky shores to which the castaways still clung. Through the marvelously clear air the smoke of the pastoral village of Poker Flat rose miles away. Mother Shipton saw it, and from a remote pinnacle of her rocky fastness hurled in that direction a final malediction. It was her last vituperative attempt, and perhaps for that reason was invested with a certain degree of sublimity. It did her good, she privately informed the Duchess. "Just you go out there and cuss, and see." She then set herself to the task of amusing "the child," as she and the Duchess were pleased to call Piney. Piney was no chicken, but it was a soothing and original theory of the pair thus to account for the fact that she didn't swear and wasn't improper.

When night crept up again through the gorges, the reedy notes of the accordion rose and fell in fitful spasms and long-drawn gasps by the flickering campfire. But music failed to fill entirely the aching void left by insufficient food, and a new diversion was proposed by Piney — storytelling. Neither Mr. Oakhurst nor his female companions caring to relate their personal experiences, this plan would have failed too but for the Innocent. Some months before he had chanced upon a stray copy of Mr. Pope's ingenious translation of the Iliad. He now proposed to narrate the principal incidents of that poem — having thoroughly mastered the argument and fairly forgotten the words — in the current vernacular of Sandy Bar. …

So with small food and much of Homer and the accordion, a week passed over the heads of the outcasts. The sun again forsook them, and again from leaden skies the snowflakes were sifted over the land. Day by day closer around them drew the snowy circle, until at last they looked from their prison over drifted walls of dazzling white that towered twenty feet above their heads. It became more and more difficult to replenish their fires, even from the fallen trees beside them, now half-hidden in the drifts. And yet no one complained. The lovers turned from the dreary prospect and looked into each other's eyes, and were happy. Mr. Oakhurst settled himself coolly to the losing game before him. The Duchess, more cheerful than she had been, assumed the care of Piney. Only Mother Shipton — once the strongest

of the party — seemed to sicken and fade. At midnight on the tenth day she called Oakhurst to her side. "I'm going," she said, in a voice of querulous weakness, "but don't say anything about it. Don't waken the kids. Take the bundle from under my head and open it." Mr. Oakhurst did so. It contained Mother Shipton's rations for the last week, untouched. "Give 'em to the child," she said, pointing to the sleeping Piney. "You've starved yourself," said the gambler. "That's what they call it," said the woman, querulously, as she lay down again and, turning her face to the wall, passed quietly away.

The accordion and the bones were put aside that day, and Homer was forgotten. When the body of Mother Shipton had been committed to the snow, Mr. Oakhurst took the Innocent aside, and showed him a pair of snowshoes, which he had fashioned from the old pack saddle. "There's one chance in a hundred to save her yet," he said, pointing to Piney; "but it's there," he added, pointing toward Poker Flat. "If you can reach there in two days she's safe." "And you?" asked Tom Simson. "I'll stay here," was the curt reply.

The lovers parted with a long embrace. "You are not going, too?" said the Duchess as she saw Mr. Oakhurst apparently waiting to accompany him. "As far as the canyon," he replied. He turned suddenly, and kissed the Duchess, leaving her pallid face aflame and her trembling limbs rigid with amazement.

Night came, but not Mr. Oakhurst. It brought the storm again and the whirling snow. Then the Duchess, feeding the fire, found that someone had quietly piled beside the hut enough fuel to last a few days longer. The tears rose to her eyes, but she hid them from Piney.

The women slept but little. In the morning, looking into each other's faces, they read their fate. Neither spoke; but Piney, accepting the position of the stronger, drew near and placed her arm around the Duchess's waist. They kept this attitude for the rest of the day. That night the storm reached its greatest fury, and, rending asunder the protecting pines, invaded the very hut.

Toward morning they found themselves unable to feed the fire, which gradually died away. As the embers slowly blackened, the Duchess crept closer to

Piney, and broke the silence of many hours: "Piney, can you pray?" "No, dear," said Piney, simply. The Duchess, without knowing exactly why, felt relieved, and, putting her head upon Piney's shoulder, spoke no more. And so reclining, the younger and purer pillowing the head of her soiled sister upon her virgin breast, they fell asleep.

The wind lulled as if it feared to waken them. Feathery drifts of snow, shaken from the long pine boughs, flew like white-winged birds, and settled about them as they slept. The moon through the rifted clouds looked down upon what had been the camp. But all human stain, all trace of earthly travail, was hidden beneath the spotless mantle mercifully flung from above.

They slept all that day and the next, nor did they waken when voices and footsteps broke the silence of the camp. And when pitying fingers brushed the snow from their wan faces, you could scarcely have told from the equal peace that dwelt upon them which was she that had sinned. Even the law of Poker Flat recognized this, and turned away, leaving them still locked in each other's arms.

But at the head of the gulch, on one of the largest pine trees, they found the deuce of clubs pinned to the bark with a bowie knife. It bore the following, written in pencil, in a firm hand:

BENEATH THIS TREE

LIES THE BODY

OF

JOHN OAKHURST,

WHO STRUCK A STREAK OF BAD LUCK

ON THE 23D OF NOVEMBER, 1850,

AND

HANDED IN HIS CHECKS

ON THE 7TH DECEMBER, 1850.

And pulseless and cold, with a Derringer by his side and a bullet in his heart, though still calm as in life, beneath the snow lay he who was at once the strongest and yet the weakest of the outcasts of Poker Flat.

Assignments

- Warm-up: Define local color literature.
- Students should complete Concept Builder 19-A.
- Students review the required reading(s) before the assigned chapter begins.
- Teachers may want to discuss assigned reading(s) with students.
- Teachers shall assign the required essay. The rest of the essays can be outlined, answered with shorter answers, discussed, or skipped.
- Students will review all readings for chapter 19.

The setting in the short story *Outcasts of Poker Flat* is the most important element. It shapes each element (plot, theme, characters). Discuss how the setting develops all of these elements.

The plot:

The plot:

The story evolves from a harmless outing to a deadly rendezvous with death.

The theme:

Setting

Contrast Bret Harte's view of nature with Emerson's view (chapter 10).

Nature to Emerson is friendly.

Nature to Hart is _____.

Kate Chopin

Kate Chopin (1850–1904) was known for her depictions of culture in New Orleans, Louisiana, and of the struggles of 19th-century women. Chopin's first published story was in 1889, and she was one of the first American writers to depict the manners, customs, speech, and surroundings of a people group. Two collections of her short fiction were published in the 1890s: *Bayou Folk* (1894) and *A Night in Acadie* (1897). Her later stories such as "The Story of an Hour," emphasized women's need for self-reliance.

The Story of an Hour

Knowing that Mrs. Mallard was afflicted with a heart trouble, great care was taken to break to her as gently as possible the news of her husband's death.

It was her sister Josephine who told her, in broken sentences; veiled hints that revealed in half concealing. Her husband's friend Richards was there, too, near her. It was he who had been in the newspaper office when intelligence of the railroad disaster was received, with Brently Mallard's name leading the list of "killed." He had only taken the time to assure himself of its truth by a second telegram, and had hastened to forestall any less careful, less tender friend in bearing the sad message.

She did not hear the story as many women have heard the same, with a paralyzed inability to accept its significance. She wept at once, with sudden, wild abandonment, in her sister's arms. When the storm of grief had spent itself she went away to her room alone. She would have no one follow her.

There stood, facing the open window, a comfortable, roomy armchair. Into this she sank, pressed down by a physical exhaustion that haunted her body and seemed to reach into her soul.

She could see in the open square before her house the tops of trees that were all aquiver with the new spring life. The delicious breath of rain was in the air. In the street below a peddler was crying his wares. The notes of a distant song which some one was singing reached her faintly, and countless sparrows were twittering in the eaves.

There were patches of blue sky showing here and there through the clouds that had met and piled one above the other in the west facing her window.

She sat with her head thrown back upon the cushion of the chair, quite motionless, except when a sob came up into her throat and shook her, as a child who has cried itself to sleep continues to sob in its dreams.

She was young, with a fair, calm face, whose lines bespoke repression and even a certain strength. But now there was a dull stare in her eyes, whose gaze was fixed away off yonder on one of those patches of blue sky. It was not a glance of reflection, but rather indicated a suspension of intelligent thought.

There was something coming to her and she was waiting for it, fearfully. What was it? She did not know; it was too subtle and elusive to name. But she felt it, creeping out of the sky, reaching toward her through the sounds, the scents, the color that filled the air.

Now her bosom rose and fell tumultuously. She was beginning to recognize this thing that was approaching to possess her, and she was striving to beat it back with her will — as powerless as her two white slender hands would have been.

When she abandoned herself a little whispered word escaped her slightly parted lips. She said it over and over under her breath: "free, free, free!" The vacant stare and the look of terror that had followed it went from her eyes. They stayed keen and bright. Her pulses beat fast, and the coursing blood warmed and relaxed every inch of her body.

She did not stop to ask if it were or were not a monstrous joy that held her. A clear and exalted perception enabled her to dismiss the suggestion as trivial.

She knew that she would weep again when she saw the kind, tender hands folded in death; the face that had never looked save with love upon her, fixed and gray and dead. But she saw beyond that bitter moment a long procession of years to come that would belong to her absolutely. And she opened and spread her arms out to them in welcome.

There would be no one to live for during those coming years; she would live for herself. There would be no powerful will bending hers in that blind persistence with which men and women believe they have a right to impose a private will upon a fellow-creature. A kind intention or a cruel intention made the act seem no less a crime as she looked upon it in that brief moment of illumination.

And yet she had loved him — sometimes. Often she had not. What did it matter! What could love, the unsolved mystery, count for in face of this possession of self-assertion which she suddenly recognized as the strongest impulse of her being!

"Free! Body and soul free!" she kept whispering.

Josephine was kneeling before the closed door with her lips to the keyhole, imploring for admission. "Louise, open the door! I beg, open the door — you will make yourself ill. What are you doing Louise? For heaven's sake open the door."

"Go away. I am not making myself ill." No; she was drinking in a very elixir of life through that open window.

Her fancy was running riot along those days ahead of her. Spring days, and summer days, and all sorts of days that would be her own. She breathed a quick prayer that life might be long. It was only yesterday she had thought with a shudder that life might be long.

She arose at length and opened the door to her sister's importunities. There was a feverish triumph in her eyes, and she carried herself unwittingly like a goddess of Victory. She clasped her sister's waist, and together they descended the stairs. Richards stood waiting for them at the bottom.

Someone was opening the front door with a latchkey. It was Brently Mallard who entered, a little travel-stained, composedly carrying his grip-sack and umbrella. He had been far from the scene of accident, and did not even know there had been one. He stood amazed at Josephine's piercing cry; at Richards' quick motion to screen him from the view of his wife.

But Richards was too late.

When the doctors came they said she had died of heart disease — of joy that kills.

Assignments

- Warm-up: Predict the end of this story after you read the first page. Write it down.
- Students should complete Concept Builder 19-B.
- Students should review reading(s) from the next chapter.
- Student should outline essay due at the end of the week.
- Per teacher instructions, students may answer orally, in a group setting, some of the essays that are not assigned as formal essays.

Dramatic Irony is when the words and actions of the characters of a work of literature have a different meaning for the reader than they do for the characters. Kate Chopin's "The Story of an Hour" includes two examples of dramatic irony. What are they?

The doctors thought that Mrs. Mallard died from happiness when she saw her husband was alive, but not from happiness, from disappointment and shock!

Dramatic Irony

Edwin Arlington Robinson
(Part One)

Edwin Arlington Robinson (1869–1935) was no doubt one of the finest poets America ever produced. His life was full of tragedy and this affected his writings. During the early 1890s the family's fortunes began to decline, triggering a series of tragedies that influenced Robinson's life and poetry. In 1892 his father died, and the panic of 1893 bankrupted the family. Robinson's brother Dean became addicted to morphine and returned home in failing health. Robinson was forced to leave Harvard because of the family's financial difficulties and his mother's failing health. She died in 1896 of "black diphtheria," and the brothers had to lay out their mother, dig the grave, and bury her. Robinson persevered and became the first major American poet of the 20th century, unique in that he devoted his life to poetry and paid the price in poverty and obscurity. Robinson is one of my personal favorites.

Luke Havergal

Go to the western gate, Luke Havergal,
There where the vines cling crimson on the wall,
And in the twilight wait for what will come.
The wind will moan, the leaves will whisper some
Whisper of her, and strike you as they fall;
But go, and if you trust her she will call.
Go to the western gate, Luke Havergal
Luke Havergal

No, there is not a dawn in eastern skies
To rift the fiery night that's in your eyes;
But there, where western glooms are gathering,
The dark will end the dark, if anything:
God slays Himself with every leaf that flies,
And hell is more than half of paradise.
No, there is not a dawn in eastern skies
In eastern skies.

Out of a grave I come to tell you this,
Out of a grave I come to quench the kiss
That flames upon your forehead with a glow
That blinds you to the way that you must go.
Yes, there is yet one way to where she is,
Bitter, but one that faith can never miss.
Out of a grave I come to tell you this
To tell you this.

There is the western gate, Luke Havergal,
There are the crimson leaves upon the wall. Go,
for the winds are tearing them away,
Nor think to riddle the dead words they say,
Nor any more to feel them as they fall;
But go! And if you trust her she will call.
There is the western gate, Luke Havergal
Luke Havergal.

- Warm-up: Paraphrase your favorite E.A. Robinson poem.
- Students should complete Concept Builder 19-C.
- Students should write rough drafts of assigned essay.
- The teacher may correct rough drafts.

CONCEPT BUILDER 19-C
Active Reading

Read "Richard Cory" by Edwin Arlington Robinson and answer the following questions.

Whenever Richard Cory went down town,
We people on the pavement looked at him:
He was a gentleman from sole to crown,
Clean-favoured and imperially slim.

And he was always quietly arrayed,
And he was always human when he talked;
But still he fluttered pulses when he said,
"Good Morning!" and he glittered when he walked.
And he was rich, yes, richer than a king,
And admirably schooled in every grace:
In fine — we thought that he was everything
To make us wish that we were in his place.

So on we worked and waited for the light,
And went without the meat and cursed the bread,
And Richard Cory, one calm summer night,
Went home and put a bullet in his head.

| 1 | Who is Richard Cory and what is his problem? |
| 2 | The author creates a dialectic. He contrasts Richard Cory with whom? |

www.poemhunter.com/poem/richard-cory

Edwin Arlington Robinson
(Part Two)

Credo

I cannot find my way: there is no star

In all the shrouded heavens anywhere;

And there is not a whisper in the air

Of any living voice but one so far

That I can hear it only as a bar

Of lost, imperial music, played when fair

And angel fingers wove, and unaware,

Dead leaves to garlands where no roses are.

No, there is not a glimmer, nor a call,

For one that welcomes, welcomes when he fears,

The black and awful chaos of the night;

For through it all, above, beyond it all,

I know the far-sent message of the years,

I feel the coming glory of the Light!

Assignments

- Warm-up: In chapter 9 Henry encounters the tattered man when, fleeing from his regiment, he falls in with a group of wounded soldiers. The tattered man appears to be simple and innocent. When we first meet him he is listening to a sergeant with such awe that the sergeant begins to laugh at him. The tattered man is almost pathetically eager to make friends with Henry. We meet him again in this final chapter. What is his purpose?

- Students should complete Concept Builder 19-D.

- Student will re-write corrected copies of essays due tomorrow.

CONCEPT BUILDER 19-D
tone

Tone is the mood of a literary piece. Describe the mood in E.A. Robinson's "Credo," and what words stand out that signify the light or darkness of this piece.

Edgar Lee Masters
Spoon River Anthology

Edgar Lee Masters (1869–1950) wrote *A Book of Verses* (1898) and several plays before gaining fame with *Spoon River Anthology* (1915), a collection of poems in free verse about the secret lives of the inhabitants of Spoon River, a small midwestern fictional town. Masters presents the poems as the voices of the occupants of the town's graveyard, talking honestly about their lives. In "Lucinda Matlock," Masters demonstrates the literary devices of realism (which is also a worldview). This style normally includes the devices of irony, simplicity, morals, values, and symbols.

Lucinda Matlock

I went to the dances at Chandlerville,

And played snap-out at Winchester.

One time we changed partners,

Driving home in the moonlight of middle June,

And then I found Davis.

We were married and lived together for seventy years,

Enjoying, working, raising the twelve children,

Eight of whom we lost

Ere I had reached the age of sixty.

I spun, I wove, I kept the house, I nursed the sick,

I made the garden, and for holiday

Rambled over the fields where sang the larks,

And by Spoon River gathering many a shell,

And many a flower and medicinal weed —

Shouting to the wooded hills, singing to the green valleys.

At ninety-six I had lived enough, that is all,

And passed to a sweet repose.

What is this I hear of sorrow and weariness,

Anger, discontent and drooping hopes?

Degenerate sons and daughters,

Life is too strong for you —

It takes life to love Life.

Assignments

- Warm-up: Write a short poem describing someone who has meant a lot to you.
- Students should complete Concept Builder 19-E.
- Essays are due. Students should take the chapter 19 test.

Read "Lucinda Matlock" by Edgar Lee Masters and answer the following questions.

1	Identify the speaker.
2	What are sources of joy and pain for Lucinda Matlock?
3	What is the speaker's present location?

Chapter 20

1915–1946 (Part 1):

The Modern Age: Late Romanticism/Naturalism

First Thoughts It's hard to imagine a less likely author for *Ethan Frome* than Edith Wharton, for this story of a poor, lonely, taciturn farmer was written by a wealthy, young member of New York City's high society. Edith Wharton never spent a day of her life inside the sort of poor New England farmhouse occupied by Ethan, his wife Zeena, and their boarder Mattie Silver. It's a world she visited only in her imagination. But, on the other hand, struggling with depression and a failed marriage, perhaps Wharton knew more about Frome's world than we understand. She draws a realistic picture of the dark, cramped, cheerless rooms of the Fromes' living quarters and she applies this setting to life itself.

Author Worldview Watch Edith Wharton, herself captured in an unhappy marriage, explores the same in her masterpiece *Ethan Frome*. This realistic novel is naturalistic in its tone and world view. Nonetheless, this modern novel, that rivals the stream of consciousness of a Dostoevsky, arrests our attention. One hopes that Frome and Mrs. Wharton will discover that only Christ can make us victorious over difficult, even hopeless situation, but this just does not occur in *Ethan Frome*. Though Wharton struggled with her faith for most of her life, she never fully embraced naturalism in her writing.

Chapter Learning Objectives In chapter 20 you will analyze *Ethan Frome* by Edith Wharton.

As a result of this chapter study you will be able to . . .

1. Analyze the narrative technique.

2. Discuss stream of consciousness in this novel.

3. Find examples of imagery in this book.

4. Tell what the Bible says about divorce.

5. Analyze how the author's personal life is exhibited in the text.

6. Evaluate the effect of unforgivingness on a person.

7. Explore the biblical understanding of suicide.

8. Define natural selection and explain why this scientific theory is anti-Christian.

Weekly Essay Options: Begin on page 274 of the Teacher Guide.

Reading ahead: 20th-century poetry.

 History connections: *American History* chapter 20, "The Wild West"

Ethan Frome
Edith Wharton

Ethan Frome is an exceptionally well-written novel. With barely more than 150 pages, Edith Wharton takes us into the human heart. We do not much like what we see. Her novels are psychological novels: a study of human motivation and ethos. Perhaps only the English author Joseph Conrad in *The Heart of Darkness* does a better job. In any event, Wharton is a masterful storyteller. Her story is a story of life itself — the story of a man and two women captured by the exigencies of life. Two people who make a fateful decision one day that permanently changes the lives of an entire community. Using the dialect and scenery of a late-19th-century New England rural community, Wharton takes us into her own heart of darkness.

The following is Edith Wharton's explanation of why she wrote *Ethan Frome* (Ethan Frome on barronsbook notes.com):

I had known something of New England village life long before I made my home in the same county as my imaginary Starkfield; though, during the years spent there, certain of its aspects became much more familiar to me.

Even before that final initiation, however, I had had an uneasy sense that the New England of fiction bore little, except a vague botanical and dialectical, resemblance to the harsh and beautiful land as I had seen it. Even the abundant enumeration of sweet-fern, asters and mountain-laurel, and the conscientious reproduction of the vernacular, left me with the feeling that the outcropping granite had in both cases been overlooked. I give the impression merely as a personal one; it accounts for "Ethan Frome," and may, to some readers, in a measure justify it.

So much for the origin of the story; there is nothing else of interest to say of it, except as concerns its construction.

The problem before me, as I saw in the first flash, was this: I had to deal with a subject of which the dramatic climax, or rather the anti-climax, occurs a generation later than the first acts of the tragedy. This enforced lapse of time would seem to anyone persuaded, as I have always been, that every subject (in the novelist's sense of the term) implicitly contains its own form and dimensions, to mark Ethan Frome as the subject for a novel. But I never thought this for a moment, for I had felt, at the same time, that the theme of my tale was not one on which many variations could be played. It must be treated as starkly and summarily as life had always presented itself to my protagonists; any attempt to elaborate and complicate their sentiments would necessarily have falsified the whole. They were, in truth, these figures, my granite outcroppings; but half-emerged from the soil, and scarcely more articulate.

This incompatibility between subject and plan would perhaps have seemed to suggest that my "situation" was after all one to be rejected. Every novelist has been visited by the insinuating wraiths of false "good situations," siren-subjects luring his cockle-shell to the rocks; their voice is oftenest heard, and their mirage-sea beheld, as he traverses the waterless desert which awaits him half-way through whatever work is actually in hand. I knew well enough what song those sirens sang, and had often tied myself to my dull job until they were out of hearing — perhaps carrying a lost masterpiece in their rainbow veils. But I had no such fear of them in the case of Ethan Frome. It was the first subject I had ever approached with full confidence in its value, for my own purpose, and a relative faith in my power to render at least a part of what I saw in it. Every novelist, again, who "intends upon" his art, has lit upon such subjects, and been fascinated by the difficulty of presenting them in the fullest relief, yet without an added ornament, or a trick of drapery or lighting. This was my task, if I were to tell the story of Ethan Frome; and my scheme of construction — which met with the immediate and unqualified disapproval of the few friends to whom I tentatively outlined it — I still think justified in the given case. It appears to me, indeed, that, while an air of artificiality is lent to a tale of complex and sophisticated people which the novelist causes to be guessed at and interpreted by any mere looker-on, there need be no such drawback if the looker-on is sophisticated, and the people he interprets are simple. If he is capable of seeing all around them, no violence is done to probability in allowing him to exercise this faculty; it is natural enough that he should act as the sympathizing intermediary between his rudimentary characters and the more complicated minds to whom he is trying to present them. But this is all self-evident, and needs explaining only to those who have never thought of fiction as an art of composition.

The real merit of my construction seems to me to lie in a minor detail. I had to find means to bring my tragedy, in a way at once natural and picture-making, to the knowledge of its narrator. I might have sat him down before a village gossip who would have poured out the whole affair to him in a breath, but in doing this I should have been false to two essential elements of my picture: first, the deep-rooted reticence and inarticulateness of the people I was trying to draw, and secondly the effect of "roundness" (in the plastic sense) produced by letting their case be seen through eyes as different as those of Harmon Gow and Mrs. Ned Hale. Each of my chroniclers contributes to the narrative just so much as he or she is capable of understanding of what, to them, is a complicated and mysterious case; and only the narrator of the tale has scope enough to see it all, to resolve it back into simplicity, and to put it in its rightful place among his larger categories.

I make no claim for originality in following a method of which "La Grande Breteche" and "The Ring and the Book" had set me the magnificent example; my one merit is, perhaps, to have guessed that the proceeding there employed was also applicable to my small tale.

I have written this brief analysis — the first I have ever published of any of my books — because, as an author's introduction to his work, I can imagine nothing of any value to his readers except a statement as to why he decided to attempt the work in question, and why he selected one form rather than another for its embodiment. These primary aims, the only ones that can be explicitly stated, must, by the artist, be almost instinctively felt and acted upon before there can pass into his creation that imponderable something more which causes life to circulate in it, and preserves it for a little from decay.

About the Author

Edith Wharton (1832–1937), whose real name was Newbold Jones, was a member of a wealthy New York family. Deeply influenced by naturalism and realism, Wharton still tried to place a sense of moral values in her novels. She is one of the few significant 20th-century American writers who did so.

Other Notable Works

The Age of Innocence
Tales of Men and Ghosts

Vocabulary Words

Prologue: taciturnity, exanimate

Chapter I: sardonically, oblique

Chapter III: scintillating, querulous

Chapter V: languidly

Chapter VI: ominous

- Warm-up: The setting of *Ethan Frome* is vital to all aspects of the novel. It develops the plot, tone, theme(s), and characters. In fact, some critics have said that the setting *is* a character. The very name of the town, "Starkfield," suggests barrenness and harshness. What is the setting of this novel?

- Students should complete Concept Builder 20-A.

- Students review the required reading(s) *before* the assigned chapter begins.

- Teachers may want to discuss assigned reading(s) with students.

- Teachers shall assign the required essay. The rest of the essays can be outlined, answered with shorter answers, discussed, or skipped.

- Students will review all readings for chapter 20.

	Read *Ethan Frome*, chapter one, by Edith Wharton then answer the following questions.
1	What did education do for Ethan Frome?
2	While this is not the true beginning of the novel — it begins with an introduction of the narrator — it is the first narrative chapter. Why would the naturalistic author Edith Wharton begin her book with an image of nature?
3	This passage is an example of stream of consciousness (where the reader is invited to observe the landscape from the viewpoint of one of the characters). Describe this scene through the eyes of Ethan Frome.
4	Give two examples of imagery (vivid descriptions).
5	Mattie is more than a person to Ethan. What does she represent to him?
6	This is the first time that the reader meets Mattie. Describe her.

CONCEPT BUILDER 20-A
Active Reading

Setting

The end of the introduction to *Ethan Frome* reads:

Abreast of the schoolhouse the road forked, and we dipped down a lane to the left, between hemlock boughs bent inward to their trunks by the weight of the snow. I had often walked that way on Sundays, and knew that the solitary roof showing through bare branches near the bottom of the hill was that of Frome's saw-mill. It looked exanimate enough, with its idle wheel looming above the black stream dashed with yellow-white spume, and its cluster of sheds sagging under their white load. Frome did not even turn his head as we drove by, and still in silence we began to mount the next slope. About a mile farther, on a road I had never travelled, we came to an orchard of starved apple-trees writhing over a hillside among outcroppings of slate that nuzzled up through the snow like animals pushing out their noses to breathe. Beyond the orchard lay a field or two, their boundaries lost under drifts; and above the fields, huddled against the white immensities of land and sky, one of those lonely New England farm-houses that make the landscape lonelier.

"That's my place," said Frome, with a sideway jerk of his lame elbow; and in the distress and oppression of the scene I did not know what to answer. The snow had ceased, and a flash of watery sunlight exposed the house on the slope above us in all its plaintive ugliness. The black wraith of a deciduous creeper flapped from the porch, and the thin wooden walls, under their worn coat of paint, seemed to shiver in the wind that had risen with the ceasing of the snow.

"The house was bigger in my father's time: I had to take down the 'L,' a while back," Frome continued, checking with a twitch of the left rein the bay's evident intention of turning in through the broken-down gate.

I saw then that the unusually forlorn and stunted look of the house was partly due to the loss of what is known in New England as the "L": that long deep-roofed adjunct usually built at right angles to the main house, and connecting it, by way of store-rooms and tool-house, with the wood-shed and cow-barn. Whether because of its symbolic sense, the image it presents of a life linked with the soil, and enclosing in itself the chief sources of warmth and nourishment, or whether merely because of the consolatory thought that it enables the dwellers in that harsh climate to get to their morning's work without facing the weather, it is certain that the "L" rather than the house itself seems to be the centre, the actual hearth-stone of the New England farm. Perhaps this connection of ideas, which had often occurred to me in my rambles about Starkfield, caused me to hear a wistful note in Frome's words, and to see in the diminished dwelling the image of his own shrunken body.

"We're kinder side-tracked here now," he added, "but there was considerable passing before the railroad was carried through to the Flats." He roused the lagging bay with another twitch; then, as if the mere sight of the house had let me too deeply into his confidence for any farther pretence of reserve, he went on slowly: "I've always set down the worst of mother's trouble to that. When she got the rheumatism so bad she couldn't move around she used to sit up there and watch the road by the hour; and one year, when they was six months mending the Bettsbridge pike after the floods, and Harmon Gow had to bring his stage round this way, she picked up so that she used to get down to the gate most days to see him. But after the trains begun running nobody ever come by here to speak of, and mother never could get it through her head what had happened, and it preyed on her right along till she died."

As we turned into the Corbury road the snow began to fall again, cutting off our last glimpse of the house; and Frome's silence fell with it, letting down between us the old veil of reticence. This time the wind did not cease with the return of the snow. Instead, it sprang up to a gale which now and then, from a tattered sky, flung pale sweeps of sunlight over a landscape chaotically tossed. But the bay was as good as Frome's word, and we pushed on to the Junction through the wild white scene.

In the afternoon the storm held off, and the clearness in the west seemed to my inexperienced eye the pledge of a fair evening. I finished my business as quickly as possible, and we set out for Starkfield with a good chance of getting there for supper. But at sunset the clouds gathered again, bringing an earlier night, and the snow began to fall straight and steadily from a sky without wind, in a soft universal diffusion more confusing than the gusts and eddies of the morning. It seemed to be a part of the thickening darkness, to be the winter night itself descending on us layer by layer.

The small ray of Frome's lantern was soon lost in this smothering medium, in which even his sense of direction, and the bay's homing instinct, finally ceased to serve us. Two or three times some ghostly landmark sprang up to warn us that we were astray, and then was sucked back into the mist; and when we finally regained our road the old horse began to show signs of exhaustion. I felt myself to blame for having accepted Frome's offer, and after a short discussion I persuaded him to let me get out of the sleigh and walk along through the snow at the bay's side. In this way we struggled on for another mile or two, and at last reached a point where Frome, peering into what seemed to me formless night, said: "That's my gate down yonder."

The last stretch had been the hardest part of the way. The bitter cold and the heavy going had nearly knocked the wind out of me, and I could feel the horse's side ticking like a clock under my hand.

"Look here, Frome," I began, "there's no earthly use in your going any farther —" but he interrupted me: "Nor you neither. There's been about enough of this for anybody."

I understood that he was offering me a night's shelter at the farm, and without answering I turned into the gate at his side, and followed him to the barn, where I helped him to unharness and bed down the tired horse. When this was done he unhooked the lantern from the sleigh, stepped out again into the night, and called to me over his shoulder: "This way."

Far off above us a square of light trembled through the screen of snow. Staggering along in Frome's wake I floundered toward it, and in the darkness almost fell into one of the deep drifts against the front of the house. Frome scrambled up the slippery steps of the porch, digging a way through the snow with his heavily booted foot. Then he lifted his lantern, found the latch, and led the way into the house. I went after him into a low unlit passage, at the back of which a ladder-like staircase rose into obscurity. On our right a line of light marked the door of the room which had sent its ray across the night; and behind the door I heard a woman's voice droning querulously.

Frome stamped on the worn oil-cloth to shake the snow from his boots, and set down his lantern on a kitchen chair which was the only piece of furniture in the hall. Then he opened the door.

"Come in," he said; and as he spoke the droning voice grew still. . . .

It was that night that I found the clue to Ethan Frome, and began to put together this vision of his story (Edith Wharton, *Ethan Frome*, introduction, www.gutenberg.org/files/4517/4517-h/4517-h.htm).

Assignments

- Warm-up: How is interest increased by the conversation between Mattie and Denis Eady?
- Students should complete Concept Builder 20-B.
- Students should review reading(s) from the next chapter.
- Student should outline essay due at the end of the week.
- Per teacher instructions, students may answer orally, in a group setting, some of the essays that are not assigned as formal essays.

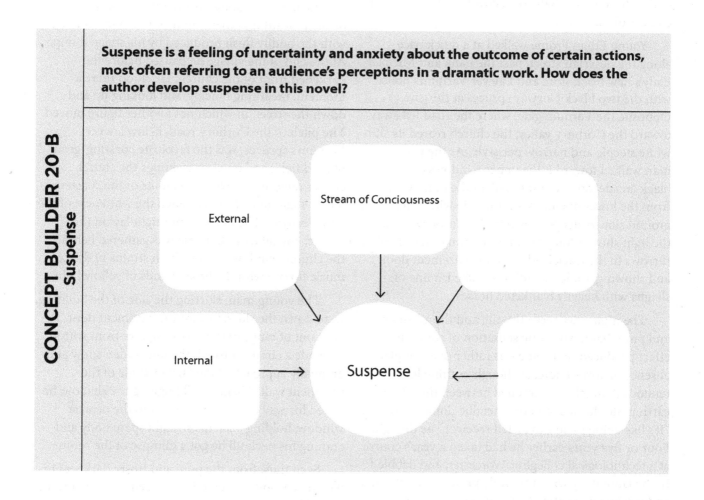

CONCEPT BUILDER 20-B
Suspense

Suspense is a feeling of uncertainty and anxiety about the outcome of certain actions, most often referring to an audience's perceptions in a dramatic work. How does the author develop suspense in this novel?

External

Stream of Conciousness

Internal

Suspense

Stream of Consciousness

The village lay under two feet of snow, with drifts at the windy corners. In a sky of iron the points of the Dipper hung like icicles and Orion flashed his cold fires. The moon had set, but the night was so transparent that the white house-fronts between the elms looked gray against the snow, clumps of bushes made black stains on it, and the basement windows of the church sent shafts of yellow light far across the endless undulations.

Young Ethan Frome walked at a quick pace along the deserted street, past the bank and Michael Eady's new brick store and Lawyer Varnum's house with the two black Norway spruces at the gate. Opposite the Varnum gate, where the road fell away toward the Corbury valley, the church reared its slim white steeple and narrow peristyle. As the young man walked toward it the upper windows drew a black arcade along the side wall of the building, but from the lower openings, on the side where the ground sloped steeply down to the Corbury road, the light shot its long bars, illuminating many fresh furrows in the track leading to the basement door, and showing, under an adjoining shed, a line of sleighs with heavily blanketed horses.

The night was perfectly still, and the air so dry and pure that it gave little sensation of cold. The effect produced on Frome was rather of a complete absence of atmosphere, as though nothing less tenuous than ether intervened between the white earth under his feet and the metallic dome overhead. "It's like being in an exhausted receiver," he thought. Four or five years earlier he had taken a year's course at a technological college at Worcester, and dabbled in the laboratory with a friendly professor of physics; and the images supplied by that experience still cropped up, at unexpected moments, through the totally different associations of thought in which he had since been living. His father's death, and the misfortunes following it, had put a premature end to Ethan's studies; but though they had not gone far enough to be of much practical use they had fed his fancy and made him aware of huge cloudy meanings behind the daily face of things.

As he strode along through the snow the sense of such meanings glowed in his brain and mingled with the bodily flush produced by his sharp tramp. At the end of the village he paused before the darkened front of the church. He stood there a moment, breathing quickly, and looking up and down the street, in which not another figure moved. The pitch of the Corbury road, below lawyer Varnum's spruces, was the favourite coasting-ground of Starkfield, and on clear evenings the church corner rang till late with the shouts of the coasters; but to-night not a sled darkened the whiteness of the long declivity. The hush of midnight lay on the village, and all its waking life was gathered behind the church windows, from which strains of dance-music flowed with the broad bands of yellow light.

The young man, skirting the side of the building, went down the slope toward the basement door. To keep out of range of the revealing rays from within he made a circuit through the untrodden snow and gradually approached the farther angle of the basement wall. Thence, still hugging the shadow, he edged his way cautiously forward to the nearest window, holding back his straight spare body and craning his neck till he got a glimpse of the room.

Seen thus, from the pure and frosty darkness in which he stood, it seemed to be seething in a mist of heat. The metal reflectors of the gas-jets sent crude waves of light against the whitewashed walls, and the iron flanks of the stove at the end of the hall looked as though they were heaving with volcanic fires. The floor was thronged with girls and young men. Down the side wall facing the window stood a row of kitchen chairs from which the older women had just risen. By this time the music had stopped, and the musicians — a fiddler, and the young lady who played the harmonium on Sundays — were hastily refreshing themselves at one corner of the supper-table which aligned its devastated pie-dishes and ice-cream saucers on the platform at the end of the hall. The guests were preparing to leave, and the tide had already set toward the passage where coats and wraps were hung, when a young man with a sprightly foot and a shock of black hair shot into the middle of the floor and clapped his hands. The signal took instant effect. The musicians hurried to their instruments, the dancers — some already half-muffled for departure — fell into line down each side of the room, the older spectators slipped back to their chairs, and the lively young man, after diving about here and there in the throng, drew forth a girl who had already wound a cherry-coloured "fascinator" about her head, and, leading her up to the end of the floor, whirled her down its length to the bounding tune of a Virginia reel.

Frome's heart was beating fast. He had been straining for a glimpse of the dark head under the cherry-coloured scarf and it vexed him that another eye should have been quicker than his. The leader of the reel, who looked as if he had Irish blood in his veins, danced well, and his partner caught his fire. As she passed down the line, her light figure swinging from hand to hand in circles of increasing swiftness, the scarf flew off her head and stood out behind her shoulders, and Frome, at each turn, caught sight of her laughing panting lips, the cloud of dark hair about her forehead, and the dark eyes which seemed the only fixed points in a maze of flying lines.

The dancers were going faster and faster, and the musicians, to keep up with them, belaboured their instruments like jockeys lashing their mounts on the home-stretch; yet it seemed to the young man at the window that the reel would never end. Now and then he turned his eyes from the girl's face to that of her partner, which, in the exhilaration of the dance, had taken on a look of almost impudent ownership. Denis Eady was the son of Michael Eady, the ambitious Irish grocer, whose suppleness and effrontery had given Starkfield its first notion of "smart" business methods, and whose new brick store testified to the success of the attempt. His son seemed likely to follow in his steps, and was meanwhile applying the same arts to the conquest of the Starkfield maidenhood. Hitherto Ethan Frome had been content to think him a mean fellow; but now he positively invited a horse-whipping. It was strange that the girl did not seem aware of it: that she could lift her rapt face to her dancer's, and drop her hands into his, without appearing to feel the offence of his look and touch (Ibid., chapter 1).

Assignments

- Warm-up: This tragic book is marked by irony. Irony is defined as a contradiction between what is said and what is expected, and is often amusing as a result. Mattie ironically becomes the opposite of what she was as a youth. How do Zeena and Ethan change by the end of the novel? What other instances of irony do you find in Mrs. Hale's conversation?

- Students should complete Concept Builder 20-C.

- Students should write rough drafts of assigned essay.

- The teacher may correct rough drafts.

The setting of *Ethan Frome* is as important as the characters. The very name of the village, "Starkfield," suggests barrenness and harshness. As you read the opening chapters, pay attention to the author's descriptions of the setting. What words do Wharton use to describe her setting?

Starkfield

Irony

Zeena's native village was slightly larger and nearer to the railway than Starkfield, and she had let her husband see from the first that life on an isolated farm was not what she had expected when she married. But purchasers were slow in coming, and while he waited for them Ethan learned the impossibility of transplanting her. She chose to look down on Starkfield, but she could not have lived in a place which looked down on her. Even Bettsbridge or Shadd's Falls would not have been sufficiently aware of her, and in the greater cities which attracted Ethan she would have suffered a complete loss of identity. And within a year of their marriage she developed the "sickliness" which had since made her notable even in a community rich in pathological instances. When she came to take care of his mother she had seemed to Ethan like the very genius of health, but he soon saw that her skill as a nurse had been acquired by the absorbed observation of her own symptoms.

Then she too fell silent. Perhaps it was the inevitable effect of life on the farm, or perhaps, as she sometimes said, it was because Ethan "never listened." The charge was not wholly unfounded. When she spoke it was only to complain, and to complain of things not in his power to remedy; and to check a tendency to impatient retort he had first formed the habit of not answering her, and finally of thinking of other things while she talked. Of late, however, since he had reasons for observing her more closely, her silence had begun to trouble him. He recalled his mother's growing taciturnity, and wondered if Zeena were also turning "queer." Women did, he knew. Zeena, who had at her fingers' ends the pathological chart of the whole region, had cited many cases of the kind while she was nursing his mother; and he himself knew of certain lonely farm-houses in the neighbourhood where stricken creatures pined, and of others where sudden tragedy had come of their presence. At times, looking at Zeena's shut face, he felt the chill of such forebodings. At other times her silence seemed deliberately assumed to conceal far-reaching intentions, mysterious conclusions drawn from suspicions and resentments impossible to guess. That supposition was even more disturbing than the other; and it was the one which had come to him the night before, when he had seen her standing in the kitchen door.

Now her departure for Bettsbridge had once more eased his mind, and all his thoughts were on the prospect of his evening with Mattie. Only one thing weighed on him, and that was his having told Zeena that he was to receive cash for the lumber. He foresaw so clearly the consequences of this imprudence that with considerable reluctance he decided to ask Andrew Hale for a small advance on his load.

When Ethan drove into Hale's yard the builder was just getting out of his sleigh.

"Hello, Ethe!" he said. "This comes handy."

Andrew Hale was a ruddy man with a big gray moustache and a stubbly double-chin unconstrained by a collar; but his scrupulously clean shirt was always fastened by a small diamond stud. This display of opulence was misleading, for though he did a fairly good business it was known that his easygoing habits and the demands of his large family frequently kept him what Starkfield called "behind." He was an old friend of Ethan's family, and his house one of the few to which Zeena occasionally went, drawn there by the fact that Mrs. Hale, in her youth, had done more "doctoring" than any other woman in Starkfield, and was still a recognised authority on symptoms and treatment.

Hale went up to the grays and patted their sweating flanks.

"Well, sir," he said, "you keep them two as if they was pets."

Ethan set about unloading the logs and when he had finished his job he pushed open the glazed door of the shed which the builder used as his office. Hale sat with his feet up on the stove, his back propped against a battered desk strewn with papers: the place, like the man, was warm, genial and untidy.

"Sit right down and thaw out," he greeted Ethan.

The latter did not know how to begin, but at length he managed to bring out his request for an advance of fifty dollars. The blood rushed to his thin skin under the sting of Hale's astonishment. It was the builder's custom to pay at the end of three months, and there was no precedent between the two men for a cash settlement.

Ethan felt that if he had pleaded an urgent need Hale might have made shift to pay him; but pride, and an instinctive prudence, kept him from resorting to this argument. After his father's death it had taken time to get his head above water, and he did not want Andrew Hale, or any one else in Starkfield, to think he was going under again. Besides, he hated lying; if he wanted the money he wanted it, and it was nobody's business to ask why. He therefore made his demand with the awkwardness of a proud man who will not admit to himself that he is stooping; and he was not much surprised at Hale's refusal.

The builder refused genially, as he did everything else: he treated the matter as something in the nature of a practical joke, and wanted to know if Ethan meditated buying a grand piano or adding a "cupolo" to his house; offering, in the latter case, to give his services free of cost.

Ethan's arts were soon exhausted, and after an embarrassed pause he wished Hale good day and opened the door of the office. As he passed out the builder suddenly called after him: "See here — you ain't in a tight place, are you?"

"Not a bit," Ethan's pride retorted before his reason had time to intervene.

"Well, that's good! Because I am, a shade. Fact is, I was going to ask you to give me a little extra time on that payment. Business is pretty slack, to begin with, and then I'm fixing up a little house for Ned and Ruth when they're married. I'm glad to do it for 'em, but it costs." His look appealed to Ethan for sympathy. "The young people like things nice. You know how it is yourself: it's not so long ago since you fixed up your own place for Zeena."

Ethan left the grays in Hale's stable and went about some other business in the village. As he walked away the builder's last phrase lingered in his ears, and he reflected grimly that his seven years with Zeena seemed to Starkfield "not so long."

The afternoon was drawing to an end, and here and there a lighted pane spangled the cold gray dusk and made the snow look whiter. The bitter weather had driven every one indoors and Ethan had the long rural street to himself. Suddenly he heard the brisk play of sleigh-bells and a cutter passed him, drawn by a free-going horse. Ethan recognised Michael Eady's roan colt, and young Denis Eady, in a handsome new fur cap, leaned forward and waved a greeting. "Hello, Ethe!" he shouted and spun on.

The cutter was going in the direction of the Frome farm, and Ethan's heart contracted as he listened to the dwindling bells. What more likely than that Denis Eady had heard of Zeena's departure for Bettsbridge, and was profiting by the opportunity to spend an hour with Mattie? Ethan was ashamed of the storm of jealousy in his breast. It seemed unworthy of the girl that his thoughts of her should be so violent.

He walked on to the church corner and entered the shade of the Varnum spruces, where he had stood with her the night before. As he passed into their gloom he saw an indistinct outline just ahead of him. At his approach it melted for an instant into two separate shapes and then conjoined again, and he heard a kiss, and a half-laughing "Oh!" provoked by the discovery of his presence. Again the outline hastily disunited and the Varnum gate slammed on one half while the other hurried on ahead of him. Ethan smiled at the discomfiture he had caused. What did it matter to Ned Hale and Ruth Varnum if they were caught kissing each other? Everybody in Starkfield knew they were engaged. It pleased Ethan to have surprised a pair of lovers on the spot where

he and Mattie had stood with such a thirst for each other in their hearts; but he felt a pang at the thought that these two need not hide their happiness.

He fetched the grays from Hale's stable and started on his long climb back to the farm. The cold was less sharp than earlier in the day and a thick fleecy sky threatened snow for the morrow. Here and there a star pricked through, showing behind it a deep well of blue. In an hour or two the moon would push over the ridge behind the farm, burn a gold-edged rent in the clouds, and then be swallowed by them. A mournful peace hung on the fields, as though they felt the relaxing grasp of the cold and stretched themselves in their long winter sleep.

Ethan's ears were alert for the jingle of sleigh-bells, but not a sound broke the silence of the lonely road. As he drew near the farm he saw, through the thin screen of larches at the gate, a light twinkling in the house above him. "She's up in her room," he said to himself, "fixing herself up for supper"; and he remembered Zeena's sarcastic stare when Mattie, on the evening of her arrival, had come down to supper with smoothed hair and a ribbon at her neck.

He passed by the graves on the knoll and turned his head to glance at one of the older headstones, which had interested him deeply as a boy because it bore his name.

SACRED TO THE MEMORY OF

ETHAN FROME AND ENDURANCE HIS WIFE,

WHO DWELLED TOGETHER IN PEACE

FOR FIFTY YEARS.

He used to think that fifty years sounded like a long time to live together, but now it seemed to him that they might pass in a flash. Then, with a sudden dart of irony, he wondered if, when their turn came, the same epitaph would be written over him and Zeena (Ibid., chapter 4).

Assignments

- Warm-up: Theme: a belief about life expressed in a prose / poetry / dramatic piece. A theme is usually subtly presented in the literary piece. A theme should not be confused with a moral. A moral is principle to apply to actual life. A theme is a comment on life. What is at least one theme in this enclosed passage?

- Students should complete Concept Builder 20-D.

- Student will re-write corrected copies of essay due tomorrow.

How does the narrator draw the reader into this story? There are several correct answers.

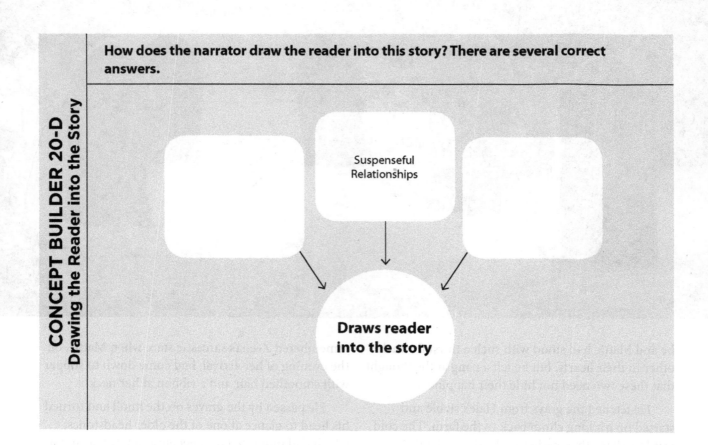

Suspenseful
Relationships

**Draws reader
into the story**

Themes

I had been told that Frome was poor, and that the saw-mill and the arid acres of his farm yielded scarcely enough to keep his household through the winter; but I had not supposed him to be in such want as Harmon's words implied, and I expressed my wonder.

"Well, matters ain't gone any too well with him," Harmon said. "When a man's been setting round like a hulk for twenty years or more, seeing things that want doing, it eats inter him, and he loses his grit. That Frome farm was always 'bout as bare's a milk-pan when the cat's been round; and you know what one of them old water-mills is wuth nowadays. When Ethan could sweat over 'em both from sunup to dark he kinder choked a living out of 'em; but his folks ate up most everything, even then, and I don't see how he makes out now. Fust his father got a kick, out haying, and went soft in the brain, and gave away money like Bible texts afore he died. Then his mother got queer and dragged along for years as weak as a baby; and his wife Zeena, she's always been the greatest hand at doctoring in the county. Sickness and trouble: that's what Ethan's had his plate full up with, ever since the very first helping."

The next morning, when I looked out, I saw the hollow-backed bay between the Varnum spruces, and Ethan Frome, throwing back his worn bearskin, made room for me in the sleigh at his side. After that, for a week, he drove me over every morning to Corbury Flats, and on my return in the afternoon met me again and carried me back through the icy night to Starkfield. The distance each way was barely three miles, but the old bay's pace was slow, and even with firm snow under the runners we were nearly an hour on the way. Ethan Frome drove in silence, the reins loosely held in his left hand, his brown seamed

profile, under the helmet-like peak of the cap, relieved against the banks of snow like the bronze image of a hero. He never turned his face to mine, or answered, except in monosyllables, the questions I put, or such slight pleasantries as I ventured. He seemed a part of the mute melancholy landscape, an incarnation of its frozen woe, with all that was warm and sentient in him fast bound below the surface; but there was nothing unfriendly in his silence. I simply felt that he lived in a depth of moral isolation too remote for casual access, and I had the sense that

353

his loneliness was not merely the result of his personal plight, tragic as I guessed that to be, but had in it, as Harmon Gow had hinted, the profound accumulated cold of many Starkfield winters.

Only once or twice was the distance between us bridged for a moment; and the glimpses thus gained confirmed my desire to know more. Once I happened to speak of an engineering job I had been on the previous year in Florida, and of the contrast between the winter landscape about us and that in which I had found myself the year before; and to my surprise Frome said suddenly: "Yes: I was down there once, and for a good while afterward I could call up the sight of it in winter. But now it's all snowed under."

He said no more, and I had to guess the rest from the inflection of his voice and his sharp relapse into silence (Ibid., Introduction).

Assignments

- Warm-up: What is the emotional mood created by the dialogue in this scene?
- Students should complete Concept Builder 20-E.
- Essays are due. Students should take the chapter 20 test.

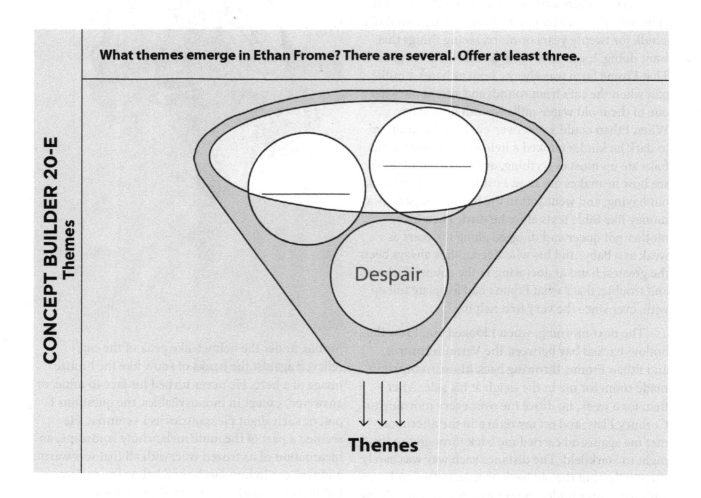

CONCEPT BUILDER 20-E
Themes

What themes emerge in Ethan Frome? There are several. Offer at least three.

Despair

Themes

Chapter 21

1915–1946 (Part 2):
The Modern Age: Late Romanticism/Naturalism

First Thoughts The famous beginning of Eliot's "Prufrock" invites the reader into tawdry alleys: "Let us go then, you and I, When the evening is spread out against the sky Like a patient etherized upon a table; Let us go, through certain half-deserted streets, The muttering retreats Of restless nights in one-night cheap hotels And sawdust restaurants with oyster-shells: Streets that follow like a tedious argument Of insidious intent To lead you to an overwhelming question . . . Oh, do not ask, "What is it?" Let us go and make our visit." Likewise, courageous readers, 20th-century poets invite you to real places and you will ask, "What is it?"

Author Worldview Watch Twentieth Century American poetry is a beautifully written testimony to the state of American modernistic culture. Strongly naturalistic, it is like a Ferris wheel. Awesome to behold, this mechanical marvel entertains the mind but teases the soul, and, ultimately, goes nowhere. One is on a ride, really, in a circle, only to return to where one began.

Chapter Learning Objectives In chapter 21 you will analyze 20th-century poetry.

As a result of this chapter study you will be able to . . .

1. Understand use of irony in poetry.

2. Find examples of anger in Langston Hughes' poetry.

3. Judge if Edna St. Vincent Millay is a second-rate poet.

4. Analyze Robert Frost's poem "Fire and Ice."

5. Decide which five American poets and poems you would use in a new anthology.

Weekly Essay Options: Begin on page 274 of the Teacher Guide.

Reading ahead: *A Farewell To Arms* by Ernest Hemingway

 History connections: *American History* chapter 21, "African American History: The Great Migration"

20th-century Poetry

Robert Lee Frost (1874–1963) was born in California but raised on a farm in New England until the age of ten. The New England countryside became Frost's favorite setting. A charismatic public reader, he was renowned for his tours. He read an original work at the inauguration of President John F. Kennedy in 1961 that helped spark a national interest in poetry. His popularity is easy to explain: he wrote of traditional farm life, appealing to a nostalgia for the old ways. His themes were universal and immutable — apple picking, stone walls, fences, country roads. His subjects were ordinary people. He was one of the few modern poets who used rhyme. This endeared him to American readers.

Frost's work is often deceptively simple. Many poems suggest a deeper meaning. For example, a quiet snowy evening by an almost hypnotic rhyme scheme may suggest the not entirely unwelcome approach of death. Beneath the falling snow and gentle raindrops are pain and unhappiness. Some critics blame Frost's bitterness on the early years of his marriage when he tried to make a living on an inhospitable New England farm. From "Stopping by Woods on a Snowy Evening" (1923):

> The woods are lovely, dark and deep, But I have promises to keep, And miles to go before I sleep, And miles to go before I sleep.

"The Death of the Hired Hand"

Mary sat musing on the lamp-flame at the table
Waiting for Warren. When she heard his step,
She ran on tip-toe down the darkened passage
To meet him in the doorway with the news
And put him on his guard. "Silas is back."
She pushed him outward with her through the door
And shut it after her. "Be kind," she said.
She took the market things from Warren's arms
And set them on the porch, then drew him down
To sit beside her on the wooden steps.
"When was I ever anything but kind to him?
But I'll not have the fellow back," he said.
"I told him so last haying, didn't I?
'If he left then,' I said, 'that ended it.'
What good is he? Who else will harbour him
At his age for the little he can do?
What help he is there's no depending on.
Off he goes always when I need him most.
'He thinks he ought to earn a little pay,

Enough at least to buy tobacco with,
So he won't have to beg and be beholden.'
'All right,' I say, 'I can't afford to pay
Any fixed wages, though I wish I could.'
'Someone else can.' 'Then someone else will have to.'
I shouldn't mind his bettering himself
If that was what it was. You can be certain,
When he begins like that, there's someone at him
Trying to coax him off with pocket-money, —
In haying time, when any help is scarce.
In winter he comes back to us. I'm done."
"Sh! not so loud: he'll hear you," Mary said.
"I want him to: he'll have to soon or late."
"He's worn out. He's asleep beside the stove.
When I came up from Rowe's I found him here,
Huddled against the barn-door fast asleep,
A miserable sight, and frightening, too —
You needn't smile — I didn't recognise him —
I wasn't looking for him — and he's changed.

Wait till you see."

"Where did you say he'd been?"

"He didn't say. I dragged him to the house,
And gave him tea and tried to make him smoke.
I tried to make him talk about his travels.
Nothing would do: he just kept nodding off."

"What did he say? Did he say anything?"

"But little."

"Anything? Mary, confess
He said he'd come to ditch the meadow for me."

"Warren!"

"But did he? I just want to know."

"Of course he did. What would you have him say?
Surely you wouldn't grudge the poor old man
Some humble way to save his self-respect.
He added, if you really care to know,
He meant to clear the upper pasture, too.
That sounds like something you have heard before?
Warren, I wish you could have heard the way
He jumbled everything. I stopped to look
Two or three times — he made me feel so queer —
To see if he was talking in his sleep.
He ran on Harold Wilson — you remember —
The boy you had in haying four years since.
He's finished school, and teaching in his college.
Silas declares you'll have to get him back.
He says they two will make a team for work:
Between them they will lay this farm as smooth!
The way he mixed that in with other things.
He thinks young Wilson a likely lad, though daft
On education — you know how they fought
All through July under the blazing sun,
Silas up on the cart to build the load,
Harold along beside to pitch it on."

"Yes, I took care to keep well out of earshot."

"Well, those days trouble Silas like a dream.
You wouldn't think they would.
How some things linger!
Harold's young college boy's assurance piqued him.
After so many years he still keeps finding
Good arguments he sees he might have used.
I sympathise. I know just how it feels
To think of the right thing to say too late.
Harold's associated in his mind with Latin.

He asked me what I thought of Harold's saying
He studied Latin like the violin
Because he liked it — that an argument!
He said he couldn't make the boy believe
He could find water with a hazel prong —
Which showed how much good school had ever done
him.
He wanted to go over that. But most of all
He thinks if he could have another chance
To teach him how to build a load of hay —"

"I know, that's Silas' one accomplishment.
He bundles every forkful in its place,
And tags and numbers it for future reference,
So he can find and easily dislodge it
In the unloading. Silas does that well.
He takes it out in bunches like big birds' nests.
You never see him standing on the hay
He's trying to lift, straining to lift himself."

"He thinks if he could teach him that, he'd be
Some good perhaps to someone in the world.
He hates to see a boy the fool of books.
Poor Silas, so concerned for other folk,
And nothing to look backward to with pride,
And nothing to look forward to with hope,
So now and never any different."

Part of a moon was falling down the west,
Dragging the whole sky with it to the hills.
Its light poured softly in her lap. She saw
And spread her apron to it. She put out her hand
Among the harp-like morning-glory strings,
Taut with the dew from garden bed to eaves,
As if she played unheard the tenderness
That wrought on him beside her in the night.
"Warren," she said, "he has come home to die:
You needn't be afraid he'll leave you this time."

"Home," he mocked gently.

"Yes, what else but home?
It all depends on what you mean by home.
Of course he's nothing to us, any more
Than was the hound that came a stranger to us
Out of the woods, worn out upon the trail."

"Home is the place where, when you have to go there,
They have to take you in."

"I should have called it

Assignments

- Warm-up: Agree or disagree with each critic below:

At his best, of course, Frost does not philosophize. The anecdote is absorbed into symbol. The method of indirection operates fully: the senses of realistic detail, the air of casual comment, are employed to build up and intensify a serious effect. (Cleanth Brooks, *Modern Poetry,* Univ. of North Carolina Pr., 1979, p. 113)

Despite his great virtues, you cannot read a great deal of Frost without this effect of the deja vu. Sententiousness and a relative absence of formal daring are his main defects. Even in his finest work, the conventionality of rhythm and rhyme contributes a certain tedium, temporarily relegated to a dim corner of the reader's consciousness. (M.L. Rosenthal, *The Modern Poets,* Oxford University Press, 1969, p. 112–113.)

- Students should complete Concept Builder 21-A.

- Teachers shall assign the required essay. The rest of the essays can be outlined, answered with shorter answers, discussed, or skipped.

CONCEPT BUILDER 21-A Active Reading	Read "The Death of the Hired Hand" by Robert Frost in the text and then answer the following questions.	
	1	From the first twelve lines, why did Silas leave Warren and Mary?
	2	If you were Warren or Mary, would you let Silas work for you?
	3	What is it that Mary knows that Warren doesn't?
	4	What does the foil Harold Wilson show the reader about Silas?
	5	Predict the ending of this poem.
	6	Using these images, what is the author telling the reader about Mary?
	7	Why won't Silas visit his brother?

Ezra Pound
(1885-1972)

Ezra Pound was one of the most influential American poets of the 20th century. From 1908 to 1920, he lived in London, where he associated with many writers, including William Butler Yeats, for whom he worked as a secretary, and T.S. Eliot, whose *Waste Land* he drastically edited and improved. He eventually moved to Italy, where he became caught up in Italian fascism. That is the rub — Pound was a racist and fascist.

Pound's interests and reading were universal. His life-work was *The Cantos*, which he wrote and published until his death. They contain brilliant passages, but their allusions to works of literature and art from many eras and cultures make them difficult. Pound's poetry is best known for its clear, visual images, fresh rhythms, and muscular, intelligent, unusual lines, such as, in Canto LXXXI, "The ant's a centaur in his dragon world," or in poems inspired by Japanese haiku, such as "In a Station of the Metro" (1916): The apparition of these faces in the crowd; Petals on a wet, black bough.

Pound's subject matter was modern and realistic. He was involved in the early stages of surrealism (Works by Ezra Pound can be found at 20th Century Poetry, www.lit.kobe_u.ac.jp/~hishika/pound.htm).

Assignments

- Warm-up: Ezra Pound was a notorious racist and supporter of the Nazi party in Germany. Do you see evidence of his racism in his poems? Should we avoid reading his poetry because he was a racist?

- Students should complete Concept Builder 21-B.

- Students should review reading(s) from the next chapter.

- Student should outline essay due at the end of the week.

- Per teacher instructions, students may answer orally, in a group setting, some of the essays that are not assigned as formal essays.

The smell of buttered popcorn on Friday night!

Home

T.S. Eliot and Langston Hughes

T.S. Eliot (1888–1965) was both an American and a British writer of unprecedented stature. He was the best! He lived on two continents but he belonged only to God. One of the most respected poets of his day, his iconoclastic poetry had revolutionary impact. He also wrote influential essays and dramas, and championed the importance of literary and social traditions for the modern poet.

Dreary imagery pervades *The Waste Land* (1922), which echoes Dante's *Inferno* to evoke London's thronged streets around the time of World War I:

> Unreal City, Under the brown fog of a winter dawn, A crowd flowed over London Bridge, so many I had not thought death had undone so many. . . . (I, 60–63)

The Waste Land's vision is ultimately apocalyptic (i.e., end times) and worldwide:

> Cracks and reforms and bursts in the violet air
> Falling towers Jerusalem,
> Athens, Alexandria, Vienna,
> London, Unreal (V, 373–377)

Eliot's vision of the world is decidedly hopeless and naturalistic — that is until he commits his life to Christ. At the end of his life, Eliot had a profound experience with Christ that profoundly changed his views of the past and future. In fact, one of the most Christian theistic pieces of literature in the English language is Eliot's *Murder in the Cathedral* that he wrote at the end of his life.

Hippopotamus

The broad-backed hippopotamus
Rests on his belly in the mud;
Although he seems so firm to us
He is merely flesh and blood.

Flesh-and-blood is weak and frail,
Susceptible to nervous shock;
While the True Church can never fail
For it is based upon a rock.

The hippo's feeble steps may err
In compassing material ends,
While the True Church need never stir
To gather in its dividends.

The 'potamus can never reach
The mango on the mango-tree;
But fruits of pomegranate and peach
Refresh the Church from over sea.

At mating time the hippo's voice
Betrays inflexions hoarse and odd,

But every week we hear rejoice
The Church, at being one with God.

The hippopotamus's day
Is passed in sleep; at night he hunts;
God works in a mysterious way —
The Church can sleep and feed at once.

I saw the 'potamus take wing
Ascending from the damp savannas,
And quiring angels round him sing
The praise of God, in loud hosannas.

Blood of the Lamb shall wash him clean
And him shall heavenly arms enfold,
Among the saints he shall be seen
Performing on a harp of gold.

He shall be washed as white as snow,
By all the martyr'd virgins kiss,
While the True Church remains below
Wrapt in the old miasmal mist.

Langston Hughes (1902–1967) One of many talented poets of the Harlem Renaissance of the 1920s in the company of James Weldon Johnson and others was Langston Hughes. He embraced African-American jazz rhythms and was one of the first black writers to attempt to make a profitable career out of his writing. Hughes incorporated blues, spirituals, colloquial speech, and folkways in his poetry. Hughes was part of the Great Migration. For many blacks, the years after the Civil War were very much like the years before the Civil War. While they were legally free, economically and socially they were still in bondage. "Jim Crow" laws made sure of this. The demon of racism manifested itself now in unjust laws promulgated by white governments to maintain its hegemony over its black population.

The Weary Blues

Droning a drowsy syncopated tune,
Rocking back and forth to a mellow croon,
I heard a Negro play.
Down on Lenox Avenue the other night
By the pale dull pallor of an old gas light
He did a lazy sway . . .
He did a lazy sway . . .
To the tune o' those Weary Blues.
With his ebony hands on each ivory key
He made that poor piano moan with melody.
O Blues!
Swaying to and fro on his rickety stool
He played that sad raggy tune like a musical fool.
Sweet Blues!
Coming from a black man's soul.
O Blues!
In a deep song voice with a melancholy tone
I heard that Negro sing, that old piano moan —
"Ain't got nobody in all this world,
Ain't got nobody but ma self.
I's gwine to quit ma frownin'
And put ma troubles on the shelf."

Thump, thump, thump, went his foot on the floor.
He played a few chords then he sang some more —
"I got the Weary Blues
And I can't be satisfied.
Got the Weary Blues
And can't be satisfied —

I ain't happy no mo'
And I wish that I had died."
And far into the night he crooned that tune.
The stars went out and so did the moon.
The singer stopped playing and went to bed
While the Weary Blues echoed through his head.
He slept like a rock or a man that's dead.

Harlem (Dream Deferred)

What happens to a dream deferred?

Does it dry up
like a raisin in the sun?
Or fester like a sore —
And then run?
Does it stink like rotten meat?
Or crust and sugar over —
like a syrupy sweet?

Maybe it just sags
like a heavy load.

Or does it explode?

- Warm-up: T.S. Eliot met the Lord late in life and wrote some of the most inspiring prose and poetry in the English language.

- Students should complete Concept Builder 21-C.

- Students should write rough drafts of assigned essay.

- The teacher may correct rough drafts.

CONCEPT BUILDER 21-C Active Reading		Read "The Weary Blues" and "Harlem (Dream Deferred)" by Langston Hughes on the previous page and then answer the following questions.
	1	In "The Weary Blues," do you sense the way the poem replicates the rhythm of the blues? Do you feel it?
	2	In "The Weary Blues," why does the blues singer sleep so soundly?
	3	In "Harlem (Dream Deferred)," Hughes compares a dream deferred to:

e.e. cummings

e.e. cummings (1894–1962) A painter, e.e. cummings, was the first American poet to recognize that poetry had become primarily a visual, not an oral, art; his poems used much unusual spacing and indentation, as well as dropping all use of capital letters. (Poems by e. e. cummings can be found at www.poets.org/poets/.)

Like Williams, cummings also used colloquial language, sharp imagery, and words from popular culture. Like Williams, he took creative liberties with layout. His poem "in Just" (1920) invites the reader to fill in the missing ideas:

In just-spring	and eddieandbill come
when the world is mud-	running from marbles and
luscious the little	piracies and it's
lame baloonman	spring
whistles far and wee	when the world is puddle-wonderful…

CONCEPT BUILDER 21-D
Active Reading

Read "anyone lived in a pretty how town" by e.e. cummings, then answer the following questions.

anyone lived in a pretty how town
(with up so floating many bells down)
spring summer autumn winter
he sang his didn't he danced his did
Women and men(both little and small)
cared for anyone not at all
they sowed their isn't they reaped their same
sun moon stars rain

children guessed(but only a few
and down they forgot as up they grew
autumn winter spring summer)
that no one loved him more by more

when by now and tree by leaf
she laughed his joy she cried his grief
bird by snow and stir by still
anyone's any was all to her

someones married their everyones
laughed their cryings and did their dance
(sleep wake hope and then)they
said their nevers they slept their dream

stars rain sun moon
(and only the snow can begin to explain
how children are apt to forget to remember
with up so floating many bells down)

one day anyone died i guess
(and no one stooped to kiss his face)
busy folk buried them side by side
little by little and was by was

all by all and deep by deep
and more by more they dream their sleep

www.poets.org/viewmedia.php/prmMID/15403

1	What happens to the children as they grow older?
2	Why does cummings repeat this phrase?

Miscellaneous Poets

Wallace Stevens (1879–1955) Stevens's poetry argues for the belief that the order of art corresponds with an order in nature. His vocabulary is rich: He writes with generous imagery.

Some of Stevens's poems draw upon popular culture, while others poke fun at sophisticated society or soar into an intellectual heaven. He is known for his exuberant word play: "Soon, with a noise like tambourines / Came her attendant Byzantines."

Stevens's work is full of surprising insights. Sometimes he plays tricks on the reader, as in "Disillusionment of Ten O'clock" (1931):

The houses are haunted By white night-gowns. None are green, Or purple with green rings, Or green with yellow rings, Or yellow with blue rings. . . .

This poem seems to complain about unimaginative lives (plain white nightgowns), but actually brings up bright images in the reader's mind. Stevens is not easy, but well worth the effort. (For more information on Stevens, including his poems, access this website: www.english.upenn.edu/~afilreis /Stevens/home.html.)

Wallace Stevens wrote many of his best-known poems while living in this house in Hartford, Connecticut. Photo by Daderot, 2007 (PD-US).

William Carlos Williams (1883–1963) William Carlos Williams was a practicing pediatrician throughout his life; he delivered more than 2,000 babies and wrote poems on his prescription pads. His sympathy for ordinary working people, children, and everyday events in modern urban settings make his poetry attractive and accessible. "The Red Wheelbarrow" (1923), like a Dutch still life, finds interest and beauty in everyday objects (Williams' poems may be found at www.library.utoronto.ca/ utel/rp/authors/wcw.html).

Hart Crane (1899–1932) Hart Crane was a disturbed young poet who committed suicide at age 33 by leaping into the sea. He left striking poems, including an epic, "The Bridge" (1930), which was inspired by the Brooklyn Bridge, in which he ambitiously attempted to review the American cultural experience and recast it in affirmative terms. His exuberant style works best in short poems such as "Voyages" (1923, 1926) and "At Melville's Tomb" (1926), whose ending is a suitable epitaph for Crane:

This fabulous shadow only the sea keeps.

Edna St. Vincent Millay (1892–1950) Millay won a Pulitzer Prize for *The Ballad of the Harp-Weaver* and other poems. While her verse was notorious for archetype images and unoriginal metaphors, it was enjoyed for its easy and lively manner, and she is noted for her mastery of the sonnet form. Her poetry was full of emotion. It seemed to belong to another age. Her poetry was more like Elizabeth Barrett Browning's poetry than some of her contemporaries.

God's World

O world, I cannot hold thee close enough!
Thy winds, thy wide grey skies!
Thy mists, that roll and rise!
Thy woods, this autumn day, that ache and sag
And all but cry with colour! That gaunt crag
To crush! To lift the lean of that black bluff!
World, World, I cannot get thee close enough!

Long have I known a glory in it all,
But never knew I this;
Here such a passion is
As stretcheth me apart, — Lord, I do fear
Thou'st made the world too beautiful this year;
My soul is all but out of me,——let fall
No burning leaf; prithee, let no bird calls.

Renascence

All I could see from where I stood
Was three long mountains and a wood;
I turned and looked the other way,
And saw three islands in a bay.
So with my eyes I traced the line
Of the horizon, thin and fine,
Straight around till I was come
Back to where I'd started from;
And all I saw from where I stood
Was three long mountains and a wood.
Over these things I could not see:
These were the things that bounded me;
And I could touch them with my hand,
Almost, I thought, from where I stand.
And all at once things seemed so small
My breath came short, and scarce at all.
But, sure, the sky is big, I said;

Miles and miles above my head;
So here upon my back I'll lie
And look my fill into the sky.
And so I looked, and, after all,
The sky was not so very tall.
The sky, I said, must somewhere stop,
And — sure enough! — I see the top!
The sky, I thought, is not so grand;
I 'most could touch it with my hand!
And reaching up my hand to try,
I screamed to feel it touch the sky.
I screamed, and — lo! — Infinity
Came down and settled over me;
Forced back my scream into my chest,
Bent back my arm upon my breast,
And, pressing of the Undefined
The definition on my mind,

Held up before my eyes a glass
Through which my shrinking sight did pass
Until it seemed I must behold
Immensity made manifold;
Whispered to me a word whose sound
Deafened the air for worlds around,
And brought unmuffled to my ears
The gossiping of friendly spheres,
The creaking of the tented sky,
The ticking of Eternity.
I saw and heard and knew at last
The How and Why of all things, past,
And present, and forevermore.
The Universe, cleft to the core,
Lay open to my probing sense
That, sick'ning, I would fain pluck thence
But could not, — nay! But needs must suck
At the great wound, and could not pluck
My lips away till I had drawn
All venom out. — Ah, fearful pawn!
For my omniscience paid I toll
In infinite remorse of soul.
All sin was of my sinning, all
Atoning mine, and mine the gall
Of all regret. Mine was the weight
Of every brooded wrong, the hate
That stood behind each envious thrust,
Mine every greed, mine every lust.
And all the while for every grief,
Each suffering, I craved relief
With individual desire, —
Craved all in vain! And felt fierce fire
About a thousand people crawl;
Perished with each, — then mourned for all!
A man was starving in Capri;
He moved his eyes and looked at me;
I felt his gaze, I heard his moan,
And knew his hunger as my own.
I saw at sea a great fog bank
Between two ships that struck and sank;
A thousand screams the heavens smote;

And every scream tore through my throat.
No hurt I did not feel, no death
That was not mine; mine each last breath
That, crying, met an answering cry
From the compassion that was I.
All suffering mine, and mine its rod;
Mine, pity like the pity of God.
Ah, awful weight! Infinity
Pressed down upon the finite Me!
My anguished spirit, like a bird,
Beating against my lips I heard;
Yet lay the weight so close about
There was no room for it without.
And so beneath the weight lay I
And suffered death, but could not die.

Long had I lain thus, craving death,
When quietly the earth beneath
Gave way, and inch by inch, so great
At last had grown the crushing weight,
Into the earth I sank till I
Full six feet under ground did lie,
And sank no more, — there is no weight
Can follow here, however great.
From off my breast I felt it roll,
And as it went my tortured soul
Burst forth and fled in such a gust
That all about me swirled the dust.

Deep in the earth I rested now;
Cool is its hand upon the brow
And soft its breast beneath the head
Of one who is so gladly dead.
And all at once, and over all
The pitying rain began to fall;
I lay and heard each pattering hoof
Upon my lowly, thatchèd roof,
And seemed to love the sound far more
Than ever I had done before.
For rain it hath a friendly sound
To one who's six feet under ground;

And scarce the friendly voice or face:
A grave is such a quiet place.

The rain, I said, is kind to come
And speak to me in my new home.
I would I were alive again
To kiss the fingers of the rain,
To drink into my eyes the shine
Of every slanting silver line,
To catch the freshened, fragrant breeze
From drenched and dripping apple-trees.
For soon the shower will be done,
And then the broad face of the sun
Will laugh above the rain-soaked earth
Until the world with answering mirth
Shakes joyously, and each round drop
Rolls, twinkling, from its grass-blade top.
How can I bear it; buried here,
While overhead the sky grows clear
And blue again after the storm?
O, multi-colored, multiform,
Beloved beauty over me,
That I shall never, never see
Again! Spring-silver, autumn-gold,
That I shall never more behold!
Sleeping your myriad magics through,
Close-sepulchred away from you!
O God, I cried, give me new birth,
And put me back upon the earth!
Upset each cloud's gigantic gourd
And let the heavy rain, down-poured
In one big torrent, set me free,
Washing my grave away from me!

I ceased; and through the breathless hush
That answered me, the far-off rush
Of herald wings came whispering
Like music down the vibrant string
Of my ascending prayer, and — crash!
Before the wild wind's whistling lash
The startled storm-clouds reared on high

And plunged in terror down the sky,
And the big rain in one black wave
Fell from the sky and struck my grave.
I know not how such things can be;
I only know there came to me
A fragrance such as never clings
To aught save happy living things;
A sound as of some joyous elf
Singing sweet songs to please himself,
And, through and over everything,
A sense of glad awakening.
The grass, a-tiptoe at my ear,
Whispering to me I could hear;
I felt the rain's cool finger-tips
Brushed tenderly across my lips,
Laid gently on my sealèd sight,
And all at once the heavy night
Fell from my eyes and I could see, —
A drenched and dripping apple-tree,
A last long line of silver rain,
A sky grown clear and blue again.
And as I looked a quickening gust
Of wind blew up to me and thrust
Into my face a miracle
Of orchard-breath, and with the smell, —
I know not how such things can be! —
I breathed my soul back into me.
Ah! Up then from the ground sprang I
And hailed the earth with such a cry
As is not heard save from a man
Who has been dead, and lives again.
About the trees my arms I wound
Like one gone mad I hugged the ground;
I raised my quivering arms on high;
I laughed and laughed into the sky,
Till at my throat a strangling sob
Caught fiercely, and a great heart-throb
Sent instant tears into my eyes;
O God, I cried, no dark disguise
Can e'er hereafter hide from me
Thy radiant identity!

Thou canst not move across the grass
But my quick eyes will see Thee pass,
Nor speak, however silently,
But my hushed voice will answer Thee.
I know the path that tells Thy way
Through the cool eve of every day;
God, I can push the grass apart
And lay my finger on Thy heart!

The world stands out on either side
No wider than the heart is wide;

Above the world is stretched the sky, —
No higher than the soul is high.
The heart can push the sea and land
Farther away on either hand;
The soul can split the sky in two,
And let the face of God shine through.
But East and West will pinch the heart
That can not keep them pushed apart;
And he whose soul is flat — the sky
Will cave in on him by and by.

Marianne Moore (1887–1972) Marianne Moore once wrote that poems were "imaginary gardens with real toads in them." Her poems are conversational, yet elaborate and subtle in their syllabic versification, drawing upon extremely precise description and historical and scientific fact. A "poet's poet," she influenced such later poets as her young friend Elizabeth Bishop. In his 1925 essay "Marianne Moore," William Carlos Williams wrote about Moore's style: "Moore guides the reader into minute details . . . in looking at some apparently small object, one feels the swirl of great events" (William Carlos Williams, "Marianne Moore" www.enotes.com/marianne-moore.../moore-marianne.../william-carlo...).

Assignments

- • Warm-up: Choose one of the poets discussed in the lesson and copy his/her style of writing in a poem of your own.
- • Students should complete Concept Builder 21-E.
- • Essays are due. Students should take the chapter 21 test.

Read "Poetry" by Marianne Moore, then answer the following questions.

I too, dislike it: there are things that are important beyond all this fiddle.
Reading it, however, with a perfect contempt for it, one discovers that there is in
it after all, a place for the genuine.
Hands that can grasp, eyes
that can dilate, hair that can rise
if it must, these things are important not because a

high-sounding interpretation can be put upon them but because they are
useful; when they become so derivative as to become unintelligible,
the same thing may be said for all of us, that we
do not admire what
we cannot understand: the bat,
holding on upside down or in quest of something to

Beat, elephants pushing, a wild horse taking a roll, a tireless wolf under
a tree, the immovable critic twitching his skin like a horse that feels a flea, the base
ball fan, the statistician —
nor is it valid
to discriminate against "business documents and

school-books": all these phenomena are important. One must make a distinction
however: when dragged into prominence by half poets, the result is not poetry,
nor till the poets among us can be
"literalists of
the imagination" — above
insolence and triviality and can present

for inspection, imaginary gardens with real toads in them, shall we have
it. In the meantime, if you demand on one hand,
the raw material of poetry in
all its rawness and
that which is on the other hand
genuine, then you are interested in poetry.

1	Moore is sympathetic with the reader who dislikes poetry but suggests there are some redeeming qualities. What are these?
2	Do you like these free verse poems? Why does Moore write this way?

Chapter 22

1915–1946 (Part 3):

The Modern Age: Late Romanticism/Naturalism

First Thoughts *A Farewell to Arms* is a powerful story. Wrought with naturalism, the vision of Ernest Hemingway is a bleak one. This is from the end of *A Farewell to Arms*:

> That was what you did. You died. You did not now what it was about. You never had time to learn. They threw you in and told you the rules and the first time they caught you off base they killed you. . . . You could count on that. Stay around and they would kill you.

Americans have journeyed a long way from the Christian theism of Jonathan Edwards. Unfortunately, the naturalism of Ernest Hemingway is closest to the contemporary American vision.

Author Worldview Watch The author once asked his daughter to write a Christian ending to A Farewell to Arms and she did: nothing changed. The wages of sin is death. Yet, in the fiery cauldron of this affair, readers glimpse some hope. These are decent people who are captured by the throes of existentialism (self-love). Existentialism, as the modern world knows all too well, does not mix well with the stark realities or an unsaved, naturalistic world. The Good News is that God so loved the world that He sent His only Begotten Son to die for it. One hopes that on the horizon there will be an American author who gets it.

Chapter Learning Objectives In chapter 22 we analyze *A Farewell to Arms* by Ernest Hemingway.

As a result of this chapter study you will be able to . . .

1. Find examples of social Darwinism in this book.

2. Compare and contrast Frederick Henry and Henry Fleming.

3. Evaluate Hemingway's view of truth.

4. Describe the foils in *A Farewell to Arms*.

5. Analyze a quote by Paul Johnson.

6. Judge the morality of Frederick Henry and Catherine Barkley.

7. Write an alternative ending to this book.

8. What effect does the power of sin have on these characters.

Weekly Essay Options: Begin on page 274 of the Teacher Guide.

Reading ahead: Review *Their Eyes Were Watching God* by Zora Neale Hurston.

History connections: *American History* chapter 22, "America Becomes a World Power"

Background

The Hemingway story is the post-World War I story. The period between the two world wars was the United States' traumatic "coming of age," despite the fact that U.S. direct involvement in World War I was relatively brief (1917–1918) and its casualties many fewer than those of its European allies and foes. Entering World War I to "end all wars," the horror of trench warfare disillusioned a generation. The American author John Dos Passos expressed America's postwar disillusionment in the novel *Three Soldiers* (1921), when he noted that civilization was a "vast edifice of sham, and the war, instead of its crumbling, was its fullest and most ultimate expression." Shocked and permanently changed, Americans returned to their homeland but could never regain their innocence. The carnage that was World War I had permanently changed the American heart.

Many returning farm boy soldiers moved into the city. Millions of southern African Americans moved into northern urban centers. For the first time, many Americans enrolled in higher education — in the 1920s college enrollment doubled. For the first time, colleges had more applicants than places to fill. Americans experienced a cultural revolution when the radio and electric lights were added to their homes. Like the businessman protagonist of Sinclair Lewis's novel *Babbitt* (1922), the average American approved of new conveniences because they were modern and because most were American inventions and American-made. Most people went to the movies once a week. Prohibition — a nation-wide ban on the production, transport, and sale of alcohol instituted through the 18th Amendment to the U.S. Constitution — began in 1919, and under-ground "speakeasies" and nightclubs proliferated, featuring jazz music, cocktails, and daring modes of dress and dance. Dancing, movie going, automobile touring, and radio were national crazes. American women, in particular, felt liberated. Many had left farms and villages for home front duty in American cities during World War I, and had become reso-lutely modern. They cut their hair short ("bobbed"), wore short "flapper" dresses, and gloried in the right to vote assured by the 19th Amendment to the Constitution, passed in 1920. They boldly spoke their mind and took public roles in society. My own grandmother, Helen Stobaugh, did something unthinkable earlier in the century: she divorced her first husband.

A new, liberated world was dawning in America. Youth, too, was rebelling, angry and disillusioned with the savage war, the older generation it held responsible, and difficult post-war economic condi-tions that, ironically, allowed Americans with dollars — like writers F. Scott Fitzgerald, Ernest Hemingway, Gertrude Stein, and Ezra Pound — to live overseas on very little money. Intellectual currents, particu-larly Freudian psychology and to a lesser extent Marxism (like the earlier Darwinian theory of evolution), implied a "godless" worldview and contributed to the breakdown of traditional values. Totalitarianism was growing in Italy and Germany and openly embraced by intellectuals like Ezra Pound. Americans abroad absorbed these views and brought them back to the United States, firing the imagination of young writers and artists. William Faulkner, for example, employed Freudian elements in all his works, as did virtually all serious American fiction writers after World War I. Faulkner was an existentialist — someone who put a lot of emphasis on experience. Americans were having for the first time "an identity crisis." Despite outward unparal-leled material prosperity, young Americans of the

1920s were the first of many of "the lost generations" — so named by essayist Gertrude Stein. As Bob Dylan expressed the soul of my generation, Hemingway's *The Sun Also Rises* (1926) and Fitzgerald's *This Side of Paradise* (1920), decried the extravagance and disillusionment of their lost generation. In T.S. Eliot's long poem *The Waste Land* (1922), Western civilization was symbolized by a bleak desert in desperate need of rain (spiritual renewal). The following is a portion of T.S. Eliot's poem "The Love Song of J. Alfred Prufrock."

The Love Song of J. Alfred Prufrock

Let us go then, you and I,
When the evening is spread out against the sky
Like a patient etherized upon a table;
Let us go, through certain half-deserted streets,
The muttering retreats
Of restless nights in one-night cheap hotels
And sawdust restaurants with oyster-shells:
Streets that follow like a tedious argument
Of insidious intent
To lead you to an overwhelming question. . . .
Oh, do not ask, "What is it?"
Let us go and make our visit.

In the room the women come and go
Talking of Michelangelo.

The yellow fog that rubs its back upon the window-panes,
The yellow smoke that rubs its muzzle on the window-panes

Licked its tongue into the corners of the evening,
Lingered upon the pools that stand in drains,
Let fall upon its back the soot that falls from chimneys,
Slipped by the terrace, made a sudden leap,
And seeing that it was a soft October night,
Curled once about the house, and fell asleep.

And indeed there will be time
For the yellow smoke that slides along the street,
Rubbing its back upon the window panes;
There will be time, there will be time
To prepare a face to meet the faces that you meet
There will be time to murder and create,
And time for all the works and days of hands
That lift and drop a question on your plate;
Time for you and time for me,
And time yet for a hundred indecisions,
And for a hundred visions and revisions,
Before the taking of a toast and tea.

Assignments

- Warm-up: How did the "new, liberated world" help shape Hemingway's writing?
- Students should complete Concept Builder 22-A.
- Students review the required reading(s) *before* the assigned chapter begins.
- Teachers may want to discuss assigned reading(s) with students.
- Teachers shall assign the required essay. The rest of the essays can be outlined, answered with shorter answers, discussed, or skipped.
- Students will review all readings for chapter 22.

The similarities between Frederick Henry and Henry Fleming (in *Red Badge of Courage*) are remarkable. Trace the development of each character.

Incident	Fredrick Henry	Henry Fleming
Decision to join the army.		
The first few battles.		
The end of the book.		

A Farewell to Arms
Ernest Hemingway

The prosperity of the 1920s was a distant memory in 1929 when the stock market crashed and *A Farewell To Arms* was published. The ensuing world depression of the 1930s affected most of the United States. Workers lost their jobs, and factories shut down; businesses and banks failed; farmers could not pay their debts and lost their farms. Midwestern droughts turned the "breadbasket" of America into a dust bowl. Many farmers left the Midwest for California in search of jobs, as vividly described in John Steinbeck's *The Grapes of Wrath* (1939). At the peak of the Depression, one-third of all Americans were out of work. Soup kitchens, shanty towns, and armies of hobos became part of national life. Hard times had hit America and deeply affected American literature and culture.

About the Author

Born in Oak Park, Illinois, in 1899, Ernest Hemingway served in World War I as an ambulance driver with the Italian army. The story in this book is approximately autobiographical. After the war, Hemingway joined other expatriates in Paris. He served as a war correspondent during the Spanish Civil War and World War II. Hemingway was a disturbed man, and in 1961 he committed suicide.

Suggested Vocabulary Words

Chapter VII: feigned

Chapter XV: felicitations

Other Notable Works

The Sun Also Rises (1926)

The Old Man and the Sea (1952)

Assignments

- Warm-up: What would a world in economic turmoil most likely produce in the lives and works of writers?
- Students should complete Concept Builder 22-B.
- Students should review reading(s) from the next chapter.
- Student should outline essay due at the end of the week.
- Per teacher instructions, students may answer orally, in a group setting, some of the essays that are not assigned as formal essays.

The setting is the time and place in which the novel occurs. It is particularly important to *A Farewell to Arms*. Discuss how the setting affects the different elements of the novel.

**Setting:
World War I Italy**

Characters:

Themes:

Plot:

The Real Story

When Hemingway was 18 he tried to enlist in the U.S. army, but was deferred because of poor vision. He therefore volunteered for non-combatant duty with the Red Cross and served in Italy.

On July 8, 1918, only a few weeks after arriving, Hemingway was seriously wounded by fragments from an Austrian mortar shell which had landed just a few feet away. At the time, Hemingway was distributing chocolate and cigarettes to Italian soldiers in the trenches near the front lines. The explosion knocked Hemingway unconscious, killed an Italian soldier, and blew the legs off another.

Hemingway's wounding along the Piave River in Italy and his subsequent recovery at a hospital in Milan, including the relationship with his nurse Agnes von Kurowsky, all inspired his great novel *A Farewell To Arms*. Agnes von Kurowsky Stanfield, an American nurse, became the character of "Catherine Barkley" in the book.

Kurowsky was a nurse in an American Red Cross hospital in Milan during World War I. One of her patients was Hemingway, who fell in love with Kurowsky. There is no evidence to suggest that his feelings were reciprocated by Kurowsky. After the war, Hemingway returned to the United States and invited Kurowsky to join him. Instead, soon after, he received a letter from her ending the relationship. Although Kurowsky did eventually return to the United States, they never met again.

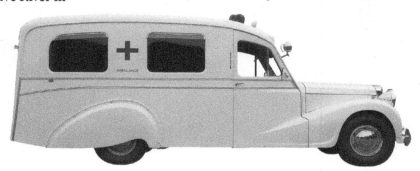

Assignments

- Warm-up: Based on what you have studied this year, in what ways does Western and American literature mirror the same stages?
- Students should complete Concept Builder 22-C.
- Students should write rough drafts of assigned essay.
- The teacher or a peer evaluator may correct rough drafts.

Literary critics call the point of view employed by Hemingway in *A Farewell to Arms* limited, first-person narrator/participant. This means that he writes from the point of view of Frederic Henry, and he tells the reader only what he himself sees, hears, feels, and thinks, never reporting scenes in which he wasn't involved, never entering other characters' minds.

What are advantages and disadvantages of this point of view? Give an example of both.

Advantage	Disadvantage
Perhaps the greatest advantage of this narrative method is that it gives readers a tremendous sense of involvement with the story. Seeing everything through the eyes of an active narrator lets readers participate in the events as they occur, real time, real effect.	The reader has every right to question Henry's credibility. He is judgmental, moody, and jaded in his views. He disrespects authority and, generally, is a typical amoral naturalist narrator.
Example	Example

LESSON 4

A Farewell To Arms

Cinema Versions

1932 — Gary Cooper and Helen Hayes

1957 — Rock Hudson and Jennifer Jones

Film poster for the 1932 Paramount
Pictures film *A Farewell to Arms* (PD-US).

Assignments

- Warm-up: Watch one of these movie versions and compare it to the book.
- Students should complete Concept Builder 22-D.
- Students will rewrite corrected copy of essay due tomorrow.

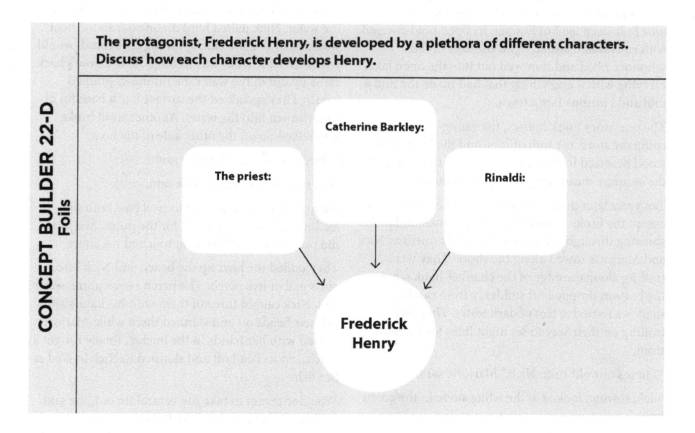

CONCEPT BUILDER 22-D
Foils

The protagonist, Frederick Henry, is developed by a plethora of different characters. Discuss how each character develops Henry.

Catherine Barkley:

The priest:

Rinaldi:

Frederick Henry

"The End of Something"
Ernest Hemingway

In the old days Hortons Bay was a lumbering town. No one who lived in it was out of sound of the big saws in the mill by the lake. Then one year there were no more logs to make lumber. The lumber schooners came into the bay and were loaded with the cut of the mill that stood stacked in the yard. All the piles of lumber were carried away. The big mill building had all its machinery that was removable taken out and hoisted on board one of the schooners by the men who had worked in the mill. The schooner moved out of the bay toward the open lake, carrying the two great saws, the travelling carriage that hurled the logs against the revolving, circular saws and all the rollers, wheels, belts and iron piled on a hull-deep load of lumber. Its open hold covered with canvas and lashed tight, the sails of the schooner filled and it moved out into the open lake, carrying with it everything that had made the mill a mill and Hortons Bay a town.

The one-story bunk houses, the eating-house, the company store, the mill offices, and the big mill itself stood deserted in the acres of sawdust that covered the swampy meadow by the shore of the bay.

Ten years later there was nothing of the mill left except the broken white limestone of its foundations showing through the swampy second growth as Nick and Marjorie rowed along the shore. They were trolling along the edge of the channel-bank where the bottom dropped off suddenly from sandy shallows to twelve feet of dark water. They were trolling on their way to set night lines for rainbow trout.

"There's our old ruin, Nick," Marjorie said.

Nick, rowing, looked at the white stone in the green trees.

"There it is," he said.

"Can you remember when it was a mill?" Marjorie asked.

"I can just remember," Nick said.

"It seems more like a castle," Marjorie said.

Nick said nothing. They rowed on out of sight of the mill, following the shore line. Then Nick cut across the bay.

"They aren't striking," he said.

"No," Marjorie said. She was intent on the rod all the time they trolled, even when she talked. She loved to fish. She loved to fish with Nick.

Close beside the boat a big trout broke the surface of the water. Nick pulled hard on one oar so the boat would turn and the bait, spinning far behind, would pass where the trout was feeding. As the trout's back came up out of the water the minnows jumped wildly. They sprinkled the surface like a handful of shot thrown into the water. Another trout broke water, feeding on the other side of the boat.

"They're feeding," Marjorie said.

"But they won't strike," Nick said.

He rowed the boat around to troll past both the feeding fish, then headed it for the point. Marjorie did not reel in until the boat touched the shore.

They pulled the boat up the beach and Nick lifted out a pail of live perch. The perch swam in the water pail. Nick caught three of them with his hands and cut heir heads off and skinned them while Marjorie chased with her hands in the bucket, finally caught a perch, cut its head off and skinned it. Nick looked at her fish.

"You don't want to take the ventral fin out," he said. "It'll be all right for bait but it's better with the ventral fin in."

He hooked each of the skinned perch through the tail. There were two hooks attached to a leader on each rod. Then Marjorie rowed the boat out over the channel-bank, holding the line in her teeth, and looking toward Nick, who stood on the shore holding the rod and letting the line run out from the reel.

"That's about right," he called.

"Should I let it drop?" Marjorie called back, holding the line in her hand.

"Sure. Let it go." Marjorie dropped the line overboard and watched the baits go down through the water.

She came in with the boat and ran the second line out the same way. Each time Nick set a heavy slab of driftwood across the butt of the rod to hold it solid and propped it up at an angle with a small slab. He reeled in the slack line so the line ran taut out to where the bait rested on the sandy floor of the channel and set the click on the reel. When a trout, feeding on the bottom, took the bait it would run with it, taking line out of the reel in a rush and making the reel sing with the click on.

Marjorie rowed up the point a little way so she would not disturb the line. She pulled hard on the oars and the boat went up the beach. Little waves came in with it. Marjorie stepped out of the boat and Nick pulled the boat high up the beach.

"What's the matter, Nick?" Marjorie asked.

"I don't know," Nick said, getting wood for a fire.

They made a fire with driftwood. Marjorie went to the boat and brought a blanket. The evening breeze blew the smoke toward the point, so Marjorie spread the blanket out between the fire and the lake.

Marjorie sat on the blanket with her back to the fire and waited for Nick. He came over and sat down beside her on the blanket. In back of them was the close second-growth timber of the point and in front was the bay with the mouth of Hortons Creek. It was not quite dark. The fire-light went as far as the water. They could both see the two steel rods at an angle over the dark water. The fire glinted on the reels.

Marjorie unpacked the basket of supper.

"I don't feel like eating," said Nick.

"Come on and eat, Nick."

"All right."

They ate without talking, and watched the two rods and the fire-light in the water.

"There's going to be a moon tonight," said Nick. He looked across the bay to the hills that were beginning to sharpen against the sky. Beyond the hills he knew the moon was coming up.

"I know it," Marjorie said happily.

"You know everything," Nick said.

"Oh, Nick, please cut it out! Please, please don't be that way!"

"I can't help it," Nick said. "You do. You know everything. That's the trouble. You know you do."

Marjorie did not say anything.

"I've taught you everything. You know you do. What don't you know, anyway?"

"Oh, shut up," Marjorie said. "There comes the moon."

They sat on the blanket without touching each other and watched the moon rise.

"You don't have to talk silly," Marjorie said. "What's really the matter?"

"I don't know."

"Of course you know."

"No I don't."

"Go on and say it."

Nick looked on at the moon, coming up over the hills.

"It isn't fun any more."

He was afraid to look at Marjorie. Then he looked at her. She sat there with her back toward him. He looked at her back. "It isn't fun any more. Not any of it."

She didn't say anything. He went on. "... I don't know, Marge. I don't know what to say."

He looked on at her back.

"Isn't love any fun?" Marjorie said.

"No," Nick said. Marjorie stood up. Nick sat there, his head in his hands.

"I'm going to take the boat," Marjorie called to him. "You can walk back around the point."

"All right," Nick said. "I'll push the boat off for you."

"You don't need to," she said. She was afloat in the boat on the water with the moonlight on it. Nick went back and lay down with his face in the blanket by the fire. He could hear Marjorie rowing on the water.

He lay there for a long time. He lay there while he heard Bill come into the clearing walking around through the woods. He felt Bill coming up to the fire. Bill didn't touch him, either.

"Did she go all right?" Bill said.

"Yes," Nick said, lying, his face on the blanket.

"Have a scene?"

"No, there wasn't any scene."

"How do you feel?"

"Oh, go away, Bill! Go away for a while."

Bill selected a sandwich from the lunch basket and walked over to have a look at the rods.

Earnest Hemingway, In Our Time, "The End of Something," (New York: Scribners, 1925), www.repeatafterus.com/title.php?i=8752.

Assignments

- Warm-up: What aspect of a fictional character helps connect you to him or her??
- Students should complete Concept Builder 22-E.
- Essays are due. Students should take the chapter 22 test

CONCEPT BUILDER 22-E Active Reading		Read "The End of Something" by Ernest Hemingway then answer the following questions.
	1	Compare this writing style to the writing style in *A Farewell to Arms*.
	2	Predict the ending of this short story.
	3	How does the history of Hortons Bay parallel the relationship of Marge and Nick?
	4	What is wrong with Nick?
	5	Ask Nick and Marge a question.
	6	Why is Nick irritated at Marjorie?

Chapter 23

1915–1946 (Part 4):
The Modern Age:
Late Romanticism/Naturalism

First Thoughts

Literary critic Sterling Brown in *The Nation*, October 16, 1937 wrote:

> Janie's grandmother, remembering how in slavery she was used "for a work-ox and a brood sow," and remembering her daughter's shame, seeks Janie's security above all else. But to Janie, her husband, for all his sixty acres, looks like "some old skull-head in de graveyard," and she goes off down the road with slick-talking Jody Sparks. In Eatonville, an all-colored town, Jody becomes the "big voice," but Janie is first neglected and then browbeaten. When Jody dies, Tea Cake, with his contagious high spirits, whirls Janie into a marriage, idyllic until Tea Cake's tragic end. Janie returns home, grief-stricken but fulfilled. Better than her grandmother's security, she had found out about living for herself (people.virginia.edu/~sfr/enam854/summer/hurston.html).

We find in this novel by Thurston something new — or rather, something old, but new again. Thurston reminds us again that something more than the ravages of naturalism will sell novels after all.

Author Worldview Watch

Zora Neale Hurston is a welcome interlude--but only that--in a long, depressing naturalistic drama that is 20th century American literature. Hurston's protagonist, like Hurston herself, do have eyes that see God, but one only wishes that one will embrace that God! Using a frame story, more popular in 19th century that it is in 20th century prose, Hurston tells a multi-layer of love and hope in a time when both were desperately needed in America. This tale is made even more poignant by the fact that African-American Hurston, working for the WPA, was relying on the largesse of a country that disenfranchised her. Nonetheless, Hurston does not give into hatred and scorn, like Langston Hughes and James Baldwin, and readers are the better for it.

Chapter Learning Objectives

In chapter 23 we enjoy Zora Thurston's *Their Eyes Were Watching God*.

As a result of this chapter study you will be able to . . .

1. Discuss the form that Hurston employs to tell her story.
2. Discuss Hurston's narrative technique.
3. Exhibit two themes in this book.
4. Draw parallels between Janie's life and Hannah's life.

Weekly Essay Options: Begin on page 274 of the Teacher Guide.

Reading ahead: *The Unvanquished* by William Faulkner.

383

Their Eyes Were Watching God
Zora Neale Hurston (1937)

Background Zora Neale Hurston was born around 1900 in Alabama but moved when she was still very young to Eatonville, Florida. For the rest of her life she explored the mystery of being born, and then lived for the majority of her life in that small town. She died on January 28, 1960.

An American folk writer whose works influenced a generation of African-American authors, she wrote an anthropological study of her racial heritage at a time when African-American culture was not a popular field of study.

Hurston was educated at Howard University, Barnard College, and Columbia University. Like Ashley Bryan, Zora Hurston collected African-American folklore. *Mules and Men* (1935), one of her best-known folklore collections, was based on her field research in the American South. *Tell My Horse* (1938) described folk customs in Haiti and Jamaica. Her best-known novel is *Their Eyes Were Watching God* (1937), in which she tracked a Southern black woman's search, over 25 years and three marriages, for her true identity and a community in which she could develop that identity.

Other Worlds

Mules and Men (1935)

Assignments

- Warm-up: Zora Neale Hurston's protagonist and her family had very little to do with the white community. In fact, Hurston says very little about interactions between the races (the main source of prejudice is exhibited by another African American, Mrs. Turner). How have other American authors handled race-mixing in American culture?
- Students should complete Concept Builder 23-A.
- Students review the required reading(s) *before* the assigned chapter begins.
- Teachers may want to discuss assigned reading(s) with students.
- Teachers shall assign the required essay. The rest of the essays can be outlined, answered with shorter answers, discussed, or skipped.
- Students will review all readings for chapter 23.

A frame story is a story within a story. What are the two stories in this novel? What advantage does that offer the author?

Characters

Assignments

- Warm-up: Identify the role of these characters: protagonist, antagonist, foil.
- Students should complete Concept Builder 23-B.
- Students should review reading(s) from the next chapter.
- Student should outline essay due at the end of the week.
- Per teacher instructions, students may answer orally, in a group setting, some of the essays that are not assigned as formal essays.

A frame story is a story within a story. What are the two stories in this novel? What advantage does that offer the author?

Insights into character through
(commentary:)

Insights into character through
(dialogue:)

Narrative Technique

Limited Omniscient

Harlem Renaissance

Hurston was a member of the Harlem Renaissance. The Harlem Renaissance was an African-American cultural movement of the late 1920s and early 1930s in the Harlem section of New York City. For the first time, African-American literature attracted significant attention. African American artists shared a strong sense of racial pride. Major prose writers in the movement were W.E.B. Du Bois and Langston Hughes. Thurston profoundly influenced the Harlem Renaissance writers of the 1930s and she herself was influenced by them. She also greatly inspired later African-American authors such as Toni Morrison. However, this theistic writer wrote with spirit and joy absent from so many writers like Ralph Ellison and Toni Morrison.

Assignments

- Warm-up: Which author has influenced you more than any other?
- Students should complete Concept Builder 23-C.
- Students should write rough drafts of assigned essay.
- The teacher may correct rough drafts.

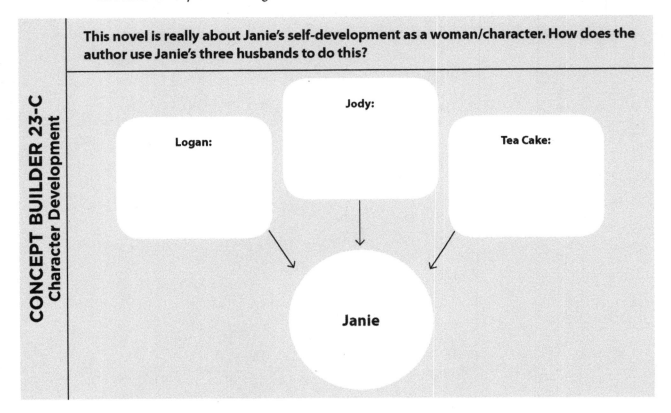

CONCEPT BUILDER 23-C
Character Development

This novel is really about Janie's self-development as a woman/character. How does the author use Janie's three husbands to do this?

Logan:

Jody:

Tea Cake:

Janie

Criticism

In *Their Eyes Were Watching God*, Miss Hurston has fulfilled the early promise of her first books. Her writing is of the essence of poetry, deeply communicative, possessed of a primitive rhythm that speaks truly to the consciousness even before thought can form. This new novel is one of warmth and humor and rich, transcendent beauty. Janie's conscious life had begun at Grandma's gate. When Nanny had spied Janie letting Johnny Taylor kiss her over the gatepost she had called Janie to come inside the house. That had been the end of her childhood. Soon after that Janie and Logan Killicks were married in Nanny's parlor. But love did not come to Janie as Nanny had told her it would. And one day Joe Starks, "from in and through Georgy," came walking down the road. Though he did not represent sun-up and pollen and blooming trees, Joe spoke for far horizons, for change and chance, and Janie at last agreed to go off with him. But in the years of their marriage Janie was never very happy with him. When Joe died, Janie was not yet forty and still a handsome woman. She had refused more than one offer of marriage before the day that Tea Cake stepped into the store. He was younger than she, so much younger that at first Janie dared not believe in the happiness he brought to her. But their life together told her all that she needed to know. This is the story of Miss Hurston's own people, but it is also a story of all peoples — of man and of woman, and of the mystery that the world holds (Zora Neale Hurston, *Their Eyes Were Watching God*, first edition, Philadelphia, PA: J.B. Lippincott Co., 1937, unsigned publisher's foreword).

The central character is Janie, born to love and look for love through three marriages. She escapes from the first marriage, with a steady but middle-aged and unsympathetic farmer, to run away with Joe Starks, an unusual and delightful Negro go-getter

Portrait of two young African American women. Photographer unknown, 1870 (LOC, PD-US).

with something in him of Babbit and a little of the Emperor Jones. How Joe becomes mayor, boss, and plutocrat of Eatonville, is a good story, humorous, eventful, and full of character. Rewarding as Joe is to the reader, he is a disappointment to Janie; when he becomes too successful he doesn't love her any more; and Janie, though she is cowed by public opinion, eventually goes off with Tea Cake, a shiftless, warm-blooded gambler who leads her a chase but makes her happy. The rest of their story is of their life and work together on a Florida plantation, until a hurricane brings on a melodramatic, but credible, conclusion.

The only weak spots in the novel are technical; it begins awkwardly with a confusing and unnecessary preview of the end; and the dramatic action, as in the story of the hurricane, is sometimes hurriedly and clumsily handled. Otherwise the narration is exactly right, because most of it is in dialogue, and the dialogue gives us a constant sense of character in action. No one has ever reported the speech of Negroes with a more accurate ear for its raciness, its rich invention, and its music. In many ways *Their Eyes Were Watching God* recalls Lyle Saxon's recent *Children of Strangers*; both of them are love stories of women with mixed blood; and in both there is an undertone, never loud enough to be isolated, of racial frustration. But Their Eyes Were Watching God has much more humor in it; and paradoxically — possibly because the author is writing unselfconsciously of her own people — it is more objective. It never comes to the verge of conscious, sentimental "sympathy." A simple and unpretentious story, but there is nothing else quite like it (Review by George Stevens, *The Saturday Review of Literature*, September 18, 1937).

Young African-American woman. Photographer unknown, 1910 (LOC, PD-US).

Assignments

- Warm-up: Agree or disagree with each critic
- Students should complete Concept Builder 23-D.
- Student will re-write corrected copies of essay due tomorrow.

CONCEPT BUILDER 23-D Motifs	Motifs are recurring themes that can develop the text's major themes. Discuss how the author develops these motifs.	
	Community	
	Race Relations	
	Husband/Wife Relationship	

Black Dialect

When *Their Eyes Were Watching God* was published in 1937, it met with mixed reviews from critics, with the most critical of these reviews coming from African-American male critics like Richard Wright. Wright was horrified that Hurston had not focused on the issue of black repression and race relations in her novel. However, Hurston was not making a statement about race relations or social injustices. Hurston herself stated that she did "not belong to the sobbing school of Negrohood who hold that nature somehow has given them a lowdown dirty deal and whose feelings are all hurt about it" (personal.centenary.edu/~agardner/Use.html).

Dialect or black English vernacular as a literary device was not merely a figure of spoken speech; rather, for Hurston, it was a reservoir of life and love. It was this love and appreciation for black culture that led to Hurston's use of dialect and folklore in her fiction. There was no political purpose.

Zora Neale Hurston. Photo by Carl Van Vechten, 1938 (PD-US).

How it Feels to Be Colored Me by Zora Neale Hurston

I am colored but I offer nothing in the way of extenuating circumstances except the fact that I am the only Negro in the United States whose grandfather on the mother's side was not an Indian chief.

I remember the very day that I became colored. Up to my thirteenth year I lived in the little Negro town of Eatonville, Florida. It is exclusively a colored town. The only white people I knew passed through the town going to or coming from Orlando. The native whites rode dusty horses, the Northern tourists chugged down the sandy village road in automobiles. The town knew the Southerners and never stopped cane chewing when they passed. But the Northerners were something else again. They were peered at cautiously from behind curtains by the timid. The more venturesome would come out on the porch to watch them go past and got just as much pleasure out of the tourists as the tourists got out of the village.

The front porch might seem a daring place for the rest of the town, but it was a gallery seat for me. My favorite place was atop the gatepost. Proscenium box for a born first-nighter. Not only did I enjoy the show, but I didn't mind the actors knowing that I liked it. I usually spoke to them in passing. I'd wave at them and when they returned my salute, I would say something like this: "Howdy-do-well-I-thank-you-where-you-goin'?" Usually automobile or the horse paused at this, and after a queer exchange of compliments, I would probably "go a piece of the way" with them, as we say in farthest Florida. If one of my family happened to come to the front in time to see me, of course negotiations would be rudely broken off. But even so, it is clear that I was the first "welcome-to-our-state" Floridian, and I hope the Miami Chamber of Commerce will please take notice.

During this period, white people differed from colored to me only in that they rode through town and never lived there. They liked to hear me "speak pieces" and sing and wanted to see me dance the parse-me-la, and gave me generously of their small silver for doing these things, which seemed strange to me for I wanted to do them so much that I needed bribing to stop, only they didn't know it. The colored people gave no dimes. They deplored any joyful tendencies in me, but I was their Zora nevertheless. I belonged to them, to the nearby hotels, to the county — everybody's Zora.

But changes came in the family when I was thirteen, and I was sent to school in Jacksonville. I left Eatonville, the town of the oleanders, a Zora. When I disembarked from the river-boat at Jacksonville, she was no more. It seemed that I had suffered a sea change. I was not Zora of Orange County any more, I was now a little colored girl. I found it out in certain ways. In my heart as well as in the mirror, I became a fast brown — warranted not to rub nor run.

But I am not tragically colored. There is no great sorrow dammed up in my soul, nor lurking behind my eyes. I do not mind at all. I do not belong to the sobbing school of Negrohood who hold that nature somehow has given them a lowdown dirty deal and whose feelings are all but about it. Even in the helter-skelter skirmish that is my life, I have seen that the world is to the strong regardless of a little pigmentation more of less. No, I do not weep at the world — I am too busy sharpening my oyster knife.

Someone is always at my elbow reminding me that I am the granddaughter of slaves. It fails to register depression with me. Slavery is sixty years in the past. The operation was successful and the patient is doing well, thank you. The terrible struggle that made me an American out of a potential slave said "On the line!" The Reconstruction said "Get set!" and the generation before said "Go!" I am off to a flying start and I must not halt in the stretch to look behind and weep. Slavery is the price I paid for civilization, and the choice was not with me. It is a bully adventure and worth all that I have paid through my ancestors for it. No one on earth ever had a greater chance for glory. The world to be won and nothing to be lost. It is thrilling to think — to know that for any act of mine, I shall get twice as much praise or twice as much blame. It is quite exciting to hold the center of the national stage, with the spectators not knowing whether to laugh or to weep.

The position of my white neighbor is much more difficult. No brown specter pulls up a chair beside me when I sit down to eat. No dark ghost thrusts its leg against mine in bed. The game of keeping what one has is never so exciting as the game of getting.

I do not always feel colored. Even now I often achieve the unconscious Zora of Eatonville before the Hegira. I feel most colored when I am thrown against a sharp white background.

For instance at Barnard. "Beside the waters of the Hudson" I feel my race. Among the thousand white persons, I am a dark rock surged upon, and overswept, but through it all, I remain myself. When covered by the waters, I am; and the ebb but reveals me again.

Sometimes it is the other way around. A white person is set down in our midst, but the contrast is just as sharp for me. For instance, when I sit in the drafty basement that is The New World Cabaret with a white person, my color comes. We enter chatting about any little nothing that we have in common and are seated by the jazz waiters. In the abrupt way that jazz orchestras have, this one plunges into a number. It loses no time in circumlocutions, but gets right down to business. It constricts the thorax and splits the heart with its tempo and narcotic harmonies. This orchestra grows rambunctious, rears on its hind legs and attacks the tonal veil with primitive fury, rending it, clawing it until it breaks through to the jungle beyond. I follow those heathen — follow them exultingly. I dance wildly inside myself; I yell within, I whoop; I shake my assegai above my head, I hurl it true to the mark yeeeeooww! I am in the jungle and living in the jungle way. My face is painted red and yellow and my body is painted blue. My pulse is throbbing like a war drum. I want to slaughter something — give pain, give death to what, I do not know. But the piece ends. The men of the orchestra wipe their lips and rest their fingers. I creep back slowly to the veneer we call civilization with the last tone and find the white friend sitting motionless in his seat, smoking calmly.

"Good music they have here," he remarks, drumming the table with his fingertips.

Music. The great blobs of purple and red emotion have not touched him. He has only heard what I felt. He is far away and I see him but dimly across the ocean and the continent that have fallen between us. He is so pale with his whiteness then and I am so colored.

At certain times I have no race, I am me. When I set my hat at a certain angle and saunter down Seventh Avenue, Harlem City, feeling as snooty as the lions in front of the Forty-Second Street Library, for instance. So far as my feelings are concerned, Peggy Hopkins Joyce on the Boule Mich with her gorgeous raiment, stately carriage, knees knocking together in a most aristocratic manner, has nothing on me. The cosmic Zora emerges. I belong to no race nor time. I am the eternal feminine with its string of beads.

I have no separate feeling about being an American citizen and colored. I am merely a fragment of the Great Soul that surges within the boundaries. My country, right or wrong.

Sometimes, I feel discriminated against, but it does not make me angry. It merely astonishes me.

How can any deny themselves the pleasure of my company? It's beyond me.

But in the main, I feel like a brown bag of miscellany propped against a wall. Against a wall in company with other bags, white, red and yellow. Pour out the contents, and there is discovered a jumble of small, things priceless and worthless. A first-water diamond, an empty spool, bits of broken glass, lengths of string, a key to a door long since crumbled away, a rusty knife-blade, old shoes saved for a road that never was and never will be, a nail bent under the weight of things too heavy for any nail, a dried flower or two still a little fragrant. In your hand is the brown bag. On the ground before you is the jumble it held — so much like the jumble in the bags, could they be emptied, that all might be dumped in a single heap and the bags refilled without altering the content of any greatly. A bit of colored glass more or less would not matter. Perhaps that is how the Great Stuffer of Bags filled them in the first place — who knows?

(xroads.virginia.edu/~ma01/grand-jean/hurston/chapters/how.html).

Assignments

- Warm-up: Which author has influenced you more than any other?
- Students should complete Concept Builder 23-E.
- Essays are due. Students should take the chapter 23 test.

CONCEPT BUILDER 23-E Active Reading		Read *How it Feels to Be Colored Me* by Zora Neale Hurston in the text and then answer the following questions.
	1	What changes occurred when the author moved to Jacksonville?
	2	The author opens this essay with a satirical statement. Satire is the use of wit to criticize behavior: the use of wit, especially irony, sarcasm, and ridicule, to criticize faults. In other words, the author is poking fun at herself! Explain.
	3	What astonishes the author? Why?
	4	What does the author mean, "Slavery is the price I paid for civilization, and the choice was not with me."

Chapter 24

1915–1946 (Part 5):

The Modern Age: Late Romanticism/Naturalism

First Thoughts

The Unvanquished is not the best book written by William Faulkner — arguably the best novelist in all of world history — but it is one of his best and one of his most readable. This story occurs in the Civil War and begins the Sartoris legends.

Author Worldview Watch

William Faulkner, like the South, the region in which he wrote and loved so fervently, is a mixed bag. Bayard, his protagonist, is clearly a theist, as are all the most admired characters in this novel (e.g., Granny). Goodness, mercy, grace--all Judeo-Christian values--are damaged in translation because, regardless of Faulkner's able stewardship, these precious gifts cannot be fully transmitted through tradition and good intentions. Judeo-Christian morality, without biblical underpinnings, are shallow, maudlin traveling companions. Faulkner and other contemporaries — e.g., Sherwood Anderson, F. Scott Fitzgerald — all learn that one cannot have one's cake and eat it too: one cannot live and believe like a godless Philistine and worship the God at Shiloh.

Chapter Learning Objectives

In chapter 24 you will analyze *The Unvanquished* and "The Tall Men" by William Faulkner.

As a result of this chapter study you will be able to . . .

1. Evaluate the point of view choice in *The Unvanquished*.
2. Discuss Faulkner's writing style.
3. In "The Tall Man," compare and contrast the worldview of the state draft investigator and the marshal.
4. State whether Faulkner's title for "The Tall Man" is correct.
5. Discuss the narrative technique in "The Tall Man."
6. Analyze the plot in "The Tall Man."
7. Compare and contrast this short story in style and substance with *The Unvanquished*.
8. Analyze the concept of family sin.
9. Discuss Faulkner's use of colloquial language.

Weekly Essay Options: Begin on page 274 of the Teacher Guide.

Reading ahead: *The Pearl* by John Steinbeck.

 History connections: *American History* chapter 24, "American Life: 1900–1940"

The Unvanquished
William Faulkner

About the Author William Faulkner (1897–1962) came from an old Mississippi family alive with Southern tradition. He created a fictional location, Yoknapatawpha County, which captured the essence of Southern life. Faulkner was a prolific writer and has left our nation with a rich corpus of literature.

Other Notable Works

The Sound and The Fury (1929)

Light in August (1932)

Vocabulary Words

Chapter I: impunity, dispensation

Chapter II: cajoling, annihilation, inviolate

Assignments

- Warm-up: Why is the setting so important to this novel?
- Students should complete Concept Builder 24-A.
- Students review the required reading(s) *before* the assigned chapter begins.
- Teachers may want to discuss assigned reading(s) with students.
- Teachers shall assign the required essay. The rest of the essays can be outlined, answered with shorter answers, discussed, or skipped.
- Students will review all readings for chapter 24.

CONCEPT BUILDER 24-A Granny	**Compare your grandmother to Granny Millard from William Faulkner's *The Unvanquished*.**	
	Bayard's grandmother, Granny, was a stubborn old woman who becomes the novel's most authentic heroine. She is a literalist. A great moral person. At the same time, she sets up a mule-stealing scam against the Yankees that lasts for almost a year, which relies on her fragile, elderly appearance and her brilliant cunning. Her death is the novel's turning point and its emotional climax.	

Nobel Prize in Literature 1949

Ladies and gentlemen,

I feel that this award was not made to me as a man, but to my work — a life's work in the agony and sweat of the human spirit, not for glory and least of all for profit, but to create out of the materials of the human spirit something which did not exist before. So this award is only mine in trust. It will not be difficult to find a dedication for the money part of it commensurate with the purpose and significance of its origin. But I would like to do the same with the acclaim too, by using this moment as a pinnacle from which I might be listened to by the young men and women already dedicated to the same anguish and travail, among whom is already that one who will some day stand here where I am standing.

Our tragedy today is a general and universal physical fear so long sustained by now that we can even bear it. There are no longer problems of the spirit. There is only the question: When will I be blown up? Because of this, the young man or woman writing today has forgotten the problems of the human heart in conflict with itself which alone can make good writing because only that is worth writing about, worth the agony and the sweat.

He must learn them again. He must teach himself that the basest of all things is to be afraid; and, teaching himself that, forget it forever, leaving no room in his workshop for anything but the old verities and truths of the heart, the old universal truths lacking which any story is ephemeral and doomed - love and honor and pity and pride and compassion and sacrifice. Until he does so, he labors under a curse. He writes not of love but of lust, of defeats in which nobody loses anything of value, of victories without hope and, worst of all, without pity or compassion. His griefs grieve on no universal bones, leaving no scars. He writes not of the heart but of the glands.

Until he relearns these things, he will write as though he stood among and watched the end of man. I decline to accept the end of man. It is easy enough to say that man is immortal simply because he will endure: that when the last dingdong of doom has clanged and faded from the last worthless rock hanging tideless in the last red and dying evening, that even then there will still be one more sound: that of his puny inexhaustible voice, still talking.

I refuse to accept this. I believe that man will not merely endure: he will prevail. He is immortal, not because he alone among creatures has an inexhaustible voice, but because he has a soul, a spirit capable of compassion and sacrifice and endurance. The poet's, the writer's, duty is to write about these things. It is his privilege to help man endure by lifting his heart, by reminding him of the courage and honor and hope and pride and compassion and pity and sacrifice which have been the glory of his past. The poet's voice need not merely be the record of man, it can be one of the props, the pillars to help him endure and prevail (Horst Frenz, editor, *Literature*, Amsterdam, NY: Elsevier Publishing Co., 1969, Nobel Lectures 1901–1967).

Assignments

- Warm-up: I think Faulkner is the greatest novelist of all time. Do you agree?
- Students should complete Concept Builder 24-B.
- Students should review reading(s) from the next chapter.
- Student should outline essay due at the end of the week.
- Per teacher instructions, students may answer orally, in a group setting, some of the essays that are not assigned as formal essays.

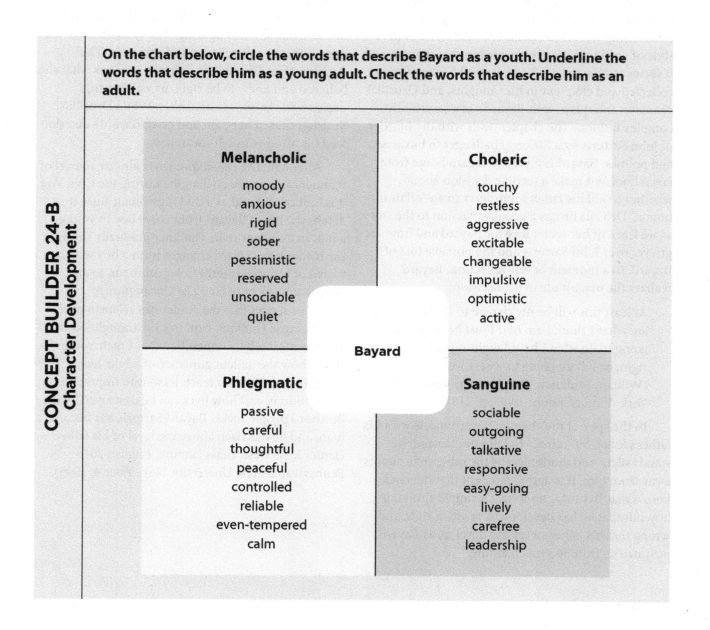

CONCEPT BUILDER 24-B
Character Development

On the chart below, circle the words that describe Bayard as a youth. Underline the words that describe him as a young adult. Check the words that describe him as an adult.

Melancholic

moody
anxious
rigid
sober
pessimistic
reserved
unsociable
quiet

Choleric

touchy
restless
aggressive
excitable
changeable
impulsive
optimistic
active

Bayard

Phlegmatic

passive
careful
thoughtful
peaceful
controlled
reliable
even-tempered
calm

Sanguine

sociable
outgoing
talkative
responsive
easy-going
lively
carefree
leadership

The Last Chapter

The last chapter of *The Unvanquished* was written to tie up the story for publication as a novel, and it is by far the most introspective. An "odor of verbena" deals with Bayard's self-realization, as well as his relationship with Drusilla and his father. Faulkner's style of writing is greatly elevated in this chapter, and it seems to come of age itself. Bayard becomes more collected and eloquent in his thoughts, and Drusilla's character interplays with Bayard's in a beautifully complex fashion. The chapter deals with the murder of John Sartoris by a lifelong challenger in business and politics. Bayard is forced to return home from law school and make a terrible decision about whether to kill his father's murderer in an "affair of honor." Drusilla brings a genuine passion to the story as we learn of her secret love for Bayard and how she grieves over John Sartoris and the possible loss of Bayard. In a moment of self-reflection, Bayard realizes the magnitude of his decision:

> At least this will be my chance to find out if I am what I think I am of if I just hope; if I am going to do what I have taught myself is right, or if I am going to wish I were (William Faulkner, *The Unvanquished*, New York: Vintage Books, 1965, p. 215).

In the apex of the chapter, Bayard meets with his father's killer, but refuses to kill him. Instead, he stands silent and motionless as the other man shoots away from him. It is at this moment that the reader knows that Bayard is no longer a simple-thinking boy, but that he has developed a sense of right and wrong that his father never did develop, as Bayard postulates, "from too much killing."

Throughout the last chapter, Faulkner uses a motif of the scent of the verbena, which is a flower Drusilla constantly wears. She says it is because it was the only flower she could smell above the odor of war while she was fighting. The symbolism of the odor is that of self-reliance and principle. The decision Drusilla made to fight the war was what she believed and knew to be right, as was Bayard's decision not to avenge his father. While Drusilla's decision caused her pain and grief, Bayard's decision feed his mind with self-awareness.

Although *The Unvanquished* is almost a novel of manners set against civilian life during the Civil War, it is best considered as a bildungsroman since it details the life of Bayard from naïve boy to young adult. In excellent style, Faulkner gradually shows the reader how Bayard changes from a boy who is scared of his grandmother's punishment, to an articulate student of law. *The Unvanquished* describes scenes that the reader can relate to over time because Faulkner captures the thoughts and feelings most adults remember about their youth. He shows how the patient guidance of adults like Bayard's grandmother teach lessons to impressionable children, and how lives can be destroyed by the decisions people make. Bayard Sartoris has become a man, and he has risen above the level of his father (James L.W. West, Class Lecture, English 261, Pennsylvania State University, November 4, 1996).

- Warm-up: The last chapter, "An Odor of Verbena," has been criticized as being an entirely different story, or a story within a story. Some critics wonder if it really belongs. What do you think?

- Students should complete Concept Builder 24-C.

- Students should write rough drafts of assigned essay.

- The teacher may correct rough drafts.

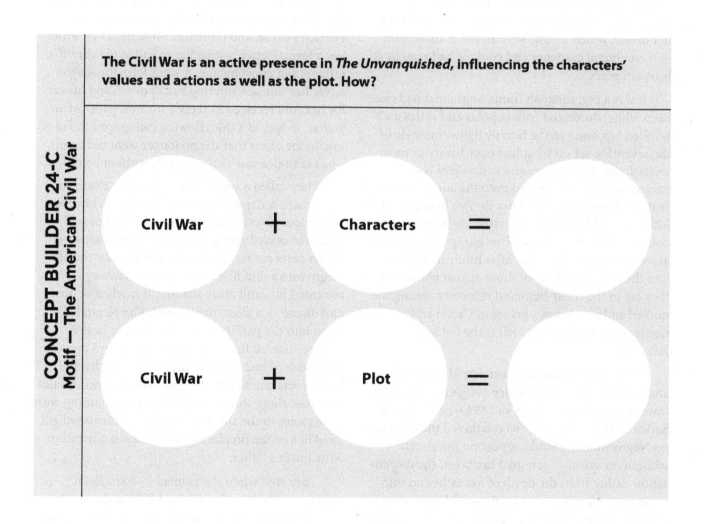

CONCEPT BUILDER 24-C
Motif — The American Civil War

The Civil War is an active presence in *The Unvanquished*, influencing the characters' values and actions as well as the plot. How?

Civil War + Characters =

Civil War + Plot =

A Rose For Emily
William Faulkner

When Miss Emily Grierson died, our whole town went to her funeral: the men through a sort of respectful affection for a fallen monument, the women mostly out of curiosity to see the inside of her house, which no one save an old man-servant — a combined gardener and cook — had seen in at least ten years.

It was a big, squarish frame house that had once been white, decorated with cupolas and spires and scrolled balconies in the heavily lightsome style of the seventies, set on what had once been our most select street. But garages and cotton gins had encroached and obliterated even the august names of that neighborhood; only Miss Emily's house was left, lifting its stubborn and coquettish decay above the cotton wagons and the gasoline pumps — an eyesore among eyesores. And now Miss Emily had gone to join the representatives of those august names where they lay in the cedar-bemused cemetery among the ranked and anonymous graves of Union and Confederate soldiers who fell at the battle of Jefferson.

Alive, Miss Emily had been a tradition, a duty, and a care; a sort of hereditary obligation upon the town, dating from that day in 1894 when Colonel Sartoris, the mayor — he who fathered the edict that no Negro woman should appear on the streets without an apron — remitted her taxes, the dispensation dating from the death of her father on into perpetuity. Not that Miss Emily would have accepted charity. Colonel Sartoris invented an involved tale to the effect that Miss Emily's father had loaned money to the town, which the town, as a matter of business, preferred this way of repaying. Only a man of Colonel Sartoris' generation and thought could have invented it, and only a woman could have believed it.

When the next generation, with its more modern ideas, became mayors and aldermen, this arrangement created some little dissatisfaction. On the first of the year they mailed her a tax notice. February came, and there was no reply. They wrote her a formal letter, asking her to call at the sheriff's office at her convenience. A week later the mayor wrote her himself, offering to call or to send his car for her, and received in reply a note on paper of an archaic shape, in a thin, flowing calligraphy in faded ink, to the effect that she no longer went out at all. The tax notice was also enclosed, without comment.

They called a special meeting of the Board of Aldermen. A deputation waited upon her, knocked at the door through which no visitor had passed since she ceased giving china-painting lessons eight or ten years earlier. They were admitted by the old Negro into a dim hall from which a stairway mounted into still more shadow. It smelled of dust and disuse — a close, dank smell. The Negro led them into the parlor. It was furnished in heavy, leather-covered furniture. When the Negro opened the blinds of one window, they could see that the leather was cracked; and when they sat down, a faint dust rose sluggishly about their thighs, spinning with slow motes in the single sun-ray. On a tarnished gilt easel before the fireplace stood a crayon portrait of Miss Emily's father.

They rose when she entered — a small, fat woman in black, with a thin gold chain descending to her waist and vanishing into her belt, leaning on an ebony cane with a tarnished gold head. Her skeleton was small and spare; perhaps that was why what would have been merely plumpness in another was obesity in her. She looked bloated, like a body long submerged in motionless water, and of that pallid hue. Her eyes, lost in the fatty ridges of her face, looked like two small pieces of coal pressed into a lump of dough as they moved from one face to another while the visitors stated their errand.

She did not ask them to sit. She just stood in the door and listened quietly until the spokesman came to a stumbling halt. Then they could hear the invisible watch ticking at the end of the gold chain.

Her voice was dry and cold. "I have no taxes in Jefferson. Colonel Sartoris explained it to me. Perhaps one of you can gain access to the city records and satisfy yourselves."

"But we have. We are the city authorities, Miss Emily. Didn't you get a notice from the sheriff, signed by him?"

"I received a paper, yes," Miss Emily said. "Perhaps he considers himself the sheriff. . . . I have no taxes in Jefferson."

"But there is nothing on the books to show that, you see. We must go by the —"

"See Colonel Sartoris. I have no taxes in Jefferson."

"But, Miss Emily —"

"See Colonel Sartoris." (Colonel Sartoris had been dead almost ten years.) "I have no taxes in Jefferson. Tobe!" The Negro appeared. "Show these gentlemen out."

So she vanquished them, horse and foot, just as she had vanquished their fathers thirty years before about the smell. That was two years after her father's death and a short time after her sweetheart — the one we believed would marry her — had deserted her. After her father's death she went out very little; after her sweetheart went away, people hardly saw her at all. A few of the ladies had the temerity to call, but were not received, and the only sign of life about the place was the Negro man — a young man then — going in and out with a market basket.

"Just as if a man — any man — could keep a kitchen properly," the ladies said; so they were not surprised when the smell developed. It was another link between the gross, teeming world and the high and mighty Griersons.

A neighbor, a woman, complained to the mayor, Judge Stevens, eighty years old.

"But what will you have me do about it, madam?" he said.

"Why, send her word to stop it," the woman said. "Isn't there a law?"

"I'm sure that won't be necessary," Judge Stevens said. "It's probably just a snake or a rat . . . killed in the yard. I'll speak to him about it."

The next day he received two more complaints, one from a man who came in diffident deprecation. "We really must do something about it, Judge. I'd be the last one in the world to bother Miss Emily, but we've got to do something." That night the Board of Aldermen met — three graybeards and one younger man, a member of the rising generation.

"It's simple enough," he said. "Send her word to have her place cleaned up. Give her a certain time to do it in, and if she don't. . . ."

". . ." Judge Stevens said, "will you accuse a lady to her face of smelling bad?"

So the next night, after midnight, four men crossed Miss Emily's lawn and slunk about the house like burglars, sniffing along the base of the brickwork and at the cellar openings while one of them performed a regular sowing motion with his hand out of a sack slung from his shoulder. They broke open the cellar door and sprinkled lime there, and in all the outbuildings. As they recrossed the lawn, a window that had been dark was lighted and Miss Emily sat in it, the light behind her, and her upright torso motionless as that of an idol. They crept quietly across the lawn and into the shadow of the locusts that lined the street. After a week or two the smell went away.

That was when people had begun to feel really sorry for her. People in our town, remembering how old lady Wyatt, her great-aunt, had gone completely crazy at last, believed that the Griersons held themselves a little too high for what they really were. None of the young men were quite good enough for Miss Emily and such. We had long thought of them as a tableau; Miss Emily a slender figure in white in the background, her father a spraddled silhouette in the foreground, his back to her and clutching a horsewhip, the two of them framed by the back-flung front door. So when she got to be thirty and was still single, we were not pleased exactly, but vindicated; even with insanity in the family she wouldn't have turned down all of her chances if they had really materialized.

When her father died, it got about that the house was all that was left to her; and in a way, people were glad. At last they could pity Miss Emily. Being left alone, and a pauper, she had become humanized. Now she too would know the old thrill and the old despair of a penny more or less.

The day after his death all the ladies prepared to call at the house and offer condolence and aid, as is our custom. Miss Emily met them at the door, dressed as usual and with no trace of grief on her face. She told them that her father was not dead. She did that for three days, with the ministers calling on her, and the doctors, trying to persuade her to let them dispose of the body. Just as they were about to resort to law and force, she broke down, and they buried her father quickly.

We did not say she was crazy then. We believed she had to do that. We remembered all the young men her father had driven away, and we knew that with nothing left, she would have to cling to that which had robbed her, as people will (www.ariyam.com/docs/lit/wf_rose.html).

She was sick for a long time. When we saw her again, her hair was cut short, making her look like a girl, with a vague resemblance to those angels in colored church windows — sort of tragic and serene.

The town had just let the contracts for paving the sidewalks, and in the summer after her father's death they began the work. The construction company came with ... mules and machinery, and a foreman named Homer Barron, a Yankee — a big, dark, ready man, with a big voice and eyes lighter than his face. ... Pretty soon he knew everybody in town. Whenever you heard a lot of laughing anywhere about the square, Homer Barron would be in the center of the group. Presently we began to see him and Miss Emily on Sunday afternoons driving in the yellow-wheeled buggy and the matched team of bays from the livery stable.

At first we were glad that Miss Emily would have an interest, because the ladies all said, "Of course a Grierson would not think seriously of a Northerner,

a day laborer." But there were still others, older people, who said that even grief could not cause a real lady to forget noblesse oblige — without calling it noblesse oblige. They just said, "Poor Emily. Her kinsfolk should come to her." She had some kin in Alabama; but years ago her father had fallen out with them over the estate of old lady Wyatt, the crazy woman, and there was no communication between the two families. They had not even been represented at the funeral.

And as soon as the old people said, "Poor Emily," the whispering began. "Do you suppose it's really so?" they said to one another. "Of course it is. What else could. . . ." This behind their hands; rustling of craned silk and satin behind jalousies closed upon the sun of Sunday afternoon as the thin, swift clop-clop-clop of the matched team passed: "Poor Emily."

She carried her head high enough — even when we believed that she was fallen. It was as if she demanded more than ever the recognition of her dignity as the last Grierson; as if it had wanted that touch of earthiness to reaffirm her imperviousness. Like when she bought the rat poison, the arsenic. That was over a year after they had begun to say "Poor Emily," and while the two female cousins were visiting her.

"I want some poison," she said to the druggist. She was over thirty then, still a slight woman, though thinner than usual, with cold, haughty black eyes in a face the flesh of which was strained across the temples and about the eyesockets as you imagine a lighthouse-keeper's face ought to look. "I want some poison," she said.

"Yes, Miss Emily. What kind? For rats and such? I'd recom —"

"I want the best you have. I don't care what kind."

The druggist named several. "They'll kill anything up to an elephant. But what you want is —"

"Arsenic," Miss Emily said. "Is that a good one?"

"Is . . . arsenic? Yes, ma'am. But what you want —"

"I want arsenic."

The druggist looked down at her. She looked back at him, erect, her face like a strained flag. "Why, of course," the druggist said. "If that's what you want. But the law requires you to tell what you are going to use it for."

Miss Emily just stared at him, her head tilted back in order to look him eye for eye, until he looked away and went and got the arsenic and wrapped it up. The Negro delivery boy brought her the package; the druggist didn't come back. When she opened the package at home there was written on the box, under the skull and bones: "For rats."

So the next day we all said, "She will kill herself"; and we said it would be the best thing. When she had first begun to be seen with Homer Barron, we had said, "She will marry him." Then we said, "She will persuade him yet," because Homer himself had remarked — he liked men, and it was known that he drank with the younger men in the Elks' Club — that he was not a marrying man. Later we said, "Poor Emily" behind the jalousies as they passed on Sunday afternoon in the glittering buggy, Miss Emily with her head high and Homer Barron with his hat cocked and a cigar in his teeth, reins and whip in a yellow glove.

Then some of the ladies began to say that it was a disgrace to the town and a bad example to the young people. The men did not want to interfere, but at last the ladies forced the Baptist minister — Miss Emily's people were Episcopal — to call upon her. He would never divulge what happened during that interview, but he refused to go back again. The next Sunday they again drove about the streets, and the following day the minister's wife wrote to Miss Emily's relations in Alabama.

So she had blood-kin under her roof again and we sat back to watch developments. At first nothing happened. Then we were sure that they were to be married. We learned that Miss Emily had been to the jeweler's and ordered a man's toilet set in silver, with the letters H. B. on each piece. Two days later we learned that she had bought a complete outfit of men's clothing, including a nightshirt, and we said, "They are married. " We were really glad. We were glad because the two female cousins were even more Grierson than Miss Emily had ever been.

So we were not surprised when Homer Barron — the streets had been finished some time since — was gone. We were a little disappointed that there was not a public blowing-off, but we believed that he had gone on to prepare for Miss Emily's coming, or to give her a chance to get rid of the cousins. (By that time it was a cabal, and we were all Miss Emily's allies to help circumvent the cousins.) Sure enough, after another week they departed. And, as we had expected all along, within three days Homer Barron was back in town. A neighbor saw the Negro man admit him at the kitchen door at dusk one evening.

And that was the last we saw of Homer Barron. And of Miss Emily for some time. The Negro man went in and out with the market basket, but the front door remained closed. Now and then we would see her at a window for a moment, as the men did that night when they sprinkled the lime, but for almost six months she did not appear on the streets. Then we knew that this was to be expected too; as if that quality of her father which had thwarted her woman's life so many times had been too virulent and too furious to die.

When we next saw Miss Emily, she had grown fat and her hair was turning gray. During the next few years it grew grayer and grayer until it attained an even pepper-and-salt iron-gray, when it ceased turning. Up to the day of her death at seventy-four it was still that vigorous iron-gray, like the hair of an active man.

From that time on her front door remained closed, save for a period of six or seven years, when she was about forty, during which she gave lessons in china-painting. She fitted up a studio in one of the downstairs rooms, where the daughters and grand-daughters of Colonel Sartoris' contemporaries were sent to her with the same regularity and in the same spirit that they were sent to church on Sundays with a twenty-five-cent piece for the collection plate. Meanwhile her taxes had been remitted.

Then the newer generation became the back-bone and the spirit of the town, and the painting pupils grew up and fell away and did not send their children to her with boxes of color and tedious brushes and pictures cut from the ladies' magazines. The front door closed upon the last one and remained closed for good. When the town got free postal delivery Miss Emily alone refused to let them fasten the metal numbers above her door and attach a mailbox to it. She would not listen to them.

Daily, monthly, yearly we watched the Negro grow grayer and more stooped, going in and out with the market basket. Each December we sent her a tax notice, which would be returned by the post office a week later, unclaimed. Now and then we would see her in one of the downstairs windows—she had evidently shut up the top floor of the house—like the carven torso of an idol in a niche, looking or not looking at us, we could never tell which. Thus she passed from generation to generation — dear, inescapable, impervious, tranquil, and perverse.

And so she died. Fell ill in the house filled with dust and shadows, with only a doddering Negro man to wait on her. We did not even know she was sick; we had long since given up trying to get any information from the Negro. He talked to no one, probably not even to her, for his voice had grown harsh and rusty, as if from disuse.

She died in one of the downstairs rooms, in a heavy walnut bed with a curtain, her gray head propped on a pillow yellow and moldy with age and lack of sunlight.

The negro met the first of the ladies at the front door and let them in, with their hushed, sibilant voices and their quick, curious glances, and then he disappeared. He walked right through the house and out the back and was not seen again.

The two female cousins came at once. They held the funeral on the second day, with the town coming to look at Miss Emily beneath a mass of bought flowers, with the crayon face of her father musing profoundly above the bier and the ladies sibilant and macabre; and the very old men — some in their brushed Confederate uniforms — on the porch and the lawn, talking of Miss Emily as if she had been a contemporary of theirs, believing that they had danced with her and courted her perhaps, confusing time with its mathematical progression, as the old

do, to whom all the past is not a diminishing road, but, instead, a huge meadow which no winter ever quite touches, divided from them now by the narrow bottleneck of the most recent decade of years.

Already we knew that there was one room in that region above stairs which no one had seen in forty years, and which would have to be forced. They waited until Miss Emily was decently in the ground before they opened it.

The violence of breaking down the door seemed to fill this room with pervading dust. A thin, acrid pall as of the tomb seemed to lie everywhere upon this room decked and furnished as for a bridal: upon the valance curtains of faded rose color, upon the rose-shaded lights, upon the dressing table, upon the delicate array of crystal and the man's toilet things backed with tarnished silver, silver so tarnished that the monogram was obscured. Among them lay a collar and tie, as if they had just been removed, which, lifted, left upon the surface a pale crescent in the dust. Upon a chair hung the suit, carefully folded; beneath it the two mute shoes and the discarded socks.

The man himself lay in the bed.

For a long while we just stood there, looking down at the profound and fleshless grin. The body had apparently once lain in the attitude of an embrace, but now the long sleep that outlasts love, that conquers even the grimace of love, had cuckolded him. What was left of him, rotted beneath what was left of the nightshirt, had become inextricable from the bed in which he lay; and upon him and upon the pillow beside him lay that even coating of the patient and biding dust.

Then we noticed that in the second pillow was the indentation of a head. One of us lifted something from it, and leaning forward, that faint and invisible dust dry and acrid in the nostrils, we saw a long strand of iron-gray hair.

The End

Assignments

- Warm-up: Is Miss Emily insane? Why or why not?
- Students should complete Concept Builder 24-D.
- Student will re-write corrected copies of essays due tomorrow.

<table>
<tr><td rowspan="8" style="writing-mode: vertical">**CONCEPT BUILDER 24-D**
Active Reading</td><td colspan="2">**Read *A Rose for Emily* by William Faulkner in the text and then answer the following questions.**</td></tr>
<tr><td>1</td><td>Why did Colonel Sartoris help Miss Emily?</td></tr>
<tr><td>2</td><td>Why is this scene humorous?</td></tr>
<tr><td>3</td><td>What do you think is the source of the smell?</td></tr>
<tr><td>4</td><td>How does Faulkner use other characters to develop Miss Emily?</td></tr>
<tr><td>5</td><td>Against regulations, why would the druggist sell Miss Emily the arsenic?</td></tr>
<tr><td>6</td><td>How are African-Americans presented in this short story?</td></tr>
<tr><td>7</td><td>Who is in the bed?</td></tr>
</table>

Sherwood Anderson
The New Englander

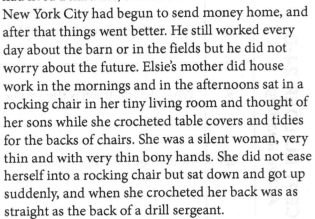

Her name was Elsie Leander and her girlhood was spent on her father's farm in Vermont. For several generations the Leanders had all lived on the same farm and had all married thin women, and so she was thin. The farm lay in the shadow of a mountain and the soil was not very rich. From the beginning and for several generations there had been a great many sons and few daughters in the family. The sons had gone west or to New York City and the daughters had stayed at home and thought such thoughts as come to New England women who see the sons of their father's neighbour slipping, away, one by one, into the West.

Her father's house was a small white frame affair, and when you went out at the back door, past a small barn and a chicken house, you got into a path that ran up the side of a hill and into an orchard. The trees were all old and gnarled. At the back of the orchard the hill dropped away and bare rocks showed.

Inside the fence a large grey rock stuck high up out of the ground. As Elsie sat with her back to the rock, with a mangled hillside at her feet, she could see several large mountains, apparently but a short distance away, and between herself and the mountains lay many tiny fields surrounded by neatly built stone walls. Everywhere rocks appeared. Large ones, too heavy to be moved, stuck out of the ground in the center of the fields. The fields were like cups filled with a green liquid that turned grey in the fall and white in the winter. The mountains, far off but apparently near at hand, were like giants ready at any moment to reach out their hands and take the cups one by one and drink off the green liquid. The large rocks in the fields were like the thumbs of the giants.

Elsie had three brothers, born ahead of her, but they had all gone away. Two of them had gone to live with her uncle in the West and her elder brother had gone to New York City where he had married and prospered. All through his youth and manhood her father had worked hard and had lived a hard life, but his son in New York City had begun to send money home, and after that things went better. He still worked every day about the barn or in the fields but he did not worry about the future. Elsie's mother did house work in the mornings and in the afternoons sat in a rocking chair in her tiny living room and thought of her sons while she crocheted table covers and tidies for the backs of chairs. She was a silent woman, very thin and with very thin bony hands. She did not ease herself into a rocking chair but sat down and got up suddenly, and when she crocheted her back was as straight as the back of a drill sergeant.

The mother rarely spoke to the daughter. Sometimes in the afternoons as the younger woman went up the hillside to her place by the rock at the back of the orchard, her father came out of the barn and stopped her. He put a hand on her shoulder and asked where she was going. "To the rock," she said and her father laughed. His laughter was like the creaking of a rusty barn door hinge and the hand he had laid on her shoulder was thin like her own hands and like her mother's hands. The father went into the barn shaking his head. "She's like her mother. She is herself like a rock," he thought. At the head of the path that led from the house to the orchard there was a great cluster of bayberry bushes. The New England farmer came out of his barn to watch his daughter go along the path, but she had disappeared behind the bushes. He looked away past his house to the fields and to the mountains in the distance. He also saw the green cup-like fields and the grim mountains. There was an almost imperceptible tightening of the muscles of his half worn-out old body. For a long time he stood in silence and then, knowing from long experience the danger of having thoughts, he went back into the barn and busied himself with the mending of an agricultural tool that had been mended many times before.

The son of the Leanders who went to live in New York City was the father of one son, a thin sensitive boy who looked like Elsie. The son died when he was twenty-three years old and some years later the father died and left his money to the old people on the New England farm. The two Leanders who had gone west had lived there with their father's brother, a farmer, until they grew into manhood. Then Will, the younger, got a job on a railroad. He was killed one winter morning. It was a cold snowy day and when the freight train he was in charge of as conductor left the city of Des Moines, he started to run over the tops of the cars. His feet slipped and he shot down into space. That was the end of him.

Of the new generation there was only Elsie and her brother Tom, whom she had never seen, left alive. Her father and mother talked of going west to Tom for two years before they came to a decision. Then it took another year to dispose of the farm and make preparations. During the whole time Elsie did not think much about the change about to take place in her life.

The trip west on the railroad train jolted Elsie out of herself. In spite of her detached attitude toward life she became excited. Her mother sat up very straight and stiff in the seat in the sleeping car and her father walked up and down in the aisle. After a night when the younger of the two women did not sleep but lay awake with red burning cheeks and with her thin fingers incessantly picking at the bed-clothes in her berth while the train went through towns and cities, crawled up the sides of hills and fell down into forest-clad valleys, she got up and dressed to sit all day looking at a new kind of land. The train ran for a day and through another sleepless night in a flat land where every field was as large as a farm in her own country. Towns appeared and disappeared in a continual procession. The whole land was so unlike anything she had ever known that she began to feel unlike herself. In the valley where she had been born and where she had lived all her days everything had an air of finality. Nothing could be changed. The tiny fields were chained to the earth. They were fixed in their places and surrounded by aged stone walls. The fields like the mountains that looked down at them were as unchangeable as the passing days. She had a feeling they had always been so, would always be so.

Elsie sat like her mother upright in the car seat and with a back like the back of a drill sergeant. The train ran swiftly along through Ohio and Indiana. Her thin hands like her mother's hands were crossed and locked. One passing casually through the car might have thought both women prisoners handcuffed and bound to their seats. Night came on and she again got into her berth. Again she lay awake and her thin cheeks became flushed, but she thought new thoughts. Her hands were no longer gripped together and she did not pick at the bed clothes. Twice during the night she stretched herself and yawned, a thing she had never in her life done before. The train stopped at a town on the prairies, and as there was something the matter with one of the wheels of the car in which she lay the trainsmen came with flaming torches to tinker it. There was a great pounding and shouting. When the train went on its way she wanted to get out of her berth and run up and down in the aisle of the car. The fancy had come to her that the men tinkering with the car wheel were new men out of the new land who had broken with strong hammers the doors of her prison away. They had destroyed forever the programme she had made for her life.

Elsie was filled with joy at the thought that the train was still going on into the West. She wanted to go on for ever in a straight line into the unknown. She fancied herself no longer on a train and imagined she had become a winged thing flying through space. Her long years of sitting alone by the rock on the New England farm had got her into the habit of expressing her thoughts aloud. Her thin voice broke the silence that lay over the sleeping car and her father and mother, both also lying awake, sat up in their berth to listen.

Tom Leander, the only living male representative of the new generation of Leanders, was a loosely built man of forty inclined to corpulency. At twenty he had married the daughter of a neighboring farmer, and when his wife inherited some money she and Tom moved into the town of Apple Junction in Iowa where Tom opened a grocery. The venture prospered as did Tom's matrimonial venture. When his brother died in New York City and his father, mother, and sister decided to come west Tom was already the father of a daughter and four sons.

On the prairies north of town and in the midst of a vast level stretch of corn fields, there was a partly completed brick house that had belonged to a rich farmer named Russell, who had begun to build the house intending to make it the most magnificent place in the county, but when it was almost completed he had found himself without money and heavily in debt. The farm, consisting of several hundred acres of corn land, had been split into three farms and sold. No one had wanted the huge unfinished brick house. For years it had stood vacant, its windows staring out over the fields that had been planted almost up to the door.

In buying the Russell house Tom was moved by two motives. He had a notion that in New England the Leanders had been rather magnificent people. His memory of his father's place in the Vermont valley was shadowy, but in speaking of it to his wife he became very definite. "We had good blood in us, we Leanders," he said, straightening his shoulders. "We lived in a big house. We were important people."

Wanting his father and mother to feel at home in the new place, Tom had also another motive. He was not a very energetic man and, although he had done well enough as keeper of a grocery, his success was largely due to the boundless energy of his wife. She did not pay much attention to her household and her children, like little animals, had to take care of themselves, but in any matter concerning the store her word was law.

To have his father the owner of the Russell Place Tom felt would establish him as a man of consequence in the eyes of his neighbor. "I can tell you what, they're used to a big house," he said to his wife. "I tell you what, my people are used to living in style."

The exaltation that had come over Elsie on the train wore away in the presence of grey empty Iowa fields, but something of the effect of it remained with her for months. In the big brick house life went on

much as it had in the tiny New England house where she had always lived. The Leanders installed themselves in three or four rooms on the ground floor. After a few weeks the furniture that had been shipped by freight arrived and was hauled out from town in one of Tom's grocery wagons. There were three or four acres of ground covered with great piles of boards the unsuccessful farmer had intended to use in the building of stables. Tom sent men to haul the boards away and Elsie's father prepared to plant a garden. They had come west in April and as soon as they were installed in the house ploughing and planting began in the fields near by. The habit of a lifetime returned to the daughter of the house. In the new place there was no gnarled orchard surrounded by a half-ruined stone fence. All of the fences in all of the fields that stretched away out of sight to the north, south, east, and west were made of wire and looked like spider webs against the blackness of the ground when it had been freshly ploughed.

There was however the house itself. It was like an island rising out of the sea. In an odd way the house, although it was less than ten years old, was very old. Its unnecessary bigness represented an old impulse in men. Elsie felt that. At the east side there was a door leading to a stairway that ran into the upper part of the house that was kept locked. Two or three stone steps led up to it. Elsie could sit on the top step with her back against the door and gaze into the distance without being disturbed. Almost at her feet began the fields that seemed to go on and on for ever. The fields were like the waters of a sea. Men came to plough and plant. Giant horses moved in a procession across the prairies. A young man who drove six horses came directly toward her. She was fascinated. The breasts of the horses as they came forward with bowed heads seemed like the breasts of giants. The soft spring air that lay over the fields was also like a sea. The horses were giants walking on the floor of a sea. With their breasts they pushed the waters of the sea before them. They were pushing the waters out of the basin of the sea. The young man who drove them was also a giant.

Elsie pressed her body against the closed door at the top of the steps. In the garden back of the house she could hear her father at work. He was raking dry masses of weeds off the ground preparatory to spading the ground for a family garden. He had always worked in a tiny confined place and would do the same thing here. In this vast open place he would work with small tools, doing little things with infinite care, raising little vegetables. In the house her mother would crochet little tidies. She herself would be small. She would press her body against the door of the house, try to get herself out of sight. Only the feeling that sometimes took possession of her, and that did not form itself into a thought, would be large.

The six horses turned at the fence and the outside horse got entangled in the traces. The driver swore vigorously. Then he turned and stared at the pale New Englander and with another oath pulled the heads of the horses about and drove away into the distance. The field in which he was ploughing contained two hundred acres. Elsie did not wait for him to return but went into the house and sat with folded arms in a room. The house she thought was a ship floating in a sea on the floor of which giants went up and down.

May came and then June. In the great fields work was always going on and Elsie became somewhat used to the sight of the young man in the field that came down to the steps. Sometimes when he drove his horses down to the wire fence he smiled and nodded. In the month of August, when it is very hot, the corn in Iowa fields grows until the corn stalks resemble young trees. The corn fields become forests. The time for the cultivating of the corn has passed and weeds grow thick between the corn rows. The men with their giant horses have gone away. Over the immense fields silence broods.

When the time of the laying-by of the crop came that first summer after Elsie's arrival in the West her mind, partially awakened by the strangeness of the railroad trip, awakened again. She did not feel like a staid thin woman with a back like the back of a drill sergeant, but like something new and as strange as the new land into which she had come to live. For a time she did not know what was the matter. In the field the corn had grown so high that she could not see into the distance. The corn was like a wall and the little bare spot of land on which her father's house stood was like a house built behind the walls of a prison. For a time she was depressed, thinking that she had come west into a wide open country, only to find herself locked up more closely than ever.

An impulse came to her. She arose and going down three or four steps seated herself almost on a level with the ground.

Immediately she got a sense of release. She could not see over the corn but she could see under it. The corn had long wide leaves that met over the rows. The rows became long tunnels running away into infinity. Out of the black ground grew weeds that made a soft carpet of green. From above light sifted down. The corn rows were mysteriously beautiful. They were warm passageways running out into life. She got up from the steps, and walking timidly to the wire fence that separated her from the field, put her hand between the wires and took hold of one of the corn stalks. For some reason after she had touched the strong young stalk and had held it for a moment firmly in her hand she grew afraid. Running quickly back to the step she sat down and covered her face with her hands. Her body trembled. She tried to imagine herself crawling through the fence and wandering along one of the passageways. The thought of trying the experiment fascinated but at the same time terrified. She got quickly up and went into the house.

One Saturday night in August Elsie found herself unable to sleep. Thoughts, more definite than any she had ever known before, came into her mind. It was a quiet hot night and her bed stood near a window. Her room was the only one the Leanders occupied on the second floor of the house. At midnight a little breeze came up from the south and when she sat up in bed the floor of corn tassels lying below her line of sight looked in the moonlight like the face of a sea just stirred by a gentle breeze.

A murmuring began in the corn and murmuring thoughts and memories awoke in her mind. The long wide succulent leaves had begun to dry in the intense heat of the August days and as the wind stirred the corn they rubbed against each other. A call, far away, as of a thousand voices arose. She imagined the voices were like the voices of children. They were not like her brother Tom's children, noisy boisterous little animals, but something quite different, tiny little things with large eyes and thin sensitive hands. One after another they crept into her arms. She became so excited over the fancy that she sat up in bed and taking a pillow into her arms held it against her breast. The figure of her cousin, the pale sensitive young Leander who had lived with his father in New York City and who had died at the age of twenty-three, came sharply into her mind. It was as though the young man had come suddenly into the room. She dropped the pillow and sat waiting, intense, expectant.

Young Harry Leander had come to visit his cousin on the New England farm during the late summer of the year before he died. He had stayed there for a month and almost every afternoon had gone with Elsie to sit by the rock at the back of the orchard. One afternoon when they had both been for a long time silent he began to talk. "I want to go live in the West," he said. "I want to go live in the West. I want to grow strong and be a man," he repeated. Tears came into his eyes.

They got up to return to the house, Elsie walking in silence beside the young man. The moment marked a high spot in her life. A strange trembling eagerness for something she had not realized in her experience of life had taken possession of her. They went in silence through the orchard but when they came to the bayberry bush her cousin stopped in the path and turned to face her. "I want you to kiss me," he said eagerly, stepping toward her.

A fluttering uncertainty had taken possession of Elsie and had been transmitted to her cousin. After he had made the sudden and unexpected demand and had stepped so close to her that his breath could be felt on her cheek, his own cheeks became scarlet and his hand that had taken her hand trembled. "Well, I wish I were strong. I only wish I were strong," he said hesitatingly and turning walked away along the path toward the house.

And in the strange new house, set like an island in its sea of corn, Harry Leander's voice seemed to arise again above the fancied voices of the children that had been coming out of the fields. Elsie got out of bed and walked up and down in the dim light coming through the window. Her body trembled violently. "I want you to kiss me," the voice said again and to quiet it and to quiet also the answering voice in herself she went to kneel by the bed and taking the pillow again into her arms pressed it against her face.

Tom Leander came with his wife and family to visit his father and mother on Sundays. The family

appeared at about ten o'clock in the morning. When the wagon turned out of the road that ran past the Russell Place Tom shouted. There was a field between the house and the road and the wagon could not be seen as it came along the narrow way through the corn. After Tom had shouted, his daughter Elizabeth, a tall girl of sixteen, jumped out of the wagon. All five children came tearing toward the house through the corn. A series of wild shouts arose on the still morning air.

The grocery man had brought food from the store. When the horse had been unhitched and put into a shed he and his wife began to carry packages into the house. The four Leander boys, accompanied by their sister, disappeared into the near-by fields. Three dogs that had trotted out from town under the wagon accompanied the children. Two or three children and occasionally a young man from a neighboring farm had come to join in the fun. Elsie's sister-in-law dismissed them all with a wave of her hand. With a wave of her hand she also brushed Elsie aside. Fires were lighted and the house reeked with the smell of cooking. Elsie went to sit on the step at the side of the house. The corn fields that had been so quiet rang with shouts and with the barking of dogs.

Tom Leander's oldest child, Elizabeth, was like her mother, full of energy. She was thin and tall like the women of her father's house but very strong and alive. In secret she wanted to be a lady but when she tried her brothers, led by her father and mother, made fun of her. "Don't put on airs," they said. When she got into the country with no one but her brothers and two or three neighboring farm boys she herself became a boy. With the boys she went tearing through the fields, following the dogs in pursuit of rabbits. Sometimes a young man came with the children from a near-by farm. Then she did not know what to do with herself. She wanted to walk demurely along the rows through the corn but was afraid her brothers would laugh and in desperation outdid the boys in roughness and noisiness. She screamed and shouted and running wildly tore her dress on the wire fences as she scrambled over in pursuit of the dogs. When a rabbit was caught and killed she rushed in and tore it out of the grasp of the dogs. The blood of the little dying animal dripped on her clothes. She swung it over her head and shouted.

The farm hand who had worked all summer in the field within sight of Elsie became enamored of the young woman from town. When the grocery man's family appeared on Sunday mornings he also appeared but did not come to the house. When the boys and dogs came tearing through the fields he joined them. He was also self-conscious and did not want the boys to know the purpose of his coming and when he and Elizabeth found themselves alone together he became embarrassed. For a moment they walked together in silence. In a wide circle about them, in the forest of the corn, ran the boys and dogs. The young man had something he wanted to say, but when he tried to find words his tongue became thick and his lips felt hot and dry. "Well," he began, "let's you and me —"

Words failed him and Elizabeth turned and ran after her brothers and for the rest of the day he could not manage to get her out of their sight. When he went to join them she became the noisiest member of the party. A frenzy of activity took possession of her. With hair hanging down her back, with clothes torn, and with cheeks and hands scratched and bleeding she led her brothers in the endless wild pursuit of the rabbits.

The Sunday in August that followed Elsie Leander's sleepless night was hot and cloudy. In the morning she was half ill and as soon as the visitors from town arrived she crept away to sit on the step at the side of the house. The children ran away into the fields. An almost overpowering desire to run with them, shouting and playing along the corn rows took possession of her. She arose and went to the back of the house. Her father was at work in the garden, pulling weeds from between rows of vegetables. Inside the house she could hear her sister-in-law moving about. On the front porch her brother Tom was asleep with his mother beside him. Elsie went back on the step and then arose and went to where the corn came down to the fence. She climbed awkwardly over and went a little way along one of the rows. Putting out her hand she touched the firm hard stalks and then, becoming afraid, dropped to her knees on the carpet of weeds that covered the ground. For a long time she stayed thus listening to the voices of the children in the distance.

An hour slipped away. Presently it was time for dinner and her sister-in-law came to the back door and shouted. There was an answering whoop from the distance and the children came running through the fields. They climbed over the fence and ran shouting across her father's garden. Elsie also arose. She was about to attempt to climb back over the fence unobserved when she heard a rustling in the corn. Young Elizabeth Leander appeared. Beside her walked the ploughman who but a few months earlier had planted the corn in the field where Elsie now stood. She could see the two people coming slowly along the rows. An understanding had been established between them. The man reached through between the corn stalks and touched the hand of the girl who laughed awkwardly and running to the fence climbed quickly over. In her hand she held the limp body of a rabbit the dogs had killed.

The farm hand went away and when Elizabeth had gone into the house Elsie climbed over the fence. Her niece stood just within the kitchen door holding the dead rabbit by one leg. The other leg had been torn away by the dogs. At sight of the New England woman, who seemed to look at her with hard unsympathetic eyes, she was ashamed and went quickly into the house. She threw the rabbit upon a table in the parlor and then ran out of the room. Its blood ran out on the delicate flowers of a white crocheted table cover that had been made by Elsie's mother.

The Sunday dinner with all the living Leanders gathered about the table was gone through in a heavy lumbering silence. When the dinner was over and Tom and his wife had washed the dishes they went to sit with the older people on the front porch. Presently they were both asleep. Elsie returned to the step at the side of the house but when the desire to go again into the cornfields came sweeping over her she got up and went indoors.

The woman of thirty-five tip-toed about the big house like a frightened child. The dead rabbit that lay on the table in the parlor had become cold and stiff. Its blood had dried on the white table cover. She went upstairs but did not go to her own room. A spirit of adventure had hold of her. In the upper part of the house there were many rooms and in some of them no glass had been put into the windows. The windows had been boarded up and narrow streaks of light crept in through the cracks between the boards.

Elsie tip-toed up the flight of stairs past the room in which she slept and opening doors went into other rooms. Dust lay thick on the floors. In the silence she could hear her brother snoring as he slept in the chair on the front porch. From what seemed a far away place there came the shrill cries of the children. The cries became soft. They were like the cries of unborn children that had called to her out of the fields on the night before.

Into her mind came the intense silent figure of her mother sitting on the porch beside her son and waiting for the day to wear itself out into night. The thought brought a lump into her throat. She wanted something and did not know what it was. Her own mood frightened her. In a windowless room at the back of the house one of the boards over a window had been broken and a bird had flown in and become imprisoned.

The presence of the woman frightened the bird. It flew wildly about. Its beating wings stirred up dust that danced in the air. Elsie stood perfectly still, also frightened, not by the presence of the bird but by the presence of life. Like the bird she was a prisoner. The thought gripped her. She wanted to go outdoors where her niece Elizabeth walked with the young ploughman through the corn, but was like the bird in the room — a prisoner. She moved restlessly about. The bird flew back and forth across the room. It alighted on the window sill near the place where the board was broken away. She stared into the frightened eyes of the bird that in turn stared into her eyes. Then the bird flew away, out through the window, and Elsie turned and ran nervously downstairs and out into the yard. She climbed over the wire fence and ran with stooped shoulders along one of the tunnels.

Elsie ran into the vastness of the cornfields filled with but one desire. She wanted to get out of her life and into some new and sweeter life she felt must be hidden away somewhere in the fields. After she had run a long way she came to a wire fence and crawled over. Her hair became unloosed and fell down over her shoulders. Her cheeks became flushed and for the moment she looked like a young girl. When she climbed over the fence she tore a great hole in the front of her dress. … In the distance she could hear the voices of the boys and the barking of the dogs. A

summer storm had been threatening for days and now black clouds had begun to spread themselves over the sky. As she ran nervously forward, stopping to listen and then running on again, the dry corn blades brushed against her shoulders and a fine shower of yellow dust from the corn tassels fell on her hair. A continued crackling noise accompanied her progress. The dust made a golden crown about her head. From the sky overhead a low rumbling sound, like the growling of giant dogs, came to her ears.

The thought that having at last ventured into the corn she would never escape became fixed in the mind of the running woman. Sharp pains shot through her body. Presently she was compelled to stop and sit on the ground. For a long time she sat with her closed eyes. Her dress became soiled. Little insects that live in the ground under the corn came out of their holes and crawled over her legs.

Following some obscure impulse the tired woman threw herself on her back and lay still with closed eyes. Her fright passed. It was warm and close in the room-like tunnels. The pain in her side went away. She opened her eyes and between the wide green corn blades could see patches of a black threatening sky. She did not want to be alarmed and so closed her eyes again. Her thin hand no longer gripped the tear in her dress … She threw her hands back over her head and lay still.

It seemed to Elsie that hours passed as she lay thus, quiet and passive under the corn. Deep within her there was a feeling that something was about to happen, something that would lift her out of herself, that would tear her away from her past and the past of her people. Her thoughts were not definite. She lay still and waited as she had waited for days and months by the rock at the back of the orchard on the Vermont farm when she was a girl. A deep grumbling noise went on in the sky overhead but the sky and everything she had ever known seemed very far away, no part of herself.

After a long silence, when it seemed to her that she was lost from herself as in a dream, Elsie heard a man's voice calling. "Aho, aho, aho," shouted the voice and after another period of silence there arose answering voices and then the sound of bodies crashing through the corn and the excited chatter of children. A dog came running along the row where she lay and stood beside her. His cold nose touched her face and she sat up. The dog ran away. The Leander boys passed. She could see their bare legs flashing in and out across one of the tunnels. Her brother had become alarmed by the rapid approach of the thunder storm and wanted to get his family to town. His voice kept calling from the house and the voices of the children answered from the fields.

Elsie sat on the ground with her hands pressed together. An odd feeling of disappointment had possession of her. She arose and walked slowly along in the general direction taken by the children. She came to a fence and crawled over, tearing her dress in a new place. One of her stockings had become unloosed and had slipped down over her shoe top. The long sharp weeds had scratched her leg so that it was criss-crossed with red lines, but she was not conscious of any pain.

The distraught woman followed the children until she came within sight of her father's house and then stopped and again sat on the ground. There was another loud crash of thunder and Tom Leander's voice called again, this time half angrily. The name of the girl Elizabeth was shouted in loud masculine tones that rolled and echoed like the thunder along the aisles under the corn.

And then Elizabeth came into sight accompanied by the young ploughman. They stopped near Elsie and the man took the girl into his arms. At the sound of their approach Elsie had thrown herself face downward on the ground and had twisted herself into a position where she could see without being seen. When their lips met her tense hands grasped one of the corn stalks. Her lips pressed themselves into the dust. When they had gone on their way she raised her head. A dusty powder covered her lips.

What seemed another long period of silence fell over the fields. A strong wind began to blow and the corn rocked back and forth. The murmuring voices of unborn children, her imagination had created in the whispering fields, became a vast shout. The wind blew harder and harder. The corn stalks were twisted and bent. Elizabeth went thoughtfully out of the field and climbing the fence confronted her father. "Where you been? What you been a doing?" he asked. "Don't you know we got to get out of here?"

When Elizabeth went toward the house Elsie followed, creeping on her hands and knees like a little animal, and when she had come within sight of the fence surrounding the house she sat on the ground and put her hands over her face. Something within herself was being twisted and whirled about as the tops of the corn stalks were now being twisted and whirled by the wind. She sat so that she did not look toward the house and when she opened her eyes she could again see along the long mysterious aisles.

Her brother, with his wife and children, went away. By turning her head Elsie could see them driving at a trot out of the yard back of her father's house. With the going of the younger woman the farm house in the midst of the cornfield rocked by the winds seemed the most desolate place in the world.

Her mother came out at the back door of the house. She ran to the steps where she knew her daughter was in the habit of sitting and then in alarm began to call. It did not occur to Elsie to answer. The voice of the older woman did not seem to have anything to do with herself. It was a thin voice and was quickly lost in the wind and in the crashing sound that arose out of the fields. With her head turned toward the house Elsie stared at her mother who ran wildly around the house and then went indoors. The back door of the house went shut with a bang.

The storm that had been threatening broke with a roar. Broad sheets of water swept over the corn-fields. Sheets of water swept over the woman's body. The storm that had for years been gathering in her also broke. Sobs arose out of her throat. She abandoned herself to a storm of grief that was only partially grief. Tears ran out of her eyes and made little furrows through the dust on her face. In the lulls that occasionally came in the storm she raised her head and heard, through the tangled mass of wet hair that covered her ears and above the sound of millions of rain-drops that alighted on the earthen floor inside the house of the corn, the thin voices of her mother and father calling to her out of the Leander house (www.online-literature.com/sherwood-anderson/1472/).

The past, or at least the interpretation of the past, is constantly changing according to new scholarship discoveries. Therefore, as new sources are discovered, and old ones re-examined, the historian understands that theories of history may change. "Every true history is contemporary history," historians Gerald Grob and George Billias write (*Interpretations of American History, Volume 1 to 1877* by Gerald N. And Billias George Athan Grob, the free press, 1967, preface). The student is asked to make the theories of historical events personal and contemporary.

Assignments

- Warm-up: William Faulkner was deeply influenced by the American short story writer Sherwood Anderson. Discuss similarities between this short story and "The Tall Men."

- Students should complete Concept Builder 24-E.

- Essays are due. Students should take the chapter 24 test.

CONCEPT BUILDER 24-E — Character Study		
Briefly describe the main characters in Sherwood Anderson's "The New Englander" and state their possible motivations.		
Character Description		Motivations

Chapter 25

1915–1946 (Part 6):
The Modern Age:
Late Romanticism/Naturalism

First Thoughts In 1940, John Steinbeck sailed along the coast of Mexico. During the trip, Steinbeck heard a legend about the misfortunes of a poor fisherman who had found a great pearl. Inspired by the legend, Steinbeck published the story in a magazine in 1945 under the title "The Pearl of the World." The story was so successful that in 1947 it was published as a book, *The Pearl*, and adapted as a film.

Author Worldview Watch John Steinbeck is a naturalist who wrote with an acidic pen. All his novels had a political agenda, and, many times, his lost protagonists alternately resemble the doomed existentialists in French novelist Albert Camus' novels and the bizarre Christian theists in Flannery O'Connor's novellas. Steinbeck, a conflicted, desperately unhappy man, with great talent, offers dramatic irony with painful effect. Still, because Steinbeck's characters are so real, and contemporary, readers will gain glimpses into the soul of modern America and will no doubt harvest important prayer points.

Chapter Learning Objectives In chapter 25 we enter the sad world of Kino and his family and experience anew the frustration and tragedy of naturalism. You will analyze *The Pearl* by John Steinbeck.

As a result of this chapter study you will be able to . . .

1. Discuss in detail how O'Neill builds suspense in this play.

2. What is the setting and how does it affect the outcome of this play?

3. Who is Smithers and what is his purpose in this play?

Weekly Essay Options: Begin on page 274 of the Teacher Guide.
Reading ahead: "The Emperor Jones" by Eugene O'Neill.

The Pearl

John Steinbeck

Background President Herbert Hoover had been in office only seven months when the stock market crashed. This great crash ended the Roaring 20s. The Great Depression followed. The American dream seemed to have gone sour. Most Americans blamed themselves for the Depression. Americans believed that if they worked hard enough they would prosper. This was no longer possible for millions of Americans. The Great Depression destroyed America's confidence in the future. This hopelessness is reflected in all of John Steinbeck's fiction.

There had been recessions and depressions in American history but nothing close to what Americans experienced in the 1930s. At one point, almost one-half of Americans were unemployed. There was no welfare "safety net" in the early 1930s. People had no food stamps or welfare checks. They had to rely upon friends, family members, and the Church. It was not enough.

In spite of President Hoover's innovative efforts, the Great Depression only worsened. When Franklin D. Roosevelt became president in 1932, Americans were ready for a change.

The Great Depression lasted from about 1929 to the beginning of America's involvement in World War II (1941). Roosevelt attacked the Great Depression forcefully and with innovative tactics. His politics of intervention can be divided into two phases. He promised a "new deal" for the American people. The first was from 1933 to 1935 and focused mainly on helping the poor and unemployed. Roosevelt authorized, with congressional support, massive spending to employ millions of people. These projects including the Civilian Conservation Corps and the Tennessee Valley Authority. While Roosevelt did not implement socialism, he did superimpose a welfare state on a capitalistic society with controversial results. Steinbeck and other intellectuals were strong proponents of socialism. Socialism advocated that the means of production were owned and controlled by the state. There was no private ownership of property. Socialists sought to champion the rights of the poor and the disenfranchised — much like the protagonist in *The Pearl*. This radical social theory gained thousands of proponents in the 1930s.

The so-called Second New Deal occurred from 1935 to 1937. During this period, Roosevelt emphasized social reform and social justice. To accomplish his goals, he established the Works Progress Administration (WPA) that helped many poor people and built massive projects (like the Blue Ridge Parkway). Next, he enacted the Social Security Act that provided a safety net and retirement income for workers.

Finally, in 1937–1938, Roosevelt implemented a third new deal. He did this mostly to help homeless farmers and agricultural workers.

The New Deal failed to stop the Great Depression. Only World War II could end the Depression. However, the New Deal convinced most Americans that their government had a moral and legal right to intervene in public and private affairs if the general good of the public demanded it. America, for better or for worse, was never to be the same. While the economic picture improved, the spiritual damage was done. Many Americans, including John Steinbeck, remained bitter the rest of their lives. Steinbeck turned his bitterness toward God and exhibited a particularly harsh form of naturalism in his writings.

Bust of John Steinbeck in Monterey, California, location of *Cannery Row*. Photo by Carol Highsmith, date unknown, www.loc.gov/pictures/item/2011634742.

Assignments

- Warm-up: Interview someone who lived during the Great Depression. What was it like?

- Students should complete Concept Builder 25-A.

- Students review the required reading(s) *before* the assigned chapter begins.

- Teachers may want to discuss assigned reading(s) with students.

- Teachers shall assign the required essay. The rest of the essays can be outlined, answered with shorter answers, discussed, or skipped.

- Students will review all readings for chapter 25.

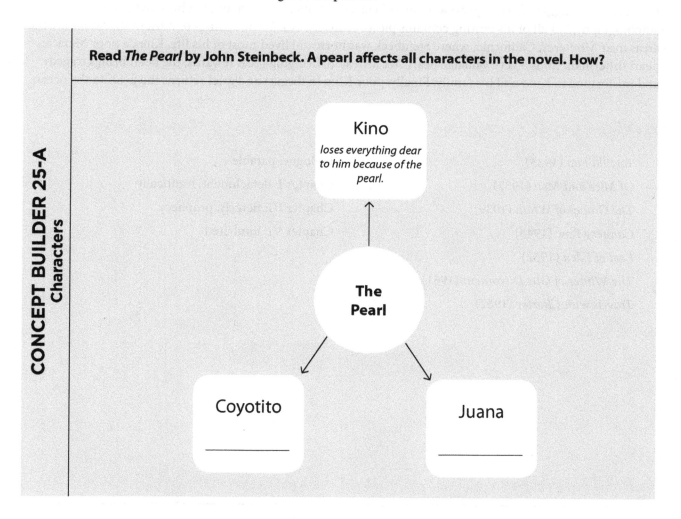

CONCEPT BUILDER 25-A
Characters

Read *The Pearl* by John Steinbeck. A pearl affects all characters in the novel. How?

Kino

loses everything dear to him because of the pearl.

The Pearl

Coyotito

_____

Juana

_____

About the Author

John Steinbeck, American writer and Nobel laureate, wrote about his life in fictional books. He described in his work the struggle of people who were marginalized in American society. Steinbeck never wrote an autobiography, but all of his writing contains pieces of his life story. The settings of most of the books are the areas near Monterey, California, where Steinbeck was born and lived most of his life. Kino, a poor Mexican pearl fisherman, finds a very valuable pearl. Yet instead of bringing great rewards, the pearl brings tragedy and misfortune to Kino and his family. Finally, poor Kino in disgust and grief returns the pearl to the ocean.

Other Notable Works

Tortilla Flat (1935)

Of Mice and Men (1937)

The Grapes of Wrath (1939)

Cannery Row (1945)

East of Eden (1952)

The Winter of Our Discontent (1961)

Travels with Charley (1962)

Vocabulary Words

Epilogue: parable

Chapter I: detachment, frantically

Chapter III: fiercely, prophecy

Chapter VI: lumbered

Assignments

- Warm-up: In what way is this novel autobiographical?
- Students should complete Concept Builder 25-B.
- Student *should* review reading(s) from the next chapter.
- Student should outline essay due at the end of the week.
- Per teacher instructions, students may answer orally, in a group setting, some of the essays that are not assigned as formal essays.

A central theme of this naturalist novel is the concept of fate, that human beings are never really free, because the course of their lives is determined by outside forces; in this novel, outside malevolent forces. How does Steinbeck create this theme? There are many correct answers.

Kino is born into a poor life.

Fate

_____

_____

_____

Quotes from *The Pearl*

classiclit.about.com/od/pearljohnsteinbeck/a/aa_thepearl.htm.

"And, as with all retold tales that are in people's hearts, there are only good and bad things and black and white things and good and evil things and no in-between. If this story is a parable, perhaps everyone takes his own meaning from it and reads his own life into it." — Prologue

"Sometimes it rose to an aching chord that caught the throat, saying this is safety, this is warmth, this is the Whole." — Chapter 1

". . . there were more illusions than realities." — Chapter 2

"A plan is a real thing, and things projected are experienced. A plan once made and visualized becomes a reality along with other realities — never to be destroyed but easily to be attacked." — Chapter 3

"For his dream of the future was real and never to be destroyed, and he had said, 'I will go,' and that made a real thing too. To determine to go and to say it was to be halfway there." — Chapter 4

"This pearl has become my soul. . . . If I give it up, I shall lose my soul." — Chapter 5

"And then Kino's brain cleared from its red concentration and he knew the sound — the keening, moaning, rising hysterical cry from the little cave in the side of the stone mountain, the cry of death." — Chapter 6

". . . removed from human experience; that they had gone through pain and had come out on the other side; that there was almost a magical protection about them." — Chapter 6

"And the music of the pearl drifted to a whisper and disappeared." — Chapter 6

Assignments

- Warm-up: What is your favorite quote?
- Students should complete Concept Builder 25-C.
- Students should write rough drafts of assigned essay.
- The teacher may correct rough drafts.

Find two examples of situational irony, an outcome that turns out to be very different from what was expected.

Situational Irony

Foreshadowing

In his work *The Pearl*, modern naturalist author John Steinbeck uses the literary technique of foreshadowing. Simply put, foreshadowing is the literary device where an author suggests plot developments that are yet to come. In *The Pearl*, Steinbeck uses the protagonist's wife, Juana, to foreshadow the destruction that the pearl will bring upon their immediate family.

Only the second night in Kino's possession of the pearl, an attempt to steal it is made — the first taste of the destruction the pearl will soon bring upon him and his family:

> . . . and then the sound came again! The whisper of a foot on dry earth and the scratch of fingers in the soil. . . . Kino's hand crept into his breast where is knife hung on a string, and then he sprang like an angry cat, leaped striking and spitting for the dark thing he knew was in the corner . . . his head crashed like lighting and exploded with pain (John Steinbeck, *The Pearl* p. 37).

Though the attempt is foiled and the pearl is safe, Kino nonetheless receives an injury. While dressing his wound, his wife, Juana, recognizes the danger which the pearl brings and attempts to warn him of it. " 'This pearl is like a sin! It will destroy us,' and her voice rose shrilly . . . 'It has brought evil. Kino, my husband, it will destroy us' " (Ibid., p. 38). Though the pearl has not brought tragedy on the scale presented later in the book, the coming doom is foreshadowed through Juana.

The consequences of owning the pearl intensify when Kino is found, beaten and left for dead by a group of thugs. After finding him bleeding and senseless in the road, she warns of the coming tragedy that the Pearl will bring: "Kino, this pearl is evil. Let us destroy it before it destroys us. . . . Kino, it is evil, it is evil!" (Ibid., p. 56).

All of Juana's forebodings are fulfilled when, later in the plot, a string of tragedies waylay Kino and his family. First, his house is burned down — "a tall edifice of fire lightened the pathway. Kino broke into a run; it was his brush house, he knew." He attempts to flee by means of the ocean, only to discover that his boat is destroyed — the most valuable possession he owns. Without the ocean, he turns to the land, hoping to evade the trackers. Finally, in the last confrontation, his baby — the most precious thing he has — is killed — ". . . he saw Coyotito lying in the little cave with the top of his head shot away."

All of this tragedy was foretold by Juana. Through Juana, Steinbeck suggested a plot device — tragedy — which was yet to come. From the beginning of the book, the eventual misery into which Kino and his family is plunged is foretold by Juana. (Daniel, Age 15 - shared with permission)

Assignments

- Warm-up: How does Steinbeck use foreshadowing in his book?
- Students should complete Concept Builder 25-D.
- Student will re-write corrected copies of essay due tomorrow.

Steinbeck, the author, is trying to make a social statement. He uses his plot and characters to make that statement. There are many correct answers.

The rich take advantage of the poor.

Theme

Through this short novel, *The Pearl*, John Steinbeck displays three themes: greed racism, and man's destiny. Steinbeck speaks of how man is susceptible quickly to becoming greedy, how tensions exist between various races, and how, in Steinbeck's view, fate is an important part of human destiny.

Initially, Kino, the main character, is a selfless, humble man caring for others. "Down the rope that hung the baby's box from the roof support a scorpion moved slowly. . . . He [Kino] could not move until the scorpion moved, and it felt for the source of death that was coming to it. . . . Kino's hand leaped to catch it [the scorpion], but it fell past his fingers, fell on the baby's shoulder, landed and struck." Kino was willing to risk his life to save the life of his son. However, this quickly changed after Kino found the pearl. " 'No,' he [Kino] said. 'I will fight this thing. I will win over it. We will have our chance.' His fist pounded the sleeping mat. 'No one shall take our good fortune from us,' he said. His eyes softened then and he raised a gentle hand to Juana's shoulder. 'Believe me,' he said. 'I am a man.' And his face grew crafty." Kino felt a strong desire to keep the pearl. He even decided to leave town to keep his dear pearl. " 'Kino,'

said huskily, 'I am afraid. A man can be killed: Let us throw the pearl back into the sea.' " Even though his wife was frightened and wanted to dispose of the pearl, Kino insisted on keeping his pearl; placing the value of the pearl over his wife's interest. Greedy Kino's love and desire for his pearl blinded him from attending to his wife's needs and fears.

In addition to greed, John Steinbeck uses racism in his story as the island doctor refused to treat Kino's injured son because of his race. "Kino hesitated a moment. This doctor was not of his people. This doctor was of a race which for nearly four hundred years had beaten and starved and robbed and despised Kino's race, and frightened it too, so that the indigene came humbly to the door." The doctor felt his race was superior to that of Kino. Even though Kino's son was injured by a scorpion, the doctor refused to help Kino because of his race. Through this, Steinbeck displays how tensions exist between various races, and how humans view each other differently simply by each other's heritage and racial background.

Steinbeck also shows how, in his view, fate plays a large role in man's destiny. Out of all the other pearlers, fate chose to bestow the pearl on Kino. "He [Kino] looked speculatively at the basket. Perhaps it would be better to open the oyster last." Out of the many pearls on the sea bed, Kino luckily chose the right oyster, containing a beautiful pearl inside. By including fate in his book, Steinbeck tries to show the reader how large of a role fate plays in shaping a human's destiny and life. Kino was a typical pearler, who by fate, was given a pearl that changed his life.

These three themes: greed, racism, and fate, provide opportunities for Steinbeck to teach the reader about various issues in human life. Steinbeck writes of how a human's behavior can suddenly turn to greed through one instance; how some humans are divided simply by their race; and how many things in human life occur by chance and are determined by fate. (Chris – shared with permission)

Assignments

- Warm-up: List several themes in *The Pearl*.
- Students should complete Concept Builder 25-E.
- Essays are due. Students should take the chapter 25 test.

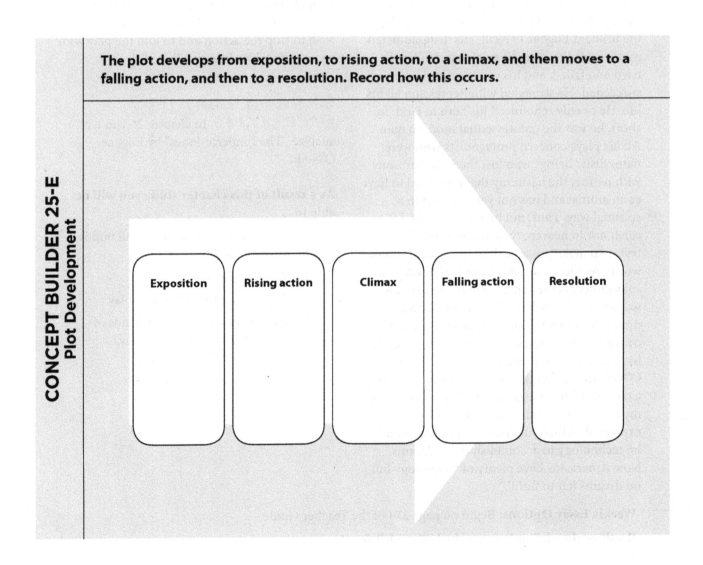

CONCEPT BUILDER 25-E
Plot Development

The plot develops from exposition, to rising action, to a climax, and then moves to a falling action, and then to a resolution. Record how this occurs.

| Exposition | Rising action | Climax | Falling action | Resolution |

Chapter 26

1946–1960 (Part 1):

The Modern Age: Realism/Naturalism

First Thoughts American playwright Eugene Gladstone O'Neill revolutionized American drama. His plays made American drama a major player on the stage of Western theater. He moved American theater from flippant comedies to earthy naturalistic plays. There is perhaps no more tragic figure in American literary history than the brilliant Eugene O'Neill. His drug-addicted mother tried to commit suicide but failed, he tried and failed, and his son tried and succeeded. He struggled with depression all his life. He openly renounced his faith in God. In short, he was the quintessential modern man. All his plays concern protagonists who were naturalistic beings who lost their old harmony with nature, the harmony that they used to have as an animal and has not yet acquired in a spiritual way. Thus, not being able to find it on earth nor in heaven, they are in the middle, trying to make peace with themselves and their world. As the critic Toby Cole explained, "The subject here is the same ancient one that always was and always will be the one subject for drama, and that is man and his struggle with his own fate. The struggle … is now with himself, his own past, his attempt 'to belong.' " (Eugene O'Neill in Playwrights on Playwriting, ed. Toby Cole, 1961 kirjasto.sci.fi/oneill.htm). As one of my professors at Harvard, Harvey Cox, explained, "Once Americans had dreams and no technology to accomplish those dreams. Now Americans have plenty of technology but no dreams left to fulfill."

Author Worldview Watch Eugene Gladsone O'Neill, perhaps best 20th century playwright, perhaps without his knowledge, writes a Christian moral expose of the effect of unforgiveness. After O'Neill rejected his faith and adopted atheism, he struggled with understanding a world that could exist with a god. Readers will continually wish to stop the action and to join the play with encouraging words to this lost soul.

Chapter Learning Objectives In chapter 26 you will analyze "The Emperor Jones" by Eugene O'Neill.

As a result of this chapter study you will be able to . . .

1. Discuss in detail how O'Neill builds suspense in this play.

2. Analyze the setting.

3. Discuss the themes in this play.

4. Comment on the several kinds of conflict that arise in this play.

Weekly Essay Options: Begin on page 274 of the Teacher Guide.

Reading ahead: "Little Foxes" by Lillian Hellman.

History connections: *American History* chapter 26, "The Vietnam War"

The Emperor Jones
Eugene O'Neill

Background "The Emperor Jones" is a 1920 play by American dramatist Eugene O'Neill that tells the haunting tale of Brutus Jones, an African-American male who kills a man, escapes to a Caribbean island, and sets up a kingdom. The play recounts his story in flashbacks as Brutus makes his way through the forest in an attempt to escape former subjects who have rebelled against him.

The play displays an uneasy mix of expressionism and surrealism, which is also characteristic of several other O'Neill plays. It was O'Neill's first play to receive great box office success, and the one that launched his career.

Assignments

- Warm-up: The Emperor Jones was haunted by unforgivingness that had been visited on him by others. Tragically, he was destroyed by that unforgivingness. Twenty years after World War II, a psychologist conducted a study of survivors of the Nazi concentration camps and their guards. To his horror, he discovered that the survivors had a higher divorce rate, suicide rate, and even higher rate of death by cancer than the concentration camp guards. In spite of the fact that the guards were guilty of heinous crimes, and the former inmates were innocent victims, it was the innocent victims who fared much poorer. Propose a reason for why this was so.

- Students should complete Concept Builder 26-A.

- Students review the required reading(s) *before* the assigned chapter begins.

- Teachers may want to discuss assigned reading(s) with students.

- Teachers shall assign the required essay. The rest of the essays can be outlined, answered with shorter answers, discussed, or skipped.

- Students will review all readings for chapter 26.

Read "The Emperor Jones" (Scene One) by Eugene O'Neill and then answer the following questions.

1	What do the readers learn about the Emperor before they meet him?
2	Why does O'Neil begin with a preface/commentary where he can speak directly to the audience?
3	Who is Smithers and how does O'Neill use him in this play?
4	Why does Jones call himself a deprecatory name?
5	How will this play end?
6	What did Emperor Jones tell his subjects about a silver bullet?

The Life of a Play

1920 Premiere "The Emperor Jones" was first staged on November 1, 1920, at the Playwright's Theater in New York City. Charles Sidney Gilpin was the first actor to play the role of Brutus Jones on stage and O'Neill said later that he was the only actor who had played the role to his satisfaction (Eoneill.com).

The 1924 Revival Although Gilpin continued to perform the role of Brutus Jones in the U.S. tour that followed the Broadway closing of the play, he eventually had a falling out with O'Neill. O'Neill replaced Gilpin with Paul Robeson as Brutus Jones in the London production. Robeson received excellent reviews and, coupled with his performance in the 1928 London production of the musical "Show Boat," Robeson went on to worldwide fame as one of the great black artists of all time (http://en.wikipedia.org/wiki/The_Emperor_Jones).

Federal Theatre Project The Federal Theatre Project of the Works Progress Administration launched several productions of the play in cities across the United States in 1938

Exterior of the Provincetown Playhouse. Photographer unknown, c1919 (PD-US).

(Federal Theatre (Memory)". *American Treasures of the Library of Congress*. Library of Congress. 2008. Retrieved 2009-02-16).

Assignments

- Warm-up: How might the Emperor Jones have ended differently if Brutus Jones had been redeemed?

- Students should complete Concept Builder 26-B.

- Student *should* review reading(s) from the next chapter.

- Student should outline essay due at the end of the week.

- Per teacher instructions, students may answer orally, in a group setting, some of the essays that are not assigned as formal essays.

The author, O'Neill, effectively builds suspense (a state of uncertainty, anxiety). How?

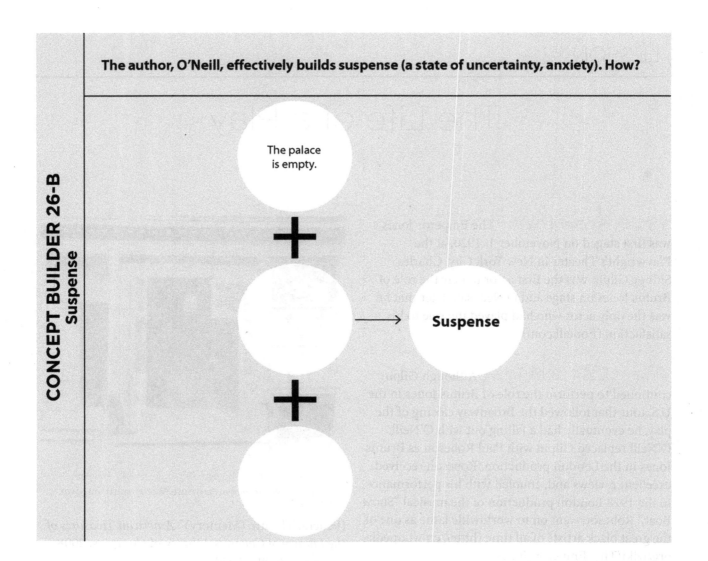

The palace
is empty.

+

+

Suspense

Movie Review

After having aroused keen interest as a drama and then as an opera, Eugene O'Neill's masterly work, *The Emperor Jones*, was presented last night at the Rivoli in talking pictorial form. And the producers, John Krimsky and Gifford Cochran, who amassed the money for producing the film from their profits on the German production, "Maedchen in Uniform," have every reason to feel proud of the screen adaptation. It is a distinguished offering, resolute and firm, with a most compelling portrayal by Paul Robeson of the ambitious Negro Pullman porter, Brutus Jones.

Although the narrative is slightly amplified, it is developed along intelligent cinematic lines and differs really but little from the sum total of the original. Instead of beginning on the island with Emperor Jones and his tottering throne, it goes into detail concerning his earlier life, his work as a Pullman car porter, his predilection for crapshoot-ing, his killing of a negro, his presence in a chain gang and his escape. It is a closely woven narrative in which there is not an instant that does not hold one's attention.

Dudley Murphy, the director, and DuBose Heyward, the author of the script, have attacked their respective tasks without any idea of catering to the box office. They realized the power of the O'Neill drama and have put forth a picture which retains the strength of the stage production. The telling of the story is just what one might expect from such competent and experienced persons. It is satisfying and absorbing, and even the beating of the drums, which one might anticipate would be done some-what extravagantly, is accomplished with the same effectiveness it was when the play first appeared in 1920 in Greenwich Village.

The interest of the drama is centred, naturally, on Brutus Jones's activities on the island where he chooses to rule over the blacks and be known as Emperor Jones. The introductory passages, however, are not without their stirring moments, particularly the amorous episodes and those depicting the gradual transition in the Negro's character. But when the scenes on the island—to which Brutus Jones swims after having made his escape from the chain gang and shipped as a stoker on a tramp—come to the screen, it is then that the picture is most stirring.

Dudley Digges portrays the cockney trader, Smithers, who is almost as ruthless in his dealings with the natives as Jones. The Negro, on proclaiming himself ruler of the territory, insists that no ordinary lead bullet will ever kill him; according to him, his life can only be snuffed out by a silver missile. Smithers and Jones go into partnership as traders and, when Jones becomes emperor, he sees to it that he has a gaudy uniform with a befeathered headgear. Being inordinately vain, he arranges to have his throne room walled with mirrors, so that he may gaze at himself as he stalks through the place.

There is an extraordinarily gripping episode when the distant beating of drums is heard for the first time. Jones is talking to Smithers, still believing that at a signal from him his many servitors will appear, despite the stillness in the building. He sounds a gong, but nothing happens, and then he realizes the meaning of the beating of tomtoms. In his uniform and high patent-leather boots, Jones decides that he will make his escape afoot, after being informed by Smithers that there are no horses left. Jones has food hidden in the woods, but when he reaches the spot, he cannot find any. He loses his way and all the time there is the monotonous beating of the drums, growing gradually nearer and nearer.

Brutus Jones sheds his uniform and tramps on, thoroughly confused. His boots are no longer comfortable, and as time passes he beholds spectres of the past—a vision of the man he killed, then others, and he shoots until the only cartridge left is his silver bullet intended for himself.

Mr. Robeson adds to the interest of one or two opening scenes by his singing. Others in the cast, which is composed wholly of Negroes, except for Mr. Digges, serve the picture with marked zeal and thoroughness. Mr. Digges's interpretation of the trader Smithers is comparable with his other efficient portrayals (Mordaunt Hall, review of *The Emperor Jones*, New York Times, September 20, 1933; movies.nytimes.com/movie/review?res=9B05E 4D61430EF3ABC4851DFBF668388629EDE).

Assignments

- Warm-up: What is your favorite quote?
- Students should complete Concept Builder 26-C.
- Students should write rough drafts of assigned essay.
- The teacher may correct rough drafts.

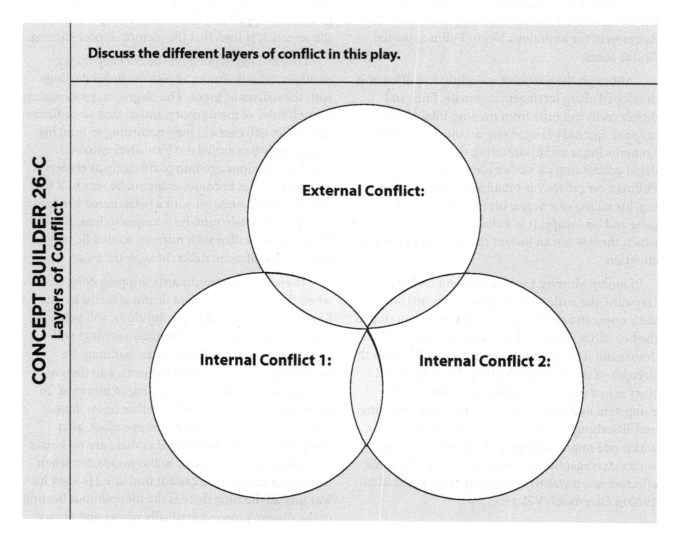

CONCEPT BUILDER 26-C
Layers of Conflict

Discuss the different layers of conflict in this play.

External Conflict:

Internal Conflict 1:

Internal Conflict 2:

Brother Palmer Garner

He was an ordinary pastor, Brother Garner, the sort of pastor you would expect a church board to send to my south Arkansas town in 1965.

South Arkansas was unprepared to face the present, much less the future. The Civil War hung like a heavy shroud on this declining railroad town. Less than 100 years before, Yankee soldiers had unceremoniously marched through our swamps to Vicksburg. To our eternal shame, no significant resistance was offered, except a brief unsuccessful skirmish at Boggy Bayou.

A pastor distinguished only by his mediocrity, Palmer Garner seemed committed to irrelevance. Despite the fact that desegregation was fracturing our fragile community and some of our neighbors and relatives were warring with the Army Reserve units at Central High School in Little Rock, Arkansas, Garner was warning us of "immoral thoughts." Most of us had not had an "immoral thought" since Elvis Presley played in the old VA gym.

The only redeeming feature of Brother Garner's sermons was that they were mercifully short. They allowed us to get to Lawson Cafe's hickory-smoked pork ribs before the Southern Baptists!

We never liked Garner's sensitivity. It seemed so effeminate — un-Christian, really. He seemed to be an incorrigible sentimentalist, and while Southern ethos was full of tradition and veiled sentimentalism, we fiercely hid our true feelings.

Garner was, however, a greater threat to our fragile equilibrium. David Scales, a African-American high school scholar and track star, had a conversion experience at one of our revival services. He foolishly thought that since Jesus loved him, we would, too. So he tried to attend our Sunday morning worship service. But he was politely asked to leave during the assurance of pardon.

Garner saw everything and was obviously displeased. Not that he castigated us. We could handle that. We enjoyed pastors who scolded us for our sins. We tolerated, even enjoyed, his paternalistic diatribes. No, Garner did the intolerable: he wept. Right in the middle of morning worship, right where great preachers like Muzon Mann had labored, where our children were baptized, Garner wept! Right in the middle of morning worship, as if it was part of the liturgy, he started crying! Not loud, uncontrollable sobs, but quiet, deep crying.

Old Man Henley, senile and almost deaf, remembering the last time he cried — when his wife died — started crying too. And then the children. How we hated Palmer Garner! If we ever doubted, Garner was obviously an outsider to our community.

Well Brother Garner did not last the year. He was moved to an obscure church in North Arkansas and I heard he died in ignominiousness.

I never forgot that day. It changed my life. As I grew older, the embarrassment of watching my pastor cry was replaced first by admiration and then awe. What a courageous man! I owe so much to Palmer Garner. He taught me how to cry and what to cry for. He showed me that the really important changes required time, courage, and tears.

— James P. Stobaugh

(Portions of the above essay appear in Stobaugh, *American History*. It also is part of the conclusion of James P. Stobaugh, *Racial Anger as an Obstacle for Racial Reconciliation*, unpublished dissertation.)

Assignments

- Warm-up: Do you have someone who deeply affected your life and encouraged you in your faith? Describe him or her.

- Students should complete Concept Builder 26-D.

- Student will re-write corrected copies of essay due tomorrow.

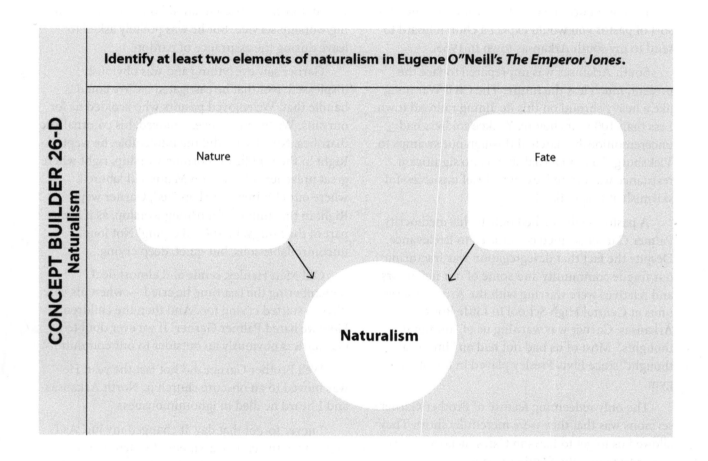

CONCEPT BUILDER 26-D
Naturalism

Identify at least two elements of naturalism in Eugene O"Neill's *The Emperor Jones*.

Nature

Fate

Naturalism

Student Essay:
Suspense in *Emperor Jones*

Eugene O"Neill, in "The Emperor Jones," uses suspense to keep the reader intrigued by the story. O'Neill uses all aspects of the story including dialogue, narration, setting, and the plot itself to create suspense. All these parts of the story work together to build suspense as the story progresses.

"In the rear of the forest is a wall of darkness dividing the world. Only when the eye becomes accustomed to the gloom can the outlines of separate trunks of the nearest trees be made out, enormous pillars of deeper blackness. A somber monotone of wind lost in the leaves moans in the air. Yet this sound serves but to intensify the impression of the forest's relentless immobility, to form a background throwing into relief its brooding, implacable silence." As this story is a play, O'Neill must tell the reader where the story is taking place, and what the setting looks like. Using carefully chosen words, the author creates a scene in which the reader expects something awful to happen.

O'Neill also uses dialogue and the plot itself, in addition to narration and the setting, to build anticipation in his story. "They'll be after you 'ot and 'eavy. Ole Lem is at the bottom o' this business an' 'e 'ates you…" Here, Smithers is telling the Emperor Jones how several people wish to harm him. Despite the risks of being caught, Jones decides to try and escape from his angry subjects. At this point, the reader wonders whether Jones will successfully escape or if his subjects will capture him, creating more suspense.

In addition to narration and dialogue, O'Neill allows the actor to create more suspense. Because the story is a play, more emotion and real reactions to the plot can create more suspense. O'Neill allows the actor to develop more suspense in the story as he or she acts it out. During the dialogue, the author inserts words such as "gutturally, mockingly, calmly, peremptorily" that suggest how scenes should be acted: what mood or tone should be created. The actor is able to take these suggestions, in addition to his or her own interpretation of scenes, and create more suspense. O'Neill provides the basic groundwork for the story, but allows the actor to insert more emotion and detail into the story. In this way, suspense is created.

O'Neill uses a combination of dialogue, the setting, narration, and the plot itself to create suspense in his play. The narrator creates a mood, expecting certain events, as he or she describes the setting. O'Neill also incorporates dialogue into the plot to builds suspense, as characters warn each other of dangers that lie ahead. Likewise, the ability for the story to be interpreted by actors allows for even more suspense and anxiety. (Chris)

Assignments

- Warm-up: How does O'Neill build suspense in this play?
- Students should complete Concept Builder 26-E.
- Essays are due. Students should take the chapter 26 test.

Through dialogue, readers can know each character's thoughts and feelings. Likewise, the author can advance the plot. There are three types of dialogue: monologue, soliloquy, and an aside. A monologue is a long speech that is spoken by a single character to himself or herself, or to the audience. A soliloquy is a monologue where the character speaks private thoughts aloud. An aside is a comment that is delivered by a character to the audience, who are on stage. Identify the following dialogue examples.

Type of Dialogue	Dialogue
	Ain't got no bullet left on'y de silver one. If mo' o' dem ha'nts come after me, how I gwine skeer dem away? … If I shoots dat one I'm a goner sho', it's black heah! Whar's de moon? …, don't dis night evah come to an end? (By the sounds, he is feeling his way cautiously forward.) Dere! Dis feels like a clear space. I gotta lie down an' rest.… I gotta rest.
	JONES — (gloomily) You kin bet yo' whole roll on one thing, white man. Dis baby plays out his string to de end and when he quits, he quits wid a bang de way he ought. Silver bullet ain't none too good for him when he go, dat's a fac'l — (then shaking off his nervousness — with a confident laugh) Sho'! what is I talkin' about? Ain't come to dat yit and I never will — … Silver bullet bring me luck anyway. I kin outguess, outrun, outfight, an' outplay de whole lot o' dem all ovah de board any time o' de day er night! You watch me! (From the distant hills comes the faint, steady thump of a tom-tom, low and vibrating. It starts at a rate exactly corresponding to normal pulse beat — 72 to the minute — and continues at a gradually accelerated rate from this point uninterruptedly to the very end of the play. Jones starts at the sound. A strange look of apprehension creeps into his face for a moment as he listens. Then he asks, with an attempt to regain his most casual manner.) What's dat drum beatin' fo'?
	In the forest. The moon has just risen. Its beams, drifting through the canopy of leaves, make a barely perceptible, suffused, eerie glow. A dense low wall of under-brush and creepers is in the nearer foreground, fencing in a small triangular clearing. Beyond this is the massed blackness of the forest like an encompassing barrier. A path is dimly discerned leading down to the clearing from left, rear, and winding away from it again toward the right. As the scene opens nothing can be distinctly made out. Except for the beating of the tom-tom, which is a trifle louder and quicker than in the previous scene, there is silence, broken every few seconds by a queer, clicking sound. Then gradually the figure of the negro, Jeff, can be discerned crouching on his haunches at the rear of the triangle. He is middle-aged, thin, brown in color, is dressed in a Pullman porter's uniform, cap, etc. He is throwing a pair of dice on the ground before him, picking them up, shaking them, casting them out with the regular, rigid, mechanical movements of an automaton. The heavy, plodding footsteps of someone approaching along the trail from the left are heard and Jones' voice, pitched in a slightly higher key and strained in a cheering effort to overcome its own tremors.

Chapter 27

1946–1960 (Part 2):
The Modern Age: Realism/Naturalism

First Thoughts "Cynicism is an unpleasant way to tell the truth," Hellman says in her play "The Little Foxes," and this more-or-less sums up her life. Lillian Hellman (1905–1984) became a writer at a time when there was no television, much less any Internet, when writers were celebrities. She more than held her own in this department. In a group that included Fitzgerald, Hemingway, Faulkner, and Hammett, Lillian Hellman was an *avant garde* radical. Hellman maintained a lavish and controversial lifestyle that offended many Americans.

She was born in New Orleans, Louisiana, and her family moved back and forth from New York City, so she was also absorbed in the New York artistic scene. Later she moved to Hollywood where she spent the remainder of her life writing for MGM, but she never forgot her Southern roots, and they reappeared in all her literary works.

Author Worldview Watch Lillian Hellman in her smash Broadway hit exposes, as Edward Albee in *Who's Afraid of Virginia Woolf?*, the facileness and ineptitude of marriage that is not centered on Christ and the Word of God. Again, Hellman borrows biblical characters--the main female character is a Jezebel double--to explore biblical themes--filial betrayal. However, Hellman, like so many of her literary peers, let's the horse out of the barn but she can't ride it because one cannot really ameliorate a sacred institution like marriage without the Bible.

Chapter Learning Objectives In chapter 27 you will analyze "The Little Foxes" by Lillian Hellman and "The Glass Menagerie" by Tennessee Williams.

As a result of this chapter study you will be able to . . .

1. Describe in great detail the relationship of Horace and his wife Regina. This relationship is a key element of the play.

2. Evaluate this play according to how well Mrs. Hellman presented a credible plot, setting, characterization, conflict, and resolution.

3. Compare Regina Giddens to Jezebel.

Weekly Essay Options: Begin on page 274 of the Teacher Guide.

Lillian Hellman

Lillian Hellman became a writer at a time when writers were celebrities and their iconoclastic behavior was admired. Like Fitzgerald and Hemingway, Hellman was a very talented and bohemian author.

A southerner to the core, Hellman's life was populated by eccentric relatives who later appeared only in her plays. By the early 1930s, Hellman was writing movies. Though she found the work dull, it provided her the opportunity to meet a wider range of creative people and to become involved in the artistic and political world of the times.

Throughout the 1940s and 1950s she continued to write plays and increase her political activism. Her anti-fascist works "Watch the Rhine" (1941) and "The Searching Wind" (1944) directly criticized America's failures to address and fight Hitler and Mussolini in their early years. Blacklisted in the 1950s for her leftist activism, Hellman continued to write and to speak out against the injustices around her.

On June 30, 1984. Lillian Hellman died in Martha's Vineyard, Massachusetts, at the age of 79. Lillian Hellman will be remembered not only as a political activist and talented playwright, but as a woman who lived life the way she sought to live it (www.pbs.org/wnet/americanmasters/episodes/lillian-hellman/about-lillian-hellman/628/).

Assignments

- Warm-up: How can a writer's "voice" on the page sometimes bring them pain as he or she works to honestly convey personal thoughts and feelings?
- Students should complete Concept Builder 27-A.
- Students review the required reading(s) *before* the assigned chapter begins.
- Teachers may want to discuss assigned reading(s) with students.
- Teachers shall assign the required essay. The rest of the essays can be outlined, answered with shorter answers, discussed, or skipped.
- Students will review all readings for chapter 27.

CONCEPT BUILDER 27-A
Character Development

Read "The Little Foxes" by Lillian Hellman, and then on the chart below, circle the words that describe Horace and underline the words that describe Regina. This relationship is a key element of the play.

Melancholic	Choleric
moody anxious rigid sober pessimistic reserved unsociable quiet	touchy restless aggressive excitable changeable impulsive optimistic active
Phlegmatic	**Sanguine**
passive careful thoughtful peaceful controlled reliable even-tempered calm	sociable outgoing talkative responsive easy-going lively carefree leadership

Horace

Regina

The Life of a Play

1920 Premiere "The Little Foxes" is perhaps the most famous achievement of Lillian Hellman. In the chicanery of the Hubbard family we have one of the best pictures of the rise of Southern industrialism in the post-Civil War period.

Its title comes from Song of Solomon 2:15, which reads, "Catch for us the foxes, the little foxes that ruin the vineyards, our vineyards that are in bloom." Set in a small town in Alabama in 1900, it focuses on the struggle between the new South and the old South.

Assignments

- Warm-up: What struggles do you see in your city, state, or country that might be the impetus of a new novel?
- Students should complete Concept Builder 27-B.
- Student *should* review reading(s) from the next chapter.
- Student should outline essay due at the end of the week.
- Per teacher instructions, students may answer orally, in a group setting, some of the essays that are not assigned as formal essays.

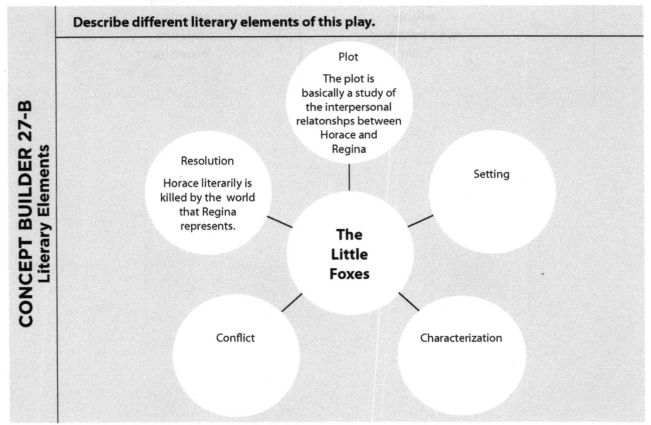

CONCEPT BUILDER 27-B
Literary Elements

Describe different literary elements of this play.

Plot
The plot is basically a study of the interpersonal relatonshps between Horace and Regina

Resolution
Horace literarily is killed by the world that Regina represents.

The Little Foxes

Setting

Characterization

Conflict

Villains in American Literature

Roger Chillingworth Roger Prynne is the husband of Hester Prynne in *The Scarlet Letter* by Nathaniel Hawthorne. He appears in town as Roger Chillingworth, and proceeds to plot against Hester and Arthur Dimmesdale. He becomes an embodiment of evil as his physical appearance shifts. He seeks to destroy Dimmesdale for impregnating his wife.

Chillingworth, an embodiment of evil, is a scientist who ignores his humanity for revenge. Hawthorne portrays Chillingworth as a classic cerebral man; even his deformed body, of which "one shoulder was slightly higher than the other," acts as a symbol of his inability to deal with the physical world.

John Claggart Claggart is the antagonist in Herman Melville's *Billy Budd*. The odd thing about Claggart is that he seems to be quite intelligent, and no one can quite figure out how he got to be in the navy. Rumor has it that Claggart was a small-time criminal in England, and that he was drafted into the navy directly from prison. But no one seems to know anything about him for sure. Like Chillingworth, then, he is mysterious. Even his citizenship is in doubt, because Claggart's accent has a hint of something foreign. This vagueness about his background is the one thing he has in common with Billy. If Billy Budd is a Christ-like figure, and he is, Claggart is Satan.

Regina Gibbens Regina Hubbard Giddens ("The Little Foxes") struggles for wealth with her two brothers, who, by virtue of their gender, were named recipients of their father's wealth. Money hungry, the two brothers control the family wealth, while Regina is supported by her disabled husband Horace. Benjamin and Oscar, the brothers, decide to build a cotton mill but are $75,000 short of the necessary funding. Asking their sister for the money, Horace refuses. Oscar suggests a marriage between his son and Regina's daughter. After being repulsed, he asks Horace outright for the money. When he refuses, a bank representative is pressured into helping Oscar steal Horace's railroad bonds stored there. When Horace discovers the theft, he decides to change his will, cutting Regina out in favor of their daughter and declaring the banker's theft of the bonds as a loan. But he is never able to do this. He dies of a heart attack because Regina will not give him his medicine. She makes no mention of the intended changes in the will but instead blackmails the banker unless she acquires majority ownership of the mill. Alienating her daughter, in the end of the play Regina is herself an outcast.

Assignments

- Warm-up: Why are some people drawn to literary villains?
- Students should complete Concept Builder 27-C.
- Students should write rough drafts of assigned essay.
- The teacher may correct rough drafts.

"The Little Foxes" influenced a literary movement that dominated American culture from about 1918 to 1950. Find examples of modernism in this play.

Modernism Element	Incident In Play
Alienation among even the most intimate friends	
Theme of change	
Use of irony	
Opposed to tradition	

Movie Reviews

The Little Foxes By Bosley Crowther (August 22, 1941)

Lillian Hellman's grim and malignant melo-drama, "The Little Foxes," which had the National Theatre's stage running knee-deep in gall and wormwood the season before last, has now been translated to the screen with all its original viciousness intact and with such extra-added virulence as the relentless camera of Director William Wyler and the tensile acting of Bette Davis could impart. As presented at the Music Hall yesterday, under the trade-mark of Samuel Goldwyn, *The Little Foxes* leaps to the front as the most bitingly sinister picture of the year and as one of the most cruelly realistic character studies yet shown on the screen.

… Henrik Ibsen and William Faulkner could not together have designed a more morbid account of inter-family treachery and revoltingly ugly greed than was contained in Miss Hellman's purple drama of deadly intrigue in the Hubbard clan. And with a perfect knowledge of the camera's flexibility, the author and Mr. Wyler have derived out of the play a taut and cumulative screen story which exhales the creepy odor of decay and freezes charitable blood with the deliberation of a Frigidaire.

Frankly, there is nothing pretty nor inspiring about this almost fustian tale of Regina Giddens's foxiness in planting figurative knives in her own deceitful brothers' backs, of her callous neglect of her good husband when he is dying of a heart attack, all because she wants to grab the bulk of the family's rising fortune for herself. The whole suspense of the picture lies in the question of who's going to sink the last knife. Even the final elopement of Regina's appalled daughter, for whom the film conveniently provides a nice romance, adds little more than a touch of leavening irony. Regina is too hard a woman to mourn much for anything.

Thus the test of the picture is the effectiveness with which it exposes a family of evil people poisoning everything they touch. And this it does spectacularly. Mr. Wyler, with the aid of Gregg Toland, has used the camera to sweep in the myriad small details of a mauve decadent household and the more indicative facets of the many characters. The focus is sharp, the texture of the images hard and realistic. Individual scenes are extraordinarily vivid and compelling, such as that in which the Hubbard brothers plot a way to outdo their sister, or the almost unbearable scene in which Regina permits her husband to struggle un-assisted with death. Only when Mr. Wyler plays obvious tricks with mirrors does a bit of pretension creep in.

And Miss Davis's performance in the role which Talluluh Bankhead played so brassily on the stage is abundant with color and mood. True, she does occasionally drop an unmistakable imitation of her predecessor; she performs queer contortions with her arms like a nautch-dancer in a Hindu temple, and generally she comports herself as though she were balancing an Academy "Oscar" on her high-coiffed head. But the role calls for heavy theatrics; it is just a cut above ten-twent'-thirt'. Miss Davis is all right.

Better than that, however, are the other members of the cast. Charles Dingle as Brother Ben Hubbard, the oldest and sharpest of the rattlesnake clan, is the perfect villain in respectable garb. Carl Benton Reid as Brother Oscar is magnificently dark, sullen and undependable. Patricia Collinge repeats her excellent stage performance as the faded flower of the Old South who tips the jug. Teresa Wright is fragile and pathetic as the harassed daughter of Regina. Dan Duryea is a shade too ungainly as Oscar's chicken-livered son, and Herbert Marshall is surprisingly British for a Southerner born and bred, hut both fill difficult roles well.

The Little Foxes will not increase your admiration for mankind. It is cold and cynical. But it is a very exciting picture to watch in a comfortably objective way, especially if you enjoy expert stabbing-in-the-back (movies.nytimes.com/movie/review?res=9E04EFD61F3BE233A25751C2A96E9C946093D6CF).

Assignments

- Warm-up: Watch *The Little Foxes* movie (1941) and write your own review. Did you like the movie or the written play better?
- Students should complete Concept Builder 27-D.
- Student will re-write corrected copies of essay due tomorrow.

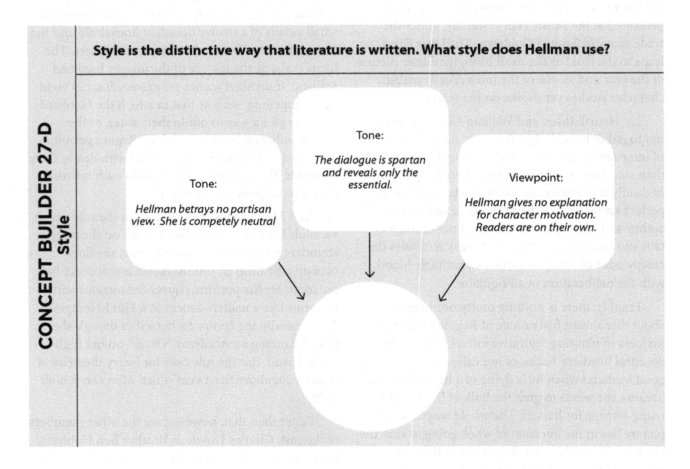

CONCEPT BUILDER 27-D
Style

Style is the distinctive way that literature is written. What style does Hellman use?

Tone:
The dialogue is spartan and reveals only the essential.

Tone:
Hellman betrays no partisan view. She is competely neutral

Viewpoint:
Hellman gives no explanation for character motivation. Readers are on their own.

444

Realism

In Lillian Hellman's "The Little Foxes," the philosophical idea of realism is strikingly obvious. The Merriam Webster Dictionary defines realism as "a concern for fact or reality and rejection of the impractical and visionary." Using both dialogue and characterization, Hellman is able to illustrate realism through the characters and their relationships in the play. The majority of the play consists of dialogue between the family members. Their lack of knowledge of and animosity towards each other is demonstrated in the conversations. As well, the characterization of the multiple family members and the relationships between them leaves nothing sugar-coated. Hellman romanticizes nothing throughout the play. This supports the clear worldview of realism in "The Little Foxes."

Dialogue is a key element in play, and through the conversations in the play, Hellman's realistic views become apparent. The dialogue is often antagonistic, with no true sense of love or compassion. One of the couples in the story, Birdie and Oscar, has a relationship with little sense of love on either side. At the beginning of the play, this is evidenced by Oscar's harsh words for his wife, after she supposedly has had too much to drink. "You have had too much wife," growls Oscar. "Get yourself in hand now." "What am I doing," protests Birdie. "I'm not doing anything. What am I doing?" "I said get yourself in hand. Stop acting like a fool." Later, a drunken Birdie is talking with her niece, Alexandra. She is harsh is discussing her future, explaining how Alexandra will end up like her. "Don't love me," snaps Birdie furiously. "Because in twenty years you'll just be like me. You know what? In twenty-two years, I haven't had a whole day of happiness. . . .

And that's the way you'll be, only you'll be worse off because you haven't got my mama to remember." At the very end of the play, Alexandra understands that she will never be happy with her family, particularly her mother, Regina. Knowing she must leave, she is quite harsh when explaining this to Regina. "Mama, I'm not coming with you. I'm not going to Chicago." "You're very upset, Alexandra." "I mean what I said. With all my heart." "We'll talk about it tomorrow. The morning will make a difference." "It won't make any difference. And there isn't anything to talk about. I am going away from you. Because I want to." "And if I say no?" "Say it, Mama, say it. And see what happens." Looking at the interactions between the three siblings, Regina, Oscar, and Ben, it is apparent that they are united by money and that there is nothing else that really matters to them in the end. "There'll be millions, Birdie, millions. ..." Lillian Hellman creates a cold family in "The Little Foxes," whose conversations with another are clearly strained.

Similarly, the characterization of the members of this family is also realistic. When Ben is explaining his family's history, he describes a family whose sole goal in life is to gain more money. "It is difficult to learn new ways. But maybe that's why it's profitable. Our grandfather and our father learned the new ways and learned how to make them pay. They work. They are in trade. Hubbard Sons, Merchandise. Others, Birdie's family, for example, look down on them. To make a long story short, Lionnet now belongs to us. Twenty years ago we took over their land, their cotton, and their daughters." The Hubbard siblings' lack of feeling is again evidenced by their scheming to arrange a marriage between Alexandra and Leo, first cousins, simply to keep their money in the family. "What's the difference to any of us if a little more goes here, a little less goes there — it's all in the family. And it will stay in the family. I'll never marry. So my money goes to Alexandra and Leo. They may even marry some day." The relationships between both married couples in "The Little Foxes" are not romanticized in any way. When Oscar slaps his wife, Birdie pretends that it is nothing. "Birdie, get your hat and coat." "Good night, Uncle Oscar." (Birdie begins to move slowly towards the door as Alexandra climbs the stairs. Alexandra is almost out of view when Birdie reaches Oscar in the doorway. As Birdie quickly attempts to pass him, he slaps her hard, across the face. Birdie cries out, puts her hand to her face. On the cry, Alexandra turns, begins to run down the stairs.) "Aunt Birdie! What happened?" "Nothing,

darling. Nothing happened." While Horace never physically hurts Regina, their relationship is also void of love. Regina: "You hate me very much." "No." "Oh, I think you do. Well, we haven't been very good together. Anyways, I don't hate you either. I have only contempt for you. I've always had." "From the very first?" "I think so." The relationships between the Hubbard siblings, Birdie and Oscar, and Regina and Horace are all without love.

Throughout "The Little Foxes," the Hubbard family members are realists. Their conversations and overall relationships with one another are mostly without love. Their main concern is money, and they are ready to do whatever it takes to gain more wealth. They are cold, calculating, and uncaring.

Assignments

- Warm-up: Find examples of realism in "The Little Foxes."
- Students should complete Concept Builder 27-E.
- Essays are due. Students should take the chapter 27 test.

CONCEPT BUILDER 27-E
Regina Hubbard

Regina is one of the most despicable characters in modern literature. Compare her to the biblical character Jezebel.

	Jezebel	Regina
Relationships		
Views of authority		
Views of God		

Chapter 28

1946–1960 (Part 3):
The Modern Age: Realism/Naturalism

First Thoughts Authors like Tennessee Williams ushered in the post-Christian age. The post-Christian age had its roots in the 1920s but really took over in the 1990s. It is dominated by anxiety, irrationality, and helplessness. In such a world, consciousness is adrift, unable to anchor itself to any universal ground of justice, truth, or reason. Consciousness itself is thus "decentered": no longer agent of action in the world, but a function through which impersonal forces pass and intersect (Patricia Waugh in Gene Edward Veith Jr., *Postmodern Times: A Christian Guide to Contemporary Thought and Culture*, Wheaton, IL: Crossway Books, 1994).

Enter now that place of tentativeness, of glass-fragile-figures, that glass menagerie that is so much a part of modern America. . . .

Author Worldview Watch Tennessee Williams, a controversial 20th century playwright, creates a timeless microcosm of world view mayhem. Christian theism, romanticism, naturalism, & realism they all clash in urban Depression era America. Readers, especially Christian readers, are inspired, discouraged, angered, and bemused by characters, especially Tom, who claim to know most everything but, it turns out, know very little about anything! They fumble, tumble, and fantasize through life and ultimately harm both themselves and those around them. At the end, readers all wonder, "What if Jesus was Lord of this home?" What a different story it would be!

Chapter Learning Objectives In chapter 28 we look at Tennessee William's "The Glass Menagerie." Students should review "The Crucible" by Arthur Miller (chapter 30).

As a result of this chapter study you will be able to . . .

1. Describe in detail the characters in this play.

2. Discuss what internal and external conflicts characters face.

3. Explain why Williams titles his play "The Glass Menagerie."

4. Compare and contrast the way that Amanda handles disappointment with the way that the biblical character Joseph handles disappointment.

5. Describe the dreams of Laura, Amanda, Tom, and Jim.

Weekly Essay Options: Begin on page 274 of the Teacher Guide.

The Glass Menagerie
Tennessee Williams

Background This remarkable play has some of the most powerful insights into the human heart that have ever appeared on Broadway. "The Glass Menagerie" was Tennessee Williams' first successful play. It won the New York Critics' Circle Award as the best play of the 1944–45 Broadway season. Less than three years later, "A Streetcar Named Desire," also by Williams, opened. It, too, captured the Critics' Circle Award and also won the Pulitzer Prize.

Tennessee Williams earned fame and became very wealthy. He really was a gifted playwright, but in many ways he was very shy and only wished to be left alone. Success depressed him. As a young man who achieved great success, he suddenly missed the challenges of life. The truth is, too, he was afraid that his best works were behind him and he wondered if he would ever write any better play in his lifetime.

Assignments

- Warm-up: Did you ever do very well at a sporting event or present a great musical recital and then did you wonder if this was the best you would ever be?

- Students should complete Concept Builder 28-A.

- Students review the required reading(s) *before* the assigned chapter begins.

- Teachers may want to discuss assigned reading(s) with students.

- Teachers shall assign the required essay. The rest of the essays can be outlined, answered with shorter answers, discussed, or skipped.

- Students will review all readings for chapter 28.

Read "The Glass Menagerie" (Scene One) by Tennessee Williams, and then answer the following questions.

1	Who is the narrator and what does he mean when he says these huge buildings are "always burning with the slow and implacable fires of human desperation"?
2	Who is the fifth character?
3	Based on these opening scenes, what sort of woman is Amanda?
4	From this dialogue, what can we infer about Laura?
5	Who is a gentlemen caller?
6	The author gives a lot of detail. What affect does this have on the play?
7	Discuss the relationship between Tom and Laura.
8	Predict the ending of this play.

The Play as Autobiography

Tennessee Williams was born Thomas Lanier Williams in Columbus, Mississippi, in 1911. His grandfather was a pastor. His dad was very much like Tom's dad. A traveling salesman, he lived out of suitcases and had little time for his children.

Tennessee's father got an office job with the International Shoe Company and the family settled in St. Louis. Rose, Tennessee's sister, and he played in low-income tenements in urban St. Louis. They also played with Rose's prized collection of small glass animals.

Tennessee's father continued to struggle with alcohol and was a destabilizing force on the family. Of the three Williams children, Rose had the hardest time growing up. In her teens, Rose was deeply depressed. She withdrew into a private world. Mrs. Williams could not accept her daughter's illness and tried repeatedly to force friends on her. She enrolled Rose in a secretarial course, but that didn't help Rose's condition either. Diagnosed as a schizophrenic, Rose was put in a mental institution.

Tom, who loved Rose dearly, heaped blame for Rose's madness on himself. Not even he understood why.

In the pathos of his family Williams found the stuff of his plays. He hardly disguised his parents, his sister, and himself when he cast them as characters on the stage. Places where he lived became settings, and he adapted plots from life's experiences. He relived the past as he wrote. "The play is memory," says Tom, the character in "The Glass Menagerie."

Assignments

- Warm-up: "The Glass Menagerie" is a play about family relationships. Write about your relationship with one of your most special family members. What makes that relationship special?
- Students should complete Concept Builder 28-B.
- Student *should* review reading(s) from the next chapter.
- Student should outline essay due at the end of the week.
- Per teacher instructions, students may answer orally, in a group setting, some of the essays that are not assigned as formal essays.

The four characters in this play are archetype characters, a typical, ideal, or classic example of a character type. Match the character with the archetype.

A	The cynical, insightful son who is obviously out of place in his role as caregiver and provider for his family.
B	The "gentleman caller," the dream every mother desires for her daughter.
C	The fragile, shy, sensitive daughter.
D	The elderly southern belle who mostly lives in a fantasy world.

____	1	Laura
____	2	Amanda
____	3	Tom
____	4	Jim

Narration

From scene I, *The Glass Menagerie*

TOM enters dressed as a merchant sailor from alley, stage left, and strolls across the front of the stage to the fire-escape. There he stops and lights a cigarette. He addresses the audience.

TOM: Yes, I have tricks in my pocket, I have things up my sleeve. But I am the opposite of a stage magician. He gives you illusion that has the appearance of truth. I give you truth in the pleasant disguise of illusion.

To begin with, I turn back time. I reverse it to that quaint period, the thirties, when the huge middle class of America was matriculating in a school for the blind. Their eyes had failed them or they had failed their eyes, and so they were having their fingers pressed forcibly down on the fiery Braille alphabet of a dissolving economy.

In Spain there was revolution. Here there was only shouting and confusion.

In Spain there was Guernica. Here there were disturbances of labour, sometimes pretty violent, in otherwise peaceful cities such as Chicago, Cleveland, Saint Louis. . . .

This is the social background of the play.

[MUSIC]

The play is memory.

Being a memory play, it is dimly lighted, it is sentimental, it is not realistic.

In memory everything seems to happen to music. That explains the fiddle in the wings.

I am the narrator of the play, and also a character in it. The other characters are my mother Amanda, my sister Laura and a gentleman caller who appears in the final scenes.

He is the most realistic character in the play, being an emissary from a world of reality that we were somehow set apart from. But since I have a poet's weakness for symbols, I am using this character also as a symbol; he is the long-delayed but always expected something that we live for. There is a fifth character in the play who doesn't appear except in this larger-than-life-size photograph over the mantel.

This is our father who left us a long time ago. He was a telephone man who fell in love with long distances; he gave up his job with the telephone company and skipped the light fantastic out of town. . . . The last we heard of him was a picture postcard from Mazatlan, on the Pacific coast of Mexico, containing a message of two words — "Hello — Good-bye!" and no address.

I think the rest of the play will explain itself.

The narrator is Tom. Tennessee Tom created a character who exists outside and inside the play's action at the same time. Standing on the fire escape adjoining the Wingfield apartment, Tom is the narrator. He is speaking directly to the crowd. Presumably no one in the play can hear him. He is personable and humorous.

It is hard to take a read on Tom. One actor's reading of Tom's lines can give you the impression that Tom regrets being a wanderer. Another actor can create the sense that Tom looks back with relief, pleased that he broke away, at least from his mother. Clearly, Tom loves Laura: "I tried to leave you behind me, but I am more faithful than I intended to be."

Tom is not a particularly reliable narrator. He writes poetry at every opportunity. Co-workers call him "Shakespeare." He is obviously emotional and often prejudiced in his views.

Ironically, Amanda tags Tom pretty well. Tom's resentful manner leads his mother to accuse him of having a "temperament like a Metropolitan [Opera] star." Tom is a self-centered man, although, admittedly he is between a rock and a hard place! He is stuck taking care of his mother and sister.

Tom lives in a dream world as complete as Laura's. He often goes to the movies and escapes into a new drama each day.

Some critics see Tom as a representative of a whole generation of young people coming of age just as World War II begins. They are full of hope and optimism but looming over the horizon are the storm clouds of war.

Assignments

- Warm-up: Laura is a young lady who cannot overcome a problem. Have you struggled to overcome a problem that you simply could not overcome? What did you do?
- Students should complete Concept Builder 28-C.
- Students should write rough drafts of assigned essay.
- The teacher or a peer evaluator may correct rough drafts.

CONCEPT BUILDER 28-C
Characterization

List the internal and external conflict that each character encounters in this play.

Character	Internal Conflict	External Conflict
Amanda		
Laura		
Jim		
Tom		

Symbolism

Critic Roger B. Stein argues that "Williams wanted his play to be more than a social and personal tragedy. To suggest the story's deeper meaning, he crowded "The Glass Menagerie" with Christian symbols. Amanda, who condemns instinct and urges Tom to think in terms of the mind and spirit, as "Christian adults" do, is often characterized in Christian terms. Her music is "Ave Maria." As a girl, she could only cook angel food cake. She urges Laura, "Possess your soul in patience," and then speaks of her dress for the dinner scene as "resurrected" from a trunk. Her constant refrain to Tom is "Rise an' Shine," and she sells subscriptions to her friends by waking them early in the morning and then sympathizing with them as "Christian martyrs. In a very small sense both Amanda and Laura are searching for a Savior who will come to help them, to save them, to give their drab lives meaning"

(Roger B. Stein, "The Glass Menagerie Revisited: Catastrophe without Violence," *Western Humanities Review*, vol. XVIII, no. 2, Spring 1964).

Here are some examples:

- Laura stumbles on the fire escape. This symbolizes the perils of entering the real world.

- When readers hear "Ave Maria," they are reminded that Amanda is a suffering martyr when she is deeply disappointed by her children.

- In a significant moment in the play the unicorn's breakage is terribly symbolic. Without its horn, the unicorn is no longer unique. During the evening Laura has broken out of her world of unreality. She, too, has become less "freakish."

Assignments

- Warm-up: What is one object that would symbolize your life? Why?
- Students should complete Concept Builder 28-D.
- Student will re-write corrected copies of essay due tomorrow.

CONCEPT BUILDER 28-D Dreams	Describe the dreams of each character.	
	Character	Dreams
	Amanda	
	Laura	
	Jim	
	Tom	

The Use of Light in the Play

AMANDA: That light bill I gave you several days ago. The one I told you we got the notices about?

[LEGEND: 'HA!']

TOM: Oh. — Yeah.

AMANDA: You didn't neglect to pay it by any chance?

TOM: Why, I —

AMANDA: Didn't! I might have known it!

JIM: Shakespeare probably wrote a poem on that light bill, Mrs. Wingfield.

AMANDA: I might have known better than to trust him with it! There's such a high price for negligence in this world!

JIM: Maybe the poem will win a ten-dollar prize.

AMANDA: We'll just have to spend the remainder of the evening in the nineteenth century, before Mr Edison made the Mazda lamp!

JIM: Candlelight is my favourite kind of light.

AMANDA: That shows you're romantic! But that's no excuse for Tom. Well, we got through dinner. Very considerate of them to let us get through dinner before they plunged us into ever-lasting darkness, wasn't it, Mr. O'Connor? (staff.bcc.edu/ faculty_websites/jalexand/Williams--The_ Glass_Menagerie.htm).

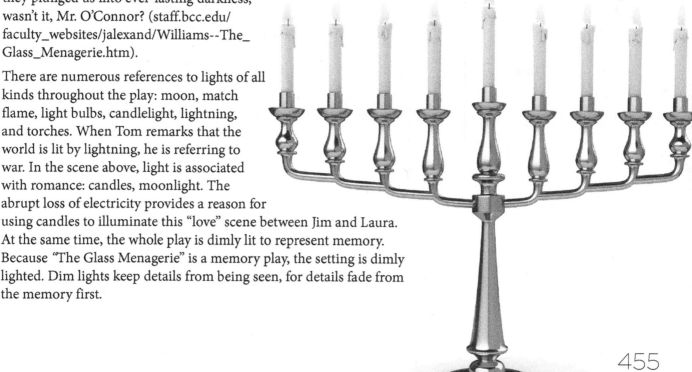

There are numerous references to lights of all kinds throughout the play: moon, match flame, light bulbs, candlelight, lightning, and torches. When Tom remarks that the world is lit by lightning, he is referring to war. In the scene above, light is associated with romance: candles, moonlight. The abrupt loss of electricity provides a reason for using candles to illuminate this "love" scene between Jim and Laura. At the same time, the whole play is dimly lit to represent memory. Because "The Glass Menagerie" is a memory play, the setting is dimly lighted. Dim lights keep details from being seen, for details fade from the memory first.

- Warm-up: Jim says, "Everyone excels in one thing. Some in many!" (Scene VII) In what do you excel?

- Students should complete Concept Builder 28-E.

- Essays are due. Students should take the chapter 28 test.

The father was absent from the entire play, yet he had a great impact. "This is our father who left us a long time ago. He was a telephone man who fell in love with long distances; he gave up his job with the telephone company and skipped the light fantastic out of town. . . . The last we heard of him was a picture postcard from Mazatlan, on the Pacific coast of Mexico, containing a message of two words — 'Hello — Good-bye!' and no address."

What does he represent to the following characters?

Character	Representation
Amanda	
Tom	

Chapter 29

1946–1960 (Part 4):

The Modern Age: Realism/Naturalism

First Thoughts In "The Glass Menagerie" the lives of the characters are touched by the history. But as critic Frank Durham states, time is used in a poetic way, too: Tom stands with us in the immediate present. . . . But through his consciousness we are carried back in time to his life in the drab apartment before his escape. . . . Within this train of memory there are two types of time, the generalized and the specific, and through the use of these two we are given a deeper insight into the lives and relationships of the Wingfields. The first scene in the apartment, the dinner scene, is an example of generalized time. It is not any one particular dinner but a kind of abstraction of all the dinners shared by the trio in their life of entrapment.

—Tennessee Williams,
Theater Poet in Prose, 1971
(books.google.com/books?id=EbZbDTgbYbYC
&sitesec=buy&source=gbs_vpt_read)

Chapter Learning Objectives In chapter 29 we finish our study of "The Glass Menagerie."

As a result of this chapter study you will be able to . . .

1. Compare Amanda Wingfield to Regina Giddens and Horace Giddens.

2. Analyze C.S. Lewis quote.

3. Discuss if Christians should support movies that help non-Christian persons prosper.

4. Compare several American literature authors.

5. Compare "The Glass Menagerie" to another Williams play.

Weekly Essay Options: Begin on page 274 of the Teacher Guide.

Reading ahead: "The Crucible" by Arthur Miller.

457

Two Themes

1. FRAGILITY
   The characters in "The Glass Menagerie" have built their lives on a fragile foundation of illusions. Take away their illusions and which of them would not break?

2. THE MYTH OF SUCCESS
   The personal failure of all the characters in the play in some ways parallel the larger social failure of America during the Great Depression.

AMANDA: Go, then! Then go to the moon — you selfish dreamer!

[Tom smashes his glass on the floor. He plunges out on the fire-escape, slamming the door. LAURA screams — cut by door.

Dance-hall Music up. TOM goes to the rail and grips it desperately, lifting his face in the chill white moonlight-penetrating narrow abyss of the alley.

LEGEND ON SCREEN: 'AND SO GOODBYE.'

TOM 's closing speech is timed with the interior pantomime. [The interior scene is played as though viewed through soundproof glass. AMANDA appears to be making a comforting speech to LAURA who is huddled upon the sofa. Now that we cannot hear the mother's speech, her silliness is gone and she has dignity and tragic beauty.

LAURA' s dark hair hides her face until at the end of the speech she lifts it to smile at her Mother. AMANDA' s gestures are slow and graceful, almost dancelike as she comforts the daughter. At the end of her speech she glances a moment at the father's picture, then withdraws through the portières. At the close of Tom's speech, LAURA blows out the candles, ending the play.]

Klara White as Laura.

TOM: I didn't go to the moon, I went much further — for time is the longest distance between places. Not long after that I was fired for writing a poem on the lid of a shoebox.

I left Saint Louis. I descended the step of this fire-escape for a last time and followed, from then on, in my father's footsteps, attempting to find in motion what was lost in space, I travelled around a great deal. The cities swept about me like dead leaves, leaves that were brightly coloured but torn away from the branches.

I would have stopped, but I was pursued by something.

It always came upon me unawares, taking me altogether by surprise. Perhaps it was a familiar bit of music. Perhaps it was only a piece of transparent glass. Perhaps I am walking along a street at night, in some strange city, before I have found companions. I pass the lighted window of a shop where perfume is sold. The window is filled with pieces of coloured glass, tiny transparent bottles in delicate colours, like bits of a shattered rainbow.

Then all at once my sister touches my shoulder. I turn around and look into her eyes.

Oh, Laura, Laura, I tried to leave you behind me, but I am more faithful than I intended to be!

I reach for a cigarette, I cross the street, I run into the movies or a bar, I buy a drink, I speak to the nearest stranger — anything that can blow your candles out!

[LAURA bends over the candles.]

— for nowadays the world is lit by lightning! Blow out your candles, Laura — and so good-bye.

[She blows the candles out.]

THE SCENE DISSOLVES

Assignments

- Warm-up: Write a letter to Laura. What would you say to encourage her?
- Students should complete Concept Builder 29-A.
- Students review the required reading(s) *before* the assigned chapter begins.
- Teachers may want to discuss assigned reading(s) with students.
- Teachers shall assign the required essay. The rest of the essays can be outlined, answered with shorter answers, discussed, or skipped.
- Students will review all readings for chapter 29.

Through dialogue, readers can know each character's thoughts and feelings. Likewise, the author can advance the plot. There are three types of dialogue: monologue, soliloquy, and an aside. A monologue is a long speech that is spoken by a single character to himself or herself, or to the audience. A soliloquy is a monologue where the character speaks private thoughts aloud. An aside is a comment that is delivered by a character to the audience, who are on stage. Identify the following dialogue examples.

Type of Dialogue	Dialogue
	I am the narrator of the play, and also a character in it. The other characters are my mother Amanda, my sister Laura and a gentleman caller who appears in the final scenes. He is the most realistic character in the play, being an emissary from a world of reality that we were somehow set apart from. But since I have a poet's weakness for symbols, I am using this character also as a symbol; he is the long-delayed but always expected something that we live for. There is a fifth character in the play who doesn't appear except in this larger-than-life-size photograph over the mantel.
	AMANDA [hopelessly fingering the huge pocketbook]: So what are we going to do the rest of our lives? Stay home and watch the parades go by? Amuse ourselves with the glass menagerie, darling? Eternally play those worn-out phonograph records your father left as a painful reminder of him? We won't have a business career — we've given that up because it gave us nervous indigestion! [Laughs wearily.] What is there left but dependency all our lives? I know so well what becomes of unmarried women who aren't prepared to occupy a position. I've seen such pitiful cases in the South — barely tolerated spinsters living upon the grudging patronage of sister's husband or brother's wife! — stuck away in some little mousetrap of a room — encouraged by one in-law to visit another — little birdlike women without any nest — eating the crust of humility all their life! Is that the future that we've mapped out for ourselves? I swear it's the only alternative I can think of! It isn't a very pleasant alternative, is it? Of course — some girls do marry!
	TOM: I didn't go to the moon, I went much further — for time is the longest distance between places. Not long after that I was fired for writing a poem on the lid of a shoebox. I left Saint Louis. I descended the step of this fire-escape for a last time and followed, from then on, in my father's footsteps, attempting to find in motion what was lost in space — I travelled around a great deal. The cities swept about me like dead leaves, leaves that were brightly coloured but torn away from the branches. I would have stopped, but I was pursued by something. It always came upon me unawares, taking me altogether by surprise. Perhaps it was a familiar bit of music. Perhaps it was only a piece of transparent glass. Perhaps I am walking along a street at night, in some strange city, before I have found companions. I pass the lighted window of a shop where perfume is sold. The window is filled with pieces of coloured glass, tiny transparent bottles in delicate colours, like bits of a shattered rainbow. Then all at once my sister touches my shoulder. I turn around and look into her eyes. Oh, Laura, Laura, I tried to leave you behind me, but I am more faithful than I intended to be! I reach for a cigarette, I cross the street, I run into the movies or a bar, I buy a drink, I speak to the nearest stranger — anything that can blow your candles out!

Form and Structure

The play has seven scenes. The first four take place over a few days. The remaining scenes occur on two successive evenings during the following spring. Williams unifies the several episodes by devising a series of projected images and words on a screen, something that was quite innovative when it first was produced.

Tom, the narrator, exists in the present and the past. He talks directly to the audience at the start of the play, at the openings of Scenes Three and Six, and again at the end.

Because the play comes from Tom's memory, time loses its usual sequence and structure. This is not a normal play where events occur in sequence, usually in a chronological sequence. Memories bounce at will between the recent and distant past. Williams' technique was popular in earlier surreal literature that emerged in Russian literature at the end of the 19th century (e.g., Dostoevsky).

The following is a flashback that Williams produces. Notice the masterful juxtaposition of music, props, and actors!

AMANDA: One Sunday afternoon in Blue Mountain, your mother received seventeen gentlemen callers! Why, sometimes there weren't chairs enough to accommodate them all. …

TOM [remaining at portières]: How did you entertain those gentleman callers?

AMANDA: I understood the art of conversation!

TOM: I bet you could talk.

AMANDA: Girls in those days knew how to talk, I can tell you.

TOM: Yes?

[IMAGE: AMANDA AS A GIRL ON A PORCH GREETING CALLERS.]

AMANDA: They knew how to entertain their gentlemen callers. It wasn't enough for a girl to be possessed of a pretty face and a graceful figure although I wasn't alighted in either respect. She also needed to have a nimble wit and a tongue to meet all occasions.

TOM: What did you talk about?

AMANDA: Things of importance going on in the world! Never anything coarse or common or vulgar.

[She addresses Tom as though he were seated in the vacant chair at the table though he remains by portieres. He plays this scene as though he held the book.]

My callers were gentleman all! Among my callers were some of the most prominent young planters of the Mississippi Delta — planters and sons of planters!

[Tom motions for music and a spot of light on AMANDA. Her eyes lift, her face glows, her voice becomes rich and elegiac.

SCREEN LEGEND: 'Où SONT Les NEIGES']

There was young Champ Laughlin who later became vice-president of the Delta Planters Bank.

Hadley Stevenson who was drowned in Moon Lake and left his widow one hundred and fifty thousand in Government bonds.

There were the Cutrere brothers, Wesley and Bates. Bates was one of my bright particular beaux! He got in a quarrel with that wild Wainwright boy. They shot it out on the floor of Moon Lake Casino. Bates was shot through the stomach. Died in the ambulance on his way to Memphis. His widow was also well provided for, came into eight or ten thousand acres, that's all. She married him on the rebound — never loved her — carried my picture on him the night he died! And there was that boy that every girl in the Delta had set her cap for! That brilliant, brilliant young Fitzhugh boy from Greene County!

TOM: What did he leave his widow?

AMANDA: He never married! Gracious, you talk as though all of my old admirers had turned up their toes to the daisies!

TOM: Isn't this the first you've mentioned that still survives?

AMANDA: That Fitzhugh boy went North and made a fortune — came to be known as the Wolf of Wall Street! He had the Midas touch, whatever he touched turned to gold!

And I could have been Mrs. Duncan J. Fitzhugh, mind you! But — I picked your father!

LAURA [rising]: Mother, let me clear the table.

AMANDA: No, dear, you go in front and study your typewriter chart. Or practise your shorthand a little. Stay fresh and pretty! It's almost time for our gentlemen callers to start arriving. [She flounces girlishly toward the kitchenette.] How many do you suppose we're going to entertain this afternoon?

[Tom throws down the paper and jumps up with a groan.]

LAURA [alone in the dining-room]: I don't believe we're going to receive any, Mother.

AMANDA [reappearing, airily] What? Not one — not one? You must be joking!

[LAURA nervously echoes her laugh. She slips in a fugitive manner through the half-open portières and draws them in gently behind her. A shaft of very clear light is thrown on her face against the faded tapestry of the curtains.]

[MUSIC: 'THE GLASS MENAGERIE' UNDER FAINTLY. Lightly.]

Not one gentleman caller? It can't be true! There must be a flood, there must have been a tornado!

LAURA: It isn't a flood, it's not a tornado, Mother. I'm just not popular like you were in Blue Mountain. [Tom utters another groan. LAURA glances at him with a faint, apologetic smile. Her voice catching a little.] Mother's afraid I'm going to be an old maid.

THE SCENE DIMS OUT WITH 'GLASS MENAGERIE'

Music

Assignments

- Warm-up: Since the play contains no formal "acts," a director can prescribe an intermission at any time. How would you divide the play if you were directing a performance?

- Students should complete Concept Builder 29-B.

- Student should review reading(s) from the next chapter.

- Student should outline essay due at the end of the week.

- Per teacher instructions, students may answer orally, in a group setting, some of the essays that are not assigned as formal essays.

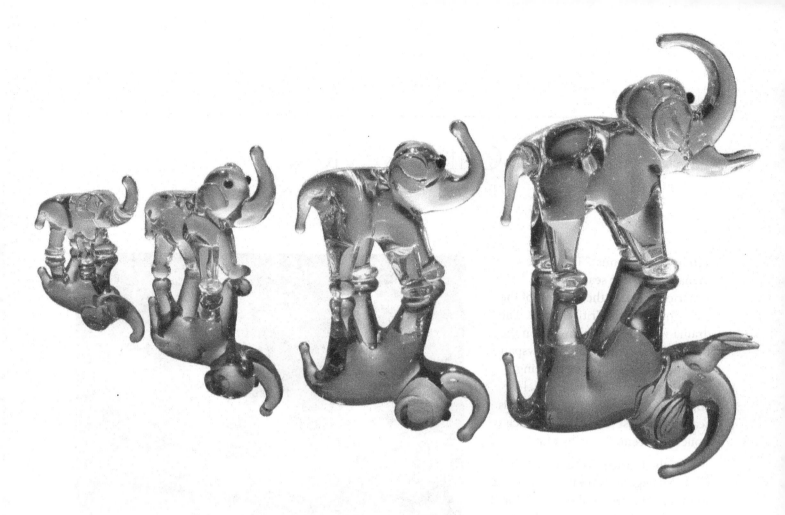

	In general there are four kinds of conflict: man vs. man, man vs. society, man vs. nature, man vs. himself. Which conflicts fit each character?			
Character	Man vs. Man	Man vs. Society	Man vs. Nature	Man vs. Himself
Amanda				
Laura				
Jim				
Tom				

Critic Review

Tennessee Williams' "The Glass Menagerie" is the season's best American play, in the opinion of the New York Drama Critics Circle. The drama won the annual award on the first ballot cast by the local newspaper and magazine reviewers, meeting yesterday afternoon at the Hotel Algonquin. No award was made this season for "best foreign play," since none was deemed worthy of it.

Of the fourteen votes cast "The Glass Menagerie" won nine. Two votes went for "Harvey" and one each for "I Remember Mama" and "A Bell for Adano." One critic voted for no award. Those in favor of the winner were John Chapman of *The Daily News*, Ward Morehouse of *The Sun*, Kelcey Allen of *Women's Wear Daily*, Wilella Waldorf of *The Post*, John Gassner of *Forum*, Tom Wenning of *Newsweek*, George Freedley of *The Morning Telegraph*, Wolcott Gibbs of *The New Yorker* and Rosamond Gilder of *Theatre Arts Magazine*. Joseph Wood Krutch of *The Nation* and Howard Barnes of the *Herald-Tribune* held out for "Harvey," Arthur Pollack of *The Brooklyn Daily Eagle* for "A Bell for Adano" and Lewis Nichols of *The New York Times* for "I Remember Mama." Louis Kronenberger of *PM* voted for no award.

In the words of the citation, the award was offered "To Tennessee Williams for his play 'The Glass Menagerie' and its sensitive understanding of four troubled human beings." According to the rules of the Critics Circle, the proceedings start with one unofficial, unsigned, nominating ballot, with Mr. Williams's play receiving eight votes at that time. On

The Algonquin Hotel at night in Manhattan, New York by Christinahle, 2007 (PD-US).

this preliminary ballot Mr. Gibbs voted for "Trio," but swung into line on the first official voting. Mr. Gibbs said he stood out for "Trio" as a protest against License Commissioner Paul Moss, who closed the show in a cause celebre earlier in the season.

"The Glass Menagerie" also is eligible for this year's Pulitzer Prize for the drama. The entries for that close April 1 and Mr. Williams's play came in from the West the night of March 31. It is his first play to receive Broadway attention, although the Theatre Guild once tried out his "Battle of the Angels," abandoning it on the road. Prior to its Broadway opening "The Glass Menagerie" had a successful run in Chicago.

The play has only four characters; its cast is composed of Laurette Taylor, Eddie Dowling, Julie Haydon and Anthony Ross. It concerns an aging woman, now impoverished, who looks back on a happy youth before she married the wrong man; her son, her crippled daughter and the Gentleman Caller who visits the house. Mr. Dowling and Margo Jones receive credit for the direction, and Mr. Dowling and Louis J. Singer are the producers. The play is at the Playhouse, where since its opening it has been in the category of a "smash hit."

Mr. Williams, members of the cast and others connected with the production will be guests of the circle at the annual dinner April 22 at the Algonquin. The circle made no award last season (Review in the *New York Times*, April 11, 1945).

Assignments

- Warm-up: Write a more satisfactory ending to this play.
- Students should complete Concept Builder 29-C.
- Students should write rough drafts of assigned essay.
- The teacher may correct rough drafts.

CONCEPT BUILDER 29-C
Dramatic Dialogue

Dramatic dialogue is dialogue that advances the plot or develops a character through dramatic interpretation.
Create dramatic dialogue illustrating the conflict inherent in each situation:

Type of Dialogue	Dialogue
Running to your car parked at the end of the church parking lot when it is raining and finding that your younger brother is sitting in the car with locked windows and he will not unlock the doors.	
Answering the telephone and finding that the phone caller is a friend whom you told you were not at home.	

The Glass Menagerie Movie 1950

Bosley Crowther of the *The New York Times* said the film "comes perilously close to sheer buffoonery in some of its most fragile scenes. And this makes for painful diffusion of the play's obvious poignancy." He added, "Apparently, Mr. Williams . . . was persuaded to 'fatten' the role of the faded and fatuous mother to suit the talents of Gertrude Lawrence . . . well known as an actress with a brilliant and devastating flair for brittle high comedy and satire, preferably Noël Coward style. So presumably it was considered advisable to give her a chance to play the old belle in this drama with a list towards the lady's comic side. If such was the story-conference reasoning, it was woefully unfortunate, for the mother . . . is the fatal weakness of the film. . . . Miss Lawrence and the screenplay make her a farcically exaggerated shrew with the zeal of a burlesque comedian to see her diffident daughter wed. . . . Furthermore, it must be mentioned that the Southern accent which Miss Lawrence affects is not only disturbingly erratic but it has an occasional Cockney strain. The character is sufficiently murky without this additional mystery. As much as we hate to say so, Miss Lawrence's performance does not compare with the tender and radiant creation of the late Laurette Taylor on the stage. On the other hand, modest Jane Wyman is beautifully sensitive in the role of the crippled and timid daughter who finds escape in her menagerie of glass, and Arthur Kennedy is intriguingly caustic as the incredibly long-suffering son. Kirk Douglas (above) is appropriately shallow as the young man who comes to call. They all do very nicely by Mr. Williams' electric scenes and lines. That is to say, they do nicely when the script and the direction permit — and that is to say when Miss Lawrence is not overwhelming the screen. It is regrettable that Director Irving Rapper was compelled, it appears, to kick around the substance of a frail, illusory drama as though it were plastic and not Venetian glass" (Bosley Crowther, review in the *New York Times*, 1950).

Assignments

- Warm-up: While the live play was a smashing success, the movie versions of *The Glass Menagerie* have failed miserably. Why?
- Students should complete Concept Builder 29-D.
- Student will re-write corrected copies of essay due tomorrow.

A play can be divided into four parts: the initial situation that introduces the conflict; the rising action caused by the conflict; the climax; the denouement or final resolution. Identify each part.

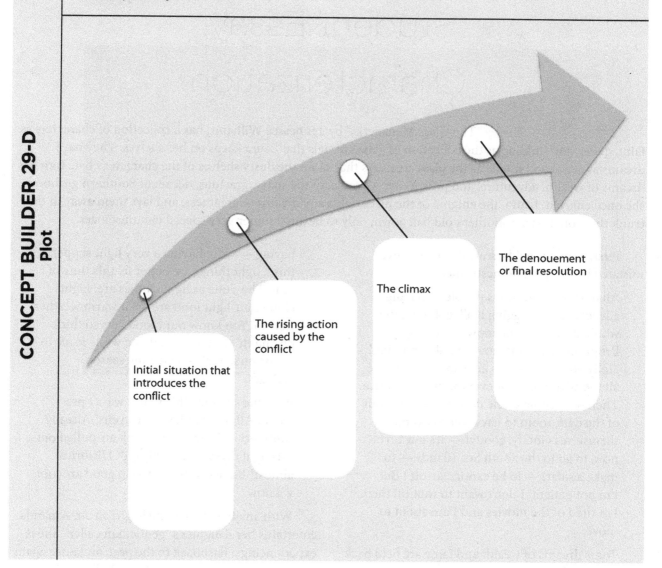

CONCEPT BUILDER 29-D
Plot

Initial situation that introduces the conflict

The rising action caused by the conflict

The climax

The denouement or final resolution

Student Essay: Characterization

Student Essay "The Glass Menagerie," by Tennessee Williams, has a collection of characters as faint, queer, and tinkling as the collection of glass animals that Laura keeps on her shelves. They have dreams as aerial and fragile as the glass creatures that sit on the dusty shelves of the character's flat. Tom has dreams of wealth, adventure, and prosperity; Amanda, of the suave, gracious, decadent Southern girlhood she once enjoyed. Laura, the enigma of the piece, folds any dreams of greatness, and lays them away in the trunk that contains her mother's old ball gown, only to be aired under very special circumstances.

First, Tom has wild dreams of adventure, unstated by his quiet domestic life.

All of those glamorous people — having adventures — hogging it all, gobbling the whole thing up. You know what happens? People go to the movies instead of moving! Hollywood characters are supposed to have all the adventures for everybody in America. Then the people in the dark room come out of the dark room to have some adventure themselves Goody, goody! — It's our turn now, to go to the South Sea Islands — to make a safari — to be exotic, far-off ! But I'm not patient. I don't want to wait till then. I'm tired of the movies and I am about to move.

Tom's dreams of wealth and fame are held back by his alcoholism. By going to the movies, he sees what he could be if unhampered by his circumstances. Tom feels held back by the dainty unreality of Amanda's dreams, and the apparent lack of Laura's. He believes that his wishes are something that must be attained because they have an apparent sense of reality.

Next, Amanda dreams of the suave, decadent Southern girlhood she once enjoyed.

Mmm, so warm already! And not quite summer, even. We're going to burn up when summer really gets started. However, we're having — we're having a very light supper. I think light things are better fo' this time of year. The same as light clothes are. Light clothes an' light food are what warm weather calls fo'. You know our blood gets so thick during th' winter — it takes a while fo' us to adjust ou'selves! — when the season changes.

It's come so quick this year. I wasn't pre-pared. All of a sudden — heavens! Already summer! — I ran to the trunk an' pulled out this light dress — Terribly old! Historical almost! But feels so good —so good an' cool, y' know. . . .

With an almost coquettish, girlish air, Amanda entertains her daughter's "gentleman caller." She is experiencing a flashback to the past, and once again becomes the enchanting Southern Belle of older days. Amanda's dreams are unreal, except to her. She wishes a return to the past, and different days to make better choices.

Finally, Laura, the quiet, contented homebody, who seems to have no dreams.

You think I'm making this up because I'm invited to dinner and have to be nice. Oh, I could do that! I could put on an act for you, Laura, and say lots of things without being very sincere. But this time I am. I'm talking to you sincerely. I happened to notice you had this inferiority complex that keeps you from feeling comfortable with people. Somebody needs to build your confidence up and make you proud instead of shy and turning away and — blushing — Somebody — ought to — ought to — kiss you, Laura! He suddenly turns her about and kisses her on the lips. When he releases her, LAURA sinks on the sofa with a bright, dazed look. He backs away and fishes in his pocket for a cigarette.

Laura's dreams remain quietly folded away until one of her glass animals breaks, and with that, the fantasy world which she lives in parts for a moment. She sees what she could be, a wife, a mother, with a home. Laura lives in a world juxtaposed between reality and dreams. Only when her ongoing dream is broken, can she find the courage to imagine a possible dream.

All the characters in *The Glass Menagerie* live in a dream world. Tom dreams of adventure, Amanda of a return to her former life, Laura of a home and a family. Their dreams are as fragile as the glass menagerie that Laura possesses — they are broken by a touch of fate's finger. (Alouette)

Assignments

- Warm-up: Laura is a young lady who cannot overcome a problem. Have you struggled to overcome a problem that you simply could not overcome? What did you do?

- Students should complete Concept Builder 29-E.

- Essays are due. Students should take the chapter 29 test.

CONCEPT BUILDER 29-E
The Use of Light

The playwright Tennessee Williams uses light to great effect. What effect do the following scenes have on the characters, theme, and plot of "The Glass Menagerie?"	
Scene	**Effect**
Because "The Glass Menagerie" is a memory play, the setting is dimly lighted.	
Light shining through little glass objects often gives off tiny spots of rainbow color.	
The electric company turns off the Wingfields' power.	
At the end of the play Tom has dreams of Laura "with candlelight."	

Chapter 30

1946–1960 (Part 5):
The Modern Age: Realism/Naturalism

First Thoughts Arthur Miller (1915–2005) was one of the finest American playwrights of the last century. Miller's play "The Crucible" (1953), although concerned with the Salem witchcraft trials, was actually aimed at the then-widespread congressional investigation of subversive activities in the United States. The drama won the 1953 Tony Award. Arthur Miller championed the worldview realism in literature and drama.

Author Worldview Watch Arthur Miller was a very talented realist who had a bone to pick with his world. As an atheist, Miller attempted to convey man's struggle with morals and evil. With his lack of biblical background, however, he failed to include a crucial factor: sin. He used the available but much maligned and misunderstood Salem Witch Trials as his setting. Ultimately, though, all the characters, John Proctor, especially, is more a 1950 martyr than a 17th century one. Oops! "John," Elizabeth Proctor says to her husband John, "I do not think you are bad--only bewildered."

Chapter Learning Objectives In chapter 30 we look at Arthur Miller's "The Crucible" and examine the Salem witch trials.

As a result of this chapter study you will be able to . . .

1. Discuss Elizabeth Proctor's role.
2. Analyze Miller's assessment of Danforth.
3. Evaluate if John Proctor is a 17th-century character or a 20th-century character.

Weekly Essay Options: Begin on page 274 of the Teacher Guide.

Reading ahead: *A Separate Peace* by John Knowles.

470

The Crucible
Arthur Miller

The Crucible is really not about the Salem witch trials. It is more about the McCarthy trials of suspected Communists in the 1950s. Early in the 1950s, America was terrified by the threat of communism taking over the world. In response, a young senator named Joseph McCarthy made a public accusation that more than 200 "card-carrying" Communists had infiltrated the United States government. Though eventually his accusations were proven to be untrue and he was censured by the Senate for unbecoming conduct, his zealous campaigning ushered in one of the most repressive times in 20th-century American politics. Arthur Miller was a target of Senator McCarthy.

But there really was a Salem witch trial. . .

Early in the year 1692, in the northern Massachusetts fishing village of Salem, a bunch of precocious young ladies fell ill, falling victim to hallucinations and seizures. In religious Puritan New England, frightening or surprising occurrences were often attributed to the devil or his cohorts. The unfathomable sickness spurred fears of witchcraft, and it was not long before the girls, and then many other residents of Salem, began to accuse other villagers of witchcraft. While there clearly was witchcraft in Salem, some vindictive accusers used this hysteria as an excuse to settle old scores. By the time the fever had run its course in late August 1692, 19 people (and two dogs) had been convicted and hanged for witchcraft. Many more lives had been disrupted.

Assignments

- Warm-up: Did John Proctor make the right decision? Why or why not?
- Students should complete Concept Builder 30-A.
- Students review the required reading(s) *before* the assigned chapter begins.
- Teachers may want to discuss assigned reading(s) with students.
- Teachers shall assign the required essay. The rest of the essays can be outlined, answered with shorter answers, discussed, or skipped.
- Students will review all readings for chapter 30.

In "The Crucible" by Authur Miller, the setting is an important part. List different aspects of Salem, Massachusetts, during the time the witch trials occurred. There are many acceptable answers.

Puritan community that believed in the existence of witches

Salem

The Wonders of the Invisible World
Cotton Mather

The Wonders of the Invisible World was published in October 1692, immediately after the Salem witch trials. Listen to what Cotton Mather, a respected leader of Puritan New England, has to say about witches and a Christian response to witches.

But now, *What shall we do?*

I. Let the Devils *coming down* in *great wrath* upon us, cause us to *come down* in *great grief* before the Lord. We may truly and sadly say, *We are brought very low! Low* indeed, when the Serpents of the dust, are crawling and coyling about us, and Insulting over us. May we not say, *We are in the very belly of Hell*, when *Hell* it self is feeding upon us? But how *Low* is that! O let us then most penitently lay our selves very Low before the God of Heaven, who has thus Abased us. . . .

II. Since the Devil is *come down in great wrath* upon us, let not us in our great wrath against one another provide a *Lodging* for him. It was a most wholesome caution, in *Eph. 4.26, 27. Let not the Sun go down upon your wrath: Neither give place to the Devil.* The Devil is come down to see what *Quarter* he shall find among us: And if his coming down, do now fill us with wrath against one another, and if between the cause of the *Sufferers* on one hand, and the cause of the *Suspected* on t'other, we carry things to such extreams of *Passion* as are now gaining upon us, the Devil will Bless himself, to find such a convenient *Lodging* as we shall therein afford unto him. And it may be that the *wrath* which we have had against one another has had more than a little influence upon the coming down of the Devil in that wrath which now amazes us. . . .

III. Inasmuch as the Devil is come down in *Great Wrath*, we had need Labour, with all the Care and Speed we can to Divert the *Great Wrath* of Heaven from coming at the same time upon us. The God of Heaven has with long and loud Admonitions, been calling us to *a Reformation of our Provoking Evils*, as the only way to avoid that *Wrath* of His, which does not only *Threaten* but *Consume* us. 'Tis because we have been Deaf to those *Calls* that we are now by a provoked God, laid open to the *Wrath* of the Devil himself. It is said in *Pr. 16.17. When a mans ways please the Lord, he maketh even his Enemies to be at peace with him.* The Devil is our grand *Enemy*; and tho' we would not be at peace with him, yet we would be at peace from him, that is, we would have him unable to disquiet our *peace*. . . .

IV. When the Devil is come down in *great Wrath*, let every *great Vice* which may have a more particular tendency to make us a Prey unto that *Wrath*, come into a due discredit with us. It is the general Concession of all men, who are not become too *Unreasonable* for common Conversation, that the Invitation of *Witchcrafts* is the thing that has now introduced the Devil into the midst of us. I say then, let not only all *Witchcrafts* be duly abominated with us, but also let us be duly watchful against all the *Steps* leading thereunto. There are lesser *Sorceries* which they say, are too frequent in our Land. As it was said in *2 King 17.9. The Children of Israel did secretly those things that were not right, against the Lord their God.* So 'tis to be feared, the Children of *New-England* have *secretly* done many things that have been pleasing to the Devil.

They say, that in some Towns it has been an usual thing for People to cure Hurts with *Spells*, or to use detestable Conjurations, with *Sieves*, *Keys*, and *Pease*, and *Nails*, and *Horse-shoes*, and I know not what other Implements, to learn the things for which they have a forbidden, and an impious *Curiosity*. 'Tis in the Devils Name, that such things are done; and in Gods Name I do this day charge them, as vile Impieties. By these Courses 'tis, that People play upon *The Hole of the Asp*, till that cruelly venemous *Asp* has pull'd many of them into the deep *Hole* of *Witchcraft* it self. It has been acknowledged by some who have sunk the deepest into this *horrible Pit*, that they began at these little *Witchcrafts*; on which 'tis pity but the Laws of the English Nation, whereby the incorrigible repetition of those *Tricks*, is made *Felony*, were severely Executed. From the like sinful *Curiosity* it is, that the Prognostications of *Judicial Astrology*, are so injudiciously regarded by multitudes among us; and altho' the Jugling *Astrologers* do scarce ever hit right, except it be in such *Weighty Judgments*, forsooth, as that many *Old Men* will die such a year, and that there will be many *Losses* felt by some that venture to Sea, and that there will be much *Lying* and *Cheating* in the World; yet their foolish Admirers will not be perswaded but that the Innocent *Stars* have been concern'd in these Events. It is a disgrace to the English Nation, that the Pamphlets of such idle, futil, trifling *Stargazers* are so much considered; and the Countenance hereby given to a Study, wherein at last, all is done by *Impulse*, if any thing be done to any purpose at all, is not a little perillous to the Souls of Men. It is (*a Science*, I dare not call it, but) a *Juggle*, whereof the Learned Hall well says, *It is presumptuous and unwarrantable, and cry'd ever down by Councils and Fathers, as unlawful, as that which lies in the mid-way between Magick and Imposture, and partakes not a little of both.* Men consult the Aspects of Planets, whose Northern or Southern motions receive denominations from a *Cælestial Dragon*, till the *Infernal Dragon* at length insinuate into them, with a *Poison* of *Witchcraft* that can't be cured. Has there not also been a world of discontent in our Borders? 'Tis no wonder, that the *fiery Serpents* are so Stinging of us; We have been a most *Murmuring Generation*. It is not Irrational, to ascribe the late Stupendious growth of Witches among us, partly to the bitter *discontents*, which Affliction and Poverty has fill'd us with: it is inconceivable, what advantage the Devil gains over men, by discontent. Moreover, the Sin of *Unbelief* may be reckoned as perhaps the chief *Crime* of our Land. We are told, *God swears in wrath, against them that believe not*; and what follows then but this, *That the Devil comes unto them in wrath?* Never were the offers of the *Gospel*, more freely tendered, or more basely despised, among any People under the whole Cope of Heaven, than in this N. E. Seems it at all marvellous unto us, that the *Devil* should get such footing in our Country? Why, 'tis because the *Saviour* has been slighted here, perhaps more than any where. The Blessed Lord Jesus Christ has been profering to us, *Grace, and Glory, and every good thing*, and been alluring of us to Accept of Him, with such Terms as these, *Undone Sinner, I am All; Art thou willing that I should be thy All?* But, as a proof of that Contempt which this Unbelief has cast upon these proffers, I would seriously ask of the so many Hundreds above a Thousand People within these Walls; which of you all, O how few of you, can indeed say, *Christ is mine, and I am his, and he is the Beloved of my Soul?* I would only say thus much: When the precious and glorious Jesus, is Entreating of us to Receive Him, in all His *Offices*, with all His *Benefits*; the Devil minds what Respect we pay unto that Heavenly Lord; if we *Refuse Him that speaks from Heaven*, then he that, *Comes from Hell*, does with a sort of claim set in, and cry out, *Lord, since this Wretch is not willing that thou shouldst have him, I pray, let me have him.* And thus, by the just vengeance of Heaven, the Devil becomes a *Master*, a *Prince*, a *God*, unto the miserable Unbelievers: but O what are many of them then hurried unto! All of these Evil Things, do I now set before you, as *Branded* with the Mark of the Devil upon them.

V. With *Great Regard*, with *Great Pity*, should we Lay to Heart the Condition of those, who are cast into Affliction, by the *Great Wrath* of the

Devil. There is a Number of our Good Neighbours, and some of them very particularly noted for Goodness and Vertue, of whom we may say, *Lord, They are vexed with Devils....*

VI. With a *Great Zeal*, we should lay hold on the *Covenant* of God, that we may secure *Us* and *Ours*, from the *Great Wrath*, with which the Devil Rages. Let us come into the *Covenant of Grace*, and then we shall not be hook'd into a *Covenant with the Devil*, nor be altogether unfurnished with Armour, against the Wretches that are in that *Covenant*. The way to come under the Saving Influences of the New Covenant, is, to close with the Lord Jesus Christ, who is the All-sufficient *Mediator* of it: Let us therefore do, *that*, by Resigning up our selves unto the Saving, Teaching, and Ruling Hands of this Blessed *Mediator*. Then we shall be, what we read in *Jude 1.Preserved in Christ Jesus*: That is, as the *Destroying Angel*, could not meddle with such as had been distinguished, by the Blood of the *Passeover* on their Houses: Thus the Blood of the Lord Jesus Christ, Sprinkled on our Souls, will *Preserve* us from the Devil....

VIII. Lastly, Shake off, every Soul, shake off the *hard Yoak* of the Devil. Where 'tis said, *The whole World lyes in Wickedness*; 'tis by some of the Ancients rendred, *The whole World lyes in the Devil.* The Devil is a Prince, yea, the Devil is a God unto all the Unregenerate; and alas, there is *A whole World of them.* Desolate Sinners, consider what an horrid Lord it is that you are Enslav'd unto; and Oh shake off your Slavery to such a Lord. Instead of *him*, now make your Choice of the Eternal God in Jesus Christ; Chuse him with a most unalterable Resolution, and unto him say, with *Thomas, My Lord, and my God!* Say with the Church, *Lord, other Lords*

have had the Dominion over us, but now thou alone shalt be our Lord for ever....

My Text says, *The Devil is come down in great Wrath, for he has but a short time.* Yea, but if you do not by a speedy and through Conversion to God, escape the Wrath of the Devil, you will your selves go down, where the Devil is to be, and you will there be sweltring under the Devils Wrath, not for a *short Time*, but, *World without end*; not for a *Short Time*, but for *Infinite Millions of Ages.* The smoak of your Torment under that Wrath, will *Ascend for ever and ever!* Indeed, the Devil's time for his Wrath upon you in this World, can be but short, but his time for you to do his Work, or, which is all one, to delay your turning to God, that is a *Long Time.* When the Devil was going to be Dispossessed of a Man, he Roar'd out, *Am I to be Tormented before my time?* You will *Torment* the Devil, if you Rescue your Souls out of his hands, by true Repentance: If once you begin to look that way, he'll Cry out, *O this is before my Time, I must have more Time, yet in the Service of such a guilty Soul.* But, I beseech you, let us join thus to torment the Devil, in an holy Revenge upon him, for all the Injuries which he has done unto us; let us tell him, *Satan, thy time with me is but short, Nay, thy time with me shall be no more; I am unutterably sorry that it has been so much; Depart from me thou Evil-Doer, that would'st have me to be an Evil Doer like thy self; I will now for ever keep the Commandments of that God, in whom I Live and Move, and have my Being!* The Devil has plaid a fine Game for himself indeed, if by his troubling of our Land, the Souls of many People should come to *think upon their ways, till even they turn their Feet into the Testimonies of the Lord.* Now that the Devil may be thus outshot in his own Bow, is the desire of all that love the Salvation of God among us, as well as of him, who has thus Addressed you. *Amen.*(www.gutenberg.org/files/28513/28513-h/28513-h.htm#Page_38).

Assignments

- Warm-up: Were there really witches in 1692 New England?
- Students should complete Concept Builder 30-B.
- Student *should* review reading(s) from the next chapter.
- Student should outline essay due at the end of the week.
- Per teacher instructions, students may answer orally, in a group setting, some of the essays that are not assigned as formal essays.

Accusations

Have you ever been accused of something that you did not do? How did it feel?

What Happened	How I Felt

Stage Directions

Arthur Miller gave stage directions to directors of his play and to actors in his play. Stage directions include props, scenery, costumes, and sound effects. These are important because they set the stage for the students to experience the characters and the world in which the characters are struggling. Along the way, Miller even offered commentaries! Many historians have taken exception to this practice, claiming quite accurately that Miller was not correct in his historical reenactment of the Salem witch trials. But, of course, that is completely beside the point. Miller was not writing history; he was writing drama.

In summary, Miller's stage directions at the beginning of each Act provide critical information about:

- Characters
- Setting
- Mood

For instance, in the first scene, lighting is an important staging element used to create the time and atmosphere of each Act. Light (or darkness) is also symbolic. It is early morning and a single candle is burning. The implication is that that fragile candle will be blown out and bad days are ahead for Salem.

Assignments

- Warm-up: Mary, Abby, and their friends were simply enjoying a childhood game but by ACT II it is no longer a game — people are being accused and arrested for witchcraft! Describe a situation when you played a joke on someone and it got out of hand. This would be a time when you were kidding around with someone who was hurt and you did not mean to hurt him/her.

- Students should complete Concept Builder 30-C.

- Students should write rough drafts of assigned essay.

- The teacher may correct rough drafts.

Identify 4 themes in "The Crucible." There are considerably more than four!

Superstition

Themes

Soliloquies and Monologues

A monologue is a speech made by one person speaking his or her thoughts aloud or directly addressing a reader, audience, or character.

Here is a monologue in "The Crucible":

ABIGAIL: I cannot bear lewd looks no more, John. My spirit's changed entirely. I ought to be given Godly looks when I suffer for them as I do. Look at my leg. I'm holes all over from their … needles and pins. The jab your wife gave me's not healed yet, y'know. And George Jacobs comes again and again and raps me with his stick — the same spot every night all this week. Looks at the lump I have.

Oh John, the world's so full of hypocrites! They pray in jail, I'm told they pray in jail! And torture me in my bed while sacred words are coming from their mouths! It will need God Himself to cleanse this town properly. If I live, if I am not murdured, I will surely cry out others until the last hypocrite is dead!

But John, you taught me goodness, therefore you are good. It were a fire you walked me through and all my ignorance was burned away. It were a fire, John, we lay in fire. And from that night no woman called me wicked any more but I knew my answer. I used to weep for my sins when the wind lifted up my skirts; and blushed for shame because some old Rebecca called me loose. And then you burned my ignorance away. As bare as some December tree I saw them all — walking like saints to church, running to feed the sick, and hypocrites in their hearts! And God gave me strength to call them liars and God made men listen to me, and by God I will scrub the world clean for the love of Him! John, I will make you such a wife when the world is white again! You will be amazed to see me every day, a light of heaven in your house!

In a soliloquy in a play or film, the speaking actor need not be alone on the stage or scene; however, none of the supporting cast (in theatre or film) speaks or even hears what the actor is saying.

Soliloquy, *The Crucible* — after Conflict with Abigail, Act I (from the viewpoint of John Proctor)

The child lies to me. I saw the mockery in her eyes; the slight upturn of her soft, tantalizing mouth; knowing that we share the same secret. And yet she dares show the same cheek as Mary Warren. … Am I one to spit shame upon the word of deceit, when it was I who instilled such empowering emotions into this girl? Abigail burns for me, much like I once longed for her comforting presence. I, long ago, paused in passing with each star-filled evening below her window. To catch a mere glimpse of her youthful, slender figure dancing in the flickering candlelight set fire to my soul. My heart was filled once more with elation and faith in the God when she and I touched. It was a revelation of all things wild and unpredictable, yet my soul was released from all tides of worry. Was this the feeling of true happiness?

Abigail has again displayed her familiar wild streak by dancing naked in the forest. I can imagine the little vixen bathing in moonlight almost if I were there beside her. Skin like porcelain pirouetting through fallen leave, herself almost like a ghost. . . . How I must falter in order to bequeath maturity upon her fair brow, and to bestow a quality she may only learn from those more wise around her! Abigail, forgive me for condemning you to this hatred world of infidelity. Forgive me, my Holy God, for I have sinned. . . .

I bade goodbye in earlier times to a life filled with materialistic things, and arrived in Salem. From then on, I had watched in silence as this growing tempest of madness encompassed the village. Even my wife Elizabeth has showed immense strain recently. Our marriage is slowly withering; her patience with me is torn to shreds. How angered I am by Abigail's naïve and hatred words! Can such a breathtakingly beautiful, passionate example of a girl suggest that I be wedded for years on end, made love with, kissed and comforted, fathered children with a "cold and sniveling woman"? Does she not see the reality of our futile affair? That it could taint my name and Elizabeth's when for so long I and she have held such a pure name as "Proctor"? And what would my sons say to discover such a scandalous incident? That the girl I had so madly fell for was as young as they be? There must be an end to her terms of endearment, her juvenile, unseeing ways; I cannot stand for it much longer. But Abigail will show her worthiness; she always does when I least expect it. Those blue eyes will no longer be clouded with worry, and I will continue living with Elizabeth. Nothing more will I expect; and neither will she. . .

Assignments

- Warm-up: How can one stand for the Lord when he or she becomes hurt by hypocrisy?
- Students should complete Concept Builder 30-D.
- Student will re-write corrected copies of essay due tomorrow.

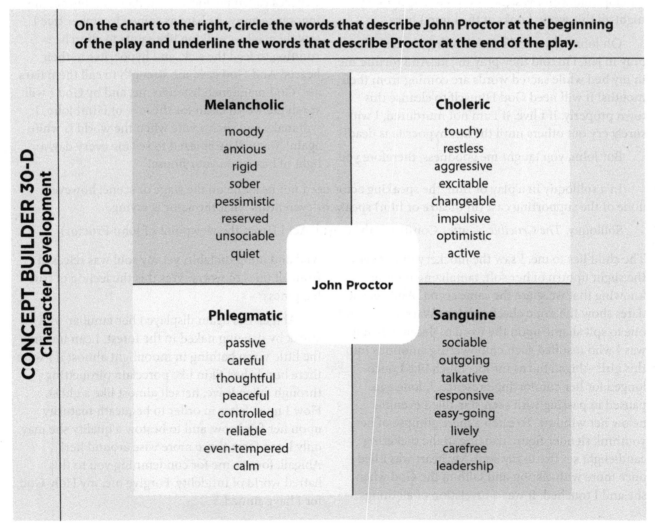

CONCEPT BUILDER 30-D
Character Development

On the chart to the right, circle the words that describe John Proctor at the beginning of the play and underline the words that describe Proctor at the end of the play.

Melancholic

moody
anxious
rigid
sober
pessimistic
reserved
unsociable
quiet

Choleric

touchy
restless
aggressive
excitable
changeable
impulsive
optimistic
active

John Proctor

Phlegmatic

passive
careful
thoughtful
peaceful
controlled
reliable
even-tempered
calm

Sanguine

sociable
outgoing
talkative
responsive
easy-going
lively
carefree
leadership

Political Agenda

In the first blank, rate how you feel about these statements. In the second blank, rate how Arthur Miller feels. 1 = strongly agree, 5 = strongly disagree

	Me	Arthur Miller	
1.			Nothing should be done for the weak and homeless. They get what they deserve.
2.			The president has too much power.
3.			We must not allow young people access to immoral material.
4.			All terrorists should be locked up and we should throw away the key!
5.			We must be careful to protect everyone's rights.
6.			America! Love it or leave it!
7.			Courts should be instructed to offer no mercy to criminals.
8.			We must elect more religious and moral leaders.
9.			We must keep the Church and state separate.
10.			No art should be banned, no matter how harmful or obnoxious.

Assignments

- Warm-up: Clearly, Arthur Miller had a political agenda when he wrote this play. State what sort of agenda Arthur Miller has.
- Students should complete Concept Builder 30-E.
- Essays are due. Students should take the chapter 30 test.

One of the most powerful scenes of dramatic irony in American literature occurs when Elizabeth Proctor is questioned in court. Why?

=

Dramatic Irony

Chapter 31

1960–Present (Part 1):
Contemporary Writers

First Thoughts John Ellis writes, "To read *A Separate Peace* is to discover a novel which is completely satisfactory and yet so provocative that the reader wishes immediately to return to it (John Ellis, www.bookrags.com/criticisms/A_Separate_Peace). Why is the novel so popular? The theme of this novel is universally applicable and universally important. It concerns growing up, making mistakes, and forgiving oneself for those mistakes. Perhaps no American author so eloquently and thoroughly gives insight into these themes.

Author Worldview Watch John Knowles wrote this theistic novel in the early 1960s. Before the world was turned upside down in the turbulent race riots and drug infused music concerts of the later 1960s, *A Separate Peace* was a much needed respite and a foreshadowing of future theistic offerings that were not long in coming. In the literary world, at least, America had turned a corner and was speeding back to its theistic, it not at times, Christian, roots. In that sense, A Separate Peace belongs to the 18th more than the 20th century.

Chapter Learning Objectives In chapter 31, we analyze John Knowles' *A Separate Peace*.

As a result of this chapter study you will be able to . . .

1. Analyze the narrator of the novel.
2. Assess the importance of the setting.
3. Give one or two themes of this novel.
4. Determine if Gene caused Finny to fall from the tree.
5. Predict what themes, characters, and plots will emerge in 20 years.

Weekly Essay Options: Begin on page 274 of the Teacher Guide.

Reading ahead: *Everything That Rises Must Converge* by Flannery O'Connor, "A Worn Path" by Eudora Welty, "The Jilting of Granny Weatherall" by Katherine Anne Porter

483

Post-World War II Literature

Perhaps nothing captures the essence of post-World War America more than the interstate highway system.

Americans were going with increased speed and frequency to no place in particular.

In 1945 American and her allies won World War II. By 1990 America and her allies had won the so-called Cold War. In 1956, President Dwight Eisenhower authorized the largest public works project in the history of the world. In 1919, it took Eisenhower 62 days to travel over mostly unpaved roads from Washington, D.C. to San Francisco. Today, the same trip takes 72 hours.

Instead of taking trains or buses, workers commuted by cars from neat suburbs. Suburbs flourished, and so did suburban problems. Shopping centers appeared, then malls, and presently Americans are shopping in surrogate city-like strip malls like Tanger Outlets (www.digitalhistory. uh.edu/database/article_display.cfm?HHID=504).

Americans wanted their transportation to be fast and cheap and their literature to be light and existential. With the paperback age and then digital age, Americans were spoiled by countless quantities of superficial, but affordable, literature and art. The net result was that commerce drove art, not vice versa.

Thankfully, though, some Americans, notably John Knowles, wrote quality, substantive works. Gene Forrester is, then, the model, quintessential post-World War II American: moral, shy, intelligent, but lost (or searching). He is somewhat confident because he has accomplished much, but limited by the exigencies of maturation and the perniciousness of fate. In short, America in its culture returns for a season to Theism but still retains a hint of Naturalism. This creates in essence, a sort of Hell: Americans hope for the best, believe in goodness, only to be reminded that the world, at least without God, is nefarious and treacherous.

Assignments

- Warm-up: World War II had a great impact on this novel. Is there one event that affected your life more than any other?
- Students should complete Concept Builder 31-A.
- Students review the required reading(s) *before* the assigned chapter begins.
- Teachers may want to discuss assigned reading(s) with students.
- Teachers shall assign the required essay. The rest of the essays can be outlined, answered with shorter answers, discussed, or skipped.
- Students will review all readings for chapter 31.

Describe the point of view of the narration. What are the advantages of this choice?

Point of View	Advantages

A Separate Peace
John Knowles

About the Author John Knowles was only 33 years old when *A Separate Peace* was published, in 1959 in England, and then in 1960 in the United States. The book was an immediate and stunning success, receiving the William Faulkner Foundation Award and the Rosenthal Award of the National Institute of Arts and Letters. But John Knowles had begun writing seriously a decade before the success of *A Separate Peace* enabled him to abandon full-time employment. He was assistant editor for the *Yale Alumni Magazine* where he'd attended college, he worked as a reporter and drama critic for the *Hartford Courant*, and then he wrote his first novel, *Descent into Proselito*, while living in Italy and France. That novel was never published; his friend and teacher, the playwright Thornton Wilder, felt it was not good enough. Knowles was born in Fairmont, West Virginia, on September 16, 1926, the third of four children. At age 15, during World War II, he went away to boarding school, the Phillips Exeter Academy in New Hampshire. The pressures of this environment at such a dire and impressionable time laid the foundation for *A Separate Peace* — and even before that novel, for a short story called

Knowles attended Phillips Exeter Academy. Photo by James Garner Williams, 2003 (CC BY-SA 2.5).

"Phineas," which takes us through the events of the first half of the novel. What makes this novel so unique is that it celebrates many old-fashioned values: honesty, hard work, and integrity.

Assignments

- Warm-up: In what ways was this novel autobiographical?
- Students should complete Concept Builder 31-B.
- Student *should* review reading(s) from the next chapter.
- Student should outline essay due at the end of the week.
- Per teacher instructions, students may answer orally, in a group setting, some of the essays that are not assigned as formal essays.

Finny is a tragic hero, on the same level as Achilles in Homer's *The Iliad*. Achilles, while being a very capable man, was also very prideful. This pride led to his eventual destruction. In what way is Finny a tragic hero?

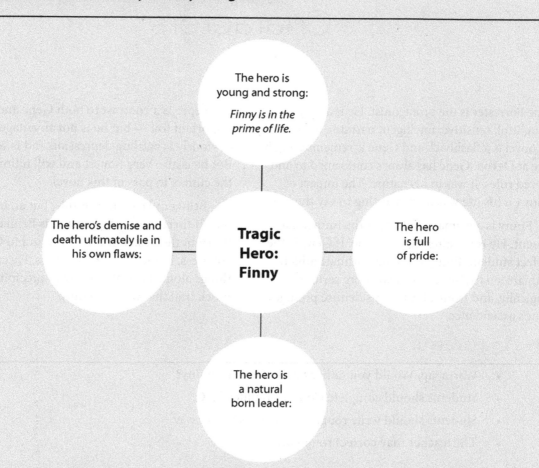

The hero is young and strong:

Finny is in the prime of life.

Tragic Hero: Finny

The hero's demise and death ultimately lie in his own flaws:

The hero is full of pride:

The hero is a natural born leader:

Characters

Gene Forrester is the protagonist. He is a very thoughtful, sensitive, intelligent narrator. Structurally, the novel is a flashback and Gene is remembering his time at Devon. Gene has always conformed to and obeyed rules. It was in his nature. The impact of Finny on his life was disconcerting to say the least.

Finny is a primary foil. He is the immediate present. He is the alter-ego to Gene. If Gene is the perfect student, Finny is the penultimate athlete. Both are smart, but Gene is far more serious. Tragically, and ironically, Finny's demise presages Gene's ascendance.

Leper is a contrast to both Gene and Finny — an important foil — but he is not an antagonist. He obviously is battling depression and is very unstable. But he is also very honest and will ultimately bring the climax to pass in this novel.

Brinker plays a minor role, but an important one. If there is an antagonist, it is Brinker. He is a thorn in the flesh both to Finny and to Gene. He is colorless, humorless, and ruthless. He cannot let things alone. He is the one who precipitates the mock trial that will kill Finny.

Assignments

- Warm-up: Would you rather be like Gene or Finny?
- Students should complete Concept Builder 31-C.
- Students should write rough drafts of assigned essay.
- The teacher may correct rough drafts.

CONCEPT BUILDER 31-C
Setting

The setting has layers, each one affecting the other one. Label these layers.

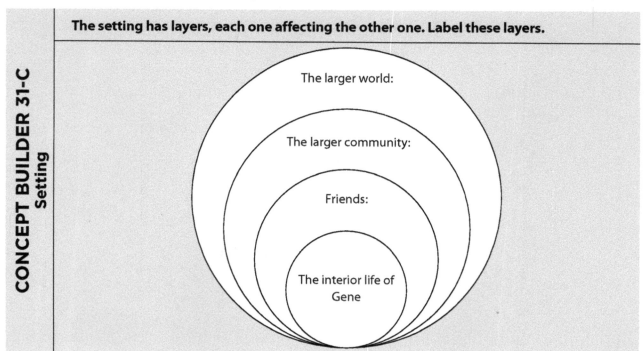

The larger world:

The larger community:

Friends:

The interior life of Gene

LESSON 4

Climax

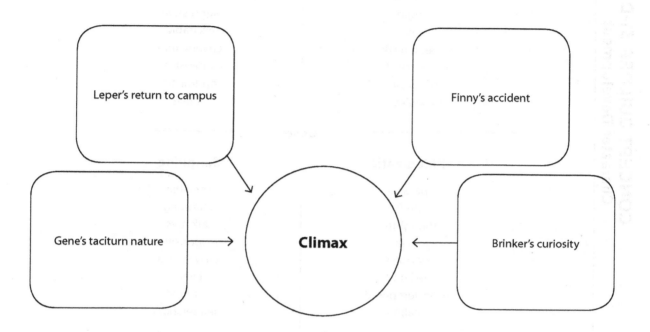

Assignments

- Warm-up: What if Finny lived? How would this change the story?
- Students should complete Concept Builder 31-D.
- Student will re-write corrected copies of essay due tomorrow.

CONCEPT BUILDER 31-D
Character Development

On the chart below, circle the words that describe Gene at the beginning of the novel and underline the words that describe Gene at the end of the novel.

Melancholic	**Choleric**
moody	touchy
anxious	restless
rigid	aggressive
sober	excitable
pessimistic	changeable
reserved	impulsive
unsociable	optimistic
quiet	active

Gene

Phlegmatic	**Sanguine**
passive	sociable
careful	outgoing
thoughtful	talkative
peaceful	responsive
controlled	easy-going
reliable	lively
even-tempered	carefree
calm	leadership

The Final Chapter

The last chapter exposes the problems with Gene's credibility as a narrator: Can readers believe him? We hear that he is never accused of Finny's death although he feels responsible for the longest time. Gene is attempting to be transparently honest — but can we believe him? If he is innocent, why does he constantly think of Finny? "Finny had a vitality which could not be quenched so suddenly," we read.

Finally, Brinker's father and his comments represent the chasm that has opened up between Gene and the war. He will fight in it, but he will not be angry at the enemy. His own war ended before he put on a uniform — thus, the "separate peace."

Assignments

- Warm-up: Did you like the ending of the novel? If not, what ending would you like?
- Students should complete Concept Builder 31-E.
- Essays are due. Students should take the chapter 31 test.

CONCEPT BUILDER 31-E
Credibility

Is Gene a credible narrator?	
Credibility	**Gene**
Is the narrator an intelligent, insightful person?	
Does the narrator lie or exaggerate?	
Is the narrator unstable, prone to fits of temper?	
Is the narrator a participant in the event?	
Does something negative in the plot happen to the narrator?	
Is the narrator responsible for this negative thing?	

Chapter 32

1960–Present (Part 2):
Contemporary Writers

First Thoughts Henry James, William Faulkner, and many other American writers experimented with fictional points of view (some are still doing so). James often restricted the information in the novel to what a single character would have known. Faulkner's novel *The Sound and the Fury* (perhaps the greatest novel ever written) breaks up the narrative into four sections, each giving the viewpoint of a different character (including a mentally retarded boy). *As I Lay Dying* employs a similar approach. These three short stories employ some of the most sophisticated stream of consciousness techniques in American literature.

Author Worldview Watch These three short stories evidence that the theistic revival among literature is well underway. Flannery O'Connor, a solid Christian, especially places the theistic banner back on the top of American literature. Katherine Anne Porter celebrates the powerful of forgiveness and the endurance of grace. These are not characters who are victims of hateful circumstances (e.g., *The Pearl*) or cruel happenstances (e.g., *Billy Budd*). Even foolish Julian in O'Connor's short story, and all others, find that in theism, living in within biblical perimeters, one finds life. One hopes that other future authors will follow this worn path.

Chapter Learning Objectives In chapter 32 you will analyze "Everything That Rises Must Converge" by Flannery O'Connor, "A Worn Path" by Eudora Welty, and "The Jilting of Granny Weatherall" by Katherine Anne Porter.

As a result of this chapter study you will be able to . . .

1. Compare Julian and his mother.
2. Discuss how Welty uses the journey motif in this short story to advance the action.
3. Analyze the use of foils in O'Connor's short story.
4. Explain how Porter uses stream of consciousness and dialogue to advance the action.
5. Describe what kills Julian's mother.
6. Explain what universal truth is revealed in "A Worn Path."

Weekly Essay Options: Begin on page 274 of the Teacher Guide.

Reading ahead: *Cold Sassy Tree* by Olive Ann Burns

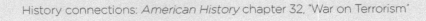 History connections: *American History* chapter 32, "War on Terrorism"

Southern Renaissance

Background In the early and middle part of the 20th century there was a renaissance of Southern literature that was unprecedented since the New England renaissance occurring a century before. Southern literature, deeply affected, ironically, by the Ohio writer Sherwood Anderson, emphasized the grotesque and unique. More than that, though, Southern prose literature was just plain good story telling.

Southern literature took to task the modernist tendency to reject everything traditional. The large cultural wave of modernism, which gradually emerged in Europe and the United States in the early years of the 20th century, expressed a sense of modern life through art as a sharp break from the past, as well as from Western civilization's classical traditions. This movement set the stage for the art and philosophies that predominate today. Modernism embraced changes in technology.

In literature, Gertrude Stein (1874–1946) developed a literary analogy to modern art. A resident of Paris and an art collector, Stein once explained that she and Picasso were doing the same thing, he in art and she in writing. She flatters herself! Her main influence was through writers and artists who came to her house and joined in her numerous parties. This group included Ernest Hemingway and F. Scott Fitzgerald.

Technological innovation in the world of factories and machines inspired new attentiveness to technique in the arts. Posters and advertisements of the period are full of images of floodlit skyscrapers.

Photography was important to the modern artist. Metaphor was out. The real, in-your-face art was in. Even surrealism, which was itself strange, invited sensory expressions that were often earthy.

Arguably, Flannery O'Connor was one of the best authors of all time. She would rival the British writer Virginia Woolf. Katherine Ann Porter, too, was a master. She was very good at writing short novels. My personal favorite was Eudora Welty, a friend of my grandmother, and one of the greatest short story and short novel authors in American literature. Her acerbic style is famous.

Assignments

- Warm-up: How is the proliferation of online writing, connecting people instantly all over the world, influencing today's society?
- Students should complete Concept Builder 32-A.
- Students review the required reading(s) *before* the assigned chapter begins.
- Teachers may want to discuss assigned reading(s) with students.
- Teachers shall assign the required essay. The rest of the essays can be outlined, answered with shorter answers, discussed, or skipped.
- Students will review all readings for chapter 32.

From ancient to modern, what is your favorite genre of writing, and what does this reflect about you as a reader?

Everything That Rises Must Converge
Flannery O'Connor

Flannery O'Connor (1925–1964) was born in Savannah, Georgia, on March 25, 1925, and died of lupus in Milledgeville, Georgia, on August 3, 1964. In those 39 years, she contributed a brief, powerful canon (2 novels, 32 short stories, plus reviews and commentaries). O'Connor is considered one of the most important voices in American literature. Her short novels and short stories are some of the best in American literature. A born-again Christian, O'Connor, to a certain measure, reintroduced Christian theism into American literature at a time when naturalism, realism, and existentialism dominated the literary landscape. "Everything That Rises Must Converge" was written a year before O'Connor's death and reflects the racial tensions endemic to 1960 America.

The narrator is Julian, a recent college graduate who is frustrated because he is underemployed. He lives at home with his bossy, widowed mother. The setting is the recently integrated, uneasy South of the 1960s. One critic observes, "Events unfold during a ride on an integrated bus, in which all of the story's complex relationships are played out: the vindictive, self-deluding dependency of Julian on his mother; the insightless yet well-intentioned doting of his mother, who is tied to the societal conventions in which she was raised; the condescension of "enlightened" whites toward blacks; the resentment of blacks toward well-meaning whites — all depicted with great skill and humor" (litmed.med.nyu.edu/Annotation?action=view&annid=86).

Everything That Rises Must Converge by Flannery O'Connor

HER DOCTOR had told Julian's mother that she must lose twenty pounds on account of her blood pressure, so on Wednesday nights Julian had to take her downtown on the bus for a reducing class at the Y. The reducing class was designed for working girls over fifty, who weighed from 165 to 200 pounds. His mother was one of the slimmer ones, but she said ladies did not tell their age or weight. She would not ride the buses by herself at night since they had been integrated, and because the reducing class was one of her few pleasures, necessary for her health, and free, she said Julian could at least put himself out to take her, considering all she did for him. Julian did not like to consider all she did for him, but every Wednesday night he braced himself and took her.

She was almost ready to go, standing before the hall mirror, putting on her hat, while he, his hands behind him, appeared pinned to the door frame, waiting like Saint Sebastian for the arrows to begin piercing him. The hat was new and had cost her seven dollars and a half. She kept saying, "Maybe I shouldn't have paid that for it. No, I shouldn't have. I'll take it off and return it tomorrow. I shouldn't have bought it."

Julian raised his eyes to heaven. "Yes, you should have bought it," he said. "Put it on and let's go." It was a hideous hat. A purple velvet flap came down on one side of it and stood up on the other; the rest of it was green and looked like a cushion with the stuffing out. He decided it was less comical than jaunty and pathetic. Everything that gave her pleasure was small and depressed him.

She lifted the hat one more time and set it down slowly on top of her head. Two wings of gray hair protruded on either side of her florid face, but her eyes, sky-blue, were as innocent and untouched by experience as they must have been when she was ten. Were it not that she was a widow who had struggled fiercely to feed and clothe and put him through school and who was supporting him still, "until he got on his feet," she might have been a little girl that he had to take to town. "It's all right, it's all right," he said. "Let's go." He opened the door himself and started down the walk to get her going. The sky was a dying violet and the houses stood out darkly against it, bulbous liver-colored monstrosities of a uniform ugliness though no two were alike. Since this had been a fashionable neighborhood forty years ago, his mother persisted in thinking they did well to have an apartment in it. Each house had a narrow collar of dirt around it in which sat, usually, a grubby child. Julian walked with his hands in his pockets, his head down and thrust forward and his eyes glazed with the determination to make himself completely numb during the time he would be sacrificed to her pleasure.

The door closed and he turned to find the dumpy figure, surmounted by the atrocious hat, coming toward him. "Well," she said, "you only live once and paying a little more for it, I at least won't meet myself coming and going."

"Some day I'll start making money," Julian said gloomily — he knew he never would — "and you can have one of those jokes whenever you take the fit." But first they would move. He visualized a place where the nearest neighbors would be three miles away on either side.

"I think you're doing fine," she said, drawing on her gloves. "You've only been out of school a year. Rome wasn't built in a day."

She was one of the few members of the Y reducing class who arrived in hat and gloves and who had a son who had been to college. "It takes time," she said, "and the world is in such a mess. This hat looked better on me than any of the others, though when she brought it out I said, 'Take that thing back. I wouldn't have it on my head,' and she said, 'Now wait till you see it on,' and when she put it on me, I said, 'We-ull,' and she said, 'If you ask me, that hat does something for you and you do something for the hat, and besides,' she said, 'with that hat, you won't meet yourself coming and going.'"

Julian thought he could have stood his lot better

if she had been selfish, if she had been an old hag who drank and screamed at him. He walked along, saturated in depression, as if in the midst of his martyrdom he had lost his faith. Catching sight of his long, hopeless, irritated face, she stopped suddenly with a grief-stricken look, and pulled back on his arm. "Wait on me," she said. "I'm going back to the house and take this thing off and tomorrow I'm going to return it. I was out of my head. I can pay the gas bill with that seven-fifty."

He caught her arm in a vicious grip. "You are not going to take it back," he said. "I like it."

"Well," she said, "I don't think I ought. . . ." "Shut up and enjoy it," he muttered, more depressed than ever.

"With the world in the mess it's in," she said, "it's a wonder we can enjoy anything. I tell you, the bottom rail is on the top."

Julian sighed.

"Of course," she said, "if you know who you are, you can go anywhere." She said this every time he took her to the reducing class. "Most of them in it are not our kind of people," she said, "but I can be gracious to anybody. I know who I am."

"...," Julian said savagely. "Knowing who you are is good for one generation only. You haven't the foggiest idea where you stand now or who you are."

She stopped and allowed her eyes to flash at him. "I most certainly do know who I am," she said, "and if you don't know who you are, I'm ashamed of you."

. . .

"Your great-grandfather was a former governor of this state," she said. "Your grandfather was a prosperous land-owner. Your grandmother was a Godhigh."

"Will you look around you," he said tensely, "and see where you are now?" and he swept his arm jerkily out to indicate the neighborhood, which the growing darkness at least made less dingy.

"You remain what you are," she said. "Your great-grand-father had a plantation and two hundred slaves."

"There are no more slaves," he said irritably.

"They were better off when they were," she said. He groaned to see that she was off on that topic. She rolled onto it every few days like a train on an open track. He knew every stop, every junction, every swamp along the way, and knew the exact point at which her conclusion would roil majestically into the station: "It's ridiculous. It's simply not realistic. They should rise, yes, but on their own side of the fence."

"Let's skip it," Julian said.

"The ones I feel sorry for," she said, "are the ones that are half white. They're tragic."

"Will you skip it?"

"Suppose we were half white. We would certainly have mixed feelings."

"I have mixed feelings now," he groaned.

"Well let's talk about something pleasant," she said. "I remember going to Grandpa's when I was a little girl. Then the house had double stairways that went up to what was really the second floor — all the cooking was done on the first. I used to like to stay down in the kitchen on account of the way the walls smelled. I would sit with my nose pressed against the plaster and take deep breaths. Actually the place belonged to the Godhighs but your grandfather Chestny paid the mortgage and saved it for them. They were in reduced circumstances," she said, "but reduced or not, they never forgot who they were."

"Doubtless that decayed mansion reminded them," Julian muttered. He never spoke of it without contempt or thought of it without longing. He had seen it once when he was a child before it had been sold. The double stairways had rotted and been torn down. Negroes were living in it. But it remained in his mind as his mother had known it. It appeared in his dreams regularly. He would stand on the wide porch, listening to the rustle of oak leaves, then wander through the high-ceilinged hall into the parlor that opened onto it and gaze at the worn rugs and faded draperies. It occurred to him that it was he, not she, who could have appreciated it. He preferred its threadbare elegance to anything he could name and it was because of it that all the neighborhoods they had lived in had been a torment to him — whereas she had hardly known the difference. She called her insensitivity "being adjustable."

"And I remember the old darky who was my nurse, Caroline. There was no better person in the world. I've always had a great respect for my colored friends," she said. "I'd do anything in the world for them and they'd. . . ."

. . .

"You're mighty touchy tonight," she said. "Do you feel all right?"

"Yes I feel all right" he said. "Now lay off."

She pursed her lips. "Well, you certainly are in a vile humor," she observed "I just won't speak to you at all."

They had reached the bus stop. There was no bus in sight and Julian, his hands still jammed in his pockets and his head thrust forward, scowled down the empty street. The frustration of having to wait on the bus as well as ride on it began to creep up his neck like a hot hand. The presence of his mother was borne in upon him as she gave a pained sigh. He looked at her bleakly. She was holding herself very erect under the preposterous hat wearing it like a banner of her imaginary dignity. There was in him an evil urge to break her spirit. He suddenly unloosened his tie and pulled it off and put it in his pocket

She stiffened. "Why must you look like that when you take me to town?" she said. "Why must you deliberately embarrass me?"

"If you'll never learn where you are," he said, "you can at least learn where I am."

"You look like a thug," she said.

"Then I must be one," he murmured.

"I'll just go home" she said. "I will not bother you. If you can't do a little thing like that for me. . . ."

Rolling his eyes upward, he put his tie back on. "Restored to my class," he muttered. He thrust his face toward her and hissed, "True culture is in the mind, the mind," he said, and tapped his head, "the mind."

"It's in the heart," she said, "and in how you do things and how you do things is because of who you are."

. . .

"I care who I am," she said icily.

The lighted bus appeared on top of the next hill and as it approached, they moved out into the street to meet it. He put his hand under her elbow and hoisted her up on the creaking step. She entered with a little smile, as if she were going into a drawing room where everyone had been waiting for her. While he put in the tokens, she sat down on one of the broad front seats for three which faced the aisle.

A thin woman with protruding teeth and long yellow hair was sitting on the end of it. His mother moved up beside her and left room for Julian beside herself. He sat down and looked at the floor across the aisle where a pair of thin feet in red and white canvas sandals were planted.

His mother immediately began a general conversation meant to attract anyone who felt like talking. "Can it get any hotter?" she said and removed from her purse a folding fan, black with a Japanese scene on it, which she began to flutter before her.

"I reckon it might could," the woman with the protruding teeth said, "but I know for a fact my apartment couldn't get no hotter."

"It must get the afternoon sun," his mother said. She sat forward and looked up and down the bus. It was half filled. Everybody was white. "I see we have the bus to ourselves," she said. Julian cringed.

"For a change," said the woman across the aisle, the owner of the red and white canvas sandals. "I come on one the other day and they were thick as fleas — up front and all through."

"The world is in a mess everywhere," his mother said. "I don't know how we've let it get in this fix."

"What gets my goat is all those boys from good families stealing automobile tires," the woman with the protruding teeth said. "I told my boy, I said you may not be rich but you been raised right and if I ever catch you in any such mess, they can send you on to the reformatory. Be exactly where you belong."

"Training tells," his mother said. "Is your boy in high school?"

"Ninth grade," the woman said.

"My son just finished college last year. He wants to write but he's selling typewriters until he gets started," his mother said.

The woman leaned forward and peered at Julian. He threw her such a malevolent look that she subsided against the seat. On the floor across the aisle there was an abandoned newspaper. He got up and got it and opened it out in front of him. His mother discreetly continued the conversation in a lower tone but the woman across the aisle said in a loud voice, "Well, that's nice. Selling typewriters is close to writing. He can go right from one to the other."

"I tell him," his mother said, "that Rome wasn't built in a day."

Behind the newspaper Julian was withdrawing into the inner compartment of his mind where he spent most of his time. This was a kind of mental bubble in which he established himself when he could not bear to be a part of what was going on around him. From it he could see out and judge but in it he was safe from any kind of penetration from without. It was the only place where he felt free of the general idiocy of his fellows. His mother had never entered it but from it he could see her with absolute clarity.

The old lady was clever enough and he thought that if she had started from any of the right premises, more might have been expected of her. She lived according to the laws of her own fantasy world outside of which he had never seen her set foot. The law of it was to sacrifice herself for him after she had first created the necessity to do so by making a mess of things. If he had permitted her sacrifices, it was only because her lack of foresight had made them necessary. All of her life had been a struggle to act like a Chestny and to give him everything she thought a Chestny ought to have without the goods a Chestny ought to have; but since, said she, it was fun to struggle, why complain? And when you had won, as she had won, what fun to look back on the hard times! He could not forgive her that she had enjoyed the struggle and that she thought she had won.

What she meant when she said she had won was that she had brought him up successfully and had sent him to college and that he had turned out so well-good looking (her teeth had gone unfilled so that his could be straightened), intelligent (he realized he was too intelligent to be a success), and with a future ahead of him (there was of course no future ahead of him). She excused his gloominess on the grounds that he was still growing up and his radical ideas on his lack of practical experience. She said he didn't yet know a thing about "life," that he hadn't even entered the real world — when already he was as disenchanted with it as a man of fifty.

The further irony of all this was that in spite of her, he had turned out so well. In spite of going to only a third-rate college, he had, on his own initiative, come out with a first-rate education; in spite of growing up dominated by a small mind, he had ended up with a large one; in spite of all her foolish views, he was free of prejudice and unafraid to face facts. Most miraculous of all, instead of being blinded by love for her as she was for him, he had cut himself emotionally free of her and could see her with complete objectivity. He was not dominated by his mother.

The bus stopped with a sudden jerk and shook him from his meditation. A woman from the back lurched forward with little steps and barely escaped falling in his newspaper as she righted herself. She got off and a large Negro got on. Julian kept his paper lowered to watch. It gave him a certain satisfaction to see injustice in daily operation. It confirmed his view that with a few exceptions there was no one worth knowing within a radius of three hundred miles. The Negro was well dressed and carried a briefcase. He looked around and then sat down on the other end of the seat where the woman with the red and white canvas sandals was sitting. He immediately unfolded a newspaper and obscured himself behind it. Julian's mother's elbow at once prodded insistently into his ribs. "Now you see why I won't ride on these buses by myself," she whispered.

The woman with the red and white canvas sandals had risen at the same time the Negro sat down and had gone farther back in the bus and taken the seat of the woman who had got off. His mother leaned forward and cast her an approving look.

Julian rose, crossed the aisle, and sat down in the place of the woman with the canvas sandals. From this position, he looked serenely across at his mother. Her face had turned an angry red. He stared at her, making his eyes the eyes of a stranger. He felt his tension suddenly lift as if he had openly declared war on her.

He would have liked to get in conversation with the Negro and to talk with him about art or politics or any subject that would be above the comprehension of those around them, but the man remained entrenched behind his paper. He was either ignoring the change of seating or had never noticed it. There was no way for Julian to convey his sympathy.

His mother kept her eyes fixed reproachfully on his face. The woman with the protruding teeth was looking at him avidly as if he were a type of monster new to her.

"Do you have a light?" he asked the Negro.

Without looking away from his paper, the man reached in his pocket and handed him a packet of matches.

"Thanks," Julian said. For a moment he held the matches foolishly. A NO SMOKING sign looked down upon him from over the door. This alone would not have deterred him; he had no cigarettes. He had quit smoking some months before because he could not afford it. "Sorry," he muttered and handed back the matches. The Negro lowered the paper and gave him an annoyed look. He took the matches and raised the paper again.

His mother continued to gaze at him but she did not take advantage of his momentary discomfort. Her eyes retained their battered look. Her face seemed to be unnaturally red, as if her blood pressure had risen. Julian allowed no glimmer of sympathy to show on his face. Having got the advantage, he wanted desperately to keep it and carry it through. He would have liked to teach her a lesson that would last her a while, but there seemed no way to continue the point. The Negro refused to come out from behind his paper.

Julian folded his arms and looked stolidly before him, facing her but as if he did not see her, as if he had ceased to recognize her existence. He visualized a scene in which, the bus having reached their stop, he would remain in his seat and when she said, "Aren't you going to get off?" he would look at her as at a stranger who had rashly addressed him. The corner they got off on was usually deserted, but it was well lighted and it would not hurt her to walk by herself the four blocks to the Y. He decided to wait until the time came and then decide whether or not he would let her get off by herself He would have to be at the Y at ten to bring her back, but he could leave her wondering if he was going to show up. There was no reason for her to think she could always depend on him.

He retired again into the high-ceilinged room sparsely settled with large pieces of antique furniture. His soul expanded momentarily but then he became aware of his mother across from him and the vision shriveled. He studied her coldly. Her feet in little pumps dangled like a child's and did not quite reach the floor. She was training on him an exaggerated look of reproach. He felt completely detached from her. At that moment he could with pleasure have slapped her as he would have slapped a particularly obnoxious child in his charge.

He began to imagine various unlikely ways by which he could teach her a lesson. He might make friends with some distinguished Negro professor or lawyer and bring him home to spend the evening. He would be entirely justified but her blood pressure would rise to 300. He could not push her to the extent of making her have a stroke, and moreover, he had never been successful at making any Negro friends. He had tried to strike up an acquaintance on the bus with some of the better types, with ones that looked like professors or ministers or lawyers. One morning he had sat down next to a distinguished-looking dark brown man who had answered his questions with a sonorous solemnity but who had turned out to be an undertaker. Another day he had sat down beside a cigar-smoking Negro with a diamond ring on his finger, but after a few stilted pleasantries, the Negro had rung the buzzer and risen, slipping two lottery tickets into Julian's hand as he climbed over him to leave.

He imagined his mother lying desperately ill and his being able to secure only a Negro doctor for her. He toyed with that idea for a few minutes and then dropped it for a momentary vision of himself participating as a sympathizer in a sit-in demonstration. This was possible but he did not linger with it. Instead, he approached the ultimate horror. He brought home a beautiful suspiciously Negroid woman. Prepare yourself, he said. There is nothing you can do about it. This is the woman I've chosen. She's intelligent, dignified, even good, and she's suffered and she hasn't thought it fun. Now persecute us, go ahead and persecute us. Drive her out of here, but remember, you're driving me, too. His eyes were narrowed and through the indignation he had generated, he saw his mother across the aisle, purple-faced, shrunken to the dwarf-like proportions of her moral nature, sitting like a mummy beneath the ridiculous banner of her hat.

He was tilted out of his fantasy again as the bus stopped. The door opened with a sucking hiss and out of the dark a large, gaily dressed, sullen-looking colored woman got on with a little boy. The child, who might have been four, had on a short plaid suit and a Tyrolean hat with a blue feather in it. Julian hoped that he would sit down beside him and that the woman would push in beside his mother. He could think of no better arrangement.

As she waited for her tokens, the woman was surveying the seating possibilities — he hoped with the idea of sitting where she was least wanted. There was something familiar-looking about her but Julian could not place what it was. She was a giant of a woman. Her face was set not only to meet opposition but to seek it out. The downward tilt of her large lower lip was like a warning sign: DON'T TAMPER WITH ME. Her bulging figure was encased in a green crepe dress and her feet overflowed in red shoes. She had on a hideous hat. A purple velvet flap came down on one side of it and stood up on the other; the rest of it was green and looked like a cushion with the stuffing out. She carried a mammoth red pocketbook that bulged throughout as if it were stuffed with rocks.

To Julian's disappointment, the little boy climbed up on the empty seat beside his mother. His mother lumped all children, black and white, into the common category, "cute," and she thought little Negroes were on the whole cuter than little white children. She smiled at the little boy as he climbed on the seat.

Meanwhile the woman was bearing down upon the empty seat beside Julian. To his annoyance, she squeezed herself into it. He saw his mother's face change as the woman settled herself next to him and he realized with satisfaction that this was more objectionable to her than it was to him. Her face seemed almost gray and there was a look of dull recognition in her eyes, as if suddenly she had sickened at some awful confrontation. Julian saw that it was because she and the woman had, in a sense, swapped sons. Though his mother would not realize the symbolic significance of this, she would feel it. His amusement showed plainly on his face.

The woman next to him muttered something unintelligible to herself. He was conscious of a kind of bristling next to him, a muted growling like that of an angry cat. He could not see anything but the red pocketbook upright on the bulging green thighs. He visualized the woman as she had stood waiting for her tokens — the ponderous figure, rising from the red shoes upward over the solid hips, the mammoth bosom, the haughty face, to the green and purple hat.

His eyes widened.

The vision of the two hats, identical, broke upon him with the radiance of a brilliant sunrise. His face was suddenly lit with joy. He could not believe that Fate had thrust upon his mother such a lesson. He gave a loud chuckle so that she would look at him and see that he saw. She turned her eyes on him slowly. The blue in them seemed to have turned a bruised purple. For a moment he had an uncomfortable sense of her innocence, but it lasted only a second before principle rescued him. Justice entitled him to laugh. His grin hardened until it said to her as plainly as if he were saying aloud: Your punishment exactly fits your pettiness. This should teach you a permanent lesson.

Her eyes shifted to the woman. She seemed unable to bear looking at him and to find the woman preferable. He became conscious again of the bristling presence at his side. The woman was rumbling like a volcano about to become active. His mother's mouth began to twitch slightly at one corner. With a sinking heart, he saw incipient signs of recovery on her face and realized that this was going to strike her suddenly as funny and was going to be no lesson at all. She kept her eyes on the woman and an amused smile came over her face as if the woman were a monkey that had stolen her hat. The little Negro was looking up at her with large fascinated eyes. He had been trying to attract her attention for some time.

"Carver!" the woman said suddenly. "Come heah!"

When he saw that the spotlight was on him at last, Carver drew his feet up and turned himself toward Julian's mother and giggled.

"Carver!" the woman said. "You heah me? Come heah!"

Carver slid down from the seat but remained squatting with his back against the base of it, his head turned slyly around toward Julian's mother, who was smiling at him. The woman reached a hand across the aisle and snatched him to her. He righted himself and hung backwards on her knees, grinning at Julian's mother. "Isn't he cute?" Julian's mother said to the woman with the protruding teeth.

"I reckon he is," the woman said without conviction.

The Negress yanked him upright but he eased out of her grip and shot across the aisle and scrambled, giggling wildly, onto the seat beside his love.

"I think he likes me," Julian's mother said, and smiled at the woman. It was the smile she used when she was being particularly gracious to an inferior. Julian saw everything lost. The lesson had rolled off her like rain on a roof.

The woman stood up and yanked the little boy off the seat as if she were snatching him from contagion. Julian could feel the rage in her at having no weapon like his mother's smile. She gave the child a sharp slap across his leg. He howled once and then thrust his head into her stomach and kicked his feet against her shins. "Be-have," she said vehemently.

The bus stopped and the Negro who had been reading the newspaper got off. The woman moved over and set the little boy down with a thump between herself and Julian. She held him firmly by the knee. In a moment he put his hands in front of his face and peeped at Julian's mother through his fingers.

"I see yoooooooo!" she said and put her hand in front of her face and peeped at him.

The woman slapped his hand down. "Quit yo' foolishness," she said, "before I knock the living Jesus out of you!"

Julian was thankful that the next stop was theirs. He reached up and pulled the cord. The woman reached up and pulled it at the same time. ... He had the terrible intuition that when they got off the bus together, his mother would open her purse and give the little boy a nickel. The gesture would be as natural to her as breathing. The bus stopped and the woman got up and lunged to the front, dragging the child, who wished to stay on, after her. Julian and his mother got up and followed. As they neared the door, Julian tried to relieve her of her pocketbook.

"No," she murmured, "I want to give the little boy a nickel."

"No!" Julian hissed. "No!"

She smiled down at the child and opened her bag. The bus door opened and the woman picked him up by the arm and descended with him, hanging at her hip. Once in the street she set him down and shook him.

Julian's mother had to close her purse while she got down the bus step but as soon as her feet were on the ground, she opened it again and began to rummage inside. "I can't find but a penny," she whispered, "but it looks like a new one."

"Don't do it!" Julian said fiercely between his teeth. There was a streetlight on the corner and she hurried to get under it so that she could better see into her pocketbook. The woman was heading off rapidly down the street with the child still hanging backward on her hand.

"Oh, little boy!" Julian's mother called and took a few quick steps and caught up with them just beyond the lamppost. "Here's a bright new penny for you," and she held out the coin, which shone bronze in the dim light.

The huge woman turned and for a moment stood, her shoulders lifted and her face frozen with frustrated rage, and stared at Julian's mother. Then all at once she seemed to explode like a piece of machinery that had been given one ounce of pressure too much. Julian saw the black fist swing out with the red pocketbook. He shut his eyes and cringed as he heard the woman shout, "He don't take nobody's pennies!" When he opened his eyes, the woman was disappearing down the street with the little boy staring wide-eyed over her shoulder. Julian's mother was sitting on the sidewalk.

"I told you not to do that," Julian said angrily. "I told you not to do that!"

He stood over her for a minute, gritting his teeth. Her legs were stretched out in front of her and her hat was on her lap. He squatted down and looked her in the face. It was totally expressionless. "You got exactly what you deserved," he said. "Now get up."

He picked up her pocketbook and put what had fallen out back in it. He picked the hat up off her lap.

The penny caught his eye on the sidewalk and he picked that up and let it drop before her eyes into the purse. Then he stood up and leaned over and held his hands out to pull her up. She remained immobile. He sighed. Rising above them on either side were black apartment buildings, marked with irregular rectangles of light. At the end of the block a man came out of a door and walked off in the opposite direction. "All right," he said, "suppose somebody happens by and wants to know why you're sitting on the sidewalk?"

She took the hand and, breathing hard, pulled heavily up on it and then stood for a moment, swaying slightly as if the spots of light in the darkness were circling around her. Her eyes, shadowed and confused, finally settled on his face. He did not try to conceal his irritation. "I hope this teaches you a lesson," he said. She leaned forward and her eyes raked his face. She seemed trying to determine his identity. Then, as if she found nothing familiar about him, she started off with a headlong movement in the wrong direction.

"Aren't you going on to the Y?" he asked.

"Home," she muttered.

"Well, are we walking?"

For answer she kept going. Julian followed along, his hands behind him. He saw no reason to let the lesson she had had go without backing it up with an explanation of its meaning. She might as well be made to understand what had happened to her. "Don't think that was just an uppity Negro woman," he said. "That was the whole colored race which will no longer take your condescending pennies. That was your black double. She can wear the same hat as you, and to be sure," he added gratuitously (because he thought it was funny), "it looked better on her than it did on you. What all this means," he said, "is that the old world is gone. …" He thought bitterly of the house that had been lost for him. "You aren't who you think you are," he said.

She continued to plow ahead, paying no attention to him. Her hair had come undone on one side. She dropped her pocketbook and took no notice. He stooped and picked it up and handed it to her but she did not take it.

"You needn't act as if the world had come to an end," he said, "because it hasn't. From now on you've got to live in a new world and face a few realities for a change. Buck up," he said, "it won't kill you."

She was breathing fast.

"Let's wait on the bus," he said.

"Home," she said thickly.

"I hate to see you behave like this," he said. "Just like a child. I should be able to expect more of you." He decided to stop where he was and make her stop and wait for a bus. "I'm not going any farther," he said, stopping. "We're going on the bus."

She continued to go on as if she had not heard him. He took a few steps and caught her arm and stopped her. He looked into her face and caught his breath. He was looking into a face he had never seen before. "Tell Grandpa to come get me," she said.

He stared, stricken.

"Tell Caroline to come get me," she said.

Stunned, he let her go and she lurched forward again, walking as if one leg were shorter than the other. A tide of darkness seemed to be sweeping her from him. "Mother!" he cried. "Darling, sweetheart, wait!" Crumpling, she fell to the pavement. He dashed forward and fell at her side, crying, "Mamma, Mamma!" He turned her over. Her face was fiercely distorted. One eye, large and staring, moved slightly to the left as if it had become unmoored. The other remained fixed on him, raked his face again, found nothing and closed.

"Wait here, wait here!" he cried and jumped up and began to run for help toward a cluster of lights he saw in the distance ahead of him. "Help, help!" he shouted, but his voice was thin, scarcely a thread of sound. The lights drifted farther away the faster he ran and his feet moved numbly as if they carried him nowhere. The tide of darkness seemed to sweep him back to her, postponing from moment to moment his entry into the world of guilt and sorrow (www.thomasaquinas.edu/sites/default/.../2011-fall-ACS-reading.pdf).

Assignments

- Warm-up: Compare Julian's mother to Amanda Wingfield.
- Students should complete Concept Builder 32-B.
- Student should review reading(s) from the next chapter.
- Student should outline essay due at the end of the week.
- Per teacher instructions, students may answer orally, in a group setting, some of the essays that are not assigned as formal essays.

Read "Everything That Rises Must Converge" by Flannery O'Connor in the text, then answer the following questions.

1	Describe Julian's relationship with his mother.
2	What does the hat symbolize?
3	The author is carefully crafting two characters through dialogue. Explain.
4	In spite of the woman's racism, she has some wisdom. Explain.
5	Julian is confident. He feels that he is superior to his mother. Why?
6	Why is Julian's mother so irritated with him?
7	How will this story end?
8	Why is Julian thrilled with the lady who is sitting next to him?
9	Why does Julian's mother try to give the young child a penny? Why did the young child's mother refuse to accept it?
10	Was Julian's mother bothered by the fact that the African-American lady had the same hat as she?
11	Julian was mostly right about everything he said but he feels guilty. Why?

Theme

Race Relations Race affects where we live, the jobs we hold, the person we marry. No matter where we are, or who we are, in one way or another, our lives are affected by racial anger. To suggest that racial anger is no longer a reality in American culture is to ignore three hundred years of history. Americans inherit a history — good and bad — of racial interaction that profoundly affects our worldviews. Race as a category in politics, social welfare policy, and religion became significant for the first time in open discussions in the 1960s and 1970s. These discussions continue today. Whether it was in a conversation on the edge of an indigo field outside Columbia, South Carolina, in 1730, or in inner-city Philadelphia today, racial discussions inevitably generated anger and controversy. Racial anger is a reaction to the perceived failure of these discussions and their inability to bring measurable results. O'Connor, in her own way, captures some of this struggle in the lives her two protagonists.

Assignments

- Warm-up: How do you deal with issues of racial conflict? How does it affect you?
- Students should complete Concept Builder 32-C.
- Students should write rough drafts of assigned essay.
- The teacher may correct rough drafts.

CONCEPT BUILDER 32-C Conflicts	List various types of external and internal conflicts that often create a tension for the plot of a story:			
	External Conflict		**Internal Conflict**	
	1		1	
	2		2	
	3		3	

"A Worn Path"
Eudora Welty

Background Eudora Welty (1909–2001) was born in Jackson, Mississippi, and lived her whole life there. Her descriptions of human character and personality are legendary.

"A Worn Path," by Eudora Welty, is a heartwarming story about the arduous trip of an elderly African-American woman, Phoenix. We don't find out the real reason Phoenix struggles along the road to town. The title, "A Worn Path," evidences that Phoenix has obviously walked down this path many times before — also the fact that she can cross a creek with her eyes closed confirms her familiarity with her journey. Her trip is full of obstacles, from bushes of thorns that get caught in her dress, to her crossing of a creek. We travel in fact with her and we travel in her mind. The use of stream of consciousness is extraordinary. At the end, we discover the heart-wrenching reason for her journey.

It was December — a bright frozen day in the early morning. Far out in the country there was an old Negro woman with her head tied in a red rag, coming along a path through the pinewoods. Her name was Phoenix Jackson. She was very old and small and she walked slowly in the dark pine shadows, moving a little from side to side in her steps, with the balanced heaviness and lightness of a pendulum in a grandfather clock. She carried a thin, small cane made from an umbrella, and with this she kept tapping the frozen earth in front of her. This made a grave and persistent noise in the still air, that seemed meditative like the chirping of a solitary little bird.

She wore a dark striped dress reaching down to her shoe tops, and an equally long apron of bleached sugar sacks, with a full pocket: all neat and tidy, but every time she took a step she might have fallen over her shoelaces, which dragged from her unlaced shoes. She looked straight ahead. Her eyes were blue with age. Her skin had a pattern all its own of numberless branching wrinkles and as though a whole little tree stood in the middle of her forehead, but a golden color ran underneath, and the two knobs of her cheeks were illumined by a yellow burning under the dark. Under the red rag her hair came down on her neck in the frailest of ringlets, still black, and with an odor like copper.

Now and then there was a quivering in the thicket. Old Phoenix said, "Out of my way, all you foxes, owls, beetles, jack rabbits, coons and wild animals! . . . Keep out from under these feet, little bob-whites. . . . Keep the big wild hogs out of my path. Don't let none of those come running my direction. I got a long way." Under her small black-freckled hand her cane, limber as a buggy whip, would switch at the brush as if to rouse up any hiding things.

On she went. The woods were deep and still. The sun made the pine needles almost too bright to look at, up where the wind rocked. The cones dropped as light as feathers. Down in the hollow was the mourning dove — it was not too late for him.

The path ran up a hill. "Seem like there is chains about my feet, time I get this far," she said, in the voice of argument old people keep to use with themselves. "Something always take a hold of me on this hill — pleads I should stay."

After she got to the top she turned and gave a full, severe look behind her where she had come.

"Up through pines," she said at length. "Now down through oaks."

Her eyes opened their widest, and she started down gently. But before she got to the bottom of the hill a bush caught her dress.

Her fingers were busy and intent, but her skirts were full and long, so that before she could pull them free in one place they were caught in another. It was not possible to allow the dress to tear. "I in the thorny bush," she said. "Thorns, you doing your appointed work. Never want to let folks pass, no sir. Old eyes thought you was a pretty little green bush."

Finally, trembling all over, she stood free, and after a moment dared to stoop for her cane. "Sun so high!" she cried, leaning back and looking, while the thick tears went over her eyes. "The time getting all gone here."

At the foot of this hill was a place where a log was laid across the creek.

"Now comes the trial," said Phoenix.

Putting her right foot out, she mounted the log and shut her eyes. Lifting her skirt, leveling her cane fiercely before her, like a festival figure in some parade, she began to march across. Then she opened her eyes and she was safe on the other side.

"I wasn't as old as I thought," she said.

But she sat down to rest. She spread her skirts on the bank around her and folded her hands over her knees. Up above her was a tree in a pearly cloud of mistletoe. She did not dare to close her eyes, and when a little boy brought her a plate with a slice of marble-cake on it she spoke to him. "That would be acceptable," she said. But when she went to take it there was just her own hand in the air.

So she left that tree, and had to go through a barbed-wire fence. There she had to creep and crawl, spreading her knees and stretching her fingers like a baby trying to climb the steps. But she talked loudly to herself: she could not let her dress be torn now, so late in the day, and she could not pay for having her arm or her leg sawed off if she got caught fast where she was.

At last she was safe through the fence and risen up out in the clearing. Big dead trees, like black men with one arm, were standing in the purple stalks of the withered cotton field. There sat a buzzard.

"Who you watching?"

In the furrow she made her way along.

"Glad this not the season for bulls," she said, looking sideways, "and the good Lord made his snakes to curl up and sleep in the winter. A pleasure I don't see no two-headed snake coming around that tree, where it come once. It took a while to get by him, back in the summer."

She passed through the old cotton and went into a field of dead corn. It whispered and shook and was taller than her head. "Through the maze now," she said, for there was no path.

Then there was something tall, black, and skinny there, moving before her.

At first she took it for a man. It could have been a man dancing in the field. But she stood still and listened, and it did not make a sound. It was as silent as a ghost.

"Ghost," she said sharply, "who be you the ghost of? For I have heard of nary death close by.

But there was no answer — only the ragged dancing in the wind.

She shut her eyes, reached out her hand, and touched a sleeve. She found a coat and inside that an emptiness, cold as ice.

"You scarecrow," she said. Her face lighted. "I ought to be shut up for good," she said with laughter. "My senses is gone. I too old. I the oldest people I ever know. Dance, old scarecrow," she said, "while I dancing with you."

She kicked her foot over the furrow, and with mouth drawn down, shook her head once or twice in a little strutting way. Some husks blew down and whirled in streamers about her skirts.

Then she went on, parting her way from side to side with the cane, through the whispering field. At last she came to the end, to a wagon track where the silver grass blew between the red ruts. The quail were walking around like pullets, seeming all dainty and unseen.

"Walk pretty," she said. "This the easy place. This the easy going."

She followed the track, swaying through the quiet bare fields, through the little strings of trees silver in their dead leaves, past cabins silver from weather, with the doors and windows boarded shut, all like old women under a spell sitting there. "I walking in their sleep," she said, nodding her head vigorously.

In a ravine she went where a spring was silently flowing through a hollow log. Old Phoenix bent and drank. "Sweet-gum makes the water sweet," she said, and drank more. "Nobody know who made this well, for it was here when I was born."

The track crossed a swampy part where the moss hung as white as lace from every limb. "Sleep on, alligators, and blow your bubbles." Then the track went into the road.

Deep, deep the road went down between the high green-colored banks. Overhead the live-oaks met, and it was as dark as a cave.

A black dog with a lolling tongue came up out of the weeds by the ditch. She was meditating, and not ready, and when he came at her she only hit him a little with her cane. Over she went in the ditch, like a little puff of milkweed.

Down there, her senses drifted away. A dream visited her, and she reached her hand up, but nothing reached down and gave her a pull. So she lay there and presently went to talking. "Old woman," she said to herself, "that black dog come up out of the weeds to stall you off, and now there he sitting on his fine tail, smiling at you."

A white man finally came along and found her — a hunter, a young man, with his dog on a chain.

"Well, Granny!" he laughed. "What are you doing there?"

"Lying on my back like a June-bug waiting to be turned over, mister," she said, reaching up her hand.

He lifted her up, gave her a swing in the air, and set her down. "Anything broken, Granny?" "No sir, them old dead weeds is springy enough," said Phoenix, when she had got her breath. "I thank you for your trouble."

"Where do you live, Granny?" he asked, while the two dogs were growling at each other. "Away back yonder, sir, behind the ridge. You can't even see it from here."

"On your way home?"

"No sir, I going to town."

"Why, that's too far! That's as far as I walk when I come out myself, and I get something for my trouble." He patted the stuffed bag he carried, and there hung down a little closed claw. It was one of the bob-whites, with its beak hooked bitterly to show it was dead. "Now you go on home, Granny!"

"I bound to go to town, mister," said Phoenix. "The time come around."

He gave another laugh, filling the whole landscape. "I know you old colored people! Wouldn't miss going to town to see Santa Claus!"

But something held old Phoenix very still. The deep lines in her face went into a fierce and different radiation. Without warning, she had seen with her own eyes a flashing nickel fall out of the man's pocket onto the ground.

"How old are you, Granny?" he was saying.

"There is no telling, mister," she said, "no telling."

Then she gave a little cry and clapped her hands and said, "Git on away from here, dog! Look! Look at that dog!" She laughed as if in admiration. "He ain't scared of nobody. He a big black dog." She whispered, "Sic him!"

"Watch me get rid of that cur," said the man. "Sic him, Pete! Sic him!"

Phoenix heard the dogs fighting, and heard the man running and throwing sticks. She even heard a gunshot. But she was slowly bending forward by that time, further and further forward, the lids stretched down over her eyes, as if she were doing this in her sleep. Her chin was lowered almost to her knees. The yellow palm of her hand came out from the fold of her apron. Her fingers slid down and along the ground under the piece of money with the grace and care they would have in lifting an egg from under a setting hen. Then she slowly straightened up, she stood erect, and the nickel was in her apron pocket. A bird flew by. Her lips moved. "God watching me the whole time. I come to stealing."

The man came back, and his own dog panted about them. "Well, I scared him off that time," he said, and then he laughed and lifted his gun and pointed it at Phoenix.

She stood straight and faced him.

"Doesn't the gun scare you?" he said, still pointing it.

"No, sir, I seen plenty go off closer by, in my day, and for less than what I done," she said, holding utterly still.

He smiled, and shouldered the gun. "Well, Granny," he said, "you must be a hundred years old, and scared of nothing. I'd give you a dime if I had any money with me. But you take my advice and stay home, and nothing will happen to you."

"I bound to go on my way, mister," said Phoenix. She inclined her head in the red rag. Then they went in different directions, but she could hear the gun shooting again and again over the hill.

She walked on. The shadows hung from the oak trees to the road like curtains. Then she smelled wood-smoke, and smelled the river, and she saw a steeple and the cabins on their steep steps. Dozens of little black children whirled around her. There ahead was Natchez shining. Bells were ringing. She walked on.

In the paved city it was Christmas time. There were red and green electric lights strung and criss-crossed everywhere, and all turned on in the daytime. Old Phoenix would have been lost if she had not distrusted her eyesight and depended on her feet to know where to take her.

She paused quietly on the sidewalk where people were passing by. A lady came along in the crowd, carrying an armful of red-, green- and silver-wrapped presents; she gave off perfume like the red roses in hot summer, and Phoenix stopped her.

"Please, missy, will you lace up my shoe?" She held up her foot.

"What do you want, Grandma?"

"See my shoe," said Phoenix. "Do all right for out in the country, but wouldn't look right to go in a big building."

"Stand still then, Grandma," said the lady. She put her packages down on the sidewalk beside her and laced and tied both shoes tightly.

"Can't lace 'em with a cane," said Phoenix. "Thank you, missy. I doesn't mind asking a nice lady to tie up my shoe, when I gets out on the street."

Moving slowly and from side to side, she went into the big building, and into a tower of steps, where she walked up and around and around until her feet knew to stop.

She entered a door, and there she saw nailed up on the wall the document that had been stamped with the gold seal and framed in the gold frame, which matched the dream that was hung up in her head.

"Here I be," she said. There was a fixed and ceremonial stiffness over her body. "A charity case, I suppose," said an attendant who sat at the desk before her.

But Phoenix only looked above her head. There was sweat on her face, the wrinkles in her

skin shone like a bright net.

"Speak up, Grandma," the woman said. "What's your name? We must have your history, you know. Have you been here before? What seems to be the trouble with you?"

Old Phoenix only gave a twitch to her face as if a fly were bothering her.

"Are you deaf?" cried the attendant.

But then the nurse came in.

"Oh, that's just old Aunt Phoenix," she said. "She doesn't come for herself — she has a little grandson. She makes these trips just as regular as clockwork. She lives away back off the Old Natchez Trace." She bent down. "Well, Aunt Phoenix, why don't you just take a seat? We won't keep you standing after your long trip." She pointed.

The old woman sat down, bolt upright in the chair.

"Now, how is the boy?" asked the nurse.

Old Phoenix did not speak.

"I said, how is the boy?"

But Phoenix only waited and stared straight ahead, her face very solemn and withdrawn into rigidity.

"Is his throat any better?" asked the nurse. "Aunt Phoenix, don't you hear me? Is your grandson's throat any better since the last time you came for the medicine?"

With her hands on her knees, the old woman waited, silent, erect and motionless, just as if she were in armor.

"You mustn't take up our time this way, Aunt Phoenix," the nurse said. "Tell us quickly about your grandson, and get it over. He isn't dead, is he?'

At last there came a flicker and then a flame of comprehension across her face, and she spoke.

"My grandson. It was my memory had left me. There I sat and forgot why I made my long trip."

"Forgot?" The nurse frowned. "After you came so far?"

Then Phoenix was like an old woman begging a dignified forgiveness for waking up frightened in the night. "I never did go to school, I was too old at the Surrender," she said in a soft voice. "I'm an old woman without an education. It was my memory fail me. My little grandson, he is just the same, and I forgot it in the coming."

"Throat never heals, does it?" said the nurse, speaking in a loud, sure voice to old Phoenix. By now she had a card with something written on it, a little list. "Yes. Swallowed lye. When was it? — January — two, three years ago?"

Phoenix spoke unasked now. "No, missy, he not dead, he just the same. Every little while his throat begin to close up again, and he not able to swallow. He not get his breath. He not able to help himself. So the time come around, and I go on another trip for the soothing medicine."

"All right. The doctor said as long as you came to get it, you could have it," said the nurse. "But it's an obstinate case."

"My little grandson, he sit up there in the house all wrapped up, waiting by himself," Phoenix went on. "We is the only two left in the world. He suffer and it don't seem to put him back at all. He got a sweet look. He going to last. He wear a little patch quilt and peep out holding his mouth open like a little bird. I remembers so plain now. I not going to forget him again, no, the whole enduring time. I could tell him from all the others in creation."

"All right." The nurse was trying to hush her now. She brought her a bottle of medicine. "Charity," she said, making a check mark in a book.

Old Phoenix held the bottle close to her eyes, and then carefully put it into her pocket. "I thank you," she said.

"It's Christmas time, Grandma," said the attendant. "Could I give you a few pennies out of my purse?"

"Five pennies is a nickel," said Phoenix stiffly.

"Here's a nickel," said the attendant.

Phoenix rose carefully and held out her hand. She received the nickel and then fished the other nickel out of her pocket and laid it beside the new one. She stared at her palm closely, with her head on one side.

Then she gave a tap with her cane on the floor.

"This is what come to me to do," she said. "I going to the store and buy my child a little windmill they sells, made out of paper. He going to find it hard to believe there such a thing in the world. I'll march myself back where he waiting, holding it straight up in this hand."

She lifted her free hand, gave a little nod, turned around, and walked out of the doctor's office. Then her slow step began on the stairs, going down(www.theatlantic.com/past/docs/issues/41feb/wornpath.htm).

Assignments

- Warm-up: What does the title "A Worn Path" mean?
- Students should complete Concept Builder 32-D.
- Student will re-write corrected copies of essay due tomorrow.

Read "A Worn Path" by Eudora Welty in the text, then answer the following questions.

1	Who is the protagonist? Describe her?
2	What point is the author making with a thorny bush?
3	What affect do the physical barriers have on his story?
4	As the protagonist walks, we learn more and more information about her. For instance, what does the scarecrow teach her?
5	Clearly the entrance of a man and his dog is an intrusion. Why?
6	Analyze this meeting between Granny and the white hunter.
7	What happened to her grandson?
8	What is the state of mind of Phoenix?

The Jilting of Granny Weatherall
Katherine Anne Porter

Background Katherine Anne Porter (1890–1980) was a descendent of Daniel Boone, legendary pioneer and explorer. She was born in Indian Creek, Texas, but she grew up in Texas and Louisiana. Her mother died when Katherine was two and she was raised by her paternal grandmother. Porter was educated in convent schools. At the age of 16 she ran away and married the first of her three husbands. A few years later she left him to work as an actress. Porter contracted tuberculosis and during her recovery she decided to became a writer. Subsequently, Porter earned her living as a journalist in Chicago and Denver.

"The Jilting of Granny Weatherall" opens with Doctor Harry visiting the 80-year-old Granny during her final day of life.

Quickly Porter uses the stream-of-consciousness narration to manifest the thoughts and memories of Granny's mind. This technique is very effective with a protagonist who is dying.

In a semi-conscious state, the spirited and tetchy Granny remembers her life— disappointments, struggles, achievements, and feelings. One critic explains, "She exemplifies many heroic qualities such as endurance, fortitude, intelligence, and the ability to work unremittingly hard. In her past life she worked as a farmer, doctor, veterinarian, and she has raised her children courageously. Many nights she sat up caring for sick children and sick animals. She was proud of the fact that she never lost a child except for Hapsy, her last born. She wishes that John, her dead husband, could see her children now and that she could see Hapsy. Furthermore, she wishes that the old days were back even though she had a hard time raising her children without her husband, John. Then her jilting sixty years ago when she was abandoned by George at the altar preoccupies her thoughts and feelings. She has never been able to forgive him because of the pain and humiliation that he caused her. She had buried the memory in her mind for many years, but now it overwhelms her" (www.yale.edu/ynhti/curriculum/units/1985/3/85.03.01.x.html).

The Jilting of Granny Weatheall by Katherine Anne Porter

She flicked her wrist neatly out of Doctor Harry's pudgy careful fingers and pulled the sheet up to her chin. The brat ought to be in knee breeches. Doctoring around the country with spectacles on his nose! "Get along now. Take your schoolbooks and go. There's nothing wrong with me."

Doctor Harry spread a warm paw like a cushion on her forehead where the forked green vein danced and made her eyelids twitch. "Now, now, be a good girl, and we'll have you up in no time."

"That's no way to speak to a woman nearly eighty years old just because she's down. I'd have you respect your elders, young man."

"Well, Missy, excuse me." Doctor Harry patted her cheek. "But I've got to warn you, haven't I? You're a marvel, but you must be careful or you're going to be good and sorry."

"Don't tell me what I'm going to be. I'm on my feet now, morally speaking. It's Cornelia. I had to go to bed to get rid of her."

Her bones felt loose, and floated around in her skin, and Doctor Harry floated like a balloon around the foot of the bed. He floated and pulled down his waistcoat, and swung his glasses on a cord. "Well, stay where you are, it certainly can't hurt you."

"Get along and doctor your sick," said Granny Weatherall. "Leave a well woman alone. I'll call for you when I want you. . . . Where were you forty years ago when I pulled through milk-leg and double pneumonia? You weren't even born. Don't let Cornelia lead you on," she shouted, because Doctor Harry appeared to float up to the ceiling and out. "I pay my own bills, and I don't throw my money away on nonsense!"

She meant to wave good-by, but it was too much trouble. Her eyes closed of themselves, it was like a dark curtain drawn around the bed. The pillow rose and floated under her, pleasant as a hammock in a light wind. She listened to the leaves rustling outside the window. No, somebody was swishing newspapers: no, Cornelia and Doctor Harry were whispering together. She leaped broad awake, thinking they whispered in her ear.

"She was never like this, never like this!" "Well, what can we expect?" "Yes, eighty years old. . . ."

Well, and what if she was? She still had ears. It was like Cornelia to whisper around doors. She always kept things secret in such a public way. She was always being tactful and kind. Cornelia was dutiful; that was the trouble with her. Dutiful and good: "So good and dutiful," said Granny, "that I'd like to spank her." She saw herself spanking Cornelia and making a fine job of it.

"What'd you say, mother?"

Granny felt her face tying up in hard knots.

"Can't a body think, I'd like to know?"

"I thought you might like something."

"I do. I want a lot of things. First off, go away and don't whisper."

She lay and drowsed, hoping in her sleep that the children would keep out and let her rest a minute. It had been a long day. Not that she was tired. It was always pleasant to snatch a minute now and then. There was always so much to be done, let me see: tomorrow.

Tomorrow was far away and there was nothing to trouble about. Things were finished somehow when the time came; thank God there was always a little margin over for peace: then a person could spread out the plan of life and tuck in the edges orderly. It was good to have everything clean and folded away, with the hair brushes and tonic bottles sitting straight on the white, embroidered linen: the day started without fuss and the pantry shelves laid out with rows of jelly glasses and brown jugs and white stone-china jars with blue whirligigs and words painted on them: coffee, tea, sugar, ginger, cinnamon, allspice: and the bronze clock with the lion on top nicely dusted off. The dust that lion could collect in twenty-four hours! The box in the attic with all those letters tied up, well, she'd have to go through that tomorrow. All those letters — George's letters and John's letters and her letters to them both — lying around for the children to find afterwards made her uneasy. Yes, that would be tomorrow's business. No use to let them know how silly she had been once.

While she was rummaging around she found death in her mind and it felt clammy and unfamiliar. She had spent so much time preparing for death there was no need for bringing it up again. Let it take care of itself for now. When she was sixty she had felt very old, finished, and went around making farewell trips to see her children and grandchildren, with a secret in her mind: This was the very last of your mother, children! Then she made her will and came down with a long fever. That was all just a notion like a lot of other things, but it was lucky, too, for she had once and for all got over the idea of dying for a long time. Now she couldn't be worried. She hoped she had better sense now. Her father had lived to be one hundred and two years old and had drunk a noggin of strong hot toddy on his last birthday. He told the reporters it was his daily habit, and he owed his long life to that. He had made quite a scandal and was very pleased about it. She believed she'd just plague Cornelia a little.

"Cornelia! Cornelia!" No footsteps, but a sudden hand on her cheek. "Bless you, where have you been?"

"Here, Mother."

"Well, Cornelia, I want a noggin of hot toddy."

"Are you cold, darling?"

"I'm chilly, Cornelia." Lying in bed stops the circulation. I must have told you a thousand times."

Well, she could just hear Cornelia telling her husband that Mother was getting a little childish and they'd have to humor her. The thing that most annoyed her was that Cornelia thought she was deaf, dumb, and blind. Little hasty glances and tiny gestures tossed around here and over her head saying, "Don't cross her, let her have her way, she's eighty years old," and she sitting there as if she lived in a thin glass cage. Sometimes granny almost made up her mind to pack up and move back to her own house where nobody could remind her every minute that she was old. Wait, wait, Cornelia, till your own children whisper behind your back!

In her day she had kept a better house and had got more work done. She wasn't too old yet for Lydia to be driving eighty miles for advice when one of the children jumped the track, and Jimmy still dropped in and talked things over: "Now, Mammy, you've a good business head, I want to know what you think of this? . . ." Old. Cornelia couldn't change the furniture around without asking. Little things, little things! They had been so sweet when they were little. Granny wished the old days were back again with the children young and everything to be done over. It had been a hard pull, but not too much for her. When she thought of all the food she had cooked, and all the clothes she had cut and sewed, and all the gardens she had made — well, the children showed it. There they were, made out of her, and they couldn't get away from that. Sometimes she wanted to see John again and point to them and say, Well, I didn't do so badly, did I? But that would have to wait. That was for tomorrow. She used to think of him as a man, but now all the children were older than their father, and he would be a child beside her if she saw him now. It seemed strange and there was something wrong in the idea. Why, he couldn't possibly recognize her. She had fenced in a hundred acres once, digging the post holes herself and clamping the wires with just a negro boy to help. That changed a woman. John would be looking for a young woman with a peaked Spanish comb in her hair and the painted fan. Digging post holes changed a woman. Riding country roads in the winter when women had their babies was another thing: sitting up nights with sick horses and sick negroes and sick children and hardly ever losing one. John, I hardly ever lost one of them! John would see that in a minute, that would be something he could understand, she wouldn't have to explain anything!

It made her feel like rolling up her sleeves and putting the whole place to rights again. No matter if Cornelia was determined to be everywhere at once, there were a great many things left undone on this place. She would start tomorrow and do them. It was good to be strong enough for everything, even if all you made melted and changed and slipped under your hands, so that by the time you finished you almost forgot what you were working for. What was it I set out to do? She asked herself intently, but she could not remember. A fog rose over the valley, she saw it marching across the creek swallowing the trees and moving up the hill like an army of ghosts. Soon it would be at the near edge of the orchard, and then it was time to go in and light the lamps. Come in, children, don't stay out in the night air.

Lighting the lamps had been beautiful. The children huddled up to her and breathed like little calves waiting at the bars in the twilight. Their eyes followed the match and watched the flame rise and settle in a blue curve, then they moved away from her. The lamp was lit, they didn't have to be scared and hang on to mother any more. Never, never, never more. God, for all my life, I thank Thee. Without Thee, my God, I could never have done it. Hail, Mary, full of grace.

I want you to pick all the fruit this year and see nothing is wasted. There's always someone who can use it. Don't let good things rot for want of using. You waste life when you waste good food. Don't let things get lost. It's bitter to lose things. Now, don't let me get to thinking, not when I'm tired and taking a little nap before supper. . . .

The pillow rose about her shoulders and pressed against her heart and the memory was being squeezed out of it: oh, push down the pillow, somebody: it would smother her if she tried to hold it. Such a fresh breeze blowing and such a green day with no threats in it. But he had not come, just the same. What does a woman do when she has put on the white veil and set out the white cake for a man and he doesn't come? She tried to remember. No, I swear he never harmed me but in that. He never harmed me but in that . . . and what if he did? There was the day, the day, but a whirl of dark smoke rose and covered it, crept up and over into the bright field where everything was planted so carefully in orderly rows. That was hell, she knew hell when she saw it. For sixty years she had prayed against remembering him and against losing her soul in the deep pit of hell, and now the two things were mingled in one and the thought of him was a smoky cloud from hell that moved and crept in her head when she had just got rid of Doctor Harry and was trying to rest a minute. Wounded vanity, Ellen, said a sharp voice in the top of her mind. Don't let your wounded vanity get the upper hand of you. Plenty of girls get jilted. You were jilted, weren't you? Then stand up to it. Her eyelids wavered and let in streamers of blue-gray light like tissue paper over her eyes. She must get up and pull the shades down or she'd never sleep. She was in bed again and the shades were not down. How could that happen? Better turn over, hide from the light, sleeping in the light gave you nightmares. "Mother, how do you feel now?" and a stinging wetness on her forehead. But I don't like having my face washed in cold water!

Hapsy? George? Lydia? Jimmy? No, Cornelia, and her features were swollen and full of little puddles. "They're coming, darling, they'll all be here soon." Go wash your face, child, you look funny.

Instead of obeying, Cornelia knelt down and put her head on the pillow. She seemed to be talking but there was no sound. "Well, are you tongue-tied? Whose birthday is it? Are you going to give a party?"

Cornelia's mouth moved urgently in strange shapes. "Don't do that, you bother me, daughter."

"Oh no, Mother. Oh, no. . . ."

Nonsense. It was strange about children. They disputed your every word. "No what, Cornelia?"

"Here's Doctor Harry."

"I won't see that boy again. He left just five minutes ago."

"That was this morning, Mother. It's night now. Here's the nurse."

"This is Doctor Harry, Mrs. Weatherall. I never saw you look so young and happy!"

"Ah, I'll never be young again — but I'd be happy if they'd let me lie in peace and get rested."

She thought she spoke up loudly, but no one answered. A warm weight on her forehead, a warm bracelet on her wrist, and a breeze went on whispering, trying to tell her something. A shuffle of leaves in the everlasting hand of God, He blew on them and they danced and rattled. "Mother, don't mind, we're going to give you a little hypodermic." "Look here, daughter, how do ants get in this bed? I saw sugar ants yesterday." Did you send for Hapsy too?

It was Hapsy she really wanted. She had to go a long way back through a great many rooms to find Hapsy standing with a baby on her arm. She seemed to herself to be Hapsy also, and the baby on Hapsy's arm was Hapsy and himself and herself, all at once, and there was no surprise in the meeting. Then Hapsy melted from within and turned flimsy as gray gauze and the baby was a gauzy shadow, and Hapsy came up close and said, "I thought you'd never come," and looked at her very searchingly and said, "You haven't changed a bit!" They leaned forward to kiss, when Cornelia began whispering from a long way off, "Oh, is there anything you want to tell me? Is there anything I can do for you?"

Yes, she had changed her mind after sixty years and she would like to see George. I want you to find George. Find him and be sure to tell him I forgot him. I want him to know I had my husband just the same and my children and my house like any other woman. A good house too and a good husband that I loved and fine children out of him. Better than I had hoped for even. Tell him I was given back everything he took away and more. Oh, no, oh, … , there was something else besides the house and the man and the children. Oh, surely they were not all? What was it? Something not given back. . . . Her breath crowded down under her ribs and grew into a monstrous frightening shape with cutting edges; it bored up into her head, and the agony was unbelievable: Yes, John, get the Doctor now, no more talk, the time has come.

When this one was born it should be the last. The last. It should have been born first, for it was the one she had truly wanted. Everything came in good time. Nothing left out, left over. She was strong, in three days she would be as well as ever. Better. A woman needed milk in her to have her full health.

"Mother, do you hear me?"

"I've been telling you —"

"Mother, Father Connolly's here."

"I went to Holy Communion only last week. Tell him I'm not so sinful as all that."

"Father just wants to speak with you."

He could speak as much as he pleased. It was like him to drop in and inquire about her soul as if it were a teething baby, and then stay on for a cup of tea and a round of cards and gossip. He always had a funny story of some sort, usually about an Irishman who made his little mistakes and confessed them, and the point lay in some absurd thing he would blurt out in the confessional showing his struggles between native piety and original sin. Granny felt easy about her soul. Cornelia, where are your manners? Give Father Connolly a chair. She had her secret comfortable understanding with a few favorite saints who cleared a straight road to God for her. All as surely signed and sealed as the papers for the new forty acres. Forever . . . heirs and assigns forever. Since the day the wedding cake was not cut, but thrown out and wasted. The whole bottom of the world dropped out, and there she was blind and sweating with nothing under her feet and the walls falling away. His hand had caught her under the breast, she had not fallen, there was the freshly polished floor with the green rug on it, just as before. He had cursed like a sailor's parrot and said, "I'll kill him for you." Don't lay a hand on him, for my sake leave something to God. "Now, Ellen, you must believe what I tell you. . . ."

So there was nothing, nothing to worry about anymore, except sometimes in the night one of the children screamed in a nightmare, and they both hustled out and hunting for the matches and calling, "There, wait a minute, here we are!" John, get the doctor now, Hapsy's time has come. But there was Hapsy standing by the bed in a white cap. "Cornelia, tell Hapsy to take off her cap. I can't see her plain."

Her eyes opened very wide and the room stood out like a picture she had seen somewhere. Dark colors with the shadows rising towards the ceiling in long angles. The tall black dresser gleamed with nothing on it but John's picture, enlarged from a little one, with John's eyes very black when they should have been blue. You never saw him, so how do you know how he looked? But the man insisted the copy was perfect, it was very rich and handsome. For a picture, yes, but it's not my husband. The table by the bed had a linen cover and a candle and a crucifix. The light was blue from Cornelia's silk lampshades. No sort of light at all, just frippery. You had to live forty years with kerosene lamps to appreciate honest electricity. She felt very strong and she saw Doctor Harry with a rosy nimbus around him.

"You look like a saint, Doctor Harry, and I vow that's as near as you'll ever come to it."

"She's saying something."

"I heard you, Cornelia. What's all this carrying on?"

"Father Connolly's saying —"

Cornelia's voice staggered and jumped like a cart in a bad road. It rounded corners and turned back again and arrived nowhere. Granny stepped up in the cart very lightly and reached for the reins, but a man sat beside her and she knew him by his hands, driving the cart. She did not look in his face, for she knew without seeing, but looked instead down the road where the trees leaned over and bowed to each other and a thousand birds were singing a Mass. She felt like singing, too, but she put her hand in the bosom of her dress and pulled out a rosary, and Father Connolly murmured Latin in a very solemn voice and tickled her feet. . . . , will you stop that nonsense? I'm a married woman. What if he did run away and leave me to face the priest by myself? I found another a whole world better. I wouldn't have exchanged my husband for anybody except St. Michael himself, and you may tell him that for me with a thank you in the bargain.

Light flashed on her closed eyelids, and a deep roaring shook her. Cornelia, is that lightning? I hear thunder. There's going to be a storm. Close all the windows. Call the children in. . . . "Mother, here we are, all of us." "Is that you, Hapsy?" "Oh, no, I'm Lydia. We drove as fast as we could." Their faces drifted above her, drifted away. The rosary fell out of her hands and Lydia put it back. Jimmy tried to help, their hands fumbled together, and granny closed two fingers around Jimmy's thumb. Beads wouldn't do, it must be something alive. She was so amazed her thoughts ran round and round. So, my dear Lord, this is my death and I wasn't even thinking about it. My children have come to see me die. But I can't, it's not time. Oh, I always hated surprises. I wanted to give Cornelia the amethyst set — Cornelia, you're to have the amethyst set, but Hapsy's to wear it when she wants, and, Doctor Harry, do shut up. Nobody sent for you. Oh, my dear Lord, do wait a minute. I meant to do something about the Forty Acres, Jimmy doesn't need it and Lydia will later on, with that worthless husband of hers. I meant to finish the altar cloth and send six bottles of wine to Sister Borgia for her dyspepsia. I want to send six bottles of wine to Sister Borgia, Father Connolly, now don't let me forget.

Cornelia's voice made short turns and tilted over and crashed. "Oh, mother, oh, mother, oh, mother. . . ."

"I'm not going, Cornelia. I'm taken by surprise. I can't go."

You'll see Hapsy again. What bothered her? "I thought you'd never come." Granny made a long journey outward, looking for Hapsy. What if I don't find her? What then? Her heart sank down and down, there was no bottom to death, she couldn't come to the end of it. The blue light from Cornelia's lampshade drew into a tiny point in the center of her brain, it flickered and winked like an eye, quietly it fluttered and dwindled. Granny laid curled down within herself, amazed and watchful, staring at the point of light that was herself; her body was now only a deeper mass of shadow in an endless darkness and this darkness would curl around the light and swallow it up. God, give a sign!

For a second time there was no sign. Again, no bridegroom and the priest in the house. She could not remember any other sorrow because this grief wiped them all away. Oh, no, there's nothing more cruel than this — I'll never forgive it. She stretched herself with a deep breath and blew out the light (people.morrisville.edu/~whitnemr/html/The%20 Jilting%20of%20Granny%20Weatherall.htm).

Assignments

- Warm-up: What are the qualities that Granny possessed which helped her to live successfully?
- Students should complete Concept Builder 32-E.
- Essays are due. Students should take the chapter 32 test.

Read "The Jilting of Granny Weatherall" by Katherine Anne Porter, and then answer the following questions.

1	What sort of woman is Granny Weatherall?
2	What bothers Granny?
3	Who is John, and what does Granny want to tell him?
4	What causes Granny to remember the day she was jilted?
5	Has Granny forgiven George?
6	Granny thinks Hapsy is at her bedside. Who is really there?
7	What important truth does this short story share?

Chapter 33

1960–Present (Part 3):
Contemporary Writers

First Thoughts The novel *Cold Sassy Tree* has been compared to Mark Twain's *Adventures of Huckleberry Finn* because of Burns' use of humor, figurative language, and satire. That is going too far, of course. It is not technically the same quality as *Huck Finn*, but *Cold Sassy Tree* captures the mannerisms and folklore of Georgia in the early 1900s. It is, literally, a theistic local color novel. How refreshing!

Author Worldview Watch Olive Ann Burns, who herself will stand under a cold sassy tree and face death at an early age, explores the transcendent power of Judeo-Christian love. These characters love with biblical, sacrificial, Christ-centered love — not love tainted by selfishness. The protagonist and his family overcome genuine, catastrophic obstacles without sentimentalism or facile angst: they do it be following biblical principles of charity and grace.

Chapter Learning Objectives In chapter 33 we analyze Olive Ann Burns' *Cold Sassy Tree*. We are blessed by a wholesome, hopeful view of life that seemed to be lost but is alive after all!

As a result of this chapter study you will be able to . . .

1. Understand the central conflict in the novel.

2. Analyze Will Tweedy and judge his reliability as a narrator.

3. Discuss Will's faith journey.

4. Analyze the female characters in the novel.

Weekly Essay Options: Begin on page 274 of the Teacher Guide.

Reading ahead: *The Chosen* by Chaim Potok

519

Cold Sassy Tree
Olive Ann Burns

Olive Ann Burns (1924–1990) once described her writing in this way, "It has been said that growing up in the South and becoming a writer is like spending your life riding in a wagon, seated in a chair that is always facing backwards. I don't face life looking backwards, but I have written about past times and past people."

Cold Sassy Tree is a coming-of-age novel. Burns focuses on the processes by which Will finds his identity and learns to find his role in the adult world. The story is narrated by adult Will from the perspective of the child Will. Will reminisces about people and past experiences. This approach enables Will to maintain a child's perspective on events while incorporating the perception and wisdom of adulthood.

Assignments

- Warm-up: If the narrator was a young lady would the story be different?
- Students should complete Concept Builder 33-A.
- Students review the required reading(s) *before* the assigned chapter begins.
- Teachers may want to discuss assigned reading(s) with students.
- Teachers shall assign the required essay. The rest of the essays can be outlined, answered with shorter answers, discussed, or skipped..
- Students will review all readings for chapter 33.

CONCEPT BUILDER 33-A Meaning	What are the three levels of meaning in *Cold Sassy Tree* by Olive Ann Burns.
	Explicit Questions
	Who are the characters? The setting? The narrator?
	Implicit Questions
	The young grandson accepts the new wife before everyone. What does this tell the reader about the child?
	Deep Questions
	Does this novel deserve to be called a classic?

Symbolism

That tree was close to a hundred feet tall and the only sassafras still left of the big grove our town was named for. On a bright fall day when the sun lit up its scarlet leaves, you never saw anything to equal it. People would ride the train to Cold Sassy just to look. Usually they'd read the plaque that was nailed to its trunk: "Sassafras: family Lauraceae, genus Sassafras, species S. albidum. Note how the leaves vary in shape on the same twig, some having no lobes, some two or three." Considering the number of train travelers we had, I thought the plaque ought to tell how unusual tall the tree was and something about how Cold Sassy got its name. We used to have another big sassafras tree, which stood next to this one and had a knothole where bluebirds nested. Us boys used to rob the nest of its bluish-white eggs and blow out the insides. The railroad had taken that sassafras down some years earlier to make room for a bigger depot platform. (page 67)

The Cold Sassy tree gives the novel its title and the town its name. The tree stands for Rucker's and Miss Love's acumen. The tree also symbolizes the town's history. The town takes its name from the trees, and the shrinking sassafras grove parallels the town's bittersweet progress. When settlers first came to Cold Sassy there was a whole grove of sassafras trees. To make room for the new railroad, all but one tree was cut down. At the end of the novel, that last tree is cut so that the tracks can be widened, and the town changes the name of the town to something more modern. The town grows grow more remote from its genesis.

Assignments

- Warm-up: What is another example of symbolism?
- Students should complete Concept Builder 33-B.
- Student should review reading(s) from the next chapter.
- Student should outline essay due at the end of the week.
- Per teacher instructions, students may answer orally, in a group setting, some of the essays that are not assigned as formal essays.

The theme of a fiction work is the central idea, whether simply implied or clearly stated. What are three themes of *Cold Sassy Tree*?

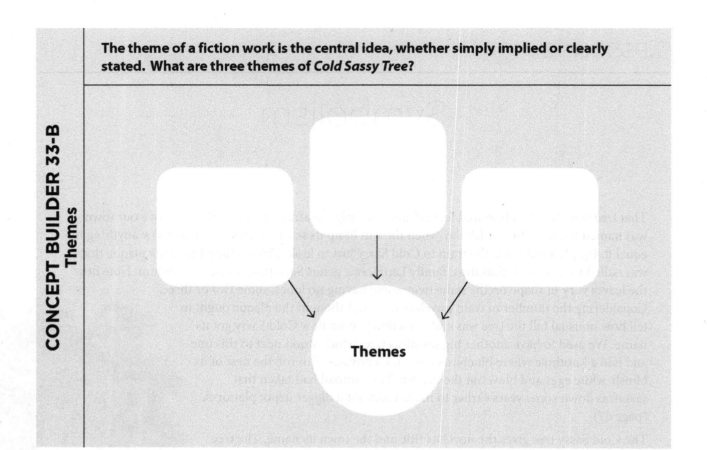

Themes

My Diary

In 1965, when I was 12 years old, I received a diary for my birthday. For three years I recorded my life and the following are a few entries.

December 20, 1965 I have formed in my mind who my favorite teacher is — Mrs. Sawyer. I like her because she understands me. (I also loved her because she was beautiful — one of my first crushes).

December 21, 1966 I went into mom and dad [sic] closet and found my Christmas presents. I thought there was no Santa Claus (I must have been the only 12 year old in America who still believed in Santa Claus).

January 29, 1967 Mom graduated from Arkansas A & M. Will be glad when she gets the first paycheck!

When my dad lost his job, Dad and Mom decided that Mom should go back to college and graduate with a teaching degree. Then my dad did the same thing and both were teachers in my local high school

Myself, Dad, Mom, John, and Bill

Assignments

- Warm-up: What insights would you write in your own diary?
- Students should complete Concept Builder 33-C.
- Students should write rough drafts of assigned essay.
- The teacher may correct rough drafts.

CONCEPT BUILDER 33-C
Character Development

On the chart below, circle the words that describe Rucker Blakeslee.

Rucker Blakeslee

Melancholic

moody
anxious
rigid
sober
pessimistic
reserved
unsociable
quiet

Choleric

touchy
restless
aggressive
excitable
changeable
impulsive
optimistic
active

Phlegmatic

passive
careful
thoughtful
peaceful
controlled
reliable
even-tempered
calm

Sanguine

sociable
outgoing
talkative
responsive
easy-going
lively
carefree
leadership

Reliable Narration

Will Tweedy is the novel's narrator and protago-nist. Will is a 14-year-old boy growing up in Cold Sassy, Georgia, at the beginning of the 20th century. Although he comes from a wealthy, conservative family, Will is a free spirit, like his grandfather, and often defies the rules. Following his grandfather's second marriage, Will struggles with issues of love and death, and his perspective changes. In many ways, this novel is about Will growing up. This story is told in first-person narration from Will's perspec-tive. Sometimes in literature, a story told in first person is unreliable because of the narrator's close-ness to the story. Other first-person narration is reliable because the narrator tells the story in an accurate, believable manner.

Assignments

- Warm-up: Is Will Tweedy a reliable narrator?
- Students should complete Concept Builder 33-D.
- Student will re-write corrected copies of essay due tomorrow.

CONCEPT BUILDER 33-D
Character Development

On the chart below, circle the words that describe Will Tweedy.

Melancholic	Choleric
moody	touchy
anxious	restless
rigid	aggressive
sober	excitable
pessimistic	changeable
reserved	impulsive
unsociable	optimistic
quiet	active

Will Tweedy

Phlegmatic	Sanguine
passive	sociable
careful	outgoing
thoughtful	talkative
peaceful	responsive
controlled	easy-going
reliable	lively
even-tempered	carefree
calm	leadership

Motifs

Motifs are recurring literary structures that develop and inform the text's major themes.

Language The Southern dialect adds authenticity. As Miss Love, who initially speaks in Yankee English, begins to speak in slang, she is accepted.

Humor as Comic Relief Will often uses humor to deal with the grief and tragedy in his life, telling funny stories to convey or dispel feelings that he does not yet understand. His naiveté adds comic relief to what might be disorienting scenes.

Family In *Cold Sassy Tree*, families are both an irritant and an invaluable support system. Family members try to force one another to behave in certain ways, but when push comes to shove they stand together. When Camp commits suicide, the family provides succor and hope.

Assignments

- Warm-up: What motifs do you find in your favorite novel?
- Students should complete Concept Builder 33-E.
- Essays are due. Students should take the chapter 33 test.

CONCEPT BUILDER 33-E Motif	Motifs are recurring structures that inform the text's major themes. In *Cold Sassy Tree*, families are both a burden and an invaluable support system. How is the family both a blessing and impediment to the major themes emerging?	
	Blessing	**Impediment**

Chapter 34

1960–Present (Part 4):
Contemporary Writers

First Thoughts It is no small pleasure for me to tell you that at least one of the great, classical pieces of American literature includes two central characters who are a Hasid and a traditional Orthodox Jew. This course moved from the theistic Puritans who embraced a metaphysical, moral worldview. The Hasidim are known for their mystical interpretation of Judaism and for their faithful devotion to their leaders. In contrast, traditional orthodoxy emphasizes a rational and intellectual approach to Judaism. But both are God centered. Rueven are Jewish first; Americans second. That is the whole strength of our nation. Something that we forgot along the way. How encouraging that Chaim Potok reminds us again that the heart of our nation is centered on God. The novel examines Jewish identity from within these contexts by telling the parallel stories of two Jewish adolescents who are similar enough to become best friends, yet different enough to change each other's view of the world.

Author Worldview Watch Finally, *The Chosen* is unabashedly a Judeo-Christian theistic novel. What a wild ride! Readers began with the sobering Christian theism of William, Bradford, journeyed through the narcissistic naturalism of Steinbeck, and end with the unabashedly and well-written theism of Potok! Readers had every reason to hope that the next century will bring more and better fruits of righteousness!

Chapter Learning Objectives In chapter 34 we finish our American literature journey by examining a delightful, theistic classic, *The Chosen* by Chaim Potok.

As a result of this chapter study you will be able to . . .

1. Analyze the ending.
2. Assess the role of women in this book.
3. Explain why Potok tells the story from Reuven's rather than Danny's point of view.
4. Evaluate if Danny should become a psychotherapist even though it violated his father's wishes.

Weekly Essay Options: Begin on page 274 of the Teacher Guide.

History connections: *American History* chapter 34, "Contemporary Issues: Part Two"

The Chosen
Chaim Potok

Background *The Chosen* is basically the story of two cultures colliding. On one level it is the story of Orthodox Judaism vs. Hasidic Judaism. On the other hand, it embraces life at many different levels. In fact, it also celebrates human virtues like respect and loyalty.

Chaim Potok (1929–2002), born Herman Harold Potok, was the son of Polish immigrants and was reared in an Orthodox Jewish home. This is important because his background deeply affected his writings. Potok began his career as an author and novelist with the publication of *The Chosen* (1967), which stands as the first book from a major publisher to portray Orthodox Judaism in the United States. Potok followed *The Chosen* with a sequel two years later called *The Promise*. Potok returned to the subject of Hasidism for a third time with *My Name is Asher Lev* (1972), the story of a young artist and his conflict with the traditions of his family and community. Potok followed this novel with a sequel, as well, publishing *The Gift of Asher Lev* (1990). Potok continued to examine the conflict between secular and religious interests in his other novels as well, which include *In the Beginning* (1975), *The Book of Lights* (1981), and *Davita's Harp* (1985). His most recent works include *I am the Clay* (1992), *The Tree of Here* (1993), *The Sky of Now* (1995), and T*he Gates of November* (1996).

Assignments

- Warm-up: Write an imaginary letter to Rueven and Danny five years after the novel ends.
- Students should complete Concept Builder 34-A.
- Students review the required reading(s) *before* the assigned chapter begins.
- Teachers may want to discuss assigned reading(s) with students.
- Teachers shall assign the required essay. The rest of the essays can be outlined, answered with shorter answers, discussed, or skipped.
- Students will review all readings for chapter 34.

In *The Chosen* by Chaim Potok, Danny and Reuven view each other as being very different. In fact, they have much in common. List ways that the two boys are similar and ways that they are different.

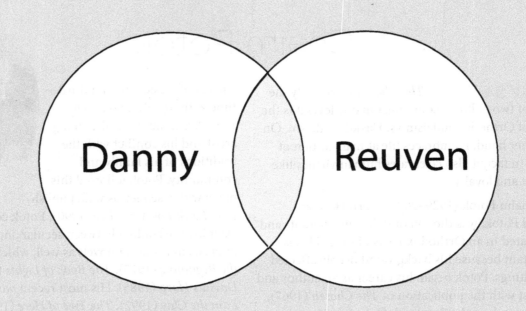

Similar	Different

Judaism

Both Rueven and Danny are Jewish. Judaism has different groups.

Three texts are sacred: the Torah, the Hebrew Bible, and the Talmud. The Torah includes the first five books of the Bible. The Torah contains Jewish law. Except in Israel, where Hebrew is the main language, most modern Jews speak the language of the nation where they live. That was the case with Rueven and Danny.

Rueven is an Orthodox Jew. Orthodox Jews in the United States use Hebrew for prayer and religious study and English for everyday conversation. Over the years, different branches of Judaism have emerged. The four main branches of Judaism include the Orthodox, Conservative, Reform, and Reconstructionist movements. Only a small percentage of Jews practice Orthodox Judaism. The way that Orthodox Jews practice their faith has changed very little over time. Orthodox Jews believe that the Torah, or first five books of the Bible, was given by God to Moses. They apply their interpretation of the Torah's laws very literally to their everyday lives.

One group of Orthodox Jews is called Hasidim. Danny is part of this sect. Danny's father is a leader, called tzaddiks.

The Hasidim are not Zionists. They do not wish to re-establish the nation of Israel. This is a conflict between Rueven and Danny.

Hasidic men dress as did their Hasidic ancestors in eastern Europe. They wear black coats, black hats, and beards. In addition to Hebrew, many Hasidim also speak Yiddish, a folk language that is akin to German.

Assignments

- Warm-up: Do religious rituals cause more divisiveness than they are worth?
- Students should complete Concept Builder 34-B.
- Student *should* review reading(s) from the next chapter.
- Student should outline essay due at the end of the week.
- Per teacher instructions, students may answer orally, in a group setting, some of the essays that are not assigned as formal essays.

Worldviews are about values. Rate the follow items: 1 equals "do not value at all"; 5 equals "value a whole lot."

	Reb Saunders	Danny Saunders	David Malter	Reuven Malter
Reb Saunders				
Danny Saunders				
David Malter				
Reuven Malter				

Two Characters

The two central characters are Rueven and Danny.

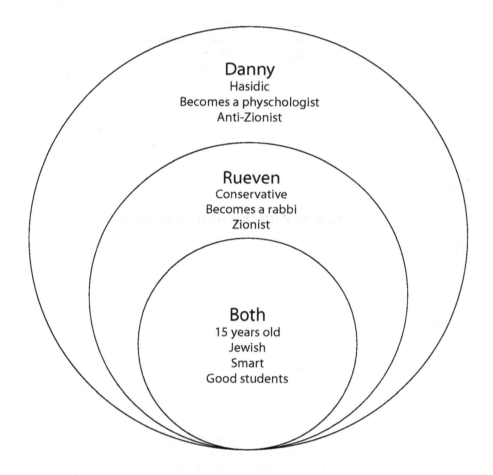

Danny
Hasidic
Becomes a physchologist
Anti-Zionist

Rueven
Conservative
Becomes a rabbi
Zionist

Both
15 years old
Jewish
Smart
Good students

Assignments

- Warm-up: Who do you like better — Danny or Rueven?
- Students should complete Concept Builder 34-C.
- Students should write rough drafts of assigned essay.
- The teacher or a peer evaluator may correct rough drafts.

One critic said of Chaim Potok's novels, "As in all good fiction, Mr. Potok makes us believe that his stories are true, that they could only have been as he has told them." In contrast, another critic said of *The Chosen* that "Reuven, the idealized first-person narrator, is too much a goody-goody to be true." Which position do you agree with? Why?

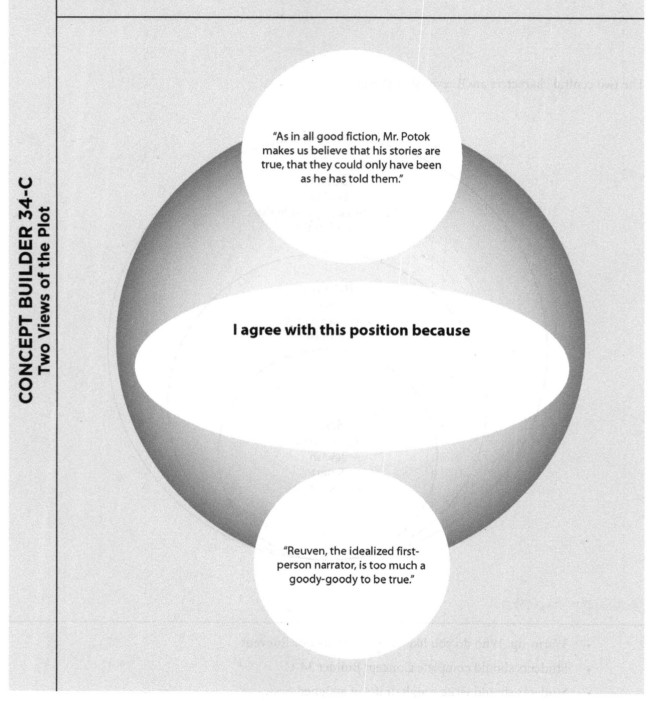

"As in all good fiction, Mr. Potok makes us believe that his stories are true, that they could only have been as he has told them."

I agree with this position because

"Reuven, the idealized first-person narrator, is too much a goody-goody to be true."

Guy Davenport, "Collision With the Outside World," in The New York Times Book Review, April 16, 1972, p. 5, 18.

Review of the Movie Version
The Chosen (1981)

The Chosen is careful to disarm its audience right away. It begins with a baseball warmup, as a team of Jewish schoolboys in Brooklyn prepares for a game. Along comes the opposition — a team of Hasidic Jews wearing side curls, austere clothing, heavy glasses and very sour, unfriendly expressions.

The first team is as put off as the audience initially must be; Hasidic Jews don't turn up in very many movies, and as sympathetic screen characters they don't turn up at all. When Woody Allen puts a Hasid into a film, it's strictly as a sight gag and nothing more. But in "The Chosen," it immediately becomes apparent that the Hasidic characters, even if they're laughed at, will also have to be reckoned with. "They should stick to praying," mutters somebody from the first team — but the Hasidim win the game.

"The Chosen," adapted from the novel by Chaim Potok, is about two Brooklyn Jewish families in the years immediately after World War II. The Malters are the more secular, a professor (Maximilian Schell) and his son, Reuven (Barry Miller), who meets Danny Saunders (Robby Benson) at the baseball game. Danny is the Hasidic son of Reb Saunders (Rod Steiger), and a stranger to most of the things that Reuven thinks familiar.

The growing friendship between the two boys is also the process by which Danny sees his first movie, wishes for his first pair of stylish eyeglasses, gets his first kiss (from a strange woman celebrating the news that the war is over) and begins dreaming of a life less cloistered than the one he is used to.

For Reuven, and for the viewer, Danny provides an introduction to the isolated world of the Hasidim, with its long silences and exceptionally strict protocol. Invited home by Danny to meet his father,

Reuven finds himself assiduously grilled in matters of Jewish law and history.

Once he passes the Reb's inspection, though, Reuven is made welcome in the Saunders family, participating in celebrations and meals and group discussions. Throughout all this, Reuven also maintains his distance, attending college with a group of Jewish friends who are less sympathetic to the Hasidic way of life. "Hasidim!" one such friend snorts. "Hasidim, but I don't believe 'em," jokes another.

"The Chosen" is partly about how these two sons of distinguished papas become friends and how their fathers' subsequent ideological disagreement (Professor Malter's Zionism is anathema to Reb Saunders) interferes with the friendship. It also describes the Hasidic culture through Danny and his reactions to the secular world, and this is what it does best.

Robby Benson, who might not be expected to be the quiet surprise of a movie like this one, nevertheless makes a fine impression as Danny. He is eager without being overeager, and full of a gentle inquisitiveness that can't help but win the audience's sympathy. He is also, and this is the one weak spot in the performance, outfitted with side curls that change from shot to shot, sometimes looking tightly wound and sometimes looking droopy. Another hair problem in the film afflicts Mr. Steiger, who sports such a long and

luxuriant beard that he seems to be speaking through a fluffy rug.

Mr. Steiger speaks with a great sonorousness and a slow, rolling delivery that is more numbing than prepossessing. His scenes tend to be a bit more overwhelming than is necessary, and Jeremy Paul Kagan, the director, intensifies this so greatly that he even, at one point, allows Mr. Steiger to dance in slow motion. Among the other principals, Mr. Miller and Mr. Schell are very good in their way, much more naturalistic and much more quietly convincing. But the performances are uniformly guarded and cool, and the story becomes less involving than it might be. The friendship between Danny and Reuven is presented carefully enough, but it doesn't have much warmth.

What "The Chosen" lacks in dramatic excitement, it tries hard to make up for in atmosphere.

Anyone interested in the time and place of this story will find a wealth of period details in the movie, all of them noticeable but none of them intrusive. Mr. Kagan, who also directed "Heroes" and "The Big Fix," locates and illustrates his story better than he tells it. Certainly, this is a gently evocative movie, with its glimpses of a strict and self-contained culture, and its memories of a time gone by.

"The Chosen" is rated PG ("Parental Guidance Suggested"). It contains brief but graphic footage of the liberation of concentration-camp inmates after World War II (Review by Janet Maslin, movies. nytimes.com/movie/review?res=9B00E6D71038F93 3A05757C0A964948260, April 30, 1982).

Assignments

- Warm-up: Watch the 1981 movie and compare it to the book.
- Students should complete Concept Builder 34-D.
- Student will re-write corrected copies of essay due tomorrow.

CONCEPT BUILDER 34-D
Character Development

On the chart below, circle the words that describe Rueven at the beginning of the play and underline the words that describe Rueven at the end of the play.

Reuven

Melancholic

moody
anxious
rigid
sober
pessimistic
reserved
unsociable
quiet

Choleric

touchy
restless
aggressive
excitable
changeable
impulsive
optimistic
active

Phlegmatic

passive
careful
thoughtful
peaceful
controlled
reliable
even-tempered
calm

Sanguine

sociable
outgoing
talkative
responsive
easy-going
lively
carefree
leadership

Norton and Gretton, Writing Incredibly Short Plays, Poems, Stories.

Father and Sons

One of the most inspiring components of this novel is the relationship between father and sons.

Reuven is a buffer between Danny and Reb Saunders when, in the novel's climax, the two friends learn Reb Saunders's purpose for raising his son in silence: Reb Saunders had discovered early on that his son's dawning intelligence was far outstripping his sense of compassion for others. He wanted his son to understand the meaning of pain, so he shut him out emotionally. Finding the grown-up Danny indeed has a heart, and cares deeply about other people, Reb Saunders is willing to give his blessing to Danny's dream of studying psychology. "He will be a tzadik for the world," Reb Saunders tells Reuven. Saunders then finally, after many years, truly talks to Danny, asking him to forgive him for the pain he caused, bringing him up as he did. The words finally spoken, he leaves the room, and both boys burst into tears ("SparkNote on *The Chosen*, SparkNotes.com, SparkNotes LLC. 2002, Web. March 21, 2012).

Can you imagine! American literature, at least in this course, ends with a father reconciling with his son and the two friends crying! What an encouraging ending.

Assignments

- Warm-up: Discuss a parent or guardian and how God has used him/her to mold you into the character you are now.
- Students should complete Concept Builder 34-E.
- Essays are due. Students should take the chapter 34 test.

CONCEPT BUILDER 34-E
Character Development

On the chart below, circle the words that describe Danny at the beginning of the play and underline the words that describe Danny at the end of the play.

Danny

Melancholic	**Choleric**
moody	touchy
anxious	restless
rigid	aggressive
sober	excitable
pessimistic	changeable
reserved	impulsive
unsociable	optimistic
quiet	active

Phlegmatic	**Sanguine**
passive	sociable
careful	outgoing
thoughtful	talkative
peaceful	responsive
controlled	easy-going
reliable	lively
even-tempered	carefree
calm	leadership

Norton and Gretton, *Writing Incredibly Short Plays, Poems, Stories.*

Glossary of Literary Terms

Allegory—A story or tale with two or more levels of meaning—a literal level and one or more symbolic levels. The events, setting, and characters in an allegory are symbols for ideas or qualities.

Alliteration—The repetition of initial consonant sounds. The repetition can be juxtaposed (side by side; e.g., simply sad).

Allusion—A casual and brief reference to a famous historical or literary figure or event.

Analogy— The process by which new or less familiar words, constructions, or pronunciations conform to the pattern of older or more familiar (and often unrelated) ones; a comparison between two unlike things. The purpose of an analogy is to describe something unfamiliar by pointing out its similarities to something that is familiar.

Antagonist—In a narrative, the character with whom the main character has the most conflict. In Jack London's *To Build a Fire* the antagonist is the extreme cold of the Yukon rather than a person or animal.

Archetype—The original pattern or model from which all other things of the same kind are made; a perfect example of a type or group.

Argumentation—The discourse in which the writer presents and logically supports a particular view or opinion; sometimes used interchangeably with *persuasion*.

Aside—In a play, an aside is a speech delivered by an actor in such a way that other characters on the stage are presumed not to hear it; an aside generally reveals a character's inner thoughts.

Autobiography—A form of nonfiction in which a person tells his/her own life story. Notable examples of autobiography include those by Benjamin Franklin and Frederick Douglass.

Ballad—A song or poem that tells a story in short stanzas and simple words with repetition, refrain, etc.

Biography—A form of nonfiction in which a writer tells the life story of another person.

Character—A person or an animal who takes part in the action of a literary work. The *main* character is the one on whom the work focuses. The person with whom the main character has the most conflict is the *antagonist*. He is the enemy of the main character (*protagonist*). Characters introduced whose sole purpose is to develop the main character are called foils.

Classicism—An approach to literature and the other arts that stresses reason, balance, clarity, ideal beauty, and orderly form in imitation of the arts of Greece and Rome.

Conflict—A struggle between opposing forces; can be internal or external; when occurring within a character is called *internal conflict*. An *external conflict* is normally an obvious conflict between the protagonist and antagonist(s). Most plots develop from conflict, making conflict one of the primary elements of narrative literature.

Crisis or **Climax**—The moment or event in the *plot* in which the conflict is most directly addressed: the main character "wins" or "loses" and the secret is revealed. After the climax, the *denouement* or falling action occurs.

Dialectic—Examining opinions or ideas logically, often by the method of question and answer.

Discourse, Forms of—Various modes into which writing can be classified; traditionally, writing has been divided into the following modes:

> **Exposition**: Writing which presents information
>
> **Narration**: Writing which tells a story

Description: Writing which portrays people, places, or things

Persuasion (sometimes also called *Argumentation*): Writing which attempts to convince people to think or act in a certain way

Drama—A story written to be performed by actors; the playwright supplies dialogue for the characters to speak and stage directions that give information about costumes, lighting, scenery, properties, the setting, and the character's movements and ways of speaking.

Dramatic monologue—A poem or speech in which an imaginary character speaks to a silent listener.

Elegy—A solemn and formal lyric poem about death, often one that mourns the passing of some particular person.

Essay—A short, nonfiction work about a particular subject; *essay* comes from the Old French word *essai*, meaning "a trial or attempt"; meant to be explanatory, an essay is not meant to be an exhaustive treatment of a subject; can be classified as formal or informal, personal or impersonal; can also be classified according to purpose as either expository, argumentative, descriptive, persuasive, or narrative.

Figurative Language—See *metaphor, simile, analogy*

Foil—A character who provides a contrast to another character and whose purpose is to develop the main character.

Genre—A division or type of literature; commonly divided into three major divisions, literature is either poetry, prose, or drama; each major genre can then be divided into smaller genres: *poetry* can be divided into lyric, concrete, dramatic, narrative, and epic poetry; *prose* can be divided into fiction (novels and short stories) and nonfiction (biography, autobiography, letters, essays, and reports); *drama* can be divided into serious drama, tragedy, comic drama, melodrama, and farce.

Gothic—The use of primitive, medieval, wild, or mysterious elements in literature. Gothic novels feature writers who use places like mysterious castles where horrifying supernatural events take place; Poe's "The Fall of the House of Usher" illustrates the influence of Gothic elements.

Harlem Renaissance—Occurring during the 1920s, a time of African American artistic creativity centered in Harlem in New York City; Langston Hughes was a Harlem Renaissance writer.

Hyperbole—A deliberate exaggeration or overstatement.

Idyll—A poem or part of a poem that describes and idealizes country life.

Irony—A method of humorous or subtly sarcastic expression in which the intended meanings of the words used is the direct opposite of their usual sense.

Journal—A daily autobiographical account of events and personal reactions.

Kenning—Indirect way of naming people or things; knowledge or recognition; in Old English poetry, a metaphorical name for something.

Literature—All writings in prose or verse, especially those of an imaginative or critical character, without regard to their excellence and/or writings considered as having permanent value, excellence of form, great emotional effect, etc.

Metaphor—(*Figure of speech*) A comparison which creatively identifies one thing with another dissimilar thing and transfers or ascribes to the first thing some of the qualities of the second. Unlike a *simile* or *analogy*, metaphor asserts that one thing is another thing—not just that one is like another. Very frequently a metaphor is invoked by the verb *to be*.

Meter—A poem's rhythmical pattern, determined by the number and types of stresses, or beats, in each line; a certain number of *metrical feet* make up a line of verse; (pentameter denotes a line containing five metrical feet); the act of describing the meter of a poem is called *scanning*, which involves marking the stressed and unstressed syllables, as follows:

> **Iamb**: A foot with one unstressed syllable followed by one stressed syllable, as in the word *abound*.
>
> **Trochee**: A foot with one stressed syllable followed by one unstressed syllable, as in the word *spoken*.
>
> **Anapest**: A foot with two unstressed syllables followed by one stressed syllable, as in the word *interrupt*.
>
> **Dactyl**: A foot with a stressed syllable followed by two unstressed syllables, as in the word *accident*.

Motif—A main idea element, feature; a main theme or subject to be elaborated on.

Narration—The way the author chooses to tell the story:

> **First Person Narration**: A character refers to himself or herself, using "I." This is a creative way to bring humor into the plot.
>
> **Second Person Narration**: Addresses the reader and/or the main character as "you" (and may also use first person narration, but not necessarily).
>
> **Third Person Narration**: Not a character in the story; refers to the story's characters as "he" and "she." This is probably the most common form of narration.
>
> **Limited Narration**: Only able to tell what one person is thinking or feeling. Omniscient Narration: Charles Dickens employs this narration in most of his novels.
>
> **Reliable Narration**: Everything this Narration says is true, and the Narrator knows everything that is necessary to the story.
>
> **Unreliable Narrator**: May not know all the relevant information; may be intoxicated or mentally ill; may lie to the audience. Example: Edgar Allan Poe's narrators are frequently unreliable.

Onomatopoeia—Use of words which, in their pronunciation, suggest their meaning. "Hiss," for example, when spoken is intended to resemble the sound of steam or of a snake. Other examples include these: *slam, buzz, screech, whirr, crush, sizzle, crunch, wring, wrench, gouge, grind, mangle, bang,* and *pop.*

Parallelism—Two or more balancing statements with phrases, clauses, or paragraphs of similar length and grammatical structure.

Plot—Arrangement of the action in fiction or drama— events of the story in the order the story gives them. A typical plot has five parts: *Exposition, Rising Action, Crisis or Climax, Falling Action,* and *Resolution* (sometimes called *Denouement*).

Précis—Summary of the plot of a literary piece.

Protagonist—The enemy of the main character (*antagonist*).

Rhetoric—Using words effectively in writing and speaking.

Setting—The place(s) and time(s) of a story, including the historical period, social milieu of the characters, geographical location, descriptions of indoor and outdoor locales.

Scop—An Old English poet or bard.

Simile—A figure of speech in which one thing is likened to another dissimilar thing by the use of like, as, etc.

Sonnet—A poem normally of fourteen lines in any of several fixed verse and rhyme schemes, typically in rhymed iambic pentameter; sonnets characteristically express a single theme or idea.

Structure—The arrangement of details and scenes that make up a literary work.

Style—An author's characteristic arrangement of words. A style may be colloquial, formal, terse, wordy, theoretical, subdued, colorful, poetic, or highly individual. Style is the arrangement of words in groups and sentences; *diction* on the other hand refers to the choice of individual words; the arrangement of details and scenes make up the *structure* of a literary work; all combine to influence the tone of the work; thus, diction, style, and structure make up the *form* of the literary work.

Theme—The one-sentence, major meaning of a literary piece, rarely stated but implied. The theme is not a moral, which is a statement of the author's didactic purpose of his literary piece. A thesis statement is very similar to the theme.

Tone—The attitude the author takes toward his subject; author's attitude is revealed through choice of details, through diction and style, and through the emphasis and comments that are made; like theme and style, tone is sometimes difficult to describe with a single word or phrase; often it varies in the same literary piece to suit the moods of the characters and the situations.

Book List for Supplemental Reading

(Comprehensive list comprised of American, British, and other authors from around the world)

Note: Not all literature is suitable for all students; educators and students should choose literature appropriate to students' age, maturity, interests, and abilities.

Jane Austen, *Emma*

Charlotte Brontë, *Jane Eyre*

Thomas Bulfinch, *The Age of Fable*

Pearl S. Buck, *The Good Earth*

John Bunyan, *Pilgrim's Progress*

Agatha Christie, *And Then There Were None*

Samuel T. Coleridge, *Rime of the Ancient Mariner*

Joseph Conrad, *Heart of Darkness*

James F. Cooper, *The Last of the Mohicans*

Clarence Day, *Life with Father*

Charles Dickens, *Great Expectations; A Christmas Carol; Oliver Twist*

Arthur C. Doyle, *The Adventures Of Sherlock Holmes*

Alexander Dumas, *The Three Musketeers*

Anne Frank, *The Diary of Anne Frank*

Edith Hamilton, *Mythology*

Nathaniel Hawthorne, *The House of the Seven Gables*

Thor Heyerdahl, *Kon-Tiki*

J. Hilton, *Lost Horizon*

Homer, *The Odyssey, The Iliad*

W. H. Hudson, *Green Mansions*

Victor Hugo, *Les Miserables*

Zora Neale Hurston, *Their Eyes Were Watching God*

Washington Irving, *The Sketch Book*

Rudyard Kipling, *Captains Courageous*

Harper Lee, *To Kill a Mockingbird*

Madeline L'Engle, *A Wrinkle in Time*

C. S. Lewis, "The Chronicles Of Narnia"

Jack London, *The Call Of The Wild*

George MacDonald, *The Curate's Awakening*

Sir Thomas Malory, *Le Morte d'Arthur*

Guy de Maupassant, *Short Stories*

Herman Melville, *Moby Dick*

Edgar Allan Poe, *Poems & Short Stories*

E. M. Remarque, *All Quiet on the Western Front*

Anne Rinaldi, *A Break With Charity: Story of the Salem Witch Trials*

Carl Sanburg, *Abraham Lincoln*

William Saroyan, *The Human Comedy*

Sir Walter Scott, *Ivanhoe*

William Shakespeare, "Hamlet," "Macbeth," "Romeo and Juliet"

George Bernard Shaw, "Pygmalion"

Sophocles, "Antigone"

Harriet Beecher Stowe, *Uncle Tom's Cabin*

John Steinbeck, *Of Mice and Men; The Grapes of Wrath*

R. L. Stevenson, *Treasure Island*

Irving Stone, *Lust For Life*

Booth Tarkington, *Penrod*

J.R.R. Tolkien, *The Lord of the Rings Trilogy*

Mark Twain, *The Adventures of Tom Sawyer*

Jules Verne, *Master of the World*

Booker T. Washington, *Up From Slavery*

H. G. Wells, *Collected Works*

FOR OLDER STUDENTS

Chinua Achebe, *Things Fall Apart*

Aristotle, *Poeticus*

Edward Bellamy, *Looking Backward*

Jorge Luis Borges, *Various Short Stories*

Stephen V. Benet, *John Brown's Body*

Charlotte Brontë, *Wuthering Heights*

Camus, *The Stranger*

Chaucer, *The Canterbury Tales*

Miguel de Cervantes, *Don Quixote*

Fyodor Dostovesky, *Crime And Punishment*

F. Scott Fitzgerald, *The Great Gatsby*

John Galsworthy, *The Forsythe Saga*

Lorraine Hansberry, *Raisin In The Sun*

Thomas Hardy, *The Return Of The Native*

SKILLS FOR LANGUAGE ARTS

From the basics of grammar to a voyage through classic literature, this 34-week, junior high course lays a foundation for students who are serious about communicating their message. Five instructive lessons weekly.

STUDENT: P 978-0-89051-859-5 $34.99
TEACHER: P 978-0-89051-860-1 $24.99

SKILLS FOR LITERARY ANALYSIS

Equips middle school students to analyze classic literary genres, discern authors' worldviews, and apply biblical standards.

STUDENT: P 978-0-89051-712-3 $34.99
TEACHER: P 978-0-89051-713-0 $15.99

SKILLS FOR RHETORIC

Help middle school students develop the skills necessary to communicate more powerfully through writing and to articulate their thought clearly.

STUDENT: P 978-0-89051-710-9 $34.99
TEACHER: P 978-0-89051-711-6 $15.99

STUDIES IN WORLD HISTORY 1

Middle school history that covers the Fertile Crescent, Egypt, India, China, Japan, Greece, Christian history, and more. Begins with creation and moves forward with a solid biblically based worldview

STUDENT: P 978-0-89051-784-0 $29.99
TEACHER: P 978-0-89051-791-8 $24.99

STUDIES IN WORLD HISTORY 2

Middle school history that covers the clash of cultures, Europe and the Renaissance, Reformation, revolutions, and more. A comprehensive examination of history, including geography, economics, and government systems.

STUDENT: P 978-0-89051-785-7 $29.99
TEACHER: P 978-0-89051-792-5 $24.99

STUDIES IN WORLD HISTORY 3

An entire year of high school American history curriculum in an easy-to-teach and comprehensive volume by respected Christian educator Dr. James Stobaugh.

STUDENT: P 978-0-89051-786-4 $29.99
TEACHER: P 978-0-89051-793-2 $24.99

STUDENT: P 978-0-89051-639-3 $29.99

STUDENT: P 978-0-89051-624-9 $29.99

Dr. James Stobaugh was a Merrill Fellow at Harvard and holds degrees from Vanderbilt and Rutgers Universities, and Princeton and Gordon-Conwell seminaries. An experienced teacher, he is a recognized leader in homeschooling and has published numerous books for students and teachers. He and his wife, Karen, have homeschooled their four children since 1985.

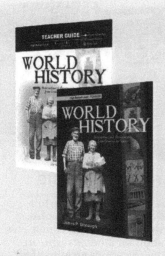

AMERICAN HISTORY

An entire year of high school American history curriculum in an easy-to-teach and comprehensive volume by respected Christian educator Dr. James Stobaugh.

STUDENT: P 978-0-89051-644-7 $29.99
TEACHER: P 978-0-89051-643-0 $19.99

BRITISH HISTORY

Examine historical theories, concepts, and global influences of this tiny country during an entire year of high school British history curriculum in an easy-to-teach and comprehensive volume.

STUDENT: P 978-0-89051-646-1 $24.99
TEACHER: P 978-0-89051-645-4 $19.99

WORLD HISTORY

This study will help high school students develop a Christian worldview while forming their own understanding of world history trends, philosophies, and events.

STUDENT: P 978-0-89051-648-5 $24.99
TEACHER: P 978-0-89051-647-8 $19.99

AMERICAN LITERATURE

A well-crafted high school presentation of whole-work selections from the major genres of American literature (prose, poetry, and drama), with background material on the writers and their worldviews.

STUDENT: P 978-0-89051-671-3 $39.99
TEACHER: P 978-0-89051-672-0 $19.99

BRITISH LITERATURE

A well-crafted highs chool presentation of whole-work selections from the major genres of British literature (prose, poetry, and drama), with background material on the writers and their worldviews.

STUDENT: P 978-0-89051-673-7 $34.99
TEACHER: P 978-0-89051-674-4 $19.99

WORLD LITERATURE

A well-crafted high school presentation of whole-work selections from the major genres of world literature (prose, poetry and drama), with background material on the writers and their worldviews.

STUDENT: P 978-0-89051-675-1 $34.99
TEACHER: P 978-0-89051-676-8 $19.99